ORGANIZATION THEORY

A Strategic Approach

FIFTH EDITION

B. J. Hodge
William P. Anthony
Lawrence M. Gales

Prentice Hall, Inc.,
Upper Saddle River, New Jersey 07458

Library of Congress Cataloging-in-Publication Data
Hodge, Billy J.
    Organization theory: a strategic approach / B.J. Hodge, William P. Anthony, Lawrence M. Gales. —5th ed.
    p. cm.
    Includes bibliographical references and index.
    ISBN 0-205-15274-0
    1. Organization. 2. Management. I. Anthony, William P.
II. Gales, Lawrence M., 1950–   . III. Title.
HD31.H542 1996
658.4—dc20   95–51122
                                                                   CIP

Acquisition Editor: Natalie Anderson
Marketing Manager: Jo-Ann DeLuca
Senior Project Manager: Alana Zdinak
Production Editor: Publishers Services, Inc.
Interior Design: Publishers Services, Inc.
Cover Design: Lorraine Castellano
Design Director: Patricia Wosczyk
Manufacturing Buyer: Vincent Scelta
Assistant Editor: Lisamarie Brassini
Editorial Assistant: Crissy Statuto
Production Coordinator: David Cotugno

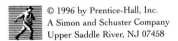 © 1996 by Prentice-Hall, Inc.
A Simon and Schuster Company
Upper Saddle River, NJ 07458

Printed in the United States of America

10 9 8 7 6 5 4 3

ISBN 0-205-15274-0

Prentice-Hall International (UK) Limited, *London*
Prentice-Hall of Australia Pty. Limited, *Sydney*
Prentice-Hall Canada Inc., *Toronto*
Prentice-Hall Hispanoamericana, S.A., *Mexico*
Prentice-Hall of India Private Limited, *New Delhi*
Prentice-Hall of Japan, Inc., *Tokyo*
Simon & Schuster Asia Pte. Ltd., *Singapore*
Editora Prentice-Hall do Brazil, Ltda., *Rio de Janeiro*

To Dottie,

B. J. Hodge

To Roz, Cathie, and Sarah,

William P. Anthony

and

To Leah, your courage, expressed in words, is an inspiration,

Lawrence M. Gales

Contents

Chapter 6   **Organizational Technology** **153**

Chapter 7   **Organizational Size, Growth, and Life Cycles** **182**

Chapter 13

Innovation, Strategic Change, and Organizational Learning 356

PART FIVE   **Integrative Cases 386**

Preface

A basic fact of organizational life is that things change. In that spirit, this fifth edition of *Organization Theory: A Strategic Approach* represents a major change over previous editions, not the least of which is a new member of the team—Larry Gales, Professor of Organization Theory at the University of Cincinnati. This new edition is consistent in both theme and content with many of the changing directions in organization theory and management today. Despite the extensive changes to this text, the strategic focus and the theoretical frameworks presented in this fifth edition can be directly traced through the previous four editions.

The material in this text is intended to be a primer in organization theory for upper-division undergraduate and introductory-level MBA students—the future managers and leaders of organizations. The book has been reengineered so that the tone and direction are focused on managerial application—how the student as a potential future manager can use the knowledge of organization theory to become more productive, both as a manager and as an organization member. Thus, the fifth edition of *Organization Theory: A Strategic Approach* continues to present a balance of theory, research, and practice. Theory and research are necessary to provide coherence, certainty, and predictability in an otherwise incoherent, uncertain, and unpredictable world. However, in presenting theory and research, we have maintained a belief that theory and research should provide practical value to the inhabitants of organizations—the managers and members of organizations. To accomplish this balance, we have provided numerous examples from organizations to illustrate the theories, concepts, and research findings throughout the text.

The book has essentially been rewritten and revised from top to bottom, with an eye toward greater readability and more emphasis on practical application. The thirteen chapters in this edition also contain new material. Material that in the past was spread across multiple chapters has been concentrated into single chapters, or, in the case of environments, two chapters. Updated cases begin and end each chapter. Numerous "real life" examples are spread throughout the chapters. The clustering of chapters has been revised to enhance the logical flow of material. The thirteen chapters are divided into four parts: "Introduction," "The Context of Organizations," "Managing the Organizational Context," and "Organizational Processes." We have created greater integration among the topics and issues covered in the text so that the reader can more easily relate material covered in early chapters with material covered later.

Part 1 (Chapters 1–2) of the text contain the basic framework for the text. Chapter 1 provides a historical background for understanding the development of organization theory; introduces a variety of theoretical perspectives; and presents the strategic approach. Chapter 2 explores the subject of organizational structure—the basic building blocks of the organization. In this chapter, we also introduce the contingency theory framework for organizations, which is central to the strategic approach. To understand the appropriate form of organization (structure and design), one must understand the conditions or context in which the organization exists. Chapter 2 presents the basic elements of structure so that the reader can think about how structure should vary with differing contextual conditions.

Part 2 (Chapters 3–7) introduces the contextual dimensions: organizational goals, environment, technology, size, and life cycle. From a contingency perspective, these are the factors that must be considered in making judgments about structure. The examination of goals in Chapter 3 has been expanded to include a discussion of ethics and ethical goals. In light of the many troubling events in the business world lately, we felt that a discussion of ethics was especially important. Although the organizational environment has been a central focus of previous editions, this new edition gives even greater attention to that subject, emphasizing the global nature of the context in which nearly every business operates. Chapter 4 describes the environment, while strategic management of the environment is the focus of Chapter 5. Chapter 6 shifts the reader's attention to technology. We present three traditional views of organizational technology based on the works of Woodward, Perrow, and Thompson. The traditional views are augmented by contemporary views of technology that examine shifts to services, demands for flexibility, and increasing automation and computerization. Part 2 concludes with Chapter 7, discussing the two related topics of organizational size and organizational life cycles. These topics have received extensive coverage in the business press due to the proliferation of mergers at the same time that many large organizations are downsizing. Coinciding with these trends are difficulties that some large, prominent organizations are encountering as they enter mature stages of their development.

The contextual conditions presented in Part 2 are the variables that managers must consider in determining the best-fitting structures, designs, and governance systems, the subjects of Part 3 (Chapters 8–9). Chapter 8 explores organizational design as a strategic response to the organizational context. The focus is on how people are grouped together in departments or divisions. The chapter also examines some recent trends in design, including virtual organizations, federal organizations, and two Asian forms—the Japanese *keiretsu* and the Korean *chaebol*. Organizational economics, an area of increasing importance in the field of organization theory, is presented in Chapter 9. Using agency theory and transaction costs economics, we examine organizational control, transactions, and boundaries in this chapter.

The theme of Part 4 (Chapters 10–13) is organizational processes. Organizational culture, introduced in Chapter 10, discusses those factors that make each organization distinctive and unique. Here, the focus is on both the observable and unobservable elements of culture. Chapter 11 introduces organizational information processing and decision making. With the advent of inexpensive high-speed computing and sophisticated tele-communications, organizations can be overwhelmed by information. Thus, managing information is a critical—some would say central—task of organizations. But information is not a final destination. Information is fuel for the decision processes that are also discussed in this chapter. The concepts of bounded rationality and garbage can decision making described in Chapter 11 provide a glimpse of the political side of organization that, along with power, are the subjects of Chapter 12.

The final chapter introduces organizational innovation, change, and renaissance—subjects that we have implicitly discussed throughout the text. Chapter 13 specifically examines a variety of organizational change perspectives. We conclude with some speculation about the nature of organizations in the 21st century and how organization theory can help managers.

The text concludes with five extensive, integrative organizational cases, three of which (Daewoo, Kodak, and General Motors) are new to the fifth edition. The IBM and

Wal-Mart cases are updated and significantly revised to reflect the changing fortunes of those two companies. The purpose of these cases is twofold: (1) to demonstrate the applicability of organization theory concepts and principles to real-life organizations; and (2) to permit the student to use these concepts and principles as problem-solving tools.

As with any complex endeavor, many people deserve thanks for their help and support in making this fifth edition possible. Though too numerous to mention, we give thanks to our colleagues and students at Florida State University and the University of Cincinnati. Special thanks are due to Erich Brockmann, Haesun Baek, and Christopher Polaszek of Florida State University and Thomas Debbink of the University of Cincinnati for their preparation of the end-of-text cases. We also appreciate the insightful and thorough reviews provided by anonymous reviewers. Special thanks are due to Natalie Anderson, our editor at Prentice Hall, and to Gene Malecki, Lori Toscano, and Gary Von Euer of Publishers Services, Inc., who have provided expert editorial assistance.

Finally, it is to our families that we dedicate this edition—without their love, help, inspiration, and support, this venture would not have been possible. It is also dedicated to our children and grandchildren, who will become the makers, managers, and members of future organizations.

PART ONE

Introduction

W hat are organizations, and why are they an important subject to study? As we will begin to see in Chapter 1, organizations are ubiquitous. They affect nearly every aspect of human existence — birth, growth, development, education, work, social relations, health, and even death. Yet the average person's understanding of the complexities of organizations and organizational life is typically quite limited. Thus, first among our goals is to provide a basis for understanding organizations. An understanding of organizations serves as a stepping-stone to our second goal, which is to provide a foundation for working successfully in organizations and for participating in or initiating efforts to change and adapt organizations to new conditions.

Organization theory and management theory are closely related concepts. A manager must understand the workings of an organization to be effective in the managerial role. Therefore, an understanding of organization theory serves as a foundation for studying management. The concepts that underlie organization theory developed hand in hand with management concepts. As people understood more about how organizations operate, they learned how managers could operate more efficiently. Moreover, although the development of organization theory is rather eclectic, it is closely related to management theory. Concepts, ideas, and research from such diverse areas as economics, engineering, psychology, sociology, social psychology, and political science appear in organization theory literature.

How do we gain an understanding of these concepts? How can we place boundaries on them and arrange them in some logical fashion? To answer these questions we use a combination of strategy and systems approaches. We examine issues in the context of real organizations and real events. We begin addressing these issues in this first chapter and return to them periodically throughout the text.

The first chapter addresses three groups of critical questions: (1) What is organization theory, how does it relate to management, and how did the field develop? (2) What is an organization, why is it important, and how can it be studied? and (3) What is a strategic systems approach to organizations?

Chapter 2 introduces the subject of organizational structure — the basic building blocks of the organization. The text takes a contingency approach: The appropriate form of organization (structure and design) depends upon the conditions or context in which the organization exists. Understanding the basic elements of structure presented in Chapter 2 provides the reader with a framework for thinking about how structure varies with differing contextual conditions. Part Two then introduces the contextual dimensions of organizational goals, environment, technology, size, and life cycle. These are the contingency factors that must be considered in making judgments about structure.

In Part Three of the text we return to focusing on the organization itself as a means for managing the organizational context. Attention is directed toward the strategic design of organizations and nonstructural means for controlling and managing the organization. We finally examine culture, the last step in managing the context. Culture has been described as the glue that holds an organization together.

Part Four explores three critical organizational processes. First, we examine the nature of information and decision making in organizations. Three models of decision making are presented and critiqued. Up to this point we will have largely regarded organizations as rational and purposeful entities. With our examination of decision making we open up the possibility that organizations and managers sometimes act (make decisions) in ways that do not fit with a rational view of the world. Chapter 12 extends the analysis by presenting a political view of organizations. Finally, we conclude the text by discussing the processes of innovation, change, and organizational renaissance. But like any long journey, the study of organizations must begin with a sturdy foundation.

Organization Theory and the Manager

CASE: THRIFTY HARDWARE COMPANY: ON-THE-JOB TRAINING*

It was early in the morning on March 4, and Mike Lawrence was both excited and concerned as he unlocked the door to Thrifty Hardware Company (Thrifty for short) in northwest Detroit. The night before he and his ailing father had signed papers transferring ownership of Thrifty to Mike. Mike had grown up in the family's retail hardware business, working summers and weekends during the school year and becoming his father's assistant after graduating from college.

As he walked into the store and turned on lights, he was soon greeted by his arriving employees. That thought, "employees," felt strange to Mike. He had known and worked with most of the workers for several years (their average tenure on the job was four years), but he had never thought of them as his "employees." Mike felt a new twinge of responsibility, which he had not felt in the past, to his eight full-time and three part-time employees.

By 8:00 A.M. the store was ready to open for business. Thrifty was a full-service hardware, lumber, and building supply store. The store carried nearly 20,000 different items from everything for minor household repairs to those needed for major renovations. The business had grown steadily through the late 1960s to the present at rates well above inflation and the industry average, and was currently doing just over $1,000,000 annually. The primary customers were local homeowners and small businesses. As Mike's father, Irv, always said, "Hardware is recessionproof. In good times you sell the frills, and in tough times when people can't afford new things or plumbers and electricians, you sell them the things they need to 'do it yourself.'"

Mike wasn't too concerned about how to run the business. As his father's assistant, he had done almost everything and knew almost everything there was to know about hardware, lumber, and building supplies. Mike had run the business when his father took rare vacations or days off and had been in charge for the last two weeks while his father was in the hospital. Doing weekly and

---

*This case is based on an actual event. Names of the people involved have been changed.

seasonal ordering, he had dealt with most of the more than twenty major suppliers. He had coordinated the small amount of advertising that they had done. And his major responsibility as his father's assistant had been to take care of the store's financial management, which involved dealing with the banks and credit card companies; managing payroll, accounts receivable and accounts payable; and preparing the books for the accountant. It was this last task that took Mike to his office early on March 4.

Once he was in his office, Mike again felt that vague uneasiness that had kept him awake the night before and had troubled him as he opened the store in the morning. As he stared at the ledger, he realized what was weighing so heavily on his mind. He had been his father's assistant, but now he had no assistant. No one else knew all the ins and outs of the business. What would happen if he got sick, or wanted to take a day off or go on a vacation? Sure, he had heard his father's stories of working seven days a week, ten hours a day. It also occurred to Mike that his father hadn't started taking vacations until Mike was twenty years old and could run the business. Mike knew that he couldn't run the business like that. He had to have an assistant. The more he thought about who to pick as an assistant, the more he began to see that what he needed was more than just an assistant. He started to think about an organizational plan. He spent the rest of the morning writing notes, talking with each of his employees, and just wandering around the nearly 20,000 square feet of sales floor and warehouse space. By the end of the workday Mike felt that an organizational plan was coming together. As his employees were leaving the store, he asked them to show up early the next day for a breakfast staff meeting. The workers looked quizzically at Mike because they'd never before had a staff meeting.

That night, after finishing the bookkeeping that he had avoided all day, Mike went to bed and slept soundly. At the staff meeting the next morning he announced his new organizational plan. First, he made Ben Slater his assistant and the store manager. Ben had been with Thrifty the longest of any of the salespeople and seemed to be the brightest and most responsible of the employees. Mike would begin today to train Ben about all the critical managerial responsibilities.

Mike then assigned each of the other full-time employees to manage specific departments. For example, Paul Schultz was responsible for the plumbing and electrical departments. He was to become completely knowledgeable about each product they sold in these two departments, each wholesaler that supplied merchandise, how and when to order, and what sold and what didn't sell. Similar responsibilities were created for lumber, paint, tools, and each additional product area.

This plan would relieve Mike of the day-to-day tasks of ordering, dealing with wholesalers, and being the primary source of product and "how-to" information. Major decisions about ordering new products or dropping slow sellers would be made by a group composed of the department head, Mike, and Ben. Bea Simms, the head cashier, also became the bookkeeper.

After dividing tasks among the employees, Mike then described what he saw as his job. He would supervise and coordinate everyone's work. He would determine Thrifty's direction, make the major decisions for the business, and provide employees with information and feedback about their jobs. Mike knew that if the company were to grow and prosper, he could not be bogged down by the day-to-day minutiae. Mike then laid out Thrifty's strategy:

- They would be a full-service hardware, lumber, and building supply company. This meant that they would stress customer service and a wide variety of products and services. Thrifty would be the premier hardware, lumber, and building supply company in its market area.
- They would treat each customer fairly and honestly. They would never sell inferior quality products and they would never use hard-sell tactics to sell something that the customer didn't want. Employees would keep in mind that it is the customer who pays their wages.
- Each employee would be respected for his or her unique contributions to the business and would be treated with fairness and respect.

Mike closed the meeting by stating that this was only the beginning. They should all expect more changes, and he welcomed suggestions from employees. As the meeting broke up, Mike felt pretty good about what had been accomplished. He thought he had laid the groundwork for the smooth operation of the business.

Although the business, in general, was running smoothly, a number of unexpected events did cause some problems. First, at 3:00 A.M. on June 1, a drunk driver rammed through the plate glass windows in the front of the store, doing over $20,000 damage to the building, fixtures, and merchandise. Fortunately, the police called Ben Slater, who arrived on the scene to begin boarding up the storefront. Then, in July, Thrifty's major hardware wholesaler burned to the ground. The immediate question that Mike faced was how to replace this supplier — quickly. Without a dependable supply of merchandise, the business would suffer and customers would go elsewhere. In the short run, he turned to several small local wholesalers. In the long run, the crisis turned into a positive event. Mike reevaluated how the store bought merchandise, and he made a major decision to join a wholesale cooperative. The major comprehensive suppliers in the hardware industry, ACE, True Value, ServiStar, and HWI, are all dealer-owned cooperatives. This change allowed him to concentrate the store's buying with far fewer wholesalers, making ordering easier and more efficient.

In September, Paul Schultz, the plumbing and electrical department manager, resigned. Next to Ben Slater, Schultz was the most competent and reliable employee. Mike knew it would be difficult to replace Schultz; but because of the changes that Mike started making in March, he knew he could clearly define the skills and responsibilities that were part of Paul's job. Finally, in November, several local auto plants announced layoffs or temporary shutdowns because car sales were slow. Mike was concerned because so many of his customers were autoworkers. Nonetheless, Mike was optimistic. The business had weathered previous economic slowdowns, increased competition, and major changes in the local neighborhood.

As the year drew to a close, Mike sat in his office and reflected on events since he had taken over Thrifty. Business had been good despite all the turmoil. Sales had increased at an annual rate of 17 percent, which was well above the rate of inflation. Profits had also increased significantly. The switch to the new wholesale cooperative had resulted in lower costs. Most important to Mike was that he now felt comfortable that he could take a few days off after the first of the year and know that the company could go on without him. What Mike did not realize was that in the last nine months he had learned a great deal about organizations.

The previous case is a real-life example of the importance of understanding the nature of organizations. Although Thrifty Hardware Company may not be the largest or most sophisticated organization, this case illustrates several key points about the nature of organizations that will be examined in greater detail in this chapter and throughout the text. First, organizations are made of *people*, whether it is the handful of employees at Thrifty or the thousands of employees at General Motors. Second, Mike learned that *division of labor* among members of the organization is critical. Everyone does not have the same task. A third aspect of organizations that Mike came to understand was the importance of *goals* to organizations. Understanding and improving the operation of Thrifty required Mike to explicitly understand each of these three elements of organization, and that is where our study of organizations begins.

ORGANIZATIONS

Organizations are ubiquitous. Nearly every aspect of our daily life is affected in some way by organizations. Work, school, family, health care, religion, entertainment — nearly every facet of life takes place in, is regulated by, or is the result of organizations and organizational action. In fact, the very concept of modern civilized society is based on the premise that people work together in formal or informal groups to complete tasks that individuals alone could not perform. Perhaps because organizations are everywhere and we are so involved in them, we give little thought to what organizations really are and how they work. Yet, most of us work in organizations. We depend on them for our livelihood and for most of the products and services we need to live. If, like Mike Lawrence in the introductory case, we wish to understand, manage, and improve the situations we face in organizations, it is necessary to study organizations.

Unlike Mike Lawrence's on-the-job education about organizations, this book takes a systematic look at organizations. Our intention is to first examine the concept of *organizations* and then explore how they are designed, how they function, and how they change over time. Our examination of organizations focuses mainly on business organizations although the basic concepts and relationships we present can be applied to nearly all complex organizations. Throughout our examination we are most concerned with explaining and understanding how organizations can operate more efficiently and effectively. We are especially concerned with what managers can do to make organizations operate better.

ORGANIZATIONAL CHALLENGES

Today's organizations face several key challenges. Even rich and powerful companies with long traditions are not immune to obstacles in meeting these challenges: Witness the recent problems faced by such industry giants as Kodak, General Motors, IBM, Sears, and countless others. While these companies face many varied challenges, five major areas represent recurrent themes in this text:

1. managing organizations in a global environment;
2. designing and structuring (or restructuring) organizations;
3. improving quality, empowerment, and competitiveness;
4. reducing complexity, increasing speed, and reacting to environmental changes; and
5. ethical and moral management of the organization.

The Global Challenge. The world is much different than it was when General Motors, for example, was first incorporated in 1908. Despite the fact that automobiles were invented in Europe, the early GM was virtually unconcerned with foreign competition. However, the world and the business environment have now changed dramatically and with increasing speed, especially in the post–World War II period. To say that organizations must be concerned with the global business environment is an understatement. The American auto industry has suffered greatly and to some extent has had to change drastically because of challenges first from Europe and then from Japan. Some business-writers and leaders have stated that businesses that fail to attend to global markets or conditions are doomed and that all businesses, either directly or indirectly, must manage in a global environment. Even Mike Lawrence had to consider global markets when he made decisions about what merchandise to buy for his store. Some foreign producers made better and/or cheaper products than his domestic suppliers. Businesses that fail to take advantage of new markets, fail to explore new potential suppliers, or fail to see changing world conditions will be surpassed or replaced by organizations with more global vision.

For example, some critics trace the problems in the U.S. automobile market to two key global factors. First, beginning in the 1960s, U.S. firms failed to perceive increasing numbers of imported cars (e.g., Volkswagen, Toyota, Datsun, and others) as a threat. Even as the number of imports increased, U.S. firms continued to ignore these indications of a serious threat. They failed to see differences in product quality and failed to discern changes in consumer attitudes. A second global event shook the auto industry and exacerbated global competition. The oil embargo of 1973 raised gasoline prices to record levels and placed a heavy premium on small, fuel-efficient cars. Like most Americans, auto firm executives failed to anticipate this event and were not in a position to respond. For many years, foreign automakers produced small, fuel-efficient cars because of the narrow streets, crowded cities, and expensive fuel in Europe and Asia. Thus, because the U.S. firms had little experience competing on the basis of small size and fuel efficiency, they were unable to compete effectively with the Japanese and European car manufacturers.

One need only look at a few newspapers or newsmagazines over the past few years to see how dramatically the world political and business landscape has changed. Communism has fallen in most of eastern Europe. The shift to market economies in these countries presents businesses with opportunities, but political instability also creates great risk. In western Europe the formation of a unified economic market has caused great concern for many businesses, particularly firms outside the European community. Several events in Asia may have important implications for business organizations.

Recent turbulence in Japan's economy has made the task of balancing trade more difficult. Because of their own recession, the Japanese are spending less on American products.

The economic and political situation in China is equally uncertain. As China has become more open and adopted a more market-based economy, it has become an increasingly important trade partner for western business. Yet, human rights organizations throughout the world have pressured the Chinese to grant greater political freedoms in exchange for favorable trade relations. Additionally, in 1997 the former British colony of Hong Kong, a major Asian economic center, reverts to the People's Republic of China. No one knows what impact this change will have on Hong Kong–based businesses.

Finally, adoption of the North American Free Trade Agreement (NAFTA) and recent revisions in the General Agreement on Tariffs and Trade (GATT) will reduce trade barriers between the U.S. and its trading partners throughout the world. This, too, will create new opportunities for American businesses, but it is also likely to increase competition. Many businesses may expand the scope of their operations; some will relocate to take advantage of lower costs of doing business; and some will be challenged by new competitors.

The point is that no business, big or small, can ignore events throughout the world. Thus, as we examine organizations in this text, we will repeatedly make reference to organizations in their global environments.

Designing and (Re)Structuring. GM, IBM, Unisys, Compaq Computer, . . . the list goes on. All of these firms are cutting back on personnel and changing the way they are organized. They are cutting the number of top managers, middle managers, support staff, and even production workers to become leaner and more efficient. To accommodate these cuts, organizations are implementing new structures. Even Mike Lawrence had to restructure Thrifty so it would run smoothly in the absence of his father. Despite these trends toward downsizing and restructuring, many firms have yet to reap anticipated benefits. We will examine the designing, downsizing, and restructuring trends at several junctures in the text to try and understand why firms may need to design, downsize, and restructure, how they should go about this process, and what firms should expect from these actions.

Quality, Empowerment, and Competitiveness. Few subjects have received more attention in the business press in recent years than the ***Total Quality Management*** movement. Organizations are realizing that quality products and services are a must if they are to remain competitive in a global marketplace. However, the formula for achieving quality products and services is complex and involves radical changes for many organizations. Foremost among these changes is employee empowerment—giving individual workers the authority and responsibility for monitoring quality. Total quality has broad and pervasive implications for organizations, and we will examine these in several chapters, including those dealing with goals, technology, structure, work groups, and culture.

Along with the total quality movement, managers have come to realize that one route to streamlined operation and greater employee involvement is to *empower* employees. The result is that employees lower in the organizational hierarchy are now being given responsibility for making decisions about a variety of job-related issues. While this may seem to be an obvious way to run an organization, it challenges traditional thinking about power, authority, and hierarchy in organizations. Like total quality, we will examine issues related to empowerment at several points in our exploration of organizations.

Both Total Quality Management and empowerment are seen as tools for organizations to become more competitive. This serves to highlight the point that businesses in almost all markets are facing increasingly fierce competition. That competition is the result of many factors including increasingly open global markets in nearly every industry, ruthless cost cutting on the part of some companies, lower economies of scale in some basic industries, such as steel, and changing consumer attitudes about price and value.

Complexity, Speed, and Responsiveness. Not only is the world changing as we noted earlier, but it appears that these changes are happening with greater speed than ever before.[1] High-speed, high-capacity computing; advanced telecommunications; and worldwide electronic media coverage have all increased the speed with which information is transmitted. The speed with which information is transferred requires that organizations be structured in ways that maximize their ability to handle information. Moreover, such innovations as ***just-in-time (JIT)*** manufacturing and inventory control systems and ***computerized integrated manufacturing systems (CIMS)*** make use of this abundant information. However, speed and responsiveness require more than bigger and faster computers. Organizations must get the right information in the right form to the appropriate people in a timely fashion. We will examine the impact on organizations of this abundant information and these demands for speed and responsiveness at several points in the text. Most specifically, we will address these issues in chapters dealing with the environment, technology, structure, information, and culture.

Moral and Ethical Management. Cynics may argue that *business ethics* is an oxymoron. We, along with numerous corporate leaders, believe that is not the case. Ethical behavior and traditional business objectives and operations can and, we maintain, should be consistent. Events such as the General Motors–NBC scandal over media coverage of supposedly exploding pickup truck gas tanks or General Electric's kickbacks to Israeli military officials point out the importance of ethical behavior in organizations. In Chapter 3 we will introduce an ethical framework for guiding the management of organizations. Periodically we will return to this ethical framework to guide discussions of issues such as decision making, downsizing, and organizational politics.

ORGANIZATIONS: A DEFINITION

It is likely that humans have always lived in organized groups. Tasks such as hunting, food gathering, protection, and migration could be more effectively and efficiently carried out in organized groups. Groups of individuals working together could accomplish goals that no individual alone could realize. Complicated tasks could be divided among several people, and people who possessed special skills, knowledge, or other attributes could work in areas that provided the best match between the individual and the group's needs. The modern organization is, in reality, an extension of the specialization and division of labor that existed in early social groups. This leads us to a preliminary definition of organizations stated on page 10.

> ## Definition
>
> An organization is defined as two or more people working together cooperatively within identifiable boundaries to accomplish a common goal or objective. Implicit in this definition are several important ideas: Organizations are made up of people (i.e., members); organizations divide labor among members; and organizations pursue shared goals or objectives.

Organizations are made up of people. Although this seems rather obvious and simplistic, to understand and appreciate the human component is important because of the complexity of social relationships and variability or diversity in humans. The human component makes organizations among the most complex systems[2] and presents managers and organizational researchers with some of their most critical challenges. Organizations such as Thrifty Hardware Company or General Motors must attract, motivate, and retain the right people. We will return to the "people" issue repeatedly throughout our investigation of organizations.

Second, when people work together a number of things become necessary. We need to *divide labor among people,* and as noted earlier, we may seek people with specialized skills or knowledge. The eighteenth-century economist and philosopher Adam Smith used the example of a pin factory to point out the value of division of labor and specialization.[3] Not all members of the organization should necessarily carry out the same tasks. For example, in Smith's pin factory, it was more efficient for laborers to specialize in specific parts of the pin production process instead of each person creating one pin from start to finish. In the introductory case, Mike Lawrence found it useful to divide responsibilities among his employees so that each one managed a different department and had specialized knowledge about its products, suppliers, and customer needs.

As we begin to divide labor and seek specialization among organizational members, it also becomes necessary to make certain that everyone continues to work toward the common goals of the organization. *Coordination and control of actions* among organization members become imperative. At Thrifty the responsibility for coordination was largely Mike's. Without coordination and control some workers may intentionally or unintentionally engage in activities that do not contribute to the organization's goals or that may interfere with them. Some people may pursue actions that further their own interests and others may simply freeload—not contribute their fair share of effort—yet still expect to share in the organization's outcomes. Moreover, some operations within organizations may require precise timing or scheduling so that actions of different workers or departments fit together. For example, Mike Lawrence found that the timing of ordering was critical. Thursday through Monday was the period of heaviest customer traffic. It was critical that orders be placed so that merchandise arrived before these busy periods. Otherwise, important merchandise may not be on display and employees would have to divert their attention from customers to stocking tasks. Similarly, an automaker must ensure that assembly workers carefully coordinate their actions so that their assembly efforts result in the efficient and effective production of a car. To exercise coordination and control, members of the organization need a formal structure that specifies roles, responsibilities, and relationships among organizational members. We will have more to say about the topic of structure shortly.

Third, *organizations have identifiable boundaries.* Defining an organization's boundaries may appear to be a simple matter. Most people think of membership as the characteristic that defines the boundaries of an organization. Employees in a business, volunteers in a voluntary organization, or students in an academic institution would all appear to be within the boundaries of those organizations. Closer inspection of the boundary issue, however, makes this determination less clear cut.

Two critical organizational tasks help us to define two different approaches to delineating an organization's boundaries. The first approach to boundaries emphasizes people and membership while the second approach emphasizes where activities take place.[4]

We already noted that organizations are made up of people, and one important task is to bring into the organization necessary employees or members willing to exchange their contributions for wages or other rewards. This task is, in part, consistent with a definition of organizational boundaries that emphasizes membership—employees, volunteers, or students. The organization's boundary is defined by those people who are official organizational members. But what about the recent trend towards using contracted labor, temporary workers, or consultants? For example, when General Motors recently downsized it released many mid- and upper-level management employees. In the aftermath of downsizing, GM realized that it had terminated some employees whose skills and knowledge it still needed. Rather than rehiring these people as regular employees, GM brought them in as independent consultants even though these people often occupied the same offices and conducted the same tasks as when they were employees. Similar events have taken place at other companies that have dramatically and quickly downsized. These changes raise two important questions. Are these contractors and temporary workers members of the organization? Where is the boundary? The answers are not clear. Basing our definition of organizational boundaries on membership suggests that these people are not true members of the organization. Yet, clearly, the work these people do for the organization is often of equal or greater importance than that carried out by true members.

A second critical task for an organization is to determine which activities it should attempt to perform and which ones it should leave to other organizations in the external environment. This is commonly referred to as the make-buy decision.[5] For example, General Motors must decide whether it should make or buy certain components, such as shock absorbers or spark plugs. While GM has decided to make many of its component parts, some competitors have decided to buy those parts from supplier companies in the external environment. This approach to organizational boundaries emphasizes activities rather than people. Accordingly, boundaries are defined by those activities that the organization chooses to pursue, regardless of whether the workers who perform the tasks are regular employees or contract laborers.

Thus, we are left with two ways of describing organizational boundaries; one emphasizing people in the organization and the other emphasizing activities that the organization conducts. Although these two views are not mutually exclusive (i.e., applying one approach does not rule out applying the other), they are not necessarily complementary views. How we choose between these two views of boundaries depends largely on the organizational question or problem we seek to answer. For example, questions dealing with positions, communication, hierarchy, or politics may be best addressed using membership as the boundary criterion. Relationships between departments, between the organization and outside customers or suppliers, and even between the organization and its employees typically focus on activities as boundary criteria.

The fourth part of our definition of an organization states that *organizations are purposeful, goal-seeking work arrangements.* They are not just temporary or transient collections of people. Organizations exist to pursue commonly held goals. Part of Mike Lawrence's strategy was a list of specific goals that his business should achieve that included serving customers, making money, and behaving ethically. In Chapter 3 we will examine in detail organizational goals. We will see, however, that the combination of the human aspect of organizations and the goal-seeking or purposeful nature of organizations may be a source of problems. We will eventually have to deal with problems of determining who sets organizational goals and what happens when goal consensus is absent. Thus, even the seemingly simple notion of organizational goals is not as simple as it would appear.

We began with a simple definition of an organization as two or more people working together to accomplish a common goal. As we began to explore this simple definition, we came to the realization that organizations are *not* simple. Therefore, we may need a more comprehensive definition. Even though debates exist about each part of the definition of an organization, it is still useful to refine our original definition: *Organizations are human systems of cooperation and coordination assembled within identifiable boundaries to pursue shared goals or objectives.* To sharpen and improve our understanding of organizations and organizational activity, researchers and managers must develop explanations of how organizations form, function, change, and survive. Such explanations are the domain of organizational theory that we discuss in this text.

ORGANIZATIONS AS SYSTEMS

Our definition of an organization also includes the term *systems.*[6] Systems theory provides a simple way to model organizations by focusing on the structure and relationships or interdependence among parts of the organization. A systems approach conveys the idea that organizations are made up of parts and that the parts interact with each other to accomplish the organization's goals. For example, at Thrifty Hardware the business must obtain inputs from the external environment. These inputs include merchandise to sell, employees, labor, and bank financing. The internal processes at Thrifty include receiving and stocking merchandise, marketing, selling, maintenance, and other activities necessary to support the day-to-day conduct of business. On the output side Thrifty must sell its goods to customers, respond to government agencies that tax or regulate the business, and deal with unexpected events, such as the drunk driver who crashed through the front window.

General Motors presents a more complex example. The purchasing department must obtain such inputs as steel, tires, paint, wire, fabrics, and many components necessary to produce an automobile. The personnel department must attract workers who have the necessary skills and then must develop training, compensation, and administrative systems to retain and motivate those employees. Production must take the material and human inputs and produce automobiles. Marketing must develop advertising, promotional, product, and sales strategies that facilitate the sale of the cars that the production subsystem produces. In a typical organization many departments or units must interact to accomplish the firm's objectives.

Critical relationships or interdependencies may exist among these departments. At GM production and personnel must work together to ensure that the organization has enough workers with the appropriate skills required by the production subsystem. Purchasing and production must plan carefully to guarantee flows of raw materials necessary to produce products. Oversupplies of raw materials can be costly, tying up capital and requiring storage. Innovative systems, such as just-in-time inventory control, change the nature of interdependence between production and purchasing and make coordination even more critical. Production and marketing must work together to plan how much of each product to produce to match expected demands and scheduled promotions. If the marketing department aggressively promotes a new product before production is fully operating, the unexpected demand may place undue stress on production. GM has experienced problems of this sort in its Saturn division. Aggressive promotion has resulted in far greater demand for Saturn than production could supply. The production department must coordinate better with personnel to ensure that they have a sufficient number of appropriately skilled and trained employees to match the anticipated demand. Similar types of coordination must take place even at Thrifty Hardware. Retailers often face serious problems when they create marketing promotions and then the manufacturers fail to ship the advertised products. The results of poor coordination among interdependent departments could be overworked employees, equipment breakdowns, defective products, unfilled orders, unhappy customers, and lost profits.

Two additional and related characteristics of systems are ***holism*** and ***synergism.*** First, *holism means that a system should be considered as a functioning whole.* Changes in any one part of the system are likely to have an impact throughout the system. If the purchasing department has difficulty obtaining raw materials, it is likely that the production department will also suffer because it has no raw materials to convert to outputs. Or if the organization implements a just-in-time inventory system, it is likely to have profound impact on the need for communication between purchasing and production. Thus, one should consider performance in all components of the organization when changes affect any one component. Second, *synergism* refers to the interactive effect of the parts of the system working together. *The sum of the interaction of the component parts of the organization working together is greater than the effect of the parts working separately,* or as it is commonly described, $2 + 2 = 5$. As each part of the system performs its role, it enhances the performance of other parts. Just as a basketball team is more than five players playing as individuals, so is an organization more than just the sum of its parts. In fact, this is usually why the parts are brought together in the first place. The organization creates separate departments in purchasing, production, personnel, and marketing because of the specialized knowledge and skills that each area requires. It is, however, only through the coordinated interaction of these departments that the organization is able to achieve its goals.

CLOSED AND OPEN SYSTEMS

Systems theorists differentiate between *closed systems* and *open systems.* Closed systems are self-perpetuating and receive no outside energy or resources. They have no need to interact with their environments. As closed systems run out of energy, they enter a state of collapse called *entropy.* A major advance in the study of organizations was the realization that organizations are *not (and cannot be)* closed systems because they depend on their external environments for energy. Open systems can avoid entropy, and create a state called *negative entropy,* by importing energy in the form of physical, human, and financial resources. The approach presented in this book emphasizes how organizations as open systems attempt to manage relationships with their environments.

Open systems models acknowledge that organizations must receive energy *(inputs)* in the form of important resources from their external environments. For example, Thrifty Hardware Company receives merchandise, labor, and customers from its outside environment. General Motors receives parts from independent suppliers, labor from the labor market, and capital from investors and lenders. Additionally, Thrifty and General Motors sell their *output* to customers who are also external to the company. Sales of products and services produce cash flow and provide additional energy for the system. Many other facets of the external environment are critical to any organization's existence, and we will explore them in detail in Chapter 4.

Figure 1.1 graphically presents the three parts of a basic open systems model: inputs, throughputs or transformation processes, and outputs. Several subsystems are also associated with these three activities and are included in the diagram.

FIGURE 1.1
The Open Systems Model

External Environment

Sources of Inputs and Constraints		Processes		Output Opportunities and Constraints
	Inputs ⟶	Transformation ⟶	Outputs ⟶	
	Boundary Spanning (Resource Acquisition): Human Resources, Material Resources, Financial Resources, and Information	Management (Decision Making, Planning, Controlling, and Structuring); Production; Maintenance; and Adaptation	Boundary Spanning (Output Transactions): Sales of Output, Advertising, and Public Relations	

Subsystems

External Environment

The input and output portions of the open systems model are critical because they represent the organization's interface with the external environment. Together, these input and output functions are part of the *boundary spanning* subsystem.[7] Input subunits of the organization are responsible for importing resources and information into the organization. In a typical business, these activities may include purchasing, receiving, personnel recruiting, and market research as well as links to investors and bankers. Output units are responsible for disseminating information about the organization and disposing of the firm's outputs. These functions may include advertising, public relations, and sales. An in-depth discussion of these activities is presented in Chapter 4, but for now the important point is that these activities require that organizational members interact extensively with people or organizations in the external environment. GM must interact with suppliers, advertising agencies, dealers, journalists, investors, bankers, government agencies, and myriad other external factors. Even a small business like Thrifty must interact with a subset of these external constituents. Remember that the external environment is a source of both energy and uncertainty for an organization, and the organization must have mechanisms for dealing with its environment if it is to survive.

The remaining process in the systems model is the throughput process. Several important activities take place in relation to throughput. First, the ***production subsystem*** is responsible for transformation of the organization's inputs into outputs. This is the means that the organization uses to take the raw materials, labor, capital, and information that it has received in the input process and convert them into outputs. In the case of a manufacturing company such as General Motors, steel, plastics, tires, batteries, glass, and countless other inputs are converted into vehicles. The transformation for a service organization such as Thrifty is less clear. Its transformation process involves the linking of customers to various services. For example, Thrifty acquires merchandise from wholesalers and then sells that merchandise to customers. The production subsystem is responsible for preparing the merchandise for sale and actual selling to customers. We will further investigate activities of the production subsystem under the heading of technology in Chapter 6.

Other activities are necessary to support the transformation process. Organizations must balance the need for stability and predictability with the need to adapt to the changing external environment. Stability and predictability are the responsibility of two key subsystems. First, as we saw in the case of Mike Lawrence, ***management*** is responsible both for coordinating and controlling activities of the various subsystems, and for setting the organization's strategic goals, design, structure, and policies. These functions provide for predictable and stable interactions within the organization. Second, smooth, trouble-free operation is the responsibility of the ***maintenance subsystem***. Activities in this subsystem include maintenance of the organization's human resources through personnel administration, maintenance of production facilities by people responsible for the cleaning and repair of equipment, and operation of support facilities, such as a legal department, clinics, information systems, and other functions necessary, but not central, to actual production of the desired outputs.

Countering the need for stability and predictability is the organization's need to respond to the changing demands of the external environment, the domain of the ***adaptation subsystem***. Departments such as research and development (R&D) and market research try to create innovations and help the firm adapt to change. In Chapter 6 we explore how organizations adapt to conditions in the external environment. Often, the organization itself needs to change to accommodate to changed conditions in the environment. These changes may include activities such as production innovations, changes in the technology of the transformation process, and changes in the organization's structure and design. Chapter 13 deals more extensively with the processes of innovation, organizational change, and learning.

■ TABLE 1.1
Subsystems and Functions

Subsystem	Function
Boundary Spanning	Input: Human Resources, Purchasing, Market Research, Investor Relations, Environmental Scanning. Output: Sales, Marketing/Advertising, Public Relations, Lobbying.
Production	Produce the goods and services that make up the organization's outputs. Examples include assembly line workers, sales staff (in a sales organization), and service providers.
Maintenance	Supports the organization by ensuring that all subsystems and physical facilities operate smoothly. Examples include plant operations, legal staff, custodians, human resource administration, and other support staff.
Adaptation	Accountable for helping the organization change to meet new opportunities and threats in environment. Includes research and development, engineering, market research, and other departments responsible for innovation and change.
Management	Responsible for ensuring that all other subsystems work smoothly together. Directs, controls, and coordinates actions of other subsystems. Sets organizational goals and strategy. Examples include top management team, department heads, and supervisors.

A STRATEGIC SYSTEMS APPROACH

The open systems model provides the first step in developing an organizing framework for this text—what we refer to as a *strategic systems approach.* The open systems model identifies or implies the existence of several key components of organizations. The next step is to systematically identify organizational dimensions. For example, the open systems model makes explicit the fact that organizations must interact with their external environment. But what other components of an organization's context or situation are critical? We must now begin to identify the set of features that scholars and managers must recognize if they are to understand the complex relationships that exist in operating organizations.

Managers select organizational structures to respond to specific conditions that the organization faces. These conditions are called the *organizational context* or *contingency factors* and include the organization's goals, environment, technology, size, and culture. Each of these contextual factors is discussed in subsequent chapters. The important point for now is that the essence of the strategic systems approach to organizations is that managers must attempt to maximize the fit between their choice of structure and the context that their organization faces.[8] Thus, Mike Lawrence at Thrifty, just like his counterparts at GM, IBM, and other organizations, tries to structure the organization to fit the various conditions it faces. Our task is to describe these different structural dimensions of the organization, the various contingency conditions or contextual factors, and how they all fit together. This is no easy task. Although the logic of strategically adapting the organization to its context is appealing, a variety of factors both internal and external to the organization make this task more difficult and complicated than we expect.

Our definition of an organization states that division of labor is a key factor in distinguishing organizations from random collections of people. Moreover, the open systems model identifies a number of key subsystems that are part of an organization. Implied in both the definition and the open systems model is the notion of *structure.* Organizational structure describes the internal relationships, division of labor, and means of coordinating activity within the organization. Structure includes such things as where decisions are made (degree of centralization), how labor is divided and departments are formed (differentiation), and the extent to which rules, policies, and procedures govern activities (formalization). One of the first things Mike Lawrence did when he took over Thrifty was to create a formal structure. Chapter 2 examines in detail organizational structure. We return to structure and the related topic of design in Chapter 8. For now it is sufficient to note that managers select or attempt to change organizational structure to fit their personal preferences and the conditions the organization faces.

It is critically important for managers to structure the organization so that internal activities are coordinated and controlled. But because organizations are open systems affected by the uncertainties, constraints, and resources available in the external environment, the structure must also be designed so that managers can control or adapt to these external conditions.

The conclusion of this approach is that the choice of an organization's structure should be **contingent,** or dependent, upon the context that the organization faces. Some contextual conditions require one type of structural response by the organization while other conditions require different structural responses. Thus, *there is no one best or most appropriate way for all organizations to structure and organize. The best-fitting structure depends on the context that the organization faces.* That is, it depends on the organization's environment, technology, goals or objectives, size, and culture. As a result, we would hardly expect Thrifty Hardware Company to have the same type of structure as General Motors, or even another retailer such as Kmart. Moreover, while not all ways of organizing and structuring are equally good, there may be more than one good way for an organization to structure or organize. This idea is referred to as *equifinality.* Thus, we will identify different types of structural configurations that work in specific situations and those that are not likely to work. More importantly, we will examine *why* those structures work or do not work. We will use *theory* to guide our study of these issues.

Definition

Contingency means that one thing depends on something else. The contingency approach states that there is no one best or most appropriate way for *all* organizations to structure and organize. The best-fitting structure depends on the context that the organization faces.

Thus, an open systems view of organizations emphasizes that organizations are open to influence and uncertainty in the environment in which they exist. Additionally, when determining how to best manage the organization, managers must consider other factors such as organizational size, technology, goals, and culture. The strategic systems approach to organization theory states that managers should consider these contextual factors when they determine the strategies for managing the firm.

The reader should be cautioned, however, that this strategic systems approach does not mean that managers will necessarily correctly survey conditions, perceive their context, and make the best decisions about organizational issues such as structure, design, and management. Other factors such as change, uncertainty, bounded rationality, faulty perceptions, and organizational politics may intervene and affect outcomes. In sum, we suggest that management decisions are likely to be better if guided by the strategic systems approach — but there is no guarantee.

Definition

The strategic systems approach to organization theory states that managers should consider contextual factors when they determine the strategies for managing the firm.

ORGANIZATION THEORY AND MANAGERIAL PRACTICE

You may still be asking yourself why we need theory to examine organizations. Theory is necessary to provide a *systematic* exploration of our topic. ***Theory*** can be defined as an explanation of some phenomenon, and it consists of principles that state relationships observed in association with that phenomenon.[9] Organization theory can be thought of as a set of related concepts, principles, and hypotheses about organizations that is used to explain components of organizations and how they relate to each other. The systems model previously presented is an example of a ***descriptive theory***.[10] It attempts to describe the nature of the relationship among the various subsystems of the organization and the environment. The goal of descriptive theory is simply to describe why and how something happens. Descriptive theory provides a means for better understanding the phenomenon of interest — in this case, organizations. Better understanding may, in turn, lead to better management. On the other hand, ***prescriptive*** or ***normative theory*** specifically suggests how things should be or what can be done about conditions identified by descriptive theory. Prescriptive theory informs managers about what they should do. The *should* in prescriptive theory is typically directed at improving various aspects of the organization: efficiency, competitiveness, profitability, adaptability, work satisfaction, or other aspects of general effectiveness. Although debate has raged about the relative merits of each approach, a general knowledge of both is necessary for us to understand organizations and how they work. We balance our approach to organization theory between descriptive and prescriptive theories. However, because this book is aimed at future managers in organizations, we concentrate on prescriptive or normative theories that suggest what managers *can* do.

A BRIEF HISTORY OF ORGANIZATION THEORY

In this section we briefly trace the development of organizational theory in order to appreciate the present state of knowledge of organizations. Although we stress organizational theory in this discussion, there is some overlap with the evolution of management study. Many concepts of organization are traceable to antiquity. There is mention of organizations and organizing in ancient China and Greece. There are even references to division of labor and delegation in the Old Testament. However, modern organizations and the systematic study of them really began with the Industrial Revolution.

DIVISION OF LABOR

As we noted earlier in this chapter, one of the earliest contributors to what is now know as organization theory was the economist Adam Smith (1723–1790), who demonstrated the greater efficiency that could be gained through division and specialization of labor. Through specialization and division of labor among ten people, a shop could produce as many as 48,000 pins per day.[11] This work laid the foundation for later organizational and industrial theorists such as Max Weber and Frederick Taylor who advocated narrowing the scope of workers' jobs so that specialization could be developed and efficiency enhanced.

WEBER AND THE RULES OF BUREAUCRACY

The German sociologist Max Weber (1864–1920) was arguably the most influential early contributor to the theory of organizations. His monumental work presented bureaucracy as the ideal form of organization. It was common in the 1800s for organizations to be simply extensions of families. Hiring and promotions were typically based on favoritism. Subjectivity took precedence over objectivity. As organizations grew larger during the Industrial Revolution, the inefficiencies of the typical organization of the day became apparent. The bureaucracy, proposed by Weber as a rational, efficient alternative, included the following characteristics:

- Division of labor was arranged so that each worker's authority and responsibility were clearly defined and were legitimate, official responsibilities.
- Positions or offices were organized in a hierarchy of authority that established a clear chain of command.
- Personnel were selected based on technical competence as established by examination, training, or education.
- Individual performance was guided by strict rules, discipline, and controls. These rules were impersonal and uniformly applied. A system of written documentation was used to record the rules and compliance with them.
- Administrative officials were not owners of the means of production. Equipment and privileges belonged to the position or office, not the person holding the position or office.
- Administrators were career officials and worked for a fixed salary.[12]

Although Weber's contributions to organization theory were immense, they went almost unnoticed in the United States until 1940. When the search for explanations of how large organizations work began in earnest, attention focused on Weber and his work.[13]

THE CLASSICAL SCHOOL

The organizational and management writers grouped under this common heading look at organizational issues from two different directions. Frederick W. Taylor focused on rationalizing jobs beginning at the lowest levels of the organization. Henri Fayol, on the other hand, focused on providing a rational model for top management of an organization. Their approaches have two things in common: (1) they proposed *one best way* to manage and (2) they attempted to develop *rational* techniques that would help in building the structure and processes necessary to coordinate action in an organization.

Today, readers of Taylor's ***Principles of Scientific Management*** may think of them as dehumanizing and exploitative of workers. That was not at all his intent. Taylor and his followers believed that the key to efficient management and positive labor relations was the scientific study of jobs performed by workers to discover wasteful steps. Furthermore, Taylor sought to simplify tasks so that workers could be easily trained to master their jobs. He believed that workers were primarily motivated by money and that, if they were narrowly specialized and had simple, narrowly defined jobs, they would be better able to pursue monetary reward. Taylor also believed that management could maximize its return on labor through his system of scientific management because of its emphasis on efficiency. Like Weber's emphasis on competence, Taylor advocated an objective system that rewarded productive labor.

At about the same time that Taylor and his followers were developing principles of scientific management, Henri Fayol was beginning his study of organizations in France. Unlike Taylor, Fayol concentrated his efforts on explaining the workings of the administrative levels of organizations. He maintained that it was possible to develop a set of universally applicable principles (i.e., one best way) that could be used to improve management practices.

According to Fayol, two management functions, ***coordination*** and ***specialization,*** are critically important.* Some disagreement exists about the exact number of principles that Fayol and his colleagues proposed as instruments for coordination and control. It is generally agreed that coordination is achieved through adherence to four of Fayol's principles. First, the ***scalar principle*** stated that coordination would be aided by a hierarchial distribution of authority in organization. Authority and control in an organization should be distributed in a pyramid-like structure. At each step up the organizational hierarchy managers would have greater authority to control activities below them. Second, the principle of ***unity of command*** stated that workers should only have to respond to one superior. Having to respond to more than one superior would be confusing and a potential source of conflict. Third, significant attention was focused on ***span of control,*** identifying the optimal number of subordinates that a supervisor could efficiently and

---

*This interpretation is based largely on Scott's (1992) writings on Fayol.

effectively supervise. Fourth, the ***exceptions principle*** stated that routine events or issues should be handled by lower-level employees. This would allow top administrators to deal with unusual problems or exceptions.

Specialization, the second management function, was achieved by virtue of how departments were formed and jobs were grouped. The ***departmentalization principle*** stated that similar tasks or functions should be grouped within the same department or unit. Fayol was also responsible for differentiating between ***line*** and ***staff functions***, another form of specialization. Line functions are those that contribute directly to the pursuit of primary organizational goals. Support activities (e.g., legal departments, information systems departments) are staff functions. According to Fayol, because staff functions are peripheral to the organization's primary goals, they should be subordinated within the organization's scalar authority structure.

Emphasis on a rational authority structure for organizations and attempts to devise a single best way to manage eventually led to the demise of the classical theorists. First, a number of researchers in what has been labeled the Human Relations School began examining the social or human aspects of organizations and shifted the focus from normative (what they thought organizations should be) to descriptive (what organizations really were like). They also began focusing on worker satisfaction, believing that the key to organizational effectiveness was a satisfied workforce. Second, contingency theorists, who viewed organizations as open systems, began to see that variations in the organizational context (i.e., variations in environment, size, and technology) would require variations in both structure and management practice.

THE HUMAN RELATIONS SCHOOL

The human relations approach to organizations explored the role of groups and social processes in organizations. Although several researchers have contributed to this perspective, perhaps the most notable works are the Hawthorne studies at Western Electric by Roethlisberger and Dickson[14] and works by Elton Mayo.[15] These studies questioned the rational, efficiency-oriented scientific management views of work. Rather, these researchers found that group interactions and social climate were also important to job performance. Other works of note in this school include Chester Barnard's book *The Functions of the Executive*[16] and Douglas McGregor's book *The Human Side of Enterprise.*[17] One point that these works emphasized was that the focus on efficiency may have been somewhat misdirected. In general, these works contested the idea that organizations were machine-like entities. They emphasized that organizations were composed of people who had roles and responsibilities beyond their work organizations. Moreover, within organizations, people had multiple and sometimes conflicting roles and objectives. While the classical theorist viewed organizations as well-oiled machines, the human relations theorist viewed organizations as shifting coalitions of people with multiple and divergent needs. According to the Human Relations School, there is more to organizational effectiveness, as we will see in Chapter 3, than efficiency.

Contemporary theorists who have adopted aspects of the Human Relations School emphasize such features as informal structure, power, and political behavior in organizations (Chapter 12), and organizational culture (Chapter 10). The human relations perspective augments our investigation of numerous issues throughout the text.

THE CONTINGENCY SCHOOL

As its name implies, the Contingency School maintains that relationships among organizational characteristics, especially the relationships between structure and size and technology and environment, are contingent or dependent upon the situation or context. Contingency theorists reject the one-best-way model of organizing proposed by earlier theorists. Thus, theorists and managers must understand the organization's context in order to prescribe the appropriate structure. The works of contingency theorists have a decidedly rational overtone and have resulted in extensive investigations of organizational technology (the work process), the external environment, goals, organizational size, and how these contextual factors are related to organizational structure. The basic premise of contingency theories is that different structural configurations are appropriate for different contextual conditions. As interpreted by managers, contingency theory suggests that they should attempt to assess the contextual conditions and select the appropriate structure and design for the organization. However, as we will see, the world of organizations is complex and uncertain. Selecting the appropriate structure and design may be much more difficult and problematic than contingency theorists indicate.

Although several contemporary approaches to organizational theory dispute many contingency theory propositions and the research support for their assertions is only modest, contingency theory has played a dominant role in organization theory in recent years. This perspective will guide much of our early discussion of environment, goals, technology, size, and structure. We will point out contradictions and differing perspectives throughout the chapters and use contingency theory as a jumping off point to explore alternative viewpoints of organizations.

CONTEMPORARY PERSPECTIVES

Recently, several new ways of viewing organizations have emerged. Some of these approaches have tried to deal with the shortcomings of contingency theory, while others take different views of organizations. Four of the more widely studied perspectives are organizational economics approaches, institutional theory, ecological perspectives, and holistic or cultural views of organizations.

ORGANIZATIONAL ECONOMICS

Two theories based in industrial and organizational economics are transaction cost economics[18] and agency theory.[19] Although subtle differences distinguish these two approaches, their central focus is similar. Both view organizations as bundles of transactions or contracts binding workers and owners together. According to agency theory, the primary interests of owners (called *principals*) and workers (called *agents*) are essentially different. Owners seek to maximize their return on investment by the most efficient use of the organization (including the workers). Agents, on the other hand, seek to minimize their efforts and maximize their remuneration. To protect their interests, principals will use various forms of contracts and organizing to ensure that agents carry out their jobs. Transaction cost economics explores transactions that take place both inside and outside the organization. These include transactions between owners and managers, managers and subordinates, suppliers and producers, and sellers and buyers. Both agency and transaction cost perspectives view the primary reason for organizing as being the reduction of uncertainty that exists in typical transactions. Agency and transaction cost theorists believe that it is human nature to act in a selfish and opportunistic fashion. Accordingly, the primary task of managers and owners of organizations is to create structure to ensure that others (e.g., employees, customers, or suppliers) do not act selfishly and opportunistically. We examine transaction and agency ideas at several points throughout the text.

INSTITUTIONAL THEORY

The perspectives presented up to this point have been infused with nearly machine-like, rational interpretations of organizations. Alternative views have emerged that treat organizations as complex groupings of sometimes conflicting rules, goals, and behaviors. Institutional theorists argue that social reality is constructed by organizational members. "The process by which actions are repeated and given meaning . . . is defined as institutionalization."[20] Institutional theory approaches to organizations emphasize the similarities among organizations. Rather than proceeding through a detailed rational assessment of a problem, organizational members bend to social pressures to conform to conventional or *institutionalized* beliefs. The result is that managers tend to imitate past practices and practices of other successful organizations.[21] We turn to the institutional perspective periodically to help explain certain seemingly nonrational actions of organizations.

CULTURAL PERSPECTIVES

The cultural perspective is, in many ways, an extension of the institutional perspective. Most other theories of organizations make many rational and simplifying assumptions about organizations. We assume that the formally structured organization that managers create *is* the organization. Additionally, many of those perspectives take a *reductionist* view of organizations. That is, they focus on only small portions of the organization at any given time. Contingency theorists largely direct attention to structure, environment, technology, and size. Organizational economics attends to transactions or contracts. Cultural approaches differ in that they are concerned with the whole organization and with informal aspects of the organization.[22] The culture is the result of organizational ideologies that produce peoples' norms, values, and beliefs. It is these norms, values, and beliefs that energize and direct peoples' actions within the organization and that provide a rationale for those actions. However, the cultural perspective differs from the institutional perspective in that it emphasizes how different and unique organizations are. We delve into the topic of culture in greater depth in Chapter 10.

ECOLOGICAL PERSPECTIVES

Up to this point, we have examined individual organizations. Two perspectives, community ecology[23] and population ecology,[24] look at groups of organizations. Community ecology approaches to organizations assume that groups of organizations can work together to control uncertainty in their environments. For example, groups of retailers or manufacturers can present a united front and influence government intervention through lobbying. Industry associations can reduce uncertainty by setting specific standards. In Chapter 5 we explore numerous other ways that organizations can attempt to control their environments through joint efforts.

Population ecologists suggest that these efforts to control environmental uncertainty may be either ineffective or deal with the wrong elements of the environment. This perspective simply states that organizations cannot, in general, determine all of the important environmental threats that need to be managed. Instead, it is the environment that selects which types of organizations will persist in the long run. Thus, population ecology focuses on organizational births and deaths. We explore this controversial view of organizations and environments in more detail in Chapter 5.

BOOK PLAN

The recurring theme throughout this text is that managers attempt to strategically manage and manipulate their organizations to be more efficient and effective. We explore the areas in which managers embark on these strategic initiatives and the limitations on their actions. The book is divided into four parts. Chapter 1 and Chapter 2 are the introductions to the organizational field, and they make up Part 1.

Part 2 describes the organizational context — those factors that organizations need to consider when decisions are to be made about how to structure and manage. Chapter 3 examines organizational goals, strategies, ethics, and assessment of effectiveness. Chapter 4 explores organizational environments with particular emphasis on global environments. Chapter 5 discusses ways in which organizations manage the environment. In Chapter 6 we investigate how organizational size, growth, and life cycles affect decisions about structure. Organizational technology is the subject of Chapter 7.

Part 3 shifts attention to how organizations use structure and design to manage their contexts. In Chapter 8 we study the basics of strategic organizational design, or how a firm assembles structural components into a design configuration. In Chapter 9 we explore a number of alternatives to formal structure and design.

Our focus shifts to organizational processes in Part 4 of the text. In particular, we examine organizational culture in Chapter 10. Chapter 11 explores the decision-making process. In Chapter 12 we review several related topics under the headings of power, authority, politics, and empowerment. As part of Chapter 12 we examine contemporary approaches to groups in organizations. In Chapter 13 we examine how organizations learn, adapt, and change over time.

Finally, we present five new, extended cases to help the student observe, analyze, and attempt to solve a number of complex organizational problems.

Questions for Discussion

1. How do you think a thorough knowledge of organization theory would help today's managers do a better job? Would this information be of most benefit to lower, middle, or top management? Why? What is the value to you of studying organization theory?
2. The subject of this book is organization *theory*. What do you think should be the relationship between theory and managerial practice (what managers do)?
3. Why is it useful to think of organizations as systems? What is the basic difference between an open systems and closed systems view of organizations? Why is it that organizations must be viewed as open systems?
4. Why is a sense of history important to the study of any field? How can understanding the historical development of organization theory help you better understand organizations and organization theory?
5. In this chapter we list five challenges to today's organizations. Select one of these challenges, and find an example of this challenge in the business press (i.e., *Fortune, Business Week, Forbes, The Wall Street Journal*, etc.). Explain how organization theory can help you better understand this issue.

CASE: FIVE RINGS FOR ATLANTA

Billy Payne, a little-known real estate attorney and former All-America defensive end for the University of Georgia in the late '60s, grew up in Atlanta. He always was a dreamer, so it was no surprise to find him dreaming the biggest dream of his life—to bring the Olympic Games to Atlanta. Starting with this dream in 1987, he began the difficult job of formulating a plan of organization that could be successful in the intense international competition for the coveted right to host the XXVI Olympiad in his hometown.

To make his dream a reality, Payne began to court members of the International Olympic Committee as well as to put together a 630-page bid package that covered every detail from the music to be played at the events to the types of flowers that would be part of dinner decorations. His training as a lawyer had prepared him well for his task, although missteps loomed.

The sentimental favorite to host the Summer Games in 1996 was Athens, Greece, but according to Payne: "... the growth of the Games and the complexity of organizing them have mitigated against a sentimental choice alone being the justification for awarding the Games."*

Armed with the United States Olympic Committee's support, Payne and his committee began their push to get the Games for Atlanta. The bid package contained mountains of information and hype for the city. Hartsfield International Airport is among the busiest in the world; Metropolitan Atlanta Rapid Transit Authority (MARTA) is a highly regarded urban rapid transit system; and the area's 50,000 hotel rooms were an important asset. Community spirit was also high. Promotional items, from the wacky

*From *The Sporting News* (November 27, 1989): 60.

mascot Whatizit to all manner of T-shirts and paraphernalia, sold well and showed broad-based, general support of a highly desirable effort.

Although the Atlanta infrastructure appeared to be in good shape to support the Olympics, Payne still had some formidable hurdles to cross. First, there was the matter of putting together an organization that would rival those of *Fortune* 500 companies, yet still be capable of being disassembled immediately after the two-week event.

To accomplish the herculean task of building an organization, Payne and his committee began assembling key players. A.D. Frazier Jr. was lured away from First Chicago Corporation to become the chief operating officer. Frazier would be no stranger to the Atlanta civic and political scenes, having been associated with Citizens and Southern National from 1969 to 1982. He also helped in staging the inauguration of President Jimmy Carter and reorganizing Carter's White House. Frazier was hailed as perfect for the job.

The broadcast of the Games is going to be a most complicated and potentially thorny issue. To address this key function, Manolo Romero, who headed broadcast operations for the Barcelona Games in 1992, was picked. His selection caps an experience that has seen him involved directly in TV coverage for every Olympics since the 1968 Games in Mexico City. He headed international operations for ABC at the Los Angeles Games.

In any Olympics, facilities are critical, and Atlanta would be no different. Where to house and feed athletes, journalists, broadcast crews, and officials and, above all, where to stage the events themselves were key issues to be resolved. Payne and his staff promised that Atlanta would be ready even though some of the sites were still in the conceptual stage. The Olympics would herald a major sports building boom in the Atlanta area, according to the committee.

Anticipated construction costs, about one-quarter of the committee's total budget, are expected to be around $250 million. Among the structures will be the Olympic Stadium ($145 million) that will be home to opening and closing ceremonies, track and field, soccer, and show jumping. Other events will be held at venues scattered around the metropolitan Atlanta area. The Olympic Village is projected to cost $5 million, and other sites and facilities will add $50 million to construction costs.

A proposal to reintroduce golf as an Olympic sport hit a snag when it was learned that the fabled Augusta National would be the site. The course, renowned as the site of the Masters tournament, is also known for its primarily white, aristocratic membership. Currently, the club has only one African-American member. The idea was abandoned because of fears of alienating the African-American community and others. To soothe ruffled feathers, Payne pledged to appoint a senior African-American administrator to the committee and to increase proposed spending at the Atlanta University Center.

How to pay for the enormous undertaking that the Olympics represent was a major challenge for Payne and his committee. The $1.4 billion price tag could be too big for the rings! The cornerstone of the finance plan is corporate sponsorships, proposed to be $40 million each. Initial optimism dimmed when many companies balked at the high price. Part of the problem was "ambush marketing," a practice followed by many companies that gives the impression of sponsorship. For example, American Express was not an official sponsor, but its heavy advertising linked to the Olympics gave many people the impression that it was an official sponsor. The committee has enlisted a team of law

firms to combat ambush marketing. Finally, five corporations, led by Nationsbank, did agree to buy into the Games.

The retirement of Atlanta's Mayor Maynard Jackson, a strong supporter of the Games, is also a setback. Jackson was a key link to a wide range of important constituents. Without Jackson in the mayor's office, the Olympic committee loses a highly visible spokesperson.

Payne's biggest challenge may be maintaining his health. An habitual workaholic, he is constantly in motion in spite of having had two coronary bypass operations in the past eleven years. Not known to rest, Payne even sleeps fast, getting by on a mere four hours per day. The high-speed, type-A Billy Payne does, indeed, face his own olympian quest — to make his biggest dream a success.

QUESTIONS FOR DISCUSSION

1. How could an understanding of organization theory help Payne and the committee better accomplish their task?
2. Relate the concept of an open systems approach to Payne and the committee's task.
3. Describe the tasks that each of the organizational subsystems (i.e., boundary spanning, management, production, maintenance, and adaptation) would perform for an organization like the Atlanta Olympic committee.

REFERENCES

1. Tom Peters, *Thriving on Chaos* (New York: Alfred A. Knopf, 1987).

2. Daniel Katz and Robert L. Kahn, *The Social Psychology of Organizations,* 2nd ed. (New York: John Wiley & Sons, 1978).

3. Adam Smith, *Selections From the Wealth of Nations,* ed. by George J. Stigler (New York: Appleton Century and Crofts, 1957).

4. W. Richard Scott, *Organizations: Rational, Natural, and Open Systems,* 3rd ed. (Englewood Cliffs, N.J.: Prentice Hall, 1992).

5. Oliver Williamson, "The Economics of Organizations: The Transaction Cost Approach," *American Journal of Sociology* 87 (1981): 548–77.

6. See note 2 above.

   See note 4 above.

7. J. Stacey Adams, "The Structure and Dynamics of Behavior in Organizational Boundary Roles," in *Handbook of Industrial and Organizational Psychology,* ed. by M. D. Dunnette (Chicago: Rand McNally, 1976), 1175–99.

8. Tom Burns and George M. Stalker, *The Management of Innovation* (London: Tavistock, 1961).

   Joan Woodward, *Management and Technology* (London: H.M.S.O., 1958).

Paul R. Lawrence and Jay W. Lorsch, *Organization and Environment: Managing Differentiation and Integration* (Boston: Graduate School of Business Administration, Harvard University, 1967).

Michael L. Tushman and David A. Nadler, "Information Processing as an Integrating Concept in Organizational Design," *Academy of Management Review* 3 (1978): 613–24.

9. H. M. Blaylock, *Theory Building* (Englewood Cliffs, N.J.: Prentice-Hall, 1971).

10. Arthur G. Bedeian and Raymond F. Zammuto, *Organizations: Theory and Design* (Chicago: The Dryden Press, 1991).

11. See note 3 above.

Adam Smith, *An Inquiry into the Nature and Causes of the Wealth of Nations,* vol. 39 of *Great Books of the Western World* (1776; reprint, Chicago: Encyclopedia Britannica, 1952).

See note 4 above.

12. A. M. Henderson and Talcott Parsons, eds. and trans., *Max Weber: The Theory of Social and Economic Organization* (New York: Free Press, 1947).

See note 4 above.

13. Daniel A. Wren, *The Evolution of Management Thought* (New York: Ronald Press, 1972), 230.

14. F. J. Roethelisberger and William J. Dickson, *Management and the Worker* (Cambridge, Mass.: Harvard University Press, 1939).

15. Elton Mayo, *The Social Problems of an Industrial Civilization* (Boston: Graduate School of Business Administration, Harvard University, 1945).

16. Chester Barnard, *The Functions of the Executive* (Cambridge, Mass.: Harvard University Press, 1958).

17. Douglas McGregor, *The Human Side of Enterprise* (New York: McGraw-Hill, 1960).

18. See note 5 above.

William Ouchi, "Markets, Bureaucracies and Clans," *Administrative Science Quarterly* 25 (1980): 129–41.

19. Eugene Fama, "Agency Problems and the Theory of the Firm," *The Journal of Political Economy* 88 (1980): 288–307.

20. See note 4 above.

21. Walter W. Powell and Paul DiMaggio, eds., *The New Institutionalism in Organizational Analysis* (Chicago: University of Chicago Press, 1991).

Lynne G. Zucker, *Institutional Patterns and Organizations: Culture and Environments* (Cambridge, Mass.: Ballinger, 1988).

22. Linda Smircich, "Concepts of Culture and Organizational Analysis," *Administrative Science Quarterly* 28 (1983): 339–58.

Harrison M. Trist and Janice M. Beyer, *The Cultures of Work Organizations* (Englewood Cliffs, N.J.: Prentice-Hall, 1993).

Joanne Martin, *Cultures in Organizations: Three Perspectives* (New York: Oxford University Press, 1992).

23. W. Graham Astley, "The Two Ecologies: Population and Community Perspectives on Organizational Evolution," *Administrative Science Quarterly* 30 (1985): 224–41.

W. Graham Astley and Andrew H. Van de Ven, "Central Perspectives and Debates in Organizational Theory," *Administrative Science Quarterly* 28 (1983): 245–73.

24. Howard E. Aldrich, *Organizations and Environments* (Englewood Cliffs, N.J.: Prentice-Hall, 1979).

Michael T. Hannan and John Freeman, "The Population Ecology of Organizations," *American Sociological Review* 82 (1977): 929–64.

Structure and Design — Basic Organizational Building Blocks

CASE: A LIMITED VIEW*

At one time, the Limited was a leader in fashion retailing. For a company that once had what appeared to be a limitless future, the Limited has recently seen a change in its fortunes. The trouble, perhaps, can be traced to founder Leslie Wexner's almost unbridled belief in entrepreneurship. Thus, the country's largest specialty store conglomerate's situation is a surprise to Wexner. Although there are many reasons for the Limited's difficulty, including a general sluggishness in the whole fashion industry, some of the problems can be traced to the company's structure.

Wexner believed that all of the Limited's division managers should operate their divisions virtually free of interference — their only guideline was to see how quickly they could get their respective divisions to the $1 billion mark in sales. But this simple guideline provided the platform for in-fighting among the divisions. Falling sales figures in all the divisions pointed out that they had lost sight of changing customer needs and habits. Wexner admits that his "hands-off" philosophy is largely to blame, and he admits that his penchant for decentralization and freedom for his managers resulted in too little support from the top. So, in order to reshape the organization, he instituted monthly meetings in which his division heads can share problems, solutions, and ideas in general. This was done in the hope that the once completely autonomous divisions could begin to build a general consensus and appreciation for the company as a whole.

Although this new approach has taken some getting use to, a concern now seems to be developing for a holistic approach to managing the entire company instead of each division head running his or her division somewhat in isolation. At the center of this attempt to broaden management's perspective is the return to

*This case is largely based on the following articles:
Susan Caminiti, "Can the Limited Fix Itself?" *Fortune* (October 17, 1994): 161–62, 166, 168, 170, and 172.
Laura Bird, "Limited Considers Splitting Operations into Two Publicly Traded Companies," *The Wall Street Journal* (March 29, 1995), A3.

defining clearly who the customer is and to building a total marketing approach suitable not only for the whole company but for each division. The Limited has, at the same time, introduced three new companies: Structure (a menswear chain); Limited Too (for girls); and Bath and Body Works (a toiletries and personal care products store).

Previous success dulled management's view of their customers and of what they looked for in a store. Customers, now older, more affluent, and perhaps more sophisticated, were turning to other outlets for quality and fashion. Even the look of the stores seemed out of date. This was especially the case with the Limited Stores division. The new president of this division, Cheryl Nido Turpin, is determined to redefine and resharpen the focus on its customers.

At the same time the chic sportswear division, Express, was also having its problems staying focused on its customers. Instead of its original emphasis on young fashion, Express turned its attention to designer clothes for older customers with similar disappointing results. Now Express has returned to young sporty merchandise, and Turpin's boss shares her enthusiasm and almost doubled the division budget.

Lerner New York, the Limited's division that had stressed low-price merchandise, is now offering pricier upscale items. The customers who were the mainstay of Lerner had turned to discounters, mail order houses, and TV to buy their goods. It is interesting to note recent changes at Lerner puts it in competition with J.C. Penney and Sears, as well as putting it head-to-head with fellow company member, the Limited. This effort by the Lerner division, however, has not been entirely successful, and as a result, it is closing about 100 of its 977 stores. Even with the cutbacks, Lerner is still the largest division of the Limited.

How has Leslie Wexner developed all this reorganization and redirection? He looked outside the retail field to see if he could transplant ideas from the industrial world into his writhing retail giant. He visited General Electric's Jack Welch and Pepsi's Wayne Galloway to find out how these proven leaders of giant nonretail organizations operate their organizations. Their ideas about decentralization might possibly fit (or be made to fit) the Limited's vast organization.

From these visits Wexner brought back the idea to put more structure into its finance meetings, for example. There is now a more or less standard way to present findings and to review results. This idea of working as a group in a structured way rather than as a loose collection of independent managers has taken hold in the Limited. The basic approach is to get managers to think brand wide instead of in terms of private labels. This approach, it is hoped, will give management a broader, more integrated way to manage.

Computer analyses have helped improve the methodology for marketing goods. These analyses center on the coordination of ordering, production, and sales efforts, a condition not previously possible. The rush to move managers around different divisions of the company (sort of robbing Peter to pay Paul) has slowed. That practice had resulted in management voids or talent gaps in divisions throughout the company.

Still the diversity of retail outlets, brands, products, and strategies may be too difficult to meld into one coherent company. The latest news from the Limited is that Wexner intends to break the company up into three autonomous companies: clothing and lingerie, bath and accessories, and everything else. Exactly how the company will be divided and how it will be managed are still unclear. Whatever happens, it is likely that the look of the Limited (and we are not just talking about clothing styles) is going to be very different in the future.

> This case points out some of the difficulties faced by a large and complex organization as it attempts to deal with changing customer demographics and a dynamic environment. It highlights the role of organization structure, differentiation, integration, and the necessity for adaptation, all concepts discussed in Chapter 2. Keep the Limited organization in mind as you read the chapter, and see if the contents of the chapter help you understand the importance of structure and design as basic organizational building blocks.

THE NATURE OF STRUCTURE AND DESIGN

As we stated in the first chapter, one of the first consequences of organizing is the need to divide labor and then coordinate among the diverse departments, work units, or groups that have been created. Some theorists suggest that structure results from choices about technology[1]; others suggest that structure is developed in reponse to environmental conditions that the organization faces[2]; and still others say that structure is the result of specific strategies (i.e., goals) that the organization seeks to pursue.[3] Whichever view one subscribes to, the first step is to understand the concept of structure and the elements of which it is composed.

The division of labor and subsequent coordination involves both the structure and design of the organization. Although these two terms—*structure* and *design*—are widely used in the organization theory literature, there is a lack of consistency and clarity in how they are used. When we speak of ***structure*** we are referring to the sum total of the ways in which an organization divides its labor into distinct tasks and then coordinates among them.[4] Some theorists also refer to structure as the arrangement of roles (i.e., jobs) within the organization. The arrangement of roles is consistent with the division of labor and coordination. The design of an organization can have two meanings because the word can be used as a noun describing the *appearance* of the organization or as a verb describing the *process* of setting up (i.e., designing) or changing (i.e., redesigning) the organization.[5] In this chapter our primary focus will be on the appearance of the organization. We return to design configurations once again in Chapter 8.

Definition

Structure refers to the sum total of the ways in which an organization divides its labor into distinct tasks and then coordinates among them.

STRUCTURE VERSUS DESIGN

The concepts of structure and design are closely related. Some confusion exists in the literature on the topic, and the terms are often used interchangeably. The definition of structure recognizes two key elements: *differentiation* and *integration.* Differentiation involves breaking up the work to be done into an array of tasks. Integration refers to the necessary coordination among these various tasks to ensure that the overall goals of the organization are achieved. The structure of the organization is usually depicted through the formal *organizational chart.* This chart displays the authority relationships (who reports to whom or the chain of command); formal communication channels; formal work groups, departments, or divisions; and formal lines of accountability.

Organization design, on the other hand, is a broader concept that includes structure but also includes other concepts. Design parameters include such things as unit grouping, unit size, planning and control systems, behavioral formalization (rules, policies, and procedures), and decision-making centralization-decentralization.[6] Thus, design is an umbrella concept that includes both process and structural issues. Think of structure as the skeleton. It is the framework upon which muscles, nerves, blood vessels, and other components are attached. These items make the structure come alive.

FORMAL VERSUS INFORMAL ORGANIZATION

In examining organization structure and design, we often speak of the *formal organization.* Organizations create an officially sanctioned structure known as the formal organization or *de jure* organization. This is the organization as it is depicted by a formal organizational chart such as that seen in Figure 2.1. The lines that connect each point on the chart show the authority or reporting relationships that exist in the organization. Typically, each point represents a position in the organization occupied by one person.

■ **FIGURE 2.1**

A Formal Organizational Chart

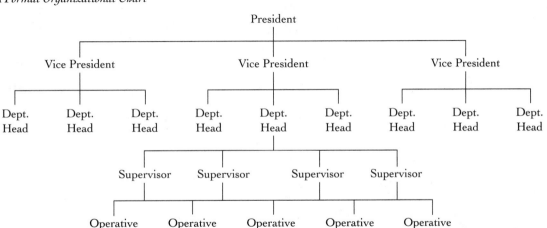

For the sake of economy, a point may be used to represent an entire unit or department. Also, not all subordinate positions in the organization are shown. In Figure 2.1, for example, each department head would have a similar complement of supervisors as those shown, and each supervisor would have a number of subordinates. Each horizontal level of points in the chart represents a level of authority in the organization. All of the department heads in this example would have essentially the same level of authority.

A formal organizational chart presents the official structure explicitly authorized by the organization. The official structure is made of the officially designated roles and relationships that exist independently of the individual person who occupies the role or the people who form relationships. This is only half of the story for superimposed on these relationships are ***informal*** or ***de facto relationships*** that are not necessarily sanctioned by the organization although they might be perceived to actually exist. (See Figure 2.2.) In the informal structure it is impossible to separate the roles and relationships from the people. Personal characteristics and patterns of social relationships that may not be captured in the formal structure are ever present and important to the informal structure.[7] The informal organization is a result of the political nature of organizations and evolves from the people working in the organization rather than from being officially established by the organization. This informal organization usually comes about, in part, because of flaws, vagueness, incompleteness, or inefficiencies in the formal design, or because of changes in conditions the organization faces. The focus in this chapter is on the formally established organization. In Chapter 12 we shift the focus to the political nature of organizations and examine the informal organization.

■ FIGURE 2.2
Some Aspects of the Informal Organization

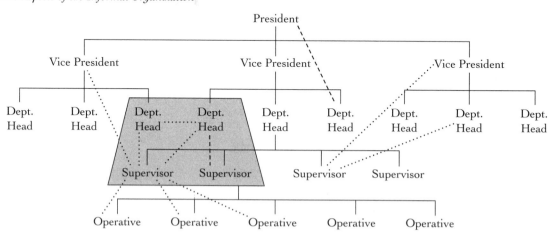

——————— Formal reporting relationship
- - - - - - Informal reporting relationship
············· Informal communication channel
◢◣ Informal group

DIFFERENTIATION AND INTEGRATION: KEY ELEMENTS OF STRUCTURE

As noted in Chapter 1 the very reason for the existence of organizations is that they can perform tasks more effectively and efficiently than individuals working alone. All organizations must split up their work into units called *tasks.* This division of labor into tasks is called *differentiation.* In most organizations today it is physically impossible and economically infeasible for one individual to do all of the tasks. To carry out its mission more efficiently, an organization will divide its work into many tasks and allocate those tasks among workers. In this way workers can specialize in their more narrowly and specifically designated task. For example, a large corporation like General Motors has differentiated tasks so that assembly people build cars; clerical workers do typing and filing; managers manage; lawyers write contracts and represent the company in legal proceedings; and top management sets the strategic direction for the firm. Within each of these groupings, tasks are further differentiated. At an assembly facility, some workers may be responsible for only narrow portions of the assembly process, for example, attaching wheels, wiring engines, or painting the cars. In fact, one of the key issues facing many organizations, including automakers, is how much tasks should be differentiated.

Just as organizations split up work, they must also coordinate this work. This coordination is called *integration.** Basically, integration involves the various means that organizations use to pull together the highly differentiated tasks into cohesive output.

As we will see in subsequent sections, differentiation and integration are key elements of organizational structure. The degree of differentiation and the methods of integration provide great insight into the structure of an organization.

NATURE AND PROCESS OF DIFFERENTIATION

Three basic types of differentiation occur in organizations. Organizations can be subdivided horizontally into an increasing number of distinct positions at the same level, vertically into increasing levels of hierarchy, and spatially by increasing numbers of distinct locations dispersed in space.[8] Although we did not use the term *differentiation* in the discussion of bureaucracies in Chapter 1, the narrowly defined tasks and narrowly defined

---

*Sometimes the same or similar terms in the organizational literature are used to express more than one idea. Integration is one such term. In the present context, the term is used to describe methods or structures used to coordinate tasks. Integration, particularly vertical, horizontal, backward, and forward, is also used to describe a firm's entry into different parts of the value-added chain of resource acquisition, production, distribution, and sales. For example, an automobile manufacturer that enters the steel fabrication business in order to supply its manufacturing facilities is involved in backward integration. A developer and distributor of shoes, such as Nike, that enters the retail business is said to be involved in forward integration. Finally, a manufacturer that adds more products to its line is involved in horizontal integration, also known as diversification. For example, Johnson & Johnson's acquisition of Neutrogena diversifies Johnson & Johnson into new areas of soap and beauty products. When discussing this type of integration, we will always use the terms backward, forward, or horizontal integration, or diversification. We take up these strategies in detail in Chapter 5.

areas of decision-making responsibility that are key components of bureaucratic organizations are prime examples of horizontal and vertical differentiation.

Horizontal differentiation refers to the division of work to be done into tasks and subtasks at the same organizational level. Horizontal differentiation is represented by the number of different individuals or units at the same level of an organization. One group of researchers refers to horizontal differentiation as the degree of occupational specialization, the specific professional activity, and the professional training required for specific tasks.[9] Thus, with increasing task specialization, increasingly specific professional credentials or certification, and increasingly focused training, we will see increasingly high levels of horizontal differentiation. In fact, some authors have used the term *specialization* instead of horizontal differentiation to describe this dimension of structure.[10] Figure 2.3 illustrates horizontal differentiation.

FIGURE 2.3
Horizontal Differentiation

Low Horizonal Complexity

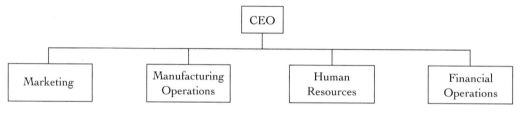

High Horizonal Complexity

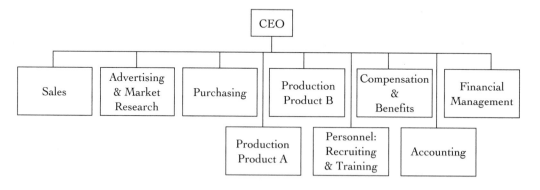

A modern hospital provides an excellent example of an organization that incorporates each of these aspects of horizontal differentiation. Among doctors and medical support personnel there exists a high degree of specialization: cardiologists, gastroenterologists, orthopedists, X-ray technicians, critical care nurses, lab technicians, and so on. Each of these task areas is specifically described and each is distinct from the other. Each area requires specific training, and each requires certification and credentials for the individual practitioner.

The horizontal division often represents a strategic decision on the part of the organization. For example, the division of a college into separate departments may be done to provide the college with greater specialized expertise or greater flexibility. Some colleges of business may divide the task of educating students into the following highly differentiated departments: management, operations management, accounting, finance, marketing, information systems, and quantitative analysis. Management faculty would only teach management courses; accounting faculty would only teach accounting; and so forth. Each department would be narrowly specialized, which should lead to high levels of specific expertise in the narrow field. Another college may decide to divide the task more broadly into the following set of departments: organizational and operations management, accounting and financial systems, and marketing. In the more broadly defined departmental arrangement, faculty would teach a broad range of courses. For example, in the combined accounting and financial systems department, a given faculty member may teach both financial accounting and finance courses. The broader task groupings may involve less specific expertise in a narrowly defined field, but such groupings would allow the departments to be more flexible and responsive to changing conditions. A sudden increase in demand for accounting courses could be met by shifting personnel from teaching finance to teaching accounting.

In the past decade the trend has been toward *less* specialization or horizontal differentiation. The term that reflects this is *broadbanding*. This refers to collapsing a large number of distinct tasks into a smaller number of positions. Each position or job involves a broad range of tasks and requires a broad range of skills. For example, a computer manufacturer may have used many discrete jobs to build computers. Each individual worker may have been responsible for only one or a few tasks in the process of building the computer. With broadbanding, individuals are trained to carry out many tasks so that one individual or a small team could be responsible for the entire task of building the computer. This gives the organization much more flexibility in assigning work. However, it has the potential disadvantage of having employees who are jacks of all trades, and masters of none.

Vertical differentiation[11] refers to the division of work by level of authority, hierarchy, or chain of command.[11] This is often referred to as the *scalar process*.[12] Here work is divided on the basis of the authority each unit or person has over each other unit or person in the organization. Vertical differentiation is represented by the number of different levels in an organization. Figure 2.4 on page 38 shows levels of vertical differentiation.

Like many other large corporations, the Union Pacific Railroad Corporation was extremely vertically differentiated. Before its 1988 reorganization, Union Pacific had nine layers of management just in its Operations Department. Each higher level had more authority. However, numerous problems can develop with extreme vertical differentiation: communication through the levels of hierarchy is slow; decision making bogs down; and top management may be detached from day-to-day events lower in the organization. Because of these problems, CEO Michael Walsh reorganized the Operations Department by reducing the number of layers from nine to five.[13] This has been a common tactic of large organizations as they downsize and remove layers of management to cut cost. This results in a *flattened* organization—fewer levels of management, with each level having more people.

▇ FIGURE 2.4
Vertical Differentiation

Low Vertical Complexity (Flat)

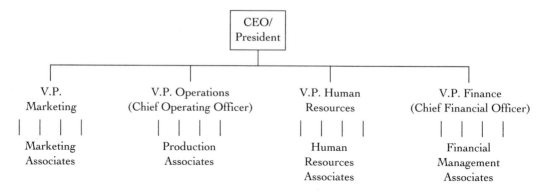

High Vertical Complexity (Tall)

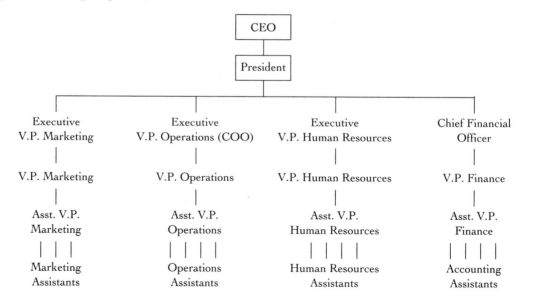

Spatial differentiation or *dispersion* can be both horizontal and vertical. This aspect of differentiation involves the geographical location of different organizational activities. This is typically the case with multinational companies that have operations in several different countries. An automobile manufacturer may have an engine-building facility in one locale and final vehicle assembly facility in another. For example, many component parts for the Honda cars manufactured in Marysville, Ohio, are made at Honda facilities in Japan. A grocery store chain may have distribution facilities throughout the country. Finally, a computer manufacturer may have its assembly operation in a separate facility from its administrative offices. Each of these is an example of spatial dispersion or differentiation. Figure 2.5 shows a spatially dispersed organization.

■ **FIGURE 2.5**
Spatial Differentiation or Dispersion

Low Spatial Complexity

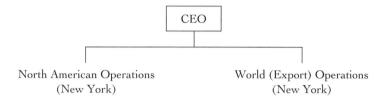

High Spatial Complexity

Exhibit 2.1   **Managing the Mobile Office**[14]

With the advent of powerful and inexpensive notebook computers, cellular phones, fax machines, beepers, and an array of electronic and telecommunications devices, the traditional corporate office is becoming a vague memory in many leading corporations. In some cases decisions to set up home and mobile offices were motivated by such natural disasters as the Los Angeles earthquake and Hurricane Andrew. Companies needed quick, on-the-spot responses to emergency situations. Temporary mobile offices met the challenge. However, many firms like AT&T, IBM, and Compaq Computers are turning to home and mobile offices as a way to conduct day-to-day business more efficiently.

A typical worker stationed in a home-based mobile office might be a sales or service representative. The employee would travel to customers or clients and log in sales or service calls on a laptop computer. When the employee returns home each day, he or she would transmit information back to the home office. In some cases, employees may receive parts or merchandise and store them in their home office for future delivery to customers. Some companies claim that mobile offices increase by 15 to 20 percent the amount of time employees spend with customers or clients. Home-based mobile offices also reduce commuting time, an advantage both to employees and employers.

Coordinating the activities of mobile office employees can be a bit of a trick. Some mobile employees return to branch offices or headquarters on a periodic basis for meetings and training. Most coordination takes place over the various telecommunications mechanisms and lacks a personal touch. However, some mobile employees feel disenfranchised because they no longer have an office in the organization. In many organizations, the size and location of an office is still seen as an important perk and symbol of power.

The home-based mobile office is not without problems. Some employers (and employees) worry about overwork. When the office is in your home, it is sometimes difficult to know when to stop working. One Compaq vice president has had to tell some home-based employees to cut back on their hours. A service representative for Perkin-Elmer, a scientific equipment company, balked at storing parts in his home office. He thought he should be compensated for the cost of space devoted to storage (approximately $120 per month), but the company disagreed.

The trend toward home-based mobile employees is bound to grow as new and better computer and communications technology break down the office barriers. The new freedom and flexibility offered by mobile technologies, however, will require new integrating skills for managers who coordinate mobile workers.

The *level of complexity* of an organization is largely determined by the amount of horizontal, vertical, and spatial differentiation that exists.[15] Complexity is often related to organizational size, but it need not be. Large organizations are often more vertically and horizontally differentiated than small ones. As we will see shortly, the trend in many organizations is to reduce both vertical and horizontal complexity. Conversely, some small organizations may be very complex. For example, a medical clinic may have narrowly specialized tasks and a clearly and steeply differentiated hierarchy. The point is that size is often associated with complexity, but this is not always the case.

CURRENT TRENDS IN DIFFERENTIATION

A source of debate among both organizational scholars and managers has been the question of how narrowly should tasks be differentiated. Early in the history of organizational studies, Weber's bureaucratic model and Frederick W. Taylor's system of Scientific Management suggested that tasks should be highly differentiated—broken down into their least common denominator. Weber believed that narrowly defined tasks and responsibilities would lead to an organization that operated with machine-like precision. Taylor believed that narrow, simplified tasks would be easy to master. Workers, even those who were poorly educated or not particularly bright, could become expert in narrow, simplified tasks. Highly differentiated tasks had the added benefit that when workers were poor performers or unreliable they could be easily replaced because the tasks were easily learned. Weber's principles of bureaucracy and Taylor's system of Scientific Management were driving forces in the industrialization of North America and western Europe in the first half of the twentieth century. Many leading manufacturing firms designed horizontally narrow, specialized tasks. Similarly, these same organizations created multilevel structures with steep vertical hierarchies.

Recently, managers and theorists alike have questioned the value of high degrees of differentiation. Theorists, researchers, and practitioners suggest that, in many situations, narrow, simple tasks are demotivating and not necessarily as efficient as once believed. In addition, high levels of complexity may result in employees who lack a vision of the overall organizational goals and purpose. We explore the issue of goals in greater detail in Chapter 3. For example, it is difficult for a person in a large organization doing a highly specialized task to identify with the overall organizational goals. This is typical of the situation that exists in traditional automobile assembly plants.

As a result, many organizations are broadening tasks so that they include operations that were formerly divided among several workers — broadbanding, as discussed previously. For example, when General Motors created its Saturn Division, the plant was designed with many fewer job titles than typical GM plants. Each worker does the work formerly divided across many different tasks in a typical GM plant. This trend has been replicated at many Ford and Chrysler facilities, too.

Similarly, many organizations are delayering their hierarchies (pushing decision making down and broadening employee responsibilities) in much the same way as Union Pacific. Many reasons are given for this movement away from highly vertically and horizontally differentiated organizations. While these broader tasks require more training, judgment, skill, and education than narrow, simple tasks, they are easier to integrate. As we will see shortly, they provide greater flexibility in responding to changing conditions.[16] Reducing complexity also facilitates communication.

In addition to the tedium and inefficiencies that sometimes result with high differentiation, many organizations find that highly differentiated tasks are often difficult to coordinate. That is, the more that work is subdivided horizontally, vertically, or spatially, the more the organization must adopt techniques or structural mechanisms to coordinate those activities. We now turn our attention to integration, the structural mechanisms for coordinating.

THE ROLE OF INTEGRATION

At the same time an organization differentiates itself, it must also integrate the activities, tasks, and sets of tasks performed throughout the organization into a coordinated whole. This coordination is the prime responsibility of people in managerial positions. The very functions of management — decision making and influence — imply coordinating and integrating activities in the organization. In addition to the management functions that integrate the differentiated parts of the organization, integration can be achieved through four broad categories of integrating structures. Keep in mind that it is management that creates or changes the organizational structure by designating levels of both differentiation and integration. Table 2.1 summarizes these integrating structures.

■   **TABLE 2.1**
Integrating Structures

Integrating Structure	Characteristics
Formalization	Rules, policies, and procedures
Centralization	Locus of decision making
Spans of Control	Number of subordinates supervised
Standardization:	Setting standards to guide processes,
Process, Input, and Output	acquisition of inputs, or desired outputs

FORMALIZATION

One method for ensuring that individuals and departments performing highly differentiated tasks coordinate their activities is through the creation of formal rules, policies, and procedures. These formal rules, policies, and procedures are referred to as ***formalization.*** Organizations typically create elaborate employee manuals, job descriptions, and other written documents to guide employee behavior. The greater the reliance on these written documents, the higher the level of formalization.

Inherent in the use of formalization to integrate tasks are a number of assumptions about people.[17] The organization that relies heavily on formalization is assuming that employees may lack the information, knowledge, skills, judgment, or self-control necessary to coordinate diverse sets of tasks in the organization. On the other hand, when management assumes that employees are informed, knowledgeable, skilled, and possess good judgment and self-control, management is likely to forgo formalization. Rather, management assumes that employees will do the right thing without the necessity of formal rules, policies, or procedures.

Spatial dispersion also affects the use of formalization. When all of an organization's operations are located under one roof, management can rely on face-to-face interactions and informal relationships to enforce expected ways of behaving. When operations are dispersed among several locations, then rules, policies, and procedures are necessary to ensure coordination.

Formalization often presents an interesting conundrum to managers. Some managers think that the way to integrate highly uncertain tasks is through rules, policies, and procedures. At first glance this may seem to be a logical thing to do—write rules, policies, and procedures to guide employees through uncertain situations. This will create certainty and predictability. However, once a manager begins this task, he or she will soon see the paradox. The more uncertain the task, the more rules, policies, and procedures are required to cover anticipated situations. But the very nature of uncertainty means that management cannot anticipate all possible situations or conditions. Thus, formalization typically is not the answer to uncertainty. Instead, managers try to rely on other means of integration for highly uncertain situations.

CENTRALIZATION: THE DECISION-MAKING LOCUS

Organizations can integrate activities through the decision-making process. Of particular importance here is the place in the organizational hierarchy where decisions are made. Decision making can be either *centralized,* with decision-making authority vested in top management, or *decentralized,* with decision-making authority vested in lower-level employees. In a highly centralized organization the president may believe that she or he needs to be involved in nearly every decision of any consequence. The president or other top managers may believe that they are the only ones with the vision and skills necessary to make decisions. For example, the president of American Home Products, the large pharmaceutical and food products company (maker of Anacin, Chapstik, and Robitussin), approves spending decisions involving as little as $1,500.[18] By contrast, many organizations today are granting authority to lower-level employees to spend money, change designs or procedures, and bend rules to meet customer demands. This is called *empowerment* and is becoming a common practice in organizations.

Much like low levels of formalization, managers in decentralized organizations are assuming that lower-level employees have the information, knowledge, skills, and good judgment to solve problems as they encounter them. In may cases, particularly in organizations involved in highly specialized and technical fields, lower-level employees have more knowledge about products, processes, and problems than do top managers. Additionally, decentralized decision making may be quicker and can reduce the burden on top management. This allows the organization to be more responsive to changing conditions and may allow management to reduce the number of top managers necessary to run the organization. This is often a key part of downsizing as organizations eliminate home office staff positions and levels of management, transferring decision-making authority down to lower levels through the delegation process.

On the other hand, centralized decision making is typically necessary when a broader organizational perspective is necessary. Lower-level employees in highly differentiated organizations may lack awareness of the more general organizational goals and may instead focus on the more localized concerns of their department or division. Under these conditions centralized decision making may be necessary. Moreover, centralized decision making can ensure consistency in the organization's actions. When decision making is decentralized, one department may treat employees, tasks, or customers in a different manner from another department. Centralization can provide consistency in treatment, but it is usually a time-consuming process to push decisions up the hierarchy.

The degree of decision-making centralization is sometimes confused with vertical differentiation. Although it is common to find decentralized decision making in flat organizations and centralized decision making in tall organizations, that does not necessarily have to be the case. Weber's ideal bureaucratic organization would be characterized by both vertical complexity and decentralized decision making. The rationale for this organizational configuration was that at each level employees should be competent to make decisions appropriate to their level (thus, no need to push routine decisions up the hierarchy). At the same time, the domain of responsibility at each level of the hierarchy was narrowly defined, necessitating a high degree of vertical complexity.

SPAN OF CONTROL

Another way to approach the issue of integration is through the *span of control.* The span of control refers to the number of immediate subordinate positions that a superior position controls or coordinates. A manager who supervises seven subordinates has a span of control of seven, which would be narrow compared to a manager who supervises twenty subordinates. The job of the manager in the supervisory position is to integrate the activities and tasks of those in immediate subordinate positions. For example, the head teller in a branch bank would supervise all the tellers and coordinate their work. The head teller may be responsible for scheduling, ensuring that each teller's cash drawer balances at the end of the day, directing tellers to relevant rules and policies, and other tasks that ensure a smooth, coordinated operation.

Much of the early management literature discussed the ideal number of subordinates a manager should supervise. The old rule of thumb was that the ideal number of subordinates for a supervisor was five to seven. Supervising fewer than five subordinates was thought to be an inefficient use of supervisors. On the other hand, it would be difficult to coordinate the activities and monitor the actions of more than seven subordinates.

This thinking on spans of control, however, has been replaced by a different approach to determining the appropriate ratio of supervisors to subordinates. No rule-of-thumb number is specified as appropriate for all managers and all situations. Rather, the approach taken now holds that the appropriate span of control depends on a number of factors. These factors include the following:

- the ability and expertise of the manager in the integrating and controlling position;
- the ability and expertise of subordinates;
- the nature of the task being performed by subordinates (i.e., routineness of tasks and interrelatedness among subordinates of tasks performed);
- the spatial differentiation (i.e., geographical dispersion) of those in supervisory and subordinate positions; and
- the amount and type of interaction required by the supervisor position with higher-level positions.

In general, the more competent the manager and subordinates, the less geographically dispersed managers and subordinates, and the less interrelated and more routine the tasks of the subordinate, the wider the span of control can be. Additionally, the less often the manager has to interact with his or her superiors and others in the organization, especially over routine matters, the greater the span can be. However, even this line of thinking is being challenged in many organizations today. For example, one line of research shows that highly professional subordinates (e.g., engineers, scientists, and accountants) require narrow spans of control because of their needs for frequent interactions with supervisors and for quick decisions.[19] Other trends toward greater delegation of responsibilities, professionalizing work forces, and self-managing groups have motivated organizations to adopt broader spans of control. For example, a medium-sized electronics manufacturer in Florida recently doubled its average span of control from seven to fourteen as a result of a restructuring. Two levels of supervision were eliminated.

Flat versus Tall Organizations. Another way of thinking about spans of control is the ***flatness*** or ***tallness*** of an organization. Earlier, Figure 2.4 contrasted flat and tall organizations. Organizations with broad spans of control tend to have few levels of hierarchy (less vertically complex) and are regarded as flat. Organizations with narrow spans of control tend to have more levels of hierarchy (more vertically complex) and are taller.

STANDARDIZATION

Integration can be achieved through process, input, and output ***standardization.*** Table 2.2 summarizes and describes each of these. Each type of standardization attempts to reduce the uncertainty and unpredictability of organizational work.

TABLE 2.2
Methods of Standardization

Method of Standardization	Example
Process	Guidelines or instructions on how to produce output: Pizza Hut's instructions on how to make each type of pizza.
Inputs:	
Raw Materials	McDonald's specifications on the type of ground beef to be used in hamburgers.
Human Resources	Specification of the type of training, certification, or degree required by job applicants: X-ray technicians must be trained and certified.
Outputs	Inspection of finished product to ensure that it meets specifications: Auto companies visually inspect finished products for flaws in fit and finish.

One commonly used form of standardization is to standardize the task or ***process*** that workers perform. For example, fast-food restaurants clearly define the process that is to be used when making a burger or pizza, waiting on customers, or cleaning restrooms. Process standardization guarantees that tasks will be performed in the same way all the time. Fast-food restaurants build their reputations on the consistency and predictability of their products. Process standardization is part of the reason for that consistency. Process standardization aids in integration by clearly outlining each task and how each task relates to other tasks. At a fast-food restaurant, standardization creates consistency in how counter workers greet customers and enter orders, how grill workers fry the burgers and deliver them to counter workers, and how the counter worker delivers the order to the waiting customer. Standardization facilitates these interactions by making interactions uniform and by removing unnecessary interactions. The same type of standardization can smooth interactions on an assembly line or in an accounting firm.

Inputs can also be standardized to aid in task integration. Input standardization is an attempt to reduce uncertainty and unpredictability of tasks by standardizing the raw material and labor inputs. The raw materials or labor can be narrowly prescribed to reduce the potential variability in the work to be done. For example, many fast-food restaurants deal with only one set of suppliers of raw materials (e.g., meat, hamburger buns, or cheese). This reduces the amount that subordinates and supervisors need to interact. Each batch of raw materials should be indistinguishable from past shipments. Thus, workers need not take any special actions or exercise any discretion in the handling of these raw materials. In fact, many fast-food chains go to great lengths to contract with specific suppliers to ensure consistency of raw material inputs. Subordinates face fewer questions or issues about these raw materials. This was a key factor for McDonald's when it opened its first restaurant in Moscow. Obtaining potatoes and beef that met McDonald's standards was difficult initially. McDonald's eventually taught farmers to grow potatoes and raise beef that met its standards.

The organization could also standardize its personnel inputs, either through training within the organization or through careful selection of educated, trained, and/or certified employees. Many organizations put employees through rigorous training when they take on new jobs. Both McDonald's and Disney operate their own "universities" for training employees in standard ways of interacting with customers or carrying out tasks. Some organizations rely instead on some outside agent to train employees and require that employees for specific jobs have a specific degree (e.g., an MBA or an engineering degree) or certification (e.g., a certified public accountant, registered nurse, or X-ray technician). Many investment banking and consulting firms in the northeastern United States will only hire graduates of specific Ivy League MBA programs. Both on-the-job training and training outside the organization help ensure that employees have the necessary information and skills to perform their jobs. This reduces the burden on supervisors to integrate.

A final method of standardization is to standardize outputs. The organization may determine that all outputs should meet the same specifications. Products or services are not customized (or the degree of customization is very limited). Output standardization is typically achieved through inspection. One common way of standardizing output is through a Total Quality Management (TQM) program that empowers employees and work teams to be responsible for verifying product and service quality. Many major corporations and even nonbusiness organizations now have some sort of quality enhancement program aimed at developing and maintaining specific quality levels — standards.

NONSTRUCTURAL MEANS FOR INTEGRATION

A number of other mechanisms can be used to provide integration in organizations. Although these are not, strictly speaking, structure, they are still important. The integrating positions of liaison roles, teams, information systems, and culture are briefly described below. We return to these subjects for more comprehensive treatment later in the text.

Liaison Roles. Organizations can create ***liaison roles*** or ***horizontal linking positions*** that link two units or departments at the same level of the organization. This is done when coordination and communication are necessary between two units. For example, an organization may create horizontally specialized departments to handle production and shipping. However, it may be necessary to coordinate between these two departments so that each knows the other's capacity, capabilities, schedules, and other constraints. Each department would create a liaison role. The persons filling those positions would be responsible for integrating between the two departments. Without the coordination and communication provided by a liaison role, each department would conduct itself without concern for the other. Production may produce more goods than shipping can effectively ship, or production may not schedule in such a way so as to make best use of the shipping department's capabilities. Thus, the liaison role can mediate potential conflicts and smooth interactions between groups.

Teams. Another way organizations are integrating work activities is by adopting a ***team-based*** form of organization. Employees and managers are organized into work and interunit teams in order to enhance communication, coordination, and control. Many organizations that have adopted TQM also adopt a team-based structure. The primary advantage of this approach is that it forces employees to think and act as a unit rather than as a set of individuals. They share information and a sense of collective responsibility for the work. Each person sees how his or her individual efforts affect those of the other team members.

As we have indicated elsewhere in this book, the Saturn unit of General Motors uses team-based management extensively to design and build the Saturn. This is completely different from the way American auto companies traditionally have operated. Usually highly specialized units do their own thing, and their work is integrated at the top of the various divisions. Of course, this takes much time as information is passed up and down the chain of command. Borrowing from the Japanese automakers, GM decided to use teams in order to shorten the time to design the car and to achieve better coordination where the work is done in building the car. GM views the team-based concept as a huge success at the Saturn operation and is adopting it in its other divisions and plants.

Culture. Culture plays an extensive role in nearly every aspect of organizational life, and Chapter 10 discusses this subject in more depth. Organization culture is composed of the informal and unwritten values, norms, and behavior patterns that are commonly accepted and observed by members of an organization. Organizations can have ***thick*** or ***thin*** cultures. Organizations with thick cultures, such as IBM, strongly enforce a detailed culture through numerous informal sanctions. Thin culture organizations have hard-to-identify, loose cultures that are not strongly enforced. Thick cultures are a means to achieve integration because people buy into a common set of shared values and operate from a common frame of reference. Things are done a certain way, not necessarily because of a rule or policy, but simply because "that's the way we do things around here." Other behaviors are avoided because "we simply do not do those things around here."

Information Systems. Finally, organizations can achieve integration through the way in which they structure their ***information system.*** This is the method they use to gather, process, analyze, and report the information necessary to operate the organization. It includes information on customers, operations, employees, and accounting information. Who has access to this information and how it is used are key parts of the system. By structuring an information system that is comprehensive, user friendly, and automated, much information can be quickly provided to people throughout the organization on a timely basis. E-mail networks, video, conference calling, and local area networks are all examples of information systems that can significantly aid the organization to achieve integrations.

PUTTING IT ALL TOGETHER: MECHANISTIC AND ORGANIC ORGANIZATIONS

Thus far we have described attributes of organizational structure. These attributes tend to group together in coherent and systematic ways. It is not an accident that flat organizations tend to be characterized by low levels of vertical and horizontal complexity, by low levels of formalization, and by decentralized decision making. By contrast, it is also no accident that tall organizations tend to be characterized by high levels of vertical and horizontal complexity, by high levels of formalization, and by centralized decision making. These arrangements are logical and consistent. This, of course, does not prevent some organizations from developing structures that are illogical and inconsistent. The result, however, is likely to be an inefficient and ineffective organization.

Two prototypical organizational types have emerged: the ***mechanistic organization*** and the ***organic organization.***[20] (The mechanistic organization is much the same as Weber's bureaucracy and is sometimes referred to as a machine bureaucracy.) These two prototypes represent extremes, and it is important to note that many organizations occupy the midrange on these structural attributes. Table 2.3 summarizes the collective attributes of these two types.

TABLE 2.3
Mechanistic and Organic Organizations

Structural Characteristic	Mechanistic	Organic
Complexity	High vertical and horizontal complexity	Low vertical and horizontal complexity
Formalization	High formalization	Low formalization
Centralization	High centralization	High decentralization
Spans of Control	Narrow spans of control	Broad spans of control
Standardization	High standardization	Low standardization

The contingency framework presented in the first chapter is based in part on the idea that these two extremes of organizational types, mechanistic and organic, are best suited for different organizational conditions. We identified five contextual factors— organizational goals, environments, technology, size, and culture—that must be considered in determining the most appropriate structural arrangement. In the following chapters we describe these contextual factors and discuss the appropriate structural responses. The reader must keep a few things in mind, however. First, the mechanistic and organic organization are prototypes or ideals. Organizations vary from these extremes. Second, some organizations do not adopt the appropriate structural attributes for their context. As a result, they *may* be inefficient and ineffective. Third, in some situations there are nonstructural means for managing the context. Thus, an organization that appears to have an inappropriate structure for its context may still be efficient and effective because it has adopted other means for coping with the context.

SUMMARY

Organizations are not random collections of people. All organizations need structure to divide labor and then to coordinate the action of the work being done. Structure provides a systematic way of dividing labor (differentiation) and coordination (integration). Structure provides reporting relationships, formal communication channels, determination of task responsibility, and delegation of decision-making authority.

We are concerned with the issue of structure because appropriate structure is required for effective organizational operations. Structure should facilitate effective performance. Characteristics of appropriate structure include clear lines of authority and accountability, effective differentiation and integration, and well-developed and clear communication channels.

The reader must keep in mind three caveats at this point. First, as the contingency framework suggests, there is not one best way to structure an organization. The most appropriate structure for an organization depends on its context (goals, environment, technology, size, and culture). We explore the relationships between structure and context in the chapters that follow. Second, we have presented the *formal* structure of the organization—that structure that management has defined and that may be recorded in organizational charts. As we stated at the outset of this chapter, the formal structure is but one side of the organization. There exists simultaneously with the formal structure an informal organization with reporting lines, communication channels, authority, power, and responsibilities that may be very different from the formal. We explore the informal organization when we investigate power and the political nature of organizations. Third, structure (and design) does not just happen. People in organizations make decisions and select specific structural arrangements. The structure (and design) of an organization is an important strategic decision. One need only look at the extensive restructuring that is going on in many organizations to understand the important strategic role that structure plays.

This chapter has reviewed the important concepts involved with structure without actually indicating how these concepts fit together into specific design configurations. How, for example, shall we decide which tasks to group together into departments or divisions? In Chapter 8 we return to structure and describe various design configurations.

Questions for Discussion

1. What is the basic difference between structure and design?
2. Basically, what is shown on an organization chart?

3. What is the informal organization, and how is it related to the formal organization? Is it possible for there to be a formal organization without an accompanying informal organization? Explain.
4. Why is differentiation necessary to build a formal organization structure?
5. What is integration, and how can it be achieved in a large organization?
6. Is spatial differentiation limited to large organizations? Explain.
7. How is the concept of span of control related to both integration and differentiation?
8. Distinguish between a mechanistic and an organic structure. When would you suggest that each be used? Can they be used together in the same organization? Explain.

CASE: SHOOT THE MOON*

General Motors thought that it was, indeed, shooting the moon when it established its Saturn Division. This move, costing some $500 million, was a major thrust by GM to give Saturn a distinctive image apart from the stoic one that the car-buying public had of the parent company. The move came at a time when the American car-making industry was facing fierce competition from abroad, especially from Japan.

Saturn has been a big hit with its buyers, but it has been a costly venture. Some $5 billion, made up of both start-up costs and operating losses, have been poured into the project. These results have been enough for GM to rethink its decision to set up the Saturn Division as a quasi-independent member of the company. It simply doesn't appear economically feasible for Saturn to add the assembly plants that are now needed to expand its product line.

In a move to curb losses and yet continue to promote the Saturn line, GM has decided to fold Saturn into its small-car group, organizationally. This decision is aimed at allowing Saturn to share both engineering and manufacturing costs with the parent company as well as to share economies of scale with other members of the newly established small-car group that includes the Chevrolet Cavalier and Pontiac Sunfire.

Saturn will remain, essentially, a separate unit of the small-car group with its own labor agreement, organization structure, and marketing strategy, which is built around a strong emphasis on customer service, no-haggle pricing, and a stress on innovation.

Basically, then, GM is attempting to reabsorb Saturn into the GM organization while preserving the uniqueness of the division. Instead of its previous degree of independence, however, Saturn will begin to share in a more integrated effort by GM to tie Saturn to the parent company in a product sense — identifying Saturn with the GM line organizationally while, at the same time, retaining Saturn's marketing strategy that has

*This case is based on the following articles:
Gabrilla Stern, "GM Puts Saturn in Small-Car Group, Shakes up North American Operation," *The Wall Street Journal* (October 5, 1994), A4.
Mike McKesson, "GM Reorganizes Units, Brings Saturn into Small-Car Group," *The Tallahassee Democrat* (October 5, 1994), 10D.
Bruce Horovitz, "Saturn Hopes Folksy Image Isn't Lost in Shuffle," *USA Today* (October 6, 1994), 1B.

produced valuable customer satisfaction with the product. As an indication of GM's intention in this regard, Saturn's president, Richard LeFauve, will head the expanded small-car division known as the Lansing Automotive Division.

The Saturn move is a part of GM's larger effort to reorganize its entire North American unit. The company is also melding its luxury car divisions in order to reduce the number of chassis required for both divisions. It is also felt that this move will avoid the design problems experienced in the midsize car products in recent years. Even though these two divisions are to be closely tied together organizationally, they will be run separately.

Thus, it appears that GM is reversing a previous decision to decentralize by moving control of operations into a smaller number of divisions in the name of efficiency and faster product introduction.

So, after a massive effort to distance itself from GM, Saturn is being "brought into the family" by GM. This is a move intended to achieve the best of both worlds—organizational control, economies of scale, and sharing of engineering and technology while preserving Saturn's niche in the small-car market.

The question of whether this organizational move will sully the Saturn image remains. Officials insist that it is possible to reap the benefits of the parent company, GM, while still pursuing the marketing strategy that has made Saturn the popular car it is today. Independence and the benefits of bigness are the anticipated outcomes of the GM reorganization efforts.

Only time will tell if these efforts will bring soaring success or bring GM back "down to earth."

QUESTIONS FOR DISCUSSION

1. How would you suggest that GM go about coordinating the Saturn Division with the rest of the small-car division? Would different techniques be needed to tie the small-car division to the parent company? Explain.
2. What do you see as the major problem(s) to be solved by this reorganization? What major problem(s) do you think it will create or aggravate?
3. What organizational factors suggest that Saturn will continue to be independent?
4. Will the spatial differentiation patterns in GM be disturbed by this move? Explain.
5. Suggest some integrating structures for the new move.
6. Would you expect the entire GM organization structure to be flatter or taller after this reorganization? Explain.
7. Is this move more toward a mechanistic or an organic structure? Explain.

REFERENCES

1. T. Burns and G. M. Stalker, *The Management of Innovation* (London: Tavistock Publications, 1961), 1.

2. P. R. Lawrence and J. Lorsch, "Differentiation and Integration in Complex Organizations," *Administrative Science Quarterly* 12 (1967): 1–47.

3. Alfred D. Chandler, Jr., *Strategy and Structure: Chapters in the History of the American Industrial Enterprise* (Cambridge, Mass.: M.I.T. Press, 1962).

4. Henry Mintzberg, *The Structuring of Organizations* (Englewood Cliffs, N.J.: Prentice-Hall, 1979), 2.

   Richard H. Hall, *Organizations: Structures, Processes, and Outcomes* (Englewood Cliffs, N.J.: Prentice-Hall, 1991).

5. Ibid., 65.

6. Ibid., 66–67.

7. W. Richard Scott, *Organizations: Rational, Natural, and Open Systems*, 3rd ed. (Englewood Cliffs, N.J.: Prentice-Hall, 1992), 18.

8. See Hall in note 4 above.

9. Jerald Hage and Michael Aiken, "Relationships of Centralization to Other Structural Properties," *Administrative Science Quarterly* 12 (1967): 72–91.

10. R. L. Daft, *Organization Theory and Design*, 4th ed. (St. Paul, Minn.: West, 1992).

11. See Hall in note 4 above.

12. Keith Davis and John W. Newstrom, *Human Behavior at Work*, 7th ed. (New York: McGraw-Hill, 1985).

13. Daniel McHalba, "Building Steam: Union Pacific Changes its Hidebound Ways Under New Chairman," *The Wall Street Journal* (January 18, 1989), A10.

14. Sue Shellenbarger, "Overwork, Low Morale Vex the Mobile Office," *The Wall Street Journal* (August 17, 1994), B1–B7.

15. See Hall in note 4 above.

16. Bill Hendrick, "Saturn Plant Hits Bumps," *Atlanta Journal/Constitution* (January 10, 1993).

    Neal Templin, "A Decisive Response to Crisis Brought Ford Enhanced Productivity," *The Wall Street Journal* (December 15, 1992), A1–A8.

    David Woodruff and Elizabeth Lesly, "Surge at Chrysler," *Business Week* (November 9, 1992): 89–96.

17. See Hall in note 4 above.

18. Elyse Tanouye and Greg Steinmetz, "Takeover Would Ease, Not End, American Home Products' Bind," *The Wall Street Journal* (August 5, 1994), A1–A10.

19. Marshal Meyer, "Expertness and the Span of Control," *American Sociological Review* 33 (1968): 944–51.

20. See Hall in note 4 above.

    See note 1 above.

PART TWO

The Context of Organizations

C hapter 1 introduced the basic concept of an organization—a group of people working together cooperatively within identifiable boundaries to accomplish a common
goal. The open systems approach to organizations further refined this definition by
establishing that organizations must interact with their environment. The contingency
framework is built on this notion of an open system. According to contingency theory,
there is not one best way to organize. Rather, there are many ways to organize, and some
are better than others. But what is "better" and under what circumstances?

Chapter 2 elaborated on the structure of organizations. That discussion provided
the foundation for understanding the building blocks of organizations. By introducing
differentiation, integration, and other aspects of structure, the reader could begin to
understand how organizations differ. Not all organizations look the same. In Part 2 we
focus on the organization's *context*—the set of circumstances that an organization faces.
By looking at the context, we begin to investigate *why* organizations adopt different
structures and how they attempt to create a better fit with their context. Understanding
the context in which an organization exists is key to understanding why there is not one
best way to organize. The best way to organize depends on the nature of the context an
organization faces.

Recall that one basic part of the definition of an organization is that it is goal oriented. In Chapter 3 we examine the related subjects of goals, objectives, and strategies.
The line of business and the manner in which an organization pursues that business are
important contextual or contingency factors that shape the requirements for organizing.
As a natural extension of our discussion of goals, we move on to issues of organizational
effectiveness. It may seem that effectiveness is a straightforward issue, but, as you will
learn, this is not the case.

The second contextual factor to be explored is the environment—the critical element in the open systems framework. Chapter 4 describes eight sectors of the environment and three general characteristics that are useful in characterizing environmental
conditions. All organizations, even those in the same industry, face different environmental conditions. It is these different conditions that organizations must recognize and
manage.

Chapter 5 is a slight departure from the examination of contextual factors. This
chapter addresses how organizations learn about, respond to, and change the environment. Some of these responses to the environment are structural and fit with our contingency framework. However, there are also many other nonstructural mechanisms for
managing the environment. These are also covered in Chapter 5.

Technology, as used in organization theory, refers to the knowledge, information,
tools, and skills necessary to complete tasks. Chapter 6 presents three different ways of
thinking about and analyzing technology in organizations. Technologies vary from one
organization to another, and the different technologies any one organization uses also

vary from department to department. These different technologies place different demands on organizations and require different ways of organizing.

Chapter 7 discusses two related contextual factors: organizational size and organizational life cycles. It may seem obvious that the ways to organize and manage small organizations differ from those that work best for large organizations. But what exactly is size? And why do large organizations require different methods of organizing? We have also been discussing organizations as if they were unchanging, static entities. You only need to pick up a copy of *The Wall Street Journal* or one of the major business periodicals to see that organizations undergo many changes. Some are planned — mergers, acquisitions, growth, divestitures, leader succession, and so on. Some are unplanned — hostile takeovers, bankruptcies, declines. All these changes require that the methods of managing and organizing also change. Our focus in Chapter 7 is the ongoing dynamic nature of organization. Later, in Chapter 13, we take up the subject of planned organizational change.

One contextual factor remains for later discussion — organizational culture. Because culture is an integrating, holistic element of organizations that includes factors such as structure and design, we save that discussion for Chapter 10.

Keep in mind as you read these five chapters that each of these factors — goals, environment, technology, size, and life cycle — places demands on the organization to be managed and organized in specific ways. That is key to the contingency framework.

CHAPTER 3

Organizational Goals and Effectiveness

CASE: MORE THAN JUST ICE CREAM

Over the last several years numerous articles in the popular and business press have profiled Ben & Jerry's Homemade, Inc., the superpremium ice cream producer in Waterbury, Vermont. Some have focused on its rapid rise from the obscurity of a "scoop shop" selling ice cream cones in Burlington, Vermont, in 1978 to nearly $132 million in sales of packaged superpremium ice cream in 1992. Others have explored its off-beat culture and unusual notion of "linked prosperity." The company promotes policies that enhance the general welfare of employees, suppliers, and community members. The company has been extensively involved (both directly and through the Ben & Jerry's Foundation) in community outreach, environmental education, and global peace programs. In addition to the typical accounting and financial performance information, Ben & Jerry's annual report includes a social audit to assess the company's social performance.

Still others have examined the problems, conflicts, and constraints that Ben & Jerry's has encountered during its rise to prominence. It has faced competitive challenges from the Pillsbury/Grand Metropolitan unit, Haagen Dazs, that used some rather questionable tactics to keep Ben & Jerry's ice cream out of retailers' freezers. The company has faced self-imposed constraints because of its compensation policy of limiting pay for top-level officers to no more than seven times the level of the lowest paid employee. Prior to 1990 the pay ratio was even more constrained at a ratio of five to one. These constraints on top management pay made it difficult when the company attempted to hire a new chief financial officer (CFO) with skills necessary to manage a $100 million company. CFO starting salaries in companies of similar size usually exceed even the more generous seven-to-one ratio now offered by Ben & Jerry's.

Finally, the intense pressures of a competitive executive labor market and the expanded needs of a growing company forced Ben & Jerry's to further modify its restrictive compensation policy.[1] The company's decision to use only Vermont dairy suppliers meeting the high quality standards may constrain growth. Currently, all Ben & Jerry's ice cream products are made in Vermont. Moreover, while shareholders have realized nice growth in their investments in the company over the past five years (low of 13¼ in the first quarter 1988 to a high of 33 in the third quarter of 1992), some may wonder what its performance would be if Ben & Jerry's did not donate 7½ percent of pretax income to charities and social action.[2]

Where do these policies come from, one might reasonably ask. In part, these actions come from an unusual **mission statement** that guides Ben & Jerry's. That mission is really a set of three related missions.

Ben & Jerry's Statement of Mission*

Ben & Jerry's is dedicated to the creation and demonstration of a new corporate concept of linked prosperity. Our mission consists of three interrelated parts:

PRODUCT MISSION: To make, distribute and sell the finest quality all-natural ice cream and related products in a wide variety of innovative flavors made from Vermont dairy products.

SOCIAL MISSION: To operate the company in a way that actively recognizes the central role that business plays in the structure of society by initiating innovative ways to improve the quality of life of a broad community: local, national, and international.

ECONOMIC MISSION: To operate the company on a sound financial basis of profitable growth, increasing value for our shareholders and creating career opportunities and financial rewards for our employees.

Underlying the mission of Ben & Jerry's is the determination to seek new and creative ways of addressing all three parts, while holding a deep respect for individuals, inside and outside the company, and for the communities of which they are a part.

Part of the uniqueness of the Ben & Jerry's organization is the result of this unusual mission statement. While meeting any one of these three broadly stated objectives could be a tall order for a young growing company like Ben & Jerry's, maximizing all three of them might be nearly impossible. Meeting social goals may negatively affect financial performance. Overemphasis on new product development and market expansion may also adversely affect financial performance. And concentrating on financial performance might jeopardize social goals and some aspects of product goals. This illustrates that, although goals are necessary to guide an organization, it is difficult for virtually any company to create a set of goals that is comprehensive, yet not inherently contradictory.

As we see in this short description of Ben & Jerry's, the company wrote a mission statement that is intended to guide the company's overall direction. It is absolutely essential for any organization to have a strong sense of its overall direction if all of its members and various stakeholder groups (i.e., groups with interests in the organization) are to know what is required and what to expect. Moreover, the mission statement establishes the legitimacy of that direction.

This chapter takes a look at the role that goals play in everyday organizational life. The material clearly shows the vital nature and place of goals and their relationship to the effective management of organizations.

---

*From Ben & Jerry's 1992 Annual Report.

ORGANIZATIONAL GOALS AND EFFECTIVENESS

A key part of our definition of an organization stated in Chapter 1 was that organizations have goals*, that they are purposeful collections of people who join together to achieve these goals. In this chapter we explore what that means. Goals are statements that identify an endpoint or condition that an organization wishes to achieve. On the surface, the idea that organizations have goals and that the members pursue those goals may seem obvious and straightforward. That, however, is not the case. As we dig below the surface and rhetoric of typical organizational goals, we begin to see problems. Organizations have many goals—some that are clear, some that are ambiguous, and some that contradict other goals. Moreover, many groups of people, both inside and outside the organization, have goals for an organization that may or may not be consistent with the official goals of the organization. Thus, even the seemingly simple idea that organizations have goals is, as we will see, deceptively complex.[3]

We begin by stating a general definition of goals, and then we examine different classes of goals or objectives in typical organizations. We next turn our attention to the process of managing goals in organizations, including setting goals, managing conflicting goals, and assessing goal attainment. Goal attainment provides us with a bridge to the second theme of this chapter—organizational effectiveness.

Like goals, organizational effectiveness is a complex and multifaceted issue. The problems that lie in answering the question of whether an organization is effective become apparent when we explore the concept of effectiveness. To a great extent, the answer to this question depends on *who* is asking the question and for *what purpose.* Thus, we present several models of organizational effectiveness that may be useful for different purposes in assessing organizational effectiveness.

GOALS AND THEIR ATTAINMENT

An organization takes on an identity of its own as a result of its specific set of goals. Even companies in the same line of business look and act differently partly because their goals differ. In general, an organization's goals or objectives serve three main purposes: (1) they establish the desired future state that the organization is trying to realize, thus setting *guidelines* for members of the organization to follow; (2) they provide a rationale for the organization's existence, what organizational theorists refer to as *legitimacy;* and (3) they provide a set of *standards* against which the organization's performance can be measured.[4]

---

*In this book, goals, purposes, and objectives are used interchangeably.

Definition

Organizational Goals: Statements that establish the desired future state an organization is attempting to achieve.

These three purposes of goals can be applied to three levels of the organization (summarized in Table 3.1). First, at the broadest and most general level, the level of the organization as a whole, overall goals are stated in *official goals* or *mission statements*. These are broad, general statements about future conditions and guiding principles, such as those of Ben & Jerry's in the introductory case. Official goals or mission statements are often so broad that they can do little more than set a general tone for the organization, but that tone may be critically important to establishing a culture. *Operative goals,* derived from official goals, are more specific statements about what the organization, division, department, or business unit intends to do. Finally, *operational goals* are the most specific and narrowly stated goals of the organization. Operational goals, contained in documents such as job descriptions, state what specific individuals in the organization should be doing. Because our level of analysis is the organization, we focus on these first two levels of goals — official goals, or mission statements, and operative goals.

TABLE 3.1
Classification of Goals

Type of Goal	Focus	Serves	Example
Official Goals, or Mission Statement	Establish broad strategy	Set guiding principles	Introduce new products; enter new markets
Operative Goals	Specific actions to enact strategy	Guide divisions, departments, or business units	Develop specific product; identify specific market to enter and take actions to realize that goal
Operational Goals	Individual jobs or tasks	Guide individuals' behaviors	Job descriptions

We must also examine a variety of other factors related to goals. These include:

- *the beneficiaries of the organization;*
- *the relevant time frame for specific goals;* and
- *the relative importance of specific goals.*

PRIMARY AND SECONDARY BENEFICIARIES

Organizations have a multitude of *stakeholders* — that is, groups of people affected by the success or failure of the organization. These groups can be divided into *primary benefi-*

ciaries and *secondary beneficiaries*. The primary beneficiaries are those people the organization serves. For Ben & Jerry's, the primary beneficiaries are the ice cream–
buying customers who purchase Ben & Jerry's products. Thus, an important part of Ben
& Jerry's mission is to produce high quality, innovative ice cream products that appeal
to its customers. Without satisfied customers or clients, a business cannot exist for long.

In addition to the primary beneficiary group, all organizations must attempt to satisfy a secondary group. This group potentially gains satisfaction through association
with the organization. For Ben & Jerry's this group includes employees, owners, retailers, suppliers, members of the local community, and many other groups. This leads us to
an important problem faced by organizations. *Because organizations have multiple stakeholders (i.e., groups with interest in the success or failure of the organization), they will necessarily have
multiple goals, some of which* may *be in conflict with one another.*[5] This has important implications for many aspects of organizations, including the assessing of effectiveness.

Exhibit 3.1

Conflicting Goals and Stakeholders at Ben & Jerry's

Earlier, we noted that two parts of Ben & Jerry's mission statement stated social
mission goals and economic goals. A specific operative goal that supports the social
mission was something called the five-to-one rule (increased to seven to one in
1990). To help spread wealth to a large segment of workers, Ben & Jerry's management instituted a rule whereby no employee could earn more than five times (or
seven times after 1990) the salary of the lowest-paid employee. If a clerical or
warehouse employee were the lowest-paid employee and earned $15,000 dollars,
the highest-paid employee could earn no more than $75,000. The objective was to
foster a sense of salary equity, particularly among low-level employees, and to
spread wealth among a wider community through contributions to community service programs.

However, the five-to-one salary rule made it difficult for Ben & Jerry's to
hire a new chief financial officer (CFO) when the incumbent left that position in
the late 1980s. At that time in the northeastern United States, typical CFOs with
even modest experience could command salaries well in excess of $75,000. Top
managers and the investors were concerned because a CFO was crucial to guiding
Ben & Jerry's through a period of rapid growth.

Clearly the social mission and associated operative goals conflicted with
those of the financial mission and the operative goals of hiring a new CFO. This
conflict was partially responsible for the shift to a seven-to-one ratio. It may be
helpful in sorting out these conflicting goals to identify the potential beneficiaries,
the relevant time frame, and the relative importance of each.

SHORT- AND LONG-TERM GOALS

Placing time dimensions on goals is also critical. Not all objectives are amenable to immediate satisfaction; some will take significantly longer to achieve than others. In fact, one
method for dealing with complex, potentially competing goals is to sequence them with

specific time frames. We can look at the various types of goals of an organization and establish some sort of time boundary for them.

Short-term goals[6] are those that the organization hopes to accomplish within a year or other specific accounting cycle. Companies may, for example, seek annual increases in sales, profits, new business, or productivity. For example, when Jack Smith took over in early 1993 as chief executive officer (CEO) at General Motors, he was confronted with monumental problems. One of the first things he had to do was establish which goals could be accomplished in the short term and which goals would have to be deferred.

A major problem at General Motors was its shrinking market share due in part to significantly higher production costs than competitors. Smith set and accomplished in 1993 several short-term goals that helped drive down costs. He was able to cut corporate staff from 13,500 to 2,500; centralize purchasing and reduce the cost of materials by $4 billion; cut 16,500 hourly workers through early retirements; eliminate models; freeze executive salaries and cut some perks; and sell noncore businesses.[7] Even with these extensive changes, GM still has a long way to go to regain its former stature in the automobile industry. A look at long-term goals indicates how much still remains to be done.

Long-term goals[8] are those that cannot be accomplished within the short run. These goals may be for periods of more than one year or one accounting cycle, but may be as long as ten or twenty years, although rapid changes in environments may make it difficult or unwise to plan beyond a three-to five-year period. Whatever the length of the defined time period, long-term goals provide the overall direction for an organization beyond a single year or accounting period.

Jack Smith faced many goals at General Motors that could not be attained in the short-term time frame. Streamlining and restructuring GM's stifling bureaucracy is a daunting task that will take significant time and effort to accomplish. Similarly, streamlining manufacturing to bring costs closer to those of competitors and reducing new product development time are necessary goals that will take additional time.[9] All of these goals are important to GM's competitiveness in the increasingly tough automotive market, but they are goals that will take considerable time to achieve.

GOALS AT THE HIGHEST LEVEL: THE ORGANIZATION'S MISSION

All organizations, whether they are businesses, not-for-profit organizations, or sociopolitical entities, have officially chartered purposes. ***Mission statements, official goals,*** or, as they are sometimes called, ***strategic objectives*** set forth those purposes. A statement is generally broad and general, but it states the direction the organization is taking and, often, the philosophy of the organization. For example, General Electric, under CEO Jack Welsh, has stated that the company should be number one or number two in everything it does. If GE cannot achieve a number one or number two ranking, it will abandon those lines of business. Mission statements typically identify the product or service, market niche, production methods, and financial objectives of the organization. Welsh's goal of being number one or two motivated GE to sell its small appliance business to Black and Decker in the early 1980s. Other organizations, typically those in high technology or changing markets, use mission statements as the basis for setting specific goals for new product or service innovations. Some organizations, like Ben & Jerry's in the introductory case, include other classes of goals that go beyond the business of the organization to include objectives such as employee development and general social responsibility.

The two sample firms in Table 3.2 illustrate the diversity of mission statements in two very different industries. These statements are important to establishing the general, long-term direction of these firms.

■ TABLE 3.2
Sample Mission Statements

Utility Company	Mutual Insurance Company*
Houston Industries	**The Principal Financial Group**
The mission of Houston Industries Incorporated is to maximize shareholder value and satisfy its customers' needs, while providing its employees a rewarding and productive work environment and conducting its affairs responsibly in the community. Houston Industries will accomplish this mission by creating a corporate vision of successful growth, by carefully managing its assets and by integrating its businesses through effective planning and allocation of resources.†	The Principal Financial Group is a diversified family of companies offering a wide range of insurance and other financial products and services for businesses, groups and individuals. For 114 years, stability and performance in a changing world have meant security and protection for millions of people. Helping people meet their financial needs is our goal . . . . Over time, *gradual change* and improvement produce *dramatic results*. The Principal provides *stability by balancing* financial risk with a sound investment policy. Our *philosophy of mutuality* means we operate on *behalf of customers*.‡

A mutual company operates on a different set of principles than a typical for-profit business. Mutual insurance companies are forms of cooperatives that are owned by the customers. Rather than trying to create wealth by amassing profits, these firms have as their primary goal benefit to customers through reduced costs of goods or services. Other examples of cooperative organizations include State Farm Insurance, Sunkist Oranges, and Recreational Equipment Incorporated (REI).
†Houston Industries Incorporated Annual Report, 1992.
‡The Principal Financial Group Annual Report, 1992.

Clearly an electric power generating utility and an insurance and financial services company are very different. To some extent, those differences are expressed in the different goal statements of Houston Industries and The Principal Financial Group. In addition to differences in business type, these mission statements, like that of Ben & Jerry's, express elements of a basic philosophy of the firm. At the top of Houston Industries' statement is its goal to "maximize shareholder value" while meeting customer needs and providing rewarding careers for employees. The Principal Financial Group emphasizes stability, gradual change, and mutuality. In the absence of a profit motive (mutual companies are *not* in business to maximize shareholder value), the focus is placed on satisfying customers (who are also owners). As the introductory case showed, Ben & Jerry's attempted to simultaneously meet three goals: product, social, and financial.

GOALS FOR ACTION: OPERATIVE GOALS

Operative goals are typically stated in terms of measurable outcomes. These goals cover all of the organization's subsystems described in Chapter 1. Different schemes have been developed for categorizing types or areas of operative goals.[10] Common to all of these is that they set standards and guide what people in the organization should be doing on a day-to-day basis. We use, with some modifications, Peter Drucker's eight key goal areas to delineate the scope of operative goals.[11]

Market Goals. Organizations may set goals to increase market share or to enter new markets. These goals may indicate new products to be developed or modifications to existing products. Such goals can serve as guidelines for product development, production, acquisitions, or divestitures, among others. Goals for increased market share may include guidelines for advertising and promotion of products, pricing, packaging, and other actions aimed at getting further market penetration. Goals for new product niches may guide research and development or acquisitions.

Financial Performance Goals. Typical businesses are guided by specific objectives for profitability, cash flow, stock market performance, and other indicators of the organization's financial soundness. Businesses may set goals of increasing profits or operating revenues of a specific amount. Investors and analysts pay particular attention to the degree to which businesses achieve these goals. Top executive compensation and, increasingly, lower-level employee salaries and bonuses are often directly tied to a firm's financial performance.

Resource Goals. As noted in Chapter 1, because organizations are open systems, they are dependent on the external environment for important resources. They must obtain resources from outside, and resource goals state objectives for obtaining external financial, physical, and human resources. Businesses must attract financial resources from investors or financial institutions. Even nonprofit organizations are not immune to the task of obtaining financial resources. In nonprofit organizations a great deal of attention is typically directed to lobbying, fund-raising and revenue-generating activities. Public television or radio stations, for example, continually ask viewers or listeners to contribute to fund-raising drives. Managers of public universities and other state agencies lobby state legislators in an effort to enhance their organization's share of revenues. In addition, business and nonbusiness organizations must obtain other resources from the environment. These include the raw materials needed to create outputs as well as the equipment and facilities necessary for the transformation process.

Innovation Goals. Another consequence of adopting an open systems view of organizations is the recognition that the environment is constantly changing. To meet those changing environmental demands, organizations must also change. Innovation goals may be objectives for changing virtually anything, including the products and services sold, the processes used to create those outputs, the people in the organization, and the organization itself. Clearly, innovation is critical to success in such high tech industries as computer hardware, software, electronics, and telecommunications.[12] However, organizations in settings as diverse as retailing, automobile manufacturing, education, health care, and consumer products adhere to the belief that they must innovate in order to survive.[13] One reason for the difficulties faced by IBM, GM, and Sears is their failure in recent years to successfully innovate and meet changing environmental conditions.

Productivity Goals. Concerns for the quality, cost, and amount of output are included under productivity goals. An important issue facing nearly every organizations is how to simultaneously increase product or service quality while reducing waste and inefficiency. Some critics have pointed to poor product quality and low productivity as reasons why American manufacturers have difficulty competing with foreign, particularly Japanese, companies. Many organizations have turned to ***Total Quality Management*** (TQM) as a means for creating specific productivity goals that address quality, cost, and amount of output. TQM involves the setting of extensive sets of goals, many of which go well beyond productivity. The interested reader can find many articles and books that specifically deal with TQM.

Management Development Goals. Not only must organizations think to the future when planning new products and services, they must also consider the managerial personnel and skills that will be necessary to lead the company in the future. As technologies and environmental conditions change, different demands will be placed on managers. With the advent of inexpensive and readily available computers and information technologies, managers must acquire many new skills. Downsizing and the elimination of middle management in many organizations have also placed new demands on remaining managers. Organizations must also anticipate employment changes brought about by retirements, dismissals, promotions, or new opportunities. Organizations must develop comprehensive plans for attracting, retaining, training, promoting, and compensating managers. In fact, many organizational and management scholars have extended these development goals to all levels of organizations. These ideas form the foundation of the book *Strategic Human Resources Management.*[14]

Employee Performance and Attitudes. Obviously, organizations set specific goals for individual employees or groups of employees. These may include sales goals for salespeople, production goals for production employees, or recruiting goals for human resources managers. These goals are tied to the specific tasks that individuals or work units perform.[15] Like management development goals, these goals are part of a comprehensive strategic human resources system.

Perhaps less clear is the idea that organizations may have goals concerning employee attitudes. The fact is that many companies spend significant amounts of time and money assessing employee attitudes and attempting to create conditions conducive to development of more positive attitudes about work and the organization. These goals are motivated in part by the mistaken belief that happy workers are productive workers. In reality, the relationship between worker satisfaction and worker performance is far more complex and has been the focus of extensive research for many years. At a minimum, we can say that positive worker attitudes contribute to the quality of work life, and that may be a desirable end in itself. Thus, as we will see later in discussions of organizational climate and culture, goals for improved employee attitudes may be important to establishing internal organizational conditions.

In distinguishing between management development goals and employee performance and attitude goals, organizations must be careful to not create an overly stratified workforce. Identifying one group as "managers" and another as "employees" has the potential to create alienation and disharmony. Moreover, many organizations pursue "promotion from within" strategies. Employees at every level who show great potential are identified early for special training and grooming as future managers. Many organizations boast of managers or leaders who rose through the ranks from mailrooms, stockrooms, or other other low-level positions to assume leadership positions. Progressive management practice should focus on developing all employees to their fullest potential and should be concerned with the attitudes and performance of all employees.

Social Responsibility and Ethical Behavior. As the Ben & Jerry's case illustrates, organizations often expend considerable effort in pursuit of various ethics and social responsibility goals. McDonald's spends valuable corporate resources promoting recycling, nutritional education, and Ronald McDonald House. For many years, J.C. Penney has been guided by the Penney Way, which advocates the fair and equitable treatment of employees and customers.[16]

Some businesses even make ethics and social responsibility fundamental to their entire approach to business, marketing themselves as "green" (i.e., environmentally responsible) or in other ways socially responsible. A case in point is The Body Shop International, the British franchisor of soap and cosmetic shops.[17] The company actively supports the animal rights movement and avoids using animal testing of its products. Instead, the company avoids testing by using ingredients that have been already established as safe. The Body Shop also extensively uses recycled materials in packaging and advocates recycling or reuse of containers. Lastly, the company has tried to stimulate local economies of poorer nations by producing and purchasing in those locales. Rather than paying at the lower local rates, the company has paid prices and wages comparable to those in Europe. Recently, a number of critics have challenged The Body Shop, suggesting, on the one hand, that some of its policies do not contribute to the well-being of local third world economies and, on the other hand, that the company's policies have detracted from its profitability.[18] This successful business is based not only on the profit motive, but, like Ben & Jerry's and a growing number of other firms, on "doing good." This leads us to examine the meaning of "doing good." For that we turn briefly to the issue of ethics.

ETHICAL PRINCIPLES

Much of what organizational members do on a day-to-day basis involves ethics. Issues such as decisions about who to lay off during downsizing, how to market products, how to dispose of potentially hazardous waste, or how many and what type of defects in products are acceptable involve ethical choices. In general, ethical dilemmas have the following five characteristics.[19]

1. *Actions taken have extended consequences.* For example, a decision to downsize a company affects those people who lose their jobs, the morale of workers remaining on the job, the community's tax base, the local economy, and so forth.

2. *Managers have alternatives and can make choices about which course of action to pursue.* There may be more than one way to reach a desired goal. Instead of downsizing, for example, a firm may decide to cut wages or worker hours across the board.

3. *Outcomes are mixed.* Not all of the consequences of most actions are totally positive or totally negative. We have noted the negative consequences of downsizing. Downsizing may, however, make a company more efficient and more competitive, thus saving the company from eventual failure.

4. *Consequences of actions are uncertain.* Managers making decisions about a problem like downsizing do not know for sure whether their actions will have the intended consequence. Were the right people laid off? Will layoffs really make the company more efficient? Most decisions that managers make are fraught with uncertainties.

5. *Decisions that managers make have personal implications; they affect people.*

Exhibit 3.2

An Ethical Dilemma in the Malt Liquor Industry[20]

Several large and small brewing companies have aggressively marketed malt liquor beverages to inner city youths. Malt liquor is similar to beer but packs considerably more punch. Typical beers contain 3.5 to 4 percent alcohol whereas malt liquors have 4.5 to 6 percent alcohol. There is nothing unethical about making strong malt beverages. The ethical dilemma arises from the manner in which producers market their products and the market niche they are pursuing.

Some brands like St. Ides, produced by G. Heileman Brewing under contract for McKenzie River Corporation, have used rap stars to promote their products, emphasizing the brew's greater strength and sexually enhancing characteristics. Rapper Ice Cube, who appeared in the movie *Boyz N The Hood* drinking from 40-ounce cans of St. Ides, was featured in a number of St. Ides ads highlighting the brew as a fast way to "get my buzz on" and get "your girl in the mood quicker . . . " King Tee, another rapper, advertises the brew's strength, "I usually drink it when I'm out just clowning, me and the home boys, you know, be like downing it. Cause it's stronger but the taste is more smooth. I grab me a 40 when I want to act a fool."

McKenzie River is not alone. Heileman was set to release its own malt liquor called PowerMaster, emphasizing the brew's strength. Pabst Brewing promoted Olde English malt liquor using the phrase "It's the Power," and Stroh Brewing alluded to the power of its product.

The commercials have not been without controversy. The Bureau of Alcohol, Tobacco and Firearms (ATF) has pressured McKenzie River, Heileman, and Stroh to withdraw controversial commercials and print ads, and to change product names because they violate ATF rules forbidding references to the strength of alcoholic beverages in commercials.

The results of these advertising campaigns, however, were dramatic. Malt liquor sales have grown at rates of 25 to 30 percent over the last few years at the same time that beer sales have declined 2.4 percent. Much of this sales increase has

> been in inner city neighborhoods and to underage drinkers. Treatment centers and community organizations in many New York City neighborhoods report startling increases in teenage alcoholism and attribute the problem to cheap, readily available malt liquor that is now the hip thing to drink.
>
> Brewers claim it was not their intent to skirt government regulations or to encourage underage drinking. McKenzie River has begun making contributions to several community groups and has developed ads promoting responsible drinking. Clearly, the actions of these brewers involve ethical questions.

Organizations use ethical codes or guidelines to social responsibility to help employees make difficult decisions. Many different frameworks cataloging different types of business ethics have been developed over the years. One of the most straightforward is that presented by F. Neil Brady in his book *Ethical Managing: Rules and Results*.[21] Brady proposes an ethical framework that balances two views of ethics: ***ethical utilitarianism*** and ***ethical formalism.*** The two perspectives are described in Table 3.3.

■ TABLE 3.3
Two Views of Ethics

Utilitarian Ethics

- ***Utilitarianism,*** based on works of British philosopher Jeremy Bentham (1748–1832), means the ethical correctness of actions is judged by ***consequences.*** Utilitarian ethics are guided by the "greatest happiness" principle. This principle states that those actions that produce the greatest good for the greatest number of people are ethical. Actions that produce good outcomes, however defined, are ethical. Because consequences occur after a decision is made or an action is taken, one cannot judge the ethics, according to utilitarianism, until *after* the fact.
- Actions that produce pain or suffering are unethical. Acting in a selfish manner would be unethical because good outcomes would not be distributed to the greatest number of people.
- The process of ethical judgment is essentially that of cost-to-benefit analysis. Managers would weigh the costs (pain or suffering) against the anticipated gains (pleasure). If the positive outcomes outweigh the negative outcomes, then the action is deemed ethical.
- Utilitarianism tends to be flexible, situational, tolerant, and liberal. Individuals are left to judge what is best for them as long as those actions do not create pain and suffering for others. Utilitarianism emphasizes a rational decision process for arriving at ethical outcomes. Problems arise because people may not agree on whether certain outcomes are positive or negative and on whether certain groups of people are affected by actions of others.
- For example, a business manager may go through an elaborate cost-to-benefit analysis to determine whether to dump potentially toxic waste material into sewers. It may not be clear whether this action is legal. Factors to weigh would include the possible damage, the cost of fines if the action is found to be illegal, the potential loss of business, and the cost of alternative means of disposal. After weighing

all of these factors, a manager would make a decision based on maximizing good outcomes (continued profitability of firm, maintaining jobs, providing goods and services) and minimizing bad outcomes (damage to the environment and threats to human health).

Ethical Formalism

* *Ethical formalism* is based largely on the writings of the eighteenth century philosopher Emanuel Kant. Whereas utilitarian ethical judgments are tied to the consequences of actions, Kant believed that we can know what is ethical *before* we know the consequences. By the application of universally recognized rules or principles, we can know what actions are ethical. These rules or principles may be formally stated laws, doctrine, or widely held beliefs or values. For example, state legal codes forbid the taking of a life (defined variously as murder or manslaughter). Many religious or personal codes also forbid such action. Holders of these rules or values will attempt to apply them consistently and universally.
* Actions that violate laws, rules, and generally held values are unethical. Making oneself an exception to the rule is unethical.
* The process of ethical judgment is something Kant called ***pure reason.*** Ethical judgments are independent of what an individual or group thinks. We recognize the authenticity of an ethical law without necessarily agreeing with it. Ethical principles are absolute, universal, and consistent.
* Formalism emphasizes universal and consistent application of rules. Emphasis is placed on a prior knowledge of rules. Problems arise when rules are confusing or when sets of rules conflict with each other.
* For example, we may have universally applicable rules that state that businesses cannot dump toxic waste materials into the sewer system of the city. Without knowing the consequences of an action, the business manager knows beforehand that to dump toxic waste down the sewer is unethical. Knowledge of these rules or laws, not knowledge of potential consequences, will guide the manager's actions.

Increasingly, organizations are using ethical codes to specify acceptable and desirable conduct for employees and the organization. We revisit the issue of organizational ethics when we explore organizational culture in Chapter 10.

PURPOSES OF GOALS AND OBJECTIVES

Clearly, goals and objectives at different levels serve different purposes. The broad, general statements of a mission statement are different from the more specific operative goals. Nonetheless, a number of features of goals are common to, or overlap, both levels. These are discussed below.

Guidance or Direction. Official goals or mission statements give general *guidance* or *direction* to employees. Employees at each of the companies featured earlier are motivated to focus on different behaviors: efficiency contributes to greater profitability at Houston Industries; customer service enhances the benefits provided to customer-owners of The

Principal Financial Group; and product innovation, community involvement, and employee development create value at Ben & Jerry's. Mission statements, however, are not specific enough to show individual employees how they should implement these guidelines in their day-to-day actions. The mission or goal statements help create a **culture** (the prevailing philosophy and values of the organization) that should support the achievement of these goals, and the operative goals provide more specific mechanisms for achieving these goals.

Motivation. The achievement of goals does not just happen *because* goals are set. The guidance component of goals tells employees what they should do and how to do it. The motivation component *encourages* workers to do those things. Frequently, goals are set to challenge employees, and often rewards accompany achievement of these goals. When General Motors created its Saturn Division, it was clear that to be competitive the division would need to be more productive and innovative than other GM divisions or the competition, and that profitability of the division would be sometime in the future. Although the Saturn cars have been a sales success, the division lost $700 million as recently as 1992. General Motors has maintained goals of high product quality, high productivity, continuous improvement, and eventual profitability by offering bonuses when the division shows an operating profit. In June, 1993, Saturn showed its first operating profit and rewarded workers with $1,000 bonuses.[22]

Legitimacy. A third purpose of goal statements is to create **legitimacy** for the organization. These statements communicate to people inside and outside the legitimate reason or justification for the organization's existence. For example, Ben & Jerry's Mission Statement provides legitimacy for the company as a producer of superpremium ice cream. The company is justified in producing and marketing this product. Early in the company's history, legitimacy was challenged by the Häagen Dazs unit of Pillsbury (now Grand Metropolitan, PLC). Pillsbury tried to pressure grocers into giving little or no freezer space to Ben & Jerry's products. Grocers and the courts saw this as a challenge to a legitimate competitor, and Pillsbury was order to stop this practice. The mission statement or official goals state the legitimate intentions of the organization. Similarly, operative goals state the legitimate means that employees should use to achieve the official goals.

Standards. It would seem logical that if organizations set goals to legitimize, guide, and motivate, then these goals can be used as standards of achievement. Quantifiable goals, like Saturn's goal of profitability, can be clearly stated, and progress toward that goal can be measured. Thus, goals may serve as standards for performance. We return to this subject shortly when we discuss organizational effectiveness.

Structure and Design. The number, diversity, and complexity of an organization's goals should play an important role in decisions about how it should be structured or designed. For example, companies with goals to produce many different products or services may require different types of structure and design than those of companies that set goals to produce only a few related products or services. Organizations having goals that require extensive interaction between departments or divisions (a concept known as interdependence) require different structures or designs than those organizations in which departments or divisions can carry out tasks more or less autonomously. Organizations that have goals dealing with environmental scanning, adaptation, or manipulation will be structured in ways that maximize boundary-spanning activities and environmental planning. Thus, the nature of the goals an organization sets should be an important consideration in decisions about how the organization should be structured, as we noted in Chapter 2, or designed, as we see in Chapter 8.

Unification of Effort. Goals, especially broad goals, can serve to unify efforts among diverse groups inside and outside an organization. Certain goals can serve as overarching mechanisms to link disparate groups together. During the Gulf War in 1992, the U.S. and its allies, a group that often failed to agree on major issues, were able to put aside differences and work together to drive Iraq out of Kuwait. This sometimes uneasy alliance included Saudi Arabia, Israel, Turkey, Germany, England, France, the United States, and others.

Companies frequently use the same technique by expressing broad goals that are difficult to oppose, for example, goals such as improving customer service or raising profits. (Unanimous support of goals is often rare in organizations as we will see shortly and again in Chapter 12.) Diverse groups in the organization can agree on these motherhood-and-apple-pie goals more easily than goals of retrenchment or downsizing.

MANAGING GOALS AND OBJECTIVES

In a perfectly rational world, managing the diverse goals of an organization might not be a significant problem. If everyone agreed on the goals and agreed on the relative importance of each goal, the organization would simply direct its efforts at sequentially fulfilling these goals in order of importance. Organizations do not, however, operate in a perfectly rational world. Organizational reality is far more complex. The process of setting organizational goals is at best ambiguous and uncertain. Moreover, goal setting is a ***political process*** whereby individuals or groups may pursue self-interest rather than what is best for the organization as a whole. Different groups within and outside the organization, referred to as ***coalitions*** or ***stakeholders,*** may have different ideas about what are the most important goals to pursue. Stakeholders with interests in the organization (e.g., customers, suppliers, investors, and others) may also have different goals or different priorities for the organization. Instead of perfectly rational agreement on an organization's goals and priorities, organizations typically have many goals, some of which may conflict with others, and managers may disagree on the relative importance of these goals. After all, what seems perfectly rational to one person or group may appear to be misguided, wrong, or irrational to others. Finally, individuals and groups may operate on the basis of a hidden agenda. For example, a manager may advocate and pursue a particular goal because it enhances his or her self-interest rather than the organization's overall interests. That process is depicted in Figure 3.1 on page 71. However, even Figure 3.1 gives the impression (sometimes a mistaken impression) that the goal-setting process yields one final set of objectives. Conflict may produce a disparate set of goals for the different coalitions and stakeholders.

Given these conditions of multiple and conflicting goals, how do managers proceed? Officially, organizations often have formal and explicit means for establishing goals whether by top management, by a vote of stockholders, by the board of directors, or by some other specified means. In actuality, the setting and managing of goals is often quite different from the formal means that the organization espouses. Internal politics is often the key to understanding the goal-setting and management process. Several techniques for managing goals are discussed below.

- If we acknowledge that the process of setting and managing goals in organizations is a political rather than a rational process, then it should become clear that the process of managing goals is one of managing conflict. When top managers responsible for goal setting disagree on an organization's goals, it is typical that the disagreeing parties will **negotiate** or **bargain** in an attempt to resolve differences. Negotiation may result in some goals being abandoned and others being pursued as the primary goals of the organization. Compromises may result when groups give and take. Some groups may come out as winners in negotiations while others are losers—a so-called win-lose negotiation. Occasionally, the bargaining process can be conducted in a way that promotes compromises or changes in the nature of the goals so that all parties regard themselves as winners—a win-win negotiation.
- Another consequence of the human and political nature of organizations is that members of the organization may be satisfied with something less than perfect or complete goal achievement. This phenomenon is referred to as *satisficing*.[23] Managers may set lofty goals for many aspects of the organization. Because some of these goals may be contradictory, it may be impossible to fully meet each of them. For example, in the early '90s Apple Computer set goals for increasing market penetration, sales, innovativeness, and profitability. The costs associated with market penetration, sales, and innovativeness caused serious declines in profits. To the extent that management was satisfied with less-than-expected profits would be an example of satisficing. Management has accepted a *satisfactory* level of performance rather than a *maximal* level of performance. We explore the phenomenon of satisficing more extensively in the chapter on organizational decision making.
- Finally, two related ordering techniques for managing multiple and potentially conflicting goals are *setting priorities* and *sequencing* of events. In setting priorities, top management determines which of the diverse goals are most important to the organization. The Apple example above suggests that Apple management may have thought that satisfying customers through new, lower-priced products and developing greater sales volume was more important

■ FIGURE 3.1
Determination of Goals and Objectives

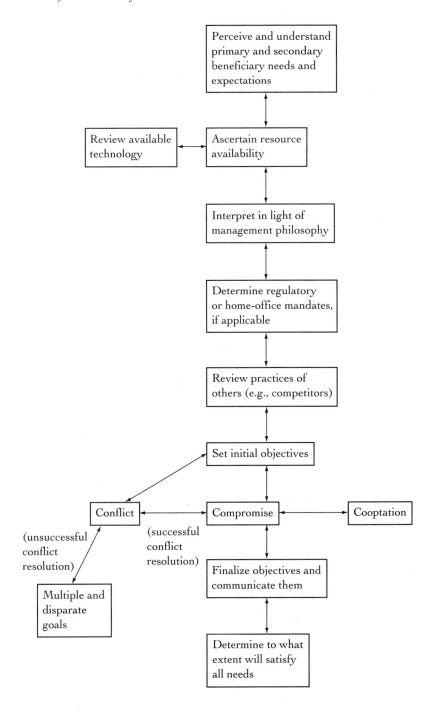

goals than satisfying investors. At the same time, Apple spent extensively on development of the Newton personal data device that may not be profitable for some time to come. Clearly, a publicly traded company cannot put too low a priority on investor satisfaction for long. The resulting decline in profitability caused turmoil at Apple that eventually led to the departure of CEO John Sculley.[24] Now Apple appears to have placed a lower priority on further development and marketing of the Newton. Sequencing, on the other hand, assumes that all goals will eventually be met; however, some will be met before others. Apple's management may have believed that it was necessary to first increase production volume and a customer base before they could pursue profitability. They may have believed that the increased size, market power, and economies of scale were necessary ingredients to future profitability. The jury is still out on profitability of the Newton at Apple.

ORGANIZATIONAL GOALS: SUMMARY AND RECAP

We began this investigation of organizational goals with the premise that organizations have goals. That is what, in part, differentiates an organization from an idle collection of people. The definition in Chapter 1 noted that *organizations are purposeful, goal-oriented entities*. As we started exploring the levels and diversity of goals that an organization may have, we began to see some problems with this idea of organizational goals. First, organizations may have multiple and conflicting goals that are broad or ambiguous so that maximization of all goals may be impossible. Next, we noted that organizations are made up of diverse internal and external constituent groups that may have different ideas about what the goals of the organization should be. This led us to the conclusion that organizational goals may not be rationally or logically constructed. Instead, organizations are political entities made up of diverse groups of people, and goals are the outcome of political processes such as bargaining, negotiating wielding power, and dominating. Thus, we began with what seemed like a straightforward idea that organizations have goals, and now we have come to realize goals are really a complex issue. As a leading organizational scholar has noted, "The concept of goals is among the most important—and most controversial—concepts to be confronted in the study of organizations."[25]

EFFECTIVENESS

Hand in hand with any discussion of goals should go a treatment of the concept of organizational effectiveness. The preceding examination of organizational goals in some respects sets the stage for exploring effectiveness. One might reasonably assume that if an organization achieves its goals, then it is effective. We will learn, however, that effectiveness is more complicated than merely achieving goals (not that achieving goals is an easy task). Thus, we now turn our attention to the subject of effectiveness.

At some point in our study of an organization or a group of organizations we probably want to ask questions about *how well the organization is doing.* On the surface this question may seem innocent and direct. And at some levels the question is rather simple. Is the organization surviving? And if it is a business, is it making money? But as you may already have guessed from the previous examination of goals, the question of effectiveness is also not as simple as it might first seem. The term *effectiveness* is itself unclear. Organizations may be more or less effective in a variety of different ways. Is effectiveness simply the amount of profits earned? Or is it the number of units produced or customers served? What about worker satisfaction? And what about definitions of *effectiveness* proposed by stakeholders of the organization? Are customers satisfied with the organization's products or services? Is the broader community satisfied with the manner in which the organization has conducted itself? Has the company polluted the air and water? Has the company provided some value to the community?

All of the above questions may be relevant to our assessment of an organization's effectiveness. Thus, the answer to our question, is Organization X effective?, may partly depend on who is asking and the reason for the question. The implication is that there is a variety of ways in which to measure an organization's effectiveness. In the following sections we look at several approaches to the assessment of organizational effectiveness and discuss their applicability, strengths, and weaknesses.

Internal Effectiveness. Some of the earliest organizational theorists focused on internal effectiveness as the key to organizational effectiveness. Two different subgroups of theorists emerged and looked at different characteristics of organizational effectiveness, or "health": internal efficiency and human relations.

The *efficiency* approach to internal effectiveness, a legacy of the industrial engineering and time-motion studies of Frederick W. Taylor, measures the efficient use of resources.[26] An organization is effective to the extent that it maximizes outputs with respect to the costs of inputs and the costs of the transformation of those inputs into outputs. For example, automakers pay great attention to the cost of producing a given car. General Motors has been judged to be a less effective car maker because its costs of production are greater than those of Ford, Chrysler, and Japanese rivals. Similarly, downsizing in many industries (e.g., Apple and IBM in the computer industry and Procter & Gamble in consumer products) has been aimed at reducing the cost of production to improve internal effectiveness. The underlying assumption is that an organization that more efficiently transforms inputs into outputs is more effective than an organization that is less efficient. Although that logic is appealing, effectiveness typically involves more than merely being efficient. Figure 3.2 on page 74 shows the relationship between efficiency and effectiveness.

Internal efficiency may be an important element in organizational effectiveness, but it provides only a limited perspective on effectiveness. A company may greatly improve its internal efficiency by substituting lower quality inputs, cutting corners on production, or using less expensive but questionable means for disposing of waste materials. All these tactics may *reduce* overall effectiveness. Additionally, a company may be efficient in producing outputs, but there may be no market for those products.

■ **FIGURE 3.2**
Efficiency and Effectiveness

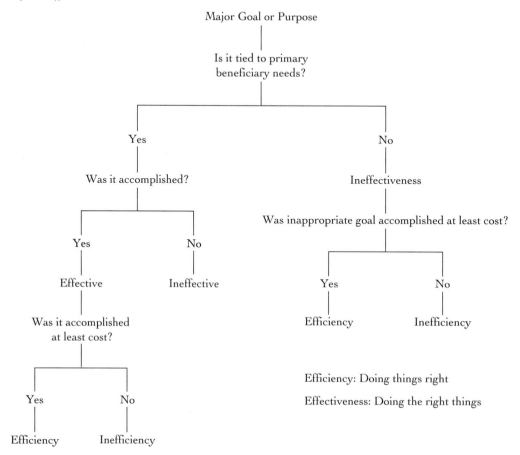

The ***Human Relations School*** of organization theory, mentioned briefly in Chapter 1, provides the foundation for a second internal process view of organizational effectiveness. Theorists from this school are concerned with the ***emotional*** or ***affective health*** of an organization and have focused on internal stress and strain as indicators of effectiveness. An effective organization is characterized by smooth vertical and horizontal information flows, a near absence of conflict, and the presence of trust and benevolence. In sum, an effective organization is one in which workers are happy and satisfied.[27]

As is the case with efficiency, the human relations approach provides only a partial, and sometimes inaccurate, picture of organizational performance. Ample evidence suggests that worker happiness does not necessarily lead to productivity—let alone effectiveness. Happy workers may become complacent and fail to see the need to adapt to changing external conditions. Even if workers are happy and efficient, they may not be producing desired outputs. Moreover, the elimination of conflict may *reduce* effectiveness. Workers may fail to challenge inefficient or misdirected efforts, thus reducing effectiveness. Thus, you can begin to see that effectiveness is more complex than efficiency and worker satisfaction and a lack of conflict.

Goals and Effectiveness. The ***goal approach*** defines effectiveness in terms of if and how well an organization accomplishes its goals. To the extent that an organization has defined its goals in ways that permit observation and measurement, effectiveness can be judged by the extent to which the organization meets its goals. The closer the organization comes to meeting its goals, the more effective it is. An advantage of the goal approach is that the effectiveness of each organization can be judged independently. The goal approach does not depend on comparative judgments of effectiveness.

Although this approach has a certain logical appeal, our earlier examination of goals should suggest to the reader that this approach is also problematic. First, if an organization has ill-defined, complex, or inappropriate goals, this approach may lead to erroneous conclusions. In the mid-1980s Kmart embarked on a goal of acquiring specialty store chains. It was successful in meeting that goal through several acquisitions: Builders Square building supply warehouse stores, Walden Books, Borders Books, Pace Membership Warehouse stores, Pay Less Drug Stores, Sports Authority, and OfficeMax. If Kmart's effectiveness were measured simply by its attainment of its acquisition goals, then cleary Kmart would be judged effective. However, by several other measures of effectiveness Kmart's performance falls short. The company's profits are down; the price of Kmart stock is down; and it is losing marketshare to Wal-Mart. Recently, Kmart has been selling several of these specialty businesses.[28]

Second, an organization's goals may not represent the diverse interests of the many stakeholder groups (e.g., community, employee, government) that have interests in the organization. An organization's goal to grow and expand may conflict with the interests of the local community that fears the potential increases in traffic, congestion, and pollution. Wal-Mart has encountered just this sort of problem in a number of rural communities in which it desires to locate new stores.[29] Wal-Mart's goals include expanding into new, untapped markets. Yet, many residents, especially in rural communities, fear that Wal-Mart's entry will degrade the quality of life in those communities. An organization's goals to streamline operations, increase productivity, and downsize may conflict with employees' goals to maintain a high quality of work life. A company may move production to another country to meet goals of low-cost labor. Federal, state, and local governments may object because such a move counters their goals of maintaining levels of employment and the tax base.

Third, the very nature of goals, that they may be ambiguous or conflict with one another, may mean that meeting some goals is not possible or that meeting some goals means that others will go unmet. We examined this problem earlier in the chapter in our discussion of goals. The point here is that it may be difficult to determine whether an organization has met its goals if the goals are ambiguous, and it may be difficult to judge effectiveness if goals are conflicting.

Thus, even though the practice of judging effectiveness by the degree to which an organization reaches goals is commonly used, it is a method that is problematic. A company that reaches its goals may not, in a more general sense, be effective.

Resources and Effectiveness. A basic premise of the open systems view of organizations presented in Chapter 1 is that organizations must acquire resources from the external environment. Materials and labor necessary to create the intended outputs of the organization are found in the external environment. The *systems resource model* claims that effectiveness is attained to the extent that the organization acquires from the environment those resources necessary to carry out its purpose. The reasoning behind this model is based on the belief that there is a clear connection between inputs to the system and its performance. An organization must have inputs to create outputs. For example, in east coast urban centers such as New York City, Washington, D.C., and Boston, many fast-food franchises have had difficulty obtaining workers willing to work at near minimum wages. The outlets cannot function without this critical labor input. Acquiring inputs, in this case labor inputs, is *necessary* for successful operation. The mere presence of this input is not, however, *sufficient* to guarantee the effective operation of the restaurant, and that is a significant weakness of the systems resource model of effectiveness. Many other factors may inhibit the performance of the franchise. Obtaining the highest quality inputs is no guarantee of superior performance. Sports teams lacking superstar players have often won championships.[30] Similarly, there is no guarantee that a business will make the best use of the inputs it acquires. While acquiring resources is clearly necessary and may be a precursor to success, resource acquisition alone does not give a comprehensive picture of organizational effectiveness.

Performance and Stakeholders.   Satisfaction of key ***constituent groups*** or ***stakeholders*** represents another major method of assessing organizational effectiveness. The belief is that organizations are effective to the extent that the key groups of individuals (i.e., constituents or stakeholders) are at least minimally satisfied. Constituents or stakeholders are those groups of individuals with a definite and immediate interest in the organization's performance. Typical of these groups are stockholders, managers, employees (and perhaps their unions), creditors, suppliers, customers, regulators, and community members, to name just a few concerned groups. These groups attempt to influence the organization to perform in certain ways and judge effectiveness by the degree to which the organization responds to this influence. Shareholders seek to maximize their return on investment and judge effectiveness accordingly. Creditors judge effectiveness by the firm's creditworthiness and its ability to meet debt obligations. Employees judge effectiveness on the basis of job security and the quality of the work environment.

Much like the problems of conflicting and inappropriate goals, stakeholders or constituent groups hold diverse expectations for a typical company. Often it is not possible to satisfy all the demands of all constituent groups. The resulting dilemma is which constituent groups are most important. Unfortunately, there is no clear answer to that question. The importance of any given constituent group will vary over time and circumstances and will be a function of the power that group holds over the organization.

Effectiveness: A Synthesis.   You may be wondering what is an effective organization? After exploring the above views of effectiveness, you may have the uneasy feeling that there is no clear-cut, surefire way to comprehensively measure organizational effectiveness. And you are correct. Each of the previously mentioned views provides only a partial, skewed vision of effectiveness. That brings us to two additional perspectives on effectiveness. These perspectives do not propose different measures of effectiveness. Instead, they suggest different ways of using some of the previously stated methods.

The ***contradictions model*** of effectiveness states that the idea of trying to characterize a whole organization as totally effective or ineffective is problematic.[31] In any complex organization there may be parts of the organization that function well and suggest effectiveness while other aspects of that same organization perform poorly. The juxtaposition of effective and ineffective segments of an organization constitutes the contradictions to which this model refers. Is that organization effective? More importantly, as noted with goals and the goal approach, the effectiveness of some parts of an organization may mean that other parts will of necessity perform suboptimally. Satisfying certain key stakeholders may mean unsatisfactory performance in the eyes of others.

Four central assumptions drive the contradictions model[32]:

1. Organizations face complex environments that place multiple and conflicting demands and constraints on them. It may not be possible to succeed in meeting all the environmental conditions an organization faces.
2. Organizations have multiple, conflicting goals. It is impossible to maximize achievement of all goals.
3. Organizations face multiple internal and external stakeholders or constituent groups that make competing or conflicting demands. It may be impossible to satisfy all groups of people who express interest in a company.
4. Organizations must manage multiple and conflicting time demands. Satisfying short- or long-term demands at the expense of the other may result in suboptimal performance.

The contradictions model merely suggests that we make note of these potential contradictions in our assessment of performance and acknowledge that *any* assessment of performance must, of necessity, be constrained or limited.

The ***competing values model*** takes a different approach to dealing with the problems and limitations of effectiveness assessment.[33] The essential point of the competing values model is that no single measure of effectiveness is, by itself, satisfactory. Rather, different methods of assessing performance will be relevant for organizations having different underlying management values or orientations. The result is the set of four different approaches to effectiveness represented in Figure 3.3 on page 78.

The appropriate measure of effectiveness for a given organization depends upon its focus (internally focused versus externally focused) and its desires for either control or flexibility. The combination of these two dimensions yields four distinct approaches to effectiveness. Organizations that best fit in the human relations quadrant are internally focused and desire flexibility. They seek to develop employees so that they reach their highest potential to contribute to the organization. The organization pursues worker satisfaction, high morale, and cooperation as means for helping employees develop. Methods for measuring effectiveness described earlier under the heading of Human Resources would apply in this case. Flexible, externally oriented firms are described as fitting the open systems model. The organization acknowledges that it is

■ **FIGURE 3.3***

Competing Values Effectiveness Model

HUMAN RELATIONS MODEL   **OPEN SYSTEM MODEL**

Flexibility

Means: Means:
    Cohesion; morale   Flexibility; readiness

Ends: Ends:
    Human resource development   Growth; resource acquisition

Internal ——————————— Output Quality ——————————— External

Means: Means:
    Information management;   Planning; goal setting
    communication

Ends: Ends:
    Stability; control   Productivity; efficiency

Control

INTERNAL PROCESS MODEL   **RATIONAL GOAL MODEL**

---

*Adapted from Robert E. Quinn and John Rohrbaugh, "A Spatial Model of Effectiveness: Toward a Competing Values Approach to Organizational Analysis," *Management Science* 29 (1983): 363–77.

affected by events or conditions in the external environment, and it seeks to maintain flexibility in responding to the environment. This organization pursues resources to foster growth. The systems resources model described earlier would fit this quadrant. Organizations that seek stability and predictability in their internal operations are internally focused and oriented toward control. Efficiency would be an appropriate measure in this situation. Finally, the control-oriented, externally focused organization seeks to achieve the goals set by top management. Emphasis is on strategic planning and goal setting, and the measures of effectiveness would be the degree to which those goals are attained. This quadrant matches the goal model presented earlier.

Effectiveness: A Summary. We have presented a diverse set of approaches to measuring organizational effectiveness. This begs the question: Which approach is best? The answer to this question is not easy but we can begin to answer that question by asking a few questions. First, why do we want to measure effectiveness? What is our objective? An investment analyst seeking to rate the investment potential of a given company will certainly use different criteria for effectiveness than will an employment specialist seeking to identify the best companies for whom to work. Second, we may also need to set a time frame on our assessment. One lesson of works such as *In Search of Excellence*[34] is that organizations that are effective at one point in time are certainly not guaranteed effectiveness in the future. Many organizations that Peters and Waterman identified as excellent at the time the book was published are no longer in business or have fallen on hard times (e.g., Amdahl, IBM, Data General, and Wang Laboratories). Because organizations are open systems, they must deal with the external environment, and, as we learn in the next chapter, environments can change rapidly and unpredictably. Criteria for effectiveness that are appropriate today may not fit in the organizations of tomorrow. Finally, as the contradictions and competing values models suggest, different approaches to effectiveness may be appropriate for different types of organizations. Thus, we can answer our question, "Which model is best?" with a resounding, "It depends."

SUMMARY

Today's managers face an important assignment—setting goals or objectives that are aimed at satisfying the needs and desires of a complex set of constituents inside and outside the organization. Goals or objectives establish the desired future state that the organization is trying to achieve. Goals create legitimacy for the organization by providing the rationale for its existence. Goals guide members' actions and set standards against which the organization's performance can be measured.

Goals are multifaceted and may apply at different levels of the organization. Mission statements or official goals state the broad ambitions of the organization as a whole in rather general terms. Operative goals are more specific and may be tailored to individual departments, divisions, or work groups. Eight categories of operative goals were introduced (market, financial performance, resource, innovation, productivity, management development, employee performance and attitudes, and ethical or social responsibility goals). An area of goals to which organizations are devoting increasing attention is ethical behavior. Utilitarian (consequence-based) and formalist (rule-based) ethics provide two potentially complementary frameworks for viewing ethical problems in organizations.

Goals also vary by the intended beneficiaries (primary and secondary). Primary beneficiaries are those the organization intends to serve (e.g., customers). Secondary beneficiaries are those who benefit because of their association with the organization (e.g., employees, suppliers, or owners).

The organization must establish a hierarchy of short- and long-term goals. Some objectives may be critical to achieve quickly. Other goals may require more time or may be sequentially linked to the achievement of prior goals. An essential managerial task is assigning a time frame to the various goals an organization seeks to fulfill.

Goals serve a number of important functions for organizations. Employees look to goal statements for guidance and direction. Goals can motivate employees to achieve specific outcomes. The organization obtains legitimacy for its actions from its mission or goal statement. Goals provide standards for judging an organization's performance. However, as was noted in the discussion of effectiveness, one must be cautious in using goals alone to measure effectiveness. The organization must take into consideration the number, diversity, and complexity of goals when seeking to create an appropriate structure or design. Last, goals can serve as a rallying point to unify or consolidate organizational members.

With the diversity of goals and the potential for conflict among goals, the task of managing goals becomes critical. Several techniques for managing goals that include sequencing, setting priorities, satisficing, and bargaining or negotiation were explored. We concluded by noting that goals are a deceptively complex issue in organizations.

The manager's job does not end with the setting of goals or objectives. At some point people inside and outside the organization want to know how effective the organization is. The question of how effective an organization is becomes, like goals, deceptively difficult and complex. Several methods can be used, but none give a comprehensive picture of effectiveness. Internal approaches focus on efficiency and/or satisfaction of employees. These approaches typically ignore the external environment or external constituent groups. The goal approach judges effectiveness by the extent to which an organization achieves its stated goals. However, goals may be ambiguous, conflicting, or inappropriate. Thus, fulfilling goals may not indicate effectiveness. Acquiring resources is essential to an organization's effectiveness, and resource acquisition has been used as a measure of effectiveness. But even if an organization is successful acquiring resources, there is no guarantee that it will use those resources appropriately. Satisfying the diverse groups of stakeholders of an organization also may be used as an indicator of effectiveness. The problem is that, like goals, there are typically many stakeholders of an organization and their demands or requirements may conflict.

We concluded by presenting two models, the contradictions model and the competing values model, which try to accommodate the shortcomings in typical models of effectiveness. The contradictions model states that any model of effectiveness is inherently flawed. When using any model of effectiveness we must take into consideration our purpose and the limitations of the model. The competing values model is a contingency model that suggests different models of effectiveness for different types of organizations.

This chapter has analyzed organizational goals and effectiveness, two critical issues in the study of organizations. These two concepts, seemingly quite straightforward, turn out to be complex and difficult but essential to our understanding and management of organizations.

Questions for Discussion

1. Explain in detail the role of goals in the formation and operation of organizations.
2. What, if any, role do/should goals play in the downsizing of a major firm?

3. Explain the reasons for sequencing in the setting of mission, operative, and operational goals.
4. Write a long-term goal dealing with innovation for your university, and propose a derivative short-term goal for your department.
5. What can cause a conflict of organization goals? How would you propose to reconcile or resolve this conflict?
6. What role would you suggest that ethics play in both goal setting and goal measurement?
7. What role do goals play in legitimacy?
8. Define effectiveness and explain which organization members should be responsible for managing the organization to achieve it.
9. How can the contradictions model and the competing values model be used to determine organization effectiveness? Apply these models to measuring the effectiveness of your college or university.

CASE: BLUE LIGHT SPECIAL

"We have a special on brand name cosmetics today on aisle three. Yes, for a limited time only you can buy three of a kind for the price of two. But hurry, the supply is limited, and this fantastic offer cannot be repeated!"

Blue Light Specials are familiar sounds in the retail giant that is Kmart today. But the once fast-growing chain has been forced to rethink its scope and direction recently due to fierce competition, legal issues, and the general state of the U.S. economy.

From its meager beginning in Michigan in 1916 as the S. S. Kresge Company, Kmart enjoyed success in achieving its objective of becoming a force to be reckoned with in the world of discount merchandising. As the announcement above indicates, the appeal to customers has been from the start low prices and fast, friendly customer service. Kmart's price-promise advertising clearly states that it will meet or beat competitors' advertised prices on identical items. And this technique propelled the company to second place on the list of successful giant discount retailers.

But things have begun to go sour, and the big discounter is struggling to cope with a variety of blips on its management radar screen.

LEGAL TROUBLES

In March of 1992, Kmart was named in a lawsuit that alleged the corporation had used bait-and-switch tactics to entice customers to buy photo portraits. The suit charges that Kmart took two sets of pictures, one of poor quality and the other of high quality color. Ads claimed that fifty-five copies of portraits could be purchased for $14.45; however, when the customer arrived, the suit contends, he or she was pressured to buy the high quality pictures for $60.

Reebok International, Ltd. claimed in 1992 that Kmart placed a Reebok look-alike stripe on the sides of its athletic shoes. In this trademark-infringement lawsuit Reebok maintains that the stripe is just too "Reebok."

Kmart has also been charged with age discrimination. At the root of this charge are twenty-three current and former employees who charge that the company systematically gets rid of its highly paid, older employees. The suit charges that Kmart created a "20-40-60" scheme that targeted employees with twenty or more years of service who were forty years or older, and who made $60,000 or more a year for "dehiring."*

COMPETITION

How has competition affected Kmart's drive to be its industry leader? From the beginning, Kmart set out to be number one in its field, but so far its drive has been unsuccessful. Leading the opposition is the megadiscount retailer, Wal-Mart, the storybook success that is the brain child of the late Sam Walton. Along with Wal-Mart, Kmart faced the perennial industry stalwarts, Sears, J.C. Penney, and lately, Toys "R" Us. In 1991 Wal-Mart surpassed Sears to become the top retailer in the U.S. It gained its position atop the industry through relentlessly searching for ways to cut costs, improve inventory control, and update distribution systems (based on quite sophisticated computer-driven innovations).

Sensing the mounting competitive pressure in the industry, Kmart, in 1988, began a $2.5 billion repositioning effort under the leadership of Joseph Antonelli, Kmart's former chairman and CEO. This effort included the remodeling of nearly all of Kmart's 2,300 stores; the addition of pharmacies in all stores; and, very important, the replacement of existing inventory and distribution systems with the Central Merchandising Automated Replenishment System. It also included taking a proactive stance on environmental issues; diversifying into mass marketing "category-killer" specialty stores; expanding into foreign (especially Canadian) markets; and experimenting with the Super Kmart concept that includes a grocery and retail discount store under one roof.

NEED FOR TURNAROUND

In the January 6, 1994, edition of *The Wall Street Journal*, however, were some alarms instead of blue light specials for Kmart. Kmart has recognized that its earnings have not been what analysts called "special" and its store renovation project has simply not been enough to allow the giant retailer to achieve its goal of becoming number one in the discount retail industry. Indeed, the corporation announced a pretax charge of $1.3 billion for the closing and relocating of some 500 of its stores.

In its bid to become leader, Kmart branched into specialty divisions — Borders and Walden bookstores, Builders Square home improvement chain, OfficeMax office supply chain, and the Sports Authority sporting goods group. But conditions warranted a decision to reverse these moves, and Kmart first made a public offering of 20 to 30 percent of these divisions through four separate stock offerings and later sold some divisions outright. Kmart would retain control but allow the divisions to trade separately. (The list below from *The Wall Street Journal* summarizes Kmart's recent moves to rebuild itself.)

---

*Detroit Free Press, January 10, 1993.

KMART'S RESTRUCTURINGS

Actions taken by Kmart since 1990 to bolster its core discount store operations:

- **February 1990:** Unveils plans to spend $2.3 billion over next five years— $1 billion more than earlier forecast—to expand and relocate more stores than previously projected and to do it more quickly. Took a $422 million after-tax ($640 million pretax) charge to cover the cost.
- **August 1991:** Sells $1 billion of a new security to ensure that its store expansion effort is not crimped by lenders' wariness to lend to developers.
- **May 1993:** Agrees to sell fourteen of its ailing Pace Membership Warehouse division stores to rival Wal-Mart Stores, Inc. Discloses it might sell minority interests in one or more specialty store chains.
- **June 1993:** Tests Super Kmart stores where groceries are sold along with general merchandise. Rival Wal-Mart already has forty such combination stores.
- **August 1993:** Puts it 560-store Pay Less Drug Stores unit on the auction block in hopes of getting as much as $1 billion for it.
- **November 1993:** Agrees to sell Pay Less unit for over $1 billion to a Los Angeles investment firm, and also arranges sales of ninety-one more Pace Warehouse clubs to Wal-Mart.
- **January 1994:** Increases to 800 from 300 the number of core discount stores it will close and relocate, and to 700 from 620 the number of store expansions. Says it intends to sell stock in four specialty store divisions, and announces an $850 million after-tax (1.3 billion pretax) charge.
- **October 1995:** Some investment analysts suggest that Kmart and its investors would be best served by the company declaring Chapter 11 bankruptcy.

Flat seasonal earnings during year's end in 1993 did not compare favorably with a $2.06 per share earnings for 1992, and the $850 million after-tax loss was in contrast to a net income of $941 million on sales of $37.7 billion a year previous.

Antonelli believed that these offerings would increase shareholder value as well as provide more flexibility for raising needed capital and building employee incentive plans to suit individual units. Those who watch the industry, however, are not convinced. According to Margo McGlade, Paine Webber analyst and long-time Kmart watcher, even the shiny new stores have not proven that Kmart can execute well. Nor are Kmart stockholders convinced. Antonelli was stripped of his position as chairman of the board and eventually replaced. The difficulty that the board had finding a replacement for Antonelli indicated how difficult the situation was at Kmart.

QUESTIONS FOR DISCUSSION

1. What external factors should Kmart have considered before setting a goal to become number one in its industry?
2. Should Kmart have established individual goals for each of its divisions? Explain.
3. Explain how Kmart's "sell off" program can affect goal attainment in its aftermath.
4. Explain how both effectiveness and efficiency can play a part in determining whether Kmart's moves will be successful.

5. Write a realistic long-term goal (for any level of operation) to be accomplished within the next two to five years for the new, lean Kmart.
6. Visit a local Kmart store, and ask employees if they know Kmart's goals for the next year.
7. Assume you are asked to set three specific objectives for Kmart for the next twelve months. What should they be?

REFERENCES

1. Lesile Kaufman-Rosen, "Being Cruel to Be Kind," *Newsweek* (October 17, 1994): 51–52.

2. *Ben & Jerry's Annual Report,* 1992.

3. W. Richard Scott, *Organizations: Rational, Natural and Open Systems,* 3rd ed. (Englewood Cliffs, N.J.: Prentice-Hall, 1992).

   Amitai Etzioni, *Modern Organizations* (Englewood Cliffs, N.J.: Prentice-Hall, 1964).

4. See Etzioni in note 3 above.

5. Richard H. Hall, *Organizations: Structures, Processes, and Outcomes,* 5th ed. (Englewood Cliffs, N.J.: Prentice-Hall, 1991).

6. Leslie W. LaRue and Lloyd D. Byars, *Management: Theory and Application,* 4th ed. (Homewood, Ill.: Richard D. Irwin, 1986), 432–33.

7. "Can Jack Smith Fix GM?" *Business Week* (November 1, 1993): 126–31.

8. Ibid.

9. Ibid.

10. Charles Perrow, "The Analysis of Goals in Complex Organizations," *American Sociological Review* 26 (1961): 854–66.

    Peter F. Drucker, *The Practice of Management* (New York: Harper & Row, 1973).

    Luther Gulick and L. Urwick, eds., *Papers on the Science of Administration* (New York: Institute of Public Administration, Columbia University, 1937).

11. Arthur G. Bedeian and Raymond F. Zammuto, *Organizations: Theory and Design* (Chicago: The Dryden Press, 1991).

    See Drucker in note 10 above.

12. G. Pascal Zachary, "Agony and Ecstasy of 200 Code Writers Beget Windows NT," *The Wall Street Journal* (May 26, 1993), A1, A6.

13. David Woodruff and Elizabeth Lesly, "Surge at Chrysler," *Business Week* (November 9, 1992): 88–96.

    Brian Dumaine, "How Managers Can Succeed Through Speed," *Fortune* (February 13, 1989): 54–59.

Ronald Henkoff, "A High-Tech Rx for Profits," *Fortune* (March 23, 1992): 106–107.

Lori Bongiorno, "A Case Study in Change at Harvard," *Business Week* (November 15, 1993): 42.

14. Charles J. Fombrun, Noel M. Tichy, and Mary Anne Devanna, *Strategic Human Resources Management* (New York: Wiley & Sons, 1984).

Anne B. Fisher, "Morale Crisis," *Fortune* (November 18, 1991): 70–80.

15. Myron Magnet, "The Truth About the American Worker," *Fortune* (May 4, 1992): 48–65.

16. See note 13 above.

17. William A. Sodeman, "The Body Shop International PLC," in *Business & Society*, 2nd ed., by Archie B. Carroll (Cincinnati, Ohio: Southwestern, 1993), 637–41.

18. See note 1 above.

19. F. Neil Brady, *Ethical Managing: Rules and Results* (New York: Macmillan Publishing, 1990).

Robert D. Hay, Edmund R. Gray, and Paul H. Smith, *Business and Society: Perspectives on Ethics & Social Responsibility* (Cincinnati, Ohio: Southwestern Publishing, 1989).

Rogene A. Buchholz, *Fundamental Concepts and Problems in Business Ethics* (Englewood Cliffs, N.J.: Prentice-Hall, 1989).

20. Kathleen Deveny, "Strong Brew: Malt Liquor Makers Find Lucrative Market in the Urban Young," *The Wall Street Journal* (March 1, 1992), A1.

21. F. Neil Brady, *Ethical Managing: Rules and Results* (New York: MacMillan Publishing Co., 1990).

22. Neal Templin, "GM Unit Posts Operating Profit for First Time," *The Wall Street Journal* (June 14, 1993), A4.

23. James G. March and Herbert A. Simon, *Organizations* (New York: John Wiley & Sons, 1958).

Herbert A. Simon, *Administrative Behavior,* 3rd ed. (New York: Free Press, 1976).

Richard M. Cyert and James G. March, *A Behavioral Theory of the Firm* (Englewood Cliffs, N.J.: Prentice-Hall, 1963).

24. Charles McCoy, "As Scully Leaves Apple, Image Lingers of a Leader Distracted by His Mission," *The Wall Street Journal* (October 18, 1993), B8.

25. See Scott in note 3, page 19, above.

26. See note 5 above.

Daniel Katz and Robert L. Kahn, *The Social Psychology of Organizations*, 2nd ed. (New York: John Wiley & Sons, 1978).

27. See note 5 above.

Kim S. Cameron, "The Effectiveness of Ineffectiveness," in Barry M. Staw and L. L. Cummings, eds., *Research in Organizational Behavior* (Greenwich, Conn.: JAI Press, 1984), 235–86.

J. Barton Cunningham, "Approaches to the Evaluation of Effectiveness," *Academy of Management Review* 2 (1977): 463–74.

28. Christina Duff, "Blue-Light Blues: K-Mart's Dowdy Stores Get a Snazzy Face Lift, but Problems Linger," *The Wall Street Journal* (November 5, 1993), 1–6.

29. Bob Ortega, "Aging Activists Turn, Turn, Turn Attention to Wal-Mart Protests," *The Wall Street Journal* (October 11, 1994), A1–A6.

30. See Cameron (1984) in note 27 above.

31. See note 5 above.

32. See note 5, pp. 288–93, above.

33. Robert E. Quinn and John Rohrbaugh, "A Spatial Model of Effectiveness: Toward a Competing Values Approach to Organizational Analysis," *Management Science* 29 (1983): 363–77.

34. Thomas J. Peters and Robert H. Waterman, Jr., *In Search of Excellence: Lessons From America's Best-Run Companies* (New York: Harper, Row & Co., 1982).

CHAPTER 4

The Global Environment for Organizations

CASE: TAKE A HIKE*

Two middle-aged executives, Bill Stuart and Fred Hallop, were musing over the American craze for physical fitness as they finished their customary lunchtime five-mile run. Hallop, whose knees had been bothering him for the past few weeks, complained, "I still can't believe we're doing this! We've been pounding the pavement now for over twenty years. I hate to think what our knee joints look like. I think we should just admit that we aren't twenty- or even thirty-something anymore."

Stuart was an elite masters class (over forty) runner who had once qualified for the U.S. Olympic trials in the marathon and held several age group records for a number of road races. He suggested, "All you need, Fred, is a new pair of shoes. And stop buying that cheap, closeout stuff. Spend some money, and get a decent pair. You're only as good as your shoes let you be." Even though he didn't make the Olympic team, Stuart had been receiving free shoes from one of the major shoe companies for many years.

Hallop shot back, "That's easy for you to say. When was the last time you *bought* a pair of running shoes?" Then Hallop sarcastically added, "It's all because of these freebies to stars like you that we mortals have to pay a hundred bucks for running shoes."

Hallop had a point. The first pair of running shoes he purchased in 1972 cost less than $20. There were no superstar endorsements, and back then the shoe companies did only modest advertising. Clearly, technical improvements and inflation would drive up the price of shoes, but a five-fold increase seemed a bit ridiculous. These new shoes didn't seem to last much longer than some of Hallop's early ones, and he seemed to have more injuries and problems recently than he did when he first started running. He had grown tired of the nearly constant model changes that the shoe companies foisted on consumers. He had once complained to Stuart, "Every time I find a shoe that fits and feels right, the

---

*Statistics about the footwear industry are based on an article by Joseph Pereira titled "Footwear Firms, Hit by Fashion Change, Face Disappointing Quarterly Earnings," that appeared in *The Wall Street Journal* (January 17, 1994), p. A5B, and the book on Nike by Donald Katz, *Just Do It* (New York: Random House, 1994).

company drops it. I have to search all over just to find a new model that's right for me. Now I'm having trouble just keeping up with the names of all of them!" On the other hand, Stuart always had the latest in shoe technology—the cutting edge—and he rarely seemed to suffer from injuries. As Hallop headed for the shower, he vowed to stop at the local athletic shoe store on the way home that evening.

Across town at Greenwood Middle School, eighth grade students sat in the cafeteria enjoying their few minutes between lunch and the beginning of the first afternoon class. Conversations shifted among many topics—music, bikes, sports, friends, food, and fashion. Thomas boasted about his latest acquisition, the most recent pair of shoes endorsed by NBA superstar Shaquille O'Neal. These $125 shoes looked intimidating— the latest high-tech variation on the old basketball shoe. The ironic thing was that Thomas wasn't even "into" basketball anymore.

The scene at Greenwood Middle School was beginning to change. A glance around the lunchroom gave evidence of several new trends. A few years ago everybody had to have the latest shoes endorsed by Michael Jordan, Charles Barkley, Bo Jackson, or some other superstar. Although there were still many students like Thomas sporting the latest in basketball, cross training, running, or some other form of athletic footwear, many students had gone in other directions. Sandra was sporting the grunge look, right down to old style Converse All Stars—retro canvas basketball shoes that were popular in the '50s and '60s. Across the lunch table Elizabeth propped up her Doc Martin leather boots. At over a hundred dollars they weren't cheap, but they were virtually indestructable. Several students wore variations on hiking boots from companies such as Timberland, a few wore Treks or other brands of all-terrain rubber sandals, and a few "skaters" wore special skateboarding shoes, such as Airwalks, Vans, or Etnies.

The scene shifts again, this time to the local shopping mall. Fred Hallop has embarked on his shoe-shopping mission. On his way to the local Foot Locker store, he noticed the mall walkers. Every time he visited the mall, he was struck by the number of senior citizens and others who made regular trips to the mall to exercise. He guessed that mall walking must be much like running was for him, a combination of exercise and socializing. Because Fred was on a shoe-shopping mission, it was not surprising that he noticed the mall walkers' shoes. Some were decked out in typical running or cross training shoes, but a large number of the seniors were wearing what looked to be special leather walking shoes. It appeared that even walkers had specialized shoes.

Hallop finally turned a corner and entered the Foot Locker store. Almost immediately he was thrown into a state of shock. This was the first time in a few years he had been in such a store. Previously, he purchased his shoes from mail order companies that catered to runners or occasionally from shoe closeout stores. He was overwhelmed by the large variety of shoes—running, aerobics, cross training, basketball, soccer, walking—and by the prices. One pair of flashy Nike running shoes caught his eye. They seemed to be state of the art in design. They even looked fast. Then Fred looked inside and saw the $129 price tag. After trying on shoes from several different companies, he finally settled on a pair of Asics for $89, the most he ever paid for a pair of running shoes. There was a certain irony in this purchase. The very first pair of running shoes Fred purchased back in 1972 was made by the precursor to Asics, a Japanese company called Onitsuka, and marketed as Tigers by Phil Knight, the founder of Nike.

What Fred Hallop, Bill Stuart, the students at Greenwood Middle School, and the mall walkers may not have realized was the turmoil and turbulence in the athletic footwear industry. Industry observers have begun to note that shifts in consumer tastes, demographics, the economy, and culture are slowing athletic shoe sales. Earnings are among the first signs of trouble. Competition in the industry has been cutthroat, and the leaders, Nike and Reebok, have spent extravagantly on advertising, promotions, and celebrity and superstar endorsements. L.A. Gear has struggled just to stay in the market. It's a common practice among the athletic shoe companies to give out free shoes to people they consider to be highly visible in their given sport. Bill Stuart was a highly competitive masters runner, so he merited free shoes. It is essentially a form of advertising. One extreme version of this practice is contracting with college and professional sports teams through coaches. A coach at a top university basketball or football program can earn a great deal of money through a shoe contract. The shoe company will then provide shoes to the team's players. At the professional level, contracts with specific players are common. Contracts for superstars like Michael Jordan, Bo Jackson, Shaquille O'Neal, David Robinson, Ken Griffey Jr., Barry Sanders, or Emmett Smith can be for several million dollars. The teams and players become walking (or running) billboards for the shoes.

Not only are advertising costs up, but the companies are running into a variety of production problems. In the 1960s and 1970s most of the top quality shoes were made in Japan. (Most of the major athletic shoe companies don't even make their shoes. For example, Nike and Reebok contract with shoe companies throughout the world to make their shoes.) As production costs rose in Japan, the major companies shifted to Korea and Taiwan, but the cost of manufacturing in those countries has also been rising. Companies are continuing to seek low cost producers. China, Singapore, Thailand, and Indonesia are the current hot spots. But problems result from these shifts. Nike, for example, has experienced difficulty maintaining the security of innovative designs. Some manufacturers in China make shoes for both Nike and Reebok. A Reebok representative visiting the factory couldn't miss seeing the latest Nike model. Another problem is counterfeiting. Because of loose controls and inadequate legal protection, some of these contract manufacturers are selling counterfeit products in the black markets of China, Hong Kong, and other places. Maintaining quality has also been difficult in some of these locations. It takes time and money to build a manufacturing infrastructure and for local workers to develop a strong work ethic. The result is that the brand identity that companies such as Nike and Reebok spend millions to develop can be threatened by conditions across the Pacific.

On top of all of these problems, the athletic shoe companies have to contend with labor unrest and other problems in professional sports. Baseball strikes, hockey lockouts, injuries, retirements, or relocations of major franchises can diminish the marketing appeal of teams and players. Thus, the best laid plans can evaporate overnight.

As a result of all of these problems, the cost of many popular shoe styles has risen well above the $100 level. Consumers are beginning to rebel. Reebok reported a 9 percent drop in estimated earnings, Stride Rite showed a 24 percent drop, while L.A. Gear has already reported a 31 percent earnings slide. But there's more to the story than just consumer resistance to high prices. All this happened in the running shoe industry while Timberland, a specialist in outdoor wear, reported a healthy 43 percent increase in profits and Nine West, a maker of casual leather shoes, enjoyed a 24 percent uptick in profits for the last quarter of 1993. Clearly, survival in the shoe industry requires a combination of swiftness, creativity, and durability!

As this description reveals, changes in the footwear industry environment are not only occurring but are hitting the manufacturers in the pocketbook. The major companies are struggling to maintain their edge. Reebok, Stride Rite, and L.A. Gear experienced losses while "leather" makers Timberland and Nine West are enjoying healthy profits as a result of changing consumer tastes, the economy, and culture.

Members of the footwear industry must constantly monitor their environment if they are to stay (as they must) in tune with it. And their environment is far more complex than one might initially think. This chapter examines this environment, its components, and explains why organizations must look outside their borders to understand and deal effectively with their outside environment. Organization success without this understanding and perspective simply is unattainable today.

THE GLOBAL ENVIRONMENT FOR ORGANIZATIONS

The idea that organizations are *open systems* was presented in Chapter 1. Although the idea that organizations are affected by and must interact with the environment may seem obvious and straightforward, we see in this chapter just how complex and important the environment is to any organization. All organizations exist within an environment that affects their operations. For some organizations the environment is rather local, such as the neighborhood area for a family restaurant. For others, such as Ford, General Motors, Nike, or Reebok, the environment is essentially worldwide. The environment is the source of resources, including customers, necessary for survival. Both opportunities for success and threats to existence arise from the environment. Thus, we can begin to see the importance of understanding what factors constitute an organization's environment. In Chapter 5 we turn our attention to tactics that organizations can use to protect themselves from or harness the environment — in other words, how organizations try to manage the environment.

This chapter focuses on describing characteristics of environments. We explore all of those external conditions that could potentially affect an organization — the *organizational environment.*[1] The organizational environment is made up of those things *outside* the organization's boundaries. The organizational environment is comprised of eight sectors or areas that are described in detail below. In addition to these eight specific sectors, one should keep in mind that organizations and their environments exist in a *global* context.

Organizations are affected by events throughout the world. When we consider each sector of the environment, we must not only look at local, regional, or national aspects of that sector, we must also consider the global implications. Obviously, it would be foolish to examine competition in the automobile industry if we did not include Japanese, European, and other producers. The introductory case in this chapter highlighted some international features of the athletic shoe industry. While these examples are obvious, nearly every organization and every sector of the environment is, in some way, affected by events or conditions around the world. Thus, while some organizational theory texts choose to treat international or global business as a distinct sector of the environment, we take the approach that every sector has international or global aspects. To treat global or international forces as discrete or separate issues downplays their pervasiveness.

Although every organization exists within a general organizational environment, each organization is affected differently by that environment because organizations differ in size, industry, goals, technology, location, strategy, and in many other ways. Elements of the environment centrally important to an automaker may be unimportant or only peripherally important to a bank or a shoe manufacturer. The term *task environment* refers to the specific parts of the environment that affect a given organization. Table 4.1 depicts the general organizational environment that potentially affects all organizations and suggests a task environment that could exist for a typical organization.

▧　TABLE 4.1
Sectors of the General Environment

Sector of the Environment	Description
Industry Sector	Competitors and substitute products; the ease or difficulty entering and leaving the industry
Cultural Sector	The local cultural and social conditions in the consumer and labor markets in which the firm operates
Legal and Political Sector	The political system, legal and political institutions, laws, and regulations that affect a firm
Economic Sector	The economic system and the general economic conditions that a firm faces
Technology Sector	The available and emerging technology that a firm can use to transform inputs into outputs
Human Resources Sector	The labor market, available skills, labor unions or organizations, and work ethic of available workers
Physical Resources Sector	Physical conditions (including weather, terrain, supply of natural resources, and natural catastrophes) that may affect an organization
Consumer and Client Sector	The market for the organization's outputs

THE NATURE OF THE GENERAL ORGANIZATIONAL ENVIRONMENT

The modern organization is shaped by components of its environment — from its purpose to the technology it employs, to the resources it needs, to its customers or clients, to its very definition of success. No organization can ignore its environment. In this section we systematically investigate sectors of organizational environments.

The environment contains both *opportunities* and *threats*. Opportunities exist in the form of markets, resources, and other external conditions that the organization can exploit to grow and prosper. Threats, on the other hand, are forces in the environment that may constrain the organization, jeopardize growth or effectiveness, or even threaten the very survival of the organization. Threats, for example, may come from new competitors that challenge a firm's market niche or position, legal or political conditions that place new burdens on a firm, or changing demographic conditions that may erode a previous market base. However, it is important to keep in mind that each organization faces a distinct environment. Factors in the environment that threaten one organization may provide opportunities for another. An example of this dual nature (both opportunities and threats) should be useful.

Companies in a variety of industries are concerned about new environmental protection standards that will become law in the United States in 1996 as a result of the Clean Air Act. The new stricter limits on toxic emissions for everything from manufacturing to operation of automobiles pose a serious threat to companies such as automakers, power generators, oil refiners, and chemical producers, to name a few. These companies must find new ways to produce their products that conform to the constraints emanating from the legal and political sector of the environment. If they fail to conform to these constraints, their very survival could be threatened. These same laws that place burdens on many companies may also provide opportunities for companies such as Catalytica, Inc., a small California firm that develops catalysts that control or speed up chemical reactions.[2] These catalysts help petroleum refiners and chemical manufacturers develop fuels and chemicals that meet new clean air standards. Thus, the threat to one set of firms provides an opportunity for Catalytica.

The message for managers is clear: They have little choice but to pay close attention to the environment and to devise mechanisms for coping with and even influencing that environment.* An organization that is out of touch with its environment would soon use up all its resources; would rely on dated, inaccurate information for decision making; and would lose contact with consumer wants and needs. In the long run an organization that fails to attend to its environment will not survive. To survive and prosper over time, organizations must react to and control the environment.

We begin by examining each of eight sectors of the general organizational environment. The reader should keep in mind that not all organizations are affected equally or in the same way by each of these sectors. We will have more to say about this issue shortly when we examine the task environment and *environmental complexity.* You should also remember that these sectors are not static. Rather, environmental sectors experience *turbulence* or *change.* For some organizations such as the railroads, environmental change is slow compared with the fast pace of change in the computer industry. Thus, it is important not only to identify various sectors that affect an organization but to monitor how those sectors change over time.

Environments also differ with respect to the availability of necessary resources and opportunities—what theorists have referred to as *munificence.*[3] For example, periods of low mortgage interest rates and high levels of employment produce a munificent environment for homebuilders and real estate companies trying to sell residential real estate. Market niches that are crowded by many competitors or that are shrinking because of changing consumer preferences also demonstrate reduced munificence. Thus, athletic shoe companies are experiencing declining munificence.

---

*In Chapter 5 we explore in detail specific mechanisms that organizations use to gain information and attempt to control the environment. We also introduce a theoretical perspective called population ecology that suggests that organizations are nearly powerless to adequately, systematically, and completely control their environments. Rather, it is the environment that does the controlling of organizations.

Finally, one must continue to keep in mind that we live in a global environment. Each of these eight sectors that we highlight has international ramifications. For some organizations, for example, Nike, IBM, or GM, the international ramifications are direct and immediate. They manufacture and market their products throughout the world. For others, like the hardware store featured in the introductory case for Chapter 1, the international ramifications are indirect and more remote. Some of the products they sell may be manufactured in other countries, and economic conditions in other countries may affect prices as well as local interest rates.

INDUSTRY SECTOR

Organizations must be cognizant of conditions within their own industry. The most obvious area of importance is competition. One need only look at the heated competition in the computer industry to see the effects of competition. Extensive competition among IBM and clone PC makers like Compaq, Dell, Gateway 2000, AST, and numerous no-name companies has dramatically driven down the cost of computers at the same time that speed, technical sophistication, and quality have made startling advances. As a result, companies like Compaq and IBM, which were once able to receive a premium price for products perceived as having higher quality than other PCs, have been forced into extensive strategic shifts and cost cutting. Compaq, which once concentrated on a small number of highly sophisticated, highly reliable, high-quality products and commanded a premium price, now cuts prices extensively on PCs and offers a wide array of models to capture the low end of the computer market.

The extensive increases in computing power and quality and accompanying cost cutting affect companies in related markets. Apple has been forced to significantly cut costs and consolidate models of Macintosh computers even though it frequently does not compete head to head with IBM or the clones. Also, the increased power and sophistication of PCs has adversely affected IBM's mainframe computing business. Many computer users who once relied on large, expensive mainframe computers can now perform the same operations on relatively inexpensive PCs. On the other hand, more powerful and sophisticated PCs have provided opportunities for software companies to produce more powerful, sophisticated, and easier-to-use products for a wider market of potential users.

Although many of the leading players in the PC business are American companies, these firms must consider important international issues within the industry sector. For example, one factor in the recent downward pressure on prices has been the influx of foreign-made machines, particularly Korean, such as Leading Technologies, Leading Edge, and Hyundai. Conversely, when American companies try to sell computers in Japan, they must deal with a character-based language that is difficult to convert to conventional keyboards. Additionally, Group Bull, a French company that purchased Zenith's computer business, should be well positioned to compete in Europe as computer firms vie for a share of that market.

Competition today is an international phenomenon. The global marketplace accounts for a major part of the competitive environment for most moderate- to large-size organizations. And it is not just high tech companies like the computer companies above that operate in this international environment. The shoe companies in the introductory case for this chapter demonstrate a somewhat lower tech variation on this theme. Nike, Reebok, Asics, Converse, and L.A. Gear are U.S.–based companies, but their shoes are made and marketed throughout the world. Two of their major competitors are Adidas and Puma, both based in Europe. The pharmaceutical industry is dominated by large, multinational companies. GlaxoWelcome, based in England, has facilities in the U.S. and several other countries. Merck and Johnson & Johnson are U.S.–based, but have facilities in numerous locales. Nearly every major industry is characterized in some way by globalization. As we examine other sectors of the environment (e.g., culture, markets, and regulations), we see that international aspects of environmental sectors make each sector more complex.

Although competition is an important aspect, there is more to the industry sector than competition. Michael Porter[4] has developed a useful framework that elaborates on industry competitiveness and provides a basis for analyzing the industry sector. He identifies five elements of the industry sector: (1) threats of new entrants, (2) substitutability threats, (3) rivalry among firms, (4) buyer bargaining power, and (5) supplier bargaining power. We will examine the first three of these elements in this section. Buyer bargaining power will be discussed in the section on the market sector, and supplier bargaining power will be presented in the section on the resource sector.

Threats From New Entrants. An important aspect of the industry sector is the relative ease or difficulty with which new firms can enter an industry. Porter calls this ***"threats from new entrants"*** while others speak of **barriers to entry.** Several factors contribute to the ease or difficulty of entry, including economies of scale, capital requirements, product differentiation, switching cost, distribution channels, government policies, and various other cost disadvantages.

Economies of scale determine the minimum size at which a type of business can be efficiently run. High economies of scale (i.e., the requirement that a firm must be large in order to be competitive) reduce threats of new entrants. New methods of production and management have reduced economies of scale for some industries. Recent innovations and changes in management have allowed companies like Nucor, a specialty steel producer, to be competitive at a smaller size than conventional wisdom suggested was possible. Nonetheless, certain types of business, such as automobile or chemicals, must of necessity be large because economies of scale are very high.[5]

Closely related to economies of scale is the ***capital required*** to enter an industry. Significant investment in capital equipment and human resources raises barriers to entry. Businesses that require minimal capital investment to start remove one obstacle to entry. For example, building personal computers essentially involves purchasing off-the-shelf technology, then assembling and marketing it. Low-entry barriers result in greater competition because of the potential flood of new companies. Clearly, these companies require expertise in computer assembly and marketing — no small task — but the capital requirements for entry are comparatively low. These low-capital requirements explain in part the proliferation of such PC clone makers as Dell, Gateway, AST, Compaq, Packard Bell, Zeos, and no-name makers too numerous to list. (To get a better indication of this situation, examine the advertising in a typical PC magazine or check your *Yellow Pages* to see how many local companies assemble and market PCs.) By contrast, designing and building supercomputers requires significantly more capital investment in research and development and specialized assembly facilities. There are comparatively fewer supercomputer makers. (There is also a much smaller market for supercomputers.)

Highly *differentiated products* create the perception among customers and potential competitors of uniqueness and raise entry barriers. Patents, copyrights, proprietary knowledge, and brand loyalty can all contribute to product differentiation and raise entry barriers. For example, although toothpaste is relatively easy to make (low-capital barriers), a new company would have to compete with strong existing brands like Crest and Colgate that dominate the market. Sometimes firms will find ways to differentiate. The emphasis on features like baking soda and peroxide toothpastes promoted by several companies and natural toothpastes like Tom's of Maine are examples.

Switching costs refers to costs to buyers associated with shifting to products of a different producer. For example, new entries into computer manufacturing that chose to produce systems that do not use existing operating systems or application software would face high entry barriers. Potential customers would face the extra costs of acquiring software. These extra costs are the costs of switching to a new product and are a barrier to new entrants. IBM has faced extensive competition in the personal computer business because the central processing chips and the disk operating system (DOS) are widely available to competitors. By contrast, Apple holds copyrights for its operating system and, until recently, did not license it to potential competitors. Potential customers would have had substantial switching costs associated with the purchase of new hardware or software. Some critics in retrospect point to IBM's failure to acquire exclusive rights to DOS as a primary reason for its difficulty in the highly competitive personal computer market.[6] On the other hand, recent critics of Apple suggest that it should have licensed its hardware and software to clone makers to ensure a large enough market. The potentially high switching costs may deter potential purchasers.

Access to distribution channels can also lower barriers to entry. The presence of distribution channels removes one entry barrier. When General Motors created the Geo line of cars, market entry was facilitated by using the existing Chevrolet distribution and dealer network. Conversely, an organization that must establish a new distribution system for a new product will encounter an entry barrier. For example, when the Saturn, Lexus, Accura, and Infinity car lines were introduced, their respective companies established new networks of dealers to sell and service these cars. The cost of creating this dealer network raised entry barriers. This cost was one of the factors that discouraged Mazda from pursuing that same strategy. New entrants into the airline industry face two substantial distribution problems. They must acquire gates in airports, and they must gain entry into the computerized reservation systems that travel agents use to sell tickets.

In many industries *government policy* plays an important role in establishing or removing entry barriers. Governments create barriers or remove barriers through domestic and foreign policies, regulatory behavior, and as a customer. For example, government licensing of radio and television stations limits the number of new entrants and controls competition. The awarding of government contracts restricts entry and competition. Defense policy and government purchasing play important roles in defense industries. Without a government contract, it would make little sense to enter into the manufacturing of jet fighter aircraft. Similarly, governments can facilitate the development of industries and specific firms through policies. The governments of England,

France, Germany, and Spain coordinated efforts to form Airbus Industries, a multinational maker of commercial aircraft. Governments can also restrict entry through controlled allocation of scarce resources such as oil drilling or timber rights on government property. Although the recent history of deregulation in industries such as banking and airlines has been mixed, the removal of government regulations in these industries through policy changes has removed some entry barriers.

Entry into foreign markets, either as a seller or manufacturer, may be restricted by government policy. During the height of the Cold War, U.S. firms were forbidden to sell certain types of products in specific countries. For example, until recently, U.S. companies could not sell computers to the former Soviet Bloc countries. Countries may also restrict foreign competitors from doing business in their country in order to protect domestic companies. Japan's policies of restricting foreign retailers and rice shipments are partially aimed at protecting small local retailers and rice farmers. Finally, government trade policies such as the North American Free Trade Agreement (NAFTA) and the General Agreement on Tariffs and Trade (GATT) reduce international barriers to trade. The effects of government go beyond barriers to or facilitation of entry. We return to the discussion of the role of government in the environment when we elaborate on environmental sectors later in this chapter.

Several other *cost disadvantages,* which are unrelated to economies of scale, can also raise entry barriers. Potential new firms in an industry may lack proprietary knowledge (i.e., trade secrets) possessed by existing firms. Entry into a new industry may also require significant time to learn the intricacies of the new business. This learning process is referred to as a *learning curve.* The learning curve reflects the idea that the more time an individual or firm practices a skill or gains experience, the easier (and/or cheaper) it is to do the task. The steepness of the learning curve an organization faces may be affected by the time at which a firm enters a new market. Companies that are *first movers,* the first firm to enter a market, face a steeper learning curve than later entrants into the field. This first mover strategy is referred to as an *r-strategy.*[7] Later entries to the market can typically learn indirectly from the experience of the first movers and avoid problems and obstacles. The late entry strategy is referred to as a *K-strategy.*

New firms may also face problems attempting to acquire scarce resources or favorable locations. For example, as the fast-food market niche becomes more crowded with competitors, new entries are finding that existing franchises have already locked up prime locations.[8]

Each of the above seven factors can substantially raise (or lower) the entry barriers that potential new firms (or existing firms entering new markets) face. High entry barriers will reduce competitiveness by discouraging, or making difficult, entry into an industry. Two other industry characteristics that remain to be examined are substitutability from similar products or services and competitive rivalry among firms.

Substitutability Threats. The nature of an industry is affected by the extent to which substitute products or services exist. Competitiveness increases with the availability of substitute products. Substitutability plays an important role in competitiveness within the pharmaceutical industry. When a company patents a newly developed drug, the company gains some measure of protection from competition. Rival firms cannot produce copies of that same drug. However, nothing prevents a competitor from developing a substitute product to replace existing drugs. For example, for many years the leading prescription for ulcer treatment was the drug Tagamet, produced by Merck. Patent protection reduced competition for a time, but eventually Glaxo Pharmaceuticals produced a substitute drug, Zantac, and dominated the ulcer treatment market. Recently, Merck has reduced the price of Tagamet in anticipation of the expiration of its patent and is now selling it as an over-the-counter (nonprescription) medication.

Competitive Rivalry. Attempts by industry members to improve their position intensifies rivalry within that industry. A variety of factors contribute to increased rivalry within an industry. Large numbers of competitors, or competitors that are of nearly equal size, are likely to face intense rivalry. Limited growth opportunities intensify rivalry. Rivalry is also intensified in industries characterized by high fixed costs and when the costs of exiting the industry are high.

The airline and commercial aircraft industries illustrate different levels of rivalry. The U.S. airline industry is dominated by a small number of large carriers (American Airlines, Delta, United, Northwest, and U.S. Air). Yet, because each firm sees opportunities to expand at the expense of other firms and no single firm is dominant, rivalry among firms is extensive. Moreover, the airlines have high fixed costs that must be covered regardless of how many passengers fly.[9] By contrast, rivalry among commercial aircraft manufacturers is considerably less. Boeing enjoys a dominant position, and its closest competitors are significantly smaller. While Boeing faces less within-industry competition than the airlines, it still faces some rivalry from McDonald-Douglas and Airbus Industries.

In addition to his identification of industry characteristics, Porter also identifies three generic strategies for managing the industry sector: ***overall cost leadership, differentiation strategy,*** and ***focus strategy.*** We discuss these as well other strategies for controlling environments in Chapter 5. Before examining strategies, however, we must complete our description of the environment. Thus, we now move to the second sector of the environment.

CULTURAL SECTOR

Organizations are embedded within a larger environment that extends far beyond a single industry. Perhaps the environmental sector that best represents that embeddedness is culture.* Culture is the foundation that guides much of what happens in a social system. "Culture filters the ways in which people see and understand their worlds. Culture prescribes some behaviors and forbids others. Culture colors the emotional responses that people have to events."[10] Culture is the glue that holds a society together. It contains the values, norms, traditions, and artifacts of a society. Organizations and their members are both affected by and have an effect on culture.

Culture affects the way organizations operate. The societal values held by consumers, for instance, are determined to a great extent by the values society at large holds important.

---

*In this section we use the term *culture* to represent the values, norms, and beliefs of the larger society within which an organization exists. The term *culture* (more specifically, organizational culture) is also used to describe the values, norms, and beliefs that exist *within* an organization. Some overlap between the general use of the term and the organizational-specific use are apparent in concepts such as Japanese management. Chapter 10 specifically examines organizational culture.

Businesses entering new markets as both employers and vendors must consider the local culture. For example, in the U.S. consumers are used to shopping at all hours, any day of the week. However, U.S. firms doing business in other countries often confront different beliefs and values about the appropriate hours for conducting business. For example, Germany has laws that restrict the hours retail stores can be open.[11] Retail stores must close at 6:30 P.M. on most weekdays and 2 P.M. on Saturdays. In 1989 the laws were modified to allow businesses to remain open until 8:30 P.M. on Thursdays. Stores remain closed on Sundays. Similar laws are present in other European countries. These restrictive business hours were the result of several factors, including powerful unions trying to preserve leisure, religious institutions trying to preserve the Christian sabbath, and political institutions trying to preserve the unique local culture. One can imagine the difficulty American firms like Toys "R" Us, Kmart, or Wal-Mart might have operating under these constraints. However, to violate these laws and norms would not only result in legal challenges from the German government but would likely alienate and offend the local citizens — the customers these companies seek to attract. It is important to note that as the Germans become increasingly exposed to U.S. business either directly or through the new media, they are gradually changing some of these business practices.

Laws are not the only force that may dictate behavior, and restrictive retail business hours are only one example of cultural differences in business practices. Other examples, some more dramatic and fundamental, abound. Local cultures can affect such things as styles of dress, manners, conduct of negotiations, and even how business cards are exchanged. For example, many U.S. companies have recently adopted more casual dress codes for employees. IBM, which was long known for the conservative attire of its employees (e.g., blue suits and white shirts), adopted policies and practices that permitted employees to dress more casually. However, this trend has not taken hold at IBM Japan. This is in part because conservative business attire is a more generally and strongly held norm across nearly all Japanese firms. To the Japanese, appearance, or *tatemae,* is critically important.[12]

Societal norms are those standards that mold the behavior, attitudes, and values of those members who constitute a society.[13] Norms come from laws, customs, religious teachings, and common practice. Members of the society take them into consideration in decisions about behaviors. Behaviors such as business hours, manners, speech, and dress reflect the prevailing culture of the community. Businesses must pay heed to the culture if they want to be part of that local community. The growing globalization of business has meant that many local cultures have been exposed to new and different ideas and practices, and many businesses have been exposed to new values, beliefs, and customs. In fact, many business organizations have themselves become microcosms of multiculturalism. ABB Asea Brown Boveri, a Swedish-Swiss maker of train engines, generators, and other large items, does business throughout the world and has taken great pains to establish a uniquely Swedish culture while at the same time accommodating the local culture in which the company's business units reside.[14] Similarly, when Honda first started building motorcycles and cars in the U.S., it carefully modified its distinctive Japanese style of doing business to accommodate American values, beliefs, norms, and behaviors. In fact, Honda chose to locate in central Ohio because of the specific local culture and the resulting positive work ethic of the residents.[15]

Violating local norms or customs can be costly. The Disney Company decided to continue its longstanding prohibition against serving alcohol when it opened EuroDisney World in France. However, local customs supported consumption of alcohol. One result was that many French visitors to the park brought their own beverages, depriving Disney of much needed concession revenues. Disney has since changed that policy to accommodate European tastes.[16]

As the examples above indicate, values, beliefs, norms, and behaviors, although durable, are not resistant to change. Businesses must monitor their environment to detect threats or opportunities from changing values, beliefs, norms, and behaviors. Clearly, producers of tobacco products have been adversely affected by changing attitudes toward the use of tobacco products. Conversely, changed attitudes about health, sports, and fitness, beginning in the 1970s, virtually created new business opportunities for companies such as Nike and Reebok. Schools, churches, political institutions, and the media play critical roles in molding, transforming, and disseminating culture.[17]

These diverse examples illustrate that culture is a critical component of the environment with which managers must reckon. While we typically think of culture creating constraints on organizations, closer inspection suggests that culture may also be an important source of opportunities. We return to culture in Chapter 10 when we focus more specifically on the internal culture of individual organizations.

LEGAL AND POLITICAL SECTOR

All organizations are affected to some degree by the diverse legal and political systems in their environments. The political system—the government, political, and legal processes—is an important variable in virtually all aspects of managerial decision making and activity. Like other aspects of the environment, the legal and political sector provides both constraints and opportunities to organizations.

The legal and political sector is important to the study of organizations because it is the source of laws and regulations that govern the operation of businesses. This sector includes local, regional, national, and international legal and political systems. In the case of an American firm, this could include city, county, state, and national laws and regulations. Additionally, a typical firm may also be affected by international agreements or the laws of other countries, especially if such a firm does business outside the U.S. or competes with foreign firms. In addition to the legal and regulatory functions of governments, they also affect organizations through the collection and provision of information, through research activities, and through governmental direct or indirect consumption.

Perhaps the most obvious impact of government is through its powers to tax and regulate. Governments often attempt to spur economic activity through tax cuts or suppress demand through the application of taxes. For example, local governments may offer tax abatements (i.e., elimination or reduction of taxes) to businesses willing to locate within the government's jurisdiction. In 1993 several states engaged in heated competition for new Mercedes Benz and BMW manufacturing facilities. The competing states typically offered elaborate plans that involved relief from property taxes for as much as ten years.[18] As a result of these tax breaks, Alabama was able to lure a Mercedes Benz plant and South Carolina obtained a BMW plant. This use of taxation powers provides business opportunities not only for the targeted firms but may also provide benefits for supplier organizations selling to BMW or Mercedes Benz. Similarly, many U.S. companies have relocated to Puerto Rico because of specific federal tax advantages granted to Puerto Rican companies.[19] On the other hand, several states and the federal government have used nuisance taxes to inhibit consumption of certain products including tobacco, alcohol, and gasoline. Increases of taxes on cigarettes have had significant impact on the tobacco industry. Guzzler taxes on inefficient luxury cars suppressed the sales of those cars.

Managers need to become familiar with applicable laws and regulations because nearly every facet of their operation is affected by legal and political considerations. In the United States organizations must, for example, heed the Equal Employment Opportunities Commission (EEOC) personnel guidelines in hiring, training, promotion, compensation, and firing. The Americans with Disabilities Act (ADA), passed by Congress in 1992, not only set personnel standards for the employment of disabled Americans, it also stated requirements for access by disabled individuals to all sorts of organizations. Businesses and other organizations are required to take into consideration the accessibility of their physical facilities to potential customers and employees. The Occupational Safety and Health Act (OSHA) sets requirements for the safe operation of facilities, including regulations protecting workers from exposure to toxic chemicals, dangerous noise levels, and other threatening conditions. The Securities and Exchange Commission (SEC) and the Internal Revenue Service (IRS) regulate the ways in which businesses are chartered, traded, monitored, and taxed. The above examples are only a few of the alphabet soup of laws, regulations, and government agencies that cover nearly every aspect of business operation.

Government's impact on business extends beyond domestic policy and domestic businesses. Another area of rapid change in recent years is international trade. The signing of NAFTA has removed or substantially reduced trade barriers among the United States, Canada, and Mexico.[20] Much debate raged over the anticipated impact of NAFTA on the three trade partners, but the real impact is uncertain. Shortly after NAFTA was signed into law, the leading trading nations of the world wound up seven years of often intense and bitter negotiations over GATT.[21] This agreement will also significantly reduce international trade barriers. Like NAFTA, the real impact of GATT is uncertain, but it will certainly change the way business acts. Both NAFTA and GATT are the result of governmental action, but these treaties also demonstrate that it is not only the actions of the domestic government (i.e., the home government of an organization) that affect a firm. Actions of foreign governments can open or close potential markets, place restrictions on the conduct of businesses, or offer incentives and opportunities to firms.

Communications and transportation have made the world a much smaller place. The events of governments in far-flung corners of the globe can have extensive consequences on organizations. Few people would have predicted the downfall of the eastern European communist block including the former Soviet Union, reunification of Germany, peace agreements between Israel and Palestinians, disintegration of the former Yugoslavia, or many other startling events in the global political arena. Management has a responsibility to monitor its environment, familiarize itself with the political climate, and adjust to it. Opportunities also exist to influence the political system.

Lobbying is a fact of political life; corporations and organizations attempt to influence government policy through lobbying. We examine lobbying and other means of environmental control in greater detail in Chapter 5.

The following section deals with the economic sector, a companion to the legal and political sector. In reality, these two elements of the environment are practically inseparable because actions taken in one generally has some impact on the other.

ECONOMIC SECTOR

Organizations exist within some form of economic system that exerts tremendous influence on them. There are, of course, many forms of economic order, ranging from mixed private-enterprise (i.e., capitalist) systems of North America, western Europe, and Japan to centrally planned economies like that of China, North Korea, and Cuba. In between, numerous economies are undergoing fundamental transformations from central planning to some form of market-based economy. Regardless of their form, however, all economic systems are concerned with resource allocation and distribution of goods and services. Market-based economies allocate through pricing. The vagaries of weather, physical catastrophes, or world events can cause havoc in markets for commodities such as oil, grains, or minerals. In market-based economies, prices, to a great extent, should reflect the relative supply and demand. U.S. oil companies, for example, prospered during oil embargoes of the 1970s because of the high price of oil but suffered more recently because of the glut of oil on the world market and the resulting price competition. Centrally planned economies attempt to deal with these pricing problems through government policy and industry control. Scarce items may be rationed or prices may be artificially manipulated, but the price of central control may be inefficient organizations that lack the discipline of markets. Moreover, it is not unusual for black markets to emerge in centrally planned economies despite the best efforts of governments to control all allocation of goods and services.

The extent of government control has an important effect on the types of organizations that exist and how those organizations are managed. Central planning often dictates the specific form of organizations as well as how those organizations will be managed. One problem many former communist countries faced as they moved from centrally planned economies to market economies was that they lacked financial institutions such as banks, brokerage firms, and equity markets. In market economies owners and managers decide on the specific characteristics of organizations.[22] Even in the relatively free market environments of North America, western Europe, and Japan, government still exerts significant control over the economy. Political debate in the United States typically focuses on how much control over business and the economy the federal government should exercise.[23]

The nature of the economic system is not the only aspect of the economic sector that is important to organizations. The general condition of the economy is also of great importance. Economic conditions refer to a wide array of factors including the unemployment rate, inflation rate, currency stability, currency exchange rates, capital availability, interest rates, cost of labor, and population demographics (i.e., age, sex, and education levels of the populace). These factors affect many aspects of organizational existence, including the competitive advantages firms may enjoy in certain economies, the cost of doing business, and the stability of the business environment.

Like every other element of an organization's environment, the economic sector is constantly changing. We have already noted the movement toward market-based economic systems in the former communist countries of eastern Europe. More subtle changes in economic conditions can also have profound effects. The German economy, renowned for its robustness, experienced some difficulty in the early 1990s as a result of reunification. Unemployment rates increased to levels unknown since World War II. Tight monetary and fiscal policies helped to drive up the value of German currency, making German products expensive in the U.S. Some companies, such as BMW and Mercedes Benz, have relocated manufacturing outside Germany while others have attempted to purchase U.S. companies.[24] In the mid-1990s, the Mexican economy is stumbling badly and the value of the peso has dropped, causing the price of imports to increase and the country's balance of trade to become negatively skewed.[25] As a result, many foreign firms have reduced investments in Mexico and have altered plans to do business there.

Part of the change in the economic sector is that economics has become more of a global issue and less restricted to local or national economies. Products that were traditionally developed and manufactured in the United States, such as steel, motor vehicles, electronics, and heavy equipment, are now made in many other locales. Many companies operate in multiple locations throughout the world. Sometimes products are developed in one nation, manufactured in another, and sold in still a third location. General Motors, Ford, Volkswagen, Honda, and Toyota, for example, manufacture and sell cars throughout the world and are affected by economic conditions in each of the countries where they operate. Recent ratification of NAFTA and GATT, along with the European Community's (EC) proposed move to a single European currency and unrestricted trade among EC members, increases the importance of global economics. Although local economies are still important — just ask retailers in a market where a large employer has laid off thousands of workers — businesses cannot ignore global economic conditions.

| **Exhibit 4.1** | **How Global Economics Plays on Main Street, America[26]** |

You might not think that things like international trade talks or changes in the value of foreign currency would have much effect on life in a small, rural town like Troy (population 19,000), Ohio, in the southwestern part of the state not far from Cincinnati and Dayton. But nothing is further from the truth. The 15 percent rise in the value of the yen in 1993, the latest move that has brought the exchange rate from over 300 yen to the dollar in the early 1970s to just over 100 yen to the dollar in late 1993, means that shoppers in local businesses face steeply higher prices for Japanese goods including cultured pearls, cameras, and cars. For example, an 18-inch strand of imported cultured pearls jumped from just under $900 a few years ago to nearly $3,000 today. Anyone who has shopped for a car recently knows that the prices of Japanese imports skyrocketed compared to prices in the 1980s. The price advantage the Japanese once enjoyed over American manufacturers turned into a disadvantage in 1994.

The currency fluctuations have also adversely affected local firms that are involved in importing and exporting Japanese goods. Hobart Bros. Company, a local machinery company, has a joint venture with Yaskawa Electric. Hobart buys robots from its Japanese partner and adapts the machines for users. The price of those robots has risen steeply with the rise in the yen. Moreover, Hobart was selling these machines in Sweden, but a significant drop in the value of the Swedish krona priced Hobart out of the European market.

Not all of the news is bad for Troy residents. Local farmers believe that recent currency fluctuations should make their soybeans and corn more attractive in Japan. Southwest Ohio is home to many Japanese transplant companies including Honda, Matsushita (Panasonic), Gokoh Corporation, and Kao to name a few. The weak dollar and strong yen may be the best incentive to lure other Japanese firms to the region, which would bolster the local economy. But with weak economies in Japan and western Europe, these transplant firms may still have difficulty selling their goods.

It should be clear that even in small towns of middle America the world economy can have a profound impact on life.

TECHNOLOGY SECTOR

The term *technology* has a very specific meaning in organization theory. The term refers to *specific skills, knowledge, tools, and abilities necessary to complete a job.*[27] This includes making and delivering a product or service. (This conceptualization of technology should be clearly differentiated from the development of new high tech consumer products, what we refer to as product innovations.) We explore this concept in greater detail in Chapter 6.

For now, it is important to understand that all organizations use technology to do their work. Given the common use of the word, we may typically think only about things such as computers and automation, but technology is a much broader concept and also refers to such diverse factors as whether work is done by individuals or by groups, the level of training or skill needed to complete a task, and the number of different tasks people in an organization or work unit perform.

The relevance of technology to the discussion of external environment is the fact that the environment is a significant source of technological innovations—new ways for members of organizations to do their jobs. To be able to compete successfully, organizations must have access to technological improvements that potentially provide greater efficiency, superior quality, or products or services that would otherwise not be possible.[28] A roofer using conventional hammer and nail technology to put shingles on a house would have great difficulty competing against one using a pneumatic staple gun and staples. The latter tool allows the roofer to work several times faster. Kmart has had great difficulty competing against Wal-Mart because Kmart's inventory control system is an antique compared with Wal-Mart's state-of-the-art computerized system inventory tracking and delivery system.[29] These two examples emphasize how new equipment—pneumatic staplers and computerized inventory control systems—can improve efficiency.

Technological innovations may also involve how people interact to carry out their jobs.[30] One of the most startling innovations at GM's Saturn plant was *not* the equipment but the team approach that was used to assemble cars — something very different from the techniques used at typical GM assembly lines.[31]

Economics plays a critical role in technological decisions. As noted earlier in this chapter in the discussion of the industry sector, factors such as capital requirements and economies of scale can be deterrents to entry into an industry. Such industries as automobile manufacturing and steel production require extensive investments in part because of the technology used. However, one of the dramatic changes in some industries is that new technologies — new approaches to assembling cars and new methods for smelting iron ore — produce new, lower economies of scale.[32]

Managers must scan the environment and investigate new technologies to find the best methods for transforming inputs into outputs. Failure to do so eventually results in inefficiencies and an inability to compete successfully.

HUMAN RESOURCES SECTOR

Recall that a key part of the definition of an organization is that it is made up of people. Organizations must go outside their boundaries to obtain these human inputs. The nature of the organization determines to a large extent the kinds and amounts of abilities that are required of potential workers. The human resources sector is the source of these human inputs.

There is more to the human resources sector than just the mere availability of labor. Levels of training and education, local wage and benefit standards, presence or absence of labor unions, and prevailing worker values or attitudes are a few examples of human resources sector variables that organizations must consider in their human resources policies and their decisions on where to locate. Earlier, it was mentioned that Honda's decision to locate its American auto and motorcycle assembly facilities was largely motivated by the cost of labor and local worker values.[33] Other key factors that motivate firms to locate in specific places are the average level of education of the populace and the availability of educational facilities. In a recent study, *Fortune* magazine noted that businesses that depend on innovations and new technology seek to locate where the workforce is highly educated.[34] In the United States, the Raleigh/Durham, North Carolina, area ranked number one, largely because of the proximity of three major research universities: the University of North Carolina–Chapel Hill, Duke University, and North Carolina State University. In fact, as organizations move toward broadening worker responsibilities, downsizing, and greater automation of routine tasks, worker knowledge and education are becoming more important factors in decisions concerning human resources.

Several human resources trends are worth noting and demonstrate the critical nature of this sector. First, with the trend toward downsizing and a leaner, more flexible workforce, many organizations are beginning to hire more part-time, temporary, or contract workers.[35] These workers can be used during periods of peak demand or for the completion of specific, specialized tasks. When demand slackens or when special needs cease, temporary, part-time, or contract workers are released. While such arrangements may reduce an organization's overhead (these workers receive only minimal benefits), they may also result in less stability and reduced worker commitment. Second, as organizations become leaner and flatter, they are requiring workers to become more flexible, perform more and different tasks, and take greater responsibility.[36] This, as noted earlier, requires that workers be better educated, but it may also mean that workers suffer greater on-the-job stress. This may come about as full-time workers work longer hours while worrying about downsizing, restructuring, and their job security. These trends to leaner and flatter organizations also frequently create situations in which managers know less about specific technical problems than their subordinates. This demands that managers learn new skills in managing highly trained technical and professional workers. Third, trends toward the globalization of organizations suggest that managers will frequently face situations in which they manage workers from different cultural backgrounds than their own. In discussing the socio-cultural sector, we noted that at ABB Asea Brown Boveri, Swedish managers sometimes face the difficult human resources task of managing workers from different backgrounds who speak different languages and have different values. Additionally, changing trade and immigration laws that increase companies' access to new markets will likely make the labor market more complex. Obviously, managers must consider carefully the human resources sector when making a wide range of strategic decisions about their firms' future.

PHYSICAL RESOURCES SECTOR

This sector of the environment contains all the physical resources an organization needs to operate. A prime feature of the physical resources sector are those raw materials that serve as inputs to an organization. For example, the steel, plastic, rubber, electronic components, paint, and so forth that a car manufacturer needs to build cars are part of the physical resources sector. Wide fluctuations in the cost and availability of crude oil have caused problems in a broad cross section of businesses either directly involved in oil exploration and refining or indirectly involved as consumers of crude oil. The degree to which critical resources are concentrated in the hands of a few suppliers can be a critical factor in the success or failure of organizations attempting to acquire those resources. Concentration of resources gives suppliers significant bargaining leverage.

The physical conditions an organization faces are also a critical part of the resource sector. These may include climatic conditions and geography. In the highly competitive fast-food industry, a prime factor in the success of a restaurant is geographic location. Yet, in that mature industry the number of prime locations still available to newcomers is rather limited.[37] New firms must either manage with less advantageous locations or find ways to compensate for their inferior sites. Subway manages with strip mall or other high-traffic locations. Rally's hamburger chain has prospered using small parcels of land that are not in high demand.

Weather conditions can cause significant problems for many organizations. In the summer of 1988 the problem in the U.S. was drought. Prices of agricultural products soared, and the diminished supply of water threatened many communities. Because of the significant price increases for agriculture products, the following years saw a dramatic increase in plantings and demand for farm supplies. In the summer of 1993 U.S. farmers faced too much rain. Flooding of the upper Mississippi River caused massive problems in agriculture and in many other businesses in Illinois, Iowa, and Missouri.

Some aspects of the physical environment, such as climate and physical disasters, are unpredictable and/or uncontrollable. Other aspects, such as the supply of raw materials, are somewhat more amenable to control. Nonetheless, it is critical that managers monitor the physical environment and attempt to manage or at least respond to developing conditions in the physical environment. It is also important that managers have disaster plans in place to cope with such unpredictable natural disasters as hurricanes, earthquakes, tornados, floods, and other events. The 1995 earthquake in Kobe, Japan, a key shipping terminus, caused innumerable problems for companies in Japan depending on the transshipment of supplies. Local businesses as well as imports and exports were seriously disrupted by this disaster.[38]

CONSUMER AND CLIENT SECTOR

The systems model of organizations, introduced in Chapter 1, highlighted that organizations acquire resources (both human and physical) from the environment, internally transform those resources through the use of technology, and then try to dispose of those resources in the external environment. Essentially, the organization is concerned with converting resources into products or services that are desired by consumers or clients. Marketplace success depends on careful analysis and a thorough understanding of market conditions.

It is imperative for managers to identify characteristics of the consumer and client market that an organization serves. Large cookie companies like the Nabisco division of RJR Nabisco Holdings Corporation, Keebler Company, and Sunshine Biscuit, Inc. are learning that lesson all too well. Recent trends including an aging population of baby boomers, preferences for either healthy products or premium products, and competition from private label store brands have resulted in a changed marketplace for these industry leaders.[39] Both Nabisco and Keebler experienced significant sales declines of cookies in the early 1990s. To recapture market share, these companies have embarked on market strategies aimed at bringing customers back and enticing new customers through new low-fat and premium products, new packaging, and more aggressive promotion. These strategies are all aimed at managing the consumer and client sector.

Organizations must also be aware of the potential power of buyers. Buyers who are the largest or most significant customers of an organization can exercise significant control, much like the resource suppliers mentioned earlier. For example, Wal-Mart can influence its supplier firms because of the large volume of business it does. Wal-Mart can win special pricing concessions, better service, or even special products. Sears has also done this in many areas and has been especially successful selling private label Kenmore washing machines and dryers produced for them by Whirlpool.

Organizations must continue to be aware of changing consumers' and clients' preferences in order to serve those needs. The survival of an organization that fails to stay abreast of its marketplace is likely to be precarious. The above example from the snack foods industry suggests some techniques — new products, new market niches, and advertising and promotional activity — that can be used to control the marketplace. In Chapter 5 we more systematically examine a wide array of techniques that can be used in some or all sectors of the environment.

SECTORS OF THE ENVIRONMENT: A RECAPITULATION

Each of the eight sectors of the environment—industry, culture, legal and political, economic, technology, human resources, physical resources, consumer and client— can have a profound impact on an organization. However, each organization—even similar organizations in the same industry—has a unique environment. Clearly, the more similar the organizations, the more likely they are to share similar environmental elements. These eight sectors make up the ***general environment.*** The configuration of sectors and elements within sectors that are most important to a given organization make up that organization's ***task environment.*** There is more to the environment, however, than the sectors. We turn our attention now to painting a more dynamic view of environments.

ENVIRONMENTAL COMPLEXITY, CHANGE, AND MUNIFICENCE

The environment creates problems for organizations because it is a source of uncertainty and constraints. ***Uncertainty*** arises because organizations face difficulty finding information and because situations change unpredictably. Two factors, ***environmental complexity*** and ***environmental change,*** contribute to uncertainty. Limitations or constraints also arise because of the limited capacity of the environment to support organizations. The term ***munificence*** refers to the availability of resources or the environment's capacity to support organizations.[40]

ENVIRONMENTAL COMPLEXITY

Environmental complexity refers to the *number* and *relatedness* of environmental elements that affect an organization. Some organizations are directly affected by only a few environmental sectors, or elements within those sectors, and the elements and sectors are closely related. An environment characterized by a few related elements or sectors is defined as *simple.* Organizations that must interact with many sectors, or elements within those sectors, in which the elements or sectors are unrelated face a *complex* environment.[41]

Two examples illustrate differences in environmental complexity. A company like Mrs. Field's Homemade Cookies may face a relatively simple environment, especially compared with an aircraft company or an automaker. Mrs. Field's requires only a few physical resources—baking ingredients and store equipment. Human resource demands are not great; industry competition, while increasing, is not a major problem; clearly, consumer demand must be present; and the impact of the economy would be two-fold— the availability of capital to finance expansion and general consumer confidence. The net result is a fairly simple environment. By contrast, a company like Boeing faces a complex environment. Nearly every sector is important, and each contains multiple elements to which Boeing must respond. For example, the legal and political sector affects Boeing because the government, through the military, is one of Boeing's largest customers. The government also affects Boeing through its regulation of the airline industry and through restrictions on trade with foreign countries. Moreover, things like employment and pollution regulations are more likely to have impact on Boeing than on Mrs. Fields. The point is that Boeing has a complex environment and must attend to far more of its environment than a company such as Mrs. Field's. Complexity means that organizations must gather more information about their environments. Greater complexity raises the amount of information that is required to successfully manage.

ENVIRONMENTAL CHANGE

By now it should be obvious that environmental conditions that affect organizations change. Economic conditions change: Interest rates fluctuate; employment levels change; consumer confidence moves; and government economic policies are modified. New technologies are introduced in many industries. Consumer preferences are fluid. Styles that were popular just a few years ago are now regarded as in poor taste. New competitors may enter an industry. All of these changes create **turbulence.**[42] Like complexity, environmental change or turbulence means that managers have to pay close attention to the environment and gather much information. Strategies that worked in the past may not fit the changing conditions. Old technologies may no longer be efficient and competitive. Organizations and their managers must be flexible and responsive to changing conditions. When an organization faces a calm or placid environment, one characterized by little change, yesterday's methods or plans are acceptable and tried-and-proven strategies suffices. The organization does not need to carefully monitor the environment and gain new information because things probably have not changed much since the last time the environment was monitored.

Computer companies live in a rapidly changing environment. Technology, competition, software, and customer preference all change and change rapidly. Firms dealing in this industry must not only constantly monitor these changing conditions, they must also try to forecast and predict future conditions and develop strategies to cope. They must respond quickly — speed may be the most important factor in coping.

MUNIFICENCE

We have repeatedly mentioned that the implication of an open systems view of organizations is that organizations must turn to the environment for resources. However, the environment is not an infinite store of resources. Some resources are abundant while others are quite scarce. **Environmental munificence** takes into consideration that abundance or scarcity of resources presents opportunities or places constraints on organizations.[43] More specifically, munificence refers to the capacity of the environment to support organizations. Munificence may be applied to the availability of financial support, access to prime locations, presence of key human resources, or possession of critical physical resources. The earlier example of competition for scarce prime restaurant locations in the fast-food industry is an example of an environment that would be low in munificence for new firms entering the business. In general, low munificence makes success for organizations far more difficult. Think how difficult it would be to get into the diamond mining industry. DeBeers of South Africa controls 95 percent of the diamond supply. Table 4.2 summarizes these environmental conditions.

■ TABLE 4.2

Environmental Dimensions	Description
Environmental Complexity:	The *number* and *relatedness* of environmental elements that affect an organization
Environmental Change:	The *amount* and *speed* with which elements of the environment *change* (turbulence)
Munificence:	The abundance of resources present in an organization's environment

CONTEMPORARY ENVIRONMENTS

Even though we presented the environment sector by sector, in reality, organizations face the entire environment. Some parts may be more important or salient than others, and this may even change over time. The trend in environmental conditions in recent years has definitely been toward increasing environmental turbulence. Alvin Toffler's classic, *Future Shock,* stands as witness to the unprecedented change with its all-encompassing impact on virtually every institution in society. In business many writers have argued quite convincingly that *all businesses* are facing increasingly complex and turbulent environments.[44] Management has a new and challenging responsibility—to monitor environmental conditions and to develop and implement effective strategies for dealing with those conditions. Organizations must also learn. More effective adaptation requires that organizations learn better. A key point of the contingency framework introduced in Chapter 1 is that different conditions in the organizational context—and environment is part of that context—require different ways of organizing and managing. Much of the focus in both academic organizational theory and popular management literature has been on how organizations should respond. Chapter 5 takes up the issue of specific methods or strategies for managing environments.

SUMMARY

■ All organizations exist within a larger environmental context. That larger environmental context is composed of eight sectors, and each of those sectors has an international or global component. Although all organizations exist in a general environment, each organization faces a unique environmental domain that is specific to that firm.

The industry sector contains the set of similar and competing firms. In addition to the extent of competition within an industry, the sector also involves the barriers to new entrants in an industry. Students of organizations should realize that these industry concepts—competition and barriers to entry—can be applied to all types of organizations, including public, private, profit, and nonprofit.

Culture, composed of the values, norms, artifacts, and accepted behavior patterns in a society, affects the way the organizations operate. One must recognize that cultures vary widely, and they place differing demands or constraints on organizations. We will return to the idea of culture later in the text to examine specific organizational cultures.

The effects on organizations of the legal and political sector are pervasive. Laws, regulations, policies, tax levees, tariffs, trade agreements — the list of legal and political elements of the environment is nearly endless. As organizations face global environments, the traditional boundaries of legal and political influence are reduced. Now organizations must confront a vast array of legal and political factors.

We noted that the economic sector is closely tied to the legal and political sector. Much of the activity in the economic sector is linked to government policy and action. Once again, this could refer to local, regional, national, and foreign government action. The economic sector consists of the type of economic system that an organization must confront, as well as the general economic conditions.

Organizations use technology to convert inputs into outputs. The environment is a source of new technologies that may make work easier, more efficient, or simply make some task possible.

The notion of an organization as an open system means, by definition, that organizations must go outside their boundaries to acquire resources. Two critical resource sectors that organizations must manage are human resources and physical resources. The human resources sector contains the set of human characteristics firms may need while the physical resources sector contains the specific resources and general physical conditions that firms face.

The final sector of the environment is the customer and client sector. Without customers or clients no organization would last long. The consumers are the ultimate arbiters of an organization's success. Organizations must identify and respond to customer and client demands.

Finally, the concepts of environmental complexity, change, and munificence are useful in characterizing the uncertainty and resource availability present in a given environmental domain. The trend today is toward increasingly uncertain environments and decreasing munificence. For organizations to succeed in these uncertain and scarce environments they must monitor and manage environmental conditions, and that is the focus of Chapter 5.

Questions for Discussion

1. Describe fully the environment that a typical local business (e.g., fast food, pizza, computer retail, bank, etc.) might face, and explain why it is important for managers to be aware of that environment.
2. Why is it important to view organizations as open systems?
3. Describe typical barriers to entry that a business like the one you chose in question one might face.
4. It may be obvious how government actions can constrain or put limits on businesses. How can government create opportunities for businesses?

5. This chapter focuses on the global environment. It was stated that even small, local businesses can be affected by global environmental conditions. Discuss how this may be so.
6. Give some examples of how conditions in the physical environment may affect businesses.
7. Describe the environmental factors (both positive and negative) that affect your university. What sectors of the environment appear to be most important?
8. Select an event in the recent world, national, and/or local news, and analyze its environmental impact on business.

CASE: TAKE OUT THE TRASH*

What to do with the hamburger wrapper and the soft drink cup? This is a question that's answered by thousands of people every day around the world. For many of us the answer is all too simple and fast and quite harmful — simply toss them out the window or on the ground. This way, however, has come under scrutiny and question lately as we have become aware of the shear magnitude of wrappers, cups, and myriad other kinds of trash that we take out every day.

Economics, the environment, government regulations, and cultural pressures have interacted to cause this awareness. What at one time was a cheap and efficient way — use of the garbage dump — is now being questioned on all these grounds. Recycling has also entered the trash picture as what at one time was thought to be the cure-all for the problem of trash disposal.

In 1987 the *MOBRO*, a garbage barge, spent weeks searching for a spot to unload its cargo of municipal solid waste generated in Islip, New York. It seemed that no one wanted this unsightly cargo. As the odyssey ended, it was learned that the cargo was the result of a private hauler's trying to dump Islip's waste. The eventful journey, nevertheless, served to focus the nation's attention on what was then thought to be a garbage crisis. But today we see that the nation is really far from running out of space to put our refuse.

SHORTAGE OF TRASH

Many communities are facing what in 1987 would have seemed improbable — they do not have enough trash! As one means of dealing with garbage, many local governments built incinerators that would serve two purposes — to dispose of trash by burning and to provide the fuel for the generation of cheap electricity. These generators were hailed as the battleground where technology prevailed over trash. Environmental officials at all levels encouraged the building of these trash-burning saviors. Not only would they get rid of trash, they would assure communities of a long-term source of cheap electricity. Thus, there was a splurge of incinerator building in the 1980s to the point that they now burn about 16 percent of the nation's trash.

---

*This case is based in part on the following article: Jeff Bailey, "Up In Smoke," *The Wall Street Journal* (August 11, 1993), pages A1–A2. The article "Recycling, Is It Worth The Effort?" *Consumer Reports* (February 1994), pages 92–98 also was helpful.

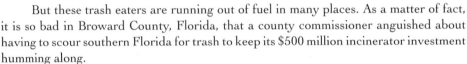

But these trash eaters are running out of fuel in many places. As a matter of fact, it is so bad in Broward County, Florida, that a county commissioner anguished about having to scour southern Florida for trash to keep its $500 million incinerator investment humming along.

At the height of concern about running out of landfill for garbage disposal, little attention was paid to the economics of trash disposal; however, the situation is now so bad in many communities that local taxpayers are being asked to subsidize the operation of incinerators because of lack of trash. To demonstrate the seriousness of the economic side of disposal, the average cost of incinerator disposal is about twice that of dumps. Incinerators were not designed to be cheap but rather to help address the problem of how to obtain a long-term source of cheap electricity and to replace unsightly dumps.

RECYCLING

The national emphasis on recycling is another factor that must be considered when trying to deal with the trash problem. The push to recycle everything from tin cans to hamburger wrappers and drinking cups has been responsible for sharp reductions in the amount of trash available for incineration. Economic conditions in recent years have also signaled less trash with the result being that local governments are now frequently in the position of literally bidding for trash. Some have even gone so far as to place guards along riverfronts to prevent trash from being smuggled out to other users!

COMPETITION

Among other results, these conditions have produced tension between private waste management companies such as WMX Technologies, Ogden Corporation, and Westinghouse Electric Corporation, and government entities. In order to stimulate private investment, local governments would typically provide municipal financing and guarantee a given amount of trash as fuel, and the companies took the assignment of making the entire project work.

When the market price for garbage plunged, friction was inevitable because the local governments had taken the risk, and the companies stood to reap the benefits. And so the trash shortage began what industry watchers have termed the *death spiral*. The shortfall causes higher dump fees to cover fixed costs and thus drives away local haulers. For example, in Claremont, New Hampshire, the incinerator is in full operation with a $96.50 fee per ton for local trash and $40-a-ton fee to attract outside trash. It looks like an endless cycle according to Allen Dusault, head of the New Hampshire–Vermont Solid Waste Project.

Air pollution stemming from the burning of waste is a growing concern both for environmentalists and government officials. To adapt incinerators with effective control devices is extremely expensive, causing an upward pressure on rates. Consequently, some utilities are fighting a federal law that forces them to obtain their electricity from incinerators at prices that are above that which market forces would suggest.

Then there is the matter of the *definition* of hazardous waste, the residue of ashes often left when trash is burned in the generation of electricity. A Federal Appeals Court

in Chicago maintains the ashes should be treated as hazardous waste while one in New York says they should not be. If the ashes are ultimately defined as hazardous, it could triple the disposal fee incinerators would have to pay to dispose of the ashes, which frequently contain heavy metals, among other things.

Another issue facing trash disposal is the matter called flow control, a common practice that allows a municipality to legally require all the trash within its boundaries to be directed to a given disposal site. This is done to enable incinerators to remain in operation by charging higher prices than nearby dumps. Truckers argue, however, that this practice flies in the face of Interstate Commerce Commission rules and regulations, and some lower courts have agreed.

Price wars could be the result of a decision against flow control. While giant haulers, such as WMX Technologies and Browning-Ferris that control large amounts of dump space, could survive a price war, many financially-strapped incinerators simply could not.

Incidentally, the very question of title is important in the trash picture. What happens to title, for instance, when commercial haulers cross municipal boundaries as they routinely do?

All of this has led some municipalities to engage in what is called economic flow control. Here, disposal fees are set at the incinerator low enough to attract trash, and the remaining costs are passed along to citizens in the form of higher local taxes to the point that Columbus, Ohio, tried for ten years to keep its incinerator competitive, but the subsidies required were on the order of $100 million, no small cost in the disposal of trash.

Incinerators are attractive—there are no rats, gulls, or smells. Some people think they don't even look like dumps, but more like engineering labs. Trash trucks rumbling over city streets, damaging roads, and creating sleep-disturbing noise are the only reminders of trash problems. So, who is to take out the trash? Whose trash is it, and whether to dump or burn all remain questions that today's organizations and citizens face. Questions that were perhaps not even on the action agenda twenty years ago are begging for answers and are becoming a dominant force in today's organizations. Hamburger wrappers and drinking cups, indeed!

QUESTIONS FOR DISCUSSION

1. How can you use the open systems concept to build a sound position for today's manager to take on the issue of trash disposal?
2. Does the trash disposal industry face many significant barriers to entry? Explain in detail.
3. Discuss the factors that bear on your university's trash problem. Be specific to your university.
4. Can Porter's Strategies (as presented in this chapter) be used to solve problems of trash disposal? Demonstrate.
5. Show by example how cultural changes have caused major impacts on trash disposal.
6. How do you think international trade agreements, such as NAFTA and GATT, will affect managerial decisions in the area of trash disposal?

REFERENCES

1. R. L. Daft, *Organization Theory and Design,* 4th ed. (St. Paul, Minn.: West, 1992).

   Richard H. Hall, *Organizations: Structures, Processes, and Outcomes* (Englewood Cliffs, N.J.: Prentice-Hall, 1991).

2. Gene Bylinsky, "Catalytica: How to Leapfrog the Giants," *Fortune* (October 18, 1993): 80.

3. Gregory G. Dess and Donald W. Beard, "Dimensions of Organizational Task Environments," *Administrative Science Quarterly* 29 (1984): 52–73.

   Mark P. Sharfman and James W. Dean, Jr., "Conceptualizing and Measuring the Organizational Environment: A Multidimensional Approach," *Journal of Management* 17 (1991): 681–700.

4. Michael E. Porter, *Competitive Strategy: Techniques for Analyzing Industries and Competitors* (New York: The Free Press, 1980).

5. Richard A. Melcher, "How Goliaths Can Act like Davids," *Business Week* (Special Enterprise Issue, 1993): 192–201.

   James B. Treece, "Sometimes, You Still Gotta Have Size," *Business Week* (Special Enterprise Issue, 1993): 200–201.

6. Paul Carroll, *Big Blues: The Unmaking of IBM* (New York: Crown Publishing, 1993).

7. J. Brittain and J. Freeman, "Organizational Proliferation and Density Dependent Selection," *Organizational Life Cycles* (San Francisco: Jossey-Bass, 1980), 291–338.

8. G. Burns, "Bye-bye to Fat Times," *Business Week* (January 9, 1995): 89.

9. Timothy K. Smith, "Why Air Travel Doesn't Work," *Fortune* (April 3, 1995), 43–56.

10. Harrison M. Trice and Janice Beyer, *The Cultures of Work Organizations* (Englewood Cliffs, N.J.: Prentice-Hall, 1993), xiii.

11. Daniel Benjamin, "Some Germans Pin Hopes on Service Jobs," *The Wall Street Journal* (November 10, 1993), A18.

12. E. Updike, "The Land of the Rising Eyebrow," *Business Week* (March 27, 1995): 8.

13. W. Jack Duncan, *Organizational Behavior* (Boston: Houghton Mifflin, 1978), 177–82.

14. Paul Hotheinz, "Yes, You Can Win in Eastern Europe," *Fortune* (May 16, 1994): 110–12.

15. Peter Behr, "Honda Is Rolling Success Off Its Ohio Assembly Line," *Washington Post* (May 3, 1987), H1, H2.

16. Stewart Toy, Mark Maremont, and Ronald Grover, "An American in Paris: Can Disney Work its Magic in Europe," *Business Week* (March 12, 1990): 60–64.

Julie Solomon, "Mickey's Trip to Trouble," *Newsweek* (February 14, 1994): 34–39.

17. D. Katz, *Just Do It* (New York: Random House, 1994).

18. Alex Taylor III, "The Auto Industry Meets the New Economy," *Fortune* (September 5, 1994): 52–60.

19. "Drugs — Manufacturing Jobs in Puerto Rico," *Monthly Labor Review* (March 1995): 19.

20. D. Harbrecht, "What Has NAFTA Wrought? Plenty of TRADE," *Business Week* (November 21, 1994): 48–49.

21. D. Harbrecht, "How Business CAN Manage the Backlash," *Business Week* (December 5, 1994): 37.

22. H. Mintzberg, "Managerial Work: Analysis from Observation," *Management Science* 18, no. 2 (1971): 97–110.

23. L. Walczak, R. S. Dunham, H. Gleckman, and S. B. Garland, "The Conservative Agenda," *Business Week* (November 21, 1994): 26–34.

24. P. Dwyer, K. Lowry Miller, and R. Neff, "Suddenly, It's Time to Buy American," *Business Week* (March 27, 1995): 58.

25. A. DePalma, "Economy Reeling, Mexicans Prepare Tough New Steps," *The New York Times* (February 26, 1995), 1, 6.

26. Valerie Reitman, "Global Money Trends Rattle Shop Windows in Heartland America," *The Wall Street Journal* (November 26, 1993), A1.

27. C. Perrow, "A Framework for the Comparative Analysis of Organizations," *American Sociological Review* 32 (1967): 194–208.

    J. D. Thompson, *Organizations in Action* (New York: McGraw-Hill, 1967).

    D. Gerwin, "Relationships Between Structure and Technology," *Handbook of Organizational Design*, vol. 2 (New York: Oxford University Press, 1981), 3–38.

28. Lowell W. Steele, *Managing Technology* (New York: McGraw-Hill, 1989).

    Eric Von Hippel, *The Sources of Innovation* (New York: Oxford University Press, 1988).

29. Christina Duff, "Blue-Light Blues: K-Mart's Dowdy Stores Get a Snazzy Face Lift, but Problems Linger," *The Wall Street Journal* (November 5, 1993), 1–6.

30. See Thompson in note 27 above.

31. W. J. Cook, "Ringing in Saturn," *U.S. News & World Report* (October 22, 1990): 51–54.

32. See note 2 above.

33. See note 15 above.

34. Kenneth Labich, "The Best Cities for Knowledge Workers," *Fortune* (November 15, 1993): 50–78.

35. Otis Port, "The Responsive Factory," *Business Week* (Special Enterprise Issue, 1993): 48–53.

    Christopher Farrell, "A Wellspring of Innovation," *Business Week* (Special Enterprise Issue, 1993): 56–62.

    Michael Hammer and James Champy, *Reengineering the Corporation: A Manifesto for Business Revolution* (New York: Harper Business, 1993).

36. Thomas A. Stewart, "Reengineering: The Hot New Managing Tool," *Fortune* (August 23, 1993): 40–48.

    Joseph Weber, "A Big Company that Works," *Business Week* (May 4, 1992): 124–32.

37. See note 8 above.

38. M. Magee, "Japanese Quake Sends Ruin Through Business," *San Francisco Chronicle* (February 6, 1995), D1.

39. Suein L. Hwang, "Healthy Eating, Premium Private Labels Take a Bite Out of Nabisco's Cookie Sales," *The Wall Street Journal* (July 13, 1992), B1–B3.

40. See Gregory G. Dess and Donald W. Beard in note 3.

    H. Aldrich, *Organizations and Environments* (Englewood Cliffs, N.J.: Prentice-Hall, 1979).

    F. E. Emery and E. L. Trist, "The Causal Texture of Organizational Environments," *Human Relations* 18, 1 (1965): 21–32.

41. See Aldrich in note 40; see Emery and Trist in note 40.

42. See Aldrich in note 40; see Dess and Beard in note 3; see Emery and Trist in note 40.

43. See Dess and Beard in note 3.

44. Tom Peters, *Thriving on Chaos* (New York: Alfred A. Knopf, 1988).

    Fortune (Special Issue: "The Tough New Consumer: Demanding More and Getting It," Autumn/Winter 1993).

    Business Week (Special Issue: "Reinventing America: Meeting the New Challenges of a Global Economy," 1992).

    John W. Verity, "Deconstructing the Computer Industry," *Business Week* (November 23, 1992): 90–100.

■ CHAPTER 5

Managing the Environment

CASE: WOULD YOU LIKE FRIES WITH YOUR ORDER?*

The Golden Arches of McDonald's have been the scene of many orders for hamburgers and fries. These arches are among the world's best known trademarks—practically everyone has eaten at a McDonald's at one time or another. But it seems this habit is beginning to stunt McDonald's growth in the U.S.

It was not too many years ago that industry watchers thought the company faced a mature industry—there was just so much that could be done with hamburgers and french fries, after all. Operating profits and same-store sales showed little growth, and the company culture was even being blamed for its apparent inability to deal effectively with its competition (like Taco Bell and Wendy's among others) that was leaner and more agile. There just didn't seem to be another menu breakthrough to follow Big Mac or the Quarter Pounder.

In order to deal with its sluggishness, McDonald's has turned its attention overseas, and with a vengeance. It is opening overseas shops at the rate of three a day, and this effort is intensifying. Presently, there are some 3,600 stores in Japan, Canada, Britain, Germany, Australia, and France. The company believes that there are some 5,000 other shops that can be built to achieve even a minimum market potential in these countries. And if the vast unpenetrated markets of such countries as China, Russia, and India are "attacked," the overseas potential approaches some 42,000 outlets. So McDonald's is shipping its smiles, standards, values, and, oh yes, its fries, overseas.

Today, McDonald's is truly a global corporation with one of the world's most recognizable names. This global presence accounts for some 80 percent of its current income. Sales are the result of a $1.4 billion advertising budget with its catchy slogans

*This case is based on the following articles:
Andrew E. Serwer, "McDonald's Conquers the World," *Fortune* (October 17, 1994): 103–16.
Steve H. Hanke, "Dancing on a Volcano," *Forbes* (January 2, 1995): 293.
Lee Smith, "Can You Make any Money in Russia?" *Fortune* (January 1, 1990): 103–107.
R. Jacob, "Where's the Beef?" *Fortune* (January 24, 1994): 16.

("Get up and get away," for example) and the featuring of Ronald McDonald, recognized by kids as rapidly as Santa Claus.

The company is focused on a single target—service. The whole thrust is to provide a standardized service package around the world. Under the direction of Mike Quinlan (or Q as he is called), McDonald's has succeeded in building up its menu, quality standards, friendliness, and atmosphere into quite an attractive package that is popularly priced in what is truly a global market.

From this global market have come several recent developments. For instance, from the Dutch, McDonald's adopted a prefab shop design that allows a shop to be moved, literally, on a weekend, and Singapore was the site for the company's first mini-McDonald's.

Nowhere is McDonald's global presence more evident, however, than in Poland.

POLAND

In Warsaw there are four stores that have succeeded in serving McDonald's food. Although the training that company officials receive at world-famous Hamburger University, McDonald's training center in Illinois, gave management its basic approach, it has been adapted to fit the Polish environment quite well. An intense preparation program preceded McDonald's entrance into the Polish market. This preparation included such things as location studies, facilities construction, supply, personnel, and dealing with government regulations. After bringing in a team of fifty in 1992 to begin operations, all but one have been replaced by Poles.

There has been no shortage of those who want to be a part of the Polish team either. The $1.70-per-hour wage for beginners represents an income that is 75 percent above the $2,000-a-year income that is typical for Poles. In order to instill basic company practices, managers (paid some $900 a month) receive training at Hamburger U. According to the company, the only resistance that it faced to its presence came from those who didn't want the political change that came in the 1980s. By the end of 1998 when it pulls its lone manager home, McDonald's hopes to have one hundred stores in Poland under the management of local personnel.

ISSUES

McDonald's has faced unique problems in its overseas operations, however. In Germany, for instance, it is against the law to offer "two-for-one" specials; France has accused the company of shortchanging workers on overtime payments; in Denmark government permission had to be sought to work on weekends; and most recently, McDonald's lost its long-term lease on its Beijing, China, restaurant. These issues are dealt with on a country-specific basis, a key to global success for any company.

Supply can be a nightmare for the overseas company also. Varying freight rates, different currencies, and fluctuating exchange rates are just a few of the headaches faced. For example, currency restrictions in Russia have hampered McDonald's. Whenever possible, therefore, McDonald's has encouraged its U.S. suppliers to follow it overseas. OSI, its chief meat supplier based in Chicago, has formed joint ventures in seventeen countries in order to get around some of these problems while ensuring that McDonald's high standards are met. However, the former Soviet government and its Russian successor have insisted that McDonald's use local suppliers of meat, chicken, produce, and potatoes. The initial problem was that the quality of Russian supplies was far below McDonald's standards. Extensive work with farmers and suppliers has raised the quality of these critical raw materials to acceptable levels. Thus, there appears a willingness on the part of local businesses to form alliances with McDonald's. In Saudi Arabia, for instance, even a member of the royal family heads the local operation (a political connection, indeed!). The Chinese government has allowed McDonald's to start some twenty-three more stores there, but after the company's Beijing experience of losing a prime lease site, the company may approach expansion in China cautiously.

McDonald's even adapts its menu to local tastes. In India, hamburgers are made from lamb rather than beef. Cattle are regarded as sacred among the Hindu people. McDonald's in Japan serves a variation on local cuisine that includes fish, rice, and noodles.

How does McDonald's keep what could well be tangled communication lines to its far-flung operations open? Rather than relying on technology, as one might expect, the company emphasizes old-fashioned face-to-face interaction. There is no E-mail in company headquarters, and the CEO doesn't even have a computer on his desk! Perhaps no company moves its executives to meetings more than McDonald's. These meetings, organized on the basis of organization function, are held monthly around the world so that problems and successes can be the base for an integrated management approach throughout the company.

To offset the lack of new products, McDonald's is placing its innovation thrust on unique locations. It has opened stores on trains, on an English ferry, in Wal-Mart stores, and on college campuses, among other locations. It is standardizing even further its kitchen equipment, a move that saved an estimated $40,000 per store in 1993.

It is also continuing to emphasize employee training. Everyone, from first-timers (who get two to three days' training) to managers (who are required to attend Hamburger University, which offers what some call the equivalent of an executive MBA program) is imbued with company philosophy and technique. Even its suppliers attend H.U., and some of them have McDonald's as their sole customer. Former Mom-and-Pop operations, such as OSI (meat suppliers) and french-fry chief, J. R. Simplot Company, are major companies thanks to their contracts with McDonald's. Of course, the company has large contracts with H. J. Heinz, Kraft, General Foods, and Coca-Cola. The Coke contract makes McDonald's the largest customer for fountain sales of Coca-Cola products.

The company is also taking a lead on environmental issues, using brown (rather than bleached-white) bags and reducing the use of styrofoam. A pilot program in Holland that recycles 100 percent of its stores' waste may well be adopted in other countries. Smoking has been banned in company-owned stores in the U.S., and the company encourages a similar practice elsewhere. And McDonald's doesn't use beef from cattle grown on cleared rainforest land. Attention has also been given to health concerns when they center around fat and calories. No-fat bran muffins, McLean burgers, and salads have been added to the menu.

So McDonald's has become a highly focused global company that is attempting on many fronts to manage its environment. Although the obstacles are many and varied, don't count McDonald's out. And remember all the environmental complexities that have been addressed by McDonald's when you are next asked, "Would you like fries with your order?" regardless of the language used.

The McDonald's case shows us how a large corporation is trying to control its ever-expanding outside environment, including the international environment. McDonald's uses training (McDonald's Hamburger University), face-to-face meetings, U.S. suppliers moving off-shore, negotiations with foreign governments, contracting with new suppliers, and other means to manage its international environment. In this chapter you will read about actions that firms can use to manage their environment. As you read this chapter, keep in mind the overriding importance of organizations attempting to manage their environment. This environment must be constantly monitored (or scanned) if an organization is to stay in consonance with this outside world that provides the inputs and absorbs the outputs that are the lifeblood necessary for the long-term survival of all organizations.

MANAGING THE ENVIRONMENT

We take for granted that organizational leaders can adapt their organizations to meet environmental demands and even change the very environment that they face. These assumptions are at the foundation of a strategic perspective on organizations — managers formulate strategies and conduct their organizations to maximize the organization's "fit" with the environmental conditions the organization faces. We assume that when managers discover new and different environmental conditions, they take action to change the organization to better match the environment or, in some instances, change the environmental conditions to better fit their organization's strengths. Contained within this view of the organizational world are the assumptions that managers can and will obtain valid and reliable information about the environment; that organizations are flexible and can be made to respond to the environmental conditions; and that managers can knowingly and meaningfully manipulate the environment to create conditions that are advantageous to their organization.

Our primary focus in this chapter is on how managers try to accomplish these tasks. First, we examine how managers come to know their environment. What can managers do to gather information; what are the obstacles to gathering information; and what happens to that information? Second, we explore how organizations adapt or respond to environmental conditions. Once managers learn about the environmental conditions, what kinds of changes can reduce uncertainty and make the organization more effective? The third step is to understand how managers can take actions that actually change the environmental conditions to make them more amenable to the organization's strengths.

There can be little doubt that organizations do each of the three things mentioned above: gather information about the environment, adapt to the environment, and change the environment. Increasingly, however, some organizational theorists are challenging these fundamental assumptions that managers can *meaningfully* and *significantly* adapt to or change the environment. We conclude this chapter by introducing the rather controversial organizational perspective called ***population ecology*** that asserts that managers are more or less powerless to knowingly and meaningfully change organizations or the environment. Fundamental to this view is the belief that environments are so complex and unpredictable that managers can never know enough or anticipate conditions appropriately to meaningfully adapt either the organization or the environment.

KNOWING THE ENVIRONMENT

The open systems view of organizations highlights the critical nature of the environment. The environment is the source of ***opportunities*** for an organization in the form of necessary resources and markets; and ***threats*** in the form of uncertainty, dependency, and scarcity. Organizations learn about these external conditions through ***boundary spanning*** and ***environmental scanning*** activities.

Boundary spanning activities are those functions that require members of the organization to spend all or part of their time interacting with people and organizations outside the boundaries of their own organization.[1] Boundary spanning units aid the organization in adjusting to the conditions that exist in the environment. The boundary spanning activities serve two general functions: (1) they gather information and provide feedback about the environment to the organization, and (2) they represent the organization to the outside world. Let us look at the first of these two functions. For example, sales or service representatives who visit customers can be an important source of information not only about the customers needs, but also about competitors. Customers and competitors represent only two parts of the environment, albeit important ones. Purchasing, sales, human resources, finance, government relations, public relations, investor relations, advertising, and countless other departments may encounter important information through interactions with suppliers, bankers, investors, government, and the general public — people and organizations outside their own boundaries. Figure 5.1 depicts the positions that boundary spanning units occupy with respect to the organization and its environment.

■   FIGURE 5.1

Boundary Spanning Units and the Environment

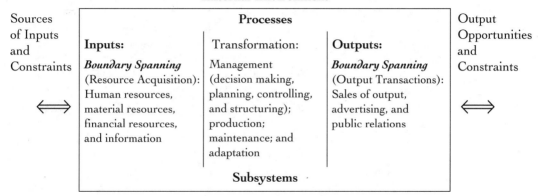

External Environment

Sources of Inputs and Constraints	Processes			Output Opportunities and Constraints
	Inputs:	Transformation:	**Outputs:**	
	Boundary Spanning (Resource Acquisition): Human resources, material resources, financial resources, and information	Management (decision making, planning, controlling, and structuring); production; maintenance; and adaptation	***Boundary Spanning*** (Output Transactions): Sales of output, advertising, and public relations	
⟷		**Subsystems**		⟷

External Environment

It is important to keep in mind that boundary spanning activities are not restricted to those individuals or units whose roles are explicitly designed for boundary spanning. Chief executive officers of major corporations or other types of organizations often fulfill the role of boundary spanner. When Lee Iacocca led Chrysler Corporation through difficult periods in the 1980s, he played a highly visible and prominent role interacting with government, bankers, investors, and even customers. Other CEOs have played similar high visibility roles either conveying information about their companies or gathering information. Examples include Bill Gates of Microsoft, who currently authors a syndicated newspaper column, and Jim Cook of Samuel Adams Brewing, who is prominently featured in the company's advertising. When the CEO appears before stockholders or analysts to report on the firm's past performance and future direction, he or she is acting as a boundary spanner. When a university dean or president appears before the community or the state legislature, he or she is acting as a boundary spanner. Indeed, CEOs, presidents, and deans are often selected because of their connections to the external environment, prestige, or status. These figurehead and liaison roles are often among the most important roles of organizational leaders.[2]

As shown in Exhibit 5.1, the CEO or president of an organization sometimes plays a critical boundary spanning role in representing the organization to the external environment. In the example given the president attempts damage control—minimizing the harm done—when a serious environmental threat occurs. The president tries to reestablish the university's legitimacy and positive image in the community.

Exhibit 5.1	**The President Attempts Damage Control**

Since development of the first atomic bomb during World War II, the U.S. government has been interested in determining the effects of radiation exposure on humans. Recently, the public has learned of questionable ethical behavior by the federal government, public institutions, and medical researchers. It appears that the federal government directly and indirectly conducted radiation exposure experiments on humans, even though a growing body of knowledge at the time suggested that exposure could lead to serious illness and death.

One such experiment was conducted in the late 1960s and early 1970s at a large mid-western university hospital. Terminal cancer patients were exposed to large doses of full-body radiation. The purpose of the experiment was ostensibly to provide the Department of Defense with data on the effects of radiation exposure. Numerous questions about the ethics and wisdom of this experiment were raised at the time of the study, but, in the midst of the Cold War, critics were silenced. Nearly all patients in the experiment died shortly after exposure, but it is unclear whether they died from their illness or from radiation.

Nearly twenty-five years after the experiments, the public has learned the lurid details. Questions have been raised about whether patients were given full information, whether they gave informed consent to participate, and whether the experimenter conducted the study in an ethical and scientifically sound fashion. Surviving family members, legislators, doctors, researchers, and the general public were outraged and demanded a full accounting of what happened. Some families threatened to sue the university and the researchers.

One can imagine the public relations nightmare that this scenario presents. Initially, the university attempted to deal with this crisis in a conventional fashion. Hospital administrators and the university public relations office issued press releases and set up a hot line to respond to questions. Still, the community was not satisfied and thought the university was stonewalling. Finally, the university president went on TV news programs and met with community leaders to assure everyone that the university was doing its best to get to the bottom of this mess. The belief was that the prestige and legitimacy of the president would calm fears and appease an angry public. This may, however, be a case of too little, too late.

Boundary spanning may also be conducted by units that are not within the organization's boundaries at all. For example, a law firm, employment agency, or advertising firms may gather environmental information or represent an organization's interests to outsiders.

ENVIRONMENTAL SCANNING

Information gathering may be a primary, explicit role or a secondary, implicit role for individuals in organizations. These are the boundary spanning roles referred to above. In addition to collecting information through boundary spanning, organizations must process this information. ***Environmental scanning*** is a particular type of boundary spanning concerned with collecting and processing information, and assessing or projecting change in various sectors of the environment.[3] The central functions of environmental scanning activities are to gather and interpret important environmental information and to introduce the results of analyses into the organization's strategic planning process. The goal of scanning is to help the organization reduce the amount of environmental uncertainty it faces.

As organizations face increasingly complex and uncertain environments, they create more numerous and specialized boundary spanning units and they engage in more scanning activity. Organizations often examine changes in demographics, competition, technology, customer needs and requirements, regulations, and a variety of other environmental forces. Information gained from scanning is used to make projections about likely conditions the organization will encounter and to aid in planning the future direction of the organization. Scanning data are the input for product development, advertising, personnel planning, production scheduling, and myriad other functions. For example, market research can yield information about changing consumer demographics, emerging buying patterns, and dying markets. Studies of local labor markets may help the personnel department anticipate labor shortages and increasing labor costs.

Research evidence suggests that, in general, the most important sectors to monitor, in the eyes of top management, are the market sector, the economic sector, and the sociocultural sector.[4] Clearly, in some industries other sectors of the environment may be equally or more important than these three sectors. For example, product innovations would clearly be important to monitor in the computer and electronics industry, and regulatory changes and supplier prices are likely to be critical factors to examine in health care–related businesses. The task facing managers is how to focus the organization's limited scanning resources in environments that are complex and uncertain. No organization can hope to cover everything. Although the specific answer to the question of what to monitor may differ from one setting to another, we can generalize that organizations that scan more of their environment and do so more often are likely to perform better than organizations that ignore the changing conditions in their environment.[5] Additionally, organizations that are facing increasingly uncertain and complex environments will create organizational designs that include more specialized units to engage in boundary spanning and scanning.[6] Thus, organizations attempt to manage environmental complexity with structural complexity.

Some scanning activities involve closely monitoring the actions of competitors. Retailers may use comparison shoppers to monitor competitors' pricing. Manufacturers may engage in reverse engineering (disassembling products to understand how they are engineered, designed, and constructed and how they can be duplicated), and some companies even use spying to gain critical information. Exhibit 5.2 provides some examples of corporate spying activity. Many lawsuits have been fought in the computer industry over reverse engineering and cloning of products.

Exhibit 5.2	### Corporate Cloak and Dagger: Scanning of Another Sort[7]

Now that the Cold War is over, you may think that spying is a thing of the past. But that is not at all the case — especially in the corporate world. It is estimated that U.S. businesses lose as much as $20 to $30 billion a year as a result of spying by domestic and foreign competitors. Some executives and political leaders have taken these threats as the impetus for clandestine warfare against competitors. Consider the following examples.

- The FBI arrested two Koreans who allegedly purchased blueprints of a new Dow Chemical polymer plant in Texas.
- Mitsubishi and Hitachi officials were arrested in the early 1980s for purchasing IBM trade secrets.
- A unit of the French government, the Direction Générale de la Sécurité Exterieure (DGSE), actively engages in surveillance. French students in the U.S. and French workers in European divisions of foreign companies have been used to ferret out trade secrets. French engineers visiting the U.S. posed as French government officials in an effort to acquire radar-evading stealth technology. French diplomates rummaged through the garbage of a U.S. computer industry executive, searching for secrets that could aid French manufacturers.
- The Japanese Ministry of International Trade and Industry (MITI) coordinates the country's largely legal information gathering that includes monitoring foreign competitors throughout the world and seeking industries ripe for Japanese challenge.
- U.S. firms doing business in the former East Bloc communist countries must be concerned that the military intelligence agencies of those countries are now turn- |

ing their attention to industrial spying. Many former agents are now for hire as freelancers and use many of the same wiretapping and photo reconnaissance techniques of the Cold War for business customers.

- Domestic competitors are not beneath spying on each other. Agents working for Avon Cosmetics were caught rummaging through dumpsters at Mary Kay. Spies have posed as students, university researchers, and journalists all in an effort to pry trade secrets from competitors.
- Perhaps one of the most widely used techniques in high technology fields is reverse engineering. Firms purchase competitors' products and take them apart to uncover engineering and design secrets. This is common practice among chip manufactures, computer makers, and software developers. Intel has encoded computer chips with cryptic messages such as "steal the best" to discourage copycats.

It's not all illegal and it's not all cloak and dagger, but corporate spying is pervasive and is a critical, costly threat that must be taken seriously.

Even with sophisticated scanning and product development, we are all aware of product flops and other ill-conceived attempts to manage the environment. Ford's infamous Edsel was the result of intensive market research; yet it is the epitome of a flop. The company surveyed car buyers in the earlier and mid-1950s to determine features that buyers valued the most. The Edsel was supposed to include all these features. However, the result in this case was an example of the whole being less than the sum of its parts. The car was poorly designed, and its eclectic collection of features was not pleasing to car buyers. More recently, the Beech Starship, a radically innovative general aviation aircraft, represents a similar failure.[8] The plane was such a radical departure from standard aircraft that potential buyers were scared away.

BOUNDARY PERMEABILITY, RESILIENCE, AND MAINTENANCE

The message is that boundary spanning and environmental scanning are critically important functions if an organization hopes to be responsive to its environment. Failure to respond to the environment will result in organizational decline and, eventually, failure. An organization must, however, strike a balance in boundary spanning and scanning. The concepts of boundary *permeability, resilience,* and *maintenance* are useful in understanding the nature of the balance that an organization must maintain.

Permeability refers to the extent to which the organization facilitates the inward and outward flow of information. Which information and how much information does top management need to make decisions? Which information and how much information should management release to the outside world? These are critical questions that management must address and that affect the permeability of the organization's boundaries. The answer to this question depends in part on the uncertainty of the environment the organization faces. Increasing levels of uncertainty call for increasing permeability.

If the organization fails to monitor and screen incoming information, there is the danger that the organization as a whole may be overwhelmed by information, some of which may be irrelevant. For example, the U.S. Commerce Department produces extensive reports on the economy, labor market, consumer demand, weather conditions, and a multitude of other environmental sectors that *could* affect a business. A critical management task is to determine how much of this information is relevant and filter out the remainder. Failure to make such a determination could result in a flood of information that could easily overwhelm even a very large firm. Similarly, some individuals in organizations play the role of *gatekeepers.* They restrict access to managers by filtering out information they deem to be irrelevant and unnecessary while forwarding information that is important and useful. For example, secretaries and administrative assistants often screen incoming information so that their bosses are not overwhelmed with trivial information. These activities are likely to involve screening mail, phone calls, and potential visitors.

Some parts of the organization may need to be protected or *buffered* from information.[9] For example, the production department of a computer company may need information on consumer demand to aid in production scheduling, but additional information about environmental conditions may be irrelevant and may even adversely affect production. Management should buffer the production department from information that could cause undue concern or even raise uncertainty.

Resilience refers to the degree to which boundary spanning units respond to changes in the mission and goals of the organization, as well as changes in the environment. Suppose that a company decides to change its goals by pursuing a new market niche. Such a shift necessitates the collection of new information relevant to that new market niche and dissemination of new information to people and organizations in the environment. Resilience refers to the ability of boundary spanning units to shift and change in ways that allow them to collect the appropriate information.

The Cadillac Division of GM provides both negative and positive examples of resilience. In the mid-1970s and early 1980s the luxury car market was undergoing extensive change. Small sports and luxury imports like BMW, Audi, Volvo, and Saab were carving out a new entry-level luxury niche. Cadillac had enough resilience in its boundary spanning units to recognize the market changes and to realize that the change was consistent with the division's mission as a luxury car manufacturer. Cadillac Division of General Motors marketed the Cimarron, a new type of car aimed at the new market niche. This small, entry-level Cadillac was supposed to compete with the early upscale imports. Unfortunately, the Cimarron was unsuccessful, and auto industry critics point to the Cadillac Division's unfamiliarity with its import competition and with the potential customers as factors in this failure. The car was small and had many of the luxury appointments typical of Cadillac products, but it lacked the refinements characteristic of the import competitors. It was also a different type of car from the ones that typical Cadillac customers would consider. In other words, Cadillac's boundary spanning departments—marketing, product development, and dealer relations—had enough resilience to recognize changing conditions and new opportunities, but lacked the ability to convert the information into appropriate actions.

In the late 1980s and early 1990s, Cadillac tried again, with greater success this time, to deal with the import threat. This time, Cadillac focused on the upper end of the market, a niche that was more familiar to management. The Seville STS was aimed at the luxury sport coupe and sport sedan market. The result was a car that has successfully competed with the large BMW, Mercedes, Lexus, and Infinity cars.[10]

The blame for failure or credit for success cannot all be placed on the boundary spanning units. The concept of resilience depends, to a great extent, on a smooth and close relationship between top management setting the new goals and mission and the boundary spanning units that are responsible for collecting and disseminating new information. Boundary spanners must be aware that the goals or environmental conditions have changed and that new and different information must be sought. In the Cadillac example boundary spanners recognized that environmental changes had taken place. Consumers were shifting to a different type of product, but boundary spanners and top management failed to recognize exactly the specific nature of the market changes that had taken place. In order for boundary spanning units to respond effectively — to be both permeable to information and to be resilient to change — it is necessary to monitor and maintain these units.

Maintenance is especially important in boundary spanning units. Because boundary spanners oftentimes operate outside the organization's boundaries, these people and departments must be carefully managed. A typical boundary spanning role, such as that of a sales representative, requires that the role occupant leave the organization in order to carry out his or her job. When the person leaves the organization, especially when departures are often and extensive, that person may lose some contact with the organization's mission or goals. The boundary spanner may also be influenced by people outside the organization and either fail to properly represent their organization or fail to acquire appropriate and relevant information. The term *going native* is used to refer to situations where people in boundary spanning roles take on characteristics of their customer or target organization rather than their own organization.[11] This is a particular problem for drug enforcement agents, corrections officers, and others in law enforcement, but it can also happen in more typical business organizations among sales and service personnel who spend extensive amounts of time with customers. Careful monitoring and periods of resocialization (i.e., retraining and refamiliarization with organizational goals) are necessary to counter this tendency.

Maintenance of boundary spanning units requires that they maintain or periodically reestablish links to decision-authority centers (e.g., top management) in the organization. This is important so that boundary spanners can renew their commitment to the organization, learn about new goals and priorities, and identify appropriate areas of the environment to scan. Maintenance of boundary spanners may take place in periodic meetings where field representatives return to headquarters, share information they have acquired, and learn about new directions the organization may be pursuing.[12]

ENVIRONMENTAL UNCERTAINTY AND DEPENDENCE

As noted in Chapter 4, organizations can potentially encounter uncertainty or problems from three aspects of the environment: (1) complexity — the number of sectors or elements of the environment relevant to an organization; (2) change — the extent or speed with which elements in the environment undergo change; and (3) munificence — the availability of critical resources in the environment.

The net result of a complex and changing environment is uncertainty. The more environmental elements that a firm needs to monitor, the more likely it is that the environment will push the organization's limited capacity to monitor. Because of the increasing demands on an organization's monitoring abilities, complexity can cause uncertainty. Similarly, the more and the faster the environment changes, the more a firm needs to closely watch the environment and take actions to adapt to changed conditions. Once again, because every organization has only a limited capacity to monitor the environment, increasing levels of change will cause uncertainty. Organizations must take some actions to manage environmental uncertainty.

Munificence creates a somewhat different problem and different type of uncertainty. Clearly, all organizations must acquire critical resources. When resources are abundant, acquisition is not much of a problem. When resources are scarce, the potential exists for an organization to become dependent upon one or a few suppliers.[13] Scarcity and the resulting dependence create problems for an organization. The firm's ability to act independently and decisively may become restricted. A firm that is dependent on the pricing and availability of supplies cannot freely and independently set production schedules, arrange shipping and receiving, or set its own pricing. As scarcity increases, dependence increases. As dependence increases, a firm's autonomy decreases. Its ability to independently and freely design and implement strategy is jeopardized. Organizations, in general, will take actions to either entirely avoid dependencies — which is often impossible — or they will take actions to manage dependent relationships.

Dependence also occurs when power is asymmetrically distributed between organizations. This is apparent in buyer-supplier relationships. Wal-Mart, for example, has grown so large in the market that it has enormous power relative to supplier companies. Suppliers, even large ones, have become dependent on Wal-Mart's business. To lose Wal-Mart as an account would be devastating to most firms. As a consequence, Wal-Mart is able to exercise its power to achieve lower prices and better terms from suppliers.

The following sections describe strategies and techniques that organizations use to adapt to or reduce uncertainty and avoid or manage dependencies. These strategies and techniques are incomplete or imperfect. Organizations will always face some uncertainty and some dependence on others. Additionally, these strategies and techniques are not necessarily mutually exclusive. Organizations will typically use several techniques or strategies in concert.

ADAPTING TO THE ENVIRONMENT

Gathering information about the environment is merely the first step toward successfully managing it, which requires that an organization take further action. Boundary spanners have scanned the environment and detected some conditions for which the organization may be unprepared, or they may anticipate new conditions for which the current organization is ill suited. To better manage these new or anticipated conditions, management may choose to change or adapt the organization. In this section we examine the variety of ways in which the organization can adapt to meet these new or anticipated changes.

It is important to remember that environmental adaptation refers to strategies that focus on the organization's attempts to change in response to the environment. One must keep in mind that there are many ways the organization can change, and more than one method of adaptation may be successful — but not all methods of change or adaptation are equally appropriate. Moreover, as we discuss at greater length in Chapter 13, change itself can cause problems for an organization.

FORECASTING AND STRATEGIC PLANNING

Strategic management deals with the future. Scanning the environment is perhaps most important as an ingredient to forecast the future. Any strategic plan is only as good as the forecasts that predict the future. To the extent that predictions are accurate, the building blocks for plans and decisions will be solidly constructed. A complete discussion of forecasting is beyond the scope of this book. The following brief discussion describes two popular methods of forecasting: trend analysis and scenario analysis.

Most forecasts are based on a *trend analysis.* Trend analysis uses historic data to determine future conditions. For example, a hardware-home center may examine sales of snow shovels and snowblowers over the past five years. It uses those trends, along with weather trends and long-range weather forecasts, to predict future snow shovel and snowblower sales. Some trends are predictable. Trends may be straight lines representing steady growth, no change, or decline; or trends may be curvilinear cycles. Snowblower sales may have decreased gradually over the past five years because of the combination of warm winters, environmental concerns, and a sluggish economy. By analyzing this trend, the retailer can predict that sales will probably continue to decline. Trends may also be cyclical. The retailer may find that snow equipment sales are tied closely to weather trends. An examination of weather trends may suggest cycles of bad winters. Thus, the retailer may forecast greater demand because the region is due for a bad winter. Some trends or cycles can be punctuated by unpredictable events. Unpredictable cycles make forecasting and planning difficult. The winter of 1993–94 was one of the most severe on record in the East and Midwest. Record cold temperatures combined with unrelenting snow and ice storms. No amount of scanning and forecasting could have predicted those weather conditions and the resulting demand for snow removal equipment. As a result, retailers and local government agencies were caught without adequate inventories of snow removal equipment.

Not all trends are as unpredictable as weather. Population or demographic trends are comparatively rather predictable. Business forecasters follow closely the tastes and trends among baby boomers, busters, and Generation X members to discern changing tastes, work habits, and living conditions. Phenomena like the boom in mini van and truck sales, movements toward self-employment, and growth in aging-related industries can be traced to population trends.[14]

Scenario forecasting is a method that presents alternative trends or events and attaches probabilities to those alternatives. The hardware–home center retailer could project the likelihood of a mild winter, an average winter, and a severe winter. A payoff matrix can be constructed for each scenario, and planners can make decisions based on these expected outcomes. Table 5.1 provides an example of scenario forecasting and contingency planning based on the scenarios.

■   TABLE 5.1
Scenario Forecasting and Contingency Planning

Scenario	Probability	Plan	Financial Benefit a. if correct b. if incorrect
1. Mild winter	30%	Small inventory	a. $5,000 b. −$5,000
2. Average winter	65%	Average inventory	a. $10,000 b. −$2,000
3. Severe winter	5%	Large inventory	a. $30,000 b. −$20,000

Forecasting presents managers with a bit of a paradox in trying to adapt to environments. The most accurate forecasts can be constructed in a simple and stable environment. When environments become increasingly complex and increasingly unstable, forecasting becomes increasingly difficult, time consuming, and inaccurate. The paradox exists because forecasting is not particularly important when the environment is simple and stable. What works today should work tomorrow. Forecasting becomes a *potentially* important tool when the environment is complex and unstable—when management needs new ways to deal with the environment—but the forecast may not be accurate or useful. However, in extreme uncertainty, forecasting and planning may be difficult and costly to accomplish successfully *because* of the uncertainty, and the results of the forecasting may be inaccurate and unreliable.

WITHDRAWAL: PROTECTING THE ORGANIZATIONAL CORE

Organizations may adapt a strategy of sealing themselves off from portions of the environment. The key to this strategy is developing means for keeping the environment from interfering with the organization's core operations.[15] Temporarily, withdrawal or taking a defensive posture may protect an organization from some environmental uncertainty. In the long run, withdrawal, especially if carried to an extreme, will place an organization out of "sync" with its environment and will likely damage the organization. How can an organization be successful if its products or services are inconsistent with the diverse demands and pressures of the environment?

Organizations typically accomplish this insulation from environmental uncertainty by focusing on narrow, specialized, and/or stable portions of the environment. For example, early in the development of the personal computer market, Compaq Computer was able to defend itself from some of the environmental uncertainty in its industry by concentrating its efforts only on a narrow market segment—premium-priced portable computers. Similarly, Apple Computer focused early attention on educational computing, a niche that was less crowded and more stable than business computing. As a result, Compaq and Apple were able to avoid some of the environmental uncertainty that befell companies such as IBM and Digital Equipment Company. However, this strategy back-fired for Apple because the majority of growth has been in the business market.

It is not only in the market or industry sectors that organizations attempt to avoid uncertainty through partial or complete withdrawal. ***Buffering,*** as noted earlier, can be used to protect parts of the organization against environmental uncertainty. Purchasing, marketing, and customer service departments are examples of units that buffer the core of the organization from uncertainty. For example, the purchasing department can pro-tect operations from shortages or seasonal fluctuations of supplies through stockpiling. Customer service protects operations from uncertainty resulting from customer demands or complaints.

It should be obvious that protecting operations from these sources of uncertainty may be counterproductive in the long run. Ignoring or insulating oneself from environ-mental uncertainty will likely just delay the inevitable. How else will the operations department know about supply problems or customer dissatisfaction unless it is exposed to that uncertainty? Many new management techniques, such as total quality manage-ment and just-in-time inventory control, require that managers of most or all depart-ments be exposed to environmental uncertainty and that they respond to it.[16] This occurs because these methods provide a strong focus on the customers and suppliers, and requires that people in the organization work together as teams, thus sharing experi-ences and exposure.

DIFFERENTIATION AND INTEGRATION

The very reason for the existence of organizations is that they can perform tasks more effectively and efficiently than individuals working alone. We noted in Chapter 2 that organizations can use differentiation (horizontal, vertical, and spatial) to divide the over-all task to be accomplished into subtasks and assign those tasks to departments or indi-viduals throughout the organization. This specialization allows the organization to perform more efficiently and with greater expertise. As the environment presents the organization with greater and greater complexity and uncertainty, the organization can respond with greater differentiation.[17] The greater specialization that differentiation yields brings specific expertise to bear on problems but requires integrator mechanisms to ensure coordination of effort.

Many reasons may be used to justify a horizontally differentiated or complex orga-nization, but the present focus is on the environment. A basic principle of organization theory is that organizations should be structured to best meet the demands of their envi-ronment. A key to managing environmental complexity is to create an organization that is structurally complex. Horizontal differentiation is one way to achieve that complexity.

If an organization faces a complex environment characterized by many important and relevant environmental sectors, it should have a structure that reflects that environ-mental complexity. If an organization faces numerous potential legal woes, it should cre-ate a department to deal with those problems. If a firm has entered many market niches, it will need a marketing department (or, perhaps, marketing departments) that is large enough and diverse enough to manage those many niches, conduct market research, and design selling strategies. Organizations facing complex environments should also create more numerous boundary spanning roles to link and coordinate with sources of uncertainty in the environment. The idea is that the organization will create departments or positions in the organization to deal with specific areas of environmental uncertainty. The more complex the environment is, the more complex the organization should be, with more departments and more positions.

The case of vertical differentiation and environmental conditions is less clear cut. As we learned in Chapter 2, high vertical complexity means that an organization has many layers of hierarchy and individuals at any given level of the hierarchy have only narrow decision-making authority or responsibility. As one moves up the hierarchy, each subsequent level of the organization should be associated with increasingly important decisions.

The problem with increasing levels of vertical complexity or differentiation is that decisions tend to get pushed up the hierarchy because individuals or departments do not want to take responsibility for possible problems. Pushing decisions up the hierarchy slows down decision-making and response time to environmental crises. The current thinking is that organizations should match environmental uncertainty with decentralized decision making and *less* vertical complexity. This allows the organization to push decisions down to those departments or individuals who encounter the sources of complexity and uncertainty.

Organizations may use *spatial differentiation* to respond to an environment that is geographically or regionally fragmented. For example, regional differences in consumer tastes, worker training and skills, or conditions in the physical environment may present problems for an organization. To manage these varied conditions, the organization creates departments or divisions based on location or region. For example, beverage companies often create local and regional distribution units so that they can respond to local and regional differences in consumer preferences.

Increasing amounts of differentiation necessitated by an uncertain and resource-starved environment place increasing importance on integration mechanisms. The key to integration is selecting mechanisms that are consistent with the environment. Although mechanisms such as formalization and standardization may play some role, organizations should seek methods, such as professionalism and decentralization, that promote flexibility. Additionally, informal mechanisms, such as liaison roles, integrator roles, and team leaders, are important in linking diverse departments together so that an organization can create a unified response to the environment.

STRUCTURING FOR THE ENVIRONMENT

In Chapter 1 it was noted that modern contingency perspectives on organizations take exception to the one-best-way view of organizing and suggest instead that structure must match the organizational context. Environment is one of these contextual factors. In the early 1960s two British researchers, Tom Burns and G. M. Stalker, described two polar examples of organizations that fit different environmental conditions.[18] In Chapter 2 we introduced the mechanistic and organic organizations as prototypical structures. The *mechanistic* organization, characterized by a strict centralized hierarchy of decision-authority, heavy reliance on rules, narrowly divided labor and specialized tasks, and emphasis on vertical (upward and downward) communication, is best suited for a stable and simple environment.[19]

The *organic* organization, with its characteristic decentralization of decision-authority, few rules, broad integrative tasks, and emphasis on horizontal communication, is suited for unstable and complex environments. Organizations facing shifting environments with many relevant sectors find that an organic structure permits greater coordination (similar to the integrator mechanisms mentioned earlier) because of lower levels of specialization and greater horizontal communication and quicker response to problems because of decentralization. Organic structures also allow for flexibility in responding to new conditions because they are less constrained by rules.[20]

The choice between a mechanistic or organic structure is the essence of the *contingency framework* introduced in Chapter 1. Neither structure is necessarily better than the other. Rather, it is important that managers recognize and understand the environment they face and select the *appropriate* organizational structure for that environment. These characteristics are summarized in Exhibit 2.10 of Chapter 2. In general, mechanistic organizations are best suited for stable, simple environments, and organic organizations are best suited for complex and unstable environmental conditions.

In Chapter 4 we noted that contemporary environments are becoming increasingly complex and unstable. The revolution in information and communication technology coupled with easier travel make the business environment uncertain. Thus, it is not surprising that more and more organizations are adopting organic structures. Downsizing and flattening organizations remove much mechanistic hierarchy. Reducing the number of job descriptions, as most U.S. automakers have done, eliminates the narrow specialization of mechanistic organizations and replaces those jobs with broadly defined jobs that require many skills. Does this mean that the mechanistic organization is an antique? Probably not. Mechanistic organizations may be less common today, but there are still environments in which they can operate efficiently and effectively.

IMITATION

The previous section suggested that managers scan the environment and select designs that are appropriate to the conditions they detect. An alternative viewpoint is that managers do not scan the environment just for sources of environmental uncertainty to address, but that they also seek examples of successful organizations, operating in similar environments, to imitate.[21] The rationale for imitation is both pragmatic and defensive. From a practical standpoint, an organization struggling to manage in a highly uncertain environment may borrow the strategies or structures of successful competitors just because the competitors were successful. Managers also imitate other successful firms to protect themselves from accusations of managerial incompetence. If a poorly performing company fails to imitate successful firms in its industry, management may be accused of not exercising *due diligence* (i.e., exercising prudence and good business judgment).[22] The result of imitative behavior is that organizations within an industry tend to look more similar than different.

An example of a management imitative strategy is the widespread adoption of total quality management (TQM) techniques in many industries. Many U.S. manufacturing companies, particularly in automobile-related areas, were unable to successfully compete in the 1980s and early 1990s with Japanese manufacturers. Although American and Japanese firms differ in many ways, many U.S. companies focused on the various quality-enhancing programs that companies like Toyota used. Now TQM programs are a common feature in many U.S. companies, particularly those competing in the auto industry.[23] One interesting feature of TQM helps to perpetuate imitative behavior. This process, called **benchmarking,** is the search among competitors and others for the *best practices* that will lead to superior quality and performance.[24] The process of searching for the best practices among competitors and firms in other industries leads directly to imitative behavior.

Additional forces motivate managers to imitate successful organizations rather than initiating novel responses to the environment. Investors and others who have a stake in a company are unlikely to want management to engage in behavior, develop strategies, or create designs that are radically different from the standards set by other successful companies. Radical deviations would be viewed as risky. Stockholders investing in a company and bankers loaning money are likely to be risk averse and may insist that a firm adopt behaviors, strategies, and designs that are consistent with those practiced by the most successful firms in the industry.[25]

CONTROLLING THE ENVIRONMENT

Strategies for adapting to the environment assume that an organization is more or less a passive recipient of the environment. The organization can change or adapt to fit environmental conditions. Now we advance a step further in managing the environment by actively manipulating the environment itself. The strategies presented in this section assume that an organization can through its actions change the environment. Two general categories of actions, described below, are typically used to control environments: niche or domain selection and interorganizational linkage strategies or, as they are often referred to, strategic alliances.

NICHE OR DOMAIN SELECTION

When we study a given organization at a specific point in time, we often take for granted that an organization's top management actively selects, and sometimes changes, the environmental niche in which the company operates. As a particular portion of the environment becomes too complex, unstable, or resource starved, a firm may choose to exit that market and search for an environment that is simple, stable, and munificent. These changes can be realized through internal product development, acquisition of other companies, or in the case of exiting a domain, divestiture of a division or product line.

In the latter part of the twentieth century the tobacco industry has been characterized by extensive uncertainty and resource scarcity. Problems for the industry began in the 1960s with the emergence of evidence suggesting a link between cigarette smoking and health problems. The subsequent Surgeon-General's report outlining the risks associated with smoking provided justification for the banning of televised cigarette commercials and attaching warning labels to cigarette packages. In the years following the Surgeon-General's report, the tobacco industry has had to face mounting scientific evidence documenting the various tobacco-related health risks, vigilant antismoking public relations and lobbying activities, rising public awareness of smoking-related problems, restrictions on smoking, increased taxation, and threats of further restrictions on all of these fronts. One strategy that tobacco companies have used to deal with the uncertain and resource-scarce environment is to enter new domains. Nearly every tobacco company has diversified into domains unrelated to tobacco, including food products and assorted consumer goods. Perhaps the best example of this strategy is Philip Morris, maker of Marlboro — the largest selling cigarette in the world — which is now the largest diversified food products company in the United States.[26] The Philip Morris food division includes Kraft General Foods. The company also owns Miller Brewing. Similarly, R. J. Reynolds diversified its holdings by acquiring Nabisco several years ago.

In the extreme, a company may entirely abandon a market niche or enter a new domain when the existing domain becomes too uncertain or the supply of resources becomes too scarce. For example, Motorola is a highly successful developer and manufacturer of computer chips, telecommunications equipment, and other electronic components. However, early in the company's history its core business was manufacturing radios and televisions, neither of which it produces today. Similarly, as noted in Chapter 2, General Electric abandoned its small appliance and television businesses in the 1980s when the company's top management determined that they could no longer be competitive in those markets. In each of these cases companies adjusted niches to avoid uncertainty and resource scarcity. By contrast, when companies find munificent environments and acceptable levels of uncertainty, they may enter new niches or domains as Honda, Toyota, and Nissan did in the late 1980s when they created luxury car divisions. This was a niche that each of the companies had previously avoided, but the combination of consumer demands, sparse competition, reduced regulatory pressure, and available capital provided the necessary inducements to enter the niche.

LINKAGE STRATEGIES

Organizations can use a wide array of strategic alliances to link with other players in the environment to actively control uncertainty and scarce resources.[27] As we noted in Chapter 4, uncertainty and resource constraints arise because other organizations or people in the environment place demands on an organization and because an organization becomes dependent on others in the environment. Every organization must go outside its boundaries to acquire some key resources. When members venture outside the boundaries, the organization becomes dependent on others and must deal with uncertainty. Moreover, these demands and dependencies shift and change over time, sometimes in an unpredictable manner. Linkage strategies are ways of connecting an organization with a source of uncertainty or with a controller of resources so that uncertainty is reduced and resources are more accessible. Figure 5.2 on page 136 identifies conditions that foster the formation of various types of interorganizational linkage strategies. The strategies, described below, can be used to control uncertainty and resources in one or more of the environmental sectors that a given organization faces.

■ **FIGURE 5.2**

Conditions that Foster Interorganizational Linkage Strategies

High Benefit Relative to Costs	+	Increased Power	+	Resource Scarcity or Performance Distress	+	Superordinate Force or Goal	+	Structural Conduciveness	+	Boundary Permeability	+	Norms and Physical Proximity

```
                                    │
                                    ▼
                        ┌───────────────────────┐
                        │ Interorganizational    │
                        │ Relationships          │
                        └───────────────────────┘
```

Agreements, Norms, and Contracts. Perhaps the simplest mechanisms that an organization can use to control uncertainty and guarantee the supply of critical resources are informal agreements or norms. Over a period of time and with repeated interactions several organizations may develop helping relationships based on ***reciprocity*** and ***mutual benefit.*** One organization agrees to do something to help another, not necessarily with the belief that there will be an immediate payback. Later on, however, the helping organization may seek a favor from the former recipient of a favor. For example, a firm may agree to purchase a key raw material, such as coal, from only one supplier for a specified period of time provided that the supplier guarantees delivery dates and quantity even in periods of shortages. When coal is in short supply the supplier is obliged to deliver, but the supplier may also demand that the purchaser buy coal, perhaps at a high price, even in periods of abundance. Sometimes these informal agreements involve swaps of knowledge, information, or expertise. In the United States organizations must exercise caution in these agreements, particularly those between wholesalers and retailers, to avoid violation of the Robinson-Patman Act, which outlaws certain types of agreements that may reduce competitiveness. The act prohibits agreements whereby a retailer agrees not to carry a product from a supplier's competitor or requires a retailer to purchase one undesired product in order to purchase a product the retailer really wants. These rules are often circumvented through informal agreements, although such agreements may also prove to be illegal.

Clearly, not all informal agreements are attempts to violate (either in spirit or principle) rules or laws. Other informal agreements may involve barter or resource sharing. The main problem with informal norms or agreements is that they only work in situations in which there are repeated interactions with partners and the partners can be trusted to act fairly.

Contracts or formal agreements make official and document interactions among organizations. For example, oil refiners purchase contracts with oil drillers or shippers to guarantee price, quantity, quality, and delivery of crude oil. The contract removes uncertainty about the supplier's behavior and ensures the refiner access to a critical resource. That same contract also removes uncertainty in the marketplace for the seller. The seller need be less concerned about the unpredictability of demand for its product.

Contracts or agreements can be used to guarantee the supply of labor, consulting work, construction, shipping, advertising, and nearly every facet of organizational existence.

Although contracts or agreements can be used to control many sorts of uncertainty and resource scarcity, problems are inherent in their use. First, contracts and agreements are expensive and time consuming to write. A legal department or outside legal counsel must research and prepare documents. When the environmental conditions are complex and unstable, it is difficult to write contracts or agreements that adequately cover all possible situations and remove all uncertainty. When resources become exceedingly scarce, a contract or agreement may not adequately protect an organization. For example, if the current price of crude oil far exceeds the price specified in a contract, the contract may not prevent the supplier from noncompliance. Finally, contracts and agreements must be monitored. An organization must observe the behavior of a contract partner for compliance. Monitoring is costly, and when the contract is complex or extensive, it may be difficult to monitor. Although contracts are widely used, they are imperfect mechanisms for controlling environments.

Joint Ventures. Sometimes organizations form a strategic alliance for a specific purpose or project. A joint venture is a specific strategy in which two or more organizations join together, pool resources, and spread risk to accomplish a goal that is mutually beneficial. A large number of joint ventures have been formed (and, in some cases, disbanded) in recent years. For example, General Motors joined with Toyota to produce small cars (the Toyota Corolla and GEO Prism) at a joint venture in California, called New United Motors Incorporated (NUMI). General Motors got access to Toyota's expertise in manufacturing small cars while Toyota established an American manufacturing presence, prior to the company's larger investment in Kentucky where it now makes the Camry. That early move also helped partially diffuse some initial resentment against Japanese imports. Chrysler had a similar relationship with Mitsubishi. However, now that market conditions have changed (most notably the rising value of the Japanese yen and Chrysler's increased capabilities in manufacturing small cars), the two companies have terminated the relationship. In many communities hospitals form joint ventures to purchase expensive equipment and provide costly diagnostic and treatment services. Such moves spread costs and risk among participants. In some cases no single hospital could efficiently operate the equipment. One of the largest construction jobs in history, the building of the Alaskan pipeline, was done by a joint venture consortium called Alyeska, formed by a group of oil companies. No single company possessed the skills or resources necessary to accomplish this job alone. Finally, IBM and Apple, two rivals in the computer industry, joined forces with Motorola to produce a new generation of microprocessors (the brains of a computer). The PowerPC chip that resulted reduced IBM's dependence on Intel, the chipmaker that provided the traditional line of chips for IBM PCs, and provided Apple with a new, more powerful chip for computers that could challenge the DOS and Windows market.

In each case, the joint venture was formed to manage environmental uncertainty. Organizations joined together to share information, expertise, resources, and risk. However, by forming a joint venture, the joined organizations must now deal with each other's unpredictability and idiosyncratic behavior. In a joint venture no one party exercises complete control over the others. Thus, this strategy may be suited for only removing some uncertainty and resource scarcity, but it will not completely eliminate those problems.

Mergers and Acquisitions. Mergers and acquisitions occur when two or more organizations become one. In a *merger* two or more companies join together to form a new third company. For example, pharmaceutical makers Marion Laboratories and Merrell-Dow merged to become Marion Merrell Dow. In an *acquisition* one company purchases another. The acquiring company becomes a parent company, and the acquired company may become a subsidiary, branch, or division. In the publishing industry Paramount acquired Prentice-Hall, Macmillan, and others. Paramount was then acquired by Viacom. Recently, Novell, a computer network software maker, acquired WordPerfect, the largest producer of word processing software and the Quattro Pro portion of Borland, another software company. WordPerfect and Quattro Pro formed the applications software subsidiary of Novell.[28] Sometimes the acquired company is fully absorbed within the acquiring company while sometimes the acquired company becomes a division or subsidiary of the acquiring company.

These strategies can be used to control several sources of uncertainty, including competitive uncertainty within an industry, market uncertainty within a niche, supplier uncertainty, and customer uncertainty. When an organization acquires or merges with a supplier, distributor, or customer, it is called *vertical integration.** The organization is bringing within its boundary functions or operations that were formerly carried on outside the boundary. Vertical integration can be either *backward* to suppliers or *forward* to users, distributors, or customers. Figure 5.3 describes the *value-added chain* of activities that an organization may require and the types of vertical integration that can take place.

■ **FIGURE 5.3**

Integration and the Value-Added Chain for a Petroleum Refinery

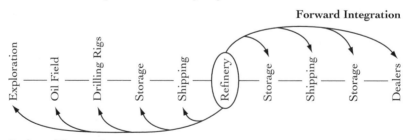

When an organization merges or acquires competitor firms, it is called *horizontal integration.* In the United States the banking industry has been the site of several horizontal mergers during the 1980s and early 1990s. For example, NationsBank (formerly

---

*Recall that in Chapter 2 we introduced the concepts of structural integration and differentiation. At that time we noted that the term *integration* was used in two distinctly different ways in the field of organization theory. Here we introduce the second use of the term. Integration in the current context refers to a business's entry into another area of business through mergers, acquisitions, or the creation of a new business.

NCNB) and First Union, two North Carolina banks, have emerged as strong regional bankers in the Southeast as the result of several acquisitions of other banks. Such moves are usually motivated by the desire to increase economies of scale, improve the efficiencies of operations, gain larger market share, and reduce competition. Horizontal mergers or acquisitions can also occur outside a firm's primary market or industry. This is called *diversification.* Some diversification is into related areas, for example Novell's purchase of WordPerfect (described in Exhibit 5.3). Both companies make software but for different market niches (network software and word processing software, respectively). Novell believed that it would be able to tie in sales of its network software with various applications software, such as word processing and spreadsheets. Other diversification may be into unrelated fields. Earlier, we noted that Philip Morris, a tobacco company, diversified by acquisitions into food and consumer goods to reduce risks resulting from the 1964 Surgeon-General's report on smoking and health, the subsequent ban on television advertising, the required warning labels, and the resulting public concern over smoking. Philip Morris now includes Miller Brewing, Kraft General Foods, and other nontobacco businesses. That move exemplifies unrelated diversification and its attempt to diminish the effects of uncertainty in tobacco by spreading risk to other market sectors.

Companies merge or acquire other companies for many reasons, including:

- growth and enhanced power and competitive status in the market;
- enhancement of economies of scale, efficiencies, and profitability;
- improved access to supplies of critical resources;
- reduction of environmental uncertainty; and
- risk management.

Exhibit 5.3   **Profile of a Failed Acquisition: Novell and WordPerfect**[29]

The software industry of the 1980s was full of gritty rags-to-riches stories of young entrepreneurs, lucky and creative "techies," and others who struck it rich by producing innovative software packages that fit the burgeoning business and personal computer industry and consumer demands. The adventures of Bill Gates and his tremendous success at Microsoft are well known. Perhaps less well-documented, but more illustrative of the new problems and opportunities confronting software companies, is the cautionary tale of WordPerfect.

WordPerfect was the brainchild of two former Brigham Young University employees, Bruce Bastian, a former marching band director, and Alan Ashton, a former computer science professor. The company they formed experienced dramatic growth after they developed an easy-to-use word processing program. But the market has changed radically since the late 1970s when Bastian and Ashton started. Technology changes quickly. Consumers and business users are becoming more sophisticated and demanding. And competition has increased. On top of these issues is the shadow that Microsoft casts over the industry. As the developer of the leading operating system (DOS) and of Windows, Microsoft has built-in advantages over competitors in producing application software that works more easily and efficiently in the DOS and Windows environment. All software that is to run on DOS- and Windows-based computers must be designed to be compatible with DOS and Windows. However, since DOS and Windows are the properties of Microsoft, independent competitive developers such as Novell and WordPerfect are dependent on Microsoft. Thus, when Microsoft developed Windows '95, it had a distinct advantage over these competitors in creating and supplying application software such as networks, word processing, and spread sheets. Microsoft is also able to bundle together application software when selling DOS and Windows to computer makers and consumers. Because of its power and success with DOS and Windows, Microsoft can bring applications to market faster and price them more aggressively.

To combat the power of Microsoft, Novell acquired WordPerfect. Novell hoped to capitalize on the apparent synergies of the two companies. Both companies realized that they could not successfully compete on their own. Unfortunately, even the union of Novell and WordPerfect was not enough to counter Microsoft's dominance, and this marriage appears to be headed for a breakup.

Space does not permit us to explain the legal, economic, political, and financial forces affecting mergers and acquisitions. Table 5.2 summarizes some of the terminology used in this field. It is important to note that mergers and acquisitions are complex phenomena that have important organizational and environmental ramifications. Often these

■ TABLE 5.2
Merger and Acquisition Terminology

Term	Description
Leveraged buyout	Acquisition of a company with little money down and a large amount of debt financed by a lending institution, the debt to be paid back from earnings of the acquired company
Hostile takeover	When a company is acquired against its will
Greenmail	The buying back of stock involved in a hostile takeover, often at a premium price not offered to all shareholders, so the target company can regain control
Golden parachute	A large salary benefit in the form of severance or termination pay guaranteed to a top executive of the acquired company by the acquiring company, should the acquiring company eventually decide to terminate the executive
Poison pill	Taking on a large load of debt or some other obligation by a company to make it less attractive to a hostile takeover bid
Shark repellents	Actions to strengthen management's control to avoid a hostile takeover. Example: issuing a new class of stock with greater voting rights than the stock widely held by outsiders
Junk bonds	Low-rated (i.e., high risk) corporate debt used to finance mergers and acquisitions that have high interest rates compared to the rates for more secure (less risky) bonds
Pac-man	A company that is a target of a hostile takeover taking the offensive and becoming the acquirer of the previous pursuer
White knight	A friendly company summoned by a company that is the target of a hostile takeover in hopes that the friendly company will out-bid the hostile pursuer

forces go beyond one organization's attempts to control its environment. Some critics argue that the flurry of acquisitions and buyouts of the mid-1980s were motivated by greed and avarice rather than attempts at environmental control and efficiency. Nonetheless, our focus here is on management of the environment. Indications are that the forces that push companies toward mergers and acquisitions still exist in the environment and that organizations will continue to view these as viable alternatives for managing environmental uncertainty and resource constraints. One of the issues that we have thus far ignored is the difficult task of integrating formerly separate organizations into one. At this point it is sufficient to say that merely because a firm merges with or acquires another does not guarantee that it will be better able to control the environment. The merged organization or acquired firm must be successfully integrated and structured to fit the environment.

A recent variation on vertical integration is the *virtual organization,* also called the network organization.[30] Through a series of agreements, contracts, and other arrangements, an organization achieves relationships with other organizations that provide many of the advantages of vertical integration without the economic costs and reduced flexibility that true vertical integration involves. Athletic footwear companies, such as Nike, form alliances with several manufacturers who make shoes. Nike designs, distributes, and markets shoes, but it does not manufacture them. Instead, Nike (and many of its competitors) relies on a network of independent manufacturers throughout Asia to make the shoes. These relationships may involve partial ownership by the parent company, but the relationships remain in place only as long as the parent company and supplier companies find it profitable. The same parent company may have other temporary alliances in other areas, such as shipping and marketing. The hallmarks of the virtual organization are its temporary nature and partial integration into the parent company. We return to this subject in Chapter 8.

Boards of Directors. The primary function of a board of directors (or, in the case of non-profit or voluntary organizations, a board of trustees) is to act as a *fiduciary* for owners by helping manage or govern an organization. (A fiduciary attempts to protect the interests of stockholders.) The board functions to oversee management's actions and make recommendations to or direct management. Beyond these specific tasks boards often carry out other jobs that link an organization to its environment and help reduce uncertainty and resource constraints. To understand these linkage functions it is necessary to understand two specific types of board members.

Boards are typically composed of both *insiders* and *outsiders.* Inside directors are individuals who are also officers or employees of the organization. For example, it is common for the president or chief executive officer (or both officers of a firm) to be insider members of the board of directors. Outsiders can come from just about anywhere. Typical categories of outsiders include bankers or venture capitalists, retired executives, executives from other businesses, consultants, academics, retired politicians or military personnel, or religious leaders. These outsiders may be chosen for their expertise, their access to scarce resources, or their links to critical outside communities or constituents. A number of large corporations have bowed to investor pressure and included more outsiders in leadership positions on boards. General Motors and Kmart, for example, appointed outsiders to the position of chairman of the board.

Two other terms used to describe board of director linkages are *interlocking directorates* and *cooptation. Interlocking directorates* form when one or more individuals serve on two or more boards of directors. This is done for two reasons: (1) to facilitate interorganizational communication and coordination and (2) to increase organizational effectiveness through sharing of expertise and resources.[31] For example, it is common for supplier and buyer organizations to have board members on each other's board of directors. It is also common for banks and large users of capital to exchange board members. In the automobile industry boards of directors often include executives from large banks that do business with the auto company and executives from supplier companies. Although board of director interlocks are common, the practice in the United States is discouraged and monitored by the antitrust division of the Justice Department.

Cooptation takes place when an organization tries to influence representatives of specific sectors of the environment. The belief is that as key outsiders gain familiarity and understanding with the conditions, opportunities, and problems that an organization faces, these outside representatives will become more receptive to the organization. For example, in the aftermath of urban riots in the late 1960s and early 1970s, many organizations tried to improve race relations and influence key African-American community leaders by including them on the firms' boards of directors. When Chrysler began having serious financial difficulties in the early 1980s, it became clear to management that one key to reducing costs and improving operations was to change the company's relationship with its union laborers. One step to accomplishing this task was to include Douglas Fraser, the United Auto Workers Union president, on Chrysler's board where other board members could attempt to influence him into more favorable treatment of the company. Through his work on Chrysler's board, Fraser came to understand that the union's failure to compromise on certain demands could result in the company's failure.[32] It is important to note that influence and cooptation are two-way streets. Outsider members of boards can also influence management to change in ways that are consistent with the outsiders' demands. Such was the hope when John Smale, an outsider and former CEO of Procter & Gamble, became chairman of the board at GM.

Management Recruiting. In the early 1990s Kodak, the photo and imagining giant, suffered through several years of dismal performance. Many of the problems facing the company were traced directly to the CEO, Kay Whitmore. Kodak was facing increasing competition in nearly every market it entered: photographic film, copiers, medical imaging, and data recording medium. Under Whitmore's leadership the company had lost ground to competitors, failed to cut costs, and managed to alienate employees and investors. Whitmore's replacement was George Fisher, formerly at Motorola, a company that had succeed dramatically in uncertain and competitive markets.[33] Kodak's board used *executive recruiting* as a mechanism to bring into the company necessary management expertise to control uncertainty. The Kodak board hired George Fisher to reinvigorate the company. The belief is that an outsider like Fisher can bring in expertise and proven management skills.

Kodak is by no means unusual in the practice of raiding other successful companies, either within an industry or outside an industry, to find the necessary talent, skills, expertise, and knowledge as well as information about the former employer-competitor required to control an organization's uncertain environment. The practice is common in many industries.

Associations. In the United States the federal government has, through antitrust laws, attempted to control the amount of cooperation and coordination among competitors within an industry. However, firms are often able to work together to control uncertainty and resource availability through *trade associations* and other types of cooperative groupings. Trade associations can reduce some competitive uncertainty by setting industry-wide technical standards so that products of various manufacturers are compatible. Perhaps the most pervasive and far-reaching activity of trade associations is lobbying government. Trade associations can leverage the strength of an entire industry to influence the legislative process at any level of government to receive more favorable treatment for their industry through *lobbying* activities. During negotiations over the North American Free Trade Agreement (NAFTA) and the General Agreement on Tarriffs and Trade (GATT), several trade associations vigorously lobbied the federal government. For example, the U.S. textile industry sought greater protection from imports while representatives of various U.S. agricultural and food products sectors sought freer access to foreign markets. Although any CEO can (and many do) individually lobby government agencies and representatives, the strength of trade or industry associations in this area is undeniable. It is no coincidence that nearly every major trade association has some office or representation in Washington, D.C.

Other forms of association can be important in garnering scarce resources for member organizations. In several industries it is common practice for potential competitors to group together into formal or informal buying groups, marketing groups, and cooperatives. In several agricultural product markets formal cooperatives play key roles in sales and distribution. Sunkist, Sunsweet, Blue Diamond, and Ocean Spray are well known trade names of cooperative marketing organizations. These companies are wholly owned by the citrus, dried fruit, nut, and cranberry producers, respectively. In the hardware and building supply business, retailers have removed some supply uncertainties by either joining buying groups like Pro and Trustworthy or by joining distribution cooperatives like Ace, True Value, Servistar, or HWI (described in Exhibit 5.4). In each case the cooperative or buying group is a mechanism to remove some uncertainty in input or output markets. In the retail pharmacy business the National Association of Chain Drug Stores (NACDS) has formed a cooperative network to help members compete with large "managed care" systems such as PCS Health Systems and Medco Containment Services that sell prescription drugs under contract for insurance plans and employers. NACDS uses the leverage created by pooling the buying power of its member retail pharmacies to obtain pricing from pharmaceutical companies comparable to that obtained by the large managed care providers.[34]

Exhibit 5.4 | **Anatomy of a Distribution Cooperative**

One problem many small businesses face is a lack of power when negotiating with suppliers or buyers. For example, a traditional neighborhood hardware store would have great difficulty competing with Builders Square, Wal-Mart, Home Depot, or other large retailers in part because of the power that these large retailers have to negotiate favorable prices from suppliers. Home Depot may buy as many as fifty or one hundred of a specific model of lawn mower for just one of its many stores while a neighborhood store may buy only ten or twenty lawn mowers in total. Not surprisingly, Home Depot can obtain more favorable pricing and terms of payment from the lawn mower manufacturer than the neighborhood retailer can receive.

Small businesses in some industries have developed a powerful mechanism to compete and receive favorable treatment from manufacturers and suppliers. In the retail hardware–home center industry, retailers have formed distribution cooperatives. These cooperatives, the largest distributors in the industry, are among the one hundred largest service companies in the United States and their trade names are widely recognized among shoppers: ACE, True Value (Cotter Company), HWI, and Servistar are the top four. The companies are *cooperatively* owned by retailers, meaning that the distributors are not profit-making businesses. Nearly all excess revenues are returned to the customer-owners (i.e., the retailers). The combined buying power of the member businesses (ranging from around 2,000 members each for HWI and Servistar to about 6,000 for True Value), along with the nonprofit nature of these companies, results in merchandise costs for the retail members that are close to the prices that large retailers such as Builders Square, Wal-Mart, or HQ pay for their goods. The cooperatives have nearly as much leverage in bargaining with manufacturers as do their large competitors.

Cooperatives also provide retailers with advertising, expertise, counseling, and other support services that help the retailers successfully compete against giant "category killers" and mass merchandisers. The cooperative tie between buyer and seller helps retailers control much uncertainty in their environment.

Advertising and Public Relations. Most of the linkage mechanisms described thus far involve links to specific organizations or groups of people. One method for linking with the general public is through advertising and public relations activities. Firms use advertising and public relations to influence the public perception of the organization, to differentiate the company from competitors, and to focus the firm on a specific market niche. For example, Anheuser-Busch spends extensively on advertising and public relations focused on alcohol education subjects, such as safe drinking ("Know when to say when"), drunk driving (designated drivers), and underage drinking as well as conventional advertising intended to sell specific products. These efforts attempt to blunt public criticism of the brewing industry. Similarly, the tobacco industry has mounted a vigorous campaign aimed at protecting smokers' rights in the face of increasing attacks from government and antismoking groups. Many companies contribute to public television and radio to enhance their public image. In each case these companies are using advertising and public relations to reduce uncertainty and increase munificence. From an environmental control standpoint, advertising and public relations are both used to increase a firm's visibility, create or modify its image, and identify or solidify its niche.

SUMMARY

Thus far this chapter has reviewed first how organizations come to know about the environment through scanning and boundary spanning and then how organizations can adapt to or change the environment that they face through a wide variety of activities. Organizations can match the environment with the appropriate level of structural complexity, plan and forecast for the future, withdraw from or avoid uncertain environments, carefully select munificent niches, imitate other successful organizations, or employ one or more linkage strategies to form relationships with other organizations. These activities are not necessarily mutually exclusive. Organizations can and do use several strategies together to manage environmental uncertainty and resource scarcity. In fact, scanning the environment and forecasting may be critical ingredients that fuel other methods of environmental adaptation or control. Scanning and forecasting may drive the selection of supplier relationships, organizational restructuring, or advertising campaigns. Moreover, management may apply certain of these strategies to specific departments or divisions while using a different set of strategies in other areas. A manufacturing department may be buffered from the environmental uncertainty that affects many other departments. Buyers may rely on contracts, while top management uses board interlocks to control uncertainty. The important issue that these strategies raise is *how* to adapt to or control the environment. Not all strategies are equally suitable for all organizations or all environmental conditions. The key task is to determine the most suitable set of strategies for the organization and the environment. This is key to a contingency framework. In general, more uncertain and resource-starved environments may require more aggressive and proactive adaptation and control strategies.

POSTSCRIPT

This contingency framework, however, leaves unanswered two critical questions. First, how aggressive should an organization be in attempting to adapt and control environments? In discussions of buyer-supplier relationships and board of director interlocks we broached the legal issues related to manipulation of the environment. In the section below we further investigate the relationship between environmental conditions and *illegal activity.* In the final section we address a controversial theoretical issue: What are the consequences of management's attempts to adapt to and control environments? Some organizational theorists suggest that managers may select responses to environmental conditions, but their ability to *successfully* adapt and control is highly questionable. The final section of the chapter presents this controversial view under the heading of *population ecology.*

Illegal Activity It must be clear at the onset that we are not advocating that organizations skirt the law to deal with scarcity or uncertainty in the environment. However, the reality is that as organizations face increasingly difficult environments, the likelihood increases that they will resort to illegal activity to control the environment.[35] Markets characterized by much competitive uncertainty may encourage managers to offer kick-backs, bribes, or other illegal inducements for favorable treatment. Firms have at times paid bribes to various foreign government officials in order to win contracts, gain favorable treatment, or simply expedite imports through customs. Where potentially large markets exist, firms may illegally cooperate to fix prices or agree to not compete so as to reduce competitive pressures. For example, several large dairy companies illegally cooperated to divide the school lunch market because they believed competition would simply drive down profits and hurt all the companies. As a result, school districts throughout Ohio and Kentucky overpaid for milk. Several companies have already admitted guilt and are paying steep fines as well as reimbursing the affected school districts for damages. Collusion, bribery, price fixing, and other forms of illegal activity may reduce some uncertainty, but the risk of detection and subsequent damage to the firm may be considerable. The Foreign Corrupt Practices Act now makes it a crime for a U.S. company to break U.S. laws in conducting business in foreign countries—even if those acts are not illegal in the foreign country. These represent only a few of the potential illegal activities that firms do conduct.

Population Ecology. The population ecology view of organizations is largely adopted from the study of animal ecology and evolution. The focus is on *organizational forms,* which are broadly defined to include *unique configurations of structure, ownership, boundaries,* and *goals.* This viewpoint applies the Darwinian notion of natural selection and survival of the fittest to organizations—those organizational forms that are the most efficient and that fit best with the prevailing environmental conditions will persist.[36] The problem, in light of the preceding discussion of adapting and controlling environments, is that population ecology is unconcerned with the forces that make an organization more efficient and a better fit with the environment. Population ecologists refer to *variations* among firms. Variations may be planned, or they may be unintentional, random, or accidental. Variations include differences or changes in structure, ownership, boundaries, or goals of the organization—many of the very characteristics that we discussed earlier in this chapter as means for responding to or controlling the environment. Additionally, some population ecologists maintain that the environment, even for the simplest of organizations, is so complex and dynamic that it is impossible for managers to know all there is to know and to anticipate critical changes. Any sector of the environment may produce unanticipated conditions that threaten the very existence of an organizational form.

It is the environment that *selects* those forms of organizations that best fit, regardless of whether change was intentional or accidental. One must keep in mind that the population ecology definition of *organizational form* is not identical to the conventional understanding of *organization* or *form.* Traditional full-service gas stations may be disappearing as an organizational form (i.e., a cluster of goals, structure, boundaries, and ownership), but the remaining gas stations may be owned and operated by the same groups that formerly ran the full-service gas station. It is the full-service form that is disappearing—not the specific organization. Finally, organizational forms that are successful fits with the environment are *retained.* Ironically, retention is fostered by forces that support stability and replication or imitation of a form. Those very factors that support retention are, in fact, the same forces that work against frequent organizational change and adaptation. Thus, frequent restructuring and changing may be destabilizing and result in failure, according to population ecologists.

This is merely a brief, thumbnail sketch of population ecology. The subject has been the focus of much research, writing, and misunderstanding among organizational theorists. The interested reader should consult the references listed at the end of this chapter. The important point is that this view presents an interesting, deterministic image of organizations that contrasts with the proactive strategic view of management adapting to and controlling environments that we have presented in this chapter. Some scholars have argued that the population ecology may be relevant for ***populations of organizations*** (all organizations of a similar type occupying the same niche) but not for individual organizations. Others have argued that the population view may be accurate for the long term, but they question whether this view fits the short-run changes and adaptation. Nonetheless, mounting research evidence suggests that the population ecology perspective has at least some value in predicting or explaining the emergence and disappearance of organizational forms.

Questions for Discussion

1. Why is it more important for today's managers to cope with the external environment than it was for managers of, say, twenty years ago?
2. Distinguish between boundary spanning and environmental scanning. Should these activities be the sole responsibility of management? Explain.
3. Interview a manager in your locality, and see what he or she knows about the topic of managing the environment. If this manager does not know a great deal (in your opinion), what would you tell him or her to stress the significance of this topic? What strategies for managing or controlling the environment would you suggest that the manager use?
4. What do permeability, resilience, and maintenance have to do with environmental management?
5. "I never waste time forecasting and making strategy. I just react to conditions of the moment." React to this quote from a CEO of a successful manufacturer of consumer health care products.
6. How can structure be used in the management of the environment? Give an example.
7. What is a linkage strategy, and how can one be used to help an organization deal with its environment?
8. What effect(s) do you think the signing of the North American Free Trade Agreement (NAFTA) and the General Agreement on Tariffs and Trade (GATT) will have on the agricultural combines located in southern Texas? Suggest how they might deal with this legislation's effect on their environment.
9. Define *population ecology*. Do you agree with this concept? Why or why not? Pick an example of a type of organization that you think is unlikely to survive. Why? What does population ecology say about the role of top management and strategic planning?

CASE: BUTT OUT*

Increasingly, smokers are coming under "fire" in the United States. What was once considered a fashionable and chic habit that was glamorously depicted in movies, TV, and almost all periodicals is now the subject of ridicule, national publicity, and litigation nationwide.

Offices, conference rooms, and other workplaces are now forbidden sites for lighting up — their smoker occupants are being forced to restricted areas and even outdoors to take their customary smoke breaks. And this trend is being accentuated everyday and in all walks of life. No longer can travelers smoke on most public transportation nor do they feel free to smoke in most public buildings. Ashtrays no longer adorn the desks and coffee tables of U.S. offices. Thank-you-for-not-smoking signs now are their replacements.

This trend is the result of an awakening public awareness of the dangers of cigarette smoking that began when the Surgeon-General of the U.S. published the now-famous report in 1964 that linked smoking to all sorts of cardiovascular diseases, especially lung cancer. In June of 1994, David Kessler, commissioner of the Food & Drug Administration, disclosed before a U.S. House of Representatives subcommittee that in the 1980s, the Brown & Williamson Company had developed and kept secret a tobacco plant that contained twice the amount of nicotine found in commonly used types of tobacco. This testimony could open the doors for cigarettes to be regulated as vehicles for the delivery of the drug nicotine. This, if it were to happen, could put cigarettes in the same category as hypodermic needles sold by prescription and could cause a severe blow to the sales of cigarettes.

COUNTERATTACK

But cigarette manufacturers are not taking this multifront attack on their industry lying down. They are mounting a broad-based counterattack aimed at legislation and even cultural pressures pointed at them. On February 1, 1994, Philip Morris (PM) filed court papers that challenged a San Francisco smoking ban and, in March, sued ABC for defamation. The company replaced resigned CEO Michael Miles (who wanted to split PM into separate food and tobacco companies) with Geoffrey Bible, who is an unashamed cigarette smoker. R. J. Reynolds features ads with its chief executive officer, James Johnson, holding a lighted cigarette. These actions were apparently taken on the assumption that these executives would appear more credible if they were shown using their company products in the belief that they were not, in fact, harmful.

The counterattack has also found its way into the rooms of editorial boards of newspapers across the country. National tours of major city newspapers have featured visits by the chief executives of R. J. Reynolds who attempted to win support for the company's position.

The industry has made serious efforts to polish its image — to change it from a negative, health-hazard behemoth. Advertising campaigns, cross-country editorial boards'

---

*This case is based on the following article: Linda Himelstein, "Tobacco: Does It Have a Future?" *Business Week* (July 4, 1994): 24–29.

visits, appeals to freedom of choice, and outright denials of the alleged health risks associated with their products are all part of the counterattack that is funded by the rich coffers of the industry members. These members appear optimistic in spite of the fact that cigarette consumption among those eighteen and over has declined from a high of 42.4 percent in 1965 to about 25 percent in 1994.

Even though tobacco companies are facing about a 50 percent reduction in profits from 1993 totals, they still have considerable financial strength. One of the big contributors to this financial condition is overseas sales. For instance, Philip Morris and RJR earned $3 billion from these sales in 1993. Companies are looking to China, eastern Europe, and Latin America, whose smokers can't seem to get enough of U.S. tobacco products. Thus, the industry looks overseas to keep its total sales up. Although this might turn out to be a temporary respite, at least the companies have for the moment staved off some of the pressures from their environment.

So, while the industry is under severe attack from many sources, it is safe to say that it is not only keenly aware of the seriousness of these assaults, it has begun a vigorous counterattack.

Will the industry succeed? Or will it simply be forced to butt out?

QUESTIONS FOR DISCUSSION

1. From which environmental sectors (see Chapter 4) are the tobacco companies receiving the most pressure? What types of strategies for managing the environment does the case illustrate?
2. What would the benefits likely be for companies like RJR Nabisco and Philip Morris in separating the tobacco business from the food and other business areas? What are the likely negative consequences of such action?
3. What other strategies would be appropriate for the tobacco companies to use to control their environments?

REFERENCES

1. J. Stacey Adams, "The Structure and Dynamics of Behavior in Organizational Boundary Roles," in *Handbook of Industrial and Organizational Psychology,* ed. by M. D. Dunnette (Chicago: Rand McNally, 1976), 1175–99.

2. Henry Mintzberg, *The Nature of Managerial Work* (Englewood Cliffs, N.J.: Prentice-Hall, 1980).

3. Andrew C. Boynton, Lawrence M. Gales, and Richard S. Blackburn, "Managerial Search Activity: The Impact of Perceived Role Uncertainty and Role Threat," *Journal of Management* 19 (1993): 725–47.

   Mary J. Culnan, "Environmental Scanning: The Effects of Task Complexity and Source Accessibility on Information Gathering Behaviors," *Decision Sciences* 14 (1983): 194–206.

Richard L. Daft, J. Sormunen, and D. Parks, "Chief Executive Scanning, Environmental Characteristics, and Company Performance: An Empirical Study," *Strategic Management Journal* 9 (1988): 123–39.

Liam Fahey and William R. King, "Environmental Scanning for Corporate Planning," *Business Horizons* 63 (August 1977): 61–71.

A. Keflas and P. Schoderbek, "Scanning the Business Environment," *Decision Sciences* 4 (1973): 63–74.

4. See Daft, Sormunen, and Parks in note 3 above.

Sumantra Ghoshal and Seok Ki Kim, "Building Effective Intelligence Systems for Competitive Advantage," *Sloan Management Review* 49 (1986): 53.

5. See Daft, Sormunen, and Parks in note 3 above.

6. R. T. Lenz and J. L. Engledow, "Environmental Analysis Units and Strategic Decision-Making: A Field Study of Selected Leading-Edge Corporations," *Strategic Management Journal* 7 (1988): 69–89.

7. Based on the following articles:

Roderick P. Deighen, "Welcome to Cold War II," *Chief Executive* (January/February 1993): 42–46.

Norm Alster, "The Valley of the Spies," *Forbes* (October 26, 1992): 200–204.

Stephen A. Carlton, "Industrial Espionage: Reality of the Information Age," *Research Technology Management* (November/December 1992): 18–24.

8. Alan Farnham, "It's a Bird! It's a Plane! It's a Flop!" *Fortune* (May 2, 1994): 108–10.

9. James D. Thompson, *Organizations in Action* (New York: McGraw-Hill, 1967).

10. C. Van Tune, "Class Action: BMW 540i versus Cadillac STS," *Motor Trend* 45, no. 12 (1993): 46–52.

S. Mitani, "Elite Eights," *Road & Track* (March 1995): 96–107.

11. See note 1 above.

R. H. Miles and W. Perreault, "Organizational Role Conflict: Its Antecedents and Consequences," *Organizational Behavior and Human Performance* 17 (1976): 19–44.

12. Richard H. Hall, *Organizations: Structures, Processes, and Outcomes* (Englewood Cliffs, N.J.: Prentice-Hall, 1991).

13. Jeffery Pfeffer and Gerald R. Salancik, *The External Control of Organizations: A Resource Dependence Perspective* (New York: Harper & Row, 1978).

14. L. Zinn, J. Berry, K. Murphy, S. Jones, M. Benedetti, and A. Z. Cuneo, "Teens: Here Comes the Biggest Wave Yet," *Business Week* (April 11, 1994): 76–86.

J. Treece, S. Anderson, G. Sandler, and K. Murphy, "Why We Love Trucks," *Business Week* (December 5, 1994): 70–80.

K. Labich, "Kissing Off Corporate America," *Fortune* (February 20, 1995): 44–52.

15. See Thompson in note 9 above.

    Raymond E. Miles and Charles C. Snow, *Organizational Strategy, Structure and Process* (New York: McGraw-Hill, 1978).

16. James W. Dean, Jr., and James R. Evans, *Total Quality: Management, Organization and Strategy* (St. Paul, Minn.: West Publishing, 1994).

17. P. R. Lawrence and J. W. Lorsch, *Organization and Environment* (Boston: Harvard Business School, 1967).

18. T. Burns and G. M. Stalker, *The Management of Innovation* (London: Tavistock Institute, 1961).

19. D. S. Pugh, D. J. Hickson, and C. R. Hinings, "An Empirical Taxonomy of Structures of Work Organizations," *Administrative Science Quarterly* (1969): 115–26.

20. See note 18 above.

    See note 19 above.

21. W. Richard Scott, *Organizations: Rational, Natural and Open Systems*, 3rd ed. (Englewood Cliffs, N.J.: Prentice-Hall, 1992).

    John W. Meyer and Brian Rowan, "Institutionalized Organizations: Formal Structure as a Myth and Ceremony," *American Journal of Sociology* 83 (1977): 340–63.

    Christine Oliver, "Strategic Responses to Institutional Processes," *Academy of Management Review* 16 (1991): 145–79.

    Paul J. DiMaggio and Walter W. Powell, eds., *The New Institutionalism in Organizational Analysis* (Chicago: University of Chicago Press, 1991).

22. Commerce Clearing House Business Law Editors, *Responsibilities of Corporate Officers and Directors Under Federal Securities Laws* (Chicago: Commerce Clearing House, 1993), 14.

23. See note 16 above.

24. Ibid.

25. See DiMaggio and Powell in note 21 above.

    See Oliver in note 21 above.

    L. G. Zucker, ed., *Institutional Patterns and Organizations: Culture and Environment* (Cambridge, Mass.: Ballinger, 1988).

    P. S. Tolbert and L. G. Zucker, "Institutional Sources of Change in the Formal Structure of Organizations: The Diffusion of Civil Service Reform, 1880–1935," *Administrative Science Quarterly* 28 (1983): 22–39.

26. "The *Fortune* 500," *Fortune* (April 19, 1993): 173–284.

27. J. C. Jarillo, "On Strategic Networks," *Strategic Management Journal* 9 (1988): 31–41.

R. R. Kamath and J. K. Liker, "A Second Look at Japanese Product Development," *Harvard Business Review* (November–December 1994): 154–158.

28. G. Pascal Zachary, "Novell Pact with Word Perfect Followed a Secret Bidding War Initiated by Lotus," *The Wall Street Journal* (March 24, 1994), A3–A6.

29. Based on G. Pascal Zachary, "Consolidation Sweeps the Software Industry; Small Firms Imperiled," *The Wall Street Journal* (March 23, 1994), A1–A8.

30. John A. Byrne, "The Virtual Corporation: The Company of the Future Will Be the Ultimate in Adaptability," *Business Week* (February 8, 1993): 98–102.

   Hans B. Thorelli, "Networks: Between Markets and Hierarchies," *Strategic Management Journal* 7 (1986): 37–51.

   O. E. Williamson, "Comparative Economic Organization: The Analysis of Discrete Structural Alternatives," *Administrative Science Quarterly* 36 (1991): 269–96.

31. See note 13 above.

   B. D. Baysinger and R. E. Hoskisson, "The Composition of Boards of Directors and Strategic Control: Effects on Corporate Strategy," *The Academy of Management Review* 15 (1990): 72–87.

   E. Fama and M. Jensen, "Separation of Ownership and Control," *Journal of Law and Economics* 26 (1983): 301–25.

   J. Pfeffer, "Size and Composition of Corporate Boards of Directors: The Organization and Its Environment," *Administrative Science Quarterly* 17 (1972): 218–29.

32. See note 13 above.

33. Mark Maremont and Gary Williams, "Kodak: Shoot the Works," *Business Week* (November 15, 1993): 30–32.

34. Elyse Tanouye, "Pharmacy Trade Group Creates Firm to Compete for Prescription-Drug Plans," *The Wall Street Journal* (April 11, 1994), 3–4.

35. B. M. Staw and E. Szwajkowski, "The Scarcity–Munificence Component of Organizational Environments and the Commission of Illegal Acts," *Administrative Science Quarterly* 20 (1975): 345–54.

   See note 13 above.

36. H. Aldrich, *Organizations and Environments* (Englewood Cliffs, N.J.: Prentice-Hall, 1979).

   G. Carrol, "Organizational Ecology," *Annual Review of Sociology* 10 (1984): 71–93.

   M. T. Hannan and J. Freeman, "The Population Ecology of Organizations," *American Journal of Sociology* 82 (1977): 929–64.

C H A P T E R   6

Organizational Technology

CASE: "HELP YOU WITH YOUR LUGGAGE?"*

Everyone who has ever traveled by commercial air carrier has heard those words countless times. For the harried, tired, and frustrated airline passenger, however, they can be most welcomed words, indeed. The flight has been long, filled with delays, and now, at last, the baggage carousel is just ahead!

You wait anxiously while countless other bags career up the conveyor and fall haphazardly onto the carousel waiting for their owners to claim them. You know that the odds of your bag being first are about like those of winning the lottery, but still you have hope. After all, someone's bag has to be first!

Finally, your battered suitcase appears as if by magic. Just as you reach to pick it up, the skycap greets you with the welcome words, "Help you with your luggage?" Neither of you gives a second thought to just how your bag reached this point. Nor did you give any consideration to the advances in the technology of luggage handling in the airline industry that have occurred since your first flight. Not too long ago all bags were literally, one by one, placed on airplanes by hand; were unloaded in line fashion; and finally were carried to the baggage claim area by baggage handlers. Today, thanks to advances such as bar codes, motorized carts, and conveyors, the baggage handler's job has been changed. Instead of physical might, mechanized and computerized equipment provides a substitute for physical labor.

DENVER'S BAGGAGE HANDLING SYSTEM

Generally, these modern baggage-handling systems work efficiently, with speed and accuracy being the keystones of daily activities. But such was not initially the case at the new Denver International Airport (DIA), a $3.2 billion facility.

DIA's opening was delayed three times in 1994 due to the failure of its state-of-the-art automated baggage system. The

---

*Sources: John Ritter, "Mile-high in Debt, Disfavor," *USA Today* (August 15, 1994), 3A.
Marj Charlier, "Denver Plans Backup Baggage System for Airport's Troubled One," *The Wall Street Journal* (August 5, 1994), A10.

system, made up of computer-controlled carts on rails, saw so many glitches, gremlins, and goblins that some Denverites were beginning to wonder if the system would ever work well enough to allow DIA to open for business. The city of Denver was losing some $1.1 million for every day of delay. This burden took the form of debt service, operating, and maintenance costs. The city council had to decide whether to spend some $55 million for an old-fashioned back-up system to get the airport ready to accept its first passenger.

In 1988 city officials were quite excited about the prospects for DIA. Stapleton, although conveniently located only seven miles from downtown, had reached its saturation point. The sixty-year-old facility was the sixth busiest in the U.S. However, the new baggage-handling system was not cooperating, and DIA sat idle while tempers and debt rose daily.

SYSTEM EATS BAGGAGE

In test runs the new system sent bags to wrong carousels, chewed up bags, and was generally a study in frustration, not only to BAE Automated Systems (the manufacturer) but also to virtually everyone who had anything to do with it. All this happened in the testing phase.

With frustration at a peak, an alternative $50 million project using a conventional technology system was proposed. The alternative system would use carts and conveyors like those used in most airports around the world.

United Airlines, the dominant carrier serving Denver, opposed the alternative system because its contract with the city called for the new airport to have an automated system. This hitch came on the heels of Continental's reduction of its service to Denver to only 23 flights a day, down from 139. It appeared that United didn't think the alternative system would work fast enough to serve its needs. Now it seems that it is possible that overall traffic at Denver will decline as a result of United's and Continental's actions.

It is also important to note that optimistic projections of increased air travel into and out of Denver are just that — optimistic. The projections were based on the economic impact of a slump in the oil industry's support of Denver and the expected results of the deregulation of the airline industry. The very bases for the new airport are in question. Reduced expectations, rising costs, and frustrations with the automated baggage-handling system have put a damper on the initial enthusiasm for the new Denver International Airport.

The DIA debacle is having a sweeping impact on Denver. Even Denver Mayor Wellington Webb's reelection may very well depend on the success of the new automated baggage system. As DIA opened for traffic in early 1995, it was still unclear how much the new baggage system contributed to the skycap's cry of, "Help you with your baggage?"

This case points out how technology can be a force in and of itself as well as become entangled with the political and economic forces in the environment to serve as a major factor in organizational decision making. Every organization has technology — whether the work of the organization involves handcrafted, one-of-a-kind items; mass-produced goods; or services such as insurance, legal counseling, or the purchase of retail goods. In fact, depending on how we view technology, every organization has many technologies.

We usually view technology, especially when it involves computerization and automation, as a positive force on organizations. However, in the Denver International Airport case, technology was initially failing and causing delays that led to huge economic losses. Technology plays a critical role in organizations. As you read this chapter on technology, keep the case in mind and see if the concepts and ideas discussed in the chapter apply to the Denver International situation. Also keep in mind that technology is a critical contingency factor that must be considered when determining how to organize.

ORGANIZATIONAL TECHNOLOGY

Technology has a profound impact on organizations. Like goals, environment, and organizational size, variations in the types of technology that organizations use require different methods of management and different types of organizational structure. In this chapter we begin by examining the basic construct—what is technology—and then explore the ways in which organizations must structure to manage their technology.

In fields as diverse as organization theory, organization behavior, management, operations, economics, ergonomics, and industrial engineering, researchers and practitioners have searched for better tools and methods for performing work in organizations. The eighteenth century economist Adam Smith wrote in *The Wealth of Nations* (1776) that the manufacturing efficiency of a simple pin factory could be dramatically increased through division of labor *(specialization)* and better machines. In the early twentieth century, the writings of Frederick W. Taylor and the Scientific Management School advocated improved efficiency through a similar pattern of specialization and better use of tools and people. Both of these early works, although separated by over one hundred years, essentially dealt with the same topics—technology and its relationship to structure.

We briefly introduced the concept of technology in Chapter 1 as part of the discussion of the contingency framework. We again touched on the concept in Chapter 4 when we identified the technology sector of the environment as an important part of the environmental domain. In this chapter we explore some of the effects that technology has on organizations. All organizations employ technology—ways of carrying out jobs or tasks. In fact, there are several ways of looking at technology, and organizations typically have multiple technologies.

Because the term *technology* has a current, everyday meaning, its use and meaning in the context of organization theory may at first seem somewhat confusing. Such terms as *high tech* and *low tech* that grace our everyday language are not useful in organization theory. These terms may in fact mislead us about the nature of work. The essential questions that should guide our thinking about technology are:

1. How does the organization get its work done? and
2. How can management properly control that technology?

These questions are embedded in the larger and more central question of what technology is. That is where our journey begins.

WHAT IS TECHNOLOGY?

Definitions of *technology* vary widely among organizational writers.[1] One reason for the diversity of definitions of *technology* is that technology researchers have focused on different aspects or levels of the organization (e.g., the whole organization, departments or work units within the organization, or the relationships among individuals, groups, or departments). Additionally, some researchers have focused on inputs or materials used in tasks. Others have examined the operations used to transform inputs or materials into outputs. And still others suggest that the knowledge or information needed to complete tasks is an indicator of technology. Synthesizing these varied approaches, we define technology in the following way. First, ***technology is the term used to refer to the work performed by an organization.***[2] Second, and more specifically, technology refers to the ***knowledge, tools, machines, information, skills, and materials used to complete tasks within organizations, as well as the nature of the outputs of the organization.***

> ### Definition
>
> *Technology* is the term used to refer to the work performed by an organization. Technology refers to the knowledge, tools, machines, information, skills, and materials used to complete tasks within organizations, as well as the nature of the outputs of the organization.

This definition implies that technology incorporates the idea of the *way* an organization uses resources to produce products and services. In other words, technology deals with the *throughputs* or *transformation processes* in our systems model, with the application of knowledge, skills, and tools to problems or tasks. Technology deals with how people in an organization carry out their tasks to produce the products and services of the organization. Technology, however, applies to more than just those tasks directly involved with the transformation process. It also deals with how products and services are distributed, the supporting activities necessary to bring services and products to market, and every other activity within an organization. Some versions of technology can be used to describe the nature of any task or job within an organization.

For example, we can envision the technology used in a typical automobile assembly line. Certain tasks are performed that use machinery, worker knowledge, and worker skills to produce large numbers of nearly identical automobiles. Machinery must be placed in an appropriate configuration to enhance coordination among workers. Various raw materials, semifinished goods, and products are needed at specific times in the appropriate quantity and quality. People with the necessary knowledge and skills to operate the machines and handle the raw materials must be present. All of these factors make up the technology of automobile manufacturing. But in addition to these people and tasks, people in other departments of an auto manufacturing facility (e.g., marketing, accounting, human resources, and clerical staff) also have specific technologies associated with their tasks. The market researcher uses peoples' opinions or perceptions as raw materials. He or she must have knowledge of market research, statistics, computers, and an array of other areas in order to do the job. Thus, every job or task in an organization involves some conceptualization of technology. Not only does each of these operations involve technology, but technology also comes into play when we consider the coordination of all of these activities so that the organization works smoothly. Although some writers on technology look strictly at the production-transformation process, we are interested more broadly in the technology of any organizational task. We are interested in the methods as well as the machinery. Some writers refer only to machinery, but methods also define the technology.

One might ask why technology is associated with structure. The *technology imperative* argues that technology drives structure.[3] In other words, the technology used in an organization causes an organization to structure or organize in a certain way. The decision about the type of technology an organization uses dictates the most appropriate structure. Compare the structure of an automobile assembly plant with that of a university or a hospital. In an auto plant people are organized around process. But even this organizing may vary. The transformation process in a conventional assembly line auto plant is different from the team-based assembly used by General Motors in the Saturn factory. The structuring of the Saturn plant is also different from that in conventional auto assembly plants. In a university, people are organized around disciplines or subjects (e.g., marketing department, management department). In a hospital, people are structured around procedures performed. By organizing around technology, organizations often achieve better coordination and reduce uncertainty because work procedures, methods, and machinery become the basis for setting up internal relationships and policies. Structure is necessary to reduce uncertainty and aid in information gathering; coordinate efforts across groups, work units or departments; and direct people.

Viewpoints on technology abound. Thus, placing each perspective in a readily understandable framework is not easy. The simplifying framework that we apply is to examine the various *levels of technology*. Organizational or *core technology* concepts are used to characterize the whole organization, and these views are examined in the following section. Although core technology is a useful idea for making broad generalizations about an organization, it may not capture the complexity and diversity of the organization's tasks. To understand this complexity and diversity we focus on smaller portions of the organization — *work unit* or *departmental technology*. However, these typically do not work in isolation. For an organization to accomplish its goals, work units or departments must coordinate and work together. Thus, our final level of focus is on the *interdependent relationships* that result from the flow of work among departments or work units because of the technology used to carry out the organization's tasks. Figure 6.1 on page 158 illustrates these three levels of technology.

ORGANIZATION-LEVEL TECHNOLOGY: THE TECHNICAL CORE

One of the first systematic studies of the relationship between technology and organization was completed by British sociologist Joan Woodward in the early 1950s.[4] Woodward intended only to study organizational and administrative aspects of British

■ **FIGURE 6.1**
Three Levels of Technology

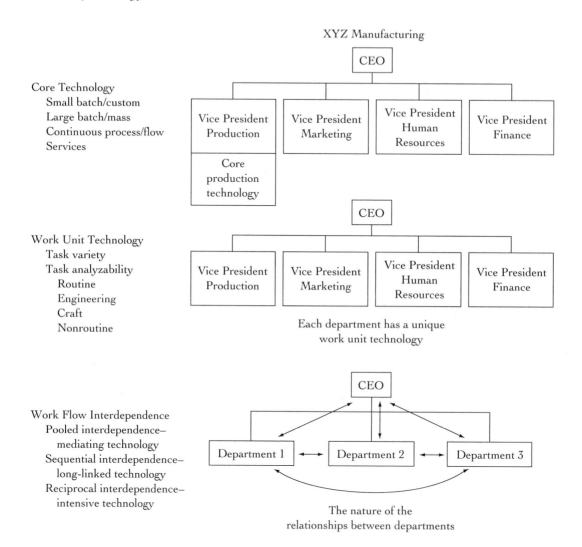

manufacturing firms. However, her study of the administrative structure of these firms failed to confirm the conventional management thinking at that time. Rather than finding one ideal form of organization, Woodward found wide variations in an array of structural components of organizations, including the amount of direct versus indirect labor, the number of levels in the hierarchy, and the spans of supervisory control. It was only after Woodward's research team began looking at technology that they discovered the relationship between technology and structure. The result was a three-category scheme for classifying organization-level technology:[5]

UNIT OR SMALL BATCH

Production runs consist of only a few units at a time, such as those found in a specialty job shop. Production is often customized to the specific needs of individual customers, which makes stockpiling finished goods impractical. Production requires significant direct labor (labor intensity). Examples include a custom tailor shop where garments are made to specific customer measurements and preferences, a machine toolmaker that designs tools to the needs and requirements of manufacturers, or an aircraft jet engine maker that makes small quantities of different engines, each of which may be modified for specific applications.

MASS OR LARGE BATCH

Many units of the same or similar products are produced at one time in long production runs. Production involves both moderate mechanization (capital intensity) and moderate amounts of direct labor (labor intensity), is more or less undifferentiated, and can be inventoried or stockpiled for future sale or use. Examples include assembly line production of automobiles, personal computers, and most clothing manufacturing.

CONTINUOUS PROCESS OR FLOW

Production runs continuously with infrequent start-ups or shut-downs. Start-ups, breakdowns, or shut-downs can be dangerous, costly, and time consuming. Production is the most highly mechanized (high capital intensity) and standardized. Output is highly uniform, and the process often has a flow-like quality. This process involves little direct labor. Examples include petrochemical refineries, breweries, and electric power generation.

CORE TECHNOLOGY AND STRUCTURE

In addition to providing a system of classifying organizational core technologies, Woodward also identified a ***contingency relationship*** between technology and structure. Her research showed that no single organizational structure best fit all organizations. Instead, she noted that structure varied with technology in the following fashion:

1. ***Unit or Small Batch*** — Organic (flexible and adaptable): moderate size span of control, highly skilled workforce, low degree of formalization, low degree of specialization, and decentralized decision making
2. ***Mass or Large Batch*** — Mechanistic-bureaucratic (stable and somewhat rigid): large size span of control, low level of workforce skill, high degree of formalization, high degree of specialization, and centralized decision making
3. ***Continuous Process or Flow*** — Organic (flexible and adaptable): small span of control, highly skilled workforce (professionalized), low degree of formalization, low degree of specialization, and decentralized decision making.

Woodward's classification scheme has been useful in the development of a contingency framework for examining organization structure. Her work was the first to clearly document that there was not one best way to structure or manage an organization. Recently, work by Hull and Collins[6] expanded on Woodward's framework by adding a fourth core technology that subdivides small batch or unit technology into two categories. *Traditional small batch technology* includes operations that are low in knowledge complexity such as custom tailoring or dressmaking, while *technical batch technology,* such as the manufacturing of jet aircraft engines or aerospace components, requires high knowledge complexity. Table 6.1 presents Hull and Collins' elaboration of Woodward's core manufacturing technology framework. The main structural implications of Hull and Collins' view of small batch technology are that traditional small batch technology requires skilled craftspeople in a simple organic structure, and there is little opportunity for automation or computerization. Technical batch technology requires highly skilled professional workers in an organic-profession *adhocracy* and presents greater opportunities for automation and computerization. An adhocracy is a highly flexible structure that can be altered or changed as needed. Hull and Collins have improved upon Woodward's typology by recognizing the diversity of technologies and their effects on the organization.

The types of core manufacturing technologies that Woodward and Hull and Collins present represent prototypes. Some core technologies may involve combinations

■ TABLE 6.1
Revision of Woodward's Typology of Production Systems with Structure and Innovative Activity

	Technical Batch	Continuous Process
High	Example: aerospace electronics Capital equipment: computer controlled, general purpose Human resources: professional and technical experts, skilled and semiskilled operatives Structure: organic-professional adhocracy Innovative activity: high R&D and innovation	Example: petrochemical plant Capital equipment: automated, sometimes computer controlled; integrated Human resources: skilled operatives, large percentage of engineers Structure: mixed, professional bureaucracy Innovative activity: medium-high R&D and innovation
Knowledge Complexity	**Traditional Batch**	**Mass Production**
Low	Example: dressmaking, printing Capital equipment: nonautomated, general purpose Human resources: skilled or unskilled operatives Structure: traditional-craft, simple structure Innovative activity: low R&D and innovation	Example: carburetor assembly Capital equipment: automated, repeat-cycle, sequential Human resources: semiskilled operatives, small proportion research and engineering Structure: mechanistic-bureaucratic, machine bureaucracy Innovative activity: low-medium R&D and innovation
	Small **Scale of Operations** Large	

Source: Frank M. Hull and Paul D. Collins, "High-Technology Batch Production Systems: Woodward's Missing Type," *Academy of Management Journal* 30, no. 4 (December 1987): 788.

or aspects of all these types. Parts of steel and sheet glass production are flow technology, yet the end products are discrete pieces much like large batch or mass technology. Moreover, this body of research is not without shortcomings. Woodward largely ignored the confounding effects of organizational size on technology. Studies of core technology resulted in a ***technology imperative***—that technology should be the principal factor in determination of the appropriate structure. Yet, size, as we noted in the previous chapter, can be a potent factor in structuring an organization. In addition, a number of other relevant issues must be examined. First, these works focus solely on manufacturing and ignore technology employed in the increasingly large and important service sector of the economy. Second, innovations in technology, such as computer integrated manufacturing (CIM), flexible manufacturing, computer-aided design (CAD)/computer-aided manufacturing (CAM), and various group or team approaches to manufacturing, challenge some of the conventional wisdom of Woodward's framework. Third, this approach to technology is useful only for classifying core (whole organization) technology. It does not deal with the varied technologies used by people in other parts of the organization but not involved with the technical core. We will examine all three of these issues. We first examine the technology of service organizations.

SERVICE AS A CORE TECHNOLOGY

In recent years, increasing attention has been focused on the service sector of the economy. Some writers suggest that the future strength and job growth in the United States' economy will be in the service sector. Regardless of the future, the reality today is that services constitute a major segment of the organizational landscape. Thus, it is important to understand how and why service technology differs from manufacturing technology. Definitions of *service* typically allude to the *intangible* nature of the output. That is, in the extreme, ***services are intangible offerings of value that do not have a physical form and are provided to a customer or client.*** Teaching, medical services, legal services, banking, insurance, restaurants, and retail stores are a few examples. In reality, however, a continuum or range of technologies exists from pure services involving no tangible output (e.g., legal services, insurance, education, and transportation) to pure manufacturing technologies such as those discussed earlier in this chapter.[7] In the midrange are technologies that involve both services and manufacturing (e.g., restaurants, banks, and retail stores). Figure 6.2 on page 162 provides examples of the full range of core technologies.

The differences between service and manufacturing technologies can best be seen by examining the extreme or prototypical cases on five dimensions: tangibility, standardization, customer participation, timing, and labor intensity.

1. **Tangibility.** Tangibility refers to the concreteness or abstractness of output. As one moves from pure manufacturing technology to pure service technology, the degree of *intangibility* increases, so that with pure services there is no tangible or concrete output. Compare manufacturing an automobile to servicing one. Manufacturing an automobile involves a clearly identifiable tangible output—the car. Servicing an automobile involves some tangible output—new oil, filters, and spark plugs—but the primary output of interest to the customer is a

■ FIGURE 6.2

*Service Technology**

Prototypical Service	Combined Service and Manufacturing	Prototypical Manufacturing
Intangible output	Some tangibility	Tangible output
Customized output	Some customization	Standardized output
Customer participation	Some customer involvement	Technical core buffered
Simultaneous production and consumption	Some inventory	Inventory of goods to be consumed later
Labor intensive	Labor and capital intensive	Capital intensive

* From David Bowen, Caren Siehl, and Benjamin Schneider (1989), "A Framework for Analyzing Customer Service Orientations in Manufacturing," *Academy of Management Review* 14 (1989): 75–95.

car that runs better than it did prior to servicing. The intangibility of this out-put creates uncertainty for both the organization providing the service and the consumer. Because there is no concrete, tangible output, judgments about the quality and appropriateness of the output are more subjective and debatable than is typically the case with tangible outputs.

2. **Standardization.** Services tend to be less standardized and more tailored to customer needs than do manufacturing technologies. Although we noted that small batch or unit technology tends to emphasize customization, a key differ-ence with services is that customization takes place at the point of sale or exchange. Compare auto manufacturing to counseling services. Although there are standard guidelines for counseling, how it is delivered depends very much on characteristics of the individual receiving the counseling.

3. **Customer Participation.** Services directly involve the customer in the produc-tion process. This is a boundary issue. In manufacturing technology the core technology is protected or buffered from customers. The production and exchange of a service requires that the customer enter into the technical core of the organization. This lack of buffering increases the potential for uncertainty. Compare making a movie to viewing one. In the latter case, the service can only be rendered in the presence of the consumers. Making the movie does not require direct customer participation.

4. **Timing.** Services require *simultaneous production* and *consumption.* Producer and consumer must be present for production to take place. Production of services requires customers to consume the output. Unlike manufacturing technology, services cannot be inventoried or stockpiled for later consumption. Even small batch manufacturing technologies do not require the immediate presence of customers. Outputs of small batch technology can be held for later consump-tion. Compare manufacturing a computer to a software development class. The computer can be manufactured and then stored in inventory for later con-sumption. A class cannot be stored. Production only takes place when students are present.

5. **Labor Intensity.** Services tend to be more labor intense than manufacturing technologies. Services require that workers interact directly with customers. Conversely, manufacturing technologies tend to be more capital intensive. Compare the mix of labor and machinery necessary to make a car with the labor intensity to service one.

MANAGING SERVICE TECHNOLOGY

The nature of services presents the organization with a significant challenge. The above-noted characteristics of service organizations create a technology that is fraught with uncertainty and unpredictability.[8] The results are often ambiguous; timing is critical; boundaries are highly permeable; work defies a high degree of standardization; and services are not easily automated. Think of the typical college class. What is the product? If you miss a class, you miss the service. Timing is critical. Students come and go. There is great variability in instructional methods and quality. Finally, it is difficult to automate the instruction and learning process found in the classroom.

How does one manage under these conditions? Research by the Aston Group from the University of Aston in Birmingham, England, provides some preliminary answers to this question.[9] They developed a scale for classifying both service and manufacturing technologies that was based on the following three factors:

1. **Automation of equipment:** the extent to which machinery and equipment is *self-operated* (i.e., automated) versus the extent to which work must be performed directly by workers;
2. **Work flow rigidity:** degree of flexibility in both human skills and machinery capabilities; and
3. **Specificity of evaluation:** the degree to which work flow can be measured quantitatively as opposed to the need for subjective evaluation.

The Aston researchers combined these factors into a general measure called **work flow integration,** which provides a fundamental basis for classifying organizations. Organizations with technologies that scored high on work flow integration were characterized by high levels of automation, greater rigidity of work, and more precise measures of operations (e.g., auto assembly plants or refineries). Low scores indicated the opposite—low work flow integration—difficulty automating tasks, greater flexibility of work, and ambiguous or unclear measures of operations (e.g., college teaching, legal practice, or medicine). Not surprisingly, services score low on work flow integration.

The Aston research suggested that increasing levels of work flow integration should be matched with increasingly bureaucratic or mechanistic structures. Low levels of work flow integration, on the other hand, require more organic organizational structures. Thus, service organizations should be managed with organic structures that include low formalization, low specialization, and decentralization. Additional research suggests that service organizations can adapt to their conditions through geographical dispersion—locating facilities close to customers—another form of decentralization.[10] This strategy is being tried in Florida and several other states in health, welfare, and human services departments. Regional district offices are being established close to clients, and the power of the headquarters office in the Florida state capital is being reduced. The belief is that those employees closest to the customers can deal best with local problems and idiosyncracies.

RECENT ADVANCEMENTS IN MANUFACTURING TECHNOLOGY

Technology is not static. Organizations develop new methods of production internally or acquire new technology from the external environment. For example, advanced manufacturing technology (AMT) includes an array of computer-based production systems, such as computer-aided design and manufacturing (CAD/CAM), robotics, flexible manufacturing systems, and fully computer-integrated manufacturing (CIM). These techniques are being implemented in the automobile and paper industries, to name just two examples. Other types of advances in the production core technology of organizations rely on changes in the people aspect of production. For example, *group* or *team approaches* emphasize a high degree of coordination among production team or group members who may be responsible for an entire manufacturing process, where previously individuals had responsibility for small, isolated tasks.[11] GM has adopted this approach in designing and operating the Saturn Division. Group and team approaches highlight the interdependent nature of many operations in organizations. Accomplishment of tasks often requires skills, knowledge, and expertise from diverse functional areas. Including people from different areas or disciplines in a group or on a team facilitates coordination. Group and team approaches to production have had significant impact on traditional large batch or mass core technologies such as autos, steel, rubber, and electronics.

Common to all the AMT approaches is an extensive reliance on computers and information technology to support the production process.[12] Although debate still exists over the full range of implications of AMT, a few consequences are clear. Each of these techniques increases the automation of tasks, thus reducing the number of people required to produce the same amount of output as under traditional large batch techniques. In many cases, these technologies have increased manufacturing flexibility. Assembly processes that once supported production of only a single type of output can, through AMT, support numerous variations in outputs. For example, AMT can be used to produce several car models on a single assembly line. Computer controls ensure that the correct parts and components are routed to the appropriate location at the right time. Much of the individual decision-making responsibility in the production process is taken over by computers. AMT reduces the amount of direct labor involved in production, and although some production tasks may now require *less* skill because of computerization, the new jobs required to program, operate, and monitor AMT require greater levels of skill and professionalism. Thus, AMT resembles a combination of technical small batch and continuous process technologies. Using AMT, the Ford Chicago Heights, Illinois, stamping plant can change dies in a matter of hours. It used to take several days.

Research shows that these technologies are associated with greater decentralization in decision making—much like small batch and continuous process technologies— but increased formalization.[13] Decentralization is necessary and possible because operators now have greater access to information because of computer-based information and they have the professionalism to execute decisions. That same computer-based system, however, also supports and requires greater formalization. Greater formalization is possible because more information is available to convey and support rules, and greater formalization may be necessary to counterbalance the risk and uncertainty resulting from decentralization. In other words, computers allow us to gather and use more information to make policy, which is used to coordinate decentralized units.

Group- or team-based approaches to production emphasize a movement away from the narrow specialization present in traditional large batch or mass production technologies. Instead, production teams include members with a broad range of skills necessary for the entire production process. The belief is that this holistic cooperative approach to production results in greater flexibility, increased coordination, better quality, and more innovativeness. The net result is that group or team production processes make traditional large batch operations function more like traditional or technical small batch production. Such approaches require a greater range of skills on the part of team members. They must now be able to communicate effectively, solve problems, monitor quality, perform calculations, and implement solutions. The philosophy behind using groups must also be congruent with the local management and culture, as the discussion in the box below suggests.

Exhibit 6.1

Groups in the U.S. and Japan[14]

The use of teams or groups in manufacturing has become quite popular in the United States in recent years following successes in Japan and Sweden. However, the record of success in the implementation of group- or team-oriented manufacturing in the United States has been rather uneven. One suggested reason for the mixed record for team and group production in the U.S. is that groups and teams, as they have been used in Japan and Sweden, run counter to basic American work philosophy. In particular, U.S. and Japanese cultures differ in five critical areas that affect groups and teams.

1. *Individualism and collectivism:* American culture and American business glorify individual creativity and industry. Success is dependent on the skills, knowledge, and motivation of individuals. By contrast, Japanese culture emphasizes membership, unity, and harmony. Group or team approaches to management and production would appear to be a natural outgrowth of Japanese culture; whereas, American culture may inhibit harmony and cohesiveness.

2. *Conflict and conformity:* A natural extension of the emphasis on harmony mentioned above is that Japanese culture emphasizes conflict avoidance. Group harmony and conformity are key elements of the culture. American culture emphasizes individuality and independence. Conflict is a natural outgrowth of this situation. Again, American culture may inhibit group- or team-oriented approaches while Japanese culture aids in their use.

3. *Power:* Japanese workers tend to be more respectful of the power and authority of managers than do American workers. Thus, status hierarchies are likely to develop within Japanese groups. American groups are more likely to emphasize democratic or egalitarian approaches to management. As a result, American teams or groups may have greater difficulty achieving cohesiveness and consensus.

4. *Time orientation:* U.S. culture tends to emphasize the present and reward fast results. Conversely, Japanese culture places greater emphasis on the past (tradition) and the future. The result is an acceptance of slower and more incremental change. This approach to investing in capital and infrastructure is referred to as *patient capital.*

5. *Homogeneity and heterogeneity:* Much has been made of the fact that Japan is a homogeneous culture. It is dominated by one cultural, racial, and ethnic group. By contrast, the U.S. is a heterogeneous culture that is highlighted by racial, cultural, ethnic, and religious diversity. In fact, recent trends in the U.S. have been in the direction of emphasizing diversity. The result is that it is more difficult to use collectivism, cohesion, and commonality of purpose in American groups or teams compared with those in Japan.

Three factors are key to successfully using groups or teams in the American cultural setting. First, managers should value and encourage dissent. Differences and disagreement can be valuable tools in producing creative solutions. Second, managers should encourage fluid and shifting group or team membership. In this way groups or teams are more likely to reflect the shifting and changing nature of U.S. culture. Overemphasis on stability and cohesiveness runs contrary to U.S. culture and may inhibit group functioning. Finally, groups must be empowered to make decisions. For team or group approaches to be successful, the group or team must be given the power and authority to implement its decisions or suggestions. Forcing groups to go through the organizational hierarchy removes much of the rationale (and motivation) for using groups.

The key point is that group or team approaches to organizational tasks may be useful and effective ways of altering technology, but management must make certain that the approach is consistent with the large culture and philosophy in which the groups or teams are embedded.

CORE TECHNOLOGY: A SUMMARY

Woodward's study of manufacturing firms represents the first attempt to classify the core technology of organizations and to determine the relationship between technology and structure. The primary criterion used in Woodward's scheme is technical complexity, or the degree to which the core operation can be automated. Subsequent studies have broadened the scope of the framework to cover other technologies besides the three described by Woodward. Absent from this framework is service technology.

Approaches to service technology have progressed on two fronts. First, some researchers have attempted to determine the characteristics of service that distinguish it from manufacturing technology. These characteristics include output tangibility, degree of standardization, timing of production, consumption, and labor intensity. However, the more closely one looks at services, the more one realizes that similarities exist between some aspects of services and the core manufacturing technologies. Moreover, services vary by degrees. Some organizations, such as insurance companies, have pure service technologies in which outputs lack tangibility, are consumed as they are produced, and involve extensive direct labor. Others, such as fast-food restaurants, involve some tangible output, permit extensive standardization, can be stockpiled, and can be partially automated. The second approach to services (and technology in general) identifies general characteristics of technology that apply to both manufacturing and services. Although the two approaches look at technology in different ways, they are compatible.

Advances in manufacturing technology have partly changed the way we look at technologies—particularly traditional large batch and mass technology. AMT and group or team approaches remind us that the organizational world is not static. While AMT may fit with Hull and Collins' view of technical batch technology, it is not consistent in all respects with the Aston Group's work. Contrary to the Aston Group, increased automation under AMT increases rather than decreases flexibility.[15] Thinking and theorizing on issues such as technology must be revisited and modified periodically.

The organizational core is not, however, the only place where technology is relevant. Organizations employ many technologies, as we can see if we look at how people throughout the organization contribute to organizational goals and objectives. Our attention now turns to describing work unit or departmental technology.

WORK UNIT OR DEPARTMENTAL TECHNOLOGY

It was noted in the introduction to this chapter that technology is a concept that can be used not only to characterize an entire organization, but also to describe work throughout the organization. The framework developed by Charles Perrow[16] and elaborated by Richard Daft and his colleagues[17] is useful for understanding not only an organization's predominant technology, but also the varied technologies that exist in departments and work units throughout organizations. Clearly, the nature of work in departments such as marketing, human resources management, accounting, and production differs. The work unit or departmental view of technology explicitly examines these differences. According to this framework, technology is defined along two dimensions of work: *exceptions* or *variety** and *analyzability.*

Originally, Perrow described task exceptions as the number of exceptions to standard procedures, unexpected or novel events, or variations in inputs or raw materials encountered during the performance of tasks. Recently, the concept has been broadened to include *task variety.* Thus, tasks that are characterized by many exceptions to standard operating procedures, that involve the performance of a large number of different or unrelated tasks, that may involve numerous novel or unexpected events, or that may use many different kinds of raw materials are defined as high in variety. By contrast, jobs that must closely follow standard operating procedures, that involve the performance of

---

*Although Perrow used the term *exceptions* in his original work on work unit technology, the term *variety* has gained wide usage in the organization theory field. We regard the terms as essentially analogous in the context of work unit or departmental technology. To avoid confusion, we will use *variety* to refer to this dimension.

a small number of different or closely related tasks, that rarely involve novel or unexpected events, or that use a limited number of raw materials are defined as low-variety tasks. The degree of variety present in jobs is associated with the degree of flexibility that a department or work unit has in carrying out its operations. Low-variety technologies permit little flexibility; whereas, high-variety technologies permit greater flexibility.

An example of a low-variety work unit would be the team responsible for the operation of a typical chain carryout pizza outlet. The number of different tasks that people perform might include taking phone orders, managing delivery people, making pizzas, waiting on customers, and stocking the supplies. Employees would normally follow a set of standard operating procedures that describes telephone manners, guidelines for supervision, specific recipes for pizzas, and quotas for stocking supplies. Exceptions could be tightly limited by requiring that customers order only those items specifically listed on the menu. In general, fast-food restaurants carefully manage jobs to maintain low variety. This makes managing such jobs relatively straightforward.

By contrast, the marketing department at the corporate headquarters for the above pizza chain will likely be characterized by high variety. The number of different types of tasks that people perform could vary widely and include such things as market research, advertising, new product development, packaging, public relations, and other related activities. Within each of these areas, individual jobs may vary greatly and the number of exceptions or novel events would likely be relatively large. Managing the corporate marketing department would be more difficult and would require greater flexibility.

The second work unit or departmental technology dimension is ***problem analyzability.*** One explanation of analyzability is the ease or difficulty encountered in searching for information to solve problems or complete tasks. Tasks that are characterized by readily available information that is easily obtained are designated as high-analyzability tasks. Tasks that are characterized by unavailable information or information that is difficult to obtain are designated as low-analyzability tasks. High-analyzability tasks are ones where information can be easily obtained to solve problems or perform tasks. Low-analyzability tasks are typically uncertain, ambiguous, and complex. Low-analyzability tasks are difficult to solve and require problem solvers to use judgment, instincts, intuition, and experience, rather than programmed solutions, to solve these problems.

Returning to the pizza company example above, the job of the work unit responsible for the store operation is generally a high-analyzability task. Readily available information guides employees in the conduct of their tasks. Menus and recipes guide the food preparation tasks. Store manuals inform employees of general policies and procedures for day-to-day operations. By contrast, the strategic planners at corporate headquarters encounter a low-analyzability task. To plan the company's direction for the next few years, they need to know about a wide range of events in the future: general economic conditions, consumer preferences, competition, labor availability, government regulations, and so on. Moreover, the planners need to know how to evaluate this information and combine it to develop a plan. These tasks are characterized by information that is difficult to identify and obtain, and is difficult to manipulate into a coherent and useful strategic plan. The planners will likely rely on their extensive experience, good judgment, and instincts or intuition to guide them.

Using the two dimensions of variety (exceptions) and analyzability, Perrow developed a four-category taxonomy of work unit or departmental technology as shown in Table 6.2. The categories are routine, engineering, craft, and nonroutine. Routine

■ **TABLE 6.2**
Work Unit or Departmental Technology: Sample Departments from a Pizza Chain

Variety (Exceptions)	
Few	**Many**
Craft	**Nonroutine**
Packaging development, test chefs	Corporate strategic planners, product development
Routine	**Engineering**
Store managers, clerical	Accounting, legal

technologies deal with few exceptions or low-variety and highly analyzable tasks — the employees at the pizza store. Engineering technologies have many exceptions or high variety, but the tasks are still highly analyzable. The accounting department at corporate headquarters would be an example. Although the accountants may perform many different tasks or encounter numerous exceptions, solving these task problems is facilitated by information or techniques that are easily available. Craft technologies deal with little variety or few exceptions, but problems are difficult to analyze. An example would be the packaging designers responsible for creating new packaging for microwave pizzas. Although they have only a few tasks to perform in packaging design, it is difficult to acquire information and to know what information is important (i.e., what packaging works best in microwaves; what packaging is easiest to handle, ship, and stock; and what packaging is most attractive to customers). Finally, nonroutine technologies combine high variety or many exceptions with low analyzability. Our strategic planners must perform many different tasks; they may encounter many exceptions, and the information they need is not clearly defined or readily available.

Much like the relationship between Woodward's core technology and organizational structure, Perrow's research suggests the need to adopt appropriate structure for departments or work units. Structure defines how work is supervised and coordinated to ensure that tasks are completed in a timely and efficient manner.

Table 6.3 on page 170 elaborates the contingent relationship between work unit or departmental technology and the appropriate departmental structure.[18] As departments move away from routine technology toward nonroutine technology, they require increasingly organic structure to operate efficiently. Selecting inappropriate structures for specific technologies results in departments or work units that perform suboptimally. A second important point to emphasize is that a given organization may have examples of each of these four types of technology. At the departmental level, an organization may have a variety of structures. Such conditions may make the overall management of the organization difficult — people in each unity are structured differently. It is difficult to establish overall corporate policy that applies to each unit. In the next section we examine how organizations must coordinate interactions that arise from these variations in technology.

■   **TABLE 6.3**
*Work Unit or Departmental Technology and Structure**

Craft Technology
Mostly Organic Structure:
Moderate formalization
Moderate centralization
Experienced workers, moderate
specialization
Moderate span of supervisory control
Requires horizontal communication
Examples: Designers, advertising

Nonroutine Technology
Organic Structure:
Low formalization
Low centralization
Highly trained and experienced
workers, generalists
Small span of supervisory control
Requires extensive horizontal communication
Examples: Strategic planners, top management

Routine Technology
Mechanistic Structure:
High formalization
High centralization
Low skill, narrow specialization
Wide span of supervisory control
Requires little vertical communication
Examples: Maintenance, clerical

Engineering Technology
Mostly Mechanistic Structure:
Moderate formalization
Moderate centralization
Formal training, moderate specialization
Moderate span of supervisory control
Requires vertical and horizontal communication
Examples: Accounting, legal research

*Based on Richard L. Daft, *Organization Theory and Design* (St. Paul, MN: West Publishing, 1992), 130.

WORK FLOW AND TECHNOLOGICAL INTERDEPENDENCE

James Thompson developed a technology framework, elaborated by others, that focuses on the nature of *interdependence* and *coordination* among departments or work units that results from the technology.[19] Thompson's view acknowledges that various parts of an organization must come together and interact for the organization as a whole to accomplish its goals. Technologies in organizations vary in how much they require or depend on individuals or departments to interact with one another in order to complete tasks. Technologies with low interdependence require little interaction and coordination; those with high interdependence require comparatively high levels of interaction or coordination. ***Thus, the essential questions about technological interdependence are: (1) how much is one unit or department dependent on another to complete work; (2) what is the nature of that interdependence; and (3) how can we achieve the necessary coordination?***

Thompson identified three types of technologies that result in three different levels of interdependence. These three technologies and the resulting interdependence are best managed by different methods of coordination. Each is described below.

MEDIATING TECHNOLOGY

This technology brings together individuals, departments, or organizations with complementary needs. For example, banks bring together borrowers and lenders, real estate agencies bring together homebuyers and home sellers, and employment agencies bring together potential workers and employers. In each case some part of the organization (or individuals in the organization) mediates between the organization and the external environment. The bank example above illustrates mediating technology. Branch offices of a bank interact with customers. In carrying out their jobs, personnel in a branch office may not be particularly dependent on the bank's central office. Questions or problems that may arise during the conduct of business can usually be answered by following standard procedures, obeying rules, or consulting policy manuals. Standardization of jobs can create consistency across units of the organization. Thus, horizontal communication between units at the same level (i.e., other branch offices) does not need to be extensive. In general, communication needs are low, and it is not necessary to locate departments or units (in this case, branch banks) close together. However, the performance of the bank as a whole is dependent on the performance of each individual branch. This type of interdependence is called ***pooled interdependence*** because the organization's technological output is the pooled total of all units (i.e., the branch banks). Little coordination among branch offices, units, or departments is necessary.

Mediating technology and pooled interdependence can be depicted as follows:

Bank Branch 1	*Bank Branch 2*	*Bank Branch 3*	*Bank Branch 4*	*Overall*
^	^	^	^	*Bank*
Customers	*Customers*	*Customers*	*Customers*	*Performance*

LONG-LINKED TECHNOLOGY

The typical assembly line operation exemplifies long-linked technology. Operations within the organization proceed in a serial or stepwise fashion. One step must be completed after another in a specific order, much like links in a chain. Each department must be able to anticipate inputs from the unit occupying the prior position in the chain, and each unit must be able to schedule the disposition of its output. For example, on an automobile assembly line the group responsible for installing the engine on the chassis is dependent upon the group that delivers nearly completed engines to the assembly line. The next group that attaches controls and wiring on the engine must wait for the installers to complete their job. The result is ***sequential interdependence*** because of the required sequencing of tasks.

Long-linked technology and sequential interdependence can be coordinated by locating interdependent individuals, departments, or units close together or adjacent to one another; by allowing for communication and feedback between interdependent individuals, departments, or units; and by using schedules or plans.

Long-linked technology and sequential interdependence are depicted below.

Step 1	*Step 2*	*Step 3*	*Step 4*	*Completed Product*
→	→	→	→	

INTENSIVE TECHNOLOGY

The third form of technology that Thompson describes involves situations in which the outputs of one individual, unit, or department become the inputs of another individual, unit, or department. Typically, a variety of different skills, techniques, and methods is brought together for a specific time period to accomplish a specific purpose that may involve several products and services. For example, the intensive care unit of a hospital requires that doctors, nurses, X-ray technicians, inhalation therapists, dietitians, and other specialists interact extensively to deliver treatment to a patient.

The nature of the interdependence that results from intensive technology is what Thompson called *reciprocal interdependence.* In the example of the intensive care unit, the doctors' work may create inputs for the X-ray technician and a radiologist. The work of the X-ray technician and radiologist then may become inputs for the doctors. Similar reciprocal relationships are likely between other members of the intensive care team, such as nurses, physicians, dietitians, and physical therapists. Coordination of intensive technology and reciprocal interdependence can be achieved by locating individuals, departments, or units close together so that communication is facilitated. Communication is critical to the *mutual adjustment* of individuals or groups. Mutual adjustment means that individuals or groups are able to understand and adjust to the conditions or needs of others. Reciprocal interdependence can also be managed through teamwork and through frequent face-to-face meetings.

Below is a graphic example of intensive technology.

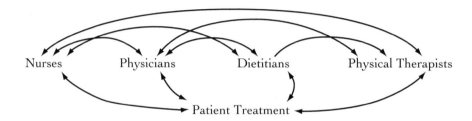

Exhibit 6.2	**Technological Interdependence at Dell Computer**[20]

Dell Computer is the number one direct marketer of PCs. Although the company does sell computers through retail stores, the bulk of its sales are through telephone orders. By tracing a typical order from the time Dell receives it until the finished product is shipped to the customer we can clearly identify examples of mediating technology and sequential technology. Shifting our focus to Dell's top management team provides an example of intensive technology.

Mediating Technology. When a customer places an order with Dell Computer that order is received and processed by one of several sales reps. The sales rep mediates between the customer and Dell Computer. The rep enters the order on the computer but does not need to interact with other Dell employees to carry out his or her job. The sales rep's actions are guided by rules and the specific computer-based order entry system the company uses. The sum total productivity of the sales department is the pooled output of all the sales representatives.

Sequential Technology. After checking the customer's credit, an order sheet is created that contains all the components to be included in the customer's computer and an order identification number. This order is sent to the assembly area where the computer is produced in a stepwise or sequential fashion. At each station along an assembly line different components, such as the specific type of processor (486SX, 486DX, Pentium), hard drive, and modem are built into the computer. Each task must be completed according to an orderly sequence of steps. Skipping a step or failure to complete a step results in a defective machine. The final steps include loading the software, testing the computer, packing it, and shipping it to the customer. Production schedules, the layout of the assembly facility, and the order sheet help to coordinate these activities.

Intensive Technology. At the same time that the above order is being processed, top management is studying the market and planning for the future. This planning may involve gathering past sales and financial performance data, economic data, and market research data; examining the results of ongoing research and development activities; surveying the competition; negotiating with suppliers or potential partners; meeting with investors and investment analysts; and numerous other similar activities. Extensive interaction is required among members of the top management team. This may involve both planned and unplanned meetings, face-to-face and telephone conversations, and other exchanges of information. Information flows in many different directions. Coordination or agreement on the strategic direction of the firm is achieved through these interactions.

Thompson's framework is one that can be used to examine any type of organization, and, while it can be used to characterize the technology and interdependence of an entire organization, it is most useful as a model of the social interactions necessary for individuals, departments, or work units to coordinate their work efforts to accomplish the organization's mission. This model of technology and interdependence does not just give suggestions about structure in the ways that we have come to think about structure (i.e., formalization, standardization, centralization, etc.). Rather, Thompson addresses mechanisms necessary to coordinate departments or units. He addresses how interdependent departments work together. We have also examined issues such as the location of interdependent departments and the amount of communication necessitated by the interdependence. Table 6.4 on page 174 summarizes Thompson's work flow interdependence framework and the suggested means for managing interdependence.

TASK DESIGN AND TECHNOLOGY: SOCIOTECHNICAL SYSTEMS

The use of a particular technology in an organization results in a particular set of tasks. These tasks are then grouped together into a particular set of jobs. A job is a grouping of tasks within a prescribed unit or department. A job encompasses a set of duties, functions, and responsibilities. Secretary, supervisor, engineer, electrician, sales clerk, and vice president are all examples of jobs.

In this section we do not provide a complete overview of task and job design; that is a more appropriate subject for books on organizational behavior, work motivation, or human resources management. Our objective is briefly to examine how technology

■   TABLE 6.4
Thompson's Work Flow Technology and Interdependence Framework *

Type of Technology	Nature of Interdependence	Methods for Coordination	Communication Requirements	Physical Location Requirements
Intensive	Reciprocal: high interdependence	Teamwork, meetings, face-to-face conversations, mutual adjustment	High need for horizontal communication	Locate units close together or allow for exchange of personnel across departments
Long-Linked	Sequential: moderate interdependence	Planning, work schedules, scheduled meetings, verbal feedback	Moderate communication needs; horizontal communication with adjacent work units; vertical communication for oversight	Locate units with adjacent functions close together; other units can be dispersed
Mediating	Pooled: low interdependence	Rules, policies, and procedures; work standardization	Low communication needs; mostly vertical	Low need to locate units close together

*Based on Richard L. Daft, *Organization Theory and Design* (St. Paul, MN: West Publishing, 1992) and Andrew H. Van de Ven, Andre Delbecq, and Richard Koenig, "Determinants of Communication Modes within Organizations," *American Sociological Review* (1976): 41.

affects the way tasks and jobs are designed. The most traditional approach is to *fit people to jobs*. A second approach is to *fit jobs to people*. A third view, *the sociotechnical perspective*, takes the middle ground and *considers both the person and the technology simultaneously*.[21]

FITTING PEOPLE TO JOBS: THE TRADITIONAL INDUSTRIAL ETHIC

Using this approach, a technology that is best from the standpoint of productivity and economic efficiency is employed. This results in a set of jobs to be filled. People are then selected and trained so that they can perform the jobs. People are viewed almost as an extension of the machine. The job is regarded as nearly inflexible as determined by the technology, and the person is seen as flexible enough to be fit to the job. This is the traditional manner in which jobs have been designed as a country industrializes. It is conducive to job specialization and assembly line–type operations.

Unfortunately, human beings are not infinitely malleable. Some people or groups cannot adapt to some task conditions. For example, in the 1970s General Motors opened a new highly automated factory in Lordstown, Ohio. However, in designing the plant GM did not take into consideration the needs of workers to communicate as part of their jobs. The new automated equipment created unnatural barriers to worker interaction. Although there were many factors that caused significant productivity and morale problems, the emphasis on technical solutions without consideration of human consequences added to Lordstown's poor performance. GM sought to avoid this problem when it designed the Saturn plant with the help of work teams that would operate the facility.

Other examples include repetitive motion problems among clerical workers who perform the same limited set of tasks many times each day and back problems among workers doing heavy lifting. In general, the low rate of successful adoption of new technologies is likely to be because many organizations fail to adapt organizational and work practices (i.e., people) to the requirements of new technologies.[22]

FITTING JOBS TO PEOPLE: THE POSTINDUSTRIAL SOCIETY

Under this approach the capabilities of an available labor force take precedence over the technology to be employed. The skills, abilities, and aspirations of the available labor force are first analyzed, and a technology is adopted that results in jobs consistent with the available skills and abilities. The job is viewed as flexible and the person, with his or her complement of skills, abilities, and aspirations, is viewed as rather rigid and unbending. This view of jobs and workers has spawned a movement toward job redesign (creating jobs with a greater variety of tasks that tap into the diversity of workers' skills and interests) and job enrichment (creating jobs with greater variety and with more responsibilities). The idea is to create jobs that are more challenging and inherently more motivating because they better fit the abilities, needs, and desires of workers.

Although much debate persists about the merits of job redesign and job enrichment, the argument is made that jobs of the future should be designed to tap the higher skills, abilities, and aspirations of a developed workforce. Unchallenging, routine jobs should be done by machines, robots, and computers. People in a postindustrial society should be left to do the challenging jobs, especially those involved with service aspects of the economy. On the other hand, evidence suggests that some people prefer highly structured jobs with little responsibility—what many people regard as routine, unchallenging jobs. Moreover, years of research fail to support the notion that a satisfied workforce is necessarily more productive.[23] Thus, job redesign and job enrichment may not always be the answer to the person- or technology-fit question or to improving organizational performance.[24] The sociotechnical approach suggests that the set of relationships between individual, organization, task, and technology may be more complex.

SOCIOTECHNICAL SYSTEMS: A MIDDLE GROUND?

Sociotechnical systems is an approach that explicitly considers both the people (socio) and the technology (technical) aspects of jobs simultaneously. This explicit recognition of each factor considers each as equally occurring and important within a holistic systems framework. The whole person is considered, and the range of factors that impinge on the human-machine interface is explicitly considered.[25]

The sociotechnical approach has its roots in the study of group dynamics (the study of human behavior in group settings) and ergonomics (the study of how tools and equipment can be adapted to human use). A basic assumption of this approach is that technology cannot be fully understood in an organization apart from its relationship to people. The design of tools, equipment, and even the entire manufacturing process must consider various human aspects, including the strength, durability, range of motion of the human body, and ability to socially interact in the conduct of one's job. Simultaneously, the design must also take into consideration the degree to which humans can adapt to the job requirements through learning, conditioning, and experience.

The sociotechnical approach is not a panacea for increased productivity or worker satisfaction. Earlier in this chapter we briefly mentioned several technology innovations under the heading Advanced Manufacturing Technologies that are beginning to prove fruitful. Tremendous advances in computer and communications technology are also beginning to change the very nature of work. Shoshanna Zuboff suggests that the changes in the workplace that will eventually be realized as the result of computerization are likely to equal those brought by mechanization during the Industrial Revolution.[26] She describes the great transformation that computerization has brought to the paper industry. Computerized paper mills differ greatly from traditional mills. Few workers walk through the hot, smelly plant. Dials, gauges, and levers on machines have been replaced by computerized sensing nodes, and people work at computer terminals in air-conditioned comfort. One of the most difficult adjustments people had to make was believing what the computer screen told them. Initially, they would run out to the factory floor to verify what was on the screen. Gradually, they began to trust the computer and ceased running out to the machine to "see it with their own eyes."

SUMMARY

Technology is a major factor in the contingency model of organizations. (Although each perspective was initially created to totally capture organizational technology, recent views regard core technology, work unit or departmental technology, and work flow interdependence as addressing different aspects of technology.) We present the reader with a three-level framework for understanding technology: Woodward's core technology describes the central technology of the whole organization; Perrow's work unit or departmental technology describes the variety of technologies that may exist in the diverse collection of departments and work units throughout the organization; and Thompson's work flow interdependence describes the technological relationships that exist among work units or departments that need to interact for the organization to accomplish its overall mission. We have also explored recent views on service technologies.

In addition to describing these various levels of technology, we explored the contingency relationships. Technology may be interesting in and of itself; however, it is of particular interest to organizational theorists and managers because of the specific demands it places on the organization. Thus, we examined the structural and managerial requirements that each type of technology presents to the organization. Our goal (and management's goal) should be to understand the need to match or fit organizations to their technology.

Finally, we briefly investigated the person–technology relationship. The current organizational wisdom is that management must simultaneously understand the demands that technology places on the individual and that the individual places on the technology. The sociotechnical approach suggests that ignoring either the technological aspects of the job or the social aspects of the job may result in suboptimal performance for the organization.

Questions for Discussion

1. The *technological imperative* suggests that technology drives structure. What does this mean? Why and how does technology drive structure?

2. Why do you suspect that the subject of technology has come to occupy so much attention in the popular management literature as well as in management practice?

3. In which industry do you see the most dramatic technological advances in the next ten years? Which characteristics of that industry invite such advances?

4. How can one distinguish between service and manufacturing technologies? Why is it important to make this distinction?

5. "Most large organizations employ not one technology, but many technologies." Do you agree with this statement? If not, why not? If so, what are the implications for organization theory and management practice?

6. Describe the work flow and technological interdependence relationship. What are the implications of this relationship to building and maintaining a sound organization structure?

CASE: IT'S NOT WHETHER YOU WIN OR LOSE . . .*

Our fascination with video games is now a basic plank in our culture. We have seen an entire generation grow up playing all sorts of games—from mechanical, coin-operated games involving contests (car races and horse races) to today's highly sophisticated electronic versions that approach what is termed *virtual reality.*

Although the industry enjoyed phenomenal growth from its beginning a generation ago, the business of games hit a major snag in the early 1980s. Arcades, once the place where mostly young people poured their allowance money into mechanical machines to hit baseballs or shoot rifles, began to lose their appeal, as did the home market in the U.S. The market, dominated by Nintendo, Sega, and Atari, reached what some called the saturation point.

But at last one of the major players in the industry is fighting back—for its own survival as well as for regaining its place in the game market. This began in 1954 when David Rosen began to put his idea "Better Technology Wins Markets" into practice. In 1956, Rosen began to import into Japan mechanical, coin-operated machines that proved to be popular. But he wasn't satisfied with the performance that the machines gave; so in 1965 he began to manufacture his own versions. Through the purchase of a Tokyo jukebox and slot-machine maker that stamped *Sega* (for Service Games) on its games, Rosen began to make the game Periscope. This game allowed players to fire torpedoes at ships by using a periscope. The abbreviation *Sega* stuck, and so did the company's commitment to technological advances in the video game industry.

While Nintendo, the major competitor, is sticking with its cartridge-based games, cutting expenses, and reducing prices to remain competitive, Sega is moving ahead on

---

*This case is based in large part on the following article: Richard Brandt, Neil Gross, and Peter Coy, "SEGA!" *Business Week* (February 21, 1994): 66–74.

two fronts—building compact-disk machines, called Saturn, that play more realistic games and building entertainment parks to rival Disney. These parks will be built around the virtual reality concept and are intended to be an eventual entry onto the information superhighway and interactive television entertainment.

Sega also hopes to enter the business world by developing the means of experiencing reality in, say, construction without the necessity of architect walk-throughs to measure progress. The company is also toying with the idea of developing video training games to help prepare those who will work with dangerous and hazardous materials without the risk of actual on-the-job training, the traditional method now used. All this seems possible to Sega through the transfer of technology built and applied to the entertainment business that it now sees as its core.

In the virtual reality theme parks, visitors will actually experience the thrill of driving a car over winding mountain passes, the excitement of winning the national stock car championship and the exhilaration of being at the helm of Starship Sega as it hurtles through the galaxy. It seems like a logical step for Sega to bring this technology, once fully developed, into the business world and thus broaden the horizons of the company.

The technology of electronics is cheaper, more efficient, and by far more reliable than the old mechanical machines that not only cost money for maintenance, but also in lost revenue when they were down. But the entire industry is concerned with the potential long-term health effects of constant game use. All agree that more research on the subject must be funded for the industry to be considered socially responsible.

The funding of such ambitious ventures as those contemplated by Sega is a major challenge, and its venture into adult-oriented games backfired under pressure from Congress and advocates for children. But Sega remains steadfast in its belief that entertainment will dominate the interactive communication in the home in the future.

Sega plans a joint venture with Time Warner and Tele-Communications to devise a system of downloading video games into game machines over a pay channel. A venture with AT&T involves Edge 16, which will play video games over telephone lines. By combining its expertise at software development with established members of the telecommunications industry, Sega hopes to accentuate its role in the entertainment of the game-hungry public. All this technology is intended to be extremely user-friendly—no manual will be necessary to get the games going.

Sega's challenge seems to be product differentiation—to create software that is hard to imitate—and this has powered its move toward the information superhighway and virtual reality theme parks. As mentioned before, Sega is betting heavily on the success of the Saturn, a machine that will play both compact disks and cartridges, and will create three-dimensional figures that move through three-dimensional space.

To keep ahead of others' technology, Sega is devoting enormous efforts to this research and to development labs in Japan. Their programmers, writers, and musicians form teams to work together to push the technology-of-games envelope to its virtual limit. And the company is growing quite rapidly, now numbering some 5,200 employees located throughout the world. About two-thirds of these employees work in research and development, a striking example of Sega's commitment to advancing the technology of the games segment of the entertainment industry.

So, as Sega works at a fever pitch to advance its technological core, one has to wonder whether it is, indeed, how the company will play its game in the future.

QUESTIONS FOR DISCUSSION

1. How would you describe (or categorize) Sega's organization-level technology? Are there other types that might suit Sega as well or better? Explain.
2. What forces would you speculate have caused Sega's passion for innovation?
3. Are these forces peculiar to the games-entertainment industry? Explain.
4. How should Sega adjust its boundary spanning system to accommodate its technical core?
5. How do you believe Sega's technical core can affect the social structure of the company? Must they form a *perfect* fit? Why or why not?
6. If you were the decision maker for Sega, what general directions would you give to your personnel department?

REFERENCES

1. R. C. Ford, B. R. Armandi, and C. P. Heaton, *Organization Theory: An Integrative Approach* (New York: Harper & Row, 1988).

2. W. Richard Scott, *Organizations: Rational, Natural and Open Systems,* 3rd ed. (Englewood Cliffs, N.J.: Prentice-Hall, 1992).

3. Charles Perrow, *Complex Organizations: A Critical Essay,* 3rd ed. (New York: Random House, 1986).

4. Joan Woodward, *Industrial Organization: Theory and Practice* (London: Oxford University Press, 1965).

5. Joan Woodward, *Management and Technology* (London: Her Majesty's Stationery Office, 1958).

6. Frank M. Hull and Paul D. Collins, "High-Technology Batch Production Systems: Woodward's Missing Type," *Academy of Management Journal* 30 (1987): 788.

7. D. E. Bowen, C. Siehl, and B. Schneider, "A Framework for Analyzing Customer Service Orientations in Manufacturing," *Academy of Management Review* 14 (1989): 75–95.

8. R. B. Chase and D. A. Tansik, "The Customer Contact Model for Organizational Design," *Management Science* 29 (1983): 1037–50.

9. D. Hickson, D. Pugh, and D. C. Pheysey, "Operations Technology and Organizational Structure: An Empirical Reappraisal," *Administrative Science Quarterly* 14 (1969): 378–97.

10. See note 8 above.

    G. B. Northcraft and R. Chase, "Managing Service Demand at the Point of Delivery," *Academy of Management Review* 10 (1985): 66–75.

11. A. Nahavandi and E. Aranda, "Restructuring Teams for the Re-Engineered Organization," *Academy of Management Executive* 8, no. 4 (1994): 58–68.

12. J. W. Dean, Jr., S. J. Yoon, and G. I. Susman, "Advanced Manufacturing Technology and Organizational Structure: Empowerment or Subordination," *Organization Science* 3 (1992): 203–29.

    C. A. Beatty and J. R. M. Gordon, "Advanced Manufacturing Technology: Making It Happen," *Business Quarterly* (Spring 1990): 46–53.

13. See Dean, Yoon, and Susman in note 12 above.

14. Based on article in note 11 above.

15. See Dean, Yoon, and Susman in note 12 above.

16. C. A. Perrow, "A Framework for the Comparative Analysis of Organizations," *American Sociological Review* (April 1967): 194–208.

17. M. Withey, R. L. Daft, and W. C. Cooper, "Measures of Perrow's Work Unit Technology: An Empirical Assessment and a New Scale," *Academy of Management Journal* 25 (1983): 45–63.

    R. L. Daft and N. Macintosh, "A New Approach to Design and Use of Management Information," *California Management Review* 21 (1978): 82–92.

18. R. Daft, *Organization Theory and Design* (St. Paul, Minn.: West Publishing, 1992).

    Christopher Gresov, "Exploring Fit and Misfit in Multiple Contingencies," *Administrative Science Quarterly* 34 (1989): 431–53.

    Jerald Hage and Michael Aiken, "Routine Technology, Social Structure, and Organizational Goals," *Administrative Science Quarterly* 14 (1969): 368–79.

    Lawrence G. Hrebiniak, "Job Technologies, Supervision, and Work Group Structure," *Administrative Science Quarterly* 19 (1974): 395–410.

    Michael Tushman, "Work Characteristics and Subunit Communication Structure: A Contingency Analysis," *Administrative Science Quarterly* 24 (1979): 82–98.

19. James Thompson, *Organizations in Action* (New York: McGraw-Hill, 1967).

    A. H. Van de Ven, A. L. Delbecq, and R. Koenig, Jr., "Determinants of Coordination Modes Within Organizations," *American Sociological Review* 41 (April 1976): 322–38.

20. Stephanie Losee, "Mr. Cozzette Buys a Computer," *Fortune* (April 18, 1994): 113–16.

21. William Passmore, Carol E. Francis, and Jeffery Haldeman, "Sociotechnical Systems: A North American Reflection on the Empirical Studies of the '70s," *Human Relations* 35 (1982): 179–204.

    Eric Trist and K. Banforth, "Some Social and Psychological Consequences of the Long Wall Method of Coal-getting," *Human Relations* (1951): 3–38.

22. A. B. Shani, "Advanced Manufacturing Systems and Organizational Choice: Sociotechnical Systems Approach," *California Management Review* 34, no. 4 (1992): 91–111.

23. Cynthia D. Fisher, "On the Dubious Wisdom of Expecting Job Satisfaction to Correlate with Performance," *Academy of Management Review* 5 (1980) 607–12.

24. Louis Davis, "The Design of Jobs," *Industrial Relations* (October 1966): 21–45.

    J. Richard Hackman, "Work Design," from *Motivation and Work Behavior*, 5th ed., ed. by Richard M. Steers and Lyman W. Porter (New York: McGraw-Hill, 1991), 418–44.

25. Kenneth R. Brousseau, "Toward a Dynamic Model of Job-Person Relationships: Findings, Research Questions, and Implications for Work Systems Design," *Academy of Management Review* 8 (1983): 33–45.

    See Passmore, Francis, and Haldeman in note 21 above.

    See Trist and Banforth in note 21 above.

    See note 22 above.

26. Shoshanna Zuboff, *In the Age of the Smart Machine* (New York: Basic Books, 1988).

CHAPTER 7

Organizational Size, Growth, and Life Cycles

CASE: A PENNEY FOR YOUR THOUGHTS*

Since its beginning, the J.C. Penney Company has been a mecca for value-conscious shoppers in the United States. But that is about to change—and in a big way.

Relying on price, value, and house brands, the company has carved a big niche in the U.S. retail shopping market. But in doing so, according to several top-level managers of the company, it has earned the reputation of being a lethargic giant, slow to recognize the vast opportunities that lie in the international marketplace while trying to compete in what many consider an "overstored" domestic marketplace. Accordingly, these executives, at the urging of Terry Prindiville, an executive vice president of the company, are overseeing an ambitious expansion plan aimed at becoming a major player in the international market.

To kick off this effort, Penney has stores under construction in Mexico; has entered into an agreement to sell its private label apparel in some 300 stores owned by Aoyama Trading Co. (Japan's largest seller of men's suits); and is now looking for sites for stores in Chile. This latter move is in response to surveys that show that a sizable number of Chileans were so anxious to buy American goods that they regularly flew to the U.S. to meet their needs.

Penney is also doing quite well through its license agreements in the United Arab Emirates and Singapore. Similar agreements are being considered in Portugal and Greece, and there is the possibility of an anchor store in a regional mall in Taiwan. Thailand and Indonesia are also on the company's expansion agenda. The traditional catalog, so long a part of the American shopping scene but now abandoned in the U.S., is being translated for use in the huge Latin American market. This effort complements catalogs already in use in Iceland, Brazil, and Russia.

Among the forces powering these moves by Penney are the North American Free Trade Agreement and the ever-increasing

---

*This case is largely based on an article by Bob Ortega, "Penney Pushes Abroad in Unusually Big Way as it Pursues Growth," *The Wall Street Journal* (February 1, 1994), A1 and A6.

awareness of the globalization of the retail market. Companies that once were highly skeptical are joining in the move. Wal-Mart, Toys "R" Us, Dillard, Saks Fifth Avenue, and Federated Stores' Bloomingdales division are eyeing possible locations from Mexico to Europe. Penney's thinking is that to meet competition it simply must grow in these largely untapped lodes of consumer purchasing power.

J.C. Penney will doubtless encounter unique problems in its ventures onto the international scene. Fluctuations in currency exchange rates and political and cultural barriers abound. For example, Penney's plans to build hypermarts in Belgium were met head on by fierce opposition from what would be zoning boards in the U.S. These boards, loaded with local merchants, simply saw the Penney invasion as the demise of what they considered to be their turf. This left Penney with only small, crowded outlets in downtown areas, thus thwarting efforts for any real growth, according to Narina Vaira, a vice president for Penny's international division.

Local labor laws also prevented Penney from taking such drastic actions as reducing employee numbers and increasing productivity in both Italy and Belgium. In a recognition of such powerful local barriers, Penney sold its Belgium chain, taking a $16 million loss.

These early ventures put a damper on the Penney plan. Increasing pressures from outside and inside the company finally resulted in a renewed interest in the international market. The world of Penney was simply changing, and it could no longer be ignored or marred by its earlier actions. But according to company officals, the real spur to action came from Liz Claiborne Inc., Estee Lauder, and Elizabeth Arden that were strictly opposed to the Penney "middle-brow" image. So its attempts to upgrade its image were diverted to enhancing its own labels such as Hunt Club, Worthington, and Arizona jeans by converting them into brand names. This brand-name approach and extensive advertising have become the main reasons for Penney's renewed efforts at the off-shore market.

In 1990, the company formed a small group to reinvestigate the possibilities for the company overseas, and what the group found in its travels really sparked the company into action.

A seeming total lack of retail savvy was the key finding. So the company tried again. But instead of buying property, Penney decided to go the lease route and to link up with local partners who knew the local scene politically, economically, and perhaps above all, culturally. These partners were brought to the Plano, Texas, headquarters to learn the "Penney-wise" way of doing business so that it could be adapted to fit local conditions to everyone's benefit.

As a result of a company study and interactions with local partners, Penney has adopted four basic strategies for capturing its share of the international market:

1. Where local conditions were favorable, Penney would open and operate stores itself.
2. Penney would license local retailers to operate its stores where regulations were considered too restrictive.
3. Where costs and regulations were prohibitive, in Singapore and Japan for instance, Penney licensed other retailers to sell certain brand names in local stores.

4. And in the most difficult of markets, Penney would use catalog sales by distributing goods through third parties who would buy Penney's goods in the U.S. and ship them to the buyer.

Mexico presents a little different picture for Penney. There, the company has decided that it does not need local partners and is issuing credit cards (made easy because of the general lack of governmental regulations restricting their use). Penney believes that the Mexican consumer's familiarity with its goods augurs for going it alone in the Mexican market.

So all its previous failures and multifaceted current attack are behind Penney beginning a serious effort to move into the international market. But based on sales along the U.S.–Mexico border, the free-trade atmosphere and a supersaturated U.S. market, Penney is encouraged.

Thus, it appears that J.C. Penney's thoughts are firmly focused toward growth and expansion overseas.

This case shows how one company's desire for growth, competitive advantage, and survival has taken it overseas in search of its objective. Managing the complexities of an international business, however, takes considerable resources and expertise. Moreover, the need for coordination and control can be affected by foreign political, economic, and cultural forces. Even with its early failures in foreign markets, Penney's management realizes that to continue growing and prospering, the company must reenter foreign markets. In this chapter we explore the related issues of organizational size, growth, and life cycles. The Penney experience, to some extent, is a product of each of these forces. Growth is an ongoing need of organizations. Opportunities for domestic growth are few; thus, Penney has turned its attention to international markets. Participation in international markets, however, requires substantial resources that are likely to be more readily available in a large organization. Finally, the growth needs, the ability to tap opportunities, and the vitality of a company like J.C. Penney are partly the result of its position in the life cycle model. We examine each of these areas in detail in this chapter.

ORGANIZATIONAL SIZE, GROWTH, AND LIFE CYCLES

Perhaps one of the most obvious features of organizations that casual observers recognize is organizational size. This attention to organizational size is furthered by the number of leading business periodicals that list the largest and fastest growing firms across a number of different categories (e.g., the *Business Week* 100, the *Fortune* 500 largest industrial companies, the *Fortune* 100 largest service companies, or the *Inc* 100 largest privately held businesses). The size of business organizations is not the only thing in which the public is interested or about which it is concerned. Concerns about organizational size extend beyond business organizations. In academic institutions we constantly hear arguments about the comparative value of large versus small universities and colleges.

Perhaps most notably, politicians, journalists, and the public debate the supposed evils of big government.

By the amount of attention and the volume of the concerns about "bigness," one would think that there is universal agreement as to what constitutes a large or small organization and the relative value of size. That, however, is not the case. As we begin to see, many methods can be used for measuring size. We will also discover that size (and its companion, growth) may be a mixed blessing to an organization. Some organizations may be particularly adept at managing their large size while others may struggle under the weight. Moreover, we will see that in some industries large size is a necessity for economies of scale and competitive purposes.

By tackling the issues of organizational growth and size, we indirectly open the door to the dynamic nature of organizations. In particular, we confront the notions of ***negative entropy, growth,*** and ***organizational life cycles.*** Inherent in these discussions is the idea that organizations are not static or stagnant entities. They grow, shrink, and otherwise change over time. In this chapter we examine the life cycle perspective on organizational change—that organizations change sequentially over time as a function of their growing size, changing conditions, and organizational maturation. These sequential changes differ from the planned organizational change that is the focus of Chapter 13. Planned organizational change is change that management intentionally undertakes to improve conditions in the organization. The changes associated with shifting life cycles may overlap to some extent with planned organizational change, but that is not necessarily the case. Some life cycle changes are the result of evolutionary changes in the organization while some of the changes are the result of the organization's attempt to deal with crises that it faces as it progresses through the various stages of the life cycle. We reserve a more detailed discussion of those planned changes for Chapter 13. For this chapter, our focus is on size, growth, and life cycles.

With increasing size comes complexity. As an organization grows, its operations and structure invariably become more difficult to manage. A manager's challenge thus becomes the task of balancing the advantages of size with the demands of complexity.

WHAT IS ORGANIZATIONAL SIZE?

One may think that the definition of organizational size is rather simple and straightforward. However, by now you probably realize that little in organizational life is simple and straightforward. There are in fact many ways to measure the size of an organization. The particular measure that is picked to assess the size of an organization should be related to *why* one is asking about size.

If you are interested in an organization's role in its industry or in the economy in general, you may want to focus on financial and market measures such as the firm's asset value, revenues, or market share. For example, *Fortune* magazine's ranking of the 500 largest industrial firms is based on firm sales revenue. The listing also includes rankings of profits and asset value. Note in Table 7.1 that the largest firms in sales revenue may lag in other categories. General Motors, the largest firm in terms of sales, ranks third in profits; Ford Motor, the profit leader, is second in revenues and third in assets; and IBM, number seven in sales, ranks ninth in profits (losses).

■ TABLE 7.1

Ten Largest U.S. Firms from Fortune 500 *for 1995**

Company	Sales $ millions	Profits $ millions (rank)	Assets $ millions (rank)	Employees†
1. General Motors	154,951.2	4,900.6 (3)	198,598.7 (6)	711,000
2. Ford Motor	128,439.0	5,308.0 (1)	219,354.0 (3)	322,213
3. Exxon	101,459.0	5,100.0 (2)	87,862.0 (27)	91,000
4. Wal-Mart	83,412.4	2,681.0 (12)	32,819.0 (76)	528,000
5. AT&T	75,094.0	4,676.0 (6)	79,262.0 (30)	308,700
6. General Electric	64,687.0	4,726.0 (4)	194,484.0 (7)	222,000
7. IBM	64,052.0	3,021.0 (9)	81,091.0 (29)	256,000
8. Mobil	59,621.0	1,079.0 (47)	41,542.0 (60)	61,900
9. Sears, Roebuck	54,559.0	1,454.0 (33)	91,896.0 (25)	249,000
10. Philip Morris	53,776.0	4,725.0 (5)	52,649.0 (44)	173,000

*Source: The *Fortune 500, Fortune* 131, no. 9 (May 15, 1995): 216–313.
†Source: *Million Dollar Directory: America's Leading Public and Private Companies* (Bethlehem, Penn.: Dun & Bradstreet, 1995).

If we are studying a particular industry, we may also want to know the *relative* size of a firm compared with others in the industry. In that case, measures such as *market share* and *concentration ratios* become important indicators of size. Market share will tell the proportion of the market that a particular firm has. For example, General Motors, the top-ranked firm on the 1995 *Fortune* 500 list, had 34.3 percent of the domestic U.S. automobile and light truck market (19.1 percent worldwide) in 1993.[1] Ford, the number four company on the *Fortune* 500 list had only 24.8 percent of the U.S. market (14.7 percent of the world market). Both firms are very large, but the sales revenue measure gives only a partial indicator of size. Market share adds to this picture. Market measures may also be useful for nonbusiness organizations. For example, universities are often described by the number of students enrolled — a measure of market share. Hospital size may be measured by the number of patients served or the number of patient beds. Hotels and motels typically use the number of rooms as indicator of size.

Another set of market-oriented measures of size addresses the number of markets in which a firm operates. One may be interested in the number (and diversity) of products and markets that a company serves. The number of different markets a firm captures has implications for how the firm is managed, how it allocates resources, and its potential for growth. For example, Coca-Cola and Pepsi compete vigorously for entry into new markets in such emerging economies as China, India, eastern Europe, and the former Soviet republics. Much of Coca-Cola's growth in recent years is because it has been better positioned than Pepsi to enter these new markets.[2] In addition to the number of markets in which the firm sells, we may also want to examine the location of various facilities. A company with manufacturing and distribution facilities scattered

■ **TABLE 7.2**

The Ten Largest Firms in the World for 1995*

Company (Country)	Sales $ millions	Profits $ millions (rank)	Assets $ millions (rank)
1. Mitsubishi (Japan)	175,835.6	218.7 (311)	109,256.0 (83)
2. Mitsui (Japan)	171,490.5	263.8 (283)	82,461.8 (107)
3. Itocho (Japan)	167,824.7	81.6 (400)	74,062.9 (117)
4. Sumitomo (Japan)	162,475.9	73.2 (408)	58,973.6 (133)
5. General Motors (U.S.)	154,951.2	4,900.6 (4)	198,598.7 (40)
6. Marubeni (Japan)	150,187.4	104.4 (373)	78,802.8 (113)
7. Ford Motor (U.S.)	128,439.0	5,308.0 (2)	219,354.0 (33)
8. Exxon (U.S.)	101,459.0	5,100.0 (3)	87,862.0 (102)
9. Nisho Iwa (Japan)	100,875.5	52.7 (419)	56,412.6 (137)
10. Royal Dutch/Shell Group (U.K./Netherlands)	94,881.3	6,235.6 (1)	108,300.0 (84)

*Source: "Fortunes Global 500," *Fortune* 132, no. 3 (August 7, 1995): F1.

throughout the world presents different organizational problems and opportunities than a firm that concentrates its operations in one location.

Concentration ratios, mentioned briefly in Chapter 2, indicate the degree to which an industry is concentrated in the hands of a few giants or dispersed among many smaller firms. Typically, industries are described according to three-firm or five-firm concentration ratios: the percentage of the market dominated by the top three or five firms, respectively. Before the import boom of the 1970s, the Big Three U. S. auto companies (GM, Ford, and Chrysler) accounted for nearly 80 percent of the domestic U.S. auto market. GM alone accounted for over 50 percent of U.S. car sales. This suggests that in the 1970s these were large firms compared to foreign competitors and that domestic firms dominated the industry. By contrast, in 1994 the same three firms account for about 74 percent of the U.S. automobile market. While these firms are still big (note GM's position at the top of the *Fortune* 500 list), the industry changes suggest that other large firms have entered the market as challengers and that factors leading to success in the industry may have changed. For example, Toyota's share of the U.S. market has been as high as 8.1 percent in the 1990s.

Exhibit 7.1

Sometimes a Large Pizza with Everything Doesn't Amount to Much

We all recognize the major national chains in the pizza industry: Pizza Hut (a division of Pepsico), Domino's, and Little Caesar's are the three largest. All three are large by any standard measure of size. These three companies have battled heatedly over market share in the pizza business and have spent millions of dollars on advertising. Pizza Hut and Little Caesar's have experienced modest increases in market share in recent years. Domino's has lost market share. The top three firms, however, still do not dominate the pizza market. Look at your local *Yellow Pages* under the Pizza heading, and see how many independent small businesses crowd the market. For example, in the Greater Cincinnati, Ohio, *Yellow Pages* seventy-one other pizza restaurants crowd the pages. Most of these are small single-location operations or local and regional chains. A few upstarts, such as Pizza Papa John's, are attempting to penetrate the national market. This suggests that large size may not be a critical feature in the success of a pizza restaurant, and large size may not confer great competitive advantage at the local level. On the other hand, most of the international expansion in the pizza business is through the efforts of these large firms. Few small operations could afford to effectively compete in the international markets.

Financial and market measures are important indicators of size, but they represent only a partial picture. A comparison of the number one and number three firms in the *Fortune* 500 list suggests the importance of exploring other aspects of size. Although Exxon is first in profits, third in revenues, and fourth in assets, it is comparatively small if our measure of size is the number of people employed (95,000 employees compared with 750,000 for GM). These size differences are partially due to differences in the technology used by these firms.

Continuous process technology most closely fits Exxon's core technology (high-capital intensity, low-labor intensity) while GM's core technology is large batch (comparatively high labor intensity). If we are interested in size because we want to design control systems to manage people in the organization—a key objective of applied organizational theory—we would likely focus on the number of people in the organization. Although all of the above-mentioned measures of size are used in the organizational literature, measuring the number of employees is one of the most commonly used.[3]

This section began with the question, What is organizational size? Like so many other issues in organization theory, the answer depends on why one is asking the question. This section has presented some of the most widely used measures of size, all of which are useful in answering the question, How large is an organization? One must be careful to select a measure that is consistent with the reason for asking the question. Because organization theory is most specifically interested in the management, coordination, and organization of people in the organization, people-oriented measures of size are of particular interest.

WHERE ORGANIZATIONS TEND TO GROW FIRST

In order to place the beginning of growth in perspective, let us follow the case of someone who starts an automobile repair shop. The person who begins such a business usually possesses the skills required to work on cars. Although this person may have a wide range of skills and expertise, he or she may not possess the skills necessary to manage the entire operation, particularly as the business begins to prosper and grow.

When repairs are done, they must be properly recorded; invoices must be prepared; taxes must be computed and paid; inventories of parts and supplies must be maintained; and as employees are needed to deal with the increasing demand for repair services, they must be hired, trained, managed, and compensated. These are just a few of the tasks associated with running the business that require different skills than those necessary to repair automobiles.

In the beginning when the business is small, these activities might be simple and undemanding on the owner-mechanic. As the business experiences success and begins to grow, however, these activities require increasing time and greater expertise. With increasing business the owner usually finds that he or she is unable to carry out all these support tasks, as well as performing the repair work itself. With the increasing demands of a larger business, it is now time for some specialization and delegation of responsibilities. Where in the past the owner-mechanic did a little bit of everything, it is now appropriate to bring in someone with specialized bookkeeping or accounting skills to take care of the financial management of the business; then someone to answer the phone and schedule appointments; someone to take people to their workplace while the car is being fixed; someone who specializes in transmission repairs; and so on.

Success can also bring about the need for other specialized support activities including marketing to plan advertising strategies and personnel to hire, train, promote, and, if necessary, fire employees. Growth may also require operational specialization. Mechanics with special expertise on particular models of cars (e.g., domestic, Japanese, German, etc.) or specific types of repairs (e.g., transmissions, mufflers, or brakes) may improve the efficiency and effectiveness of the business.

In short, as the business grows, the owner (and the organization) is faced with the need for the specialized knowledge required to support the main operations and the need to coordinate activities among the growing number of people in the organization. Thus, the effects of success and growth can be seen on task differentiation (increasingly narrow specialization) and on increasing emphasis on support functions (e.g., clerical, accounting, and marketing functions) not directly involved in the core operation of automobile repair.[4]

WHY GROW? THE MIXED BLESSING OF LARGE ORGANIZATIONAL SIZE

Organizational researchers have long been intrigued by organizational growth. Debate has focused on such issues as whether growth is inevitable or intentional and on the consequences of growth.[5] Earlier, many organizational theorists thought that growth was inevitable—a consequence of *the open systems view and negative entropy.* One interpretation of the open systems perspective is that organizations must continue to import resources from the environment to grow and change in order to avoid a state of **entropy** (i.e., decline and collapse of the system). More recently, perhaps in the shadow of the widespread downsizing of organizations, theorists have suggested that growth is more likely an intentional action pursued by owners and managers. Clearly, organizations can continue to prosper in the face of downsizing—perhaps because of downsizing. On the other hand, the by-product of growth, large size, has certain undeniable advantages. Thus, if growth is an intentional and advantageous action, it is important to examine the reasons for and consequences of growing larger.

GROWTH, COMPETITIVE ADVANTAGE, AND SURVIVAL

Management may pursue a strategy of growth to give an organization a better competitive position in its industry. Growth can be achieved from strategies directed at expanding production and sales, entering new markets, mergers, acquisitions, and other linkage strategies. As we noted in Chapter 4, these strategies can increase an organization's power to control its environment. Greater power in the environment provides strong motivation to pursue growth.

Large organizations can exert significant power over suppliers, buyers, regulators, and nearly every facet of the environment. While government agencies may have little or no interest in supporting a failing small business, it was politically and economically unwise for the U.S. government to abandon Chrysler during its financial troubles in the early 1980s. Chrysler's large size gave it significant clout when dealing with the government and creditors. No politician wanted to be held responsible for the tremendous loss of jobs and the general economic instability that would have resulted if Chrysler had failed. Similarly, large firms, because of their market power, are often able to pressure suppliers for special treatment. Large mail-order prescription drug insurance companies and retailers like PCS and Medco have been able to pressure doctors into prescribing certain drugs that are believed to be more cost-effective and pressure pharmaceutical companies into lowering prices.[6] For example, there are several drugs available to treat stomach ulcers. The largest seller is Zantac, produced by the British pharmaceutical giant, Glaxo (now called GlaxoWelcome PLC). Glaxo invested heavily in advertising and promoting this drug with doctors. Such companies as Medco and PCS have been able to influence doctors to substitute a less expensive drug, Tagamet. Even though Zantac is a newer drug, Medco and PCS believe that Tagamet is equally effective for most patients; further, it is significantly cheaper. Because these two prescription providers are so large, they can influence doctors to change their prescription-writing habits. The U.S. government, the largest medical insurer through Medicare and Medicaid, has played a similar role in influencing hospitals, doctors, and pharmaceutical companies to hold the line on prices. In the appliance business, large chain stores such as Circuit City are able to get manufacturers to make special models of appliances with model numbers and features that are unique to that chain. A customer trying to comparison shop will have difficulty comparing brand-name products because each large chain will have its own model numbers. Thus, products may be similar but not identical. Small firms are unable to obtain such special treatment from suppliers and are thus likely to feel more competitive pressure. Look at how Wal-Mart has driven out the smaller hardware stores, drugstores, and other small businesses in the various towns it has entered. Wal-Mart's size gives it discount buying power with manufacturers and allows it to offer greater variety at a lower cost compared to small family-owned businesses.

The notion that "big is good" has been most clearly illustrated by ***economies of scale.*** The economies of scale argument states that the larger the organization, the more goods or services it can produce at a lower fixed cost per unit—up to a certain point. This idea applies not only to production, but also to marketing, research and development, and sales efforts as well. For example, the proposed merger of Chase Manhattan and Chemical Bank will create the largest retail banking operation in the U.S. This combination of assets will allow the merged companies to cut the number of branch banks, cut service personnel, and consolidate many operations that are duplicated in the two banks. The result should be more efficient operations. Similarly, Disney's acquisition of Capital Cities/ABC will give the company unparalleled access to network television outlets and cable television. The acquisition, combined with Disney's presence in television and theatrical film production, theme parks, and a variety of related entertainment businesses, makes the company a formidable force in the industry.[7]

An important limitation on the economies of scale argument is that there is a point of diminishing returns at which increasing size no longer brings about lower costs—and may even raise costs of doing business. Recently, questions have been raised about how large an organization needs to be to achieve economies of scale.

It has been suggested that, because of technological and environmental changes, smaller organizations can achieve the economies of scale formerly reserved for large organizations. An example can be seen in the steel industry. Through the 1960s the model organization in the steel industry was large with many large mills that operated in a near-continuous fashion. Giants, such as U.S. Steel (now USX) and LTV, dominated the industry. During the 1970s and 1980s, the large traditional U.S. steel mills went through a period of serious decline because of their inability to compete with Japanese and European manufacturers. Many U.S. mills closed. Now because of changing technology in the production of steel, changes in the supply of raw materials (availability of recycled scrap), and changes in market demand, it is economically feasible to run minimills such as Nucor or Birmingham Steel. The old mills used huge coal- or gas-fired blast furnaces. The new mills use electric furnaces and are much smaller—Birmingham had sales of $344 million in 1989 compared to $7.6 billion for LTV. They operate more like small batch technology, producing specialty steel on demand.[8] The economies of scale for steel production have been lowered, and small firms can now compete.

Despite eroding economies of scale in some industries, there are still situations or conditions in which large size gives organizations clear advantages. Theodore Levitt of Harvard University, quoted in *Business Week*, succinctly stated the case for bigness:

> *Some things can only be done by large organizations. Who's going to be the general contractor to go to the moon or build a massive pipeline in Alaska? If you had to commit money for a project that takes five years to complete, like building a plant, would you turn it over to a small company? Some things inherently require scale.*[9]

For example, businesses that require large capital investments (e.g., automobile manufacturing or oil refining); extensive distribution networks (e.g., beer and soft drinks); large marketing budgets (e.g., athletic footware, consumer products); or intensive research and development activities (e.g., pharmaceuticals and semiconductor technology) still benefit from large size.[10] It would be difficult for small organizations to compete with the capital facilities of GM or Exxon, the distribution networks of Anheuser-Busch or Coca-Cola, the market power of Nike or Procter & Gamble, or the

R&D budgets of Merck or Intel.[11] It has been argued that as large companies learn to be more flexible and to subcontract out more actual manufacturing, they will continue to dominate as an organizational form well into the twenty-first century.[12] Still, the trends toward downsizing and reengineering suggest that small size may provide organizations with certain advantages in some industries.

WHAT HAPPENS WHEN ORGANIZATION SIZE INCREASES: LIFE CYCLES

Much the way people change as they grow and mature, organizations experience different passages or stages as they move through periods of growth. Organizations emerge, prosper, grow, stagnate, decline, and sometimes die. However, the human maturation process is tightly constrained by human genetics and biology. We all emerge as newborn infants, and those who survive become, by turns, toddlers, children, adolescents, teens, young adults, and onward toward our eventual death. Accidents or disease can stop the progress at any time, but each stage of human development is marked by well-defined physiological, emotional, and cognitive developments.

Organizations differ from humans in a few respects as will become clearer as the stages of development are described in the following sections. One important difference is that not all organizations emerge in the same way. Our auto repair business may be the prototype for birth—an entrepreneurial venture started by some individual with an idea and a willingness to take a risk. However, some businesses emerge as more or less fully formed large operations. For example, Lexmark was a "new" business when it was formally established in 1991. This was not, by any stretch of the imagination, a new entrepreneurial venture such as the auto repair business described earlier. Yet, this spin-off of IBM—Lexmark is the former printer and typewriter division of IBM—is a new company.[13] A spin-off company faces problems of its own that are different from an entrepreneurial venture. Most importantly, it must establish an identity that is separate from its former parent company. But this type of organization does not suffer the same *liability of newness* that plagues start-up new ventures.

A second critical difference between organizations and humans is that organizations can "backtrack." Old, mature organizations can recapture some of their youth through reorganization, downsizing, and other forms of organizational change. Unfortunately we humans are quite limited in the degree to which we can recapture our youth. Certainly, we can change our life style, exercise and change our diets, embark on new careers, and make many other changes, but the fountain of youth is still illusive. Organizations can, albeit not without difficulty, recapture characteristics of earlier phases of the life cycle. We introduce the ideas of organizational change and renewal as strategies for dealing with the stagnation of the elaboration stage. We return to those issues in Chapter 13 in which we discuss organizational change in greater detail.

Generally speaking, the trend is for organizations to become *more formalized* and *more complex* as their size increases and they mature. Recall that formalization refers to the rules, policies, and regulations used to govern people in the organization, and complexity refers to three aspects of division of labor: horizontal division of tasks, vertical (or hierarchical) division of responsibility, and spatial separation of departments or divisions.[14]

Formalization and complexity are the direct result of the need to divide the increased work in the organization and the desire to achieve greater specialization. There comes a point, as described earlier in the auto repair business example, when one person (or even a few people) can no longer do all the jobs that must be done to make the organization work effectively and efficiently. The addition of people usually means that the organization becomes more formal and structured. Rules and policies are implemented to guide people so that their efforts are consistent with the organization's goals, to achieve coordination among people and tasks, and to avoid waste and inefficiency. People's jobs become more narrowly defined and more specialized — horizontal differentiation. Work becomes more segmented. Administrative layers must eventually be added to supervise and coordinate activities across the growing number of departments and to control the behaviors of the increasingly large work force — vertical differentiation. Early in its existence, the few employees of the auto repair business may have been generalists — each one did a little of everything. As the company grew and prospered, it became increasingly formal and differentiated. The business may eventually add new repair locations throughout its expanding market. This contributes to spatial dispersion. Should management become more ambitious and decide to open facilities in other countries, this would vastly increase the spatial dispersion and resulting complexity.

In the following sections we examine the typical pattern of stages through which an organization passes. Although much has been written on organizational growth and life cycles, the field has not yet reached universal agreement on the stages and processes. We provide an integration of three perspectives.[15]

ORGANIZATIONAL BIRTH

In this stage, primary focus is on the entrepreneur's attempts to invent or develop a new product or service, create a new technology for producing a product or service, or simply to improve upon existing products, services, or technologies. The entrepreneur sees an opportunity — an available niche and the necessary resources — and attempts to fill that niche. Often the organization has not yet been officially created and may not be recognizable as an organization. Henry Mintzberg has used the term *adhocracy* to describe the organization at this stage.[16] The organization is informal; structure is created, implemented, or changed as needed and often in response to rapid growth and expansion — hence, the name adhocracy. The structure that is present tends to be highly organic. Leadership and control are vested in the owner entrepreneur; some theorists refer to this as the ***entrepreneurial stage***.[17] Entrepreneurs spend much of their time in unscheduled meetings and touring facilities.[18] This differs somewhat from the pattern of activities engaged in by managers of more firmly established firms. In fact, the hands-on leadership and heavy involvement of founders is in many respects a substitute for formal structure. This is the situation that exists in the early years of many organizations. The loose informal atmosphere in the early days at companies like Ben & Jerry's or Apple Computers and the prominent role that the founders played initially are indicative of the entrepreneurial stage.

The critical task that organizations face in this first stage of development is survival. Although statistics on new business failures vary widely, a majority—between 60 percent and 75 percent—of new business ventures fail within the first six years.[19] They fail for many reasons: Lack of adequate capital, inexperience, poorly conceived ideas, and hostile environments are just a few. The term *liability of newness* has been used to describe the nearly overwhelming odds against success for new business.[20] New organizations face the daunting task of establishing legitimacy, creating or discovering new knowledge, learning new roles, training new employees, and developing new markets.[21] To survive, the organization must bring in management knowledge and business leadership to begin creating some permanence to the organization. Typically, the entrepreneurial founders turn over the day-to-day management of the organization to someone with business and leadership skills. This is not always an easy transition for founders. It is often difficult for founders to place their *baby* in the hands of a virtual stranger. Steve Jobs and Steve Wozniak, cofounders of Apple, experienced just that problem and eventually had to leave the company after outside professional managers arrived. The short example below describes the problems John Walker, founder of the software maker Autodesk, experienced as the company grew and required outside management expertise.

Exhibit 7.2   **The Strange Case of Autodesk**[22]

Autodesk is hardly a household name even though it is among the largest firms in the crowded PC software market. Autodesk's lack of recognition is due in part to its market—inexpensive computer-aided design (CAD) software for engineers. That market lacks the high-consumer visibility of word processing or spreadsheets. However, another reason for Autodesk's obscurity is the behavior of its founder, John Walker.

Walker is a brilliant software engineer who has an uncanny knack for identifying industry trends. Walker's skill in refining and marketing low-cost CAD software for use on PCs is without question. As a result, Autodesk has grown rapidly, with sales increasing tenfold in its second year and increasing by a magnitude of ten over the next four years. Over the years Walker has played many roles in the company, including writing press releases and ad copy, working trade shows, and offering philosophical pronouncements.

However, Autodesk's growth has not been without problems. One person can't do everything, and Walker notes, "I'm an engineer. I'm a programmer. I'm a technologist. I have no interest in running a large U.S. public company . . . ."[23]

In 1986, Walker turned over management responsibility to Alvar Green, the firm's chief financial officer. But this relationship was an uneasy and contentious one. The real power in the company still remained with Walker and his programmers. These eccentric freethinkers often quarreled among themselves and severely attacked managers through highly critical electronic mail messages. They held Green, who had essentially no background in computers, in low regard. The proverbial straw that forced Green out of the company was a scathing forty-four page letter from Walker that attacked Green's management philosophy and strategic direction of Autodesk.

The critical question Autodesk faced was whether any manager could succeed in reigning in the creative and idiosyncratic nature of Autodesk, which was its source of early success, while preserving the financial stability. Enter Carol Bartz, a former executive with Sun Microsystems. Thus far, Bartz's combination of tough management and experience in the computer industry has helped her and Autodesk succeed. Walker has promised to support her and let her manage. Perhaps Autodesk can now move past the entrepreneurial phase and continue to prosper in the competitive software industry.

EMERGENT STRUCTURE

The odds against an organization surviving the entrepreneurial stage are steep. If the venture solves the financial, market, and managerial problems of its birth, it will need two characteristics of a formal organization. Mike Lawrence at Thrifty in Chapter 1 and John Walker at Autodesk each realized that they could no longer do a little bit of everything to run their organizations. As the firm grows, management must provide leadership, establish clear goals, differentiate departments, divide labor, delegate responsibilities, and develop a hierarchy. This stage, referred to as the ***collectivity stage,*** represents the emergence of structure with some degree of stability.[24] Although the organization is beginning to be formally structured, it still retains an air of informality and flexibility. Members are likely to rely on shared values, commitment, and informal communication means to accomplish the organization's goals.[25] For example, Ben & Jerry's Homemade, the premium ice cream maker, announced the commencement of a search for a new CEO to replace cofounder Ben Cohen.[26] In fact, it placed ads in newspapers asking people to nominate themselves and write an essay on why they would make a good CEO. Of course, this was primarily an advertising ploy, but it did aid in solidifying Ben & Jerry's values. Cohen and the board of directors realized that the size and complexity of the growing ice cream company had outstripped his interest and ability to manage. The ideal candidate for the job should combine management acumen and the ability to maintain the offbeat culture of Ben & Jerry's that has been so important to its early success.

The critical tasks that the organization faces at this point are balancing the needs for some formal structure with the needs to continue growing and adapting to external conditions. Additionally, the top management team that has been brought in to run the former entrepreneurial venture must successfully delegate responsibilities to lower-level employees. Otherwise, decision making and problem solving will quickly overwhelm top management, and lower-level employees will become frustrated or leave the organization.

THE FORMAL ORGANIZATION

Over time and with continued, but slower, growth, an organization continues its march toward formalized structure and bureaucracy. The slower growth creates an environment of greater stability and predictability than that which existed in previous stages.

The *formalization stage* is marked by greater reliance on traditional bureaucratic mechanisms of control: rules are implemented; tasks become more narrowly specialized; domains of responsibility become more clearly articulated; hierarchy and formal communication channels become institutionalized.[27] Mintzberg notes that organizations often expand into new markets or begin to operate in new locations at this stage.[28] To hold the organization together it may be necessary to create a more elaborate and complex divisional structure with divisions representing markets, products, or geographical regions. Managers will spend the majority of their time in scheduled meetings and performing desk work.[29] This contrasts with the earlier emphasis on the unscheduled meetings and touring of facilities of the entrepreneurial stage.

Organizations must balance the greater need for structure at this stage with the continuing need to remain flexible and responsive to changing environmental conditions. Examples abound of companies such as Sears, IBM, and General Motors that created exceedingly complex and bureaucratic structures to deal with the multitude of products, markets, and operations. However, overreliance on complex formal structure and bureaucratic mechanism may result in inefficiencies and unresponsiveness to internal and external conditions. The organization fails to respond in a timely fashion to changing conditions in the environment, and employees become stifled by bureaucracy.

Exhibit 7.3

The Weight (or Wait?) of Bureaucracy

The stories are legendary and, unfortunately, all too common at large bureaucratic organizations. A customer makes an unusual request—a custom product, individualized service, special shipping instructions, or maybe an unusual installation. The technical staff low in the organizational hierarchy knows that the customer's request can be met, but it may require that several departments that are unaccustomed to cooperating work together, or it may mean bending a few rules. However, the bureaucratic organization works by rules and standard procedures. Special requests often mean exceptions to rules and standard procedures. When bureaucracies become burdensome, it may take a long time to coordinate across departments or to get permission to bend the rules. Many forms or reports must be completed to document the unusual request. Often requests for variances from standard operating procedures must travel up many layers of the hierarchy. Weeks may pass before action is taken. The customer may get impatient; employees may get frustrated; competitors may intervene; and a sale is lost. This is the weight (or wait) of bureaucracy. Try registering for a course at your university after the registration period ends or try taking a class for which you lack prerequisites. How easily does your school respond to such out-of-the-ordinary requests? Or even try something as simple as ordering a nonstandard item at a fast food restaurant like McDonald's.

Growing organizations must balance the need for control and consistency in their operations—hallmarks of bureaucracies—with the need for flexibility and timely responsiveness. Weber developed the notion of a bureaucracy as an efficient and effective organization, but too much of a good thing may cripple an organization.

"DINOSAURS" AND TURNAROUNDS

The organizational landscape is populated by many well-recognized behemoths. We need only to look back at the *Fortune* 500 list at the beginning of this chapter for examples. Many of these organizations have reached the point at which bureaucratic controls no longer work. Rules and policies become too numerous and cumbersome. Because of their size and complexity, bureaucratic controls designed for one part or division of the organization often are inappropriate for other parts or divisions. To deal with the complex multidimensional organization, managers write more rules and more complex rules. Thus, the rules themselves inhibit control and communication rather than enhance it. People spend increasing time learning the rules, petitioning for exceptions to the rules, monitoring and enforcing the rules, or devising schemes to skirt the rules.

This stage has been labeled the ***elaboration stage*** by some authors because of the need to elaborate on bureaucratic mechanisms.[30] Often organizations at this point in development utilize teamwork and the self-management by shared values and norms to replace bureaucratic rules and procedures. Managers of organizations at the elaboration stage often speak of reinventing their firm, delayering, downsizing, reengineering, or in other ways restructuring the organization to better fit its environment and its internal conditions.[31] The changes necessary to avoid decline at this phase often also involve changes in goals, people, and technology. Change may include restructuring, reengineering work processes, and rethinking the basic nature of the organization.[32] ***Restructuring*** refers to reconfiguring organizational units or departments. The organization may subdivide into smaller units and rely on control mechanisms other than bureaucracy. At this stage, organizations often institute complex structural solutions including multidivisional structures or matrix structures. In effect, the single large organization is trying to act like many smaller organizations. Changing the structure is typically an important element to maintaining or restoring a thriving organization. One need only look at the top ten *Fortune* 500 companies to see the prevalence of change efforts among large corporations. General Motors, Ford, IBM, General Electric, and Chrysler have each instituted major organizational restructuring to increase efficiency, improve communication, and enhance responsiveness to environmental conditions. These structures are discussed in greater detail in Chapter 8, but for now it is important to note that structurally defined lines of communication and responsibility reduce some of the need for bureaucracy. ***Reengineering*** refers to reconfiguring the work process. This may involve restructuring, but it also involves altering technology. ***Rethinking*** refers to a reevaluation of the organization: its identity (what the organization is and what it stands for); its purpose (who the organization benefits); its values or philosophy; and its methods or capabilities (how the organization achieves its purpose and identity).[33]

Another important feature of the late-phase organization is the nature of its workforce. Studies on workforces are referred to as ***organizational demography.***[34] Demographers try to characterize an organization's workers with respect to such factors as age, gender, work experience, skills, training, and education level. These average worker characteristics can be used to make judgments about the potential productivity and commitment of workers, and the need for training. Older workers and workers with longer experience at one organization are more likely to stay on the job and be committed to the organization, thus reducing costly turnover. However, younger workers and workers who have been on a specific job for a short period of time may bring into the organization more training and current knowledge. Unfortunately, they may lack the commitment of the older workers and thus may be more likely to leave after only a short stay.

Demographers have also noted that greater uniformity of workers (i.e., greater similarity in age, training, skills, etc.) may aid social interactions in the organization, thus facilitating task coordination and control. The assumption here is that workers who share a similar background are more likely to hold similar values. Having employees who share similar values should improve the communication necessary to coordinate and control tasks and is likely to reduce conflict.

One must be careful interpreting the above findings. This does not necessarily mean that uniformity in the workforce is good and diversity is bad. Although it may be true that uniformity makes communication and coordination easier, too much similarity or uniformity may lead the organization to stifling conformity and a lack of creativity. Demographic diversity may, however, produce conflict. An example of this conflict can be seen in organizations that have downsized by using early retirement. Older workers who remain in the organization often lose their cohort group and are at odds with their new, younger bosses or managers.[35] Younger bosses or managers sometimes fail to respect the experience and history of their older coworkers and subordinates. Much of the miscommunication is based on the different values of the different groups of workers and the stereotypes and biases that sometimes result from those value differences. But even this conflict and miscommunication can be constructive in moving the organization forward. Diversity, conflict, and discussion can help an organization realize new and creative directions.

The example of ConAgra below describes an organization that was clearly in the elaboration stage. ConAgra has implemented many new strategies to reverse the typical stagnation that can set in at the elaboration stage.

Exhibit 7.4   **ConAgra is Cooking Again[36]**

ConAgra, the Omaha-based food giant, has successfully implemented a turnaround to cut costs and increase internal cooperation and communication. CEO Philip B. Fletcher sought to implement programs to increase stagnant operating income and increase the firm's stock price.

Fletcher saw that poor organization resulted in many inefficiencies, poor communication, and weak coordination. For example, ConAgra's two popcorn makers, Golden Valley and Orville Redenbacher, were buying plastic packaging from the same vender. Golden Valley was paying 15 percent more while buying four times as much. Fletcher created executive councils in which division heads meet periodically to discuss pooling resources, reducing and consolidating purchasing, improving warehousing, and cutting transportation costs. A computerized supplier cost network has also been implemented so each division can see what other divisions are paying for various supplies.

In order to get managers to pay attention to this new cooperation and efficiency effort, 25 percent of their bonuses is tied directly to savings targets through the "Get the Family Money" program to encourage executives to act as a single family.

ConAgra's changes are beginning to show results. Frozen food sales rose 2 percent in fiscal 1994 after a decline of 12 percent in 1993. Operating margins have increased to 4.7 percent in 1994 from 3 percent in 1993. And stock share prices have increased to $112 on July 11, 1994, from $100 on December 31, 1993.

There is still more to do. International sales make up an anemic 10 percent of sales. New acquisitions, new markets, and new or revised products are needed. However, by first focusing on changing the organization's structure, ConAgra has managed to stop the slide that so often affects old-line companies in mature industries.

TABLE 7.3
Organizational Life Cycles

Stage	Characteristics	Challenge
1. Birth — entrepreneurial	Rapid growth, liability of newness	Survival
2. Emergent structure — collectivity	Continued growth, balance, stability and flexibility	Delegation of responsibility, professional management
3. Formal organization — formalization	Slow growth, formal organization, beginning of bureaucracy	Balance needs for coordination and control with needs for flexibility and responsiveness.
4. Dinosaurs and turnarounds — elaboration	Slow growth or stagnation, large and complex; highly bureaucratic	Restructure; reinvent, downsize

ORGANIZATIONAL DECLINE

Decline is not a separate stage of organizational development; rather, it is the negative outcome of an organization's failure to effectively resolve the respective crises of each stage. Definitions of decline focus on the ***organization's inability or reduced capacity to cope with its environment.***[37] For example, the organization may be unable to adapt to changing consumer demands, changing markets for raw materials, changing regulatory constraints from government agencies, or changing labor market conditions. Bankruptcy (either Chapter XI reorganization or Chapter VII liquidation of the Federal Bankruptcy Code) are obvious indicators of decline, but organizations may be in distress well before they are legally labeled as such by the bankruptcy designation.[38]

Typically, the failure of an organization is not a swift fall. The failure is likely to be a slow, agonizing retreat, described as a downward spiral[39] that has its own set of characteristic stages.[40] By its very nature, decline is a difficult process to reverse.[41] As a firm's fortunes begin to decline, it may face difficulty attracting a wide array of resources. Investors generally shy away from a declining firm. Employees who are able to leave — sometimes the best and brightest workers — leave for greener pastures. The organization is left with a less skilled and demoralized workforce. Suppliers, fearful about the financial instability of the declining firm, may be reluctant to service the firm. These problems typically plunge the declining organization further down the road of decline, and thus, the downward spiral continues.

The five stages of decline are characterized by five distinct sets of organizational actions described in Table 7.4. During the first four stages the organization can take corrective actions to reverse the trends. The final stage of decline is the point of no return, and the organization eventually ceases to exist. Chapter 13 provides a more comprehensive examination of strategies that organizations use to avoid or reverse decline.

■ **TABLE 7.4**
Stages of Organizational Decline *

Stages	**Decline-Related Actions**	**Attempts to Reverse Decline**
1. Blinded	Failure to detect environmental pressure	Gather information
2. Inaction	Failure to decide on corrective actions; misinterpretation of information; noticeable decline in performance	Prompt action
3. Faulty Action	Faulty decision and/or faulty implementation of solutions; steepening decline	Corrective action
4. Crisis	Given faulty action in a hostile environment: last chance for reversal Given a favorable environment: slow decline unless corrective actions are taken	Major restructuring or reorganization
5. Dissolution	Given a hostile environment: quick demise Given a favorable environment: slow decline	No choices

*Adopted from W. Weitzel and E. Jonsson, "Decline in Organizations: A Literature Integration and Extension," *Administrative Science Quarterly* 34 (1989): 97–102.

ADVANTAGES OF SMALL SIZE: A TREND FOR THE FUTURE

As noted earlier in this chapter, organizations pursue growth and the resulting large size for many reasons. Until recently, the prevailing wisdom was that bigger is better. However, the discussion of organizational life cycles and the tendencies of large organizations to become increasingly bureaucratic suggest that there may be some problems associated with managing large organizations: increasing administrative overhead, increasing red tape, slowness to respond, difficulty coordinating among disparate units of the organization, lack of responsiveness to employee and customer needs, difficulty communicating, and more. Countering the bigger-is-better philosophy is a growing movement toward thinking small.[42]

Thinking small does not necessarily mean that companies want to reduce financial or market performance indicators such as revenues, market share, or profits. Rather, thinking small may mean many different things: downsizing the human resources component of the organization (i.e., doing more with fewer people); splitting an organization into several smaller divisions that run more or less autonomously; selling off unprofitable divisions or divisions that do not mesh well with a firm's core business; or changing the structure and culture of the organization so that people behave more like employees in small businesses.[43] Each of these strategies is briefly described below. We return to each of them periodically throughout the text because they are also related to topics such as organizational change (Chapter 13), design (Chapter 8), control (Chapter 9), and culture (Chapter 10).

DOWNSIZING

One result of the progression through the life cycle model is development of a significant administrative staff whose purpose is to service the organization. The administrative staff becomes responsible for fulfilling the requirements of a bureaucracy—documentation of actions, completion of paperwork, and supervision of workers. Coincidental with the above trend is the increasingly narrow specialization of jobs.

At the auto repair shop described earlier in the chapter, the founder was originally responsible for all varieties of repairs: brakes, mufflers, transmissions, fuel injection systems, ignition systems, and so forth. As the business grew, it became apparent that some economies and efficiencies could be gained by specialization. Brake and muffler repairs did not require great training or skill to perform, while fuel injection and ignition repairs were quite complex and required significant amounts of skill and training. Specialization ensured that adequately trained (i.e., specialized) employees performed the appropriate tasks. In a perfect world, this sort of specialization may work. Unfortunately, the repair traffic at the shop was unpredictable. Some days all of the repairs were brake and muffler jobs; other days were all fuel injection problems. On any given day some part of the workforce might be idle because there was no demand for their expertise.

One solution to this problem was to downsize—eliminate some of the employees—and broadly train the remaining employees in all facets of auto repair. Additionally, the remaining employees could work in teams with one member more expert in brake and muffler work and the other more expert in fuel injection and ignition work. As a team, their strengths would complement each other and, because they are more broadly trained, they would lack the weaknesses of the former system. Similar sorts of teamwork and broadening of jobs could be accomplished in other areas of the organization.

Under the old system, the shop relied extensively on supervisors to assign work and to ensure its satisfactory completion. The brake and muffler repair division supervisor would assign repair jobs, make certain that employees were making timely progress toward completing the job, and inspect work to ensure that it was properly completed. The supervisor, however, did not perform any actual repairs. After downsizing, the supervisor's job was eliminated. Under the new system, the repair teams were responsible for monitoring and guaranteeing their own work. In addition to downsizing, other changes in design, control, and culture were necessary to make the new system work.

REDESIGN

As the auto repair business grew larger and as the structure grew more complex and bureaucratic, the firm started losing its personal feel. In the early days, the founder knew all the customers or quickly learned about them. The founder also knew all the employees and consider them friends. But as the company grew, the founder was no longer able to know each customer or employee. As CEO, the founder's responsibilities were also more specialized—setting the strategic direction of the firm and meeting with investors, bankers, and suppliers. In fact, this trend was duplicated throughout the organization's top management. There was a feeling that managers had lost touch with the day-to-day operation of the business. The solution, made possible in part by downsizing, is to redesign the formerly bureaucratic organization into a flatter, more organic organization. The redesigned firm would need fewer layers of hierarchy because people were now supervising their own work, and coordination would be easier because people were working in teams.

Another step in redesigning (and downsizing) may be the elimination of certain divisions. As the auto repair business grew, the management decided to integrate backwards in the auto parts distribution business. The belief was that by buying an auto parts wholesale company the auto repair business would have a more dependable and cheaper source of parts. This purchase also involved some diversification. The firm began selling auto parts to other repair shops. Management soon learned that the skills and expertise necessary to run the parts business were different from that necessary to run the auto repair business. After a few years of losing money, management decided to sell the parts business so that they could focus on their core business—auto repair.

Management could have made a different decision concerning the parts business. If they thought there was still potential to profitably operate the parts business independently of the repair business, they could have spun it off as a separate autonomous unit of the company. It would have had its own management team and it would have operated nearly independently of the repair business. The result of the spin-off would have been that both remaining businesses would have operated more like small companies. These are called *strategic business units (SBUs)* to reflect the autonomy of each division. Companies such as General Electric and Johnson & Johnson operate many of their divisions in this fashion. For example, Johnson & Johnson has approximately 166 operating units that operate as small independent companies.[44]

VIRTUAL ORGANIZATION

More and more, organizations are subcontracting out much of their work in order to achieve the advantages of smaller size and flexibility. It is possible that an organization could contract out so much of its work that it becomes a shell or umbrella organization. This is sometimes referred to as a *virtual organization.* We discuss this in more detail in subsequent chapters. Its relevance here is that the virtual organization allows the firm to concentrate on those business areas for which it is best suited and contract with outsiders for everything else.

An example of a virtual organization is a large electric utility company in Florida that does not generate its own power. It buys power from other companies. It subcontracts with another company to maintain utility poles and rights of way. Lawn maintenance at headquarters and meter reading are also performed by subcontractors. The company sticks with its core competence — building and maintaining power lines. It is a specialist in this area and is very efficient.

COORDINATION AND CONTROL: CHANGING THE CULTURE

Culture, the principal focus of Chapter 10, embodies the basic philosophy and values of an organization. Without going into a detailed discussion of culture, it is important now only to note that large organizations can act much like small ones by changing their culture — their basic values and philosophy. To some extent, changing the culture is an extension of the rethinking mentioned earlier. Instead of valuing largeness, hierarchy, authority, and power, the large firm can shift its values and philosophy to mirror small firms — think small. The dominant values become entrepreneurship, risk taking, closeness to customers, decentralized authority, individual responsibility, and other similar values that contribute to innovativeness and responsiveness.[45] In many industries that are heavily dependent on new technological developments, new information, and new skills or training, the old hierarchical bureaucratic system no longer works. Employees low in the organization may possess more information about how to solve the problems and accomplish the goals of the organization than do top managers. Thus, hierarchical bureaucratic control over employees will not be efficient and effective. Instead, the organization must rely on clearly communicating its basic values and attracting employees who share those values — an approach called ***clan control.***[46]

The transformation from large organization to a small-thinking, small-acting large organization is not easy. None of the above-mentioned changes is easy to accomplish. One need only follow the recent experiences of General Motors and IBM as they try to downsize and redesign to see the great difficulty in reversing years of bureaucratic largeness and excess. It is still difficult for employees to adopt the values and philosophy of small firms. But there are success stories. We have already mentioned GE and Johnson & Johnson as successful large businesses that act much like smaller firms.[47] Other success stories include Emerson Electric, Dana Corporation, and Hewlett-Packard, all of which are *Fortune* 500 companies.

SUMMARY

Organizations, if they are successful, can generally expect to grow and change over time. The growth can be measured by a number of indicators, such as market share, profits, revenues, geographical dispersion, number of products, or number of employees. The appropriateness of a given measure depends upon one's intended purpose. All these measures can play an important role in organization theory; however, our primary emphasis is on the number of people in the organization.

Growth can appear in nearly any portion of the organization, but it is common for growth to first appear in the administrative or support staff. As the organization grows, it tends to become more specialized and differentiated. Technical support staff multiplies, and supervisors are added. Eventually, this leads to an increasingly complex and bureaucratic organization.

Growth and the resulting large size are associated with several competitive advantages. Large size may produce economies of scale, market power, political power, and other desirable outcomes. In some industries, large size is a requirement in order to be competitive. However, we also noted that large size is not always a clear advantage. Large size may burden an organization with inflexibility, rigidity, bureaucracy, and lethargy.

We presented a life cycle model that is useful in describing the general trend of development that organizations typically follow. Unlike human models of development, organizations do not necessarily start with the conventional entrepreneurial birth. Some, like spin-offs, start farther along the developmental path. Also, unlike humans, organization can revitalize themselves and return to earlier phases of development through various change efforts.

At any stage of development an organization can slip down the path to decline. Decline itself has a series of unique stages with specific problems and potential solutions. Unfortunately, the organization that repeatedly fails to turn itself around continues the downward spiral of decline.

The concluding section of this chapter suggests a trend toward acting like a small business. Many organizations have undertaken downsizing, restructuring, and culture changes in an attempt to capture the entrepreneurial spirit and management style of small firms.

Questions for Discussion

1. Must all organizations either grow or die? Explain.
2. What would you suggest to be the best measure of a university's growth? Would this be the same if you were to measure the growth of a local high school? Explain.
3. What would you expect to be the big differences between a large and a small organization?
4. For a growing small business, why do you think growth begins in the support areas?
5. How are size and complexity related? Explain.
6. This chapter describes five stages of organizational decline. Using an organization with which you are familiar, see where they fit it now. What actions (if any) can the organization take to prevent its dissolution? Who is responsible for taking these actions?
7. Is growth always good? Why might you as the president or chancellor deliberately try to keep your company or university from growing?
8. What can happen to the culture of a growing organization? A declining one?

9. How is the downsizing trend related to growth? Why is downsizing undertaken? Is it usually permanent?

CASE: FADING MEMORIES*

It's the dream of nearly every entrepreneur: Come up with a simple idea that quickly captures the market. Legends of successful entrepreneurs are filled with rags-to-riches stories of individuals who plunked down their life savings to start a business out of a basement, garage, or storefront and went on to great success. Names such as Ford Motor Company, Apple Computers, and Performance Cycle are examples of such entrepreneurial ventures that grew from humble beginnings to later catch fire and win significant market share in their respective markets. Harvey Harris had similar dreams for his company, Grandmother Calendar Co.

The idea behind Grandmother Calendar was quite simple. Harris marketed elaborately customized calendars that featured personalized artwork and photographs supplied by the customer. Calendars could include detailed collages, birth certificates, traffic tickets, and other official documents that were scanned into the finished product. Special dates in the body of the calendar could also be personalized. Harris offered his high quality product at a starting price of $20, about $5 less than the closest competitive product, although special features added to the price.

Greeting card retailers, gift shops, drugstores, and even discounters such as Kmart sold the Grandmother Calendar mail order kit to hopeful customers. The kit included instructions for the calendar layout and for designation of special dates. Customers would complete the instructions, enclose photos, drawings, or documents they wanted included on the calendar and send these materials to the Grandmother Calendar headquarters in Oklahoma City.

When a calendar order was received at the Grandmother Calendar plant, photos, artwork, and documents were scanned into a computer, arranged, and edited to meet the customer's request. At the same time, information about special dates, such as anniversaries and birthdays, was entered into the computer. To produce the calendar, graphic images and information were electronically merged. The calendar was then printed, spiral-bound, and mailed to the customer.

The idea was really quite simple, and the technology was not terribly difficult too manage . . . at least under normal circumstances it was not too difficult. The problem was too much success, too fast. One retailer, Paragon Gifts, sold nearly 25,000 kits in six months. This was three times more sales than Harris had anticipated. As the Christmas holiday season approached, orders flooded in faster than they could be processed. To deal with the influx of orders, Harris added some new state-of-the-art equipment and he pushed employees to speed up production, but it was a case of too little, too late. At the height of the Christmas season, the 300-calendar-per-day production lagged far behind the incoming order rate of 1,000 per day. Thousands of orders went unfilled.

---

*Based on an article by Louise Lee, "Picture This! A Firm Failing From Too Much Success," *The Wall Street Journal* (March 17, 1995), B1, B6.

The press of orders spelled the beginning of a disaster. Equipment started to break down from overuse and workers began to make mistakes. The quality of those calendars that did get made suffered from poor color reproduction and spelling errors. Retailers selling the calendar kits were unaware of problems and kept selling to unsuspecting customers. This further fueled the backlog. Keep in mind the time-sensitive nature of this market and product. Calendars, especially customized ones like these, are gift items and keyed to the holiday season and the new year. Sales lost in December are not likely to be made up in January, and dissatisfied customers are unlikely to be patient.

By December, it was clear to Harris that he had serious problems. The company wrote to customers trying to reassure them that they would get their calendars but not in time for Christmas. Late in December, paychecks to many of Grandmother's employees bounced. Finally, in early January, the company shut down entirely—not from a lack of customers, but from an inability to meet customer demand.

In the aftermath, retailers who sold the Grandmother Calendar packets were trying to make certain that photos, documents, and other materials were returned to customers. Most customers received refunds of the base charge of $20, but charges over $20 paid for special features were not refunded. Creditors and suppliers are sifting through Grandmother's remains for anything of value to cover their claims. The state attorney general's office is also investigating Grandmother's failure.

What went wrong at the Grandmother Calendar Co.? At some level, Harris was a victim of his own success. He clearly had a good idea, a good product (at least before the rush of orders came in), and a good market niche. However, Harris lacked the management and organizational skills necessary to manage this venture. He did not plan for this level of success. Grandmother was undercapitalized. The company lacked the resources to add enough equipment and enough people to serve the avalanche of orders. Harris admitted, "I made mistakes . . . I'm not an attorney. I'm not an accountant . . . (I) did not track receivables, payables, and funding. I should have made, well, better decisions." One former employee discussing the demise of Grandmother alluded to the fact that it was just a small company.

QUESTIONS FOR DISCUSSION

1. At what life cycle stage was the Grandmother Calendar Co.? What evidence suggests that the company was at that stage?
2. Could Harris have avoided the eventual failure of his company? What should he have done to avoid failure?
3. Do you agree with the former employee's judgment that the company's problems were the result of its small size? Why? Why not?

REFERENCES

1. Ansen J. Darney and Marlita A. Retty, eds. *Market Share Register* (Detroit, Mich.: Gale Research Inc., 1994). "Vital Signs: Checking the Auto World's Pulse," *Ward's Auto World* 29, no. 12 (December 1993): 22.

2. Nathaniel C. Nash, "Coke's Great Romanian Adventure," *The New York Times* (February 26, 1995), 10 (Sect. 3).

3. J. D. Ford and J. W. Slocum, Jr., "Size, Technology, Environment and Structure of Organizations," *Academy of Management Review* 2 (1977): 561–75.

4. John Child and Roger Mansfield, "Technology, Size and Organizational Structure," *Sociology* 6 (1972): 369–93.

5. J. Pfeffer and G. R. Salancik, *The External Control of Organizations: A Resource Dependence Perspective* (New York: Harper & Row, 1978): 131–39.

   W. Richard Scott, *Organizations: Rational, Natural, and Open Systems*, 3rd ed. (Englewood Cliffs, N.J.: Prentice-Hall, 1992), 82–85.

6. T. M. Burton, "Eli Lilly Accepts FTC Curbs, Clearing Way for its $4 Billion Purchase of PCS," *The Wall Street Journal* (November 4, 1994), B1.

   S. N. Mehta, "In Shadow of Medco and PCS, Other Firms Are Busy," *The Wall Street Journal* (July 13, 1994), B2.

7. M. J. Mandel, "Land of the Giants," *Business Week* (September 11,1995): 34–35.

   K. Holland, "Wow! That's Some Bank," *Business Week* (September 11, 1995): 36–39.

8. John A. Byrne, "Why a Big Steelmaker Is Mimicking the Minimills," *Business Week* (March 27, 1989): 92.

9. John A. Byrne, "Is Your Company Too Big?" *Business Week* (March 27, 1989): 85–90.

10. Richard A. Melcher, "How Goliaths Can Act Like Davids," *Business Week* (1993 special Enterprise issue): 192–201.

11. Ibid.

12. Bennett Harrison, *Lean and Mean: The Changing Landscape of Corporate Power in the Age of Flexibility* (New York: Basic Books, 1994).

13. Paul B. Carroll, "Culture Shock: Story of an IBM Unit That Split Off Shows Difficulties of Change," *The Wall Street Journal* (July 23, 1992), 1.

14. Richard H. Hall, *Organizations: Structure, Processes, & Outcomes* (Englewood Cliffs, N.J.: Prentice-Hall, 1992).

15. Henry Mintzberg, *The Structuring of Organizations* (Englewood Cliffs, N.J.: Prentice-Hall, 1979).

   Robert K. Kazanjian, Relation of Dominant Problems to Stages of Growth in Technology-Based New Ventures," *Academy of Management Journal* 31 (1988): 257–79.

   Robert E. Quinn and Kim Cameron, "Organizational Life Cycles and Shifting Criteria of Effectiveness: Some Preliminary Evidence," *Management Science* 29 (1983): 33–51.

   K. S. Cameron and D. A. Whetten, "Models of the Organizational Life Cycle: Applications to Higher Education," *Review of Higher Education* 6 (1983): 269–99.

16. See Mintzberg in note 15 above.

17. See Quinn and Cameron in note 15 above.

18. S. Dunphy, "An Ethnographic Study Comparing the Nature of Managerial Work to the Nature of Entrepreneurial Work," *Journal of Business & Entrepreneurship* 8, no. 2 (1993): 37–44.

19. Justin G. Longnecker, Carlos W. Moore, and J. William Petty, *Small Business Management: An Entrepreneurial Emphasis* (Cincinnati, Ohio: South Western Publishing, 1994).

20. Arthur L. Stinchcombe, "Social Structure and Organizations," in *Handbook of Organizations,* James G. March, ed. (Chicago: Rand McNally, 1965), 142–93.

21. See Scott in note 5 above.

22. G. P. Zachary, "Theocracy of Hackers' Rules Autodesk Inc., A Strangely Run Firm," *The Wall Street Journal* (May 28, 1992), A1.

23. Ibid, p. 1.

24. See Quinn and Cameron in note 15 above.

25. R. L. Daft, *Organization Theory and Design,* 4th ed. (St. Paul, Minn.: West Publishing, 1992), 164.

26. William M. Bulkeley, "Ben & Jerry's Is Looking for Ben's Successor," *The Wall Street Journal* (June 14, 1994), B1–B2.

27. See Quinn and Cameron in note 15 above.

28. See Mintzberg in note 15 above.

29. See note 18 above.

30. See Quinn and Cameron in note 15 above.

31. Thomas A. Stewart, "Re-Engineering: The Hot New Managing Tool," *Fortune* 128, no. 4 (August 23, 1993): 40–48.

    Michael Hammer and James Champy, *Reengineering the Corporation: A Manifesto for Business Revolution* (New York: Harper Business, 1993).

    Noel M. Tichy, "Revolutionize Your Company," *Fortune* 128, no. 15 (1993): 114–18.

32. R. W. Keidel, "Rethinking Organizational Design," *Academy of Management Executive* 8, no. 4, (1994): 12–28.

33. See note 32 above.

34. R. Ely, "The Power of Demography: Women's Social Constructions of Gender Identity at Work," *Academy of Management Journal* 38 (1995): 589–634.

    A. Lomi, "The Population Ecology of Organizational Founding: Location, Dependence, and Unobserved Heterogeneity," *Administrative Science Quarterly* 40 (1995): 111–44.

35. Sue Shellenbarger and Carol Hymowitz, "Over the Hill: As Population Ages, Older Workers Clash with Younger Bosses," *The Wall Street Journal* (June 13, 1994), A1–A8.

36. Greg Burns, "How a Boss Got ConAgra Cooking Again," *Business Week* (July 25, 1994): 72–73.

37. W. Weitzel and E. Jonsson, "Decline in Organizations: A Literature Integration and Extension," *Administrative Science Quarterly* 34 (1989): 91–109.

38. L. M. Gales and I. F. Kesner, "An Analysis of Board of Director Size and Composition in Bankrupt Organizations," *Journal of Business Research* 30 (1994): 271–82.

39. D. C. Hambrick and R. A. D'Aveni, "Large Corporate Failures as Downward Spirals," *Administrative Science Quarterly* 33 (1988): 1–23.

40. See note 37 above.

    D. A. Whetten, "Organizational Growth and Decline Processes," *Annual Review of Sociology* 13 (1987): 335–58.

41. R. I. Sutton and A. L. Callahan, "The Stigma of Bankruptcy: Spoiled Organizational Image and Its Management," *Academy of Management Journal* 30 (1987): 405–36.

    See note 39 above.

42. E. F. Schumacher, *Small is Beautiful; Economics as if People Mattered* (New York: Harper & Row, 1973).

43. See note 10 above.

44. See note 10 above.

    Joseph Weber, "A Big Company That Works," *Business Week* (May 4, 1992): 124–32.

45. See note 10 above.

46. William G. Ouchi, "Markets, Bureaucracies and Clans," *Administrative Science Quarterly* 25 (1980): 129–41.

47. See note 10 above.

PART THREE

Managing the Organizational Context

W e began this text by introducing the contingency framework — no one method of organizing or managing is inherently superior. Rather, the best way to organize or manage depends on the context an organization confronts. In Part Two, we identified in considerable detail the nature of the organizational context: the goals, environment, technology, and size of an organization. These conditions are likely to vary considerably from one organization to another — even for different organizations within a single industry.

Part Three explores the ways in which organizations can respond to these diverse conditions. In Chapter 8, we examine an organizational design as a strategic response to the organizational context. In that chapter, we first focus attention on how people are grouped together in departments or divisions. Functional groups place people together based on the nature of the tasks they perform. For example, people performing marketing-related tasks are grouped into a marketing department. An alternative way to group is on the basis of output. We explore three distinct types of output groupings: products or service, markets or customers, and geography. Functional and output grouping can be combined in designs such as the matrix and hybrid forms. Each type of design has specific strengths and weaknesses that match particular contextual conditions.

Chapter 8 also introduces recent trends in design. Many organizations are adopting looser affiliations, such as the virtual organization and the federal organization. In addition, several distinctly national organizational forms have emerged. We present two of these from Asia, the Japanese *keiretsu* and the Korean *chaebol*.

Design is not the only mechanism for managing the context of an organization. Chapter 9 introduces the concept of governance as it has developed in the organizational economics field. Two theoretical frameworks, agency theory and transaction cost economics, deal with how owners and managers of firms deal with critical problems of governing. Agency theory addresses the problem of how owners manage the contractual relationship with their managers. Transaction cost economics delves into the problem of managing transaction for goods and services both within the firm's boundaries and across them.

The governance mechanisms described in Chapter 9 are a stepping-stone to the broader concept of organizational culture. Culture, discussed in Chapter 10, is what makes organizations distinct and different. Think, for example, of organizations such as Kmart and Wal-Mart that are in the same industry. Yet, these two retailing giants are very different. Part of what distinguishes them are the different values, norms, and beliefs of the key people in these two companies. Culture plays a crucial role in an organization's response to its context.

Patterns of Strategic Organizational Design

CASE: WHERE HAVE THE PYRAMIDS GONE?*

Where have the pyramids gone?
When one thinks of the design of organization in U.S. industry, the pyramid comes to mind. Like the pyramids in Egypt, they have a broad base that tapers to a sharp point at the top. That is to say, there are more members located at the bottom of the organization who are "governed" by a decreasing number of managers as one shifts focus toward the top. The essence of such design is centralization with a few managers making most, if not all, the critical decisions on behalf of numerous subordinates.

These designs stress control, place little emphasis on subordinate development, and emphasize effectiveness over empowerment. These designs reflect the values that U.S. managers have traditionally placed high on their decision agenda.

But there is a move today to change the design of organizations—a move that is aimed at stressing opposite values. Decentralization, involvement, and personnel development are believed to be better means to gain the essential value of all organizations—coordination and customer satisfaction. Although there are perhaps many driving forces for this movement (though still in its infancy), cultural change has produced a workforce that almost demands involvement in the life of the organization.

This new organization form is horizontal rather than vertical in its basic shape. It results from the elimination of layers of management and the granting of more responsibility to employees. The focus is on the customer as opposed to loyalty to a particular functional grouping. The Total Quality Management movement has been largely responsible for this new shape of organizations.

Organizing around process stresses that attention be given to customer satisfaction and product development from a holistic perspective rather than stressing individual functions, such as product planning and statistical control. It is, in short, a type of

---

*This case is based on the following source: John A. Byrne (with bureau reports), "The Horizontal Corporation," *Business Week* (December 20, 1993): 76–81.

organization-culture revolution, a revolution that is unsettling, to say the least, for traditional managers schooled in the culture of the pyramid organization.

The move to the horizontal organization has so far been concentrated at the lower levels where teams of employees work together on the entire process needed to get the product to the customer. In other words, the customer is the overarching focus on the teams' efforts. The benefits attained from this beginning, however, are expected to find their way to the top.

The few managers who traditionally guided the pyramid will perhaps be replaced by teams of managers who will operate similarly to employees in lower ranks. This means that decision-making work will be the responsibility of a group of managers, all of whom are focused on the customers' needs and expectations of the product or service that the organization renders.

This horizontal organization form seems well adapted to both small and large organizations as well as old and new companies. For example, Astra/Merck Group, a new stand-alone company set up to market antiulcer and high blood pressure drugs licensed from Sweden's Astra, is built around about a half dozen market-oriented processes instead of using a more traditional functional design. Modicon, Inc., a company that makes automation control equipment, sees product development as a process that involves a team of fifteen managers instead of seeing product development as an engineering function.

Eastman Chemical Company, a spin-off of Eastman Kodak Company, is built around self-directed work teams instead of the senior vice presidents who would otherwise be in charge. Kodak sees this as the most dramatic change in the seventy years that it has been in business. The company even sees its organization chart as an "organization pizza," with a lot of "pepperoni" sitting on it in place of the usual boxes and lines of the pyramidal design. American Telephone & Telegraph, DuPont, General Electric, Motorola, and Xerox have also employed the horizontal structure, to some degree at least.

Basically built on managing laterally rather than vertically, the horizontal structure is based on seven principles or concepts:

1. Organize around process, not task.
2. Flatten the hierarchy.
3. Use teams to manage everything.
4. Let customers drive performance.
5. Reward team performance.
6. Maximize supplier–customer contact.
7. Inform and train all employees.

It should be pointed out here, however, that companies have not yet abandoned the pyramid altogether. There still appears to be a need for specialists, especially in finance and in manufacturing as well. Even if the horizontal organization form is beginning to find its way into corporate organization structure forms, it will probably not completely replace the vertical, functional structure, at least in the foreseeable future. The firm that will finally evolve will probably be a hybrid one in which managers manage process and teamwork.

In any event, both theorists and practitioners are beginning to craft what will likely replace the "ancient pyramids" of organization design. For the student of organization theory, this is a move well worth watching.

> This introduction brings attention to a developing movement in the design of organizations that could revolutionize not only the way that structures are built, but the way of thinking and working in them. This chapter describes in more detail some of these developments with which today's student should be familiar. Keep these examples in mind as you study the chapter material, and see if they change the way you think about organizations and how they might be shaped to better suit their reason for existence—customer satisfaction.

PATTERNS OF STRATEGIC ORGANIZATIONAL DESIGN

In Chapter 2, we introduced the subjects of structure and design. The focus was primarily on structural differentiation and integration—that is, how finely or broadly to segment tasks and how to coordinate those same tasks. We discussed how structural characteristics tend to cluster into identifiable organizational prototypes: the mechanistic organization (machine bureaucracy) and the organic organization. In this chapter, our focus shifts to the related issue of design configuration—how tasks and people are grouped together in the organization. We examine specific organizational forms.

In our strategic systems approach to organizations, organizational design is part of the transformation process in the input-output analysis. Proper design should facilitate the acquisition and use of inputs, management of the transformation process (i.e., the technology), and disposal of outputs. In short, good design should lead to organizational efficiency and effectiveness. Although good design may not be sufficient to provide for efficiency and effectiveness, it is clearly a key factor.

Essentially, design involves strategic decisions about the grouping of individuals or tasks into work units, departments, or divisions of the organization. An organization faces a basic dilemma with regard to design. The very reason an organization exists is that people working together can accomplish more than people working individually. Synergy is achieved through specialization (differentiation) so that people become proficient in specific areas. That is how differentiation is reflected in the organization's design. But the more the organization differentiates, the more difficult it becomes to coordinate effort. In Chapter 2, we discussed integration mechanisms that can bring about some integration. The design of the organization can also play a critical role in integration. In making decisions about the appropriate design for an organization, top management seeks to find the configuration that permits the optimal mix of differentiation and integration while allowing the organization to adapt to its surroundings.

Like the world in which organizations are embedded, the tasks and decisions concerning appropriate designs are becoming complex. As we have noted repeatedly, the advent of inexpensive, high-speed computing and telecommunications technology has radically changed the world of organizations. Not only have these technologies made more information available cheaper and faster, they have, in effect, made the world smaller. These technologies have had dramatic impact on the emergence of new organizational designs that make use of the technologies as coordination mechanisms.

We begin by discussing bases for grouping work and designing organizations. These bases for grouping lead to two basic design configurations, the functional and product or market organizations, and to two combination design configurations, the hybrid and matrix organizations. We conclude by examining recent design trends brought about by the joint pressures of information technologies and globalization.

BASES FOR ORGANIZATION DESIGN

The essential question one asks when making decisions about grouping workers and forming departments or divisions is: Should workers be grouped together based on what they do (tasks and equipment) or based on the outcomes they hope to achieve (products, services, or markets)? There are specific advantages and disadvantages to both rules. Grouping workers together according to the nature of the work (tasks and equipment) is called *functional grouping,* while grouping according to outcomes is called *product or market grouping.* These two principles for grouping result in two fundamentally different designs.

FUNCTIONAL GROUPING

This common form of differentiation results in the classification of work done by the organization into the primary functional components that need to be carried out for the organization to operate. People are grouped together on the basis of the functions they perform and/or the equipment they use. Functions such as production, marketing, finance, accounting, personnel, or human resources management often serve as broad categories for differentiation.

The following examples show different ways in which functional grouping can be achieved. In a personnel or human resources division, positions could be further subdivided into units such as compensation, benefits, recruiting, and training. Each of these subfunctions requires specialized knowledge, skills, and information necessary to accomplish the personnel or human resources function. Workers in each subunit of the personnel or human resources department perform essentially the same or similar tasks using the same skills, knowledge, and equipment. Similarly, in a manufacturing setting, workers who use the same equipment or skills may be grouped together. For example, workers in an auto plant may be grouped into units such as assemblers, painting technicians, and welders. These groupings are based both on the functional skills the workers possess (e.g., knowledge of welding) and the equipment they use (e.g., welding equipment).

The general principle of functional grouping is that workers in each unit would be performing the same or similar tasks or activities, using the same equipment, or possessing the same sets of skills and knowledge. No single department bears full responsibility for the organization's outputs. Figure 8.1 illustrates a functional manufacturing organization.

◼ FIGURE 8.1

Differentiation on the Basis of Similarity of Work or Function

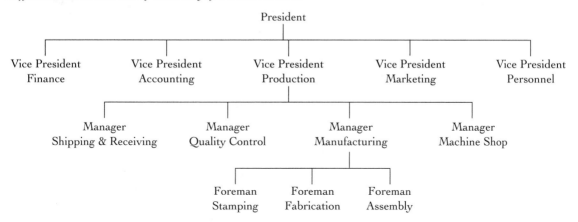

The functional organization has a characteristic set of strengths or advantages. First, by grouping people together based on functions, skills, or knowledge an organization is likely to develop a high degree of functional expertise, and individual department members will be able to develop highly refined functional skills. Moreover, communication within a functional department is facilitated by a common knowledge and language base. Functional areas often develop jargon that aids communication among experts but which may also keep outsiders in the dark. For example, in the personnel or human resources department mentioned above, the department would be able to enhance its collective human resources skills through the synergies of working together. Employees in the department could develop specific human resources expertise (e.g., compensation) while being exposed to the full range of human resources functions. This aspect of functional grouping is also important in career development. Newly hired employees can more easily develop functional skills and training. The career path from new human resources assistant to human resources vice president is clearly defined. Second, functional departments are more likely than other types of grouping to enhance economies of scale. By grouping together people who share information, skills, equipment, and facilities, the organization is able to carry out the function more efficiently. As we will see, combined forms of grouping, such as product and market, often necessitate redundant functions and facilities that reduce economies of scale. These two qualities, functional expertise and economies of scale, can lead to highly efficient departments with high levels of technical competence.

Certain weaknesses are also associated with the functional design and, as we see shortly, limit its usefulness to specific conditions. First among these weaknesses is the difficulty of coordinating across functional lines. All the factors that make communication within the functional areas easier — common tasks, knowledge, language, and training — are likely to inhibit communication between different functional departments. Cross-functional coordination is critical because the overall tasks and goals of the organization are rarely functional. Thus, a second weakness of the functional design is that it is likely to produce a functional view of the organization. A classic study of managers' perceptions of the organization suggested that managers viewed as most important the functions of their specific departments.[1] The problem is that organizational goals and objectives are rarely stated in terms of functions. For example, the goals of an automobile manufacturer are likely to be to produce and sell the best cars, not to have the best human resources department. Achievement of the company's goal requires extensive cross-functional coordination, which may be difficult when functional departments think narrowly in terms of functions.

Poor coordination and the narrow, functional view of the organization may lead to further difficulties in managing the organization. Because many of the problems and decisions the organization faces involve several different functional areas, decision making must be pushed up the organizational hierarchy to top management. This results in slower decision making. Information must wend its way up through each functional department to where managers have an overview of the organization. In addition to slowing decision making, this may overload top managers with trivial decisions. One final weakness of the functional form is that it is likely to inhibit innovation. New products, services, and processes typically require an integrative, cross-functional view of the organization especially when they must be developed quickly, as is usually the case these days. Functional grouping makes integrative, cross-functional thinking difficult.

These combined strengths and weaknesses limit the applicability of the functional organization. This design is best suited for small- or medium-sized organizations with a single product or a few closely related products. This helps functional departments focus on a common overall organizational goal. Because of the difficulties with decision making, functional organizations are best for low-uncertainty (stable and simple) environments. The problems with cross-functional coordination indicate that functional designs are best suited for organizations with low-interdependence, routine technologies.

Some of these limitations of functional organizations can be overcome through structural mechanisms described in Chapter 2. Cross-functional coordination can be attained through horizontal linking techniques such as liaison roles, integrator roles, and horizontal information systems. Cross-functional teams or task forces can also be used on an ad hoc basis to deal with cross-functional coordination. Heavy reliance on these means of coordination may signal the need to restructure the organization.

OUTPUT GROUPING: PRODUCTS, MARKETS, AND GEOGRAPHY

Grouping can also be based on outputs. Three types of output groupings are products (or services) produced, markets served, or geographical regions served.* Differentiation is based on output, and the resulting designs are characterized by departments or divisions dedicated to specific products, services, customer groups, or geographic regions of customers. Departments or divisions are essentially semiautonomous organizations with people and positions representing all functional areas. Figure 8.2 illustrates each of the three output-based designs.

---

*Geographical groupings could also be used in functional organizations, especially if the availability of specific skills or facilities were limited to specific locations. For example, inexpensive or skilled labor may be more readily available in an identifiable country or region. Thus, production facilities would be located in those regions. Rail lines or deep water ports may be necessary for the location of certain shipping facilities. Still, however, the primary rationale for grouping is function.

■ FIGURE 8.2
Output-Based Designs

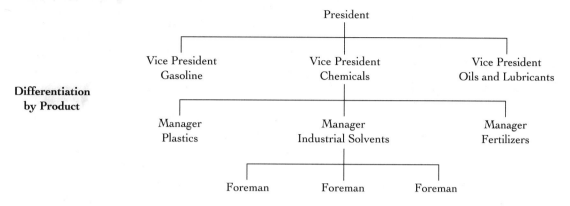

Differentiation by Product

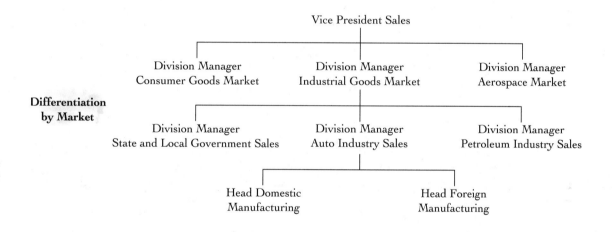

Differentiation by Market

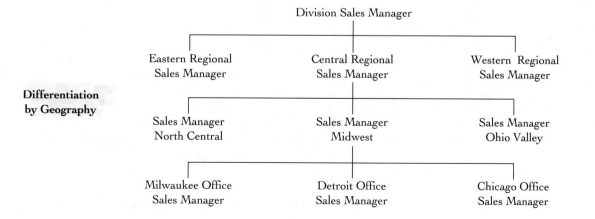

Differentiation by Geography

In large, multiproduct, geographically dispersed, multimarket organizations, grouping by output has become increasingly common. The classic example of product-based grouping was General Motors with its Chevrolet, Pontiac, Oldsmobile, Buick, Cadillac, and GMC Truck and Coach divisions. Each product group was essentially a self-contained division. Chevrolet, for example, had its own design, production, marketing, human resources, and accounting departments. Procter & Gamble, the consumer products giant, also used a product-based design for many years. Divisions included Tide, Crest, and Duncan-Hines. Many companies involved in defense contracting or other areas of government contracting have specific divisions assigned to different markets. Some computer hardware and software companies have specific federal government divisions. Johnson & Johnson is an example of an organization that uses both product and market differentiation simultaneously. Different divisions produce and sell baby products, over-the-counter medicines, surgical supplies, and other of the company's myriad products. These divisions, which are semiautonomous units, represent both different products and different groups of customers. Increasingly, as businesses become more global in their reach, they are adopting divisional designs based on geography. Ford Motor Company, which in the past was mainly a product design (Ford, Lincoln-Mercury, Ford Tractor, Ford Aerospace), is moving to a geographical design with North American, European, South American, and Asian divisions.

The primary advantage of these output-oriented designs is that they focus attention and effort on the specific requirements of the product and customers. The departments or divisions are multifunctional groups that work together, allowing business functions to more easily and effectively coordinate. Thus, they are a good match for non-routine, high-interdependence technologies. Because the design is more product- and customer-oriented, adaptability to new product designs, product requirements, new customer demands, or market conditions is easier than in a functionally designed organization with more than a single product, market, or region. Because these divisions are largely self-contained, decision making can be decentralized, relieving the burden on top management and aiding in responsiveness to changing environmental conditions. Thus, the design is particularly well suited for uncertain environments. These designs also provide a method for placing responsibility for efficiency and profitability at the divisional level. If a product, market, or region is underperforming, it is easier to identify and trace responsibility.

Although there are numerous advantages to the product, market, and geographical forms of output designs, there are also disadvantages. Although functional designs may create functionally biased views of the organization, output-based designs can create product, market, or geographic biases. This can, for example, lead to conflict between product groups. Some internal competition may be useful in forcing divisions to become more efficient; however, extensive competition may jeopardize the viability of the entire company. Additionally, dividing a company into many divisional units may reduce the potential for economies of scale. A product, market, or geographical organization typically must duplicate many functions and facilities to meet each division's needs. This lack of economies of scale can be reflected in such things as inefficient use of facilities and suboptimal use of human resources. Because each division may need marketing expertise, for example, it is likely that no single marketing department will grow large enough to develop the economies of scale and level of aggregate competence that a single marketing department for the entire organization would achieve. The organization must weigh the comparative advantages of specialization for a specific division versus the efficiencies offered through economies of scale.

A divisional design based on products, markets, or geography may also reduce the company's ability to share information and resources across divisions. We noted that cross-functional coordination is often a problem in functional organizations. Coordination across different products, markets, or regions can be problematic in the output-oriented organization. Some lack of sharing may be the result of internal competition, but much of it may be simply the result of ignorance and poor communications.

Some of these disadvantages are reflected in a number of recent restructurings. For example, GM and Procter & Gamble have altered their former product-based groupings to improve efficiency and cross-product coordination. We can see how problems associated with output-based designs can become dysfunctional by examining General Motors' operations in the early and mid-1980s. Because of a lack of coordination among different product divisions, in addition to loose controls at the top management level in corporate headquarters, GM suffered greatly in the marketplace as customers became disenchanted and confused by the various GM products.

Although the various car lines were targeted at different market segments, they were nearly indistinguishable in appearance. Yet, GM failed to achieve any economies of scale through shared functions or facilities. In many respects GM was in a worst-case situation. It operated with a product structure that was intended to yield distinctive products, but the products lacked uniqueness. At the same time, GM's efficiency suffered because of the duplication of functions and facilities. Chrysler and Ford were able to exploit GM's inefficiencies and the market's confusion about GM's offerings. As a result GM has been moving away from its traditional product-oriented design, a change that has been difficult and time consuming.

COMBINING FUNCTION AND OUTPUT: HYBRID AND MATRIX DESIGNS

A careful examination of most large organizations shows that some combination of functional grouping and output grouping is typically used. Outside of single-product organizations, it is increasingly uncommon to find strict functional designs. Similarly, divisionalized organizations using some form of output grouping are finding that it is often more efficient and effective to maintain some functional units to serve all divisions. Some organizations, particularly those in areas that demand both technical precision and responsiveness to market conditions, are finding that it is important to differentiate and integrate across *both* functional and output areas. The result is that many organizations are creating designs that incorporate elements of both functional groupings and output groupings. Two such prototypical designs are the hybrid design and the matrix design.

Hybrid Organizations. A careful examination of typical large, multiproduct organizations shows some combination of all the forms of groupings discussed thus far. Few organizations maintain strict output-oriented divisional designs without retaining some centralized functional areas. Figure 8.3 illustrates the ***hybrid organizational design,*** which combines both functional and output groupings (product, market, and/or geographical). The rationale for this mixed form of grouping is that certain functional areas

■ **FIGURE 8.3**
Hybrid Design

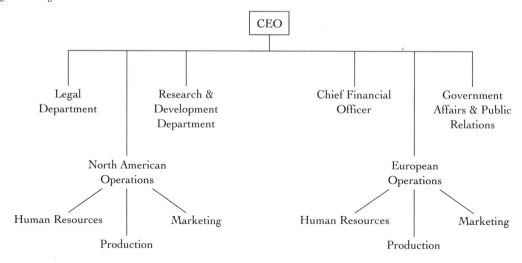

may not vary across the organization and/or may require a comparatively large size to operate efficiently. These areas are contained within functional departments. At the same time, it may be important for other areas of the organization to be tailored to meet specific product, market, or geographical requirements. Thus, the organization may want to create product, market, or regional divisions with self-contained production, marketing, and human resources activities. A critical question that the organization must face is which areas to maintain as functional units and which to assign to products, markets, or regions.

It is common, for example, for large organizations to maintain a single functional legal department to serve the legal needs of all divisions or departments of the organizations. This is because of the cost associated with maintaining a legal department — economies of scale can be achieved by a centralized functional legal department — and the opportunity to develop high levels of technical sophistication. It is also becoming increasingly important to maintain a functional information systems department that serves the entire company so that diverse and geographically scattered departments or divisions can be linked together. Otherwise, individual departments or divisions may adopt different hardware and software that cut them off from the rest of the organization. However, in an area such as information systems it is important that specific needs and requirements of departments and divisions be taken into consideration when adopting a company-wide standard. Failure to do so may mean that some parts of the organization are using equipment or techniques that are poorly suited to their tasks.

A large, hybrid, multiproduct, multimarket organization operating in widely dispersed regions will still be able to retain separate cross-functional divisions to deal with distinctive products, markets, or regions. This allows the organization to respond to the specific conditions in diverse environments and to utilize an array of technologies that have different design requirements.

In most respects, the hybrid design retains most advantages of both the functional design and the output design. The organization achieves economies of scale and expertise in functional areas while maintaining responsiveness to product, market, or regional differences in other areas. Thus, the hybrid is well suited to both environmental and technological uncertainty. Simultaneously, the presence of a core headquarters organization in the functions allows for greater coordination.

The most significant problem that hybrid organizations face is that the functional headquarters operation may become distant and detached from divisional units. There is a tendency for a lack of shared vision between divisions and functional units. Great care must be exercised to maintain links between the divisions and headquarters. Nonetheless, the hybrid is a highly desirable form with advantages that appear to outweigh the disadvantages for many large organizations.

Matrix Organizations. A design that became increasingly common in high tech organizations of the 1970s and 1980s is the ***matrix design.***[2] Figure 8.4 on pages 220–21 shows an array of matrix organizations. The essence of the matrix is the joint existence of functional (vertical or column) groupings and output (horizontal or row) groupings that overlap. The output groupings may be products, projects, or programs. The functional managers and product, project, or program managers are also referred to as ***matrix managers.*** Functional resources are allocated among the products, projects, or programs on the basis of need. Projects may go through a development cycle in which different areas' functional expertise is needed at different times. People with different functional skills can be moved from one project to another as each project progresses. Similarly, product managers may have varied functional needs based on things such as production cycles, product changes, or seasonal marketing campaigns. For example, a marketing expert assigned to a particular product group may be temporarily moved to another product as specific needs develop. Similar types of moves can be made across program groups. The allocation process points up one of the conditions to which matrix organizations are well suited. Matrix organizations work well when functional resources are in short supply.

The rationale behind the matrix design is that it is uniquely suited to respond to two sets of competing demands. First, the organization, through its project, product, or program managers, can be responsive to environmental conditions. Second, at the same time, the organization, through its functional managers, provides high levels of scarce functional expertise. In fact, it has been argued that, in order for the matrix design to work effectively, the organization must face nearly equal pressures for responsiveness to the environment (e.g., markets) and for functional precision or expertise. Without these nearly equal pressures to balance the power of the vertical and horizontal axes, one side will dominate and the organization will lose effectiveness. It is the responsibility of top management to maintain the balance and mediate among the horizontal and vertical matrix bosses.

A second key feature of the matrix design is that it violates a basic principle of management—unity of command. In typical designs each worker is responsible to one, and only one, boss. In a matrix design, a portion of the workforce called ***two-boss managers*** must be responsive to two bosses, a functional boss and a product, project, or program boss. This arrangement is often called a dual authority structure.[3] It is important to note that not everyone in the matrix organization has two bosses; it is only the two-boss manager who must deal with two bosses. It is the two-boss manager who must implement

FIGURE 8.4
Matrix Designs

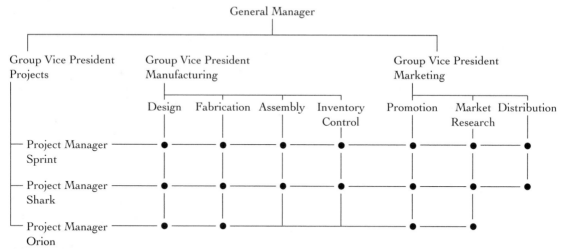

Project Matrix Structure

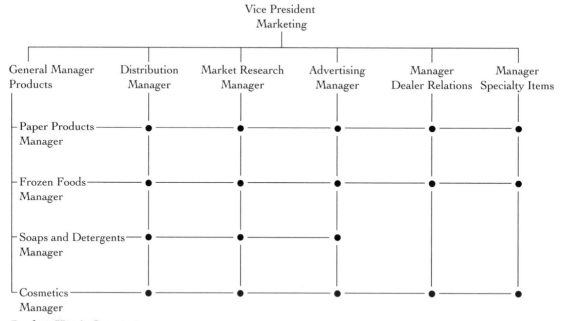

Product Matrix Structure

FIGURE 8.4
Matrix Designs (continued)

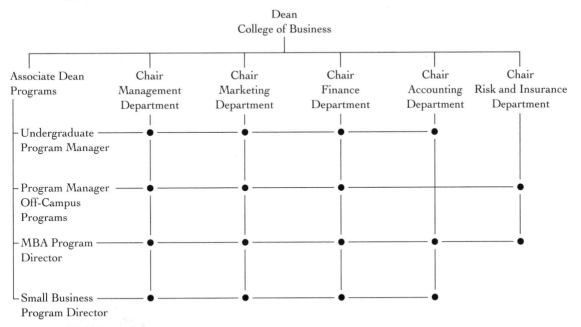

Program Matrix Structure

actions that take into consideration functional and output-oriented demands. It is also the two-boss manager who may suffer the stress over potentially conflicting demands placed upon him or her by the matrix bosses.

The chief advantage of the matrix organization is that it allows the proper technical advice, expertise, and other functional resources to be present at the proper location and at the desired time. The matrix design is flexible. Thus, the matrix may be appropriate when the external environment is complex and changing. It allows for changes in shifting emphasis on product, projects, or programs as needs or conditions dictate.

A second advantage is that the organization can be simultaneously responsive to the demands for functional expertise and precision and the demands of the marketplace for varied and specialized outputs. The combination of a functional focus and an output focus in the matrix permits greater coordination around specific problems or tasks. For this reason the matrix design tends to be well suited to tasks that are nonroutine and highly interdependent. That is why the design is often used in organizations that specialize in research and development or high tech areas.

Because of the competing functional and product, project, or program dimensions of the matrix, potential for conflict is inherent in the design, and that is a chief disadvantage. The dual functional and output-oriented pressures that must exist for a matrix to work also require extensive cooperation and the ability on the part of managers to handle conflict. The design requires that managers be skilled negotiators and be able to mediate between conflicting parties. Additionally, the matrix design places the two-boss manager at the nexus of these conflicting functional and output demands. The people who occupy these roles must be able to manage the stress of potentially conflicting role demands from two bosses. Moreover, because the two-boss managers may be periodically moved from projects, products, or programs, they must also be able to deal with the role stress and traumas that frequent relocation entails (e.g., breaking and forming work and friendship groups, forming new supervisor–subordinate relationships, and possibly even relocating one's family).

Finally, there exists a potential paradox in the matrix design. We noted that the design is particularly well suited to complex, changing environments. But the design *may* be problematic when swift responses are required. The potential for conflict, the need for frequent meetings, and the extensive negotiation and mediation required to manage functional and product demands are cornerstones of the matrix design and may slow responses to the environment. Thus, when rapid responses are of paramount importance, the matrix may not be the best design. However, when the speed of response must be balanced with a high-quality or high-precision response, a matrix may be appropriate.

ORGANIZATIONS FOR THE TWENTY-FIRST CENTURY: EVOLVING DESIGNS

The previous four designs are prototypes that organizations have modeled for many years. Recently, many organizational leaders and theorists have come to realize that the conditions facing organizations have changed dramatically. The chapters on environment and technology have already alluded to these changing conditions. Three related sets of changes are presenting managers and theorists with new challenges in designing organizations. First, inexpensive, fast, and pervasive computer and telecommunications technology (information technology) has dramatically changed the way people work. These technological changes have made information more readily available to more people. They have permitted extensive automation and, in some areas, reduced the direct human component in tasks. Moreover, these technologies have made communication easier. Information technologies are directly involved in the other two areas of change: task technology and globalization. Information technologies have been important factors in many of the advanced manufacturing techniques, such as flexible manufacturing, customization, and just-in-time inventory and production. Finally, the advent of advanced information technologies has made the world marketplace more accessible to more organizations. These conditions both require and allow organizations to adopt new design configurations.

Before describing these contemporary designs, a note of caution is in order. A visit to any substantial bookstore will disclose an extensive collection of books (not including conventional textbooks) that deals with issues related to organization design. There is no shortage of writers suggesting new twists on design. There is, however, considerable overlap in what most of these authors propose. On the one hand, that consistency is comforting—it suggests that there is some order to the universe of organizations. On the other hand, many of these authors use different labels to identify their new design configurations. Thus, the reader should be aware that several different terms are used to describe the same or similar organizational forms.

THE VIRTUAL ORGANIZATION

The label that has won widespread use in both the popular and academic literature is the ***virtual organization.***[4] At the heart of the virtual organization is a core organization that carries out some critical functions to which the organization is particularly well suited. Functions outside this core area of competence may be performed by temporary or contract workers, or farmed out to other organizations with which the core organization has formed alliances or affiliations. The core organization maintains these relationships only as long as they are productive and beneficial. In many respects the virtual organization is an extension of the interorganizational external control strategies discussed in Chapter 5. Two other terms used to describe similar designs are *shamrock*[5] and *network organizations.*[6]

A good example of a virtual organization is Nike, the athletic footware and apparel marketer.[7] Nike's core competencies are product development, marketing and distribution. In its history, the company has done very little manufacturing of its products. Those products can be produced more efficiently through a vast set of supplier companies throughout Asia and elsewhere that specialize in shoe or apparel manufacturing. This arrangement allows Nike to avoid much of the capital cost of investing in production facilities while at the same time giving the company flexibility. Should a particular type of product lose favor in the marketplace, Nike can move out of its alliance with the producer. Such a move would avoid the costs of either selling or retooling a manufacturing facility that Nike owned. The major advantage is that Nike can concentrate on the things it does best: designing, marketing, and distributing its products. Nike has mastered the art of selling its products through prominent personalities such as Michael Jordan, Charles Barkley, and Bo Jackson.

The downside to the virtual organization is that the core organization has less control than in a conventional organization. It may be difficult to monitor and control supplier companies and contract or temporary employees outside the core than it would if these functions were carried on inside the organization's boundaries by regular employees. An organization must balance its needs for control with needs for specialization and flexibility. Another criticism of the virtual organization is of a broader nature. Some critics have claimed that these new organizations are, in effect, hollow organizations.[8] These organizations concentrate their efforts on high-skill technical and professional work. Productive labor often takes place elsewhere, typically in the developing economies of other nations. The fear is that organizations (and nations) that do not actually produce things will lose their economic clout and skills to producer companies (and nations).

Even short of these competitiveness issues, there are other social and economic concerns.[9] First, the core work of the virtual organization requires increasingly higher levels of education. Some critics question whether current educational systems are capable of producing the requisite education levels among the pool of employees. Second, the entire nature of jobs will change. Because the virtual organization requires a cadre of temporary and part-time workers, future workers will move between more jobs and often hold several jobs simultaneously. Third, there is fear that the organizational stratification of workers into core and others will result in further economic stratification of society. All these issues are critical and will need to be answered as the virtual organization gains increasingly wide use in the workplace.

THE FEDERAL ORGANIZATION

A second design that has become widely used in various forms is what Charles Handy has labeled the *federal organization.*[10] This design is, in many respects, an extension of the product-based divisional design. It is characterized by a small central organization that provides overall leadership and planning and a number of loosely affiliated subsidiaries. Although the central organization provides tight financial controls over the subsidiaries, the subsidiaries maintain extensive freedom and flexibility in the general conduct of business.

Johnson & Johnson provides a good example of the federal design.[11] Johnson & Johnson is well known to consumers for Band-Aid brand products and Johnson's baby products, all produced by the Johnson & Johnson Consumer Products division. Other divisions include McNeil Consumer Products, maker of Tylenol; Ethicon surgical products; and Ortho Pharmaceutical, a prescription drug company. In fact, Johnson & Johnson is made up of 166 separately operating units that are, in most respects, independent companies. Interestingly, although the notion of a federal organization may be new to the organization theory lexicon, Johnson & Johnson's founder Robert Wood Johnson created an organization of small, decentralized units in the 1930s because he believed that this design would promote accountability and market responsiveness.[12] Those same ideals are still central to the federal design. Johnson & Johnson's success with the federal design is mirrored by General Electric, Formosa Plastics, and the Swedish-Swiss conglomerate ABB Asea Brown Boveri.

Two distinctly Asian versions of the federal organization are the Japanese *keiretsu* and the Korean *chaebol.* Although the nature of each of these designs and of firm ownership is different, the *keiretsu* and the *chaebol* are similar in that they involve large numbers of affiliated organizations that are rather loosely tied together through cross ownership.

Keiretsu. The *keiretsu* are major families or groups of independent organizations that have been the key to Japan's post–World War II redevelopment and economic success.[13] Prior to World War II, Japan's economic and political system was dominated by the *zaibatsu.* The *zaibatsu* were extremely powerful family-centered holding companies. A small number of large *zaibatsu* dominated the Japanese economy. Equally as important, the *zaibatsu's* power extended beyond business to government and politics. Many *zaibatsu* leaders played leading roles in government. Some critics argue that the *zaibatsu's* drive for market expansion and domination was a key factor in Japan's imperialistic tendencies leading up to World War II. At the conclusion of World War II, the United States occupation forces in Japan broke up the *zaibatsu,* but some of the former *zaibatsu* companies regained some economic clout as the industrial groupings we now know as *keiretsu.*

At the core of the *keiretsu* are major banks and trading companies. These core companies act very much like holding companies do in the United States. The member companies are independent entities tied together through cross holding of shares, overlapping boards of directors, and formal or informal agreements. The largest *keiretsu* — the Big Six — are, in order of size, Mitsubishi, Mitsui, Sumitomo, Fuyo, Dai-Ichi Kangyo Bank (DKB), and Sanwa.

Each of these six groups of firms has larger revenues than either General Motors or Exxon.[14] Figure 8.5 depicts the member companies of the Mitsui group.

FIGURE 8.5
The Mitsui Group

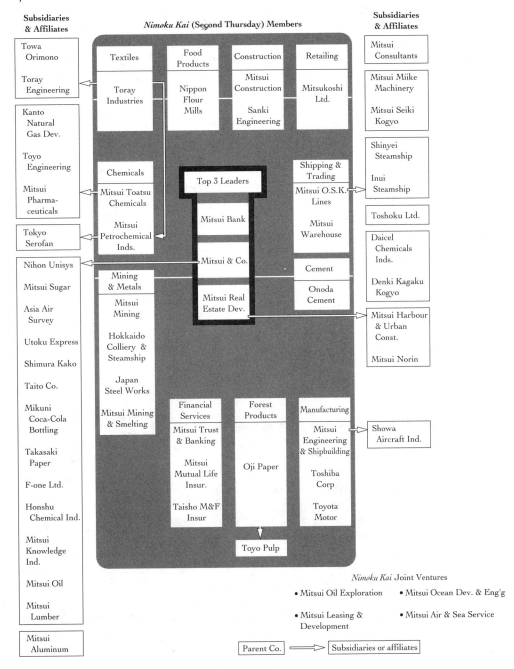

Source: Adapted from Max Eli, *Japan Inc.* (Chicago: Probus Publishing & Company, 1991), 25.

In addition to the formal ties that bind member companies together, top executives of the affiliated companies often interact extensively in social and business settings. For example, Mitsubishi, the largest *keiretsu*, grew out of a post–World War II organization known as *Kinyo Kai*, or Friday Conference. *Kinyo Kai* developed as a forum to discuss the post-war reindustrialization of Japan. Today, the conference is a mechanism for the presidents of most important member companies to discuss policy issues that affect the *keiretsu*.[15] Thus, the core companies may even play a role in strategy development for member firms.

The value of the *keiretsu* to member firms is that they work together cooperatively to ensure each other's viability and competitiveness. For example, Toyota is a member of two *keiretsu* that also include a wide array of supplier companies critical to its just-in-time production and inventory control systems; banks that supply debt to finance operations; advertising firms that market Toyota products; and shipping companies that transport Toyotas. Toyota has an ownership stake in many of these companies, and these companies often have small ownership stakes in Toyota. Joint ownership holdings provide a basis for cooperation among these companies. Regardless of ownership, however, managers realize that it is in everyone's best interest to work together. When Toyota, for example, requests a design change in certain electronic components, the supplier knows that creating better parts in a timely fashion at a competitive cost and with extremely high quality will improve not only Toyota, but also the supplier firm.

The *keiretsu* is not a perfect solution or the only solution to interfirm coordination. Sony, for example, is essentially independent of the *keiretsu* system. Moreover, recent economic uncertainty in Japan has caused some problems for the tightly linked *keiretsu* companies.[16] The tight links between suppliers and manufacturers may prove to be inefficient and too rigid during times that call for flexibility and cost cutting. Nonetheless, the *keiretsu* have provided tremendous clout to the Japanese economy.

Chaebol. The Korean **chaebol**, formed with the cooperation and support of government, are largely family-based collections of businesses. The collection of companies is typically large and diverse. Cross ownership and longstanding family ties are at the core of the chaebol.[17] Its basis in family ownership is similar to the *zaibatsu* in Japan. However, in Japan the pre–World War II *zaibatsu* played a controlling role in government. The role is reversed for the *chaebol*. Its continued operation depends on government support and acceptance.

The *chaebol* system is characterized by six distinctive features.

1. *Family controlled and managed:* Large number of leaders of divisions and subsidiaries are family members.
2. *Paternalistic leadership:* One central leader with near-absolute authority; separation between CEO and the lower divisions of the organization; a father-like figure; concern for welfare of employees.
3. *Centralized planning and control:* Centralized oversight of the diverse holdings; centralized decision making.
4. *Entrepreneurial orientation:* High value placed on ambition, clear vision, and political skills.

5. *Close ties with government:* Success dependent on cultivating strong links to people with political power; extensive government financial support; many former government workers employed to help manage relationships with government; government leads and business follows.

6. *Strong ties to schools:* Going to the "right" school (both high school and college) is important to success.

The four largest *chaebol* are well-recognized names in the world marketplace: Samsung, Hyundai, Lucky-Goldstar, and Daewoo.[18] Although the names may be familiar to consumers, the wide diversity of products and companies affiliated with each company may not be apparent. The diverse companies that make up the Samsung *chaebol* produce food products, aircraft engine parts, computer chips, consumer electronics, and many other products and services. Table 8.1 lists the five largest *chaebol* and their array of products. Table 8.2 lists the companies that are part of the Samsung *chaebol*.

■ **TABLE 8.1**

Five Largest South Korean Chaebol*

Company	Products
Samsung	Electronics, semiconductors, aerospace, food products, insurance, advertising, shipping, and trading
Hyundai	Construction services, automobiles, shipbuilding, electronics, heavy equipment, railroad locomotives, semiconductors, shipping, insurance, and advertising
Lucky-Goldstar	Electronics, semiconductors, telecommunications, oil, chemicals, trading, insurance, and advertising
Daewoo	Automobiles and auto parts, electronics, shipbuilding, machinery, financial services
Sunkyong	Oil refining, chemicals, synthetics

*From Laxmi Nakarmi and Robert Neff, "Korea's Powerhouses Under Siege," *Business Week* (November 20, 1989): 52.

The large-sized *chaebol* accounted for over 60 percent of Korea's GNP in the 1980s, and links with government have made the *chaebol* companies potent economic and political forces. The companies were able to manage competition, avoid organized labor, and obtain favorable government treatment because of the government's desire to foster economic growth. Although some of the *chaebol's* power has eroded in the 1990s, these companies still represent powerful forces in the world marketplace.[19]

These brief descriptions of the *keiretsu* and the *chaebol* give a glimpse of these Asian organizational forms. Although they are similar, important differences distinguish the two. The *keiretsu* firms are more loosely tied together than those in the *chaebol*. Control is more centralized in the Korean *chaebol* than in the Japanese *keiretsu*. *Keiretsu* managers are more likely to have more extensive professional training and credentials. We also noted the important role the government plays in the *chaebol*. In Japan, the *keiretsu* and the government interact more as political peers.[20]

■ TABLE 8.2

The Samsung Chaebol: Principal Business Areas and Descriptions *

Company	Description
Trading Co.	
Samsung Co. Ltd.	Import-Export, natural resources
Electronics	
Samsung Electronics Co., Ltd.	TVs, VCRs, audio equipment, appliances
Samsung Electronic Devices Co., Ltd.	Picture tubes, CRTs, monitors
Samsung Electro-Mechanics	VHF and UHF tuners, ceramics
Samsung Corning Co., Ltd.	TV glass products
Samsung Semiconductors Co., Ltd.	Semiconductors, computers
Samsung Telecommunications Co., Ltd.	Fiber optics, fax machines
Heavy Industry & Chemicals	
Samsung Shipbuilding & Heavy Industries	Shipbuilding, structural steel, marine structures, industrial machines
Samsung Petrochemicals Co., Ltd.	Chemicals
Samsung Construction Co., Ltd.	Civil construction, large-scale projects
Korea Engineering Co., Ltd.	Plant engineering
Chonju Paper Manufacturing Co., Ltd.	Paper and pulp products
Precision Instruments	
Samsung Aerospace Industries, Ltd.	Jet engines, cameras, optical equipment, robotics, computers, control systems

*Based on R. Steers, Yoo Keun Shin, and Gerardo R. Ungson, *The Chaebol: Korea's New Industrial Might* (New York: Harper & Row, 1989).

There is much more of importance about both forms that is beyond the scope of this text. The purpose here is only to show that both are variations on the federal form of organization. Both involve collections of semiautonomous organizations that work together for extraordinary market and political power, and both are products of the national cultures in which they are imbedded.

CHARACTERISTICS OF EFFECTIVE STRUCTURES

Up to now, this chapter has described various ways of grouping work in organizations to create specific design configurations. What we have not yet addressed, however, are the characteristics of an effective design.

We must point out at the outset that ***there is no one right design*** that is best for all organizations.[21] There are designs that are more appropriate for a particular organization, given the circumstances it faces. A federal design may work for Johnson & Johnson, but it may prove disastrous for a firm that seeks synergies from its diverse product groups. Major determinants of the most appropriate designs are the environmental conditions the firm faces, the technology (or technologies) that the firm uses, the firm's strategic goals or objectives, its size and point in the organizational life cycle, and finally its culture — an area we will explore in Chapter 10.

Regardless of these circumstances, all organization designs should have certain characteristics if they are to be effective. These are efficient operation, encouragement of innovation, flexibility and adaptiveness, facilitation of individual performance and development, facilitation of coordination and communication, and facilitation of strategy formulation, implementation, and achievement.

EFFICIENCY

An organization's design should encourage the efficient pursuit of the organization's goals. Efficiency, *doing things right*, is a critical factor for the survival and success of an organization, and the appropriateness of the organization's design is among the key factors.[22] One need only look at struggling organizations of the late 1980s and early 1990s such as IBM, Kmart, and General Motors. In each case, among the first actions these companies took to restore efficient operation was to implement a new design. It is not only struggling firms that modify their designs to enhance efficiency. Many firms change design configurations to eliminate duplication, improve responsiveness, and achieve economies of scale. Efficient design should provide a skeleton or network of task differentiation and integration for the allocation and utilization of an organization's resources.

INNOVATION

Even organizations in static, simple environments need innovation — the ability to generate more effective and efficient ways of operating and new products or services to offer. Design should encourage innovation by providing the pooling of resources and the necessary communication for innovation to take place. This important concept is discussed further in Chapter 13.

Campbell's Soup had an image as a stodgy, old-fashioned company. Its performance into the mid-1980s was lackluster. The company had grown slow and inefficient. Change was clearly needed if the company was to remain viable and competitive into the twenty-first century. The company instituted a number of operational and technological changes to improve the efficiency of its operation. However, to implement these changes, it was also necessary to reconfigure the company into a combined geographic and product-oriented design. Organizing in this manner facilitated the communication necessary to coordinate new technologies.[23]

Organizations facing dynamic, complex environments require even more innovation if the organization is to stay in tune with and respond to its environment. Design should thus facilitate scanning of the environment, boundary spanning, and innovation. In these environments, designs that keep the organization in close contact with elements of the environment are critical to survival. Links between the environment and top decision makers who formulate and implement strategy are critical.

FLEXIBILITY AND ADAPTIVENESS

All organizations need to be flexible and adaptive. Fewer and fewer industrial environments can be characterized as stable and simple. As noted above, the ability to change and respond to new environmental conditions is critical to survival. It is not only necessary to innovate in areas of operations and products or services, but the organization itself, as the Campbell's example suggests, must also be in a position to change itself and respond. An effective design must balance the needs for consistency and predictability with the needs for flexibility and responsiveness.

Designs can facilitate flexibility and adaptiveness in two ways. First, the design and supporting structure can act as a conduit to transmit information from boundary spanners and environmental scanners to top decision makers, allowing management to formulate and implement new strategies, including redesigning the organization. Second, the design itself can create units, departments, or divisions close to the environment that can respond. For example, in matrix organizations resources can be moved around as needed in response to changing conditions. This can happen without much involvement of top management.

FACILITATION OF INDIVIDUAL PERFORMANCE AND DEVELOPMENT

Probably the most common complaint about organizational designs made by organization members is that, instead of facilitating performance, they often block effective performance and stifle the individual.

While many of these complaints are directed at bureaucratic structures, the design configuration may also be a problem. Functional designs may pigeonhole people into narrowly defined functional tasks. Some functional departments, such as human resources or information systems, may, in some firms, be the organizational backwaters far from the action because these functions are not directly involved in producing output. People in these departments may become alienated. More recently, progressive organizations are realizing the importance of these support services. On the other hand, output-oriented and federal designs may hinder personnel movement among divisions, which may stifle advancement within the organization.

Whatever the design, it should offer the individual the opportunity to perform at his or her highest level of ability in areas of interest and competence. The design should encourage employees to grow on the job by learning new skills and accepting increasing responsibilities as they become more experienced. The design should provide a clear career path or ladder of organization jobs or positions and a system whereby employees can get necessary training to qualify them for higher level jobs.

FACILITATION OF COORDINATION AND COMMUNICATION

At the core of structuring and designing organizations is the effective execution of tasks. Leaders should differentiate tasks, group employees together, and then integrate that work so that the work of the organization can be conducted in a nearly smooth and seamless manner. Key to that smooth and seamless operation is the design configuration that management selects. Managers must ask several questions. Should work be organized around functional expertise, outputs, or both? How big do units need to be to achieve economies of scale? How much do units, divisions, or departments need to interact? The appropriate design will then facilitate coordination and communication where it is most needed. It is important to note, however, that merely picking a design that fits is not enough. In Chapter 2, we discussed a number of structural and nonstructural mechanisms that play important roles in integration. These must be present along with the appropriate design if coordination and communication are to be achieved.

FACILITATION OF STRATEGY FORMULATION AND IMPLEMENTATION

The relationship between strategy and structure, or design, has been the focus of extensive investigation in the organizational literature. It should be clear by now that structure and design are both key factors in the development of strategies and are key outcomes of the strategy formulation process. As we noted earlier, the design and structure of the organization are key to the scanning of environments by boundary spanners and the transmission of information to top management. This information is fundamental in the formulation of strategy. Whether these units are functional or otherwise may depend on a multitude of factors, but it is critical that the appropriate information be transmitted to top management.

The organization, as we noted previously, may be strategically redesigned as a result of the information transmitted to top management. Organizations may move from functional groupings to some other design configuration as they grow and develop new products or services. Matrix designs may be adopted as organizations face increasing pressure for quality and responsiveness to customer demands. Federal or virtual organizations may alter their collection of affiliations as they enter new or exit old markets. The point is that strategy and design are tightly linked. As organizations adopt new strategies, they may need to modify their designs. Different design configurations may make available different information and resources that may result in shifting strategies. Designs may again need to be realigned with strategy.

SUMMARY

The basis for designing an organization is the grouping of workers into departments, work units, or divisions. At its simplest level, two different approaches can be used for grouping: by function (i.e., peoples' tasks, knowledge, skills, training, or equipment) or output (i.e., products, services, markets, or geographic regions). These two approaches to grouping lead to basic design configurations: functional and output oriented (i.e., product, market, or geographic).

The two basic design configurations can also be combined to form two additional designs. The hybrid design allows the organization to retain some functional departments serving the entire organization while creating output-oriented departments or divisions for most areas of the organization. The matrix simultaneously uses both functional and output groupings to create an organization with dual lines of authority and responsibility. The matrix creates some unique conditions and problems for organizations. Matrix bosses must head the functional and output dimensions of the design, and two-boss managers must balance the demands of both sets of matrix bosses. This configuration violates one of the basic principles of organizations—unity of command.

The virtual organization and the federal organization are two contemporary variations on organizational design made possible by telecommunications and computer technologies. The loose network of cooperating organizational units in the virtual organization create unprecedented flexibility and adaptiveness. The federal organization is, in many respects, an elaboration of the product-based, output-oriented organization. The federal organization, with its diverse collection of affiliated, semiautonomous organizations, allows large organizations to act as small ones. As was the case with the virtual organization, the federal design is well suited to a complex, changing environment.

The *keiretsu* and the *chaebol* represent two Asian variations on the federal organization. Although there are some similarities between these two forms—large sets of cooperating and interacting firms—they are as distinctively different as the two countries in which they are found. The *keiretsu* is characterized by cross ownership among numbers of cooperating, but independent, firms. The *chaebol* is a collection of diverse companies with some common family ownership ties and a strong, centralized leadership.

Finally, we examined the design-effectiveness relationship. The key points are that (1) no one design is best for all organizations and (2) the appropriate design depends on the conditions the organization faces. The most appropriate design allows the organization to pursue its goals in an effective and efficient manner. This, of course, assumes that the organization's goals are appropriate!

Questions for Discussion

1. How has the technological "explosion" affected organizational design?
2. One common form of differentiation results in what is termed *functional grouping.* Name and describe a corporation that has such an organization design. What do you see as the cause(s) or reasons for employing this type of design?
3. Describe and show possible uses for the three types of output groupings.
4. Under what conditions would a hybrid design work best? Explain.
5. Under what conditions would a matrix design work best? What basic principle of management does the matrix design violate? Explain. Does this present problems or unusual challenges in managing a matrix organization?
6. Describe the virtual organization design. Is this a new concept in design or a new label for an old one? Explain.
7. How can you explain the use of the Japanese *keiretsu* and the Korean *chaebol?* Would they work in the United States? Explain.
8. How can you tell if a company has a good organization design?

CASE: NOW YOU SEE IT, NOW YOU DON'T

As if by magic, U.S. corporations are changing their organization designs. In place of the traditional, vertical hierarchies, companies across the spectrum of U.S. industry are setting up loosely knit arrangements that are being called the virtual corporation.

These new patterns are basically joint ventures and strategic alliances that are brought together to accomplish a specific purpose and then are disbanded or are altered by the addition and/or deletion of new "partners." These temporary networks are an organizational response to the rapidly changing economic and political landscape facing today's companies. Add to this dynamic scene the rush to globalization, and the stage is set for the disappearance of the permanent and vertical design, according to forward-thinking theorists and practitioners alike.

The new arrangement blurs formal organization lines to the point where it is often difficult to see where one organization ends and another begins. The individual organizations are held together by information technology that is evident in the advent of the information superhighway and, perhaps above that, trust in the skills and abilities of partner organizations in the alliance.

The basic purpose of the concept of the virtual corporation is the pooling of core technologies (or core competencies) in order to capitalize on rapidly closing windows of opportunity in the marketplace. It is no longer feasible, the argument goes, for the traditional organizational hierarchy to own all the means of designing, manufacturing, and marketing products that are demanded by consumers who have what might be called fickle tastes. Product life cycles are shortening. This means that companies must work not only faster but more efficiently to meet this demand.

The virtual organization requires new thinking by managers. It was once fashionable to believe that, in order to produce a quality output, one company must have complete control over the entire required production-marketing processes. A company had to have its own capability to conceive, produce, and market its product or service if it was to ensure success. But now there are simply too many marketplace changes to allow this type of thinking.

Enter the virtual organization, made possible by information technology and a new kind of management thinking about the permanence of organization designs. This combination is already being employed in a variety of companies. As one might expect, companies in the information world are among the leaders in using the virtual organization. For example, AT&T has used Japan's Marubeni Trading Company to hook up with Matsushita Electric Industrial Company to quicken the production of the Safari notebook computer that was designed by Henry Dreyfuss Associates—a melding of needed core technologies of companies on a global scale.

The ability to get products out faster has been the key reason that Corning, Inc. has taken the lead in virtual arrangements. Approximately 19 percent of its 1992 earnings came from its nineteen partnerships. Fast-changing technologies are the principal reason for these arrangements, according to Chairman James R. Houghton. He says it is time for the vast majority of U.S. corporations to wake up before they are overrun by companies using the virtual, loose-knit organizational arrangements.

Apple Computers has also already made good use of the virtual corporation concept. Its alliance with Sony has enabled the company to produce its line of Powerbook

notebook computers. It has been a marriage of Apple's software with Sony's manufacturing skills.

Flexible teams of workers linked together by computer networks are able to work concurrently rather than in sequence—and they can do this at different locations, even worldwide. This workplace setup can allow companies to abandon inefficient production processes that they do not do well and outsource them to their partners for the production function. Other partners can perform the design function; others the engineering work; and still others can carry out most, if not all, of the marketing work, all from different locations.

As you can see, the virtual corporation allows companies to shed inefficient or unprofitable arms of the organization by outsourcing them and concentrating on what might be their core competence—product design, say. So competitive advantage can be gained by the symbiotic combination of skills and advantages of the members of the virtual corporation.

The virtual corporation is not without its drawbacks, however. Along with the advantages of temporary combinations of core technologies, comes the inevitable loss of control. A bond of trust must exist among the members of the alliance, and a new or sharply redefined focus on coordination by managers at all levels is a must. These requirements represent a drastic departure for most of today's managers who have spent their careers in the vertical, permanent organization of contemporary companies. The more partners that come into the virtual corporation, the greater is the possibility for error and lack of coordination.

So even though the future of the virtual corporation looks bright (some even say it is inevitable), there will perhaps always be the need for some remnants of the old organization design. And all of this bodes a drastic change for companies—from the type of organization design, to the type of equipment, to the type of space, and especially for the type of personnel needed.

The skills of Mandrake or David Copperfield might be required to make the virtual organization a reality.

QUESTIONS FOR DISCUSSION

1. What changes in the general environment for most organizations make the creation of virtual organizations both possible and desirable?
2. What are the key features and benefits of a virtual organization?
3. What might be some typical problems resulting from the design that various partners or units face in a virtual organization?
4. Under what types of conditions would a virtual organization be undesirable?
5. Is the virtual organization just another management fad, or do you think this design represents real change and real value to the linked organizations?

REFERENCES

1. D. C. Dearborn and H. A. Simon, "Selective Perception: A Note on the Departmental Identification of Executives," *Sociometry* 21 (1958): 140–44.

M. J. Wallen, G. R. Huber, and W. H. Glick, "Functional Background as a Determinant of Executives Selective Perception," *Academy of Management Journal* 38 (1995): 943–74.

2. Jay Galbraith, "Designing Matrix Organizations," *Business Horizons* (February 1971): 29–40.

   Stanley M. Davis and Paul R. Lawrence, *Matrix* (Reading, Mass.: Addison-Wesley, 1977).

3. Richard L. Daft, *Organization Theory and Design*, 4th ed. (St. Paul, Minn.: West Publishing, 1992).

4. William H. Davidow and Michael S. Malone, *The Virtual Corporation: Structuring and Revitalizing the Corporation for the 21st Century* (New York: Harper-Collins, 1992).

   W. Bridges, "The End of the Job," *Fortune* 130 (September 9, 1994): 62–74.

   Paula Dwyer, "Tearing Up Today's Organizational Chart," *Business Week* (November 18, 1974): 80–90.

5. Charles Handy, *The Age of Unreason* (Boston: Harvard Business School Press, 1989).

6. Jay R. Galbraith and Robert K. Kazanjian, "Strategy, Technology, and Emerging Organizational Forms," in *Futures of Organizations,* ed. by Jerald Hage (Lexington, Mass.: Lexington Books, 1988).

   David Limerick and Bert Cunnington, *Managing the New Organization: A Blueprint for Networks and Strategic Alliances* (San Francisco: Jossey-Bass, 1993).

7. Donald Katz, *Just Do It!* (New York: Random House, 1994).

8. See note 7 above. See note 5 above.

9. See note 5 above.

10. See note 5 above.

11. Joseph Weber, "A Big Company That Works," *Business Week* (May 4, 1992): 124–32.

12. See note 11 above.

13. Max Eli, *Japan Inc.: Global Strategies of Japanese Trading Corporations* (Chicago: Probus Publishing, 1991).

14. See note 13 above.

15. See note 13 above.

16. T. Arakawa, "Keiretsu Walls Cracking as Auto Industry Feels the Squeeze," *Tokyo Business Today* 61, no. 4 (April 1993): 14–15.

17. Benjamin Gomes-Casseres, "State and Markets in Korea," Harvard Business School (Boston: President and Fellows of Harvard College, case 9-387-181, 1987).

Richard Steers, Yoo Keun Shin, and Gerardo R. Ungson, *The Chaebol: Korea's New Industrial Might* (New York: Harper & Row, 1989).

18. Laxmi Nakarmi and Robert Neff, "Korea's Powerhouses Are Under Siege," *Business Week* (November 20, 1989): 52–55.

19. See note 18 above.

20. See R. Steers, Yoo Keun Shin, and G. R. Ungson in note 17 above.

21. Y. K. Shetty and Howard M. Carlisle, "A Contingency Model of Organization Design," *California Management Review* 15 (Fall 1972): 38–45.

22. J. Pfeffer and G. Salancik, *The External Control of Organizations* (New York: Harper & Row, 1978).

23. B. Saporito, "Campbell Soup Gets Piping Hot," *Fortune* 124 (September 9, 1991): 142–48.

CHAPTER 9

Organizational Governance and Control

CASE: FIRE UP THE GRILL*

The backyard barbecue is almost as American as apple pie. The image of a barbecue has been one of messy charcoal grills, noxious smoke, and, of course, the dreaded cleanup afterward. But the Thermos Company is attempting to change all that.

Long known for its Thermos vaccuum bottle that keeps liquids either hot or cold (how does it know which it should do?), the company is also becoming a major player in the cookout grill business. Until recently, a competitor to such well-known brands as Sunbeam, CharBroil, and Weber, Thermos had seen its annual $225 million annual sales volume as "medium rare" in a one-billion-a-year market. Clearly, a new product was needed if Thermos was to "relight" its business.

To do this, CEO Monte Peterson decided to change the traditional organization structure with its concentration on product to a teamwork pattern based on the consumer. Peterson believes that the market is experiencing a consumer revolution not unlike that which faced Henry Ford. An enlightened consumer simply is not seduced by slick packaging and glitzy ad campaigns. Instead, if a company is to sell its product successfully, it simply must build and market one that is sharply focused on what the consumer wants, not on one that is the most cost-effective or is best engineered from the manufacturer's point of view.

Peterson believes that innovation based on consumer needs is the key to winning in this new marketplace. And so he put together a different kind of organization to bring out Thermos's Thermal Electric Grill, which he hopes will capture some 20 percent of the market in the next few years. This product development team had the unreserved commitment from top management and followed a strict deadline schedule, keys to success in the product development field.

Eric Olson of the University of Colorado's College of Business cautions, however, that product teams are not necessarily the answer to all development ventures. He found in his

*This case is based on the following article: Brian Dumaine, "Payoff from the New Management," *Fortune* (December 13, 1993): 103–104, 108, 110.

research of forty-five projects at twelve or so *Fortune* 500 companies that teamwork was not best for product modification (like new handles or shapes). The forming of teams for these types of modifications simply proved too cumbersome and took too much time to assemble. The result was that competitors often were in the market perhaps even before teams could even be put together. But product modification was not what Thermos needed; it needed a brand new grill. So Peterson set out to build his "clan" organization.

The "Lifestyle" team, as it was called, was made up of six Thermos middle managers from functional fields such as engineering, finance, manufacturing, and marketing. But it was not to be a function-based group. It was to design a totally new grill that was to be just what the "customer ordered." The team was assigned the task of actually going into the field to find precisely what people looked for in their grills and to develop a product that met those needs.

To complete the "Lifestyle" team, Thermos enlisted outside help from suppliers and consultants. In this connection, Fitch, Inc., an industrial design firm, provided ten members to help in the design of the new electric grill. It is important to know that this group began with no assumptions about what the product should look like, but, rather, got involved in the total strategy necessary to bring it to market.

There was no designated leader for the team who would serve as the final decision maker. Instead, the member whose area of expertise was needed would lead the clan. So marketing experts and R&D specialists took their turns as leader as the situation demanded. And the design of the new product was to be the sole focus of the group effort. Peterson made this move in recognition of the fact that all too often, in his opinion, team efforts failed because they were working on too many projects at the same time.

As its first task in designing the new grill, the field research unit took to the road. Traveling all across the country, they interviewed people while they were barbecuing and even videotaped some sessions for later review. They found out that many women were the chief cook instead of the stereotypical man clad in his apron and chef's hat. Rusty, dirty grills were found to be incompatible with many new decks just built. Condo living and environmental regulations were big factors for people with cramped space who couldn't use smoke-belching charcoal grills.

Armed with field information, the team returned to its Schaumburg, Illinois, headquarters to share it with the rest of the group. After these meetings the team built a working model and a plastic dummy one that they took to retailers and customers to get feedback needed for final production specifications.

While the research team was in the field, the engineering group was busy doing computer runs in an effort to improve electric grill technology so that any new ideas found in the field could be incorporated into the new product. The result of these efforts was a product of Thermos's core—vacuum technology. Conventional electric grills did not get hot enough to provide the searing characteristic of barbecuing. So engineers designed a domed vacuum hood that would keep the heat inside the grill in the same way the Thermos bottle held heat. It even left the sear marks associated with barbecuing!

The product was not to be just another electric grill. It had to be seen not only as functionally different, but also as one that had features to suit the areas where it would be used. Tripod legs, a larger storage table, and a way to keep utensils out of the way of the cook were all features added as a result of talks with consumers and retailers. Manufacturing would not have known about these requirements until much later in the overall production process if it were not for the clan approach of product design that was Peterson's brainchild.

When the final product was ready for its ultimate test, Thermos gave one hundred grills to its employees with instructions to "treat them ugly." Peterson thought this was a better way to find out about the grill's acceptance than to learn about its problems from Kmart or Target customers. That would have simply been too late. Finally, Thermos loaded grills on the back of a U-Haul truck and took them to trade association conventions where they were demonstrated to potential buyers. They were now ready for market.

This new clan approach to product development has yielded what Thermos hopes will be a way to ratchet-up its market share — a new product that doesn't require its user to "fire up the grill."

> This case illustrates how the Thermos Company abandoned traditional top-down structural arrangements in favor of a type of "clan" pattern to bring out its new product, the Thermal Electric Grill. This interdisciplinary-team concept replaced bureaucracy with flexible groups who determined leaders based on situation-specific expertise rather than on the chain of command. As a result, innovation and customer satisfaction were achieved.
>
> This chapter explains the concepts of organizational control and governance. Two economic approaches to organization provide the framework for discussing several mechanisms for control. We look at contracting, boards of directors, markets, bureaucracy, and clans as ways of gaining control.

ORGANIZATIONAL GOVERNANCE AND CONTROL

In the first chapter of this text, we presented a definition of organizations that highlighted four key features: organizations are social entities made up of people; organizations are goal directed; organizations are structured; and organizations are open systems with identifiable boundaries. Several important issues are assumed within this definition that now need to be discussed explicitly. These issues come under the heading of organizational governance and control. Specifically, this chapter investigates the mechanisms that organizations use to get members to perform desired tasks that help the organization achieve its goals.

Recall that our definition emphasized that organizations are made up of people. When an organization assembles a collection of people, one problem that managers may encounter is how to ensure that this diverse group of people is engaged in activities that contribute to the achievement of organizational goals. How do owners create control systems that maximize the effectiveness and efficiency of the organization? How do owners make certain that employees do not loaf on the job, steal, or in other ways engage in counterproductive behaviors? Or, in the case of Thermos, how does an organization ensure high-quality inputs from employees? The discussions of structure and design provided some answers to this question; however, in this chapter we examine additional mechanisms for control.

AGENCY THEORY AND TRANSACTION COST ECONOMICS

Much of our discussion in this chapter is based on a segment of organization theory called organizational economics.[1] Organizational economics is actually made up of distinct theories, of which the two major branches are *agency theory*[2] and *transaction cost economics*.[3] Although these two theoretical perspectives are not identical, there is some overlap in both how they view the organization and how they view governance.

The field of organizational economics has developed a language and vocabulary of its own that may seem to the reader a bit unusual and obscure. However, because the field attaches rather specific meaning to these terms, we have tried to both remain faithful to that language and vocabulary and to clearly define terms.

Agency theory regards the organization (or firm, as is often preferred) as a series of contractual relationships between owners and workers.[4] Potential owners invest in firms to increase their wealth. This ownership may be through stock ownership in a publicly traded company or through direct ownership (e.g., proprietorship or partnership). Owners, also called *principals,* contract with managers and employees, also called *agents,* to produce goods and services. Because of a variety of factors, including basic human nature and the uncertain nature of some tasks, managers and other employees may engage in activities that are not conducive to owner wealth maximization. Instead, these behaviors may be directed at satisfying the particular goals and objectives of managers and employees. These counterproductive activities produce *agency costs.* Contracts, agreements that specify the exact duties and obligations of employees, are fashioned to guarantee that the agents perform as required. Those contracts must be written and monitored, all of which requires time and resources. In subsequent sections, we discuss why, according to agency theory, contracts are necessary and the types of contracts that owners can use to safeguard their interests.

Transaction cost theorists view the organization as a series of transactions.[5] Transactions are exchanges of goods and services among individuals and organizations. The firm has transactions with suppliers, with labor, or with customers. Some of these transactions take place within the organization, and some take place across the organization's boundaries. Because of the varying degrees of uncertainty that exist in transactions, the people and organizations involved experience *transaction costs* in executing transactions. Some transaction costs, such as brokerage fees, service charges, and points on loans, are explicit. Other transaction costs, such as monitoring the performance of transaction partners, are implicit in a transaction. Transaction costs are an indicator of inefficiency in a transaction. The greater the transaction costs to a firm, the less efficient the transaction and the less wealth available to owners. Thus, owners of a firm seek the lowest possible transaction costs. In subsequent sections we investigate the sources of these costs and the governance mechanisms that are used to control transaction costs.

Although there are important differences between these two theoretical perspectives, most of the differences are relevant to researchers and theoreticians. The important similarity between these two perspectives is that they both deal with how owners of a firm attempt to ensure that employees, suppliers, or contractors conduct themselves in ways that aid the organization in the achievement of its goals and objectives. According to both perspectives, owners should seek organizational arrangements that maximize economic efficiency; that is, those arrangements with the lowest agency costs or transaction costs. As a consequence of this emphasis on wealth enhancement through efficiency, agency theory and transaction costs economics are often labeled as *economic efficiency* views of organizations.[6] Both theoretical perspectives discuss **governance** mechanisms that can be used to ensure goal-directed behaviors, to control behaviors inside the firm, and to control the behaviors of transaction partners outside the firm. Thus, we group agency theory and transaction cost economics together.

THE NATURE OF THE PROBLEM OF ORGANIZING

Chapters 1 and 2 presented a somewhat traditional view of organizations and organizing. Organizations are created to accomplish some commonly held goal and organizations are structured — that is, tasks are divided vertically and horizontally among the people in the organization — in ways consistent with those goals, the organization's technology, its environment, and its size. Economic perspectives on organizations take a rather specific view concerning organizations and organizing. **Owners** of organizations create organizations as a means for accomplishing their rather specific goal — wealth maximization. Owners must make decisions about how to best achieve this goal of wealth maximization. To organizational economists, this question — how owners can maximize wealth — is central to how the firm should be organized.

Agency theory is primarily directed at the relationship between *principals (owners)* and *agents (employees)*. Thus, agency theory focuses on the structuring of the relationship between owners and employees *(agent-principal relationships)*. Agency theory examines the appropriate types of contracts and monitoring to ensure that owners can control the behavior of employees and reduce agency costs. Basic points are summarized in Table 9.1.

TABLE 9.1
Basic Points of Agency Theory

Organizations — series of contractual relationships between agents and principals
Principals — owners (shareholders) of a firm
Agents — people hired by the owners to run the firm (managers and workers)
Agency Costs — costs associated with monitoring agent behavior and enforcing contracts
Goal — efficient arrangement (lowest agency costs) of agent-principal relationships

Transaction cost economics focuses on the question of how to maximize the efficiency of transactions. Transaction cost theory attempts to determine the *efficient boundaries of the firm.*[7] That essentially means whether transactions should take place within the organization's boundaries, across the boundaries, or be housed within some sort of hybrid arrangement.[8] For example, is it more efficient (i.e., lower transaction costs) for a company to buy critical supplies or components from an outside supplier firm or should the company produce those supplies or components internally? Basic points of the transaction cost perspective are summarized in Table 9.2.

■ **TABLE 9.2**
Basic Points of Transaction Cost Perspective

Organization—series of transactions, some within the organization, some across the organization's boundaries
Transaction—exchange of goods and services among groups within the organization or across organizational boundaries
Transaction Costs—explicit fees or costs associated with a transaction; implicit costs of monitoring and controlling a transaction
Goal—to determine the most efficient arrangement of transactions; whether transactions should take place inside the organization or across organizational boundaries; seek lowest possible transaction costs

---

The problem an owner faces is that all forms of organizing have associated with them certain ***transaction*** or ***agency costs.*** Organizational economists use the term *cost* to refer to a wide range of problems that owners must remedy in order to create an organization that allows for wealth maximization. These costs are described below.

BOUNDED RATIONALITY

We have already examined the concept of bounded rationality elsewhere. Recall that bounded rationality means that humans (e.g., managers and owners) are limited in their ability to process information.[9] Another way of thinking about this is that owners and managers always face some uncertainty in transactions or contract relationships because they are unable to process all available information. They may lack time, attention, or ability to effectively gather and use the information needed. The situations owners face may be inherently complex and uncertain. Owners may be unable to process all potentially available information about managers; managers may likewise be unable to process all information about employees, suppliers, or customers. Additionally, because of uncertainty, some information may just not be available at any cost. Thus, a goal of organizing is to create an organization or some set of governance mechanisms that reduces as much as possible the uncertainty, that maximizes the available information, and that reduces the impact of bounded rationality.

OPPORTUNISM

Economic theorists assume that human beings operate on the bases of self-interest.[10] It is assumed that individuals attempt to maximize their positive outcomes and minimize their efforts or inputs. This results in a critical problem for organizations—a lack of goal consensus. Owners, managers, and lower-level employees often operate under different assumptions about what is important to the organization and what is important to the individual. As noted above, the goal of owners is the economically efficient operation of their firm and minimization of risk. Such a situation should lead to wealth maximization. Employees, according to organizational economic theorists, seek to minimize their work and maximize their rewards.

Economic theorists suggest that agents (i.e., managers and workers) do not perform in the manner in which they agreed because they value leisure more than hard work. Agents *shirk* their responsibilities and duties. This problem is referred to as ***moral hazard***—workers will not put forth the agreed upon effort.[11] Also, agents are likely to misrepresent themselves by claiming skills, knowledge, achievements, or other advantages that owners cannot easily verify. This condition is known as ***adverse selection.***[12]

For example, suppose you were enrolled in a large lecture class of 250 students and that you agreed as part of the class to attend every class meeting. However, it is spring term and the weather is nice, so you skip class—even though you agreed (contracted) to attend class. You have shirked on your responsibility. When the professor entered into a contract with you to attend class, she was faced with the problem of moral hazard—that you might not obey the contract. You realized that in a class of 250 students it might be difficult for the professor to monitor attendance. In entering into this contract, you portrayed yourself as an honest and dependable individual. The professor had no way of easily verifying that image of you. Consequently, the professor was faced with the problem of adverse selection. Thus, an objective of organizing and creating governance mechanisms is to reduce the opportunities for people to behave opportunistically.

INFORMATION ASYMMETRY

Information related to exchanges or transactions is not evenly distributed among participants.[13] One participant is likely to have more information than another. For example, a department or division may mislead or withhold information from top management about performance or conditions in that department or division to enhance how it is perceived. This is possible in large, complex organizations because it may be difficult to monitor the department or division. In Chapter 11, we present a brief example of just such behavior in an automobile company division.

Agency theory has used this concept to explain the opportunism and moral hazard problem. Agents (employees) are likely to have certain information about their own behavior and shortcomings that is not readily available to principals (owners). If the owners knew of these shortcomings, they would either terminate the relationship or, at a minimum, pay the agents less. Principals (owners) attempt to reduce information asymmetry by carefully monitoring and constructing contracts and by using other governance mechanisms discussed later in this chapter. Some critics of agency theory note that agency theorists emphasize information asymmetry favoring agents and contributing to opportunism. These critics suggest that principals (owners) may also possess information advantages and exhibit opportunism towards agents (employees).[14]

According to transaction cost theorists, the problem of information asymmetry is, in part, what motivates key decisions about whether to conduct certain tasks (i.e., transactions) within the boundaries of the organization (i.e., internalized) or outside the boundaries through contracts with suppliers and contractors. If management believes that potential outside suppliers and contractors have considerably more information and knowledge about issues related to a specific transaction, management may fear that the outsiders may cheat the firm through misrepresentation. Under such conditions, management may regard the cost of such a transaction—fear and uncertainty about the supplier's conduct along with the costs of gathering information and monitoring the supplier's conduct—as too high. Under those conditions, the firm's management may decide that internalizing the operation is more efficient.

A university may rely on outside contractors to perform cleaning and maintenance tasks, for example. The rationale for hiring outsiders to perform this work is that these companies specialize in cleaning and maintenance tasks. Moreover, the university administration would not have to deal with the capital costs of upkeep for cleaning and maintenance equipment or the management and supervision of these workers. A typical agreement would require that cleaning and maintenance be performed after hours. However, it may be difficult, particularly in a large university, to completely monitor the performance of the outside contractor. Thus, the contractor may withhold information and misrepresent the quality and extent of the cleaning tasks performed. Other problems might involve damage to the buildings and theft. If the cost of monitoring and enforcing the agreement with the contractor grows too large, the university may decide that it is better off (i.e., the transaction is less costly) if the task is internalized. This, of course, means that the university now has to create a cleaning and maintenance department, hire workers and supervisors, and invest in the appropriate equipment and supplies. However, the university is assuming that monitoring and disciplining the performance of internalized cleaning crews who are university employees will be easier than monitoring and disciplining the contractor.

Exhibit 9.1	**Human Nature: An Alternative View**[15]

The view of human nature painted by organizational economics, especially agency theory, is rather bleak — humans are motivated by self-interest. Whether you call it self-interest or opportunism, the result is the same. Agents will do virtually anything, including misrepresentation (adverse selection) and shirking responsibilities (moral hazard), in order to extract the best possible outcomes from principals.

Organizational theorist Charles Perrow believes this economic view is, at best, an oversimplification and, at worst, downright wrong. He identifies several problems with the economic view of the world of organizations.

First, the agency theory view of interactions between agents and principals suggests that agents are the problem. Information asymmetries favor agents in their interactions with principals. It is equally probable that principals can misrepresent themselves to agents. Agents do not always know the true value of their work to principals. Internal and external labor markets are imperfect mechanisms for valuing work. Thus, the problem of adverse selection can work both ways, but agency theory only considers agent misrepresentation. Exploitation of workers by owners is more than just an abstract possibility.

Second, Perrow notes that the opportunism, shirking, and laziness associated with the moral hazard problem may be overstated. Our work interactions often go well beyond the simplified idea of a contract between owners and workers. It is possible that employees do not have to be coerced, that they willingly take on responsibilities, and that they are capable of honest and charitable acts. Not everything we do is done simply for economic reward. Agency theory assumes that self-interest is human nature; yet, there is much that people do that is either neutral or is directed toward improving the conditions of others. Perrow warns that agency theory in its extreme may even be dangerous. He notes that it creates a lens through which we view much that goes on. We are likely to attribute our good fortune to hard work and misfortune to laziness or avarice. Often luck or circumstances come into play, and we may make faulty assumptions about the causes of people's behaviors. Moreover, viewing an organization as merely a collection of contracts oversimplifies the richness of organizations.

ASSET SPECIFICITY

Any organization has to invest in some specific assets necessary to achieve its goals. The degree to which these assets are fixed and specific (versus flexible and general) is referred to as asset specificity.[16] A high degree of asset specificity means that an organization may lack flexibility. It may be locked into certain relationships with outside suppliers, or it may be difficult to change internal tasks and relationships.

For example, a manufacturing company that invests heavily in customized milling and grinding equipment may find it difficult to change the nature of tasks in the milling and grinding department. The machinery — specific assets — restricts flexibility. That same investment may also make it costly for the company to turn to an outside company to perform milling and grinding work, even if conditions change and the outside company can do the work more efficiently. Thus, the decision to invest (or not invest) in specific assets has implications for how the organization governs its relationship with employees and other firms.

Let us return to the earlier example of the cleaning crews at the university. The university invests in cleaning equipment, employees to perform the cleaning, facilities to house the cleaning equipment, and supervisory staff. By making these investments, the university has created some asset specificity. Once these investments are made, it may be costly, difficult, or impossible to switch these assets to other uses. The cleaning equipment cannot be used for other tasks; the personnel may be limited in the tasks they can perform (e.g., they cannot teach organization theory); and the new facility may be difficult to convert to other uses. Thus, once these investments are made, the costs of switching to other options for cleaning are increased. In this way asset specificity adds to transaction costs.

SMALL NUMBERS

Another transaction problem that organizations may face is having only a small number of potential trading partners (i.e., an oligopoly).[17] For example, Aldila, a maker of graphite composite golf club shafts was the primary supplier to Callaway Golf, a premier club maker. Aldila sold nearly two-thirds of its production to Callaway and Callaway depended on Aldila for a majority of its shafts.[18] Early in this relationship there were only a few other companies manufacturing high quality graphite golf club shafts. This situation illustrates small numbers trading relationships for both Callaway and Aldila. In this case, each company is highly dependent on the other, although it is not necessary for both partners to be so dependent for there to be a small numbers trading problem. Aldila has the potential to sell its product to many other golf club manufacturers. Callaway, until recently, had only a few other potential suppliers of shafts.

The problem with small numbers is that an organization can be more easily exploited by a trading partner. Knowing that Callaway depended on Aldila for a reliable supply of shafts, Aldila could exploit the situation and raise the transaction costs for Callaway. For example, it could have forced Callaway to pay more, buy in larger quantities, or agree to less favorable terms, although there is no evidence that Aldila acted in this way. Callaway recently decided to reduce its dependence on Aldila by seeking other suppliers. By using several suppliers, Callaway reduces its dependence on any one supplier and reduces the small numbers problem. It could also have decided to **internalize** (i.e., vertically integrate) either by acquiring a graphite shaft maker or by starting its own operation. That action would have required a significant investment in specific assets, and as we noted above, asset specificity creates other transaction costs that could be a problem for Callaway.

Table 9.3 summarizes this discussion of costs. In general, firms seek ways of organizing that reduce all of these **transaction** or **agency costs**. Transaction and agency costs are sources of inefficiency. They detract from owners' goals of wealth maximization. In the following section we examine mechanisms that are used to control transaction and agency costs.

■ **TABLE 9.3**
Sources of Agency and Transaction Costs

- **Bounded rationality** — Humans (e.g., managers and owners) are limited in their ability to process information.
- **Opportunism** — Human beings operate on the basis of self-interest resulting in problems of moral hazard and adverse selection.
- **Information asymmetry** — Information related to exchanges or transactions is not evenly distributed among participants.
- **Asset specificity** — Degree of investment in specific fixed assets that cannot easily be used for other purposes makes it necessary to achieve goals.
- **Small numbers** — Organizations are faced with only a small number of potential trading partners (an oligopoly).

MECHANISMS FOR ORGANIZATIONAL GOVERNANCE

In the previous section we noted considerable overlap between the two economic perspectives. That was true with respect to identifying costs and inefficiencies. However, the overlap and similarity between agency cost and transaction cost perspectives are less when it comes to remedies. This is, in part, because of the differences in the organizational phenomenon upon which they focus. Nonetheless, there are still similarities. Both economic perspectives address, using the organization as a mechanism to support exchanges, exchanges between owner and employee and exchanges between the organization and its environment. Organizational economics seeks governance mechanisms or organizational arrangements that reduce the costs of these exchanges.[19] Agency theory emphasizes legal aspects of control — contracts and legally designated governing bodies. The transaction cost perspective emphasizes the designation of efficient boundaries for an organization—which operations should take place inside the organization and which should take place outside.

CONTRACTING AND MONITORING TO REDUCE AGENCY COSTS

According to agency theory, as we noted, problems are the result of goal differences between principals (owners) and agents (employees).[20] Principals seek to maximize wealth through the efficient operation of the firm. Agents seek to maximize their share of wealth in relation to the effort they put forth on the job (i.e., maximize pay and benefits while minimizing effort). Therein lies the first part of the problem: Owners seek maximal effort from employees at minimal cost (i.e., efficiency) while employees seek to minimize effort and maximize remuneration (i.e., pay and benefits).

Owners attempt to protect their interests by creating contracts that obligate either employee behavior (i.e., ***behavioral contracts***) or employee performance (i.e., ***outcome-based contracts***).[21] Behavioral contracts are contracts that specify that employees engage in specific activities.

For example, behavioral contracts may specify employee work hours and tasks to be performed. Employee compensation would be based on behavior—being at work during prescribed hours and performing required tasks. Behavioral contracts are used when the desired outcomes are unclear or difficult to measure, when tasks are fairly routine, and when the extent of goal conflict between owners and employees is not great.[22]

Outcome-based or performance contracts tie compensation and rewards to measurable outcomes. Piece-rate production, commissions, and pay-for-performance are all examples of outcome-based contracts. For example, in some leading corporations chief executive pay and bonuses are based on the company's overall performance. Compensation may be tied to the company's stock price, sales growth, or profits. Another example of an outcome-based contract is the sales commission paid to a salesperson. Outcome-based contracts are used when there are large differences in goals between owners and agents, when behavior on the job is difficult to monitor, and when outcomes are easily measured.[23]

BOARDS OF DIRECTORS AND CONTROL

Boards of directors potentially play an important role in the control and governance of a company. Boards are charged with the responsibilities of advising, counseling, and critically listening to reports by management; assessing firm performance; acting on designated board tasks; and suggesting means for improving the organization.[24] Stockholders select a board of directors that is supposed to represent stockholder interests in an organization. The board is charged with the ***fiduciary responsibility*** (i.e., legal trustee) of safeguarding the stockholders' investments in the company. The board of directors plays the role of intermediary between the officers of the company and the stockholders.

Boards are usually composed of two sets of representatives: insiders, who are officers, former officers, or relatives of officers of the firm, and outsiders, who may be stockholders but lack any other formal work relationship to the company (i.e., they are not employees, former employees, or relatives of employees of the company). Outsiders are supposed to be objective observers of the organization as well as potential sources of knowledge, skills, expertise, and information. Ideally, it is the outside board members who monitor and provide oversight for the organization. Inside board members can provide insight and expertise into the specific operational issues associated with running the company. Overall the board of directors should play the following key roles:

- establish policies and objectives of the firm;
- elect, monitor, advise, evaluate and compensate the corporate officers, and approve their actions;
- protect the value of the corporate assets;
- monitor, approve, and report on the financial condition of the firm, including required reports to stockholders and regulators;
- delegate selected board powers to others, as necessary;
- ensure that the corporate charter and by-laws are enforced and are revised, as necessary; and
- maintain the integrity of the board.[25]

In theory, the board of directors should provide an important system of checks and balances against opportunistic behavior on the part of management. However, practice and reality sometimes do not coincide. Often the board of directors lacks objectivity and independence. As the following executive pay example in Exhibit 9.2 suggests, some board members are beholden to the top management of the firm. One problem is that many of the potential directors are selected by management and usually run for election to the board unopposed. Stockholders are left with only limited choices to fill board positions. The result is that boards are often packed with friends and business acquaintances of the firm's top management. This situation is made more precarious when the chairman of the board of directors is also the chief executive officer — the top management position in the firm. Other members often have their own agenda that is not consistent with that of either management or owners of the firm. And sometimes boards of directors lack the skills and expertise to monitor and act in ways that improve the control and performance of the firm.[26] The net result is that, in the best case scenario, an independent and intelligent board can provide some control over management. In the worst-case scenario, boards may become merely a rubber stamp for top management or they may even be completely inept at controlling top management.

Exhibit 9.2	**Pay-for-Performance?**

It is really a very simple idea — pay people on the basis of their performance.[27] Many organizations manage to do just that with lower- and mid-level employees. Some companies pay lower-level production workers based on their productivity. This is referred to as piece-rate compensation. The employee gets paid for each piece produced. Produce more widgets; get paid more. Produce fewer widgets; get paid less. Salespeople paid commissions on sales are also receiving performance-based compensations. Sell more cars; get paid more. Sell fewer cars; get paid less.

The idea, although imperfect, is consistent with the idea of outcome-based contracting. Workers contract to perform certain tasks — produce widgets or sell cars—and receive compensation. The compensation system becomes a governance mechanism for the control of performance desired by the firm's owners. The system requires that outcomes or performance be easily measured.

But compensation of top managers, a place where pay-for-performance seems logical, is exactly where it is most problematic.[28] Top managers, particularly chief executive officers (CEOs), are responsible for the overall performance of the firm. For owners (shareholders), that performance is probably best indicated by the firm's stock value. The problem is that CEO pay typically bears little relationship to the firm's stock performance. Moreover, determining the value of a CEO's complete compensation package, which typically includes bonuses, stock grants, options, and other "rewards" in addition to base salary, is often quite difficult. It's clear that when companies do well and stock value increases, CEO compensation rises. What's not as clear is what happens when a company's value doesn't rise as fast as the industry average, or when the value falls. A few examples illustrate the point.

Fortune magazine runs annual surveys of executive compensation. *Fortune* reported that, in 1993, Travelers, Inc. CEO, Sanford Weill, received the highest total compensation package, worth $45.7 million. That huge compensation package may be justified by the 30 percent annual rate of return for shareholders over the past five years. But that return on investment for shareholders ranked only eleventh among the top 200 firms. In fact, among companies with the 200 highest paid CEOs, International Game Technology had the highest annual rate of return for shareholders (88.5 percent) in the past five years. Yet, CEO John J. Russell's compensation package of $4.4 million was only fifty-fifth on the list of highest paid CEOs.[29] These *levels* of compensation and performance also deal with the *increases* in compensation and performance.

In a 1991 *Fortune* survey, compensation expert Graef Crystal developed a model for realistically valuing executive compensation packages and for determining the match between the compensation the CEO received and what should have been received, based on the company's performance.[30] Eighty-six out of 200 CEOs received more than Crystal's model predicted they should receive. The top twenty-three compensation packages exceeded the predicted amounts of compensation by over 100 percent! The top paid CEO in the 1991 survey was Time Warner CEO Steven Ross, whose compensation ($35.1 million) exceeded the model by over 1,000 percent. Number two was Reebok's Paul Fireman, whose compensation ($20.8 million) was 960 percent over what the model predicted. Clearly, there were many CEOs whose salaries fell below the levels predicted by Crystal's model.

Why is compensation imperfect as a governance mechanism? Crystal points to several factors. First is the problem of *information asymmetry*.[31] The group responsible for setting CEO compensation is the compensation committee of the board of directors. This committee is considered to be lowest in prestige of the various board committees, which may mean that compensation committee members are not particularly committed to their task. Additionally, the committee is made up of outsiders, board members who are not officers, retired officers, or relatives of officers of the firm. This is supposed to give them independence, but they often lack key information in making compensation decisions. As a result, the CEO can selectively provide information to the committee that enhances his or her positive performance and downplays negative performance. Second, CEOs typically hire compensation consultants to craft and present generous compensation packages to the board of directors. Although the compensation expert is hired by the CEO, he or she is really under contract to the organization. This presents problems of objectivity and loyalty. Does the consultant develop a package that is best for the company (i.e., owners and principals) or best for the CEO (agent)? The consultant's arcane presentation of compensation information to the committee may also go well beyond the limited expertise of committee members. Third, outside board members are often selected by and beholden to the CEO. Thus, CEOs often select people on whom they can count to rubber-stamp generous compensation packages. These factors can result in CEO compensation packages that are overly generous and unrelated to the company's performance.

MARKETS AS DISCIPLINARY FORCES

Important sources of control that are exerted on a firm are the disciplinary force of markets.[32] What this means is that various markets, such as the stock market, labor market, and debt market, can provide feedback about a company's performance. This feedback pressure's the company's management to perform better.

The following example illustrates how markets discipline managers. Games Incorporated (GI) is a maker of electronic games. The company is traded on a stock market, and many investors own shares in the company. GI's management embarked on an aggressive campaign to expand its market and invested large amounts of money in research, facilities development, and new personnel. At the beginning of the year, the company's stock traded at $10 per share. When the company announced this new strategy, the share price went up to $13 per share. Investors were indicating their approval of the aggressive new strategy. However, at the end of the year management announced that sales were disappointingly low, and investors tried to unload shares in GI. The share price dropped to $7. Investors signaled their disapproval of management's performance. In an extreme case, owners who thought the firm had been mismanaged could try to force management out (i.e., fire them) or a potential owner could try to take over the firm by buying all the shares. The new owner of the firm would be indicating that he or she thought that the firm had potential to do better under different ownership and management.

Labor markets and debt markets can provide similar forms of discipline on managers. Successful managers should find that they are in demand in the labor market. Other firms may attempt to woo them away from their companies. However, after the expansion plans at GI backfired, it was unlikely that GI executives would be in high demand by other firms. Thus, the labor market, the potential to move among different firms, and the ability to demand higher salaries provide an incentive to perform. If prior to GI's recent expansion plan the company had performed well, it would probably not have had difficulty borrowing money. Borrowing money puts pressure on a company to become more efficient because the firm now has to pay off debt. After GI's poor performance, the debt market will discipline the company by lowering the company's credit rating and forcing it to pay higher interest.[33] In the extreme, the debt market can discipline a company that is performing poorly by forcing it into bankruptcy.

TRANSACTION COSTS AND THE EFFICIENT BOUNDARIES OF THE FIRM

According to the transaction cost economic perspective on organizations, a critical choice that a firm faces is the determination of efficient boundaries of the organization. What this phrase means is that firm owners must make decisions about which activities should take place within the boundaries of the firm and which activities should be done outside the firm's boundaries. When transactions take place outside a firm's boundaries, the firm must monitor the marketplace in search of trustworthy, reliable providers of key resources. This is referred to as *market control.* When markets fail, when these transactions are too costly or difficult to monitor, the firm will internalize the transaction. Once internalized, management has two options for controlling the transactions: *bureaucratic control* and *clan control.*

MARKET CONTROL

Early in the history of Ford Motor Company, the company purchased steel from the major steel producers. At various times during the automobile production cycle, buyers would conduct transactions with steel producers to buy quantities of steel. This type of transaction is often referred to as a market transaction or market control. The company would seek bids from competing steel companies to supply specific quantities and qualities of steel.

Market control relies on prices and competition in external markets to control transaction-related costs. With many suppliers and many buyers of steel, there should be extensive (nearly perfect) competition among sellers for customers. To attract customers, sellers of steel are forced through price competition to offer fair market value. Sellers would be unable to extract high prices because of competition. Some other seller is always willing to undercut a competitor's high price until the market reaches equilibrium. With nearly perfect competition, buyers and sellers all know the fair market price. Market control should work to produce efficient transactions as long as sufficient numbers of sellers and buyers are present in the marketplace to produce nearly perfect competition and as long as sufficient knowledge or information is present so that buyers can safeguard against seller opportunism. So, for example, Ford Motor Company needed to be able to judge accurately the quality of steel the sellers were offering. If the buyer is unable to make this type of judgment, then market controls may fail. It is also important to note that when two companies are engaged in repeated transactions over a long period of time, there is strong motivation for the supplier firm to honestly represent its goods. Otherwise, once the buyer firm learns of the deceptions or misrepresentations, it will discontinue transactions.

Market control can also be used inside a firm when an individual, department, or division has outputs that can be easily measured with respect to their price. In many respects, the outcome-based contracts mentioned earlier are examples of market control. The firm rewards performance and bids for the continuation of that performance on a market basis. Internal and external labor markets exist to fix the price of specific types of labor. However, it is difficult to price many support services and basic functions such as information systems support and accounting, but some organizations are using external bidding in the marketplace to force greater internal efficiency and control. Additionally, market control can be used to monitor the performance of divisions or departments, especially self-contained product divisions where there is a measurable outcome that can be priced in the marketplace. For example, earlier in the book we noted General Electric's drive to be number one or number two in everything it does. The company used the external marketplace to evaluate the performance of various divisions.[34] GE determined that the performance of the television and small appliance divisions was unsatisfactory and thus decided to sell those divisions. Prior to the time of the sale, the market pressure on these divisions acted to control and direct performance. Division executives knew that their performance would be judged against that of marketplace competitors.

BUREAUCRATIC CONTROL

Let us return to Ford Motor Company. In 1919, Henry Ford determined that he did not want his company to be at the mercy of large steel companies. Perhaps he feared that the few large steel companies would exploit Ford's dependence on steel and raise prices. Ford may also have worried that the steel companies would pass off inferior goods. Or perhaps the steel makers would be insensitive to Ford's specific needs. As a result of the increasing dependence on steel, Ford built the large River Rouge industrial complex that included a steel foundry where Ford processed its own steel.[35] In sum, Ford decided that the transaction costs of dealing with the large steel companies were too high; thus, he vertically integrated into the steel business. He defined the efficient boundaries of his firm so that they included steel making. This internalization of a transaction is also referred to as hierarchical or bureaucratic control.[36]

Bureaucratic control means that control of a particular transaction is done through the organization's hierarchy or bureaucracy. Recall that a bureaucracy emphasizes narrow specialization; limited areas of decision responsibility; and the extensive use of rules, policies, and procedures. Thus, when Ford Motor Company internalized steel production, the operation was controlled by the narrowly skilled specialization of employees; referral of problems up the organizational hierarchy; and application of rules, policies, and procedures. Control mechanisms often include such things as comprehensive job descriptions and performance appraisal systems, statistical or numerical control systems to monitor and control production, budgeting and accounting systems to monitor financial performance, and work rules or procedural guidelines for the conduct of tasks.[37] As you can see, bureaucratic control is similar in many respects to the behavioral contracting of agency theory. Through the use of bureaucratic control mechanisms, Ford could attempt to ensure that steel was more efficiently produced for its operations than if the company had relied on outside firms to supply steel. By directly monitoring employees and applying rules, hierarchy, and specialization, Ford could remove many of the problems of dealing with an imperfect market and external firms for steel.

CLAN CONTROL

In both Chapters 2 and 8 it was mentioned that bureaucracies can become inefficient. This is especially true when the organization faces uncertainty from the environment and the technology. Rule creation, monitoring, and enforcement require personnel, time, and money. With the creation of rules and layers of hierarchy for monitoring and enforcing rules, the organization becomes inflexible and unable to meet changing conditions. Organizational efficiency can suffer.

The organic organizational structure was proposed as an alternative to bureaucratic structure. Jobs and responsibilities are broadened; hierarchy is reduced; and decision making is pushed down to lower levels of the organization. We did not, however, discuss in detail in those earlier chapters how the organization can achieve control in the organic organization. For control in the organic organization we turn to ***clan control.***

Clan control utilizes the shared norms, values, and beliefs of organizational members to ensure that people pursue common goals and objectives.[38] At the root of these shared norms, values, and beliefs is the organization's culture. These norms, values, and beliefs are given expression through cultural mechanisms such as stories and myths about the organization, symbols, traditions, and ceremonies. We discuss these in greater detail in Chapter 10. For now it is sufficient to note that these commonly held norms, values, and beliefs, as expressed through the culture, operate to produce goal consensus and commitment to the organization.

Clan control can be implemented through the careful screening, selection, or training of employees. For example, some organizations only hire graduates of specific colleges or universities with particular degrees because the employer believes that the college or university, along with the academic discipline, instills a particular set of values or beliefs in employees. Other organizations rely on internal training, sometimes coupled with specific initiation rites to produce shared norms, values, and beliefs. The armed forces provide good examples of this approach. The combination of uniforms, boot camp, and training provide recruits with a common vision and shared identity. The armed forces combine clan control with a heavy dose of bureaucratic control. Clearly, significant numbers of rules and official procedures are also used to achieve goals in the armed forces. Fraternities, sororities, social organizations, and religious institutions use clan control. Businesses are relying more on clan control, particularly as they downsize, eliminate layers of hierarchy, and reengineer.

When members of the organization share values, norms, and beliefs and when they are committed to the commonly held goals of the organization, it is less likely that opportunism will be a problem. Employees come to realize that their well-being and the well-being of the organization are intimately linked. If opportunism is not present, then information asymmetry is less of a problem. Employees use information and knowledge in pursuit of the shared goals of the organization. Clearly, clan control does not eliminate all transaction costs, but it does reduce problems of opportunism.

One area in which Ford Motor Company successfully emphasized shared values was in its "Quality is Job #1" campaign. Like GM and Chrysler, Ford was plagued in the 1970s and early 1980s with low-quality products compared with Japanese and European competitors. In the mid-1980s, Ford instituted the "Quality is Job #1" campaign with signs placed prominently throughout factories and advertisements featuring the slogan. Workers were trained in techniques to improve quality, and quality circles were instituted to get worker insights on how the company could change procedures to increase quality. In short, quality became a shared value among Ford employees. That shared value, a foundation of clan control, became a mechanism for controlling employee behavior. Workers would monitor their own work and that of fellow workers to ensure quality. Some aspects of bureaucratic control (rules) and market controls (customer demands for higher quality) were present, but shared values were a key factor.

Similarly, in the introductory case on the Thermos Company, clan control was used to achieve teamwork. Because both Ford and Thermos were facing new and uncertain conditions, it was important that they assemble autonomous work groups that could make decisions and enact policies that dealt with the environment and technology. Reliance on bureaucracy could have been cumbersome and might have produced inefficiencies and delays. The belief is that the organization can count on team members to perform in appropriate ways because they share the basic values, norms, and beliefs of the organization. At Ford, workers shared the value that quality was critical to the success of the company and were thus committed to quality improvement. At Thermos, team members shared the basic commitment to product innovation and cross-disciplinary cooperation.

SUMMARY

This chapter has introduced organizational economics as a vehicle for describing organizational control. In particular, two theoretical frameworks have been presented. Agency theory focuses on the relationships between owners (principals) and employees (agents). Transaction costs focus on decisions about the organization's boundaries—whether certain operations should be conducted within the organization or outside its boundaries. The objective of both perspectives is to describe *efficient forms of organizing*.

Owners and managers run into problems in their quest for efficiency. These problems, also called agency costs or transaction costs, include bounded rationality, opportunism, information asymmetry, asset specificity, and small numbers of exchange partners. The objective of owners is to maximize efficiency by reducing these sources of transaction and agency costs.

Transaction and agency costs can be reduced through the use of appropriate governance mechanisms. Agency theory emphasizes legal aspects of control through behavioral and outcome-based contracting or through boards of directors. Through the use of markets, bureaucracies, or clans as control mechanisms, transaction cost theory describes the conditions under which transactions should be internalized or conducted by external suppliers. Markets, bureaucracies, and clans represent different governance mechanisms for controlling transactions.

Questions for Discussion

1. According to agency theory, how would you describe basic human nature? How does this basic human nature contribute to agency costs?
2. How do behavior contracts and outcome-based contracts differ? Describe the situations in which each would apply.

3. Transaction cost economics focuses on determining the efficient boundaries of the firm. What does this mean? According to transaction cost theory, what is the central decision that firms face?

4. What are the sources of transaction and agency costs that affect transactions and agent-principal relations?

5. Compare and contrast bureaucratic control and clan control. Under what conditions would you use each?

6. Charles Perrow voiced concern about the dangers of economic theories of organizations, particularly agency theory. What are his concerns? Do you think he is justified? Why? Why not?

CASE: SWEET TOOTH*

For anyone who has ever had a sweet tooth, Mars has tried to have the answer for this craving. With a rich mix of brand names such as Snickers, Milky Way, and M&Ms, the Mars Company seemed to have a corner on the candy market. But lately the sugar coating is melting.

Ownership of the privately-held company is vested in the hands of John, Forrest, Jr., and Jacqueline, children of Forrest Mars, Sr. Mars is a closely held and private company. Because its stock is not publicly traded, the usual performance information found in annual reports and other documents supplied to investors is not available for Mars. That which is available, however, tells of a company yielding market share to its competition (e.g., Hershey, Nestlé, and Cadbury Schweppes), both on the domestic and foreign fronts. But its $13 billion estimated annual sales still make it a potent player in the confectionery, pet food, and food-vending businesses.

The lack of innovation in the form of new product development has resulted in the fact that no new "big-sale" items have been produced. Marketing and sales arms of the company simply have not kept pace with Mars's fanatic quest for quality control. In spite of this condition, competitors are worried because, as they argue, Mars simply doesn't play by everyone else's rules. They're unpredictable, and they don't seem to be too worried about market share loss. They even seem to ignore the situation.

Instead of worrying about losing its domestic market, Mars seems bent on pursuing its global expansion strategy at full speed. Is this tack a visionary move or one based on virtually ignoring environmental information? Whatever the answer, Mars isn't saying, following its veil-of-secrecy stance.

Inside Mars, there is an air of everyone for himself or herself, and it seems everyone is afraid of John and Forrest, Jr., who run the company. Forrest, Jr. is known for his fiery temper and for seeming to enjoy publicly upbraiding Mars's managers. This atmosphere invites filtering information to the point of withholding. This secrecy has probably contributed to Mars's present condition. Managers can be loathe to share information that is either likely to help a fellow manager about to absorb an upbraiding from Forrest, Jr., or to share ideas. If they prove wrong, such ideas could get their "genius" into trouble.

---

*This case is based on the following article: Bill Saporito, "The Eclipse of Mars," *Fortune* (November 28, 1994): 82-84, 86, 90, 92.

The brothers seem to genuinely enjoy running the company. They are a kind of contradiction, of a sort, when it comes to money, however. They are willing to pay far-above-average salaries and yet demand economy rental cars and make use of discount coupons at hotels when they are on the road. This disdain for fancy spending was doubtlessly handed down from Forrest, Sr., known for his penchant for simplicity and economy.

At corporate headquarters in McLean, Virginia, perks are frowned on, and in operating headquarters in Hackettstown, New Jersey, open offices are the norm. There, there are no private offices, and desks are arranged in an open area divided into zones, from Zone Five for brand managers to Zones One and Two for senior executives. Salaries are posted for all to see, and not from the vantage point of a private dining room, which does not exist. There are no reserved parking spaces either.

This approach to management (a combination of secretiveness, openness, and frugality) has worked from the beginning, but it appears to be faltering now. The best answer to the question, Why? seems to be that the Mars brothers have simply ignored the company's changing environment.

The candy business has seen major mergers and consolidations, exemplified by Philip Morris, Nestlé, and Cadbury Schweppes acquiring smaller companies and then outdoing Mars on the advertising front as well. New products have come from these new organizations. Hershey has been active on its own in this regard with its introduction of new Hugs, Nutrageous, and Nuggets. While all this was happening, Mars simply sat back and watched while it lost significant market share to Hershey.

Mars paid little attention to similar occurrences in the European market where Philip Morris and Cadbury bought companies to consolidate their positions in that market. Result? Mars has seen its share of the German market, for example, fall from 30 percent to 20 percent in just the last three years.

Mars has not handled changes occurring in its distribution chain well either. Supermarkets and discount stores have realigned and restructured. Many have centralized and concentrated their buying. At the same time Mars has aggressively pursued a strategy of cost cutting. The result is that Mars has not been able to supply the product necessary to meet the orders it takes. Even though special committees have been established to deal with the problem, success so far has been elusive. The company's policy of asset exhaustion has caused sales to exceed production capacity. The policy is especially worrisome because managers know their pay is directly tied to asset-utilization rates. This policy also means that production facilities may be straining to fulfill orders. In the long run, this may mean equipment breakdowns and further delays.

Special discounts to retailers were abruptly canceled, and these price breaks represent a sizeable portion of retail profits. This lack of sensitivity has caused many to turn to Hershey, which has shown far more flexibility in promotional spending.

The Mars organization doesn't reward risk taking and independent thinking—seemingly necessary conditions for success in the global market that Mars seeks to serve. The company truly believes in global marketing—one market, one product, one message—for what it sees as a homogeneous environment. It has found, however, that the same market program for Spain did not work for England. Same-color labels for all of its Whiskas cat food products did not appeal to all European cat owners.

Mars's venture into "scientific" health food for dogs failed when it was introduced in supermarkets. Mars later learned that buyers bought this type of food in pet stores or vets' offices.

In view of this series of ill-founded decisions, it is no wonder that there is concern about whether the Mars brothers have the ability to lead the company into a bright future. With a history of "chewing up" executive talent, lacking innovation, ignoring the environment, and irritating personalities, could it be that Mars's ability to satisfy our sweet tooth might be turning sour?

QUESTIONS FOR DISCUSSION

1. How would you describe the methods of governance and control that the Mars brothers have used to run their company?
2. Mars is a privately held company (stock is not traded on any market). How would this affect the control of management's behavior and performance? How else could Mars use markets to discipline management?
3. Could clan control be used at Mars? How could the company adopt a clan control philosophy of management?
4. If you were brought in as a consultant to Mars, what would you recommend that the company do with respect to control in order to achieve better performance?

REFERENCES

1. A. A. Berle, and G. C. Means, *The Modern Corporation and Private Property* (New York: Macmillan, 1932).

   R. Coase, "The Nature of the Firm," *Econmica* 4 (1937): 386–405.

   E. Fama, "Agency Problems and the Theory of the Firm," *Journal of Political Economy* 88 (1980): 288–307.

   O. E. Williamson, *The Economics of Discretionary Behavior: Managerial Objectives in a Theory of the Firm* (Englewood Cliffs, N.J.: Prentice-Hall, 1964).

2. See Fama in note 1 above.

   M. Jensen, and W. Meckling, "Theory of the Firm: Managerial Behavior, Agency Costs, and Ownership," *Journal of Financial Economics* 3 (1976): 305–60.

   K. M. Eisenhardt, "Agency Theory: An Assessment and Review," *Academy of Management Review* 14 (1989): 57–74.

3. See Williamson in note 1 above.

   O. E. Williamson, "Comparative Economic Organization: The Analysis of Discrete Structural Alternatives," *Administrative Science Quarterly* 36 (1991): 269–96.

4. B. M. Oviatt, "Agency and Transaction Cost Perspectives on the Manager-Shareholder Relationship: Incentives for Congruent Interests," *Academy of Management Review* 13 (1988): 214–25.

5. See Williamson in note 1 above.

6. W. S. Hesterly, J. Liebeskind, and T. R. Zenger, "Organizational Economics: An Impending Revolution in Organization Theory?" *Academy of Management Review* 15 (1990): 402–20.

7. O. E. Williamson, "The Economics of Organization: The Transaction Cost Approach," *American Journal of Sociology* 87 (1981): 548–77.

8. See Williamson (1991) in note 3 above.

9. Herbert A. Simon, *Administrative Behavior,* 3rd ed. (New York: The Free Press, 1976).

   G. R. Jones and C. W. L. Hill, "Transaction Cost Analysis of Strategy-Structure Choice," *Strategic Management Journal* 9 (1976): 159–72.

   See Eisenhardt in note 2 above.

10. Ibid.

11. See Eisenhardt in note 2 above.

12. Ibid.

13. Ibid.

    See Jones and Hill in note 9 above.

14. C. Perrow, *Complex Organizations,* 3rd ed. (New York: Random House, 1986).

15. This discussion is based on Chapter 7 of *Complex Organizations.* See note 14 above.

16. See Jones and Hill in note 9 above.

17. Ibid.

18. Michael Gonzalez, "Stock Prices Rally to End Mixed After Sell-Off Tied to Mexico Aid," *The Wall Street Journal* (January 24, 1995), C2.

19. See note 6 above.

20. See Eisenhardt in note 2 above.

21. Ibid.

22. Ibid.

23. Ibid.

24. J. K. Louden, *The Director* (New York: American Management Association, 1982).

25. R. S. Chaganti, V. Mahajan, and S. Sharma, "Corporate Board Size, Composition, and Corporate Failures in Retailing Industry," *Journal of Management Studies* 22 (1985): 400–17.

    Conference Board, *Corporate Directorship Practices, Studies in Business Policy* (New York: Conference Board, 1967).

26. Myles L. Mace, *Directors: Myth and Reality* (Boston, Mass.: Harvard Business School Press, 1971).

Murray L. Weidenbaum, "Battle of the Boardroom: Controlling the Future Corporation," *Business and Society Review* 58 (1986): 10–12.

27. Thomas Rollins, "Pay for Performance: Is It Worth the Trouble?" *Personnel Administrator* (May 1988): 42–46.

Charles Cumming, "Linking Pay to Performance," *Personnel Administrator* (May 1988): 47–52.

28. Graef S. Crystal, "Why CEO Compensation Is So High," *California Management Review* 34 (Fall 1991): 9–29.

29. Brian Dumaine, "A Knockout Year for CEO Pay," *Fortune* 130, no. 2 (July 25, 1994): 94–103.

30. Graef S. Crystal, "How Much CEOs Really Make," *Fortune* 127 (June 17, 1991): 72–80.

31. See note 28 above.

32. O. E. Williamson, Corporate Finance and Governance," *The Journal of Finance* 43 (1988): 567–91.

See Jones and Hill in note 9 above.

Rita D. Kosnik, "Greenmail: A Study of Board Performance in Corporate Governance," *Administrative Science Quarterly* 32 (1987): 163–85.

33. See Williamson in note 32 above.

34. Stratford Sherman, "A Master Class in Radical Change," *Fortune* (December 13, 1993): 82–90.

Tim Smart, "Jack Welch on the Art of Thinking Small," *Business Week* (Special Enterprise Issue, 1993): 212–15.

35. P. Collier and D. Horowitz, *The Fords: An American Epic* (New York: Summit Books, 1987).

36. W. G. Ouchi, "Markets, Bureaucracies and Clans," *Administrative Science Quarterly* 25 (1980): 129–41.

37. R. L. Daft and N. B. Macintosh, "The Nature and Use of Formal Control Systems for Management Control and Strategy Implementation," *Journal of Management* 10 (1984): 43–66.

See note 36 above.

38. See note 36 above.

PART FOUR

Organizational Processes

Organizations are not static entities. They develop, grow, act, and change. We have already begun the process of investigating this dynamic nature of organizations under such topic headings as organizational growth and life cycles, adapting to environmental change, and altering technology. In these final four chapters, we directly examine the dynamic nature of organizational processes.

Chapter 10 introduces the concept of organizational culture. As you look around the landscape of organizations, one of the first things that will strike you is that organizations, even those in the same industry, all look different. The differences go beyond simple appearances and affect the fundamental values, norms, beliefs, expectations, and behaviors of members. Chapter 10 explores how cultures emerge, the impact they have on the organization, how they change, and how they should fit with the basic strategic focus of the organization.

Many business and organizational experts maintain that we are living in an information society today. Among organizational theorists, there are those who view organizations as essentially information processors. True, information is critical and crucial to the functioning of organizations. But information is often only an intermediate stop in the journey to a decision. The process of decision making is ubiquitous in organizations. With the flattening and decentralizing of organizations, more and more members are involved in decision making, as we discuss in Chapter 11.

As outsiders, we sometimes watch organizations do strange and unexpected things. Perhaps a company introduces a new product of dubious merit, for example, a car design that seems to appeal to no particular market. Sometimes a firm fires a person for no apparent reason—at least no apparent reason to outsiders. In Chapter 12 we explore power within organizations and the political nature of organizations. Organizations are not simple machines, but, as we noted in Chapter 1, they are made up of people—people from diverse backgrounds, with different skills, knowledge, goals, and expectations. The result is that organizations do not always act in a rational and predictable manner.

Finally, Chapter 13 formally introduces the notions of organizational innovation, change, and renaissance. Implicitly, we have discussed these topics throughout the book. A hallmark of our strategic perspective is that we have suggested how managers can use knowledge of organizations to bring about desired changes. In Chapter 13, we specifically examine a variety of perspectives on how to change organizations. Additionally, we speculate about the nature of organizations of the twenty-first century and how knowledge of organizations will help managers.

Organizational Culture

CASE: PUT ON YOUR MAKEUP*

For many women, putting on makeup is an integral part of getting dressed. Few users probably think about what is involved in getting the products to them. For Mary Kay Cosmetics, Inc., every aspect of selling products is intimately tied to the company's culture.

Mary Kay Ash, the seventy-eight-year-old chairwoman emeritus, began her career in cosmetics as a young saleswoman for Stanley Home Products, a company that sold cleaners and brushes directly to customers. After failing in 1937 to receive the annual prize for the best sales record in the company, she vowed to gain the prize the following year. Ash's recognition as the top seller at Stanley in 1938 was the beginning of her success and enthusiasm for direct selling.

Ash worked for other direct selling companies and even went into an early "retirement" before deciding in 1963 to start her own company. While she was still employed at Stanley Home Products, Ash learned of a family of particularly effective skin-care products. She invested $5,000 to purchase formulas to begin what is now arguably the most successful direct sales organization in the world—Mary Kay Cosmetics, Inc. The company's sales force numbers approximately 300,000, and many of them share Mary Kay Ash's enthusiasm for selling. That, according to Ash and many analysts, is critical to the company's success. Thus, a key factor in understanding Mary Kay Cosmetics' success is understanding how the company maintains, motivates, and nurtures that enthusiasm for selling.

Cornerstones in the Mary Kay culture are symbols and ceremonies of recognition. Annually, the company holds "The Seminar" at the Dallas headquarters. Beauty consultants (Mary Kay representatives are not merely salespeople) gladly pay their own registration fees and all expenses to be at the "greatest sales party in the United States." At The Seminar consultants learn about products and selling techniques, but the central focus is on the recognition ceremonies where sales performance is publicly rewarded. Nearly

*Based on Alan Farnham, "Mary Kay's Lessons in Leadership," *Fortune* (September 20, 1993): 68–77.

every level of performance is in some way recognized with pins and trophies, but the fiercest competition is for the top prize—a pink Cadillac—the symbol that says "You've made it in the company."

To make the sales that are the bases for these recognitions, consultants buy from Mary Kay Cosmetics a basic starter kit for about $100. The mark-up on these basic items is 100 percent. Consultants then call a few friends and hold a Mary Kay Party where they sell items and recruit their own sales force. Income for consultants is unlimited, but real increases in income and promotions typically depend on increasing one's sales force. At the top of the promotion ladder, a national sales director for Mary Kay can earn in excess of $200,000 annually.

Emotional and symbolic rewards are perhaps as important as monetary rewards to the consultants, and Mary Kay bestows them generously. At the annual seminar, color-coded badges, emblems, and even suits are unmistakable symbols of how well their wearers did in the past year. Lapel pins read "$25,000" or a diamond bracelet proclaims "$1,000,000." Many successful consultants are invited to join Ms. Ash on trips.

Shot through all of these rewards for success is the sincerity of Mary Kay Ash. Mary Kay is an icon for the success of direct selling. Moreover, she has the uncanny ability to make her consultants really feel that they are a vital part of a truly successful organization. Her genuine caring for the consultants is further reinforced by her remembering birthdays, children's illnesses, and other individual events or circumstances. The recognition of performance and recognition of the individual are critical to Mary Kay's effective motivational effort and to sustaining the Mary Kay culture. Cynicism has no part to play at Mary Kay Cosmetics.

Another critical feature of the Mary Kay culture is the values she espouses. Ash believes in putting God first, family second, and career third. She stresses this message repeatedly to consultants and to their husbands. Because most Mary Kay consultants are women, the traditional support role falls to their husbands. Mary Kay encourages her "daughters," as she refers to her consultants, to show their appreciation to their supportive spouses.

Mary Kay has created a culture that is the primary vehicle for instilling her strongly held beliefs and values into each consultant and to make each one feel that she is a genuine member of the Mary Kay family. The result is a highly successful company with a cadre of successful and committed consultants who help a lot of women "put on their makeup."

Culture is the key to understanding an organization like Mary Kay Cosmetics. It is the strong set of norms, beliefs, and values of the organization's members along with the stories, myths, symbols, and celebrations that distinguish Mary Kay. Culture is the glue that binds the sales force to the company. Culture gives the company a sense of mission and a distinctiveness. It is key to motivating the consultants, and it is an integral part of the success of Mary Kay Cosmetics.

While every organization has a distinctive culture, not every one is as strong and deep as Mary Kay Cosmetics'. Additionally, culture does not always play the positive role it does at Mary Kay. Some organizations are stifled by cultures that inhibit flexibility, responsiveness, and change.

This chapter presents the key elements of culture, and describes how those elements create that sense of purpose and distinctiveness. As you read this chapter, keep in mind that culture is a holistic, overarching phenomenon. Culture is the sum of all parts of an organization—and then some. This is unlike many of the discrete characteristics of organizations that we have examined thus far. Culture, particularly strong culture, plays a critical role in all aspects of organizational life.

ORGANIZATIONAL CULTURE

Since the dawn of human social systems, culture has existed to help people deal with the uncertainty and ambiguity of their existence. Culture develops naturally when groups of humans come together. Members of formal organizations face uncertainties and ambiguities much like those that exist in the larger social system. Thus, it is not surprising that organizations develop distinctive cultures as part of the mechanism for managing the environment.[1] Despite the central nature of culture to human endeavors, exploration of organizational culture is a recent phenomenon. Beginning in the late 1970s, organizational scholars and others realized that culture plays a large part in determining a wide variety of behaviors, attitudes, and beliefs related to work and the workplace. Two important popular books, *Theory Z* by William Ouchi and *In Search of Excellence* by Thomas Peters and Robert Waterman, Jr., marked a heightened awareness of the potential importance of culture on the part of managers, academic researchers, and the general public.[2] Culture appears to develop in organizations much as it does in other types of human groupings. We are beginning to better understand its impact in work organizations.[3]

This chapter presents a multifaceted view of organizational culture. First, culture is defined. We then examine four different perspectives on the formation of culture. Because of the newness and complexity of the concept of organizational culture, the field has not yet arrived at one consistent and widely held set of views about culture. After exploring these four perspectives on culture formation, we begin to examine characteristics of culture. After identifying characteristics of culture, a logical next step is to describe how to audit organizational culture. Finally, inherent in the discussion of culture is the idea that culture plays a role in an organization's performance. Thus, auditing culture may be an important step to adjusting, adapting, or changing a culture to better fit an organization's strategic position. The chapter concludes with a discussion of the link between culture and strategy.

CULTURE DEFINED

Scientists from the fields of anthropology and sociology have been studying culture for many years. Still they are quick to note that culture is an abstract and complex concept; thus, many definitions of culture exist. The same is true even with a narrowed focus on *organizational culture.* Most definitions of organizational culture, however, contain some common elements. Most definitions note that culture exists at two levels in organizations: the *observable* traces or indicators of the culture and the *unobservable* forces present in the organization.[4] Observable traces may include physical characteristics of the organization such as architecture, artwork, dress patterns, language, stories, myths, behavior, formal rules, rituals, ceremonies, and appearance.[5] But these physical traces are not the culture itself. They are indicators of the unobservable characteristics of culture—the norms, beliefs, assumptions, ideology, values, and shared perceptions held by members of the organization.[6] Organizational culture, as one set of scholars has defined it, is a set of broad, tacitly understood rules that tell employees what to do under a wide variety of unimaginable circumstances.[7] It is the "patterns or configurations of these interpretations" of the observable characteristics that make up the culture,[8] the taken-for-granted and shared meanings, beliefs, and assumptions that people in the organization use to cope with problems, adapt to external conditions, and develop internal integration.[9] Thus, culture is a force that orients and directs the behavior of individual organizational members so that there is consistency and predictability within the organization.[10]

> ## Definition
>
> Organizational culture is a two-level construct that includes both observable and unobservable characteristics of the organization. At the observable level, culture includes many aspects of the organization such as architecture, dress, behavior patterns, rules, stories, myths, language, and ceremonies. At the unobservable level culture is composed of the shared values, norms, beliefs, and assumptions of organizational members. Culture is the pattern or configuration of these two levels of characteristics that orients or directs organizational members to manage problems and their surroundings.

For example, because the basic values and beliefs that underlie our form of government are contained in our Constitution, it can be thought of as a reflection or product of our national culture. Many companies have credos or codes of beliefs that similarly reflect their organizational culture. Such documents are at least one indicator of culture.

THE FORMATION OF CULTURE

Culture is not static. Organizational cultures emerge and change as the organization itself changes. Several organizational scholars have written on the subject of the formation of organizational culture, each offering somewhat different views on the subject. The views of four leading scholars—Edgar Schein, Christian Scholz, Meryl Louis, and Charles Fombrun—on the formation of organizational culture are presented in the following sections.

SCHEIN'S STAGES OF CULTURE FORMATION

People form groups seeking to satisfy needs. They bring goals, values, and even hopes to the group process and endeavor to find ways in which they can achieve what they want. Schein suggests that groups progress through a series of stages that affect culture. Throughout the stages of group development, maintenance and continuation of the group depend on the group finding ways to preserve the shared values and norms that hold the group together.[11]

According to Schein, the first stage of cultural development revolves around issues of dependency and authority. The question of who will lead the group (or organization) is the focal point. The group looks for someone to give it direction. The type of person who is selected to lead is indicative of many values and norms of the group or organization. Leader characteristics such as age, training, background, gender, and experience may all be important in the formation of the culture. The group or organization must grapple with issues of who they want to lead and how they want to be led. Some issues that may surface are: He's too inexperienced to be president; No outsider can understand this business. Both these statements point out issues that surface in this first step of cultural development.

Historically, initial leaders and founders have had great impact on the future culture of their organizations. The J.C. Penney Company still reflects its founder's beliefs about customer satisfaction and fairness. The "Penney Way" codifies James Cash Penney's beliefs and values about how to conduct business. Henry Ford's ideas about building cars and treating workers influenced (both positively and negatively) the Ford Motor Company long after he died.

Schein's second stage of cultural development involves the "confrontation of intimacy, role differentiation, (and) peer relationship issues."[12] Successful first efforts to deal with the authority issue (first stage) are likely to produce a feeling of success and good feelings about membership that are likely to carry over for an extended period of time. Early success can often motivate employees to give greater commitment and effort to the organization. This can be exemplified by NASA's early success at putting Neil Armstrong on the moon or the experience of winning athletic teams. The cultures of Notre Dame's football program, the Boston Celtics and Chicago Bulls professional basketball teams, or the Dallas Cowboys and San Francisco 49ers professional football teams owe much to early and continuing success. Each of these organizations has developed unique strong cultures around winning traditions: the divine blessing of Notre Dame, the Celtic mystique, the other-worldliness of the Michael Jordan–led Bulls, the business approach to football of the Cowboys, and the finesse of the 49ers.

During the third stage of cultural development, creativity and stability issues must be confronted. The group or organization begins to cope with the innovative approaches that brought its initial success as that innovation and creativity come into conflict with the needs for order and stability. Although creative and innovative forces may be critical factors in the formation of an organization, those same forces can disrupt the order of the organization.

This clash is typical of many entrepreneurial firms. For example, Steve Jobs, the cofounder of Apple Computers, was a creative, energetic, and visionary manager. Under his leadership the company became a highly successful start-up with unique products. In many respects, Apple Computers defined the concept of personal computing. However, early in the history of Apple, the company had difficulty reining in the creative and innovative spirit. As a consequence, the company had difficulty establishing order and stability. This was most noticeable in the company's haphazard approach to early product development and its inability to successfully market its products to large business users.

Apple owners and managers finally determined that they would need to bring in a skilled business manager to bring about the order and stability the firm needed to grow and prosper. John Sculley, a former Pepsico executive, was eventually brought in to provide the professional managerial skills that were deemed necessary for Apple. It would be nice and simple if the Apple story ended here with a successful and prosperous company, but that is not the case. The arrival of Sculley caused great turmoil. His managerial style and philosophy clashed with those of Steve Jobs and many of the early Apple people. Much turnover and tumult followed over the company's need to develop a somewhat more bureaucratic management system, and many managers, including Jobs, eventually left the company. Although Sculley was able to forge a more stable and orderly organization, his tenure at Apple was rocky because of the challenge to the old Apple way of doing things, and he stepped down in 1994.

Finally, the organization or group matures only to encounter a confrontation of survival and growth issues. The organization or group learns whether it is flexible and adaptable to changing conditions in the surrounding environment or whether its very survival will be questioned.

The airline industry has been characterized by dramatic upheaval over the past several years due in part to deregulation. Some companies have successfully dealt with survival and growth issues and have made various adjustments to their cultures. Southwest Airlines has developed a unique culture that delivers relaxed, casual, inexpensive transportation to business and recreational travelers. The culture is based on a high degree of employee involvement. After several brushes with failure, Continental Airlines appears to be surviving because of its emphasis on a particular niche of the marketplace — no frills services to short-distance travelers. By contrast, two former giants of the industry, Eastern Airlines and Pan Am, were unable to adapt to the new conditions brought about by deregulation. Both companies ended up in bankruptcy liquidation.

In the early 1980s, Lee Iacocca almost single-handedly saved Chrysler Corporation from bankruptcy by leading a major cultural change. The old Chrysler culture was characterized by aversion to risk, pessimism, one-way (top-down) communication, and the insularity of different Chrysler subunits. Chrysler's culture underwent a massive transformation under Iacocca's leadership. The company became aggressive in pursuing government support, new markets, products, and technology; a new optimism pervaded management and production workers; the organization became more streamlined with emphasis on two-way communications (i.e., production workers became important sources of new ideas); and cooperation among subunits became standard procedure.

Chrysler has at times struggled and stumbled, but the company has transformed itself. The company has been an innovator. Its car designs have won praise from auto critics and consumers. The company's new product development process (the time and techniques needed to design new cars) is at the forefront among the Big Three U.S. companies and approaches the speed and efficiency of industry-leading Japanese companies. By nearly every measure, Chrysler has undergone a successful turnaround. A big part of that turnaround is the new culture that Lee Iacocca initiated in the early 1980s.

The stages of cultural development represent changed goals, values, and focus of the organization. The underlying question throughout these stages of development is whether the organization can forge the kind of culture that is needed to survive. This is true even when members are not necessarily aware of attempts to form and change the culture. Table 10.1 summarizes Schein's four stages of cultural development.

■ **TABLE 10.1**
Schein: Culture Formation in Groups

Stage	Dominant Assumption	Group Focus
1. Dependency/ authority confrontation	A leader will guide the group to its maximum benefit.	Leadership selection
2. Confrontation of intimacy, role differentiation, peer relationship issues	The group is successful and the members like each other.	Normative consensus; harmony
3. Creativity/stability issue	The group can be innovative and stable at once.	Team continuity and accomplishment
4. Survival/growth issues	The group has endured and so must be "right."	Group's attention: status quo/resistance to change

Source: Adapted from Edgar H. Schein, *Organizational Culture and Leadership* (San Francisco: Jossey-Bass, 1985), 191.

SCHOLZ'S TYPOLOGY OF CULTURE FORMATION

Christian Scholz views organizational culture as a complex phenomenon and believes that the best way to understand cultural formation is through a typology of past research efforts.[13] Scholz argues that culture develops along three dimensions: an evolutionary dimension, an internal dimension, and an external dimension. These three dimensions make up his typology.

The ***evolutionary dimension*** of cultural formation is somewhat similar to Schein's view: culture develops over time in a series of stages. Scholz proposes that a nascent culture is already in place and that subsequent stages are the result of how the organization responds to challenges to the culture. He outlines five evolutionary stages: (1) the stable stage during which no change is contemplated; (2) the reactive stage during which minimal change is accepted; (3) the anticipating stage when incremental changes are accepted; (4) the exploring stage during which large amounts of change are possible; and (5) the creative stage when continuous change is possible. According to Scholz, not all organizations follow this sequence, nor is any one stage regarded as better than another.

The focus of the ***internal dimension*** of culture is on particular internal conditions operating within the organization that affect the culture. For example, an organization that uses standardized production processes would create conditions for a culture that is constant and process oriented. On the other hand, a professional organization with employees possessing varied skills and high levels of professional expertise is likely to foster development of a culture that emphasizes individualism and professionalism.

External environmental conditions are the forces that constitute the ***external dimension*** of culture. External conditions and how organizational members perceive and respond to those conditions play a critical role in the development of the culture. A company facing a complex and dynamic environment is likely to develop a culture that values flexibility, innovativeness, and risk taking. Conversely, an organization facing a simple and stable environment is likely to adapt a culture that features conservatism, risk aversion, and bureaucracy.

Scholz's model of cultural development is somewhat more complex than Schein's. He views organizational culture as arising from these three diverse sets of pressures: time, internal characteristics of the organization, and external conditions in the environment.

FOMBRUN'S LEVELS OF CULTURE

Charles Fombrun has described the development of culture through forces at three major levels: societal, industrial, and organizational. According to Fombrun's view, organizational culture is a product of the broader culture in which organizations are embedded. Understanding the interplay between societal and industry levels of culture with characteristics of the organization is vital for an accurate analysis of culture and for guidance on how to modify culture.[14]

At the ***societal level*** culture represents the values, attitudes, and meanings that members bring to the organization. This may be influenced by such social forces as the educational system, political system, economic conditions, and the social structure of the larger society. The organization operates within this general cultural atmosphere. These conditions may influence the strategies, mission, objectives, norms, and practices in the organization in subtle but real ways. A company's strategy, products, and advertisements must be consistent with the community culture if the organization wishes to maintain legitimacy and approval.

For example, Cincinnati, Ohio, is regarded as a culturally conservative community. Movies, art exhibits, and music that raise no objection in East Coast or West Coast communities sometimes offend local sensibilities. A local rock radio station, with a tendency toward wacky advertising, offended many in the community with a recent campaign. Billboards featured the heads of two male on-air morning personalities on bodies of naked pregnant women. The billboard text referred to morning sickness. While the campaign was consistent with the station's bizarre sense of humor and its off-the-wall morning show, some people in the city found the billboards so offensive that they withdrew advertising, wrote complaints, and stopped listening to the station. The station eventually withdrew the advertising. The societal level is often an ethical, legal, and social guide to conducting business in a community.

The essence of the ***industrial level*** of culture is best realized by considering the similarities of cultures within and differences in cultures between industries. Often there are dominant values or beliefs of an organization that are espoused by a majority of organizations within an industry. Over time industries develop styles that have a remarkable influence on such things as decision making, political stances, member lifestyles, and even dress codes. For example, the banking industry has had a unique and prevalent way of doing business. At one time banks were concerned almost exclusively with efficiency, cost control, and basic standard service. Until the late 1960s many banks had limited business hours (i.e., "bankers' hours"), staying open only from 9:00 A.M. to 3:00 P.M. with some additional late hours on Fridays. Extended weekday hours, Saturday banking, and ATMs are fairly recent phenomena in the industry, but once a few banks experimented with extended hours, most others joined in. Now banking is characterized by more extensive services, more aggressive marketing, and a customer-oriented focus. Nonetheless, the industry is still characterized as conservative and formal. Managers dress conservatively, avoid risk, and generally advocate fiscal and social conservatism.

Compare banking with the industrial culture present in the entertainment business (i.e., television, recording, and films). The dominant values are for more casual or flamboyant dress, high-risk behavior, and fiscal and social radicalism.

LOUIS'S MULTIPLE CULTURES

Up to this point in the discussion we have treated organizational culture as monolithic — that is, an organization has a *single* culture. Cultural researcher Meryl Louis suggests that organizations, especially large, complex ones, often develop different cultures at different sites or ***loci*** within the organization.[15] Thus, unique cultures (perhaps *subcultures* is a better term) may develop around different levels in the organization or within different divisions or departments. Conditions, problems, or personnel at different loci can produce pressures for different cultures within the organization. Moreover, loci outside the organization may also produce conditions for different cultures. For example, in southern California many firms hire large numbers of Hispanic and Asian workers. These workers bring in values, beliefs, and norms derived from their neighborhood ethnic cultures. Another example where the cultural locus is outside the firm is legal departments. Legal departments in firms as diverse as Ford and Exxon may have similar departmental cultures because of the shared values, norms, and beliefs of attorneys.

INTERNATIONAL CULTURAL CONSIDERATIONS

The above views on culture should reinforce the idea that organizational cultures do not develop independently of national cultures. Nations tend to exhibit certain characteristics (values, norms, practices, beliefs, and standards) that are collectively created over long periods of time. These characteristics become ingrained in human nature. A culture, for example, develops a common language and ways of thinking that consciously and unconsciously direct activities performed by members of the culture. Geert Hofstede surveyed people from around the world concerning their work-related values. He found major differences across countries that had a profound impact on the way individuals within a country approach their work lives. For instance, Westerners tend to be much more concerned with individual achievement and recognition. Eastern cultures tend to be more collective in nature, and group achievement and recognition is a dominant motivator. Even among Western nations, there are differences. For example, French workers perceive a large "power distance" between themselves and their bosses. American workers perceive a more collegial work relationship with bosses, and often view bosses as peers and colleagues.[16]

In recent years, much discussion has focused on the national and organizational cultural differences that distinguish Japanese and American organizations. To fully understand Japanese management, it is important to understand the national culture in which Japanese firms are embedded.[17] Several important characteristics of Japan and Japanese culture contribute to the unique Japanese management culture. First, history and geography contribute to Japan's emphasis on protecting its borders from foreigners. Japan was essentially closed to foreigners until late in the nineteenth century. This, in turn, has contributed to the homogeneity of the Japanese population and their fear and mistrust of foreigners. Japanese culture is, to a large extent, based on Confucianism and Buddhism. By contrast, American culture is a product of largely open borders and heterogeneity. The Protestant ethic plays a central role in American culture, but the U.S. was settled by diverse immigrant groups who often brought with them their unique ethnic and national cultures. Thus, we often speak of Italian-Americans, German-Americans, Mexican-Americans, and Asian-Americans. The different national histories and cultural paths of Japan and the U.S. have produced distinct national organizational cultures. Table 10.2 highlights the differences between these two cultures.

■ **TABLE 10.2**

Contrasting Japanese and American Organizational Cultures

Japanese Culture	American Culture
Emphasis on collectivism and groups	Emphasis on individualism
Emphasis on family and respect for authority	Emphasis on individual and youth
Emphasis on cooperation and harmony	Emphasis on competition, conflict, confrontation, and differences
Emphasis on patience, long-term results	Emphasis on immediacy, short-term results
Emphasis on humility and austerity	Emphasis on self-promotion and material wealth

Source: Adapted from Harrison M. Trice and Janice M. Beyer, *The Cultures of Work Organizations* (Englewood Cliffs, N.J.: Prentice-Hall, 1993), pages 54, 342.

Organizations develop cultures within the context of their national cultures. An organization is, above all, a citizen of a particular country, and the country's dominant norms, standards, styles, and beliefs set the parameters in which an organization's culture develops. Problems likely arise when organizations develop cultures that are not congruent with societal cultures. Also, organizations are increasingly multicultural.

Many large multinational firms blend the cultures of the various national cultures in which they are embedded.

THICK AND THIN CULTURES

Organizational culture is the result of a complex interplay of forces. If the forces that contribute to the development of an organizational culture are favorable, an organization may develop a culture that is widely and broadly held by members and that strongly unifies members as they pursue organizational goals. The thickness or thinness of the culture is a measure of its strength.[18] Organizational culture is said to be **thick** if it is widespread and accepted throughout the organization. Organizational members subscribe to a shared set of beliefs, values, and norms. A **thin** culture is one that is not widely held and does not enjoy acceptance throughout the organization. The organization lacks a core of commonly held beliefs, norms, and values. Employees may find it difficult to identify with such a company or to even identify its core goals and values.

An example of a thick culture is Ford Motor Company. All employees carry a three-by-five-inch plastic card that lists the company's creed, the company's basic values. The message is a simple reminder of Ford's culture: At Ford the quality of the products and services is an extension of the employees.[19] This value is reinforced with banners and through the example of quality circles. Ford has tried to extend this culture of quality and service to its dealers with a President's Award based on service rather than on sales. In the introductory case on Mary Kay Cosmetics we saw that award ceremonies can be powerful mechanisms for spreading the culture. Company creeds and award systems are just two mechanisms for spreading a culture. Later in this chapter we explore several others.

When a company is successful in widely and broadly spreading its values, like Ford's message about quality and service, it is more likely to develop a thick culture. A thick culture is a strong tie that binds the total organizational system together. A thick culture can help organizations channel energy into productive and predictable behaviors and responses that help the organization manage ambiguity and uncertainty. For example, customers and clients, as we noted in Chapters 4 and 5, can be important sources of uncertainty. One part of that uncertainty is how those customers and clients respond to boundary spanners—for example, sales and service representatives. To manage this uncertainty, many companies develop formal and informal dress codes for their sales and service people.

Perhaps one of the most widely recognized codes was the unofficial dress code at IBM. For many years, it was nearly universal that IBM employees, especially those who dealt with customers, dressed in conservative dark suits, white shirts, and muted ties.[20] Customers could gain some reassurance from the appearance of IBM personnel—these were knowledgeable, official representatives of IBM. Such reassurance may have been particularly important for mainframe computer customers who were spending millions of dollars on IBM systems. The movement away from mainframe computing and the increasing emphasis on innovation and creativity in the information technology business is pressuring IBM to adopt a more relaxed culture with more casual dress.

CULTURAL INDICATORS AND MANIFESTATIONS

Early in this chapter we noted that culture exists on two levels: the unobserved but implied values, norms, and beliefs of the organization and the observable indicators of those values, norms, and beliefs. We turn our attention now to those observable indicators and manifestations of culture. Often it is through the study of these observable indicators and manifestations of the culture that we learn of the underlying values, norms, and beliefs. For the members of an organization, the physical manifestations of culture provide "sense-making" mechanisms by which members try to gain some common perception and understanding of events and circumstances.[21] The following sections explore these physical manifestations of culture.

RITES, RITUALS, AND CEREMONIES

Rites, rituals, and ceremonies (sometimes called *ceremonials*) are public social events that mark the passage of some event or milestone. Rites and rituals celebrate discrete individual events, while ceremonies combine several rites or rituals into a single event.[22] Typical types of rites, rituals, and ceremonies include those that celebrate entry into the organization (orientation, boot camp, or induction ceremonies); transtions (promotions); renewal and enhancement (annual meetings, Christmas parties, picnics); degradation (firings and layoffs); or parting (retirement parties, farewell parties). Some rites and rituals may be highly planned, rehearsed, and formal to the extent that they are defined and described in company documents. Others may be spontaneous, unplanned events. Ceremonies tend to be more elaborate, planned activities much like the Mary Kay Seminars mentioned in the introductory case.

Ceremonies, rites, and rituals hold the group together. In fact, many ceremonies, rites, and rituals require that the members of the organization come together to conduct them. Religious meetings, graduations, recognition events, homecomings, annual meetings, and Christmas parties are examples of events that require the organization's members to come together in order to carry them out. These events are manifestations of the beliefs and values, and the perceptions and understandings of the organization—for example, Mary Kay's rewards for selling and valuing of family. A small entrepreneurial banking firm provides a less formalized example of rituals. The bank's founder gathers employees together every day or two for informal meetings in which he dispenses his views on banking. These events provide a basis for making sense of the environment and give the organization a sense of continuity and stability that binds members together.

SYMBOLS AND SLOGANS

Firms spend considerable time and effort developing means of ready recognition of the organization and its products. "We deliver for you" is a slogan used by the U.S. Postal Service to share with the consumer the organization's desire to provide timely, convenient, dependable service. UPS uses the company's brown uniforms and brown trucks to provide employees and customers with a common vision of the company and to convey the image of efficiency. Wal-Mart uses the word "*Always*" in conjunction with advertising and in-store displays to convey to customers and employees the company's dedication to consistent low prices and quality service. Delta Airlines has used slogans extensively to transmit to employees and consumers the company's customer-oriented values. The slogans have included "We love to fly and it shows" and, more recently, "You'll love the way we fly."

The Disney Company, especially its theme park division, has an especially strong and rich culture. Slogans and symbols play important roles in sustaining that culture. In particular, Disneyland is labeled by Disney people as "The Happiest Place on Earth" where "everyone is a child at heart."[23] Symbols such as the ever-present mouse ears, the multitude of Disney animation characters, and the fantasy recreations in park locations (e.g., Fantasyland, Frontierland, Tomorrowland, etc.) and rides (e.g., Small World, Pirates of the Caribbean, etc.) reinforce the Disney values of youth, fun, and fantasy.

Logos and trademarks also indicate cultural values and beliefs. Sometimes these logos may simply be unique, readily identifiable markers of a company's products and services. Mercedes-Benz's three-pointed star is a widely recognized symbol of high-quality, luxury autos. Perhaps one of the most widely recognized sets of corporate symbols are those associated with Coca Cola—the red disk, the script logo, and the "wave."

Nike has developed a thick culture with many symbols. One of the primary symbols of that culture is the "swoosh" emblazoned on shoes, hats, and clothing. In the 1970s, the "swoosh" became identified in the minds of employees and consumers with a youthful, innovative, free-spirited company that led a national craze in fitness.[24] The "swoosh" was thought to embody the antiestablishment and antitraditional business values of the company's founder, Phil Knight. The "swoosh" became such an important identifying logo that many Nike field representatives tattooed the symbol on various parts of their anatomy as a sign of their commitment to Nike.

LANGUAGE

One of the marks of a group is its tendency to develop a language or jargon of its own. The language serves as shorthand to members and as a barrier to nonmembers. Members of the organization can quickly and easily discern the meaning of particular words or phrases that are unknown to outsiders. Members develop an organizational vocabulary, and members use it in their daily contacts with each other. Professional groups and technical professions develop sophisticated jargon as can be seen among doctors, lawyers, and computer hardware and software specialists.

A strong culture may not necessarily be a positive factor. At one accounting firm, partners used a particularly derogatory term to refer to clients.[25] The term served two purposes. First, everyone in the firm knew that the term meant *client*. Outsiders would be less clear about the meaning. Second, it conveyed to employees the firm's rather negative value toward its clients—clients were a source of problems with which the firm must deal.

Nike, with its thick culture, developed the label *Ekin* (Nike spelled backward) for its special breed of technical field representatives.[26] The Ekins are those highly committed employees noted earlier who often tattoo the Nike "swoosh" on their bodies. As described by one Ekin, they are hard-working, passionate, committed representatives who bring information about the latest Nike innovations to retailers and customers. Their passion for Nike is matched by their passion for fitness and athletics. Many are former collegiate and professional athletes. Thus, the term *Ekin* takes on an important role in conveying the values and beliefs of Nike about free spirit, sport, fun, passion, and innovation. Nike has used the "Just Do It" slogan to generate a similar level of commitment and identification in the consumer marketplace.

Disney theme parks have evolved a colorful language that is a critical element of the company's culture.[27] Language is used to reinforce the ideas that Disney theme parks are theatrical performances and that good wholesome fun is the main attraction. Some examples of the Disney lexicon are:

- Disney theme parks are referred to as "parks," not "amusement parks";
- Park visitors are referred to as "guests," never "customers";
- Employees at Disney parks are called "cast members";
- Cast members do not wear "uniforms," instead they have "wardrobes" and "costumes";
- Cast members work on "attractions," rather than "rides"; and
- "Security hosts," not police, investigate "incidents," but Disney parks do not have "accidents."

Not all of the language examples at Disney parks are officially approved.[28] "Cast members" have developed their own slang that may not further the official Disney culture but is, nonetheless, an important part of the Disney culture. For example, lower-status "cast members" are called "peanut pushers" and "soda jerks." Problem "guests" may acquire the label of "duck" or "duffess." And even "cast members" who become too imbued with the Disney culture are not immune from negative labeling. These gung-ho followers are called "Disnoids."

MYTHS AND STORIES

Groups and organizations develop a history of operations and events over time in the form of myths and stories that is handed down from one generation to another. Mary Kay Ash's rise from a sales representative at Stanley Home Products to the head of a multibillion dollar cosmetics company is a story that inspires many of the legion of sales associates at Mary Kay Cosmetics. Similar myths and stories of leaders, founders, and innovators serve to motivate and lead people through adversity and uncertainty.

A classic example of the strength and pervasiveness of a myth is the image that Lee Iacocca built during his years leading Chrysler out of chaos and financial crisis in the early 1980s.[29] Iacocca took over a deeply troubled company in 1979. Chrysler trailed GM and Ford in nearly every category imaginable: cost, product quality, innovativeness, service, and customer appeal. Iacocca, who had been fired from Ford Motor Company in a political squabble with Henry Ford II, did have a track record of success. In the 1960s, Iacocca was instrumental in the development and marketing of the Ford Mustang and the Cobra sports/racing cars. While Iacocca clearly did play a key role in the turn-around at Chrysler in the early- to mid-1980s, he did not do it singlehandedly. Many people inside and outside the company played important roles in reversing Chrysler's declining fortunes. However, the myth that prevails in many circles is that Lee Iacocca personally and singlehandedly pulled Chrysler out of its decline.

Although myths and stories typically involve elements of truth, they often get distorted or exaggerated over time. Mary Kay Ash's rise to success took many years and much hard work. Iacocca's success at Chrysler was due in part to his skill and expertise, but was also the result of hard work by many others behind the scenes. These myths and stories play a part in guiding members about the appropriate and expected behaviors. Mary Kay's story of her rise to prominence glorifies the commitment to hard work and the value of enhancing personal beauty. Lee Iacocca's story also documents the value of hard work, but also emphasizes hardball politicking, showmanship, and risk taking.

PHYSICAL ENVIRONMENT

People work in organizations that have a concrete physical presence. Organizations have buildings, factories, and grounds. Buildings and factories have ornamentation such as artwork, furniture, and other adornments. The specific architecture often affects the process of work and may give evidence of the culture or contribute to the development of culture. Often the physical grounds include parking lots, gardens, and outdoor recreation areas. These conditions may also be important elements of culture. In general, physical structure, symbols, artifacts, and other stimuli are an integral part of an organization's culture. The physical environment is composed of three basic elements: physical structures, physical stimuli, and symbolic artifacts.[30]

Physical Structure. Consider, for example, a basic aspect of the physical layout or design of a building. Layout or design determines the size and location of various offices. This can give important evidence about culture. The design of buildings and one's location in them can have a profound effect on attitudes and behavior. To some extent, buildings are designed to meet certain functional needs — to determine what can be done in the buildings and how successfully or easily it can be done. Consider the following examples.

Levi Strauss's corporate culture is characterized by openness, friendliness, flexibility, and innovation. In the 1970s, the company moved to a new headquarters building in San Francisco. The building, a high-rise glass tower, was not amenable to the Levi Strauss culture. Headquarters' offices were scattered throughout several floors; offices were closed in; and there were few open areas where workers could congregate. Such a physical environment may be a good match for a highly bureaucratic culture, but it was a poor match for the open, flexible culture of Levi Strauss. In 1982, Levi Strauss built a new headquarters' facility that matched its culture of openness and flexibility. The new facility featured a set of four-story buildings around a central, open courtyard. Offices were open, interconnected, and faced the courtyard.

At Nike, founder and chief executive Phil Knight has a large, well-appointed private office that is far off the beaten path. Few employees ever see the inside of Knight's private office. Instead, most Nike executives interact with Knight in an outer office. This office configuration perpetuates the mystery and mystique that surround Knight. On the other hand, Nike's headquarter facilities in Beaverton, Oregon, are much like an exclusive college campus with tasteful architecture, elaborate sports and recreational facilities, extensive sports-related artwork, and other artifacts that contribute to the unique Nike culture that emphasizes innovation, creativity, fun, athleticism, competition, and hard work.[31]

The executive offices at Ford Motor Company are on the top floors of Ford's World Headquarters (the "glass house") in Dearborn, Michigan. The layout of the headquarters is hierarchical with higher-level departments located on upper-level floors of the building. This configuration replicates the hierarchical culture of Ford. During Henry Ford II's presidency at Ford, his executive office suite on the top floor of the "glass house" included a private dining room (with a personal chef for Ford). Few people other than top Ford Motor executives ever had the privilege of entering this dining room. This contributed to a culture of privilege for top management and a separation of top management from lower-level employees that was characteristic of the company during Henry Ford II's leadership.[32] It will be interesting to see if this architecture continues to match Ford Motor's needs as the auto industry undergoes extensive change and Ford strives for a more participative culture.

These examples show the effects that physical structures can have on people in organizations. Friendships can be made or broken; communication can be facilitated or inhibited; work can flow smoothly or encounter barriers because of the physical layout of organizations. Thus, the physical structure of organizations can play a crucial role in the development and support of a culture.

Physical Stimuli. The second aspect of the physical environment is the physical stimuli present in the organization. These are parts of the physical environment that gradually come into members' awareness. Examples include such things as mail deliveries, time clocks, and telephone calls. The physical stimuli are often distractions to routines. For example, employees may become aware of patterns of mail delivery and structure their work around those deliveries. Employees may stop work in anticipation of mail deliveries. Much of the folklore of organizational life focuses on friendships or information exchanges around the office watercooler. These physical stimuli have a great deal of influence on culture.

Symbolic Artifacts. Finally, we must consider symbolic artifacts—"aspects of the physical setting that individually and collectively guide (our) interpretation of the social setting."[33] These things give us cues and clues about the culture. Spartan surroundings, like those characteristic of many Japanese corporate headquarters, convey an image of efficiency; the opulence of the Ford Motor chief executive suite during Henry Ford II's reign gave an image of privilege and social stratification. The presence or absence of corporate jets, executive parking spaces, executive dining rooms, and expensive artwork and furnishings can contribute to the specific culture of an organization. For example, think about the meaning conveyed by a company that provides convenient, covered parking for top executives, but relegates lower-level employees to open parking lots that stretch for acres around an office complex. Or think of the image that Nike conveys to employees and visitors to its headquarters who encounter extensive displays of art depicting sports and sports celebrities.

From this discussion of cultural manifestations, one can see that they are both a result of culture and a reflection of culture. They are an integral part of organizational culture and must be considered along with the other, more abstract, components of culture. Table 10.3 presents a comprehensive list and description of cultural manifestations.

TABLE 10.3
*Cultural Manifestations**

Manifestation	Description
Rite	Relatively elaborate, dramatic, planned sets of activities that consolidate various forms of cultural expressions into one event, which is carried out through social interactions, usually for the benefit of an audience.
Ceremonial	A system of several rites connected with a single occasion or event.
Ritual	A standardized, detailed set of techniques and behaviors that manage anxieties, but seldom produce intended, technical consequences of practical importance.
Myth	A dramatic narrative of imagined events, usually used to explain origins or transformations. Also, an unquestioned belief about the practical benefits of certain techniques and behaviors that is not supported by demonstrated fact.
Saga	An historical narrative describing the unique accomplishments of a group and its leaders.
Legend	A handed-down narrative of some wonderful event that is based in history but has been embellished with fictional details.
Story	A narrative based on true events—often a combination of truth and fiction.
Folktale	A completely fictional narrative.
Symbol	Any object, act, event, quality, or relation that serves as a vehicle for conveying meaning.
Language	A particular form or manner in which members of a group use vocal sounds and written signs to convey meanings to each other.
Gesture	Movements of parts of the body used to express meanings.
Physical setting	Those things that surround people physically and provide them with immediate sensory stimuli as they carry out culturally expressive activities.
Artifact	Material objects manufactured by people to facilitate culturally expressive activities.

*Our discussion of cultural manifestations is a representative sampling rather than an exhaustive treatment of Trice and Beyer's list.
Source: Harrison M. Trice and Janice M. Beyer, "Studying Organizational Culture Through Rites and Ceremonials," *Academy of Management Review* 9, no. 4 (October 1984): 655.

EFFECTS OF CULTURE ON ORGANIZATIONS

In our earlier discussion of thick and thin cultures, we briefly mentioned how cultures can affect organization. We now expand that theme by examining five specific aspects of culture's effect on organizations: direction, pervasiveness, strength, flexibility, and commitment.[34]

Direction refers to the way culture affects goal attainment. Culture can help push an organization toward its goals or away from them. It can either be consistent with organizational goals (a positive force) or it can be inconsistent with goals (a negative force). For example, if a firm's culture fosters a "not-invented-here" attitude toward innovation, the firm will be reluctant to go outside its boundaries for innovations. This attitude breeds a belief that any innovation not invented or developed inside the organization cannot be any good. Such a culture may be an important factor in directing the organization to maintain an active research and development division, but it also directs the firm away from potentially valuable outside innovations. The company may periodically reinvent the wheel; that is, it may spend valuable time and resources developing innovations that are already available outside the firm.

The degree to which members share a culture is an indication of its *pervasiveness*. Cultures like those at Nike and Mary Kay Cosmetics are pervasive. Adherence to the basic tenets of those cultures is widespread among members. Widespread adoption of the basic culture is key to a thick culture, while thin cultures are not pervasive.

Strength of culture refers to its impact on members. Some religious sects and political organizations have what amounts to a compelling force over their members. Take the case of the Japanese religious sect that commanded highly educated followers to engage in urban terrorism, releasing lethal nerve gas in the Tokyo subway system. We can even find strong cultures, albeit somewhat weaker than the above example, among businesses. Recall the earlier example of the Ekins at Nike who tattooed the "swoosh" emblem on their bodies. Such behavior is indicative of a strong culture.

Flexible cultures are adaptable to changing conditions. Organizations, particularly those that face changing and complex environments, must retain flexibility to accommodate. Evidence of flexibility (or inflexibility) can be seen in how organizations respond in times of crisis. Several techniques can be used to establish flexibility.[35]

One method is to establish a senior management position that is responsible for questioning proposed actions and questioning the status quo in general. This person should have considerable experience with the organization so that he or she has legitimacy in the organization and can see situations from a total organizational perspective.

A second strategy is to recruit outsiders to fill positions on governing boards and management. Outsiders can bring a fresh perspective to organizational problems and can help the organization avoid the "not-invented-here" syndrome. When IBM began to suffer serious erosion to its position in the computer industry, its initial responses were indicative of an inflexible culture. The company responded with some cost cutting, but it maintained its same conservative culture—reliance on mainframe computers, promotion from within, and risk-aversive behavior in everything from employee appearance and dress to how the company produced and marketed its computers. More recently with the arrival of Louis Gerstner as CEO, IBM has shown signs of developing a more flexible, adaptive culture. The hiring of Gerstner itself, a man who was an IBM outsider, was symbolic of the breakdown of the old culture. Outsiders, particularly on boards of directors, can also serve as boundary spanners to the environment. One cautionary note related to the recruitment of outsiders for executive positions is that it may lower morale in the organization. Some managers may feel that they have been passed over.

Finally, flexibility can be enhanced throughout the organization by cross training and frequent job reassignments. With cross training, workers learn many different jobs.

This tends to reduce the narrow provincial view that often accompanies a narrow, functional job focus. Frequent reassignments help familiarize employees with the total organization and can help reduce divisional alliances that may not be in the best interest of the total organization. Flexibility is an important factor in the integration of culture and strategy.

The culture of an organization also has impact on the degree of *commitment* shown by its members. Commitment is a condition in which members of a group give their efforts, abilities, and loyalties to the organization and its pursuit of its goals in return for satisfaction. In other words, the culture creates conditions in the organization whereby members are either willing or not willing to commit themselves to the pursuit of the organization's goals in exchange for some general state of satisfaction. A strong culture can enhance the likelihood that members will display a high degree of commitment.

Culture aids the attainment of member commitment by laying out the mission and the values to be observed in pursuit of that mission. Culture may also aid by spelling out to the member the value of the organization to the individual. By committing to an organization, the member is choosing one set of options over those offered by committing to other organizations.[36] Commitment is a type of emotional (and perhaps financial) investment in the organization.

Several factors, including salary and the physical environment, can reinforce employee commitment to the organization. Being accepted as a member of a desirable group gives an individual a strong incentive to adopt the culture as a way of life. Recall the earlier example of the Ekins and Nike. Similar examples can be found in college fraternities and sororities. Willingness to adopt an organization's rituals and way of life is essential to acculturation. Over time, the individual feels a sense of identity with the group and is even willing to make sacrifices for it. This, in turn, leads to a deeper sense of commitment. Thus, one of the prime requirements for, or conditions of, commitment is the sense of identification with the organization that culture provides.

CULTURE AND COMPETITIVE ADVANTAGE

From a strategic standpoint, a strong thick culture can even become a source of competitive advantage.[37] Competitive advantage is a means by which one company can achieve superior performance relative to another competitor organization. Because culture is a powerful influence on behavior, a culture that stimulates productive behaviors that contribute to company success can be a powerful determinant of long-term firm success. Three conditions must be met before culture can guide success over the long haul. First, the culture must be valuable. The culture must facilitate high sales, low costs, high margins, or some other outcomes that are conducive to adding financial value to the firm. Second, the culture must be rare. Characteristics of the culture must not be commonly found among other competing companies' cultures within the industry. If all companies possess the same cultural characteristics, one specific firm cannot gain competitive advantage from those characteristics. Third, imitation of the culture must be difficult and imperfect. Other firms should be unable to build or imitate the culture perfectly and thus gain the same competitive advantages. If other firms can easily imitate the culture, its value as a source of competitive advantage dwindles. However, it is important to note that it is difficult to modify or change cultures effectively.

In the following two sections, we turn our attention to the process of cultural change. It is first necessary to assess culture through a culture audit. This helps to establish the current state of the culture. We then look at the specific process of changing culture.

THE CULTURE AUDIT

Just as companies conduct financial and managerial audits, it is necessary to put culture under the microscope. The purpose of such investigations is to ensure that the organization's culture fits with the organization's other characteristics (e.g., goals or mission, structure, people, processes). A culture that fits should have a net positive effect on the organization and its mission.

Two key reasons for recent interest in culture are the increasingly turbulent environment in which organizations currently exist and the increasing attention given to the methods of non–U.S. companies — particularly the attention to Japanese management.[38] As a result, awareness of culture's role in organizational life has increased. At the same time, managers, organizational scholars, and journalists have begun to study organizational cultures in other countries to identify cultural advantages.

THE INFORMAL CULTURE AUDIT

Culture seems to creep into assumptions that organization members make every day about all manner of organizational issues. Over time, the culture becomes almost second nature, a normative consensus like wearing a tie, getting to work on time, or answering the phone. Only when changes occur do members of the organization become conscious of the values, assumptions, and norms that form the foundation of the culture.[39]

Role changes are prime causes for attention to culture. When we enter new situations, we attempt to see if our old culture fits. Think, for example, about your first days in college. We try to learn about the accepted ways of doing things in our new environment; we examine dress codes and language. We try hard to discern the pecking order and jargon so that we are not so awkward so as to stand out in the crowd.

The acculturation process involves both the newcomer's attempt to learn and adopt the prevailing culture and the old-timer's attempt to mold the newcomer to the culture. This process is often formally addressed by orientation programs aimed at teaching new members the official culture. However, there exists an informal culture that also must be learned. As we noted in the chapter on organizational politics, how things get done and how people behave is often different from what is written in the official documents of the organization.

Conflict among different subcultures within an organization may also call attention of members to the culture of the organization. Variations in culture within an organization are common across functional or product groupings. For example, it is common to see somewhat different values and norms among a company's engineering and operations groups compared with those in marketing or human resources. Value and norm differences may affect such seemingly trivial things as dress or such important issues as organizational priorities.

How top managers behave also causes members to monitor culture. What top executives say and do goes far to show the organization's culture. When IBM spun off its printer business into a separate independent business, Lexmark, top management at Lexmark took great pains to establish a culture that was unique and separate from the old IBM culture.[40] In particular, top management wanted to establish a more casual work environment. To do this, they relaxed the old norms for dress that existed at IBM with Friday dress-down days. On Fridays even top managers wore open neck sports shirts with no ties. At IBM the norm for reports for corporate strategy sessions was that managers would have extensively prepared presentations with many graphs and overhead slides. This often inhibited the free exchange of new ideas and critical evaluation of projects. Lexmark tried to change this by insisting that managers reduce the use of overhead slides. Top management's attention to these behaviors caused others in the organization to pay attention to culture.

A culture audit, then, is a look at values, beliefs, norms, behaviors, and other aspects of culture. It consists of monitoring, evaluating, and perhaps changing various components of culture. Audits show the extent to which both the formal and informal rules of the organization operate.

Culture audits can be conducted by asking questions aimed at finding out how members feel and think about the organization and their places in it. As an exercise, you can do the same for your college or university. What are the key values? What do people believe? How do students behave? How do faculty behave? These and other questions can be quite revealing in showing the underlying culture of your institution.

THE FORMAL CULTURE AUDIT

The audit outlined in the previous section describes an informal process that may be appropriate for an individual in an organization. The individual can gain great insight into an organization's culture, and individual managers may even be able to take actions to facilitate the fit between the culture and individual employees. But what if top management (or others in the organization) suspect that there may be problems with the culture? What if management is contemplating changing the culture? The simple observational process of an informal audit is not likely to be rigorous enough. Management should turn to a *formal culture audit* to gain a comprehensive picture of the culture.

The formal process of learning about a culture is difficult, and no single method is without problems.[41] Managers may themselves attempt to assess the culture through structured observations and data collection. After all, managers are likely to have access to more data about their organization than outsiders. However, insiders may be too close to the culture of their organization to accurately and objectively assess that culture. Thus, organizations often turn to outside consultants to work with insiders in conducting an audit.

Insider Audit. An audit may involve the use of surveys or questionnaires to gain information about employee behaviors, beliefs, values, and norms. Although surveys and questionnaires can sometimes provide useful information about culture, most experts discourage their use. The belief is that the resulting behaviors, beliefs, values, and norms identified by these methods are likely to be superficial and perhaps even biased (i.e., not accurate). Experts recommend that the culture be examined through systematic and "intensive group discussions to bring cultural substance to the surface."[42] This process can be used to develop a list of the various characteristics of the culture. The listed characteristics can then be analyzed for evidence of underlying beliefs, values, and norms. Once a tentative sketch of the culture is developed, it can then be validated with further observations of the organization.

Outsider Audit. An outside consultant can often provide a different perspective on the culture of an organization.[43] Edgar Schein, whose four-stage model of culture we introduced earlier, has developed the ten-step process for auditing culture that is described below.[44]

1. *Entry and focus on surprises.* The outside consultant enters the organization and begins to "feel" its culture and watch for surprises — that is, responses to things that are unexpected.
2. *Systematic observation and checking.* Consultant attempts to verify that "surprises" really are surprises.
3. *Locate motivated insider.* Outsider would probably have a difficult time analyzing culture without some key insider to provide insights. It is important to find a key insider with access to important information who is also motivated to assist in the audit process.
4. *Revealing surprises, puzzlement, and hunches.* Outsider reveals to members of organization his or her initial assessments in order to get reactions about their appropriateness and accuracy.
5. *Joint exploration to find explanations.* Consultant uses feedback to modify or change the initial assessment presented in number four above. Consultant and insiders attempt to fit observations with the assumption about culture in an attempt to explain behaviors.
6. *Formalizing hypotheses.* Consultant and insiders collaborate to form statements about the culture based on data and observations. These hypotheses become a model of the culture.
7. *Systematic checking and consolidation.* Consultant gathers additional observations, surveys, questionnaires, interviews, and other data to verify the hypothesized culture.
8. *Deriving cultural assumptions.* Once hypotheses are validated, the evaluator derives cultural assumptions and sees how the assumptions affect member behaviors and beliefs.
9. *Perpetual recalibration.* The model is fine tuned to fit it to the actual underlying assumptions that are present in the culture. Caution must be exercised in this process because some members of the organization may be unaware of the underlying assumptions that guide their behaviors or they may be reluctant to admit those assumptions.

10. *Formal written description.* Consultant reduces the model to a written description to see if a true description can be found. If the data are accurate and the logic used to develop the model is sound, then the written description should be possible; otherwise, a coherent written description may be impossible. Finally, the written description must be periodically updated and modified to keep pace with changes in the organization.

The process outlined above is just one audit method. Others are also available, but most share many of the features of Schein's system. This formal audit can be useful because it provides order and direction to the process. Management can use this systematic process to better understand and strategically adjust the organization's culture.

A note of caution is in order. Culture, by its very nature, is an elusive aspect of organizations. The second level of culture, the underlying norms, values, beliefs, and assumptions, are latent—we can never directly observe them. As a result, we must infer them from other observable aspects of the organization. The inference process we use for moving from the observable to the latent characteristics may be subject to error and bias. Thus, the resulting description of an organization's culture may be imperfect and inaccurate. Nonetheless, a systematic and rigorous audit should provide useful information in the strategic management of an organization.

CULTURE CHANGE

Cultures of organizations are, by nature, dynamic. That is, they naturally change and evolve in response to changes in the organization, the members of the organization, and its environment. However, when we specifically refer to *culture change,* we are focusing on *planned change of a more substantial and extensive nature.*[45] Management of an organization includes the idea that managers can change a culture, or parts of a culture, to be more consistent with the organization's strategic objectives. As we noted above, the audit is a key component to systematic cultural change.

Management can use two basic approaches to the task of culture change: top-down change and bottom-up change. With *top-down change,* top management plays the lead role in changing the culture. The culture may be changed by "decrees" that different norms of behavior are to be observed. For example, management at Ford Motor Company could decree that "Quality is Job #1," indicating to employees that new values, expectations, and behaviors should be observed with regard to quality. Top management can also attempt to change the culture through leadership and example. For example, a company's leadership may advocate new norms and behaviors toward customers. To indicate the company's sincerity, top management could visit key customers. This shows both members of the organization and customers that the company is serious about being customer oriented. Earlier in this chapter, Lexmark, a former IBM division that is now an independent company, was used to show the difficulty it experienced trying to shed the old IBM culture. One technique the company used was that top management served as a model for the new norms, values, and behaviors that were to be part of the Lexmark culture. This included such things as top managers dressing more casually and holding more informal meetings.

The major advantage of top-down change is that it can be implemented quickly. One particular strategy that is often used to bring about top-down change is through a change in the top management team. Bringing in new leaders often involves an implicit attempt to change the culture. One problem with top-down culture change, however, is that the changes may not be consistent with the values and norms of lower-level members of the organization. This may produce resentment and resistance, and may produce changes that are not long lasting.

With ***bottom-up*** or participative approaches to change, organizational members are involved in the change process. This type of change may be slower, but it is likely to be longer lasting because employees are involved with and committed to the change.

AT&T provides a classic example of bottom-up change.[46] The breakup of AT&T in the early 1980s into the regional telephone companies (the so-called Baby Bells) and the AT&T Company that provide long-distance service and research and technical support presented AT&T management with a unique opportunity to create a new corporate culture. Under the old monopolistic system AT&T had grown bureaucratic, unresponsive, and insular. With the breakup of AT&T and the development of long-distance competition, the company's management realized that change was needed. Management conducted surveys of several thousand employees, gathered recommendations from twenty key managers, and employed a management consultant to get an independent perspective. Changing the culture has taken nearly a decade, but the result has been a culture that emphasizes openness, customer focus, teamwork, and flexibility. No longer was AT&T lethargic, unresponsive, and bureaucratic. Now, AT&T will again have to deal with culture change as it breaks off some business units into separate companies.

In reality, the changes at AT&T involve both top-down and bottom-up approaches. Key top managers have changed since the breakup, and they have led by example. But they have also consulted with and involved many lower-level employees. A combination of approaches is likely to lead to more consistent and long-lasting culture change.

CULTURE AND STRATEGY

Because of its crucial role in organization performance, it is necessary to examine the relationship between culture and strategy. The formulation and pursuit of a strategy involves the allocation of an organization's resources (including human resources) and attention to a specific set of long-term purposes. The beliefs, values, norms, and philosophy of top management should guide the strategy formulation. These beliefs might include such fundamental beliefs as being an innovation leader or price leader in a particular market, the fair and equitable treatment of employees and customers, and doing no harm to the environment. The formulation of that strategy then sets a context or agenda for organizational action. Individuals' beliefs are the rules, norms, values, and assumptions that members observe when engaging in behaviors directed at the fulfillment of the strategy. These beliefs may include work rules; norms about interactions with peers, subordinates, or superiors; and expectations about how to interact with customers. Thus, managing the culture and strategy so that they are consistent and congruent is a key managerial task. As can be seen in Figure 10.1, culture and strategy interact with other aspects of the organization to produce performance.[47]

■ FIGURE 10.1
The Relationship of Culture to Strategy

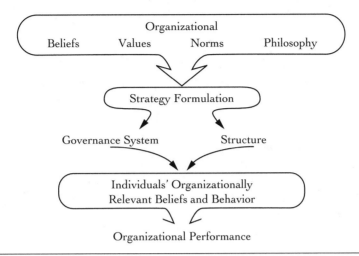

Source: From Stanley M. Davis, *Managing Corporate Culture* (Cambridge, Mass.: Ballinger, 1984), 6. Copyright 1984 by The Human Resource Planning Society. Reprinted with permission from Ballinger Publishing Company.

Taking our strategic systems view of organizations, culture is both an input that guides the strategy formulation and implementation process and is also part of the throughput process. Culture provides guidelines for strategy formulation and implementation, and culture provides a context for the organization to pursue the strategy. Thus, there must be congruency between culture, strategy, and organization.

SUMMARY

This chapter has explored the role of culture in the overall scheme of organization theory and demonstrated how organizations must know and manage their cultures for long-term survival. Culture is a complex and multifaceted concept that has a major influence on organizational life that includes two levels: observable and unobservable characteristics of the organization. The observable level includes many characteristics such as architecture, dress, behavior patterns, rules, stories, myths, language, and ceremonies. The unobservable level of culture is composed of the shared values, norms, beliefs, and assumptions of organizational members. Culture is the pattern or configuration of these two levels of characteristics that orients or directs organizational members to manage problems and their surroundings.

We presented four views on organizational culture. Schein's view of culture emphasizes the stagelike evolution of culture over time. Scholz also describes an evolution of culture but includes focus on internal and external attributes of culture. Louis's emphasis is on the location of cultural genesis. Different elements of a culture, and even different subcultures, can emerge in different parts of the organization or can even come from outside the organization. Finally, Fombrun argues that we must consider the different levels of culture and how society and the firm's industry have profound impact on the organization's culture. Fombrun reminds us that organizations are themselves embedded in larger cultural entities—communities and nations.

Not all organizational cultures are equally powerful in affecting the members. Thick cultures are ones in which the cultural forces are spread widely and deeply throughout the organization. As a result, the culture becomes a core of organizational life. A thin culture is one that does not spread so deeply and widely throughout the organization. As a result, the culture is not central to everyday organizational life.

Related to the concepts of thick and thin culture are three characteristics: direction, strength, and pervasiveness. Culture can direct behavior toward or away from organizational goals. Pervasive cultures are ones that are shared by nearly all members of the organization. A strong culture is one that has significant force or control over the behaviors of members.

One can study culture by looking at such observable features as ceremonies, rituals, symbols, slogans, myths, stories, and language. The physical environment of the organization, including offices, buildings, grounds, artwork, and other physical traces, can also give insight into an organization's culture. At the root of these observable features are the norms, beliefs, values, assumptions, and expectations that guide behaviors.

A key to managing an organization's culture is the cultural audit. The purpose of a formal audit is to ensure congruence or agreement between the culture and the *other* parts of an organization—its strategy, design, structure, tasks, and people.

When a culture is no longer congruent with other aspects of an organization, it can be changed. Top-down change is change that focuses first on changes in top-management values, beliefs, norms, expectations, and behaviors. It may even involve a change in top-management personnel. Bottom-up change begins with input from all levels of employees, including those lowest in the organizational hierarchy. Both sources of change can be critical to successful cultural change.

Culture and strategic management of the organization are closely tied together. Adjustments in one often signal the need for changes in the other. Our strategic systems approach emphasizes the need for alignment between culture and all other aspects of the organization.

Questions for Discussion

1. Under what conditions would a thick culture be desirable? Undesirable?
2. Under what conditions would a thin culture be desirable? Undesirable?
3. How would you describe the culture of your college or university? Identify key observable features of the culture. What are the basic underlying values, beliefs, norms, and expectations that are part of the culture? Is it a thick or thin culture? Why?
4. Is your college or university's culture congruent with the other key characteristics of the organization? Strategy? Structure? Design? Tasks? People?
5. Devise a plan for changing either a part or all of your college or university's culture

or that of a business with which you are familiar. Use both top-down and bottom-up approaches.

CASE: FLYING HIGH AT SOUTHWEST AIRLINES*

The airline industry today is highly competitive and turbulent. Industry members are working hard to come up with ways to gain some sort of competitive advantage. Frequent flyer programs, no-check-in boarding, no more Saturday stayovers on discount fares, and cooperative arrangements with hotels and car rental companies are just a few of the techniques that airlines are using to regain customer loyalty. In spite of all the enticements, however, industry members are losing literally billions of dollars each year. One airline, however, is bucking that trend and is doing just fine—Southwest Airlines.

Just what is this company doing differently that seems to be working? Carrying passengers on relatively short-hop trips for surprisingly low fares and building a strong company culture based on its chairman's unique personality and off-the-wall management style are just a few of the things that Southwest does. Other airlines are attempting to copy Southwest's operational strategy of efficient routing, maintenance, and turnaround, but it is doubtful if any will be able to copy Chairman Herb Kelleher's personality that has produced such a thick culture at Southwest.

Early in its short history, Southwest adopted a short-haul, point-to-point routing strategy. Southwest flies back and forth between pairs of cities, many of which are small markets not serviced by large carriers. Southwest has frequent flights between these pairs of cities that average only 375 miles apart. The company also uses many smaller airports, such as Dallas's Love Field and Chicago's Midway. This differs from the standard hub-and-spoke system used by the industry leaders. Under the hub-and-spoke system, passengers must typically travel to a hub airport (for example, Delta's hubs are Atlanta, Cincinnati, and Salt Lake City) in order to get to their eventual destination. A traveler unfortunate enough to not live in a hub city would have to fly to a hub and then to the final destination.

Cost control dominates Southwest's operations. The company has held down training and maintenance costs by using only Boeing 737 aircraft. Pilots only need to be familiar with the operations of one type of craft; maintenance workers only need to learn one set of maintenance routines; and crew members need to learn only one set of cabin preparation procedures. As a result, passengers are "treated" to peanuts and crackers and have no assigned seats. Typical flights are less than one hour, and with the short turnaround time (ten to fifteen minutes between flights) that streamlined maintenance permits, planes fly as many as ten flights per day. The ultimate consequence of this efficient use of capital is that Southwest has a significant cost advantage over competitors.

In addition, Kelleher (or Herb, as employees affectionately call him) is a stickler for cost control. He personally approves every expenditure over $1,000 and constantly monitors cost-per-mile figures, comparing them to industry averages to gain every penny's worth of advantage.

---

*Based on the following article: Kenneth Labich, "Is Herb Kelleher America's Best CEO?" *Fortune* (May 2, 1994): 44–52.

Like most businesses, Southwest's labor costs are a major concern, and most (80 percent) of its employees are unionized. Thanks to Kelleher's hands-on management, these costs are held in check and balanced with a productive work force. Average pay is about $44,000, considerably less than comparable numbers at American or United. Profit-sharing is a big part of the compensation package with 15 percent of net profits going to workers, and the company matches employee contributions to their 401(k) retirement plans.

Kelleher's folksy style can be seen throughout the company. He often lunches with employees in the company cafeteria, and he has been known to lead employees in a company cheer. His style is infectious. Pilots can be seen manning boarding gates, and ticket agents often load baggage. When Southwest acquired Morris Air in 1993, Southwest employees sent greeting cards, candy, and even T-shirts to welcome Morris employees to their new "family."

A sense of humor is a must for Southwest employees, who often amuse passengers with jokes and prizes for off-beat contests they conduct in waiting lounges and even on flights. Flight attendants have been known to greet passengers from overhead bins while the passengers board. One contest gave a prize to the passenger with the largest hole in his or her sock. All of this is aimed at making passengers feel at home on Southwest flights and to break the monotony of frequent flying.

Southwest is looking for employees who are able to work well in a collegial atmosphere. Education and experience are not nearly as important as the desire to excel and to be part of a winning team. The company believes that the necessary training can be provided to those employees who want to be part of Southwest. This sense of camaraderie is perhaps Southwest's most prized asset. The company gives more than mere lip service to the notion of *family*. Some have even observed that Southwest's culture is almost cultlike, and Kelleher is the uncontested leader.

Southwest is not the first airline to focus on short hops and no-frills flying — recall that the late People Express tried this niche in the late 1970s and early 1980s — and competitors are trying to match Southwest's operational strategy. A key question is whether competitors can challenge Southwest without adopting Southwest's culture . . . and it's not clear that competitors can adopt that culture. The ability to get the most out of employees seems to be a personal quality of Kelleher. Job descriptions and company rules do not seem to play an important role in Southwest's success.

A major worry at the company is what will happen to Southwest after Kelleher. There is no doubt that the essence of company success is due in large part to his presence and personality. Although he is only 63 and intends to be active for the foreseeable future, he has had periodic health problems due in part to his frenetic work schedule and his love of cigarettes, Kentucky bourbon, and Texas sun.

Airline analysts dismiss these concerns and argue that the Kelleher "way" is instilled in the company. Analysts also point to a cadre of able potential successors already on board at the company. Even though none of these potential successors can fill all of Kelleher's roles, Southwest is likely to keep flying high for some time to come.

Questions for Discussion

1. What are the key norms, values, beliefs, and expectations that are embodied in Southwest's culture?

2. How important is culture to Southwest's success? Why? Do a little background research. What happened to People Express? Can you speculate as to why People Express failed? Did culture play a role or were other factors important in People Express's collapse?
3. Can other airlines (or companies in general) copy Southwest's culture? How important is Herb Kelleher to that culture?
4. What are the potential dangers of a thick culture such as that at Southwest? Can you describe a situation in which this culture could cause problems for Southwest?

REFERENCES

1. Harrison M. Trice and Janice M. Beyer, *The Cultures of Work Organizations* (Englewood Cliffs, N.J.: Prentice-Hall, 1993).

2. See note 1, page 29, above.

3. Ralph H. Kilmann, Mary J. Saxton, and Roy Serpa, "Issues in Understanding and Changing Culture," *California Management Review* 27, no. 2 (Winter 1987): 92–93.

4. See note 1 above.

   J. Steven Ott, *The Organizational Culture Perspective* (Pacific Grove, Calif.: Brooks/Cole Pub., 1989).

5. Joanne Martin, *Cultures in Organizations: Three Perspectives* (New York: Oxford University Press, 1992).

   Maryan S. Schall, "A Communication-Rules Approach to Organizational Culture," *Administrative Science Quarterly* 28 (1983): 557–58.

   Andrew Pettigrew, "On Studying Organizational Cultures," *Administrative Science Quarterly* 24 (1979): 572.

   Edgar H. Schein, *Organizational Culture and Leadership* (San Francisco: Jossey-Bass, 1985).

6. Ibid.

   Sonja A. Sackman, "Cultures and Subcultures: An Analysis of Organizational Knowledge," *Administrative Science Quarterly* 37, no.1 (1992): 140–61.

7. Colin Camerer and Ari Vepsalainen, "The Economic Efficiency of Corporate Culture," *Strategic Management Journal* 9 (1988): 115–26.

8. See Martin, page 3, in note 5 above.

9. See Schein in note 5 above.

   See Sackman in note 6 above.

   Alan L. Wilkins and William G. Ouchi, "Efficient Cultures: Exploring the Relationship Between Culture and Organizational Performance," *Administrative Science Quarterly* 28 (1983): 468–69.

10. See note 1, pages 1–2, above.

11. Edgar Schein, "The Role of the Founder in Creating Organizational Culture," *Organizational Dynamics* 13 (1983): 13–28.

    See Schein in note 5 above.

12. See Schein, pages 163-65, in note 5 above.

13. Christian Scholz, "Corporate Culture and Strategy — The Problem of Strategic Fit," *Long Range Planning* 26, no. 4 (August 1987): 79–85.

14. Charles Fombrun, "Corporate Culture, Environment, and Strategy," *Human Resources Management* 22 (1983): 139–52.

15. Meryl R. Louis, "An Investigator's Guide to Workplace Culture," in *Organizational Culture,* ed. by Peter Frost, Larry F. Moore, Meryl R. Louis, Craig C. Lundberg, and Joanne Martin (Beverly Hills, Calif.: Sage Publications, 1985), 73–98.

16. Geert Hofstede, *Culture's Consequences: International Differences in Work-related Values* (Beverly Hills, Calif.: Sage, 1980).

17. See note 1, pages 340–50, above.

18. See note 13, page 81, above.

19. Arthur Flax, "Ford Brings Its Culture to Its Dealers," *Automotive News* (March 12, 1986):1.

20. Jenny C. McCune, "Who Are Those People in Blue Suits," *Management Review* 80 (September 1991): 16–19.

21. Gareth Morgan, Peter J. Frost, and Louis Pondy, "Organizational Symbolism," in *Organizational Symbolism,* ed. by Louis Pondy, Peter J. Frost, Gareth Morgan, and Thomas C. Dandridge (Greenwich, Conn.: JAI Press, 1983), 3–39.

22. Harrison M. Trice and Janice M. Beyer, "Studying Organizational Cultures Through Rites and Ceremonials," *Academy of Management Review* 9 (1984): 653–69.

    See Martin, page 44, in note 5 above.

23. John Van Maanen, "The Smile Factory: Work at Disneyland," in *Reframing Organizational Culture,* ed. by Peter J. Frost, et al. (Newbury Park, Calif.: Sage, 1990), 58–76.

24. Donald Katz, *Just Do It* (New York: Random House, 1994).

25. See Ott, page 28, in note 4 above.

26. See Ott, pages 86–87, in note 4 above.

27. See note 23 above.

28. Ibid.

29. See note 1, pages 271–72, above.

Lee Iacocca, *Iacocca: An Autobiography* (New York: Bantam, 1984).

30. Tim R. V. Davis, "The Influence of the Physical Environment in Offices," *Academy of Management Review* 9 (1984): 271–83.

31. See note 24 above.

32. Peter Collier and David Horowitz, *The Fords: An American Epic* (New York: Summit Books, 1987).

33. See note 30, page 276, above.

34. See note 3, pages 88–89, above.

    Jay W. Lorsch, "Managing Culture: The Invisible Barrier to Strategic Change," *California Management Review* 26 (Winter 1986): 105–109.

    See Pettigrew, page 578, in note 5 above.

35. See Lorsch in note 34 above.

36. See Pettigrew, page 578, in note 5 above.

37. Jay B. Barney, "Organizational Culture: Can It Be a Source of Sustained Competitive Advantage?" *Academy of Management Review* 11 (1986): 656–65.

38. Alan L. Wilkins, "The Culture Audit: A Tool for Understanding Organizations," *Organizational Dynamics* 12 (Autumn 1983): 24–25.

    William G. Ouchi, *Theory Z: How American Business Can Meet the Japanese Challenge* (Reading, Mass.: Addison-Wesley, 1982).

39. See Wilkins, pages 34–36, in note 38 above.

40. Paul B. Carroll, "Story of an IBM Unit That Split Off Shows Difficulties of Change," *The Wall Street Journal* (July 23, 1992), A1.

41. See note 1, pages 360–61, above.

42. Ibid, page 361.

43. Ibid, page 362.

44. See Schein, pages 114–19, in note 5 above.

45. This definition of culture change is based on the one used by Harrison M. Trice and Janice M. Beyer in note 1, page 395, above.

46. W. Brooke Tunstall, "The Breaking Up of the Bell System: A Case Study in Cultural Transformation," *California Management Review* 26 (Winter 1986): 110–24.

    David Kirkpatrick, "Could AT&T Rule the World?" *Fortune* (May 17, 1993): 11.

47. David Nadler and Michael Tushman, *Strategic Organizational Design: Concepts, Tools, and Processes* (Glenview, Ill.: Scott, Foresman, 1988).

Information and Organizational Decision Making

CASE: MIDWEST CITY UNIVERSITY REBUILDS ITS STADIUM*

Midwest City University (MCU) is a large (approximately 32,000 students), state-supported urban university serving the southern part of a midwestern industrial and agricultural state. MCU has several outstanding programs, including medicine, music and performing arts, engineering, and architecture. However, MCU has rarely rated anywhere near outstanding in intercollegiate football. Among the university's sports teams, football was always in the shadows of MCU's successful basketball program. Winning seasons had been a rarity in recent years. In the ten years prior to the opening of the rebuilt stadium (1983 to 1992), the team had a combined record of 32-76-2. The best season was 5-6.

Nonetheless, in the late 1980s, the university spent nearly $10 million to refurbish the on-campus stadium. The president attempted to justify this decision by noting that the continuation of a competitive intercollegiate athletic program had to include football and that the football program could not recruit potential players or attract opponents without a first-class facility on campus. The stadium was essentially useless in its current state of disrepair, and the county had threatened to condemn it. If the university wanted to continue playing football, it either had to move games five miles away to a downtown stadium used by the local NFL team or rebuild the campus stadium. Although some groups such as the board of trustees and alumni supported the decisions to rebuild, many others questioned the wisdom of this project.

Some background may help to put the stadium renovation decision in context. The late 1980s were a difficult time for many state universities, and MCU was typical in this regard. MCU faced the dual threats of declining enrollments and declining levels of state financial support. Over the period from 1988 to 1994, the state support for MCU was cut by nearly 25 percent.

*Although the name of this university has been changed, the events portrayed in this case are real.

Declining enrollments meant that tuition revenues were also falling. In general, the university was experiencing serious budget constraints.

Despite the rather dire financial conditions and protests from faculty members and others, the administration decided in the late 1980s to embark on a major stadium renovation. Funding for the stadium project was done in an unconventional manner. Typically, building funds are taken from a separate capital funds budget. The stadium project, however, was funded by a combination of bonds underwritten by the general operating budget and some funds actually taken from the general operating budget. The general operating budget is typically reserved for the day-to-day operation of the university—to pay faculty and staff salaries and to pay general operating expenses. Drawing on general funds increases the cost of running the university and reduces the funds available for educational programs and salaries. Needless to say, the funding decision was controversial and unpopular in some quarters.

During this same period the administration, through the president and provost, made draconian cuts in support services, staffing levels, and resources. Many vacant faculty positions were not filled with new faculty. A significant number of clerical workers, custodians, and other support staff were cut. Simultaneously, several union contracts expired and bitter, divisive negotiations dragged on. At one point, the faculty held a referendum resulting in a vote of no confidence in the president. Many faculty pointed to the stadium project as a major reason for their dissatisfaction with the president. It was not just the spending that bothered faculty members. Many professors objected to what they saw as a rather heavy-handed decision process that ignored any role for faculty input on the stadium project. To the dismay of the faculty, the MCU board of trustees ignored the referendum and gave the president a resounding vote of confidence. Not long after this vote, contract negotiations between the faculty and the university broke off and a strike was called. The stadium project was just one of many issues.

The strike was short lived, with faculty winning only a few concessions from the administration. The local media portrayed the faculty as petty, whiny, and out of touch with the economic and educational reality of the state. At no point was there any mention in the media of the stadium spending. Shortly after, the faculty agreed to a new contract with minimal raises (average of 2 percent per year for three years). The president was rewarded by the board of trustees with a three-year contract extension and a significant raise (an average of over 10 percent per year).

In 1993, MCU's football fortunes took a turn for the better. The team, playing in its renovated stadium, had its first winning season in over ten years (8-3) and was mentioned as a possible bowl participant. Attendance at games was up. The athletic department had begun to receive increased recognition. New sources of revenue were being developed.

It would be nice if the story ended here with a vastly improved football program that added recognition and revenue to the university. Unfortunately, intercollegiate football, like organizational life in general, is filled with turbulence and uncertainty. After the 1993 season, the head coach left for a new job. This was his reward for turning around a perennially losing team. The team also lost a core group of seventeen starting seniors, and because of the loss of their head coach, the team had a poor recruiting year. The team finished the 1994 season with a 2-8-1 record. Faculty and others in the university community were once again questioning the wisdom of spending large sums of money on a football stadium.

Information processing and decision making are critical events in organizations. Some theorists suggest that information processing and decision making are at the root of all organizational activity. We normally think of decision making as an orderly, rational process — and sometimes it is, but not always. In this chapter we first look at information as the raw material that feeds the decision-making process, and we then look at three models of decision making. The first two of these are models that suggest a rational or bounded rational approach to decision making. Decision makers identify problems and attempt, in an orderly fashion, to find solutions to problems. These two models differ in the degree of rationality present. The second model, bounded rationality, suggests reasons why rationality in decision making is bounded or constrained. Finally, we examine garbage can decision making, a situation such as that at MCU where even the pretense of rationality vanishes.

As discussed in earlier chapters, the organization must develop a linkage system to keep it in tune with its external environment. Following the establishment of such systems, the organization is in the posture of gathering and processing information in order to make proper organizational choices. This chapter examines the value of such information and describes its characteristics.

In this chapter, we describe the information process from a generic point of view. We briefly describe the management of the information process and show how information is related to decision making. We discuss the tremendous impact that high-tech information systems can have on organizational structures, processes, and relationships.

Organizations are basically information processors. They gather, analyze, synthesize, and interpret information from their environment for their own uses and for return to the environment. They use this information to make choices or decisions about what the organization does and does not do and how it does it. In short, information and the knowledge it represents are the lifeblood of the organization. No organization can exist for long if it does not have valid and reliable information on which to base its decisions and operations. Using our systems approach, we can depict the information flow through the organization as seen in Figure 11.1.

■ FIGURE 11.1

Information Flows from and to the Environment

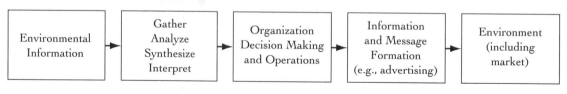

THE VALUE OF INFORMATION

Information is valuable to the organization only if it is useful in decision making and operations. The more useful the information, the more valuable it is. General Motors is certainly more interested in consumer auto preferences than it is in consumer satisfaction with toothpaste.

There are seven primary characteristics of information that make it valuable to the organization: *relevance, quality, richness, quantity, timeliness, accessibility, and symbolism.* Let's look at each of these.

RELEVANCE OF INFORMATION

The more relevant the information to the core technology of the organization, the more valuable it is.[1] Two of the key information challenges faced by the organization are deciding what environmental information is relevant and to whom in the organization the information is relevant. By using the concepts of domain and task environment, the organization decides which aspects of the environment are relevant for scanning purposes. A decision is made on scanner or sensor placement and function in order to avoid both information overload and tracking inappropriate aspects of the environment.

In addition, linking scanners or sensors to proper decision-authority centers ensures that environmental information is provided to the decision center where action can be taken, as shown in Figure 11.2. For example, the personnel unit needs to know

■ **FIGURE 11.2**
Information Links the Environment with the Decision–Authority Center

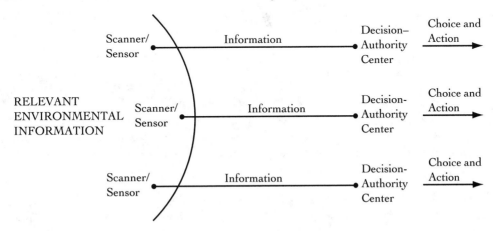

labor market availability figures and the purchasing manager needs to know raw material prices, not vice versa.

The most relevant information the organization needs is that information needed to make strategic decisions. Strategic decisions are those major decisions that affect the long-term direction of the organization. Decisions to build a new plant, develop a new product, or enter a new market with an existing product are examples of strategic decisions.

Strategic decisions made without the proper information can often lead to organizational disaster. For example, Bank of America Corporation was one of the world's most successful banking organizations until its decline in the middle and late 1980s. Although analysts have attributed numerous reasons for this organization's problems, one cannot deny that Bank America made many significant strategic decisions without first having adequate information. The bank lent heavily to Third World countries without having enough qualified credit specialists to obtain and report back vital information about these countries' abilities to repay the loans. In addition, A. W. (Tom) Clausen, president of Bank America from 1970 to 1980, neglected to hire enough auditors so that control information about the bank's myriad operations, particularly loan repayments, could be relayed to top-level Bank America officials. Clausen and his successor, Samuel Armacost, have also been criticized for not investing quickly enough in computers and telecommunications equipment. Indeed, until the end of 1984, Bank America had *forty different* computer networks that it used for different purposes.[2] Thus, while its competitors had already installed and were using powerful, integrated systems for obtaining and synthesizing information, Bank America still had to rely on separate systems for functions such as branch teller operations, automated teller operations, mortgage banking, U.S. commercial operations. Asian commercial operations, and so on. Bank America even continued to invest in "oil patch" real estate after the U.S. oil industry went into recession in the mid-1980s. In short, Bank America's failure to design, implement, and use a system for obtaining relevant and timely information for both day-to-day operations and strategic decision making is most definitely one of the causes behind this banking organization's present crisis.

QUALITY OF INFORMATION

The quality of information refers to its accuracy. Does the information accurately represent reality? The more accurate the information, the higher its quality and the more confident organizations can be when using it to make decisions.[3] The cost of information generally increases as the quality desired becomes higher. However, this cost must be balanced against the cost of having and acting on erroneous information. If Chrysler Corporation believed the market wanted sporty, high-performance cars and designed cars to meet this objective, a grave mistake would be made if, in reality, the market wanted large, luxury sedans.

Type I and Type II Errors.   There are two essential types of errors that can be committed with information quality. The first, *Type I error,* occurs when the organization accepts as *true* a piece of information that is actually *false* (e.g., believing that people want to buy expensive home computers when they do not). A *Type II error* occurs when the organization accepts as *false* something that is actually *true* (e.g., a firm believing that the purchase of home video recorders has peaked, thus leaving the market, only to realize two years later that sales continue to increase). In both cases organizations act on faulty information and make poor decisions.

"Unk-unks," "unknown-unknowns," are especially problematic. With an unk-unk, the organization does not know something but does not realize that it *should* know it. A known-unknown, on the other hand, reflects that even though the organization does not know something, at least it realizes it should know it.[4] This concept came from the early days of the space program. Envision this: A rocket is sitting on the launch pad. The countdown begins. The button is pushed. A powerful explosion immediately occurs, and the rocket disintegrates in a ball of fire on the pad. The engineers and scientists are puzzled as to what happened. As they read through their data printouts and examine the wreckage, they realize that the fuel pressure in a second-stage secondary fuel line became excessive, causing the line to break and the rocket to explode. They did not measure this pressure at the time of launch because they did not believe it to be important.

However, prior to the launching of a similar rocket, they install a sensor to measure the pressure on the secondary fuel line. As the countdown proceeds, they are reading their telemetry and they notice that they are not receiving a readout from the secondary fuel line. They then make a very important decision—they do *not* push the button for launch.

In both cases—the first one, in which the rocket exploded, and the second one, in which the launch was aborted—the engineers did not know the pressure in the secondary fuel line. But in the second case, they realized it was an important fact so they did not push the button. They had turned an unknown-unknown into a known-unknown, which resulted in their taking an entirely different course of action.

Thus, organizations face a conundrum: They must seek information to reduce uncertainty, but unk-unks are uncertainties about which the organization is unaware. An organization cannot seek information to solve uncertainties that are not known to the members. Although there are no solutions to unk-unks, organizations must scan the environment widely and broadly to discover potential problems as well as sources of information.[5] It is a reality of organizational life that uncertainty, both of the known and unknown varieties, will always be present.

INFORMATION RICHNESS

Two related aspects of information that have received considerable attention are ***information richness*** and ***information quantity*** (or amount).[6] Information quantity is discussed in the next section. Information richness refers to the "carrying capacity" of a particular method of conveying information.[7] Methods that convey great meaning are defined as ***rich*** while those that convey less meaning are ***lean.***

Perhaps the best way to explain richness is by example. You could convey the same basic message to your boss using several different communication media: reports, memos, letters, telephone calls, or face-to-face meetings. Although the basic message in each interaction—say, for example, that sales of a new product are exceeding expectations by 25 percent—is the same, the richness of the potential information that is conveyed differs.

Written forms of communication are viewed as lean communication media. The written report may be useful for conveying a large quantity of specific, precise, numerical data. You could give a precise accounting, production, or sales report of the new product's performance using computer printouts, spreadsheets, graphs, and other similar mechanisms for reporting the data. However, written reports tend to be lengthy (hence, they often include an executive summary), and they provide only for one-way communication. Reports do not include mechanisms for querying the data or for feedback. Reports take time to write, which may reduce the timeliness of the information, another related and important dimension of information. You may choose to send a memo summarizing the sales situation. This increases the richness slightly by condensing the information and addressing it to a specific target individual, but feedback is still slow. Additionally, both reports and memos lack an extensive visual component that may be important to you in judging the accuracy and confidence that you (the reporter) have in the information. Your boss's perception of the person behind the report or memo may be important to his or her assessment of that information.

Spoken communications, by phone or voice mail, add new dimensions of richness to efforts to convey information — the sound of the sender's voice. Information about the speaker's tone of voice can provide the recipient with some information about the sender's confidence in the information. A live telephone conversation allows the boss to ask you to "get to the point" so that he or she does not have to waste valuable time filtering through marginally relevant information to get to the heart of the issues at hand. A live telephone conversation also allows the receiver to query the sender. The boss may ask you about your confidence in the information, or he or she may ask about some issues that you may not have thought to put in your initial report: Will the sales trend continue and are competitors entering the market? Still, telephone and voice mail information lack the visual component that may provide other important information.

The richest form of information is that given by face-to-face communication. The recipient gets the verbal message and voice cues mentioned earlier as well as visual cues. Visual cues may be important sources of nonverbal information about both the speaker and the issues. Figure 11.3 illustrates the relationship between communication medium and information richness.

■ FIGURE 11.3
Information Richness and Communication Medium

| Lean | Computer Printouts | Reports | Letters/ E-Mail | Voice Mail | Phone | Face-to-Face | Rich |

Researchers have found important relationships between information richness and the types of tasks being carried out,[8] position in the organizational hierarchy,[9] and the type of control system used in the organization.[10]

Recall from Chapter 6 that one dimension of work unit or departmental technology is task analyzability, which is defined as either task programmability or ease or difficulty of obtaining information. Organizational members need increasingly rich information as tasks become lower in analyzability. Low analyzability tasks require rich information, particularly because of the availability of feedback and the multiple information cues that are characteristic of rich information sources.

For much the same reason, as you move up the organizational hierarchy you find that individuals need increasingly rich information. Top management jobs are generally characterized as nonroutine. As such, they require rich information to deal with the low analyzability and ambiguity typical of those roles. Much of the information that top managers receive is highly processed and highly condensed. For example, technical reports often include executive summaries — condensed versions of the report that are often only one or two pages long and simply summarize main points.

Finally, as we noted in Chapter 9, organizations differ in the types of control systems that are used to direct and control employee behavior. Market control systems emphasize measurable outcomes. Thus, information requirements are modest. All that is needed is to record individual performance levels (e.g., sales, production). The information required is primarily lean numeric information. Bureaucratic control with its reliance on rules and its emphasis on documentation and recordkeeping also requires mostly lean information, but a large amount of it. Clan control systems rely on shared values and norms to control employee behavior. To learn about the norms and values of employees and to convey the norms and values of the organization, the organization must make extensive use of rich information.

QUANTITY OF INFORMATION

Organizations walk a tightrope with respect to quantity of information. Enough information is needed to make an informed decision, but too much information causes information overload. When information overload occurs, decision–authority centers often ignore *all* the information provided. They reason, Who has time to wade through that thick report and find the information I need in my job?

Consequently, organizations must constantly monitor the linkage between scanners or sensors and decision–authority centers to ensure that the right quantity of information is provided. There is a tendency today to provide too much information, most of it irrelevant. The computer is a wonderful machine for generating printout after printout. Without careful monitoring, organizations can drown in a sea of computer printouts.

All too often, a situation is created as shown in Figure 11.4. In this figure the three boxes (information a manager receives, information a manager wants, and information a manager needs) overlap in a relatively small shaded area. A large portion of the information that a manager needs (Box 3) is not even recognized by the manager (Box 2). This is a good example of an unknown-unknown to the manager.

Assumptions. Some organizations are slow to make decisions because they think they need more information. In effect, they study an issue to death. Organizations never have perfect and complete information. In fact, Simon states that managers operate under *bounded rationality*,[11] a concept first encountered in our discussion of goals. Bounded rationality means that even though managers intend to be rational in their organizational activities, they can act rationally only to a point.

Several factors contribute to bounded rationality. First, as we noted, decision makers never get perfect information. Even in the simplest of decisions, decision makers

■   FIGURE 11.4
Information Needs of a Manager

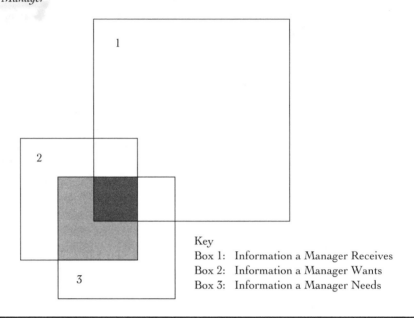

Key
Box 1:   Information a Manager Receives
Box 2:   Information a Manager Wants
Box 3:   Information a Manager Needs

Source: Sumantra Ghoshal and Seok Ki Kim, "Building Effective Intelligence Systems for Competitive Advantage," *Sloan Management Review* 49 (Fall 1986): 57. Reprinted by permission of the publisher. Copyright 1986 by the Sloan Management Review Association. All rights reserved.

experience at least some uncertainty. Also, despite the fact that we live in an information age in which large quantities of information are readily and cheaply available, human beings have limited cognitive capacity or ability to handle all of the information available. Moreover, the personal biases and emotions of decision makers affect judgments. Thus, more information is not always the key to quality decision making. We return to these issues later in this chapter when we look at different models of organizational decision making.

Organizations must make assumptions about pieces of information they know they need but do not have. They must fill in the gaps, as shown in Figure 11.5. These assumptions must be reasonable. That is, they must be based on the information available. For example, if an organization decides to introduce a new product related to fitness, such as a home exercise machine, assumptions about the future of the fitness trend, health, home exercise, and so on should be based on what it knows is occurring now and what it can reasonably project for the future.

Organizations also must know about information they need to make assumptions about. There are two key issues involved here. First, they must realize their known-unknowns. (No assumptions will be made about unk-unks because the organization does not know it needs the information.) For example, if the primary factor that determines the success of walk-in emergency facilities is future population density average over either age or income, then when a health-care organization is making an expansion

■ FIGURE 11.5
Assumptions Fill in the Information Gaps

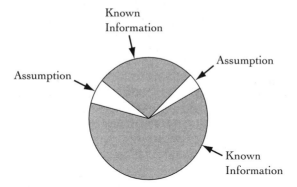

decision, it needs to make an assumption about future population density. It does this only if it knows population density is the key factor. Ignoring population density and making assumptions about future age or income patterns would be incorrect in this case.

Second, the cost of information increases geometrically as the organization tries to gather more information about a particular issue, as shown in Figure 11.6. This occurs

■ FIGURE 11.6
Information-Gathering Costs Increase Geometrically

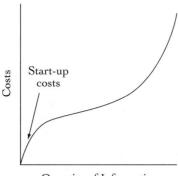

because the organization usually has some information about an issue readily available in regular reports or on file. However, as the need for more information on the subject expands, the organization may need to begin gathering new reports and gathering new data. It may be able to use secondary data sources, such as census data on markets, or it may need to conduct a special market survey, which is quite expensive. The organization must always balance the cost of this new additional information with its benefit.

TIMELINESS OF INFORMATION

There is a time value to information. Knowing after the fact that a given stock has doubled in value is not as useful as knowing of this potential prior to its actually doubling in value. Being able to know immediately the actions of a competitor is much more valuable than learning of these actions six months after they occur. Most information the organization uses is historical. Data are collected on customer buying patterns, inventory turnover, sales, assets, and so on, and these data reflect what *has* occurred. Accounting data are all historical. The usefulness of these data increases the more recent they are. A company is more interested in quarterly sales reports for the past year than in reports from two years ago.[12] Speed is a major factor for using information, and one of the major contributions of the computer is the speed it affords for information access and utilization.

Historical data can be used to project future trends. Through trend line analysis and other forecasting techniques, organizations attempt to project historical data into the future. This is fine as long as the conditions that shaped the historical data are similar to those that will shape future data. Forecasters were predicting oil prices would rise to $50 to $55 per barrel in the early 1980s, only to see the price drop below $20 per barrel in 1986. The assumptions about world oil usage, oil supply, and the power of OPEC were all flawed. In the aftermath of Desert Storm, embargoes against Iraq, shifting alliances in the Middle East, and cracks in OPEC solidarity, the price of oil has become increasingly unpredictable.

The key factor in timeliness is the need to obtain information soon enough to take or not to take action. In 1986, had the crew of the space shuttle Challenger known of the fuel leak in the right solid rocket booster during lift-off, they might have been able to jettison the craft from its rockets and fuel tank and escape the horrible explosion that occurred.

No one ever knows the future with certainty, and hindsight is always illuminating. We can all be Monday morning quarterbacks. Organizations should learn from their mistakes and try to obtain information in such a way that they do not repeat the same mistakes in the future. If it takes several hours for the results of a quality-control check to get to the production superintendent, a whole production run may need to be stopped if poor quality greatly exceeds tolerance levels. If a company continues to push a computer product that has become obsolete because it is unaware that a competitor has introduced a markedly better and less expensive product, much sales effort, time, and money that could be better spent elsewhere will have been wasted. If an organization does not have the proper information to develop a new product to meet or beat the competition, it might find itself out of business. There is a tremendous *opportunity cost* for doing the wrong thing at the wrong time. That cost is the action that *could have* been taken but was not. It is the cost of a lost opportunity.

ACCESSIBILITY OF INFORMATION

In order for information to be valuable to the organization's decision makers, it must be accessible. In other words, it must be available and relatively easy to obtain. Research has indicated that the accessibility of information, rather than its quality, might be a more important determinant of a manager's preference for information sources.[13]

Ideally, managers would select information from those sources perceived to offer the highest value (i.e., relevancy, accuracy, quantity, and timeliness). However, in practice, the less-qualified, more easily accessible information sources might be used more frequently by managers. Indeed, managers indicate that they chose information sources because of their accessibility even though the information obtained from such sources might be of a quality inferior to that obtained from less accessible sources.

Managers choose information based on accessibility for several reasons. First, managers incur both social and economic costs in searching for valuable information that might not be readily available. Because of organizational pressures on managers to produce results, the more accessible sources of information are likely to be used. Second, the structure of the organization can restrict access to higher-quality, more valued information sources. Think of a situation in which an organization's marketing managers need technical information that is readily available only to the firm's production managers. Third, organizational incentive systems can reward members for seeking information from a particular source while punishing them for seeking information from other sources. For example, in some organizations employees are forbidden to rely on certain types of information. Finally, information in organizations is often incomplete, vague, and subject to various interpretations; therefore, managers may come to rely on those sources used over a period of time that are considered both trustworthy and readily accessible. For example, coworkers can be considered by some managers to be very trust worthy and accessible sources of information. Thus, the student of organization theory should be aware that accessibility is a key factor in determining information value, even to the point where it might outweigh other factors, particularly relevance and quality.

SYMBOLIC VALUE OF INFORMATION

Finally, information has a *symbolic value*.[14] That is, the mere fact that a manager has access to or receives information may confer status or prestige on that person, even if the person does not use or need the information. For example, a middle manager may receive revised quarterly budget estimates that usually go only to the very top-level managers in the organization. Even though the mid-level manager does not need or use this information, the mere fact that he or she receives it has value to the person because it confers a status associated only with those holding high-level positions in the organization.

The authors have also noticed that the value of a strategic plan for some managers is that it is leatherbound with gold inlay and placed on the corner of the desk for display, *not* that it is actually used. The same phenomenon is also observed with the purchase of expensive coffee-table books that are never read but are used for display purposes.

Consequently, including certain people in the "information loop" has a symbolic value, even though the actual information is of little use to them. The design and management of an information system should recognize this value aspect of information.

The concepts of relevance, quality, richness, quantity, timeliness, accessibility, and symbolism of information all give information value. Organizations should manage their information in a way that enhances these attributes, at the same time realizing the costs associated with doing so. The next section discusses how this can be accomplished.

SYSTEMS FOR MANAGING INFORMATION

Information consists of a series of both stocks and flows, as shown in Figure 11.7. Information moves between the organization and its environment, and within the organization as well. It also moves from one unit to the next within the organization.[15] However, information is also stored in the environment and organization for later use. The system of gathering, reporting, analyzing, accepting, storing, retrieving, and using information in the organization is the *information system.* This system must be managed by the organization just as its production, marketing, or accounting systems must be managed.[16] Let us briefly look at the information process and then at some ways in which organizations manage it.

■ **FIGURE 11.7**
Stocks and Flows of Information

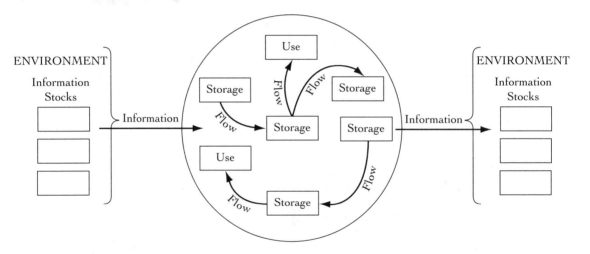

THE INFORMATION PROCESS

The information process is shown in Figure 11.8.

Gathering Information. Gathering involves obtaining necessary information from both outside and inside the organization. This information may come from *primary* data sources such as personal interviews or conversations, observation, or mailed questionnaires, or it may come from *secondary* sources such as census data, industry reports, or reports generated by the organization for other purposes.

The issues of *validity* and *reliability* are key factors when information is gathered. Because information is sometimes gathered through questionnaires, tests, or interviews, the validity and reliability of information-gathering devices become critical.

Suppose, for example, that the organization tests its job applicants for manual dexterity. The test would need to have high levels of validity and reliability if it were to be

FIGURE 11.8
The Information Process

truly useful to the organization in screening applicants. Let us assume that manual dexterity is, indeed, a job requirement. The test would be *valid* if it actually measured what it claims to measure. In this case the test would need to measure the applicant's ability and skill in using hands and fingers to do a manual task of some sort. The test would be *reliable* if it produced consistent measurements over time, that is, if applicants were retested the following day or several days thereafter, and the same results were obtained. Whenever gathering information using some measuring device such as a questionnaire or test, be very concerned with assessing the validity and reliability of the device or instrument.

Let us revisit the issue of test relevance. If the job in the above example does not require manual dexterity, then testing for it obtains an irrelevant piece of information about the job applicant. If this information is used in selecting and hiring decisions, the quality of the decisions is severely affected. A random drawing might as well be used. This situation unfortunately exemplifies an all too common situation in information gathering in organizations — information is gathered for one purpose but is used for a different, inappropriate purpose. For example, some organizations may gather information on employees' ages in order to plan retirement programs, only to use the information to discriminate against older employees. Such discrimination is illegal.

The purpose of gathering information should be clearly spelled out and understood by all involved. Checks should be made periodically to ensure that the information is being gathered for the purposes intended.

Reporting Information. Making sure that the information is reported or communicated to the right person or unit is extremely important. For environmental information, this means it must eventually be received by the decision–authority center. For internally generated information, it means that the information is sent to a unit or person for decision and operations purposes.

The problem here, of course, involves information coordination. Organizations must address the question of how to get information to proper units fast enough so that the right hand knows what the left hand is doing. Information reporting is critical for coordination. Of course, modern computer systems have enabled some organizations to ensure that the right information is reported to the right person within a matter of minutes, even seconds.

The importance of this step in the information process can be seen by the following example. If the production unit implements a new process requiring a different skill, the personnel unit needs to know this in order to design a training program and to begin using that skill as a criterion in the selection process. If marketing undertakes a heavy sales and promotional campaign, production needs to know this in advance so that it can produce enough product in order to avoid extended delivery delays; purchasing needs to order enough raw materials and semifinished goods; personnel may need to hire more people; and so on. The point is, very often a decision in one unit of an organization affects many others, and this information must be reported or communicated to these other units.

Analyzing Information. This step answers the question, What does the information mean? Often staff groups in an organization are responsible for performing detailed analyses of information for line managers. The key issue of analysis is to balance the need for it with any bias that may occur. Any time information is analyzed, there is a potential for bias. The person who analyzes the information may interpret it in such a way that personal bias intentionally or unintentionally enters the analysis. Important points may be omitted and minor points emphasized. Politicians often claim to be quoted out of context by the news media.

The problem of bias is exacerbated if the information is analyzed at each stage as it passes through the organization. Each time it is analyzed, it is reinterpreted. One ends up with a message at the end much like one receives at the end of the line when children play telephone-pass-it-on.

Therefore, the organization needs to provide guidelines for those analyzing information. Sometimes standard reporting forms, such as those frequently used for sales, production, or budget reports, help. In addition, people may be required to include original data as appendices. Care must also be taken to ensure that the information is not needlessly transferred to a unit for analysis when additional analysis is not useful.

Again, we cannot overestimate the importance of computer technology concerning the analysis of information. Executive information systems permit organizations' top-level managers to manipulate and analyze data in a multitude of ways. And the software that permits such manipulation and analysis is not available only in the executive suite. Lower-level employees with basic computer literacy and access are now able to obtain, manipulate, and analyze information as never before.

Accepting Information. Information is useless unless it is accepted by those to whom it is sent. Just because it is sent to an organizational unit does not mean it is received and accepted. There needs to be a follow-up of some sort (e.g., a phone call, return initial sheet, and so on) to indicate something was received.

Acceptance does not mean agreement. Acceptance means that the unit has received the information and should have read it. The individuals in the unit may or may not agree with the information.

Storing Information. Sometimes the information can be acted on immediately, but often it is stored. This may simply mean placing it in a pile on some executive's desk, or it may mean storing it in a file or on computer disk or tape. The key factors in storing are cost, timeliness, and access. Any time an organization stores information, it costs something. Not only are personnel costs involved with the actual storage procedure, but there are also equipment costs (e.g., computer, filing cabinet) and access costs, the costs of not having the information readily available. It costs something not to have the data when needed and to retrieve them. Of course, the computer has substantially reduced the need for storage space and thus its cost.

Retrieving Information. How accessible is the information? Again computers have made information much more accessible than ever before. As we have already seen, on-line capability allows executives to retrieve information from desktop terminals or personal computers. This has greatly expanded managers' access to information. Although this is generally viewed as good, it can cause problems if managers retrieve data and information out of their job area and attempt to tell others how to run their operations.[17]

The retrieval decision is actually made at the time the information is stored. At that point the ease and time of retrieval should be considered as factors in information storage. Information would not be stored in boxes in some faraway warehouse if the organization expected to retrieve it soon.

Using Information. Information should be gathered only if it is to be used. Too often, organizations gather information because it was determined by someone that "It would be nice to have—you never know what might come up." This contributes to irrelevant information and information overload. There should be a purpose and a goal for every piece of information. In other words, the expected use of the information should be clearly formulated *before* it is gathered.

This characteristic of information is called *user-based*. The users of the information should have the most significant say-so as to what information is to be gathered and how it is to be reported. This helps to ensure that the information is *user-friendly*, that is, the users find the information easy to use. Although this seems obvious to many people, it has not often occurred in the past. Rather, the person or unit gathering the information or the unit analyzing and storing it (e.g., the computer unit) often would determine the quality, form, and purpose of the information. The end user would have little say-so.

Frequently, this situation is particularly bad with budgetary information. Managers in an organization that the authors have worked with receive computer printouts of budgetary expenditures that are difficult to read and interpret. These printouts usually arrive several weeks late as well. When both the budget staff and computer people were asked for a different form depicting the information in a different way on a more frequent basis, the response was that "the system was not set up to do that." Consequently, no changes were made, and the managers continue to keep their budgets using pen and paper, or on their own PCs, while the computer printouts end up unused in a filing cabinet.

An *information audit* is a useful tool for determining if and how information is actually being used. An information audit reviews reports, memos, printouts, and so on to determine how they are generated, where they go, and how they are used. The goal is to streamline information flow and reporting procedures as well as to ensure that information being collected is being used as intended. It also attempts to determine if there are information needs not being satisfied and whether it would be cost effective to satisfy them.

MANAGING THE INFORMATION PROCESS

The organization should be concerned with managing information just as it manages its other resources—people, money, materials, plant, and so on. To do this, organizations must design a *management information system* (MIS). An MIS is a formalized system of making available to management timely, accurate, and relevant information for decision making.[18] It implies that the organization has established a formal system to ensure that the right information is available at the right time for the right managers so they can make the best possible decisions.

An organization has basically two options in managing information: It can either increase information-processing capacity or it can decrease it. Computer information systems are popular because they increase capacity in an organization. Because organizations face ever-increasing requirements for information, not only from the macro environment but from the micro (i.e., internal) environment as well, computers have become not only popular but essential for information management purposes.

CHARACTERISTICS OF AN EFFECTIVE MIS

An effective MIS has several characteristics. First, the information should be *user-based*. It should fulfill the needs of the user for effective decision making. Second, it should be *timely, accurate,* and *relevant*. Third, it should be *tied to a computer* for ease of analysis, storage, and access. Fourth, it should be *cost effective*. The process, as well as the information carried, should justify itself in terms of benefits. Fifth, the MIS should be a *system of systems*.* The accounting system, marketing information system, inventory control system, and so on should be viewed as a total system of information to be integrated and coordinated in order to minimize overlaps, duplicate reports, and separate systems for data gathering. Finally, the system should be *managed*. An organizational unit should be vested with the authority to manage the system and to act in a staff support capacity to line managers.

One of the main challenges facing an MIS department and its managers is to ensure that the information it provides truly benefits the entire organization, that is, that the information has value both to the organization as a whole and to various subunits

---

*Ralph Stair, *Principles of Information Systems: A Managerial Approach* (Boston: Boyd & Frazer, 1992).

within the organization. At Rayovac Corporation in Wisconsin, an Information Policy Board (IPB) comprised of representatives from each functional area within the organization was set up to provide overall direction to Rayovac's MIS department in the areas of policy, project priorities, the monitoring of progress, and the provision of clear communication channels between the MIS department and other areas. IPB members survey their individual areas for proposed projects with the emphasis on bringing forward only those that have either a high payback for a particular subunit or organization-wide support.[19]

THE EVOLUTION OF MIS

Organizations have always had a system for managing information even if it was simply a set of books, staff meetings, or occasional memos and reports. The difference in today's systems is that they have been substantially affected by the computer and are much more sophisticated. As organizations become larger and more complex, data needs increase greatly. Computers help handle these needs. This has led to the first step in the development of current information systems found in organizations—the development of electronic-data-processing (EDP) departments. The evolution of the information system is shown in Figure 11.9. Electronic data processing, the use of computers to handle information, led many organizations to formalize and systematize their information systems.

FIGURE 11.9
The Evolution of Information Systems

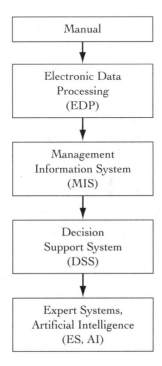

EDP departments were established, and EDP directors were appointed. Unfortunately, these individuals were often computer technicians and knew little about management or the decision-making needs of managers. Consequently, many of the early systems were not user-based, but rather were designed to satisfy the needs of the EDP department.

Because these early systems were used primarily in accounting, billing, and payroll, the EDP department's function was to gather and process data rather than to provide timely information to managers for decision-making purposes. However, the standardized reports and procedures developed, in addition to the systems concept, would serve as the basis for the next phase of MIS development—the development of MIS departments.

MIS. The growth of EDP departments caused managers to look at their information needs more systematically. Managers realized that computers were useful for more than the routine processing of masses of standardized data needed for payroll, billing, or accounting purposes. They realized that the computer was also useful for storing and manipulating data for decision making. Consequently, MIS departments were formed and MIS directors, whose job it was to coordinate the management of the organization's information flow in a systematic manner, were appointed.

DSS. The third phase of growth in information management was the development of *decision support systems* (DSS). A DSS is an interactive computer system that can easily be used by noncomputer specialists to assist them in making decisions. It is an easy-to-use system for desktop terminals or personal computers that requires little computer expertise. Information is available on a *real-time* basis, that is, there is no need to wait "until we get that report from EDP" before going ahead with the decision.[20] For example, suppose an organization is considering new transportation routes and methods for its product. Factors that must be weighed include the current delivery routes, schedules, and costs. Rather than preparing a request for this information and forwarding it to the EDP department, one can call up the information via a desktop terminal hooked to the organization's computer. Data can be read off the screen, and a hard copy can be generated. This is much faster than the old method, and its ease and speed encourage managers to use the computer for decision making much more than was the case when a specifically generated computer report had to be ordered by the manager. Wausau Insurance Company, for example, developed an outstanding DSS that allows its managers to select, analyze, and project information without having to request reports from subordinates.

Differences between DSS and MIS. There are some similarities between the MIS and DSS concepts—both are computer based and designed to supply information to managers. But there are some key differences. First, a DSS allows information *manipulation*, not just data storage and retrieval. Managers call up information they need for a particular decision. A second key difference is that a DSS allows managers to make nonroutine decisions in unstructured situations. An MIS, on the other hand, emphasizes routine, structured decisions. For example, analyzing a monthly quality control report would be a typical MIS function, but using quality control information to change training requirements would be an issue for the DSS. Interorganization conflict can be reduced with a DSS more than with an MIS. Because managers can access and manipulate data directly, they do not depend so much on the EDP/MIS unit for assistance. The clash of orientations and backgrounds between managers and technically trained computer people is reduced because they need not interact as much. Finally, the DSS may obviate the need for a separate EDP/MIS department. The proliferation of microcomputers, diverse and user-friendly software programs, and fourth-generation programming languages may reduce the need for a large number of technically trained EDP specialists in the organization.

Expert Systems. The next stage of information growth involves *expert systems*. These are knowledge-based systems that allow users to solve problems and to learn from the process. These systems may also be called *artificial intelligence* because the computer acts as if it were thinking through a problem or an issue. Although this area is still new, it may eventually replace the DSS concept as the key tool for improving decision making.[21]

Expert systems work by guiding users through problems by asking them a structured set of questions about the issue. The computer then draws conclusions based on the answers it has been given. Its problem-solving abilities are guided by a set of programmed rules modeled on the actual reasoning of human experts in the field. A human expert has specialized knowledge that is used to solve problems. This knowledge is constantly being updated through new learning and experience. The computer is actually programmed to play the role of a human expert, capable of continued learning.

The potential for expert systems is unlimited. At the Siemens plant in Germany, where Siemens produces car heaters for Fords, an expert system has been developed and used to detect defective heaters. Previously, workers had to turn on the car motors and listen for disparate sounds in order to identify defective heater units. The new expert system can actually recognize those sounds that are wrong, thus indicating which parts are defective.[22]

Although not yet widely used, artificial intelligence and expert systems could be the most exciting scientific and commercial development of the twentieth century.[23] Computers that actually think and learn certainly would be a major aid in managerial decision making and organizational information processing. Researchers are now working on the development of "neural" computers that will actually be able to mimic the human brain's vast web of interconnected neurons. This is a quantum leap from expert systems, which are programmed to solve special problems within the parameters set by the designer. The neural computer, like the human brain, will be capable of creating rational and organized thought patterns on its own.

Expert systems are being used in some areas. Besides the Siemens example above, they are used to solve problems of resource allocation, such as portfolio management and capital budgeting. They are also used to diagnose problems with accounts receivable reports, financial statements, and other reports, and to schedule and assign tasks such as personnel shifts in hospitals or timetables for delivery trucks. In the medical field they are being used to help diagnose diseases and illnesses. Finally, they can be used to manage information and data files. Schlumberger, an oil-field equipment company, uses an expert system to evaluate potential oil sites. The system interprets a much larger amount of information than can be handled by human experts.

Expert systems appear to be the next revolution in information management. The implications of this revolution are now only being speculated on. Full adoption of expert systems will change completely the way computers are used to manage an organization's information system.

INFORMATION AND THE DECISION-MAKING PROCESS

Information is the raw material that feeds decision making at all levels in the organization. To understand the role of information better, it is useful to digress briefly and examine decision making. Theorists have developed three models of decision making, and information plays important but different roles in each of these models. Table 11.1 below summarizes key points of these three models.

▨ **TABLE 11.1**
Decision-Making Models

Model	Assumptions	Decision Processes	Decision Outcomes
Rational/ Economic	1) Perfect information at no cost 2) Perfect rationality	Stepwise; linear. Begin with problem identification; end with solution implementation.	Utility Maximization
Bounded Rationality	1) Imperfect information — uncertainty — and information costs 2) Power and personal preferences affect decisions. 3) Decision makers face cognitive limitations.	Decision makers attempt to act in a stepwise, linear rational fashion, but rationality is bounded or constrained.	Satisficing
Garbage Can	1) Multiple, ambiguous and conflicting goals 2) Means for achieving goals not well understood (ambiguous technology) 3) Fluid participation of members in decision making	Nonlinear process; no clear beginning or ending points; decision process can start at any point.	Solutions where there are no problems. Problems that go unsolved. Some problems get solved.

RATIONAL DECISION MAKING

Economists have long used simplifying assumptions about human economic choices to model human behavior. One result of these simplifying assumptions is the ***rational*** or ***economic model of decision making.*** The model assumes that decision makers gather perfect information available at no cost, use perfect rationality, and arrive at ***utility maximizing*** decision outcomes. A utility maximizing outcome is one that provides the decision maker with the best possible set of outcomes.[24]

For example, a retail grocery business may try to use this approach to deal with the problem of the optimal inventory levels of various products to stock on the shelves. The proces would start with **problem recognition** or **identification:** The store must stock the right amount of inventory. Too much inventory results in storage and opportunity costs—the money tied up in inventory cannot be used for other things; too little inventory results in lost sales. The next step would be for managers to **determine the desired outcomes:** Managers must determine the appropriate levels of inventory. Once the problem has been identified and the desired outcome has been determined, managers must **collect data** about the underlying causes of the gap between the desired state and the current state: Why is the firm unable to achieve utility maximizing inventory levels? In the case of inventory levels, two obvious problems would be unpredictability in supply and unpredictability in demand for goods. Clearly, many other issues may affect supply and demand: weather conditions, competition, new products, changing consumer habits, and so on. Once the decision makers have collected data, they **develop alternative solutions** to the problem. Managers may, for example, develop expert systems to monitor inventory levels and automatically place orders as needed. The marketing department may conduct consumer surveys and focus groups to track consumers and develop a model of consumer preference to guide inventory control. The purchasing department may suggest a variety of purchasing strategies and strategic relationships with suppliers to guarantee pricing and supply of inventory. Once these solutions are developed, management **assesses** the alternatives for the one solution or set of solutions that provide a utility maximizing outcome. The final step is to **implement** the decision.[25]

Fundamental to this stepwise process are the assumptions that (1) managers will obtain perfect, unbiased information, (2) managers will use this information to act in a perfectly rational manner, and (3) managers will select the utility maximizing outcome. The decision process is linear in nature (an identifiable beginning and end) and rational. However, a close look at the above inventory control problem suggests that, although perfect rationality may be a desirable state, it is likely to be unattainable. Any number of problems are likely to make rationality bounded or constrained. Decision makers may be unaware of certain consumer trends. The purchasing department may be unable to forecast the financial well-being of certain suppliers. Unpredictable weather conditions may affect the availability of certain goods. On top of problems of uncertainty, differences of opinion among different departments involved may affect decision premises and information availability. The information systems department may believe that the bulk of resources should go toward the development of a highly sophisticated computer system and software to monitor and control flows of inventory. The marketing department may believe that the key to better inventory control is enhancing the firm's ability to predict consumer preference. Thus, they believe that the bulk of resources should be spent on surveys, focus groups, and development of a computer model of consumer preference. As we see in Chapter 12, these sorts of differences are not unusual. For now, it is important to note that such differences further constrain the organization's ability to act in a truly rational fashion. Instead, we are most likely to witness bounded rationality.

BOUNDED RATIONAL DECISION MAKING

One way to think about the decision-making process in organizations is to recognize the difference between how the organization would like to make decisions—using perfect rationality—versus how an organization actually makes decisions—using bounded rationality. The organization members' best intentions may be to make rational deci- sions, but the real life conditions place boundaries or constraints on their ability to act rationally.

Earlier in this chapter, we identified factors that contribute to bounded rationality. In summary, decision makers face uncertainty, and perfect information is not available. Information searches cost money and take valuable time. Often, decisions need to be made quickly, precluding a comprehensive information search. Decision makers have cognitive limits; they may not be able to process all available information. Individuals or departments may have biases or preferences for certain information and certain types of solutions, regardless of whether or not the outcomes are utility maximizing. Decision makers may ignore information and rely instead on intuition or gut instincts.[26]

The result of bounded rational decision making is *satisficing.* A satisficing outcome is one that is of lesser quality than a utility maximizing outcome. Typically, a satisficing outcome is the first outcome that meets some minimum level of acceptability. It may be a compromise between different departments, although it need not be. It may be the out- come preferred by the most powerful department, even though a solution suggested by a less powerful group may be better.

In the earlier example of the inventory control problem, it may be that the mar- keting department is the dominant and most powerful department in the organization. It may influence the decision process in such a way that most of the resources are devoted to surveys, focus groups, and decision modeling of consumer preference. Some smaller amount of resources may be used to develop a computerized inventory control system, and nearly no resources may be devoted to developing better relations with suppliers. The results may produce a system that improves inventory control but is far from utility maximizing.

Most decisions in organizations exhibit at least some degree of bounded rational- ity. As we see in Chapter 12, the complexity of the decisions, the degree of uncertainty present, and the decentralization of power in an organization contribute to bounded rationality. In some specific types of organizations and with some specific types of prob- lems, the norms of rationality present in bounded rationality vanish. In the following sec- tion we explore decision making in which linearity and rationality are no longer present.

GARBAGE CAN DECISION MAKING

Perhaps you've been involved in or witnessed a decision that completely defied common sense. It may be that *garbage can decision making* is at work.[27] The stepwise decision- making process that is the hallmark of rational decision making and, to a somewhat lesser extent, of bounded rationality, is no longer present. In fact, solutions may precede the identification of problems, or no problem may even exist. Decisions may be made that do not solve problems, and those problems may continue. Sometimes some problems eventually get solved, although any thought of utility maximizing should be abandoned.

Rational decision making and bounded rationality were presented as decision- making models for individual decisions. The problems of bounded rationality are exac- erbated by the fact that organizations must make many decisions. The garbage can model, unlike the first two models, is an attempt to characterize the complexity of orga- nizations faced with multiple decisions.

Garbage can decision making gets its name from the colorful way in which researchers portrayed the process. Think of peering into a garbage can and seeing problems, solutions, information, participants swirling around in a random fashion. Decision makers can enter the decision process at any point. The "decision" may start with a solution in search of a problem. The following example will shed some light on garbage can decision making.

Exhibit 11.1   **The Sports and Convocation Center**

The president of the 12,000-student private urban university sat at his desk pondering the offer—$12 million to build a new multipurpose center on campus. The only conditions of the offer were that the money be spent for a multipurpose center and that the center bear the name of the donor. That should be no problem, the president thought.

Over the next few weeks the president began to put the wheels in motion. The public relations department put out a news release announcing the donation and the tentative plans for a new multipurpose sports and convocation center. An architectural firm was hired to draw up plans. And a handpicked committee of faculty, staff, board of trustee members, and others was assembled to guide the process.

Two months after the donation, the architect presented plans to the president. The president, the donor, and the board of trustees accepted the plan and hired a construction company to begin building the center.

As the center neared completion, a number of problems rocked the university. First, the donor received extensive negative publicity in the national press because of his involvement in highly publicized criminal activities. The wealthy donor had made his millions not in the oil business, but as an international arms merchant, selling weapons to just about any government or political group that could come up with hard currency. Some of the weapons that he sold were U.S. made, and their sale in foreign markets was prohibited. Questions were raised about the propriety of an academic institution being associated with a suspected criminal, especially one associated with terrorism and unsavory political groups. Second, several prominent faculty members suggested that the university had lost sight of its educational mission. Many classroom buildings were in disrepair; educational facilities were hopelessly out-of-date; student fees had to be raised to offset cost overruns for the sports and convocation center; and faculty, whose salaries lagged behind national averages, had not received raises in several years. The final problem was that once the center opened, the local community, one of the wealthiest in the city, complained vigorously about the increased auto traffic, noise, drinking, and rowdy behavior on nights of basketball games and concerts.

Shortly after the center opened, a faculty leader at an all-university meeting asked the president a critical question: How did the university end up with this center? The president then tried to reconstruct the decision process. He noted that the old athletic and special event facilities were in terrible condition. Basketball games and graduation programs had not been held on campus since the mid-1960s. The last three basketball coaches complained that they could not recruit top-notch prospects because of the horrendous facilities. Students and physical education faculty members had voiced concern about inadequate facilities for physical education classes, intramural sports, and recreational use.

The donor presented a potential solution to these problems. The president went on to note that he had sought input from his committee, but that most members failed to respond. When asked about the other problems on campus, the president merely deflected the questions and said that there were many problems on campus and in higher education today, but those were not the problems that this donor wanted solved. Faculty and students were displeased with the president's answers to their question. But as the meeting broke up, it was clear to those in attendance that they were stuck with the new sports and convocation center.

In retrospect, the center has become a focal point of campus activity. The athletic facilities receive heavy student and faculty use. Users boast about the high quality and comprehensiveness of the sports center. The center also houses the new student bookstore and a convenience store, both of which are very popular with students and faculty. Basketball, graduation, and concerts are back on campus for the first time since the mid-1960s. Still, other problems persist. Many classroom facilities need maintenance and upgrading. Computer facilities are several years behind the current technology. Faculty have received modest raises in the past three years, but they still lag behind those at comparable schools. Most significantly, the university has a new president who has tried to build bridges to all the important stakeholder groups: students, alumni, faculty, local residents, business, and government. Whether or not he will be able to solve all of the problems of the university is still uncertain.

The above case presents many key elements of garbage can decision making. Specific organizational conditions must be present; those conditions lead to a nonlinear decision process; and the results may vary greatly. These points are summarized below.[28]

The Organization. The goals and objectives of the organization are ambiguous, conflicting, and poorly articulated. Many problems exist simultaneously. These conditions may lead organizational members to pursue different sets of problems and set different priorities. One characteristic of garbage can decision making is that many decisions are being made simultaneously. In educational institutions like the university in the above example, it is common for multiple and conflicting goals to exist and for some of the goals to be ambiguous. For example, it is unclear how a new sports and convocation center will further teaching or research goals.

A second organizational characteristic is that the means for accomplishing the organization's goals are ambiguous or poorly understood. Essentially, this means that the organization's technology is characterized by great uncertainty. For example, what means or technology does the university in the example use to increase the quality of teaching and research or to increase the prestige of the school? Building the center may add to visibility of athletic teams, but even that is questionable. The school would still need to recruit and train a highly skilled group of potential players. And as we saw, the center reduced the university's prestige among the local community members who were unhappy about increased traffic.

The third organizational characteristic is referred to as *fluid participation.* In organizations in which garbage can decision making is likely to take place, participants move in and out of the decision process frequently. This fluidity in participation may be because of employee turnover or because employee commitment to the decision and time for decision making is limited. In the example above, several different groups of people were involved in the decision process at different times with little consistency over time.

In general, this organizational situation has been labeled **organizational anarchy.**[29] The organization is highly organic and may be going through a period of rapid change. These conditions do not fit all organizations, but they may be found temporarily in many organizations. When these conditions are present, we are likely to find the type of decision making described in the next section.

The Decision Process. Whereas rational and bounded rational decision making are linear, stepwise processes, garbage can decision making is nonlinear. It can start and stop at any point. Four different streams of the decision process weave in and out in a nearly random fashion. These four streams are problems, solutions, organizational participants, and choice opportunities.

As noted in earlier decision models, problems are identified gaps between where an organization wants to be and where it is. The same is true in the case of garbage can decision making, but problems sometimes do not precede solutions and solutions may not solve problems. In fact, problems may be invented to fit solutions as in the case of the sports and convocation center. As this suggests, the sequence of problem identification leading to solutions may be reversed. Some problems may be solved, but they may not be the most important and pressing problems. Some problems continue to go unsolved.

We noted previously that the participation of organizational members in the decision process is fluid. This fluidity affects the decision process by creating inconsistency. Different participants are likely to see the set of potential problems and solutions in a different light and set different priorities. For example, the university faculty in the earlier case may have seen the solution to lagging prestige as recruiting better faculty and students. Or they may have seen an entirely different problem. Shifting decision-making participation makes it difficult to reach any consensus or common ground.

Recall from the case that this "decision event" began with an opportunity — the donor pledged money for a center. In this example, the decision process began with an opportunity. It may also be that a choice opportunity is lacking. Thus, an organization can identify a problem and a potential solution but cannot implement that solution because the appropriate set of problems, solutions, and participants is not present.

The consequences of garbage can decision making are that solutions are sometimes enacted where no problems exist. The sports and convocation center was a solution to a problem that had not yet been identified. It may also be that problems continue even after a solution has been implemented. The sports and convocation center did not increase the prestige of the university and did not improve the quality of sports teams appreciably. At the same time, other problems continued with no solutions in sight. Classroom buildings were still in disrepair, and faculty salaries still lagged behind national averages. However, even in a garbage can situation, some problems do get solved. The sports and convocation center did provide a much needed facility for recreational sports, concerts, and university events.

It is important to note that garbage can decision making is not a desired state of affairs. The chaotic and random nature of decision making is not likely to lead to high-quality decision outcomes. The garbage can model is a *descriptive model.* It describes conditions and consequences that are likely to occur in certain organizational settings. No organization intends to make garbage can decisions. Thus, the garbage can model is *not* something that one would prescribe or suggest for an organization.

INFORMATION TECHNOLOGY AND THE MODERN ORGANIZATION

The important field of information technology, primarily in the forms of computers and satellite networks, is having a dramatic impact upon organizational structures, processes, and power relationships. Although these phenomena are so new that organization and management theorists have not yet adequately studied and analyzed them, several implications are becoming evident.

The changes currently going on in organizations as a result of the introduction and use of information technology are as profound as those brought about by the Industrial Revolution two centuries ago. Indeed, the changes in jobs and organizational structures will be radical, and organizations are only beginning to experience the effects that these "smart machines" are causing.[30]

Highly automated machines that can acquire, store, analyze, and communicate information throughout the organization make such information easily accessible to all with a PC or terminal connected to the mainframe. Today, that includes many managerial, clerical, and administrative personnel. Even many factory workers now work through a computer interface rather than directly with a specific process on the factory floor. For example, at the Benetton Group's textile factories in Italy, a computer in the headquarters relays information to computers controlling various weaving machines and instructs the machines on what types of cloth to make, in what patterns, and in what colors.[31] Of course, there are workers involved in this process, but they are systems analysts and computer operators, *not* traditional textile workers. We can expect to see more of this in the auto, steel, glass, rubber, and paper industries.

The effect of these changes is that the structures and processes of organizations are being changed and will continue to change radically. Child, for example, argues that the codification (structuring) and diffusion (sharing) of information will very much affect the typical organization's hierarchy by allowing for what Peters and Waterman call the "simultaneous loose–tight coupling" of organizational members, units, and levels.[32] For example, Volkswagen is a geographically and product-diversified semihierarchy that uses INTELSAT, an international satellite network that links Volkswagen operations in Brazil, Germany, the United States, and Canada.[33] This communication and information link allows the company to take advantage of the opportunities presented by international specialization, while, simultaneously, it provides for uniformity among the different affiliated organizations and units within the Volkswagen group.

In addition, traditional status and power relationships based on hierarchy might crumble should certain trends continue. Computerization undermines traditional forms of authority and breaks down barriers between job categories and functions.[34] Thus, being part of the *network* can become more important than having a certain position in the hierarchy.[35] Knowledge is power, so the saying goes, and many people in modern organizations are gaining power to an unprecedented degree because of their access to vitally important information.

Finally, before we leave this subject, the reader should note that information technology, by being able to enhance the speed and amount of information transferred, can allow for greater control and coordination down and across organizational units. Conversely, information technology can also lead to greater decentralization and flexibility. Top-level managers' use of executive information systems often permits these executives to delegate more authority to their subordinate managers because the former have a means to check more easily on company operations. Like many other facets of organization theory, a manager's particular philosophy has a great deal to do with how power and authority are delegated and dispersed throughout the organization.

SUMMARY

Information is the lifeblood of the organization. It links the organization to its environment, and it is the oil that lubricates the internal operations. Consequently, information must be managed just as any other valuable resource is managed.

Information has several key characteristics that are important for managers to understand and recognize. These include the relevance, quality, richness, quantity, timeliness, and accessibility of information. Additionally, information, or access to information, has symbolic value in organizations. Sometimes people collect information simply because that is what is expected in the organizations. Sometimes control of information, as we see in the next chapter, becomes a symbol of power.

Information systems have evolved from manual systems through electronic data processing (EDP), management information systems (MIS), and decision support systems (DSS), to expert systems using artificial intelligence (at least in some organizations).

Regardless of the stage of information evolution of a particular organization, the information process remains basically the same. Information is gathered, reported, analyzed, accepted, stored, retrieved, and used. The system of information management must ensure that the right quantity, quality, timeliness, and relevance of internal and external information is provided to decision-authority centers.

Information is a key input in the decision-making process. When making decisions, managers in organizations try to behave in a systematic, rational fashion. However, because of a variety of factors, decision makers face bounded rationality. These conditions include the complexity of most organizational problems, the uncertainty of technology and the environment, the limitations on human cognitive processes, individual emotions, and individual preference. Under conditions of bounded rationality, decision makers attempt to act rationally, but they are bounded or constrained in the ability to do so. Under some rare conditions even bounded rationality is absent from organizational decision processes. Garbage can decision making is likely to occur when organizations have multiple goals that may be ambiguous or conflicting, when the technology is unclear, and when participation of organizational members in the decision process is fluid. With garbage can decision making, even the pretense of rationality is gone.

Finally, we are beginning to see evidence that the introduction of information technology is having an impact on structures and processes in organizations. Information technologies are permitting organizations to become more flexible and more organic. Forms like the virtual organization discussed in Chapter 8 would not be possible without advanced information technology. The interplay between information, information technologies, and organizational design is key to the strategic success of organizations.

Questions for Discussion

1. Why is information important for an organization?
2. What is bounded rationality? Why does it often happen in business decisions?
3. What are the key characteristics of information?
4. What is the relationship between information richness and task technology? Explain why you think the relationship is that way.
5. What are the differences between and MIS and a DSS?
6. What are expert systems and artificial intelligence? How do they differ from a DSS?
7. What are the key assumptions of the rational economic decision-making model? Are they reasonable assumptions in the typical organizational context?
8. Why does bounded rationality plague most organizational decisions? What is the consequence of bounded rationality on decisions?
9. Under what kinds of conditions are we likely to see garbage can decision making? Describe a situation or organization in which you think garbage can decision making is likely.
10. Think of an example of an organization that has recently automated its information technology. What effects did this have on the administrative hierarchy and processes in the organization?

CASE: SICK CALL*

In today's health-conscious society, medical costs take a front-row seat. Perhaps no other sector of the U.S. economy has been the focus on costs to the extent that the medical field has.

In general, hospital costs, prescription drug bills, and doctors' fees have risen dramatically in the last decade or so. But concern over medical costs is not new. As long ago as 1945 Kaiser Permanente was formed to provide medical care at the Henry Kaiser shipyards and steel mills on the West Coast. Thus was born the first modern-day HMO. The Kaiser plan was a complete program for health care, a plan in which Kaiser

---

*This case is based on the following article: George Anders, "In Age of the HMO. Pioneer of the Species Has Hit a Rough Patch," *The Wall Street Journal* (December 1, 1994): A1–A12.

Parmanente owned its own hospitals, provided health insurance, and even employed its own staff of doctors.

This no-frills medical care appeared to be the breakthrough that patients wanted, and based on rather remarkable success, especially in California, Kaiser spread eastward to many states in the 1970s and 1980s. The vertical-integration pattern that Kaiser used was more efficient and cost-effective than that of other HMOs that relied on contracts with physicians and hospitals.

But developments in California in the early 1990s brought a "sick call" for Kaiser. Startling advances in medical technology, an increase in specialists, and even a shift to a more conservative medical philosophy have brought Kaiser up short. These forces have combined to bring about a plunge in medical costs. For example, costs for blood tests and cardiology exams have dropped as much as 20 percent since 1991. Rival HMOs can now use contracts for services that are much lower in cost than Kaiser's charges because of the overhead that Kaiser must recoup due to its vertically integrated plan for providing services. In other words, rival HMOs have a distinct advantage now when it comes to cost control, once Kaiser's strong point.

Kaiser simply can no longer be competitive on cost alone due to its contracts with in-house doctors and hospitals. This big disadvantage is the product of Kaiser's deliberate decision to enter the HMO field as a fully-integrated member. In other words, the very essence of the cost-cutting advantage that it enjoyed at the beginning is now its biggest liability. The original cost advantage has eroded drastically over the last ten years with the result that membership coming from the California Public Employees' Retirement System, for instance, has dropped by some 475 to the current figure of 136,642. Even though this latter number is still quite sizeable, the trend of declining membership is of much concern to Kaiser management.

Part of Kaiser's disadvantage is the fact that its physicians are also owners and managers, and they are understandably reluctant to cut their own earnings by cutting costs for their services. They have, however, agreed to perform even surgery at standard rates rather than receive the premiums they once did for such services. Though signing bonuses are no longer paid, the base pay for doctors has not been cut even though it is considered too high for the market.

At the core of the vexing issue is the collegial atmosphere in which decisions such as cost cutting are made. This means that even though Oliver Goldsmith, head of Kaiser Permanente's doctors, might like to make a unilateral decision to cut costs, he is stymied by the collegial approach to setting physician fees at Kaiser.

On the hospital side of the organization, Kaiser is making better strides. Outpatient stays, made possible by surgical technologies and supporting systems, are gaining favor. Patient tracking systems and procedures now move patients more rapidly through the stages of recovery from surgery, thus shortening the hospital stays that are necessary. Edgar Carlson, the regional director for Kaiser for Southern California, has seen his hospitals cut patient days by some 11 percent and hopes to raise this figure to the 25 to 30 percent range in the near future. Thus far, however, Kaiser has stopped short of closing hospitals altogether.

The decision to use its own doctors and hospitals is also costing Kaiser on the health insurance front. Rival HMOs are allowing, even encouraging, their members to seek care from a preselected group of doctors with lower rates than Kaiser can offer through its own staff. According to Kaiser's CEO, product innovation isn't the

company's strong point. It is simply not the strategic intent to move away from its ownership concept of providing health care.

Although Kaiser has teamed up with Pacific Mutual Life Insurance Company to begin offering "out-of-network" care and thus has gained several accounts, the decision has been hard for Kaiser to accept philosophically.

Customer service has also been a bane for Kaiser. Even though they are satisfied with care for major illness, patients with minor ailments experience long waits on the phone, delays in getting test results, waiting-room delays, and problems with getting convenient appointments. A recent report on health conducted by the Bay Area Business Group confirms this condition, putting Kaiser in the lower 25 percent in terms of patient satisfaction with doctors. Better attention to phone calls, the use of postcards to mail some routine test results, and the encouragement of doctors to be nicer to their patients are all measures that Kaiser has installed to deal with these complaints.

Learning from its West Coast experience, Kaiser doesn't use its fully integrated approach in its newer regions like the mid-Atlantic states, Georgia, North Carolina, and Texas. Even though it still owns its clinics, it contracts with outside hospitals for overnight stays. But in California, problems still result from the original plan.

California's massive layoffs have taken a toll on membership with the result that it is now essentially flat in both the northern and southern regions. If this trend cannot be reversed, Kaiser will find itself with aging members who typically are more expensive to treat. And even though Wall Street watchers think that publicly-traded HMOs will do a better job, Kaiser maintains that the drive for profit will soon lose its allure and that its cash reserves and overall financial position will enable Kaiser to "ride out the storm" of price competition. Analysts and patients alike are watching to see how well Kaiser answers its "sick call."

QUESTIONS FOR DISCUSSION

1. How would you describe the decision-making process at Kaiser? What factors contributed to that type of decision making?
2. Could Kaiser use rational decision making for its major strategic designs? Why? Why not?
3. What could Kaiser do to improve the quality of its decision making?

REFERENCES

1. James O. Hicks, Jr., *Management Information Systems: A User Perspective* (St. Paul, Minn.: West, 1984), 12.

2. Jonathan P. Levine, "Bank of America Rushes into the Information Age," *Business Week* (April 15, 1985): 110–12.

3. John G. Burch, Jr., and Felix R. Strater, *Information Systems: Theory and Practice,* 2d ed. (New York: John Wiley & Sons, 1979), 16–17.

4. J. W. Dean, Jr., and M. P. Sharfman, "Procedural Rationality in the Strategic Decision-Making Process," *Journal of Management Studies* 30 (1993): 587–610.

L. M. Gales and D. Mansour-Cole, "User Involvement in Innovation Projects: Toward an Information Processing Model" (*Journal of Engineering Technology Management*, in press).

5. See Dean and Scharfman in note 4 above.

6. R. L. Daft and R. H. Lengel, "Information Richness: A New Approach to Managerial Behavior and Organizational Design," in *Research in Organizational Behavior*, vol. 9 (Greenwich, Conn.: JAI Press, 1984): 191–233.

   R. L. Daft and R. H. Lengel, "Organizational Information Requirements, Media Richness and Structural Design," *Management Science* 32 (1986): 554–71.

7. See Daft and Lengel in note 6 above.

   See Gales and Mansour-Cole in note 4 above.

8. See Daft and Lengel in note 6 above.

   See Gales and Mansour-Cole in note 4 above.

9. H. Mintzberg, *The Nature of Managerial Work* (New York: Harper-Row, 1973).

   R. L. Daft, J. Sormunen, and D. Parks, "Chief Executive Scanning, Environmental Characteristics, and Company Performance: An Empirical Study," *Strategic Management Journal* 9 (1988): 123–39.

10. W. G. Ouchi, "A Conceptual Framework for the Design of Organizational Control Mechanisms," *Management Science* 25 (1979): 833–48.

    W. G. Ouchi, "Markets, Bureaucracies, and Clans," *Administrative Science Quarterly* 25 (1980): 129–41.

11. Herbert A. Simon, *Administrative Behavior*, 2d ed. (New York: Macmillan, 1957).

12. See note 1 above.

13. Charles A. O'Reilly III, "Variations in Decision-Makers' Use of Information Sources: The Impact of Quality and Accessibility of Information," *Academy of Management Journal* 25, no. 4 (December 1982): 756–71.

    A. C. Boynton, L. M. Gales, and R. S. Blackburn, "Managerial Search Activity: The Impact of Perceived Role Uncertainty and Role Threat," *Journal of Management* 19 (1993): 725–47.

14. M. S. Feldman and J. G. March, "Information in Organizations as Signal and Symbol," *Administrative Science Quarterly* 26, no. 2 (June 1981): 171–76.

15. Don Matthews, *The Design of Management Information Systems* (New York: Petrocelli/Charter, 1976), 42–49.

16. Henry C. Lucas, Jr., *Information Systems: Concepts for Management* (New York: McGraw-Hill, 1967), 7–13.

17. Peter F. Drucker, "Playing in the Information-Based Orchestra," *The Wall Street Journal* (June 4, 1985), 32.

18. James A. E. Stoner and Charles Wankel, *Management*, 3d ed. (Englewood Cliffs, N.J.: Prentice-Hall, 1986), 622.

19. John P. Murray, "Developing an Information Center at Rayovac," *Data Management* (January 1983): 20–25.

20. Steven Alter, "A Taxonomy of Decision Support Systems," *Sloan Management Review* 19, no. 1 (Fall 1977): 39–59.

21. Robert W. Blanning, "Knowledge Acquisition and System Validation in Expert Systems for Management," *Human Systems Management* 4, no. 4 (Autumn 1984): 280–85.

22. Brian O'Reilly, "Computers That Think Like People," *Fortune* (February 27, 1989): 91.

23. Patrick H. Winston and Karen A. Prendergast, eds., *The AI Business: The Commercial Uses of Artificial Intelligence* (Cambridge, Mass.: MIT Press, 1985), preface.

24. J. G. March, "Bounded Rationality, Ambiguity, and the Engineering of Choice," *The Bell Journal of Economics* 9 (1978).

    H. A. Simon, *The New Science of Management Decision* (Englewood Cliffs, N.J.: Prentice-Hall, 1960).

    H. A. Simon, "A Behavioral Model of Rational Choice," *The Quarterly Journal of Economics* (February 1955): 99–118.

25. Danny Samson, *Managerial Decision Making* (Homewood, Ill.: Richard D. Irwin, 1988).

26. See note 11 above.

    James G. March and Herbert A. Simon, *Organizations* (New York: John Wiley & Sons, 1958).

    Richard M. Cyert and James G. March, *A Behavioral Theory of the Firm* (Englewood Cliffs, N.J.: Prentice-Hall, 1963).

27. Michael D. Cohen, James G. March, and Johan P. Olsen, "A Garbage Can Model of Organizational Choice," *Administrative Science Quarterly* 17 (1972): 1–25.

28. Ibid.

29. Ibid.

30. Shoshanna Zuboff, *In the Age of the Smart Machine* (New York: Basic Books, 1988).

31. Curtis Bill Pepper, "Fast Forward," *Business Monthly* (February 1989): 26–27.

32. John Child, "Information Technology, Organization, and the Response to Strategic Challenges," *California Management Review* 30, no. 1 (Fall 1987): 48.

    Thomas J. Peters and Robert H. Waterman, *In Search of Excellence* (New York: Harper & Row, 1982).

33. See Child in note 32 above.

34. See note 30 above.

35. Gareth Morgan, *Riding the Waves of Change: Developing Managerial Competencies for a Turbulent World* (San Francisco: Jossey-Bass, 1988).

Power and Politics: Organizations as Political Entities

CASE: POWER PLAY*

The personal computer business is global and fiercely competitive, but one company, Acer Inc., is making its way toward being a significant player in this market. Once known as a clone maker, the company is witnessing sales of Acer-brand machines lead it to the top ten in the PC market. For a company that once concentrated on making machines for others to sell under their brand names, this rise in the market is stunning the PC world.

How has Acer been able to move so aggressively in such a difficult market? Basically, the rise can be traced to two main forces—management philosophy and an accompanying highly decentralized organization structure. Observers of the industry say that Acer has, as a result, been able to anticipate market shifts and meet them with cutting-edge chips.

Stan Shih, founder and chairman of the Taiwanese firm, believes in maximum autonomy for Acer's managers and the freedom to act that goes with it. He says that, as a result of his approach, the company is more flexible and thus able to move quickly into new markets around the world.

This ability is far removed from the Acer firm of just a few years ago. Then, hurting from an ill-fated acquisition and an unjustified push to sell its brand of PCs in the American market, it faced price competition from IBM and Compaq Computer here as well. Many thought that Acer would be unable to overcome such obstacles and had virtually written off the company as a player in the PC market.

Unlike firms in Japan or South Korea, Acer could not turn to its government for subsidies. So Shih applied his approach to being competitive—slashing the number of workers and trimming other production costs. To complement these moves, Shih took another dramatic step with the use of massive decentralization

---

*This case is based on the following article: David P. Hamilton and Jeremy Mark, "Acer Emerges as Global PC Power and Asian Pacesetter," *The Wall Street Journal* (December 1, 1994), B4.

of the management structure. Instead of the typical vertical hierarchy that one might expect to find in industry, Shih virtually collapsed the structure into individual business units. These units were empowered to make their own decisions (that reflected Shih's philosophy), and they were much closer to the marketplace. Much faster, more flexible decisions were the result. This move reversed the organization trend in the company and returned it to its beginnings as a local PC maker.

The decentralized business units run strictly as individual units of the firm, making their own marketing decisions, competing against each other to make low-cost components, and being held individually accountable for their profitability. Acer's plans call for the establishment of some twenty such units locally and for listing their shares on worldwide markets. This is an attempt to establish Acer as a global company operating on a local level so as to reap the benefits of both approaches to operations and marketing.

Shih's management philosophy is also seen in the company's reward system, which is based on demonstrated merit and giving workers a financial stake in the company. This arrangement appeals to Acer's managers, many of whom returned to the company after being disillusioned by the glass ceiling that they experienced when they were employed by firms in Silicon Valley.

The actions of Acer have been complemented by a joint venture with Texas Instruments, Inc., to make memory chips. The move seems to be paying off as evidenced by its 90 percent contribution to Acer's profits in 1993. Further evidence of success is Acer's lead in Latin American and Southeastern Asian markets for PCs. The careful product design and target marketing strategy that emphasizes ease of use appears to be winning over U.S. consumers.

The localization strategy based on a philosophy of decentralization and empowerment is proving effective for Acer. The ability to determine product and its design at the local level are seen as its keys to success. It will be interesting to keep an eye on Acer to see if it can reap long-term benefits from its "power-sharing" approach to managing a company that is reinventing itself while, at the same time, gaining a larger share of the global PC market. Whether Acer's slogan, "Global Brand, Local Touch," will become more than just a slogan is the question yet to be answered.

This brief look at the Acer Company shows how the role of power and authority has been redefined. As a result of power sharing, coupled with a complementary merit program and employee ownership, Acer is proving that a company can succeed on a global front while maintaining a local focus. Many organizations are finding that traditional models of authority, based on hierarchical authority and centralized decision making, are not well suited to the turbulent and complex environments that many organizations face.

This chapter explores the concepts of power, authority, and politics. The Acer Company is an embodiment of how these concepts are being applied by one company in a highly competitive global market. This case can be the start, we hope, for a better understanding of some of the most important concepts in organization theory explained in this chapter.

POWER AND POLITICS: ORGANIZATIONS AS POLITICAL ENTITIES

Beginning in Chapter 1 and continuing through the early parts of this book, we have regarded organizations as intentional and purposeful. That is, we have assumed that organizations are intentionally structured and designed to accomplish specific, organizationally determined goals and objectives. Elsewhere, we have introduced the strategic contingency framework that suggests that managers will structure and design a company to ***best fit*** the context (i.e., goals, environment, technology, size, and culture) it faces. Implicit in the definition of organizations and in the contingency framework is the notion of ***rationality.*** We assumed that rational managers would act in ways to maximize the efficiency and effectiveness of the organization; that managers would do what is best for the collective good of the organization.

As we progressed through our study of organizations, we encountered some chinks in this rational view of organizations. In Chapter 3 we discovered that organizational goals and objectives may be incongruent, ambiguous, or otherwise problematic. Furthermore, it was noted that judging organizational effectiveness was itself problematic. Chapter 11 pointed out the human limitations brought about by ***bounded rationality.*** By now it should become clear that organizations do not always behave rationally.

In this chapter we explore in greater detail power and the political nature of organizations. We investigate authority—the rational basis of power. One way to think about the rational side of an organization is to think about what an organization *should do.* Authority is based on what individuals should be doing according to the official, formal dictates of the organization. However, we will see that not all power is associated with authority and the official, formal dictates of the organization. Instead, individuals throughout the organization can derive power from many different sources that are unrelated to authority. Often this power allows individuals to pursue goals and objectives other than those that are officially documented. Understanding the divergent nature of power in organizations leads us to a ***political perspective*** on organizations. Rather than discussing what organizations *should do,* the political perspective addresses what organizations *actually do.*

This is not a case of organizations being either rational or political. Every organization has a political side, some more so than others. Understanding the distribution of power and the political nature of organizations is critical to understanding the actions (or inactions) of organizations. We begin this examination with an overview of authority—the rational basis of power.

THE NATURE OF POWER AND AUTHORITY

This section of the chapter examines the component parts of power and authority and how they fit together to provide the influence a decision maker needs to make choices that are accepted and implemented.

AUTHORITY

The word *authority* probably brings to mind a picture of a parent scolding a child or of a sergeant giving a command to the troops. One person gives a command or issues an order in an attempt to elicit some form of desired behavior from another person or group of people. Clearly, the president of a university or the CEO of a corporation has authority to issue directives.

What happens when a superior issues an order or gives a command? First, the superior makes the decision or choice; this requires the *right* to do so. In other words, the superior must be given approval or sanction to make decisions in the name of the organization, and this requires some form of recognition by the organization itself. In the case of formal business organizations, this approval ultimately comes from the owners who have the right to direct the use of their property. Recall the discussion in Chapter 9 of governance and the problems associated with the relationship between owners and managers. The positive outcome of successfully solving the governance problems between owners and managers is that owners grant to managers the authority to make decisions and give orders or commands. The rights of owners, in turn, are based on the legal system and social norms that grant to property owners the right to use private property in ways such that its use does not infringe upon the rights of others.[1] In essence, the right of a manager to make decisions and to issue orders, instructions, and so on comes from ownership and property rights.

Directing the behavior of others is based on two "subrights": (1) the right to decide and (2) the right to issue appropriate implementing instructions or directions. Without the right to decide, no manager could be a successful planner, and without the right to issue orders and instructions, the manager's plans would be worthless because there could be no assurance of the implementation of the plans. Thus, authority is fundamental to every organization because the nature of managerial responsibility involves decision making and influence. This fact of organizational life was clearly recognized in Weber's bureaucratic model of organizations. The hierarchical division of labor and the accompanying scalar principle defined levels of authority and decision-making responsibility.

The essence of authority is rights. These rights are determined (ideally, at least) by obligations. The obligation (responsibility) should determine the nature of the right (authority), and these should be equal or in balance. As we noted in Chapter 9, the fundamental role and responsibility of management is to protect and enhance the wealth of owners. This management obligation is the source of management's authority to run the organization. A manager accepts the responsibility to use organization resources effectively and efficiently and to guide others in pursuit of the organization's goals and objectives. Critical to the management of the organization is the determination of how much and what type of authority managers must have if they are to adequately discharge their responsibilities.

In Chapter 7 the Autodesk minicase presented a clear example in which owners (in this case, the founder John Walker) did not give authority to top managers to make decisions necessary to fulfill managerial obligations. The result was an organization that floundered under the weight of constant struggles and battles over direction of the firm.

Two points emerge from the above discussion. First, authority is a right determined by an obligation, and second, authority is solely associated with the formal organization that has formal sanction or approval from society. This latter point becomes important when we discuss power, which may be independent of the formal organization.

We can define *authority* as *the rationally based formal right to make decisions and influence behavior to implement decisions based on formal organizational relationships.* The organization must be a formal one and officially recognize the organizational relationship between owners, managers, and subordinates if authority is to be granted. Influence attempts that fall outside of these formally recognized parameters involve the exercise of power.

FOUNDATIONS OF AUTHORITY

Authority is the mainspring of influence in the formal, rational organization. It has its roots in the official recognition of the organization by society at large. From a rational perspective, it is a prime mover for guiding the organization and its various membership groups toward their objectives. Several forms of authority are discussed in the sections below and are summarized in Table 12.1. Additionally, the discussion treats the components and uses of authority in order to demonstrate how this force affects organizational behavior.

TABLE 12.1
Foundations of Authority

Type	Meaning	Example
Managerial	Right to make and enforce decisions	Decision to direct a subordinate's behavior
Staff	Right to make suggestions and recommendations	Study recommending a change in job descriptions
Situational	Right to make binding decisions within a very restricted area or scope	Accountant deciding proper accounting methods
Operative	Right to work without undue supervision	Tool and die maker rejecting poor raw material

Managerial Authority. Managers of formal organizations are responsible for acquiring, deploying, and controlling resources needed to accomplish objectives. To do this, managers must have the right to make and enforce necessary decisions. This right is termed *authority* and is possessed by all who hold managerial positions. Managerial authority is composed of the right to choose among alternatives and the right to enforce those choices, based on official position. Without both of these components, no manager can successfully carry out responsibilities. This is true because managers by being so designated are charged with the responsibility to make decisions and ensure that they are carried out.

You will recall from our discussion of bureaucracies in Chapters 2 and 7 that authority is rationally allocated according to position and responsibility in the organizational hierarchy. As one moves up the hierarchy, position authority becomes broader and greater. The manager's responsibility should be a determining factor in deciding the amount and type of authority that an individual is granted. This balance between responsibility and authority is in keeping with the ***principle of parity of authority and responsibility,*** a long-recognized guide to building and maintaining a rationally sound organizational structure. The principle simply states that it is desirable to maintain balance between authority and responsibility in order to avoid the dysfunctional situation in which managers are given responsibility for some actions but given no authority to carry them out effectively. This also avoids the situation in which a manager's authority exceeds his or her responsibility. Individuals should possess authority and use it to enforce the decisions and actions needed to carry out their responsibilities for the accomplishment of organizational objectives.

Staff Authority. Every day, members of an organization make suggestions and recommendations about the solutions to various problems, procedural changes, or other improvements. Each time this happens, staff authority is being exercised. Even though we normally associated this type of authority with staff experts or professionals (e.g., attorney, information systems specialist), it is actually possessed by every member of the organization.

Everyone in an organization has the right to recommend, to suggest, to advise, and to attempt to exert influence to gain acceptance for ideas.[2] Individual job expertise is the basis of many popular management techniques including total quality management, suggestion boxes, employee empowerment, and the simultaneous flattening and decentralizing of organizations. The assumption is that individuals should know best how to carry out their jobs and that staff experts should know the most about their specific specialty.

One possibly confusing aspect of the use of staff authority is that subordinates sometimes elect to not use their staff authority for one reason or another. Sometimes superiors discourage their subordinates from using it, perhaps because exercising staff authority may contradict or diminish the supervisor's managerial authority. Whether or not the individual exercises staff authority, it is still possessed by all organizational members.

Situational Authority. Situational authority is a type of hybrid authority that contains elements of both managerial and staff authority. Generally, it is delegated to a staff expert by a manager. The staff expert is restricted rather specifically in the areas in which the authority can be exercised.

Recall that staff authority embodies the right to make suggestions and recommendations and managerial authority is the right to make and enforce decisions. Situational authority may begin as staff authority. For example, an accountant may make recommendations about changing specific accounting procedures. A manager may then delegate authority to the accountant to enact changes in the accounting system as the accountant sees fit. This authority normally resides with the manager but has been delegated to the accountant. However, the accountant's authority to make changes is limited to changes in the accounting system. He or she has no authority to make changes in other systems; thus, the authority is situational.

Operative Authority. All members of an organization have some authority to make certain decisions about how, in what order, and with which tools they will carry out their tasks. The right to work without undue supervision is also commonly considered to apply to all members. These rights, taken collectively, are operative authority.[3]

Operative authority is made up of two basic rights: the right to carry out responsibilities of the job and the right to determine, within reason, how and when it will be done. Whether one is a manager, a technician, or an unskilled laborer, one has these minimum rights. Without them, it would not be possible to plan and carry out one's personal responsibility.

Authority provides the formal, official, and rational basis for the distribution of power in organizations. One problem with the concept of authority is that in many organizations, especially those that are decentralized and where lower-level employees are empowered, the hierarchical lines of authority are blurred. For example, in the case of Acer Inc. at the beginning of this chapter, there is potential for conflicts because of the decentralization of divisions. Different divisions may end up engaging in strategies that conflict with each other either through internal competition for scarce resources or through competition in the marketplace.

In the following sections we investigate power. The reader should be cautioned that authority and power are not analogous. Authority is but one source of power. Individuals acquire and exercise power that is derived from sources unrelated to formal authority. We will see in the concluding sections of the chapter that these sources of power, which are unrelated to formal authority, are in part what gives rise to the political nature of organizations.

POWER

Power is the ability (potential or actual) to impose one's will on others;[4] ***it is the ability of one person to affect the behavior of someone else in a desired way.*** This ability can be based on a number of factors at both the individual level and the organizational level. Some of these factors include knowledge, authority, information, personality, and resource control. In subsequent sections we systematically investigate these varied sources of power.

Authority is simply power that the organization formally sanctions or recognizes. Power, on the other hand, is influence that does not necessarily depend on formal organizational recognition. Power may exist within or outside the bounds of formal organizational relationships. In other words, power is a larger concept than authority and, indeed, subsumes authority as a formal power relationship.

An example will clarify the difference between power and authority. Consider the situation in which a supervisor issues directions to subordinates that require them to carry out a normal work task. These directions are considered by both supervisor and subordinate to be legitimate or official. The supervisor in this instance can be said to be using power in the form of position authority, which is derived from his or her role as a manager and which was delegated to him or her by superiors in order to accomplish certain organizational goals.

Now assume that the supervisor directs a subordinate to do a personal errand for him or her. This errand is clearly outside the official job description for the subordinate and the relationship between the supervisor and subordinate. This command cannot be founded in the official authority vested in the supervisor. Rather, this attempt to use power is not based on the formal organization. If the subordinate performs the errand, the influence attempt is successful, and we can say that the supervisor has power over the subordinate.

In this example, there is a dependency relationship between the supervisor and the subordinate. Even though this relationship is not based on formal job relationships, the subordinate may feel compelled to carry out the requested errand because he or she depends on the supervisor for various rewards. Formal relationships often have a kind of carryover effect into informal relationships. This can be particularly troublesome when supervisor requests border on sexual harassment or demands to violate ethical codes.

The extent to which an individual can exercise power can be viewed as a function of the dependency relationship that exists between parties. If person B depends on A (for knowledge, income resources, and so forth), then A is in a position to exercise influence or power over B. The more dependent that B is on A, other things being equal, the more power A can exercise over B.

One thing that may not be obvious is that power may not necessarily be consistent with the organizational hierarchy. In the rational, bureaucratic view of organization, power should increase as one moves up the hierarchy. However, when one fully understands the nature of power and dependency in organizations, it should become clear that power (separate from authority) may be independent of position and level in the organization. Two perspectives on power are presented below. The first focuses exclusively on individual bases of power in the organization, while the second explores how individuals, groups, or departments gain power through dependency relationships.

THE FRENCH AND RAVEN POWER TYPOLOGY

The classic work by J. R. P. French and B. Raven lists and describes various bases of power found within organizations.[5] The French and Raven power typology provides insight into sources and potency of power in organizations. A summary of these sources is presented in Table 12.2.

■   TABLE 12.2

The French and Raven Power Typology

Type	Meaning	Example
Rational/legal	Accepted as legitimate by those involved	Obeying commands of police officer
Reward	Granting of benefits to others	Working hard for a promotion or recommendation
Coercive	Punishing others	Disciplinary action of a three-day suspension
Referent	Identification with person in a power position	Hero worship
Charismatic	Dynamic personality	Religious leaders
Expert	Extensive knowledge or high-level skill	Computer programmer

Rational or Legal Power. Rational or legal power stems from one person's acceptance that its exercise by another person agrees with some set of rules or protocol considered legitimate by both parties. The legitimacy of this power, in fact, provides an alternative name for this base of power—legitimate power. Rational or legal power typically results from the type of position one holds and from the position in the organizational hierarchy that one occupies. A police officer has the power to give tickets and arrest people because of the societal rules and protocol that assign that responsibility. Supervisors have rational or legal power over subordinates because of the power vested in their respective positions.

The conditions of legitimacy are a function of the culture that is instrumental in helping define societal norms. For instance, in countries of the Far East it is considered legitimate for the older members of a group to be shown more deference (and thus be given more power) than younger members. In other cultures that may not be the case. Other factors may override age and be more potent sources of power, as can be seen when power is traceable to knowledge, ability, or some other factor.

Reward Power. Power that comes from one's ability to control and dispense benefits to others is termed ***reward power.***[6] The controller of benefits has the ability to shape the behavior of others by the simple act of dispensing or withholding these benefits.

The strength of reward power is primarily determined by two major forces: the size of the reward and the belief that it will, in fact, be dispensed. In other words, A's reward power over B increases as the size of the benefit increases. Other things being equal, a larger reward gives the person granting that reward greater power over the recipient than a smaller reward.

A supervisor who has control over subordinate pay raises or bonuses gains not only the legitimate power of his or her position but also has power over subordinates because of his or her ability to grant or withhold raises or bonuses. The larger the pay raise or bonus, the more power the supervisor has to get subordinates to perform tasks that they otherwise might not perform.

In the use of reward power it is also important that the person controlling the rewards has some means for determining whether the requested task has been completed. While this may seem rather obvious, the actual process of performance appraisal is often not easy and is prone to inaccuracy and distortion. This is particularly the case with jobs or tasks characterized by uncertainty or ambiguity.

Coercive Power. The ability to coerce or punish another person is a strong foundation of power or influence.[7] This base of power often provides strong motivation and can, in many ways, be viewed as the obverse of reward power. Where reward power relies on the dispensing of rewards for its strength, coercive power depends on the meting out of punishment for its effectiveness. On many professional sports teams players who show up late for training camp or miss or show up late for practices are typically fined. Depending on the frequency and extent of the transgression, the player may be fined anywhere from a few hundred dollars to several thousand dollars. In many organizations poor performers may lose specific benefits or perquisites. For example, a sales representative whose sales decline may be moved to a less desirable territory or lose access to a company car. Continued poor performance may result in demotion. Of course, the ultimate in coercive power is the threat of firing.

Although the punishment that results from the exercise of coercive power may result in the cessation of undesirable behaviors or the performance of desired behaviors, it may also produce undesirable side effects. First, the targeted person may shift goals and behavior to doing as little as possible while avoiding punishment. Thus, the undesirable behavior may be eliminated, but the targeted person is still only a marginal contributor to the organization. Second, the person on the receiving end of coercive power is likely to feel estranged from the person using that power. The estrangement may be manifested in resentment, feelings of victimization, and possibly the desire to retaliate. This sense of resentment and latent frustration can have serious dysfunctional consequences in a relationship, especially if it is unresolved over a period of time.

The effectiveness of coercive power depends on the nature of punishment, its perceived impact, the probability that it will be used, and the measurement of desired behaviors. If punishment is not defined by the targeted person as punishing, if it is seen as relatively mild, or if the likelihood that it will be used is slight, coercive power is made less potent. For example, professional hockey games were, for many years, plagued by fighting—a behavior deemed inappropriate by the National Hockey League (NHL). The NHL tried to eliminate fighting through a combination of penalties, fines, and suspensions. Initial efforts were unsuccessful because the penalties were only mildly punishing and the likelihood of the league assessing fines or suspensions was low. The effort to cut fighting only became successful after the NHL decided to increase the severity of penalties and increase the certainty that players engaged in fights would receive stiff fines and suspensions. The coercive power was used by the NHL to enforce its formal authority as a governing body.

Referent Power. Referent power can be defined as the power A has over B because B identifies with A.[8] This sense of identification makes A capable of influencing B's behavior even though neither A nor B may be aware of the sense of identification.

This type of power can be illustrated in the case of hero worship. Star athletes are worshiped by aspiring youngsters who see that their own abilities can be enhanced by emulating the star's behavior. The controversy over athletes as role models exists because of the referent power star athletes possess. Because most people at one time or another have known this feeling of identification with success, this is a common and powerful foundation of influence.

Kirk Cottrell, the founder of Island Water Sports, a Florida surf shop chain, has this type of power with young people. "I watch this guy with young people, and believe me, it's uncanny," stated Nancy Lyman, a friend and former classmate of this young entrepreneur, who succinctly stated the case of hero worship of Cottrell by young surfers and employees.[9] People with referent power are often able to get their admirers to follow and commit to the organization in ways unavailable to other individuals.

People with whom others identify might not be aware of their own referent power. This makes tracing power relationships difficult. Secret admiration of successful people is an example. Such relationships would be difficult to identify and analyze even though they are undoubtedly common and have tremendous impact on interpersonal relationships.

Charismatic Power. Influence or power based on one's personality can be defined as charismatic power. There are those who have an almost undefinable magnetic quality about their personalities that attracts others to follow them.[10] Some would argue that Hitler had this type of influence in pre–World War II Germany. Gandhi's power in India was due in part to his charisma. In the United States John F. Kennedy was said to have been a charismatic leader.

Those who possess charisma find it relatively easy to influence their followers. One dimension of charismatic power that helps explain its potency is that charismatic leaders also help their followers attain personal goals. By following such a leader, the followers can realize their own objectives even though they might primarily be serving the leader's purposes.

Within the business world a few leaders stand out because of their charismatic power. Former Chrysler CEO Lee Iacocca clearly had charisma that extended beyond the boundaries of the Chrysler Corporation. In the early 1980s, when the company was on the verge of bankruptcy, Iacocca was able to influence the federal government to guarantee loans to Chrysler. He convinced the United Auto Workers union to make several contract concessions so that the company could reduce its costs of production. Finally, Iacocca appeared in print, radio, and television advertisements promoting Chrysler products.[11] Phil Knight, one of the cofounders of Nike, has provided his company with a similar type of personal leadership.[12]

No special effort is required to exercise charismatic power. Charismatic personalities, both positive and negative ones, often retain their power to influence even long after the person has left office or died. Such power is potent and a formidable influence in organizations. Followers of charismatic leaders follow because of the compelling nature of the leader's persona.

Expert Power. There are those who wield power because of their knowledge or special skills. They are respected for this knowledge or skill, irrespective of their position in the organization. Those who admire this expertise or who need it to solve problems are willing to subordinate themselves in return for the expert's assistance. For example, a scientist, an information systems specialist, or a technician may exert power beyond that typically associated with their position because of the expertise they possess. Academic degrees, professional certification, or other forms of official documentation are often associated with expert power. For example, consider labels such as MBA, MD, CPA, CFP (certified financial planner), CLU (certified life underwriter).

This base of power is important and unique because it is independent of the organizational hierarchy. People low in the organization can exercise power based on expertise. One consequence of the pervasive downsizing taking place today is that more and more expertise is accumulating low in the organization. Expert power, as we will note shortly, is similar to the dependency-based view of power. The more specialized and the more scarce the specific expertise one possesses, the more power one can exert.

The power typology discussed above helps identify and clarify some sources of power in and around organizations. Thus far, the focus has been on individual power. Often power resides not in individuals, but in departments or units of an organization. To understand departmental and unit power, it is necessary to understand dependencies and critical contingencies within organizations.

DEPENDENCY, CRITICAL CONTINGENCIES, AND POWER

As we noted above, power can come from many sources, but these sources at some level revolve around dependency. When individuals, departments, or organizations become dependent upon other individuals, departments, or organizations, the dependent party loses power. Similarly, individuals, departments, or organizations that can solve problems — critical or strategic contingencies — for other individuals, departments, or organizations gain power. The abilities to create dependencies or solve critical or strategic contingencies are among the most important determinants of power.[13] Although some dependency relationships and some ability to solve critical problems of the organization are associated with the formal organizational hierarchy, this need not be the case. In fact, one interesting consequence of this view of power is that some individuals lower in an organization (lower-order participants) can obtain power that would seem inconsistent with their position.

Power through Control of Resources. Every organization must have resources to convert into products or services. Without a sufficient amount and proper distribution of such resources, the organization will soon cease to exist. The control over resources thus has important power implications both inside the organization and among organizations. In Chapter 5 we addressed the issue of how organizations avoid or manage dependencies through either vertical integration or through structuring their relationships with suppliers. In this section, we focus on the internal power dependency relationships that may develop in organizations.

In general, individuals or departments who control critical or scarce resources within an organization can wield tremendous power.[14] Resources that are in short supply and resources that are central to the organization's continued success are sources of power. Individuals who or departments that possess or allocate these resources to others have great ability to influence the organization.

Think about your own university or college. Which departments on campus seem to possess the greatest power to influence the direction of the university? Typically, those departments that enjoy the greatest power are the ones that control critical resources. These days, two critical resources on most campuses are money and highly qualified students. Departments with greater access to these two key resources should be able to exert significant influence. For example, on many campuses departments that are able to acquire outside grants or funding from the federal government, businesses, foundations, private individuals, or other sources gain power to influence decisions about hiring and development of facilities. Similarly, if a university, as many are, faces a shrinking population of potential students, a department that maintains high enrollments should gain some power to influence decisions.

Power through Solving Critical or Strategic Contingencies. Broadly speaking, we may regard information, knowledge, and special skills as types of resources in an organization. Uncertainty or lack of knowledge creates the potential for power dependency relationships. Those individuals who or departments that solve key problems facing an organization or reduce uncertainty are likely to gain power as a result. For example, in many organizations the maintenance or physical plant department is not regarded as having much power. However, it might just take a machinery breakdown or a power system failure to remind an organization of the critical role that the maintenance or physical plant department plays in the organization. Solving these problems may give the department significant power to influence future decisions about machinery or plant facilities.

In general, the more pervasive the threats or uncertainty are to the organization, the more power that will result to those who can manage the threats and uncertainty. If, for example, environmental threats are felt by the entire organization and one particular department has the ability to solve those environmental threats, then that department will gain power. Because of the widespread potential for litigation that many organizations face, legal departments, with their specialized knowledge and ability to deal with the legal environment, often have extraordinary power over many key aspects of organizations. The legal department often gives final approval on product designs, packaging, labeling, contracts, policies, and public relations communications, to name just a few areas.

Substitutability. The ability to solve critical problems or supply scarce resources for an organization clearly provides a basis of power. However, when the organization can somehow substitute for those skills, expertise, or resources, individuals or departments lose power.[15] As many organizations move toward downsizing and network (or virtual) organizations, they begin to contract out many functions that they once viewed as critical in-house activities. For example, many organizations use outside suppliers of marketing, legal, human resources, accounting, and even engineering expertise.[16] Reliance on outsiders will likely diminish the power of insiders who once carried out those functions. In shifting to outsiders for solutions to critical organizational problems, the organization may have reduced insider power, but the organization now becomes more dependent on outside contractors. Organizations face key questions about tradeoffs between powerful internal coalitions or dependencies on external suppliers. The decision over internal supply versus external supply is a critical one, and the power dependency is but one of the key issues top management must face.

Power and Location in the Organization. How often have you tried to get the "ear" of some key decision maker, whether to voice a complaint, ask a question, or obtain permission to carry out some action? And how often have you been frustrated by some secretary or assistant who bars your access to that key decision maker? This scenario is fairly common in organizations. People in positions such as secretary or administrative assistant often knowingly or unknowingly exercise power because of their proximity to holders of legitimate position power and because they control access to that person. People in these roles can control the flow of information and people to their superiors. They can make appointments; set the calendar; control the agenda for meetings; and screen incoming communications.[17] In a sense, these people occupy the role of ***gate keeper,*** and they control a scarce resource. During the administration of President Richard Nixon, the assistants who controlled access to the president became extremely powerful men.

One's position in an organization's network can also be a source of power. This concept is referred to as ***network centrality.*** The power that a manager derives from network centrality is the power of information—the power of being well informed. A manager who has contacts throughout the organization may gain power because he or she knows what is going on in far-flung corners of the organization and has the ability to get a broader view of the organization. This can become useful in forming coalitions within the organization.[18]

Power and Position in the Organization. Earlier in this chapter, we noted that one source of power was a person's position in the organization. This base of power was referred to as the rational or legal (or legitimate) position power that is associated with one's position in the organizational hierarchy. In general, a person's power in the organization is related to his or her rank within the hierarchy—the higher up one resides, the more power one has. This is consistent with the bureaucratic and rational view of organizations. However, many changes that have taken place in the latter part of the twentieth century have eroded some of that rational or legal basis of power. As a consequence, middle managers and even employees lower in the organization's hierarchy have gained power to influence an organization's direction and actions.

The extensive downsizing at many organizations and the increasing reliance on new, sophisticated information technologies have given rise to more power for individuals lower in the organizational hierarchy. Downsizing has created scarcity of expertise in some organizations. It is likely that fewer people will possess specialized skills and knowledge, and it is likely that these people will not be top managers.[19] These conditions should yield power. These lower-level individuals can control the flow of information to top management, which, in turn, can affect the decision premises of top managers.

Several factors can contribute to the power of lower-level members of organizations. First, when individuals are indispensable because of skills, knowledge, or information they possess, they gain power. Additionally, the longer an individual is in an organization, the more likely he or she is to have access to sources of power: critical information, people important to the organization, or instrumentalities—aspects of the physical plant of the organization or its resources.[20]

Another important source of power for lower-level organizational members is the power vacuum created when there is a leadership transition, particularly if the new leader is from outside the organization. Under such conditions new leaders often become highly dependent on lower-level staff assistants for guidance navigating around their new organizational home. This problem may be particularly acute in large, complex organizations. Some new leaders try to counter this tendency by bringing in their own staff of assistants.

Finally, the rules of the organization can themselves be used as a source of power for lower-level employees.[21] No organization can successfully survive an exact enforcement of all its rules. By simply following the rules, lower-level employees can be quite powerful, and the more important their tasks are to the organization, the more powerful they can be. For example, in the transportation industry drivers, pilots, shipping clerks, baggage handlers, and others can exert extensive influence by insisting on following rules to a T. Sometimes such actions can be used to change archaic rules or to force other changes or actions.

Exhibit 12.1   **Purchasing Automobile Components**

An automobile is an extremely complex product, made up of many subassemblies. Some subassemblies are made internally, and others are made by outside suppliers. When a new car is designed, the design team typically gives various groups design parameters and asks them to design such components as steering systems, suspension systems, interiors, and even engines and engine control systems. The designs of many of these component systems are themselves very complex. The result is that the design team (the rational or legal authority) may be unable to evaluate the quality of component systems.

At one of the Big Three U.S. car companies, the design team for a new car model provided detailed information on steering and suspension requirements to the division that produced those components. The Steering and Suspension Division (SSD) was to bid on the job (i.e., create a design) and was to also seek external bids on the design. SSD was given this responsibility because it had more knowledge and expertise in steering and suspension design than any other group in the company—despite the fact that the head of SSD was lower in the organization than the head of the design team. Thus, SSD could control the flow of information to outside firms bidding on the steering and suspension system, and it would evaluate the incoming bids. SSD could further influence the process by controlling the flow of information back to the design team because the design team members lacked the knowledge, information, or expertise to make appropriate judgments.

As you will see in the continuation of this story, this situation is ripe for political intrigue.

HOW TO ASSESS POWER

Because power permeates the organization and all its members are, in some way, affected by it, it is important to find some means to measure or assess it—even if such assessments are informal. If people are able to assess power, they can more easily find their place in the power structure. The following sections identify several indicators of power.[22]

POWER DETERMINANTS AS INDICATORS OF POWER

To measure power by its determinants requires a judgment about how much of a particular type or basis of power a person or department possesses. Determinants (sources or origins) of power are *indirect* measures of power that a given person or department has at a particular time.

An example of the determinants of power as a measure of power should help. When people have expert power, it means that they have special expertise or knowledge about a given field; their power originates from this expertise. If they appear to have considerable in-depth knowledge, we may tend to assign disproportionate power to them. The more fields in which they effectively demonstrate expert power, the more powerful they can be as employees.

Employees, of course, can behave in a way that creates the impression that they have more power than they actually do by using double-talk and by appearing sure of their positions. Only experience with a given employee can reveal whether that power is based on legitimate expert power (or on some other basis).[23]

POWER CONSEQUENCES

Another means of assessing power is to determine the effects or consequences of the decisions made by various actors. A look at who makes the significant organizational decisions gives a good indication of who has the most power in the organization. It is important, however, to distinguish between who *makes* the decisions and who *announces* them. For example, the president of a corporation might announce a merger plan that was actually the work of a close adviser. A dean might announce a plan to allocate the school's budget that could really be the work of a staff assistant.

Those actors called on to make the decisions that cause the most severe consequences or alter the behavior of the most important actors are those whose power can be measured by the consequences of its use. Consider, for example, the various magnitudes of the following decisions: mergers, building new plants, introducing new products, allocating the budget to departments, and hiring new employees. Although there are countless other types of decisions, the point is that a hierarchy of power consequences exists. That hierarchy varies from one organization to another and may vary over time within any given organization.

POWER SYMBOLS

Those who have power often like to display the trappings of that power. This may include such things as larger offices, more luxurious office furnishings, more expensive company cars, reserved parking spaces, access to special dining or recreational facilities, or even the manner of dress. In one organization managers could discern power by counting ceiling tiles in their offices. Larger offices, which were associated with greater power, had more ceiling tiles. One manager could boast of an office with twenty ceiling tiles, a clear indication that she had more power than colleagues in offices with only fifteen tiles, even though the difference in office size was a mere twenty-four square feet.

Even though symbols signify power, it is impossible to generalize their applicability. In some organizations and in some cultures, spartan conditions (e.g., small offices, modest furnishings, etc.) may be a form of reverse symbolism. For example, some organizations avoid special treatment for managers. They forego executive dining rooms and parking spaces. They insist that managers share in moves toward efficiency by using small offices and driving modest cars. Such avoidance of perquisites is common among Japanese organizations.

REPRESENTATIONAL INDICATORS OF POWER

Membership on influential boards and committees or participation in critical teams or task forces can be indicative of an individual's power.[24] If a midlevel manager is the head of a special team or task force, this may be an indication of the individual's popularity with top management and of his or her ability to influence the organization. Every organization has key jobs or positions that are associated with possession of power. The title (executive vice president) and/or function (budget officer) of the position are sometimes good indicators of power.[25]

There appears to be no overall best way to assess power. One measure may be best in one circumstance while another measure may be best suited for a different set of circumstances. We simply describe these indicators and suggest that individuals be aware of the multidimensional nature of power in organizations.

THE USE OF POWER IN ORGANIZATIONS

We have discussed a number of concepts relating to organizational power as well as the power of individuals within organizations. Power is a complex, ever-changing force in any group. It can arise from a number of sources and be possessed to some extent by all members. Basically, though, power is used to alter events and circumstances to fit the holder's preferences. This is true whether we are concerned with organizational or individual power.

One requirement for the effective use of power is effort: Some energy, and perhaps ingenuity, must be exerted to have influence. Power vacuums (opportunities to gain resources or solve critical problems) exist in all groups and organizations; it remains for someone to spend the energy to fill the vacuum.

Some functional areas make the effort to fill a power vacuum quite worthwhile. Organizations rely on information about their financial health, and so an enterprising member of the budget department has an opportunity to store up this valuable resource. The budget officer can, for instance, devise an allocation system known only to himself or herself so that no one else can gain access to needed information without permission. This, of course, can cause problems for the organization, but it nonetheless makes the budget officer powerful. This condition can easily permit the budget officer to make *unauthorized* budgets that contradict the organization's intent.

Similarly, how the budget officer decides to report budget data can affect the perceptions of how well specific departments are doing. For example, in a nonprofit professional association (e.g., legal association, medical association, accountants association, etc.), the budget officer can affect judgments about the effectiveness of the publications department by choosing to emphasize either the cost of publications or the revenues generated. Typically, nonprofit professional associations provide publications to members as a service. A portion of membership dues is used to offset the cost of publications. Advertising revenues can be used to reduce the cost to members for this service. If the budget manager wants to emphasize the positive contributions of the publications department, he or she could emphasize the increasing revenues that publications generate, which reduce the real costs to members. If the budget manager wishes to shed a less favorable light on publications, he or she could emphasize the increasing cost of publications while deemphasizing or ignoring revenues generated.

Clearly, the control of information flows in an organization can be a tremendous source of power. People who and departments that control information can quickly develop a multitude of "friends" seeking favors. A position such as budget officer or information systems manager can be key to the allocation or diversion of resources.[26]

Coalitions of members are potent forces in an organization. Because we are all part of many different organizations, we have probably experienced observing and even participating in various coalitions. Every organization seems to have an "in" group (those in favor in the organization) and an "out" group (those who are out of favor in the organization). Regardless of the type of organization, there typically appears to be a relatively small "in" group that determines what happens. Consider your college or business school. It is likely that one group (perhaps a department or a program group) has more power than other groups. Perhaps because of the popularity of a particular major, the research productivity of a group of faculty, or faculty success obtaining grants or outside funding, a group may become powerful and influential in affecting the policies and strategic direction of the college or school. This power may be separate from the formal or official power structure of the organization, or the power may reside in top management. The power resides in these *dominant coalitions* because the group holds extensive power and authority, and as a result, they become influential to the decision-making process.

Definition

Dominant coalition: group holding extensive power and authority that may be separate from formal power; key group of decision makers with extensive influence.

THE STICKINESS OF POWER

One interesting characteristic of power is that those who hold power are reluctant to relinquish it. As a consequence, transitions of power in organizations are not smooth and seamless. Rather, transition of power is characterized by stickiness—power holders try to retain as much power as long as they can. This can produce conflict, challenge, and confrontation over power transitions.

A group or coalition that obtains power because it can solve key problems facing an organization may try to retain power by redefining all future problems in ways that fit the group's particular competence. For example, in the late 1950s and early 1960s stylists and marketers were dominant coalitions in the automobile industry. Style and marketing sold cars; thus, those groups that possessed knowledge and competence to solve styling and marketing problems gained great power. This distribution of power was fine when the external environment demanded that the automobile companies market cars based on styling.

In the late 1960s, the environment began to shift. Several factors converged to drastically change the automobile marketplace. Small, inexpensive imports began to penetrate the market at the same time baby boomers were becoming first-time car buyers. The ecology movement and the counterculture of the late 1960s and early 1970s emphasized living simply and efficiently. The final blow to the big-car mentality of the earlier generation was rising gasoline prices brought about by the embargoes and boycotts of the mid-1970s. Unfortunately for the U.S. automobile companies, the dominant coalitions tried to retain their powerful positions by redefining these problems as styling and marketing problems. Essentially, the coalitions were saying, "This is merely a marketing and styling problem that we can solve with our expertise." For example, Ford tried to deal with foreign competition by marketing existing products "dressed up" to look more like the imported competition. Many earlier attempts at fuel efficiency and pollution control were based mainly on appearance, rather than substance. No one successfully challenged the assumptions and proposed solutions of the stylists and marketers because of the past successes of these groups.

When these early, feeble attempts based on marketing and styling failed to deal with the changed environment, power finally shifted. New coalitions that possessed the unique skills, knowledge, and resources to deal with the changed environment began to emerge as power centers. However, the transition was far from smooth. It lagged far behind the environmental changes and was characterized by conflict and confrontation. This stickiness in the transition of power is characteristic of the unwillingness of power holders to give up their source of power.

Power is a dynamic force used by many organization members for many purposes. A snapshot of the power structure is not adequate—we need a high-speed, full-length motion picture of it in order to appreciate it as a part of organizational life, composed as it is of all those activities that characterize the members' efforts to use power for their benefit.

POWER AND POLITICS

Earlier in the chapter, we examined authority relationships and power in organizations. Here, we examine the relationship that power has to political forces within the organization. Our focus is on how the political processes at work in the organization affect organizational actions.

We have already laid the groundwork in previous chapters and in the earlier sections of this chapter for explaining and understanding organizational politics. In Chapter 3 we noted that organizational goals are often characterized by ambiguity and conflict. Lack of agreement about the legitimate goals of the organization leads to the formation of coalitions intent on pursuing their own views of goals. Additionally, when we examined organizational effectiveness, we noted that different constituents, both internal and external to the organization, had different perceptions of what constituted an effective organization. One of the primary messages of Chapters 4 through 6 was that organizations faced varying degrees of uncertainty from the environment and from the technologies used by the organization. Structure, design, control systems, and information can resolve some uncertainty, but, as pointed out in Chapter 11, individuals and organizations face the constraints of bounded rationality when trying to reduce uncertainty and solve the organization's problems. It is these conditions that give rise to power — power that is often unrelated to the official hierarchy of the organization. It is also these conditions that give rise to the political nature of organizations.

Most of us spend much of our lives in organizations of one form or another. But how many of us have stopped to ponder who really governs these organizations? We do not necessarily mean who holds the top management or administrative position because, as we've noted, those are not always the people in control.

Earlier, we asked you to think about who has power in your university or college. Think again about your school. Can you identify the different constituencies that exercise control over that institution? Is it the president, the deans, the provost or vice president, the faculty, the alumni or the students, the governing board or the state government if your school is public? To pose such questions is to indicate the difficulty in finding clear answers. For at the same time, we could say that no one group or person mentioned above has complete control of your college or university. This lack of clarity over control arises because of the political nature of organizations.

The alumni exert influence on the course and direction of your college or university through promising or withholding financial and moral support. At MCU in the introductory case of Chapter 11, the alumni were key to supporting the stadium project. The governing board exerted pressure through issuing and enforcing rules. In the case of a state institution the state government influences the direction of the school through legislation and financial support. The president, vice presidents, provost, and other administrators make decisions and offer directives. Yet, two things are important to understand the political nature of organizations. First, each of these groups may be pursuing very different, sometimes conflicting, goals for the institution. Second, in addition to these formal influence wielders, there exist myriad groups and individuals attempting to informally influence the direction of the organization.

These informal and unofficial power sources are able to influence the organization because of the multiple, and perhaps conflicting, goals that exist. Because the goals may be unclear or ambiguous, it may be difficult to clearly determine the effectiveness of the organization. The appropriate technology for accomplishing these goals may be unclear, and even if the type of technology is obvious, the technology may itself be characterized by uncertainty. Achieving the goals may be made more difficult and uncertain because of environmental turbulence and complexity. Furthermore, as the environment changes, the appropriateness of some goals may be drawn into question. Finally, our decision makers, both those formally recognized by the organization and those who informally and unofficially try to influence the decision process, are prone to bounded rationality. Their judgments are affected by a lack of information, personal biases, self-interest, emotions, and faulty reasoning. All these factors together produce conditions ripe for organizational politicking.

POLITICS DEFINED

These examples indicate the necessity for a clear definition of politics in organizations. Jeffery Pfeffer has suggested the following definition:

Definition

Organizational politics involves those activities taken within organizations to acquire, develop, and use power and other resources to obtain one's preferred outcomes in a situation in which there is uncertainty or [a lack of consensus] about choices.[27]

According to this definition, issues can be resolved through both the formal and informal use of power. The important factor that defines an action as political is that power is used in pursuit of one's own preferred outcomes. These may or may not coincide with the official organizationally preferred outcomes.

THE RATIONAL AND POLITICAL NATURE OF ORGANIZATIONS: A SUMMARY

Following Pfeffer, we have identified four organizational characteristics that differentiate the political and rational perspectives of organizations. They are summarized below.[28]

Goals. As we have already noted, the political view of organizations is premised on the multiple and conflicting goals that typically exist in organizations. This situation allows for the formation of coalitions around different sets of goals. For example, in colleges and universities there is often a lack of agreement about the relative importance and priorities that should be assigned to teaching and research. Different coalitions with differing priorities form around these goals. If the organization were entirely rational, there would be consensus — perfect agreement — on the nature and priority of the goals.

Power. In a sense we have already documented the differences between the rational and political views of power. The rational view of power follows the bureaucratic authority structure of the organization. Power increases as one moves up the organizational hierarchy. One's power is derived from one's official position. Thus, the bulk of power in the organization is centralized and in the hands of top management. However, the political view of power is based not just on position. Power also results from control of resources and information, and from possession of specific skills or knowledge necessary to solve key strategic contingencies. Thus, the political view indicates that power is likely to be diffused throughout the organization and decentralized. As problems and conditions shift, the political power structure also shifts.

Uncertainty and Information. It should be clear by now that organizations face uncertainty from many sources. Two views of organizations differ on the extent of this uncertainty and on the degree to which searching for information will resolve uncertainty. The rational view suggests that organizations face only low to moderate uncertainty and that uncertainty can be overcome by searching for information. From a political perspective, organizational uncertainty is problematic. Uncertainty may be extensive and not easily reduced by an information search. Sometimes it is not clear what information should be sought. And because of the power associated with information, groups or coalitions may withhold or distort information in an effort to maximize self-interest.

Decision Making. The rational view of decision making is as we described in Chapter 11 — rational-economic decision making. Decision making follows a stepwise process beginning with problem identification and ending with solution implementation and evaluation. All necessary information is available, and the utility maximizing outcome is obvious. Moreover, how desired outcomes are to be achieved is clearly agreed upon. But as we noted in Chapter 11, perfect information and perfect rationality are infrequently the case. In the political organization, decision making is characterized by bounded rationality. Groups or coalitions pursue self-interest. Conflicts may result, and negotiation will be a necessary part of the decision making process. Methods appropriate for achieving these outcomes are unclear, and coalitions may disagree about how they should be attained. The outcome will be satisficing, and some groups will retain or increase power while others lose power.

Recall the earlier example of the Steering and Suspension Division (SSD) and the problem of selecting a steering and suspension system for a new car. We noted how this division had extensive power because of its ability to transmit or withhold information and because of its specialized skills and knowledge relative to a critical organizational problem. The description below illustrates organizational politics in action.

Exhibit 12.2   **Politics and the Steering and Suspension Division**

The Steering and Suspension Division was given responsibility to design an advanced steering and suspension system for a luxury sedan. At the same time, SSD was to seek bids from outside vendors to design and build the same steering and suspension system. While the division that would ultimately build the car gave SSD general design and performance requirements for the system, it was up to SSD to set specific technical requirements and to judge the performance of any system that was submitted for bidding.

SSD held a unique position. The division had knowledge and skills about steering and suspension systems that the car-building division did not have. It could also convey and withhold critical data to outside developers that would either facilitate or inhibit design and production. SSD could maximize the likelihood that its own design would be selected by withholding or distorting information that it passed on to the car-building division.

Eventually, several firms and SSD bid on the steering and suspension job. Even to an objective observer, it was not entirely clear which design was superior. What was clear was that the SSD design was not the least expensive. However, in passing information to the car division, SSD highlighted the positive qualities of its own design and downplayed the negative qualities. At the same time, SSD emphasized (perhaps, even distorted) the negative characteristics of competitors' designs while giving little attention to any positive characteristics.

SSD's actions could, at best, be described as self-serving. To understand why SSD acted in the way it did, one must look at goals, power, uncertainty, and the decision process. SSD's goals were to preserve jobs within the division even if its steering and suspension system was more expensive and/or less technically sophisticated. To give the new steering and suspension system to an outside vendor would mean a loss of jobs for SSD. SSD was willing to suboptimize on cost and quality to save jobs.

The company had decentralized power by placing expertise and information control in individual divisions. SSD had power because of its expertise in steering and suspension systems and because of its control of information flows to supplier firms and to the car division.

The company faced uncertainty in the design of cars because of the high degree of complexity in the tasks and technology used to make them. The company faced additional uncertainty because of the external environment. The competence and reliability of supplier firms were questionable. Customer demands for advanced steering and suspension systems was uncertain. Finally, the actions of competitors were unpredictable. As a consequence, the company and the car-building division faced high levels of uncertainty. Collecting more information may not have addressed this uncertainty, especially when some information collection was placed in the hands of SSD.

The decision process for selecting a steering and suspension design was fragmented. Perfect information did not exist, and the decision needed to be made in a limited time frame. Coalitions played key roles and struggled over local goals rather than the larger organizational goal. The result was a satisficing decision—an acceptable, but not utility maximizing, steering and suspension system. The steering and suspension system provided some, but not all, of the technical and performance characteristics that were desired, and the cost was higher than desired. Design and production employees in SSD retained their jobs.

The question is not whether or not an organization is political. All organizations display some aspects of political behavior. The degree to which political behavior is present or dominates an organization depends on a number of factors that include size, complexity, uncertainty, an organization's life cycle stage and structure, to name just a few.

The larger and more complex the organization, the more likely it is that politics plays a prominent role.[29] This is clearly illustrated in the example above of the car maker and the Steering and Suspension Division. Size and complexity contributed to the political environment. The situation with SSD was also characterized by both technological and environmental uncertainty, conditions that contribute to political activities in an organization.

The four-stage view of organizational life cycles that was presented in Chapter 7 provides a foundation for examining shifting power bases and political action in organizations.[30] Essentially, during the first two stages of the organizational life cycle, most political activity emanates from the founder as he or she tries to influence and control different cadres of subordinates. Political activity is minimized by centralized control held by the founder. In the third stage, the increasingly bureaucratic nature of the organization results in diffusion of skills, resources, information, and power. As a result, coalitions form and struggle for control. In the fourth stage when the organization may be spiraling downward, coalitions that gained power in the third stage may exert themselves and try to shift the primary strategic focus of the organization. Politics often turns to outright conflicts over the very nature and future of the organization.

This life cycle framework raises an important and interesting point about political behavior in organizations. The reader may conclude that political behavior is not good or healthy in organizations. That is not necessarily or always the case. Political behavior and the conflict that it often produces can be useful in bringing forth new and divergent ideas. Coalitions may question the organizational orthodoxy. For example, in the introductory case to Chapter 11 the university may be better off in the long run to have a viable football program. A highly visible athletic program may bring positive publicity and revenues to the university. SSD's behavior may be seen as a short-run effort to save jobs. However, in the long run, keeping the steering and suspension development and production internal may help the company retain certain critical personnel and expertise. It may also allow the company to protect sensitive technology from competitors. Thus, the political nature of organizations is neither all bad nor all good; it is merely the way things are in organizations.

SUMMARY

 Because they are the prime means of influence in both formal and informal organizations, authority and power are critical aspects of organizational existence. Authority is the formal and official right to decide and act in the formal organization. Power, on the other hand, is the ability to exert influence over others that may or may not be consistent with the official organization.

When considering the formal authority structure of organizations, four types of authority were considered: managerial, staff, situational, and operative. These four types of authority constitute the formal rights of organizational members and provide the legitimate basis of power.

Power was examined at the individual and organizational level. First, a typology of individual power within organizations identified six bases of power: rational or legal, reward, coercive, referent, charismatic, and expert power. The focus then shifted to power that results from dependency relationships, control of information, control of resources, and the ability to solve key problems within the organization. Power of this sort is not necessarily distributed according to the official, formal authority structure of the organization. Individuals and coalitions at nearly any level in organizations can hold and exercise power.

Because of the decentralized nature of power, the lack of goal consensus, and the uncertainty organizations face, political behavior is a fact of life in organizations. Political behavior involves those actions aimed at gaining and using power to gain individually preferred outcomes. Although political behavior in organizations is ubiquitous, the degree of political action is related to such things as the size and complexity of the organization and the stage of the organizational life cycle. Finally, we noted that political behavior is not necessarily negative. Although political behavior may be associated with suboptimizing, the conflict and negotiating associated with political behavior may also help an organization reorient itself.

Questions for Discussion

1. Define the term *authority* and discuss the bases of authority. How does authority differ from power?
2. "Power is not necessarily consistent with the official organizational hierarchy." Do you agree with this statement? Explain.
3. Apply the French and Raven's power typology to an organization with which you are familiar. Describe how the people can derive power from each of the bases.
4. Now take the same organization as described in #3 above and show how people, departments, or subunits can gain power through control of resources, through centrality, and through solving key problems or contingencies.
5. How does substitutability affect power and its use?
6. Show how Pfeffer's concept of politics helps you understand how organizations behave. Give an example of the political nature of an organization.

CASE: DARTBOARD*

Herbert Haft and his wife, Gloria, began in 1954 what has developed into a prototype of family dynasties. When Dart Discount Drugstore was begun by the Hafts, Herbert ran the pharmacy counter while Gloria operated the front of the store. From this meager beginning the Haft family pioneered what we know today as the discount drug business. With the help of their three children, the Hafts built a network of stores and shopping centers that stretch from coast to coast. Today, the Dart Group owns major shares of Trak Auto, Crown Books, Shoppers Food Warehouse, a Total Beverage discount superstore, and vast real estate and other holdings. The family also owns some three dozen strip shopping centers in the Washington, D.C., area and Combined Properties, a valuable real estate company. These holdings, combined, are estimated to be worth between $500 million and $1 billion.

The tight-knit family carried its spirit into the operations of their companies. Herbert, age 73, has a reputation as a confrontational businessman but didn't seem to carry this attitude to his relationship with his family. Herbert seemed bent on turning over the operations of Dart to his oldest child, Robert, who had developed a reputation of his own as a shrewd mover in the world of business. So all appeared to be peaceful on the business and family fronts.

---

*This case is based on the following articles: Kara Swisher, "Father-Son Struggle Splinters Dynasty," *Washington Post* (July 25, 1993), A1. Terri Agins and Meg Cox, "Haft Feud Threatens Family's Empire," *The Wall Street Journal* (August 16, 1993), B1.

Robert brought a professional savvy to the company and was heavily involved in starting Trak Auto and Crown Books. Gloria brought a keen financial sense while daughter Linda helped run Dart's financial subsidiary. Younger brother Ronald headed Combined Properties, the real estate division. So the five members of the Haft family harmoniously pooled their talents as leaders of the huge Dart conglomerate.

But peace and harmony shattered into a family-rending feud in the spring of 1993. It began when Robert distanced himself from his father because of the latter's reputation as a difficult and unorthodox businessman. His father's reputation cost Robert social acceptance in prestigious Woodmont Country Club, even though Robert tried on numerous occasions to gain it.

Robert proposed the acquisition of Dollar Tree general merchandise stores and the Books a Million discount retailers. Even though some former board members of Dart were pleased with Robert's proposals, the idea "just didn't seem right" to Herbert. Robert also brought a more open style to the company in sharp contrast to his father's secretiveness. Thus began the rift between Robert and Herbert Haft that has erupted into a family, as well as a corporate, battle royal. Charges of Herbert's sexual infidelity and physical abuse on the family front, are matched by father-son rivalry and bitter power plays on the corporate front.

Herbert replaced heir-apparent Robert with younger brother Ronald and began major corporate strategy shifts coupled with the firings of long-time managers. Gloria, Herbert's wife and business partner of forty-six years, has taken Robert's side as has sister Linda. Herbert responding by kicking both Robert and Gloria off Dart's board and firing directors who supported them. Citing incompetence, Herbert also removed Robert from senior jobs at Dart, Crown, and Trak. In response Robert has filed a $9-million lawsuit for money he says he is owed under a long-term contract.

Herbert has decided that Robert's "incompetence" is the basis for replacing him with younger son Ronald, who many doubt has the ability to be of much assistance in running Dart. Even Gloria agrees that Ronald lacks the stuff for management. Nevertheless, Ronald is now president of Dart and a director of Dart, Crown, and Trak. Herbert also has adopted what some call a siege mentality, changing locks, installing guards at the headquarters of Combined Properties, and even forbidding Gloria from retrieving personal articles from there.

On the family front Gloria has sought legal separation from Herbert, citing years'-long adultery, physical and verbal abuse, and attempts to destroy her financially. Additionally, she is attempting to gain control of either the public companies or the closely held real estate businesses, a move to effectively break up the empire that she had such a large part in starting. A divorce settlement could easily divide Herbert's holdings between him and Gloria, sealing the fate of what was once a harmonious family and corporate "marriage."

Herbert has fired Robert's secretary and engaged in an expansion binge for Crown. For instance, he directed one Crown store to undergo a 32,000-square-foot expansion even though it was a candidate for closing because of poor sales. Herbert even refused to see Robert's children when they were supposed to see their grandfather for at least a "little time." Not even the closest observers thought Herbert would apply his tough-guy approach to his own grandchildren.

As things stand now, it is likely that the courts will be the final arbiters for the family-corporate feud because the once happy family has found itself on the bull's eye of a volatile dartboard.

QUESTIONS FOR DISCUSSION

1. How could you use the concept of organizational politics to better understand Dart Group and the Haft family's behavior?
2. Why do you think Robert Haft lost the power struggle? What factor reduced his power to influence Dart Group?
3. What are Herbert Haft's sources of power?

REFERENCES

1. B. J. Hodge and H. J. Johnson, *Management and Organizational Behavior* (New York: John Wiley & Sons, 1970), 38–40.

   Also based on Weber's notions of power in bureaucracies; M. Weber, *The Theory of Social and Economic Organization* (New York: Free Press, 1947).

2. See Hodge and Johnson in note 1 above.

3. See Hodge and Johnson, pages 145–47, in note 1 above.

4. R. A. Dahl, "The Concept of Power," *Behavioral Science* 2 (1957): 210–15.

   R. M. Emerson, "Power-Dependence Relations," *American Sociological Review* 27 (1962): 31–41.

   D. Mechanic, "Sources of Power of Lower-Level Participants in Complex Organizations," *Administrative Science Quarterly* 7 (1962): 349–64.

   H. Joseph Reitz, *Behavior in Organizations* (Homewood, Ill.: Richard D. Irwin, 1977), 463–64.

5. J. R. P. French and B. Raven, "The Bases of Social Power," in *Studies in Social Power,* ed. by D. Cartwright (Ann Arbor, Mich.: Institute for Social Research, 1959), 150–67.

   J. S. Adams and A. K. Romney, "The Determinants of Authority Interactions," in *Values and Groups,* ed. by N. F. Washburne (New York: Pergamon Press, 1962), 227–56.

6. B. Raven, "The Bases of Social Power," in *Current Studies in Social Psychology,* ed. by I. D. Steiner and M. Fishbein (New York: Holt, Rinehart, and Winston, 1965), 374.

7. B. Raven, "Legitimate Power, Coercive Power, and Observability in Social Influence," *Sociometry* 21 (1958): 83–97.

8. See French and Raven, page 162, in note 5 above.

Walter Nord, "Development in the Study of Power," in *Concepts and Controversy in Organization Behavior* (Pacific Palisades, Calif.: Goodyear, 1976), 437–38.

9. David Bailey, "Kirk Cottrell: Riding the Crest of a Retailing Wave," *Florida Trend* (May 1987): 38.

10. W. Jack Duncan, *Organizational Behavior* (Boston: Houghton Mifflin, 1978), 313.

11. Lee A. Iacocca with Wm. Novak, *Iacocca: An Autobiography* (New York: Bantam, 1984).

12. Donald Katz, *Just Do It* (New York: Random House, 1994).

13. D. J. Hickson, C. R. Hinings, C. A. Lee, R. E. Schneck, and J. M. Pennings, "A Strategic Contingencies Theory of Intraorganizational Power," *Administrative Science Quarterly* 16 (1971): 216–29.

Jeffery Pfeffer, *Power in Organizations* (Marshfield, Mass.: Pitman, 1981).

Jeffery Pfeffer and Gerald Salancik, *The External Control of Organizations* (New York: Harper & Row, 1978).

14. Jeffery Pfeffer and Gerald Salancik, "Organizational Decision Making as a Political Process: The Case of a University Budget," *Administrative Science Quarterly* 19 (1974): 135–51.

See Pfeffer in Note 13 above.

15. Rosabeth M. Kanter, "Power Failure in Management Circuits," *Harvard Business Review* (July–August 1979): 65–75.

16. Amanda Bennett, "Growing Small: Big Firms Continue to Trim Their Staffs, 2-Tier Setup Emerges," *The Wall Street Journal*, no. 12 (May 4, 1987), A1.

17. A. M. Pettigrew, "Information Control as a Power Resource," *Sociology* 6 (1972): 187–204.

18. W. Graham Astley and Paramjit S. Sachdeva, "Structural Sources of Intraorganizational Power: A Theoretical Synthesis," *Academy of Management Review* 9 (1984): 104–13.

19. See Mechanic in note 4 above.

20. Ibid.

21. Ibid, pages 362-64.

22. See Pfeffer in note 13 above.

23. V. L. Huber, "The Sources, Uses, and Conservation of Managerial Power," *Personnel* 58, no. 4 (1981): 62.

24. See Pfeffer in note 13 above.

25. Henry Mintzberg, *Power In and Around Organizations* (Englewood Cliffs, N.J.: Prentice-Hall, 1983), 68.

26. A. B. Wildavsky, "Budgeting as a Political Process," in *International Encyclopedia of the Social Sciences*, vol 2, ed. by D. C. Sills (New York: Cromwell, Collier, Macmillan, 1968), 191–93.

27. See Pfeffer, page 7, in note 13 above.

28. See Pfeffer in note 13 above. This is based on Pfeffer's discussion on page 31.

29. Don R. Beeman and Thomas W. Sharkey, "The Use and Abuse of Corporate Politics," *Business Horizons* (March–April 1987): 26–30.

30. Barbara Gray and Sonny S. Ariss, "Politics and Strategic Change Across Organizational Life Cycles," *Academy of Management Review* 10 (1985): 707–23.

CHAPTER 13

Innovation, Strategic Change, and Organizational Learning

CASE: SHACK ATTACK*

Tandy Corporation has been undergoing major change recently. During the 1980s, shareholders were calling for CEO John Roach's removal because of lagging sales and declining relative market share in the "plug-in" electronics market. Although the industry as a whole was enjoying success, Tandy's Radio Shack was floundering. As evidence of this fall Tandy stock fell 66 percent during the period between 1983 and the first quarter of 1992.

In the face of this decline stockholders and analysts alike began to question Roach's tenure. It was to Roach's great advantage that during this challenge his personal friends sat on the Tandy board of directors, and, in one case, Roach sat on the board of a friend's organization. For example, Tandy's board included an influential Forth Worth oil man and the chancellor of Texas Christian University, and Roach was on the TCU board of governors. During all the calls for change at the top of Tandy, these friends and the rest of the board stood by and supported Roach. All the while Roach devised a counterattack.

Two of Roach's initiatives have given new life to Tandy. One initiative, Computer City, is considered a "home run" as evidenced by third-year sales of $1 billion. The only other retailer to enjoy that degree of success in such a short time is Wal-Mart's Sam's Club. The other new venture is a giant superstore called The Incredible Universe whose outlets are now averaging $60 to $80 million in annual sales.

These changes and recent successes obscure the question of how Tandy found itself in need of a rebirth. Radio Shack, Tandy's original mainstay, was once called "America's Technology Store." The outlets sold all types of high tech electronic products (a result of Roach's love of gadgets) and one of the first popular home

---

*This case is based on the following article: Scott McCartney, "Tandy, After Resisting Calls for CEO's Head, Enjoys a Comeback," *The Wall Street Journal* (October 18, 1994), A1, A13.

computers, the TRS-80. The company became the U.S. leader in personal computer manufacturing and sales during the 1980s.

Perhaps Tandy's initial success in computers and technology clouded the company's vision of the future. The company made a number of major management mistakes and strategic missteps. First, rather than investing in software and marketing to stay abreast of Apple and IBM, its chief rivals, Tandy stuck with its proprietary operating system. Tandy management thought that a computer that was only partially compatible with IBM's DOS-based machines would provide the company with a competitive advantage. Tandy soon learned that the marketplace wanted complete IBM compatibility. This error in judgment severely cut into Radio Shack's market by 1992.

On the retailing side Radio Shack was attacked by discount retailers (including Wal-Mart) that began to market computers made by several different companies while Radio Shack stuck with the Tandy brand. Value-conscious consumers were lured away by the competition. The decision to make and sell only its own products was costly to Tandy.

Thus, it fell to John Roach, the detail-oriented, hands-on CEO, to revive Tandy. His two new retail ventures are pumping new life into the company.

Computer City is the answer to the beating that Tandy was suffering at the hands of discounters like CompUSA, Inc. Computer City sells Tandy products as well as products made by all the leading manufacturers. In addition to offering product variety, Computer City's clean, upscale stores have become prime examples of cost-squeezing efficiency. Tandy has used strategies that include negotiating for smaller sales commissions with American Express and pooling purchasing, advertising, and even leasing to get better deals from suppliers, advertisers, and landlords. These combined economizing moves have produced dramatic results for Tandy.

The Incredible Universe caters to a different portion of the computer and electronics market. The huge (180,000 square feet) stores have become the scene for "fun shopping" for electronics. The stores feature live entertainment and video games to entertain shoppers. Additionally, the outlets use a variety of technical advancements to make shopping easier and to make for a more efficient operation. Bar coding of products helps to record sales, track inventory, and prepare purchases for pickup at the loading dock. All these improvements earned Roach a patent, something unheard of, for retailing innovations. The Incredible Universe is expanding operations rapidly and expects to be profitable by the end of 1995, a quick pace for a retail venture.

At the same time, Radio Shack is broadening its inventory to include many gadget items along with Tandy computers and the old-line electronics components. The plan seems to be working as sales have increased by 5 percent for 1994 in stores that are more than one year old.

Although there are probably some detractors of Roach and his revitalization plan for Tandy, he and his company seem for now to be enjoying the turnaround. The renaissance certainly bears watching, given the volatile nature of computer technology and retailing.

Throughout this book we have emphasized that organizations are open systems. Tandy was open to many threats and opportunities in its environment. Initially, the company failed to respond to conditions in the environment—new computer software and hardware, new manufacturers, and new retailers. The result was that Tandy suffered to the point where stockholders lost money and the CEO nearly lost his job.

Organizational changes, learning, and innovation helped reverse the dire circumstances at Tandy. In this final chapter, we discuss how organizations face the difficult, demanding, and critical task of changing. Nothing in the universe of organizations is static, and organizations themselves must change to match changing conditions. To remain static in the face of a changing world is to invite decline and eventual failure. Change merely for the sake of change or change that is not carefully planned can also invite failure. Change must be carefully planned, and that is the focus of this chapter.

We devote attention to the process of organizational renewal through a variety of approaches to planned organizational change. In particular, we explore a number of techniques, including reengineering and Total Quality Management, aimed at making organizations more responsive to their environments. Finally, we introduce the concept of the learning organization, a concept that embodies the notion of ongoing, continuous change.

THE CONCEPT OF CHANGE

The mid-1990s is a period of unprecedented change in organizations. The popular business press constantly documents organizational restructuring, reengineering, downsizing, and other assorted changes. Even during the robust economic recovery during 1993 and 1994, many large companies such as IBM, AT&T, Digital Equipment, Boeing, and Amdahl were shedding jobs at an incredible pace. Terms such as *downsizing* and *rightsizing* may suggest a one-time fix, but many experts view this as an ongoing process for organizations of the future.[1] But the features in the popular press beg the question: What is organizational change? Can we specify a definition that is broad enough to encompass the wide range of manipulations to organizations about which we read?

 Change is simply the alteration of the status quo. In a technical sense it occurs continuously; no moment is exactly like the one that preceded it. For practical purposes, however, we are interested in significant, planned changes to the organizational system: changes to input and output relationships, changes to the technology or transformation processes, changes to structure or design, changes to coordination mechanisms, changes to people and roles in the organization, changes to culture, or basically, changes to any of the aspects of organizations that we discussed in the previous twelve chapters of this book. The forces for change are everywhere; they can be found within the organization itself and they can be found in the external environment.

Language and terminology add some confusion to the discussion of organizational change. The focus of this chapter is on *planned change;* that is, change that is intentional and guided by individuals within (or hired by) the organization. Often, discussion of change includes the term *innovation.* The definition of *innovation* is nearly identical with the above definition of *change:* " . . . a departure from existing practices or technologies and represents a significant departure from the state of the art at the time it appears."[2] *Innovation* is often used to identify changes in technology (i.e., process innovations) and new products (i.e., product innovations), but the term also is used to refer to changes in administrative practice and in the organizational structure and design. Thus, to differentiate between change and innovation is fruitless. Rather, types of changes are clearly specified in the following discussion, for example, structural change, process innovation, new product development, and so forth.

THE DILEMMA OF ORGANIZATIONAL CHANGE

Organizations face a dilemma with respect to planned change. On the one hand, organizations desire change in order to remain competitive, to adopt more effective and efficient means of operation, and to remain in harmony with their environments. On the other hand, organizations often resist change because of their desire for relative stability and predictability.[3] Organizations must have stable outputs, predictable costs, and protection of their financial integrity. One group of writers on organizational change have noted that "successful organizations have an inherent drive toward stability and increasing rigidity."[4] However, this stability and rigidity may prevent an organization from learning about its environment and adapting to changing conditions. A key question thus becomes, Can the organization meet the needs for change and responsiveness while maintaining enough stability to prevent disruption of operations? The organization must find its place along the following continua:

Stability	*Rapid change*
Predictability	*Unpredictability*
Staleness	*Innovation*
Familiarity	*Unfamiliarity*
Boredom	*Enervation*
Certainty	*Uncertainty*
Atrophy	*New strength*

An organization that maintains the status quo may find that it has a great deal of stability and familiarity, but it may also find that the status quo generates staleness, boredom, and atrophy. Change can bring new challenges, new markets, and new technology, but it can also be a source of instability, uncertainty, and unpredictability. Finding the proper point on these continua to balance the desirable and undesirable consequences of change is a critical challenge for managers. In the study of new product and process innovations, researchers typically distinguish between incremental (minor) innovations or changes to existing conditions and, at the other extreme, radical (major) innovations or changes.[5] Choosing the right point is not an easy task, and there is no one right answer for all organizations. Such factors as the nature of the organization's environment, the people in the organization, and the existing culture, to name only a few, have differential impact on how much change an organization needs and on how an organization manages change.

THE CHANGE PROCESS

The process of changing an organization may be a complex and drawn-out affair that involves many people, large amounts of organizational resources, and lots of time. Nonetheless, in many respects, organizational change is much like the processes associated with any generic decision process (see Chapter 11). As we see in Figure 13.1, the first step in the process is recognition of a need for change; recognition that a gap exists between the organization's current state of affairs and its desired state of affairs. Management may recognize changes in the external environment such as new laws, new competitors, new products, new technological advances, or other sorts of relevant change. Or management may recognize internal conditions that are undesirable. In either case, members of the organization recognize a gap between the current organizational conditions and the desired conditions. Those desired conditions could include greater profitability, greater efficiency, new products, new markets, new operations, or other changed conditions.

■ FIGURE 13.1
Planned Organizational Change Process

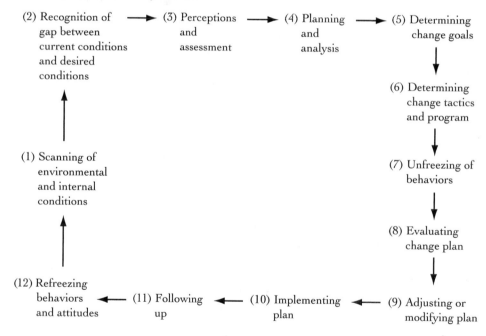

This gap between what is and what is desired becomes the impetus for change. People recognize the gap and decide that something should be done about it. If the change process proceeds in a planned fashion, the process will follow a series of specific steps. Following recognition that a problem exists, managers perceive and assess the types of changes that they think are necessary, the degree of change needed, and the speed of change required to narrow the gap. However, because of bounded rationality and the culture of the organization, the nature of problem identification and the assessment of the nature of change are likely to be biased and perhaps incomplete. How does management view change? Do they find it threatening? Do they see it as a nuisance or a challenge? How much experience does management have with change? Is the culture one that is receptive to change? All of these questions come to bear as managers attempt to assess the extent and type of change that may be performed.

It is at the planning and analysis stage that management decides how it will deal with change. This is the first step for management in designing a specific change strategy. Managers (or whoever makes up the change team) determine the parts of the organization in need of change. For example, a company may determine that it needs to improve efficiency (i.e., a gap in performance) and that this can be achieved by improving operations. At this point management often determines (either formally or informally) the scope and direction of change, whether change efforts are to be actively encouraged, redirected, amplified, ignored, or even prevented. Thus, some managers may focus attention on ways to improve efficiency (e.g., decrease labor costs, decrease waste, improve maintenance to reduce downtime, etc.). Other managers may take this efficiency mandate as license to make many other types of changes that are only peripherally related to efficiency. Still other managers may try to thwart any changes because they fear the impact the changes might have on their jobs, power, and prestige in the organization.

Once the nature of the change has been identified, it is necessary to specify the goals of the change effort. The problem may be inefficiency, but management must specify the goals of change. For example, an automaker may specify a decline in direct labor costs of 10 percent or a steel company may desire a reduction in waste material of 5 percent. The goals should be specific and verifiable. Goal specification is critical because without clear objectives it is hard to know what to change and whether the change effort has been successful.

At this point, management still has not determined the specific change tactics or program to be used to accomplish the above-stated goals. That is the next step. The organization needs to develop the specific tactics, programs, and activities that will achieve the goals.[6] If the goal is to reduce direct labor costs by 10 percent, management now needs to identify how this is to be achieved. The company could reduce the labor force and demand that existing workers work harder, faster, and smarter. The company could also adopt new technology (e.g., robotics, work teams) that increases productivity (i.e., a decrease of direct labor costs). Management may also note that workers take a long time to make cars because of the large number of parts involved or options available on the product. Thus, another type of change could be a redesign of the product itself (e.g., fewer parts and fewer options) that made it easier to produce. For any given problem or gap there are likely to be many change strategies that could prove useful—individually or in combination.

Once the change program has been determined, the organization must focus on implementation. Implementing change means that people are likely to be affected and that changes in employee behaviors will be required. Change frequently involves unlearning old ways of doing things and learning new ways to do them. This step is the unlearning or unfreezing step. Attempts must be made to ensure that employees approach change with open minds. As part of this step, the organization needs to be sure that employees know:

- what is being changed;
- why change is needed;
- what will be expected of them;
- what will be the benefits for them;
- what disadvantages or problems might crop up and how they will be handled; and
- what behavior changes will be needed in programs, tasks, and activities.

As we stated at the beginning of the chapter, the mid-1990s have been characterized by radical changes in organizations. One such type of change has been the extensive downsizing at many organizations. In the past, layoffs were largely the result of downturns in the business cycle. The latest round of downsizing, however, appears to be different. Many prosperous companies (as well as those that are underperforming) are shedding workers. A variety of complex and often interactive forces, including worldwide competition, deregulation, new technologies, and demanding stakeholders, have resulted in these changes.

The success of downsizing strategies has been mixed at best.[7] However, results of several studies suggest that when the above-listed points are followed, it is more likely that remaining employees will respond favorably to downsizing. In particular, when employees know what to expect, why it is happening, and what impact it is likely to have on them, they are more likely to respond positively to the change.

Employee receptivity to organizational change of any sort is never a sure bet. However, one way to increase the likelihood of employees accepting and embracing change is to have them participate in planning and carrying out the change strategy. Employees could help to identify gaps and potential solutions. They could also be involved in the actual implementation of the potential change strategy. This participation should occur in an open, nonthreatening, and supportive environment. It is not unusual for employees to oppose change because they feel threatened by it or do not fully understand it. Managers can to some extent overcome these concerns through employee participation.[8]

Employee participation was part of a successful change strategy for SDRC, a Cincinnati-based software corporation. When Ronald Friesam, former vice president of Unisys, took over the struggling SDRC, his task was to bring some structure and direction to the company. To accomplish this with minimum difficulty, Friesam worked closely with current and former employees. Thus, employees were consulted about major changes in goals and structure of the organization.[9]

Large size may to some extent preclude widespread employee participation in change efforts. For example, Sears began showing the signs of decline and stagnation in the 1980s. In 1988, Sears Chairman Edward Brennan unilaterally announced plans for significant changes at Sears, including moving the company's 6,000-person headquarters staff from an urban location at the Sears Tower in Chicago to a suburban location about 30 miles away, massive cuts in personnel, reduction in bureaucracy, and changes in strategy.[10] Although employee participation was limited by Sears's size, the changes have produced a modest turnaround in the company's fortunes. Linda Wachner, CEO of Warnaco, maker of intimate apparel and menswear, was also successful at inducing change in her company without extensive participation. Once employees were comfortable with Wachner in her new role as CEO, she guided her company through radical changes with a combination of tough-minded, brutal honesty and a consistent customer-oriented philosophy.[11] Wachner avoided employee participation by choice but was still able to achieve significant change at Warnaco.

Change efforts do not end with implementation. Once changes have been implemented, the organization must assess the changes to determine if they have solved the problems that motivated change in the first place. Although this may seem to be an obvious and necessary step, it is one that is sometimes missing from change strategies. Fear may keep managers from evaluating change strategies—fear that they may not have been successful. However, assessment can lead to modifications and adjustments that eventually produce successful changes in the organization. Given the complexity of organizations and the disruptive nature of change, it is likely that any change strategy needs at least some fine-tuning, and maybe even major adjustments.

The formal change process ends with refreezing of behaviors and attitudes. The new behaviors and attitudes that have been brought about by the change strategy need to become part of the institutional fabric of the organization. Through official policies such as work rules, compensation systems, and training, and through unofficial means such as the culture (e.g., language, symbols, and stories), the organization must establish the new behaviors and attitudes as the ones that are desired and appropriate. An organization that has downsized and flattened its administrative hierarchy needs to establish new rules and norms for communication between layers of the organization. Perhaps the organization has set guidelines for lower-level employees to take new responsibilities for making decisions. The organization must create an internal environment to support these new behaviors. One company that delayered failed to set new communication norms and found that lower-level employees, who were supposedly empowered to make decisions, were still asking for permission because that was the way things used to work.

An organization that wants to avoid major problems and subsequent radical change should continue to monitor change efforts long after they have been implemented and adjusted. Continuous monitoring may bring problems to the forefront before they are serious and require radical or extensive change.

INITIATING CHANGE

Not all change is initiated at the same pace. Change can be slow and deliberate or it can be quick and radical. Up to this point our focus has been on formally planned change. But change may also emerge through an unplanned and unforeseen process. We briefly review these avenues of change.

Planned incremental change is change that is evolutionary rather than revolutionary. For example, suppose an organization decides to institute a new human resources system. A human resources system involves many facets of organizational life including recruiting, training, performance evaluation, compensation, promotions, and benefits. To change all these components at one time may severely disrupt the organization. A planned incremental change strategy would approach changing the human resources system one piece at a time. The process might begin with a change in the performance appraisal system. Even that change may be phased in one department or one division at a time.

The value of this approach is that disruptions to the organization would be limited and the organization would be able to evaluate the new performance appraisal system in a limited setting. Thus, if problems developed, it might be easier and less costly to correct them on a small-scale introduction rather than if the change had been made in the entire organization.

Hewlett-Packard, the computer technology company, is an example of an organization that has used incremental changes in new product innovations to keep the company competitive in the rapidly changing computer industry. Over the past few years the company's domination of the printer market has been due in no small part to its attitude toward change and innovation. The company has avoided a crisis mentality and has continually revamped and modified its products. In 1994, new products accounted for 70 percent of revenues, but many of these new products are extensions or variations on previously existing products. The company is willing to cannibalize its products to yield incremental improvements.[12]

Radical change, sometimes referred to as framebreaking change, is brought about by major changes in the business strategy.[13] Changing strategy typically requires a change in structure, people, and organizational processes. Researchers suggest that organizations often go through long periods of stability and then face a brief period of fundamental change in the industry that requires the organization to undergo radical, framebreaking change.[14] For example, Kmart went through the period from the 1960s through the mid-1980s without undergoing much significant change. However, the challenges presented by Wal-Mart and various "category killer" stores like Toys "R" Us and Home Depot have forced Kmart to alter its basic business strategy. At present, the company is in the process of radical, framebreaking changes that are likely to affect structure, people, and processes.

Although major framebreaking changes may seem to be rare events, they are a little deceptive. What managers and consultants find is that even incremental changes often have a chain reaction in an organization. It is not unusual to find that subtle changes in one area necessitate changes in another area, and so on. Jack Welch, chairman of the board at General Electric, notes that change strategies often underestimate the impact and scope of the effects on the organization.[15] Thus, what sometimes begins as minor fine-tuning or adjustment to the organization ends up being more akin to radical change.

Unplanned change is change that just happens or emerges. Strategy and practice in the organization emerge in the course of business as a stream of actions and decisions.[16] As we have noted throughout this text, organizations are dynamic and changing entities. The environments in which they are embedded are also constantly changing. Thus, it is reasonable to assume that change takes place in organizations whether or not it is guided by management. Organizations do not just wander aimlessly, but they change and respond to events in their environment, often with only minimal conscious planning on the part of management. Recall the discussion in Chapter 7 on the sequence of natural changes through which organizations progress as part of normal organizational life cycles. These, too, constitute unplanned changes.

TYPES OF ORGANIZATIONAL CHANGE

Perhaps the greatest challenge facing modern organizations is the need to identify appropriate areas to change, to nurture those changes, and to maintain change in various aspects of the organization. We have at various times throughout this text discussed the variety of forces, particularly those emanating from the environment, that demand that the organization adapt and change. We have also implicitly, and occasionally explicitly (see Chapter 5), described aspects of the organization and its context that can be changed. Nonetheless, it is useful at this point to list the broad categories of organizational change and innovation that are possible. The following six sections identify and briefly describe discrete aspects of an organization that can be changed. Although we treat these as discrete parts of the organization, it is important to reiterate that change in one area often necessitates change in other areas.

GOALS AND STRATEGY

Most types of planned organizational change involve some modification of organizational goals and strategy. Some planned changes may emerge from lower levels of the organization in response to local problems or conditions. Although these changes may not be motivated by changing corporate-level goals or strategy, they are most likely to be driven by local department or work unit goals.

Typically, changing the goals and strategy are but the starting point for changing other aspects of the organization. Goals for new products would likely require research and development, new production, and perhaps new personnel and new structures. Improving financial performance could involve such changes as increased efficiency (i.e., less waste, greater productivity), improved marketing, less overhead, or other sorts of changes. A goal of improving quality could involve changes in virtually all aspects of the organization, from the skills and training of personnel to the culture of the organization. The point is that most large-scale planned organizational changes begin with new or modified goals and strategy, but changing the goals and strategy are just preliminary steps to further organizational change.

PEOPLE

This text began with a definition of organizations that emphasized the human social nature of organizations—that, first and foremost, organizations are made up of people. Thus, it makes sense that one element of the organization that we can change is the people who make up the organization.

One of the more pervasive forms of change that has affected organizations around the world has been downsizing. Although there are typically structural aspects to downsizing (the elimination of layers of bureaucracy, merging of departments or divisions, etc.), the most obvious aspect of downsizing is that the organization eliminates people. Management must decide on rules and strategy for determining who to cut from the organization as well as on the procedures for actually eliminating personnel. Eliminating the wrong people from the organization can be costly. Critical skills and knowledge may be lost, as was the case at General Motors. In some cases, firms that have downsized have belatedly realized that they cut the wrong people and have faced the embarrassing task of rehiring released workers.[17]

How the organization releases the eliminated workers can have profound impact on not only those who lose jobs, but also on those employees who remain on the job.[18] Keys to successful downsizing include keeping employees informed of possible job elimination, providing a fair and just system for eliminating jobs, helping to place departing workers in new jobs, allowing departing workers to retain self-esteem and dignity, and using cultural ceremonies and rites to manage feelings and attitudes of remaining workers. Creating a supportive work environment can be an important step in smoothing the difficult process of laying off workers.

Several other people changes are also available to the organization. The organization can recruit new employees with particular skills or background. For example, with the increasing emphasis on international business, many organizations are seeking potential employees fluent in several languages and familiar with diverse national cultures. The emphasis on computerization and automation has forced many organizations to seek employees with higher levels of education and with specific computer training. However, recruiting is not the only way to obtain these or other specialized skills. Many firms use extensive and ongoing on-the-job training and development to ensure that employee skills and knowledge are current and relevant.

PRODUCTS AND SERVICES

We noted in Chapter 5 that one mechanism for managing environmental uncertainty was to develop new products or services. New products and services may allow a company to enter new market niches that are less crowded and less competitive. Some industries and firms are dedicated to new product and service innovation. For example, the financial health of many large pharmaceutical companies is based on their ability to generate new patented products. Glaxo, the British pharmaceutical giant, has pinned much of its recent success to one particular product — Zantac, an ulcer medication. Once a patent expires, the company is exposed to generic drug makers who do not bear the research and development costs and who can produce generic versions of drugs at considerably lower prices. For example, Glaxo's main competitor in the prescription ulcer medication market had been Smith, Kline, Beckman, maker of Tagamet. Recently, the patent expired on Tagamet and now generic drug makers can sell their own versions of Tagamet at substantially lower prices. However, even before a patent expires, a drug company may face competition from another firm making a similar, more effective or cheaper product. Thus, pharmaceutical companies must spend considerable resources and time developing new products.[19] Smith, Kline, Beckman pursued a different strategy. It began marketing Tagamet as an over-the-counter heartburn medication.

It is not just the pharmaceutical industry that lives and dies with new products and services. Much of the computer hardware and software industry and the consumer electronics industry is driven by product and service innovations. The relative advantage of a computer maker may be the result of bigger and faster processors and memory, better customer service, or new technical twists. However, it is important to recognize that the ultimate success of product and service innovations is low. Only 31 percent of product innovations ever make it to the marketplace, and among those that do, only 56 percent are still there five years later. The most astounding statistic is that only 12 percent of new products are ever financially successful (i.e., producing a positive return on investment).[20] One need only look at the marketplace for examples of product and service flops.[21] In the early 1980s, Xerox marketed an innovative and powerful workstation that was far ahead of available computer technology. But poor timing and high price doomed the 8010 Star. Shortly after the Xerox product hit the market, IBM introduced the comparatively low-cost PC. Thus, while some industries like computers, consumer electronics, movies, pharmaceuticals, and toys depend on new products for their lifeblood, the success rate across industries is quite low.

There are no guarantees to success in product or service innovation, but a number of studies have identified several features that are likely to increase the probability of success.[22] These are summarized in Table 13.1 and include (1) close involvement with potential customers and identification of customer needs; (2) products or services that are consistent with the strategy and skill-base of the organization; (3) creativity and scientific or technical expertise necessary for product or service development and production; (4) entrepreneurial skills to sell the innovation in the organization and to market it outside; (5) appropriate organizational structure to develop, produce, and market the innovation; (6) project manager to oversee and coordinate development, production, and marketing; and (7) an innovation *champion* — a person who can advocate for and represent a product or service innovation to top management.

▦ TABLE 13.1
Keys to Product and Service Innovation Success

---

1. Identification of customer needs and customer involvement
2. Consistency with organizational strategy and skill-base
3. Creativity and scientific or technical expertise
4. Entrepreneurship; sell the innovation to top management and customers
5. Structure congruent with the innovation
6. Project manager to oversee and coordinate development, production, and marketing
7. Champion to advocate for and represent a product or service innovation to top management

---

TECHNOLOGY

In an attempt to increase productivity and flexibility in manufacturing, many firms are changing their technologies. Several trends in technology come under the broad heading of *advanced manufacturing technology* or AMT.[23] Most of these involve the use of computers and advanced communication technology. Some examples include computer-aided manufacturing (CAM), computer-aided design (CAD), material requirements planning, flexible manufacturing systems and cells (FMS or FMC), robotics and numerical control, automated materials handling, and computer-integrated manufacturing. A comprehensive discussion of these technological changes is beyond the scope of this text, but each is briefly described below in Table 13.2 on page 368.

■ **TABLE 13.2**

Examples of Advanced Manufacturing Technologies

Computer-Aided Manufacturing: Technologies that involve the computerization of various aspects of the manufacturing or production process, including numerical control (use of coded instructions to run machinery), robotics (use of computer-controlled devices or manipulators to perform specific tasks in the manufacturing process).

Flexible Manufacturing Systems or Flexible Manufacturing Cells: Two or more machines teamed together to perform cutting or forming operations along with automated materials handling. Arrangements of machines and machine pathways can be altered or changed on relatively short notice to produce varied outcomes.

Computer-Aided Design: Use of computer and computer database to create or modify product designs and engineering data. Often paired with CAM to produce CAD/CAM, in which design and production systems are closely linked and design information is used in machine control.

Material Requirements Planning: Computer-based inventory and production scheduling system used to ensure timely supply of parts for production system. This may be used as an integral part of a just-in-time (JIT) inventory control system.

Computer-Integrated Manufacturing: Combination of two or more of the above individual advances under the control of a central computer system.

Some technology changes, such as computerization or robotics, do not involve specific technical advances but rely instead on changing the deployment of people or arrangement of tasks. One approach that has gained widespread application in manufacturing and service settings is the movement to ***cross-functional teams.*** For example, a manufacturer may assemble a team of individuals with a broad range of skills to produce a product rather than using functional departments to conduct narrow tasks. The advantages of cross-functional teams are better integration and coordination of work and greater flexibility. With cross-functional teams, workers with different skills, knowledge, and perspectives are in closer contact and can exchange ideas or discuss problems more easily. In cross-functional teams, members are more likely to learn diverse skills in addition to the ones they bring to the team. This allows for flexibility in work arrangements. Finally, cross-functional teams are more likely to take a holistic view of the manufacturing or service process because the team is involved in the total process rather than just some narrow portion.

The General Motors Saturn Division has adopted cross-functional teams as a way to assemble cars. In a traditional General Motors assembly plant, workers have narrow skills and narrowly defined jobs.[24] For example, a worker may be responsible for just attaching the driver's side front door to a car. He or she would take a preassembled door panel that had the door handle, lock, and latching mechanisms already installed. This worker's only task would be to attach the door to the car body by bolting the hinge to the door opening. At most, he or she would also be responsible for completing connections for lights, warning bells, and electric locks and windows. The old way of thinking was that this worker could become expert at attaching doors to the car. Workers could easily be trained for this job. Therefore, workers who were absent or who performed poorly could easily be replaced. The new view of work is that this type of job is boring, demotivating, and dehumanizing. At Saturn, an assembly team would work together closely on all parts of the car body assembly. A team would follow a car throughout most of the assembly process.

The rationale behind the team approach is that through teamwork the company can produce a better product and produce it more efficiently.[25] Workers are taught to be more highly motivated by the broad range of tasks they perform and by identification with a completed final product. Cross-functional teams permit better communication among workers (but workers are also required to possess better communication skills) so that coordination of tasks is handled more easily and efficiently. Workers working as a team may discover a better process for assembling door panels and attaching them to the cars. Because the workers work together as a team on the entire assembly process, it is more likely that they will see and understand the larger nature of the job. Rather than seeing his or her job as attaching doors to a car, a worker is more likely to see his or her job as being part of the work of a team that builds the entire car. The results are greater quality and efficiency.[26]

Cross-functional teams are not just for manufacturing. Many service companies from banks to insurance companies to health care providers have turned to cross-functional teams as a way to improve the quality of work and the quality of work life. Like any other management practice, cross-functional teams are not without costs and are not the answer to every organizational problem. The teamwork required to make cross-functional teams work smoothly requires an educated workforce and workers who are skilled at communications, negotiations, and conflict resolution. Because workers are working together closely and because the organization's authority structure is typically decentralized with teams, there is a greater potential for conflicts and disagreements. Additionally, there are some tasks where the efficiencies and expertise gained by the old-style specialization may outweigh the benefits of teams. Finally, the use of teams (cross functional or otherwise) must fit with the prevailing culture of the organization.[27] Merely using teams because other organizations successfully use them is certainly no guarantee of success.

Process mapping is an attempt to change the technology by streamlining the process.[28] Process mapping involves describing the sequences of operations, tasks, machines, tools, people, and supplies involved in completing a process. For example, General Electric has used process mapping in its Evendale, Ohio, jet engine manufacturing facility to schematically describe all the steps involved in manufacturing a jet engine. The task of mapping is complex. GE took more than one month to map the production of just one jet engine. The paperwork for this task was so extensive that it wrapped around an entire conference room.[29] When the mapping is successfully completed, managers can see wasted or inefficient steps and bottlenecks in the process. The mapping then becomes a diagnostic tool for rearranging a production process to operate more smoothly.

With any of these changes in technology, it is important to keep in mind that the technology must be congruent with other aspects of the organization.[30] For example, implementation of Advanced Manufacturing Technology (AMT) may require additional training for personnel and extensive capital expenditures on computer systems. Technology changes may require changes in the organizational design and structure as well as the culture. One problem that many firms moving to cross-functional teams find is that recognition, rewards, compensation, and other aspects of the culture are geared toward the individual rather than the team. This situation makes teamwork difficult to maintain.

ORGANIZATIONAL DEVELOPMENT

Even before many organizations began moving in the direction of teamwork and group approaches to work, organizations faced the problem of getting people from diverse backgrounds with different needs and talents to work together. Extensive team-oriented approaches to work make working together even more important. Two additional trends in organizations today make working together both more important and more problematic: Organizational membership is becoming increasingly diverse with more women, minorities, and foreign-born workers on the job, and organizations are becoming increasingly international in focus and in operation. These trends place increasing pressure on the social aspects of organizing: being able to effectively communicate, understanding the different needs and background of fellow workers, and being able to either reach agreement or constructively disagree.

Organizational development (OD) is the area of organizational change that aims at improving the social functioning of organizations. OD is a subgroup of organizational change strategies that uses knowledge of the behavioral sciences for planned interventions into organizational processes with the goal of increasing organizational health and effectiveness.[31] Although OD change efforts could conceivably address any aspect of an organization, these approaches have typically focused on improving and facilitating interactions among people in organizations. Thus, the focus has been on such things as attitudes about trust, cooperation, acceptance, and tolerance. The goals of OD have been to improve communication among workers, to develop norms of trust and acceptance, and to move toward collaboration and consensus.[32]

Several techniques can be used individually or as part of a larger change plan. A first step in OD intervention is often a diagnostic survey of worker attitudes about jobs, supervision, and the general quality of work life that is used to identify problem areas. *Survey feedback* to organizational members can be used to initiate further change plans. Feedback may provide a basis for managers to improve their management and leadership skills.[33] Results of survey feedback may also be used by a consultant to guide *process consultation,* interventions in which a consultant would observe actual organizational processes (group meetings, teamwork, and other work events).[34] As a result of observing these processes, consultants would provide feedback on ways to improve communications, leadership, decision making, and conflict management. Consultants may also intervene with *team building* activities that deal with methods for improving communication and understanding among team or group members. As we noted above in our discussion of cross-functional teams, team approaches change the basic nature of technology (how we do the job), but they also depend on new and different interpersonal skills. Without attention to the development of these skills, team-based work is not likely to be successful. These same techniques that are used within specific groups or teams in an organization can also be used across many groups, departments, or units of an organization. A current trend in OD is *diversity training* as shown in Exhibit 13.1.

Exhibit 13.1	**Organizational Development: Diversity Training**[35]

One type of OD intervention that many organizations are using today is diversity training. Organizations have become increasingly diverse, with more women;

racial, ethnic, and religious minorities; foreign nationals; and others whose lifestyles, beliefs, or behaviors are out of the mainstream. Accommodating this diversity has not always been easy. Many large organizations face increasing managerial and even legal challenges because of sexual or racial harassment, discrimination, or other forms of perceived unfair treatment. Some problems may result from ignorance, but others are the result of ingrained dislike, misunderstanding, or even hatred. Often the first step in combating these problems is diversity training. The belief is that understanding breeds tolerance and acceptance, that tolerance and acceptance should lead to improved working conditions, and that all these forces will lead to a more productive organization.

Large numbers of companies, both large and small, have seen the benefits of diversity training. Not only does training improve individuals' understanding of their coworkers' differences, but it is also a springboard to more creative problem solving. Companies as different as Ford Motor, Rohm & Haas, Corestates Financial, and IBM have found that diverse workteams are likely to see problems and opportunities in different ways than homogeneous teams. These teams may be the source of novel solutions to critical problems.

The news on diversity training, however, is not all positive. News reports have highlighted some unscrupulous methods used by overambitious trainers. Some reports have highlighted the experiences of white males who have been *forced* to confront real or imagined racism or sexism. Force simply does not work. Real understanding and acceptance requires a supportive and trusting environment.

STRUCTURE AND DESIGN CHANGE

In Chapters 2 and 8 we identified a number of current trends in organizational structure and design: downsizing, flattening or delayering, and decentralizing. Essentially, structural changes involve changes in division of labor and coordination—changes in differentiation. Changes in design involve changes in grouping of jobs, tasks, or output. We also identified two new organizational forms—the virtual organization and the federal organization.[36] The reader should refer to those chapters that provide a more detailed discussion of these types of change. According to many popular management books and articles, the conventional wisdom is that most organizations are (or should be) moving in the direction of becoming flatter, more decentralized, and connected or networked to other organizations (e.g., suppliers, customers, regulators, and even competitors).[37]

As is the case with any of the other changes mentioned thus far, changing the structure and design of an organization is an ambitious undertaking. We have at various points in the text discussed the great difficulty experienced by many large organizations (e.g., GM, IBM, Sears, and Kmart) attempting to restructure. Changes in structure and design must be carefully managed to be congruent with other aspects of the organization; in particular, people, technology, goals, and culture. For example, downsizing and decentralization often mean that workers need new skills and need to learn new decision-making processes. The organization's culture must also support the newly found autonomy and initiative of workers.

Also managers and others involved in changing structure and design must be aware of the informal side of the organization. The informal structure may remain unaltered and may be counter to the changes made to formal structure and design. This is where careful attention to the people and culture of the organization is particularly important. Thus, as we noted at the beginning of this chapter, change in one aspect of an organization often necessitates change in other aspects.

CULTURE CHANGE

Changing an organization's culture, as we noted in Chapter 10, is an extensive and ambitious undertaking. At the deeper level of culture, we are talking about a change in the norms, values, beliefs, and expectations in the organization. Moreover, this type of change typically involves changes in all the areas previously mentioned: people, goals, technology, teams, structure, and design. Rather than restate the issues surrounding cultural change (the interested reader can refer to Chapter 10), the following description of Total Quality Management should give the reader a sense of perspective on the all-encompassing nature of cultural change.

During the decade of the seventies, many U.S. companies suffered market share declines at the hands of Japanese companies. One major reason for this was the perceived lack of quality of U.S. goods. U.S. automakers were hit especially hard. Not all the declines were suffered at the hands of Japanese competitors. Such companies as Sears, Montgomery Ward, and Kmart suffered setbacks from Wal-Mart, Target, and Nordstrom. The latter three retailers were seen as providing superior quality service. As managers and management scholars began to study the problems of these and similarly poor performing companies, it became apparent that poor quality was a significant problem.

Early approaches to the quality problem included several different techniques: quality circles, participative decision making, and decentralized decision making. Although some of these techniques produced some improvements in quality, the results were sometimes limited in scope and duration. Critics pointed out that these approaches were often piecemeal and directed only at small segments of the organization, especially production. When investigators looked more closely at the Japanese experience with quality, they found that such companies as Toyota had the whole organization focus on quality.

Several models of Total Quality Management (TQM) have guided management practice, but the two perspectives that have received the most attention are those of Deming and Juran.[38] The following are common elements of the Deming and Juran approaches to quality.[39]

First, the organization must *focus on the customer and create total customer satisfaction.* Many companies have stated an emphasis on customer satisfaction, but what differs in the TQM approach is that the customer, not the company, defines satisfaction. This means that organizations must get to know their customers better. This means listening to customers and seeking customer input during the design phase of products or services. It is important to note that TQM gives broad meaning to the term *customer.* Customers may be inside the organization. At Chrysler, for example, production is a customer of engineering. Engineering must design cars that meet the needs of the production department.

Empowerment is a second feature of TQM. Empowerment incorporates the ideas of participative management, delegation, and the granting of real power to make and enforce decisions to lower-level employees. For example, production workers at Ford can stop the assembly line if they see problems. They do not need to get permission or authorization from a supervisor. The idea behind empowerment is to give responsibility to people who are involved with the work process.

Third, TQM embodies the concept of *team-based management.* Like the earlier Saturn example, TQM takes teamwork beyond mere cooperation. Work is organized around teams rather than individuals. Teams are empowered to make most decisions, and managers serve as coaches or facilitators rather than as bosses or supervisors. As we noted in describing Saturn's use of teams, a result of the team approach is team identification with outputs. A team assembling a whole car is more likely to identify with the output than an individual who attaches a few bolts. Team-based management goes beyond the performance of tasks. The organization must be committed to team-based organizing and team-based compensation.

Continuous improvement and measurement is the fourth key to TQM. Three component processes make up continuous improvement and measurement: measurement and tracking of critical success factors, use of statistical process control, and benchmarking best practices. Error rates, output, waste, delays, customer satisfaction, manufacturing tolerances, and other important data must be measured and tracked on a consistent basis. Results of the measurement should be posted so that people know what is going on. Sometimes posting these data is enough to motivate people to pay attention to quality. Monitoring can also provide keys to improving quality. Scientific sampling is conducted during the production process so that problems or errors can be detected and fixed during the process rather than waiting until the end. The point is that changes add quality that can and should be made at any time.

Benchmarking involves identifying a competitor or another company in a similar industry that is doing something particularly well, studying that process, and then trying to emulate that process in your organization. For example, a university identified the registrar's office as a significant problem area. Students complained about the cost, delays, and errors in getting transcripts sent to employers or other schools. The registrar surveyed several universities to find registrar's offices that were particularly good at serving student needs. A team from the university visited the exemplary registrar's office to study the processes used and adapt them to their office. Surprisingly, even in the competitive business environment, companies are often willing to share best practices.

Finally, TQM entails *open communication* and *feedback.* Neither communication nor feedback is a new concept. Both have been discussed extensively under other organizational change headings. However, at the heart of TQM is the idea that people must feel free to broach sensitive subjects related to quality. Communication must be up, down, and across the organization, as must the commitment to TQM. Departments that are customers to other departments within the organization must feel free to communicate their needs and satisfaction.

TQM represents a culture change for organizations adopting it because it involves changing the core values, norms, beliefs, and expectations in the organization. (It also frequently involves other forms of change: employee skills, workteams, and structure.)

The first aspect of the new norms, values, beliefs, and expectations involves the concept of quality itself. The organization must embrace a customer-defined idea of quality. Although the old saw "the customer is always right" is time-honored, the notion of customer-defined quality takes that idea a few steps further. This devotion to quality means that the organization must do anything and everything it can to satisfy customers — even when those customers are members of the same organization. A second part of the new norms, values, beliefs, and expectations is directed at the notion of power in the organization. TQM upsets the typical expectation that power should be hierarchical. A third change, one that is often difficult in the rugged individualism of American culture, is the team approach. The organization must shift its thinking from the glorification of individuals to the glorification of teams. Another shift in beliefs is the change to measuring ongoing processes to detect errors, waste, and problems rather than measuring after processes are completed. This often goes against such traditions as production cycles and model years. Finally, honest, open communication and feedback may violate past norms of discretion, professional deference, and hierarchy. For TQM to work, it must be emphasized that the process encompasses nearly all aspects of the organization. This is not a one-time, one-shot deal. It is a continuous and ongoing process.

ORGANIZATIONAL LEARNING

Most approaches to organizational change attempt to fix or change portions of the organization. Even attempts to change the culture may only modify components of the organization — changing values, norms, beliefs, and expectations. It is true that some of these changes can be quite radical and may result in more efficient and effective organizations. *Organizational learning* offers a different perspective on change and organization that addresses the fundamental nature of an organization. The organizational learning perspective is an attempt to create an organization that is able to continually monitor the environment and adapt to changing conditions.

The organizational learning framework proposes that organizations, much like people, have memory and can learn. Clearly organizations are made up of people who think and learn, but the organizational learning framework goes a step further. Organizational memory and learning are more than just the aggregate of individual memory and learning. Organizations have a memory of what works and what does not work, as well as a rich history of past events. This memory is stored in a variety of forms including documents, policies, procedures, reports, products, databases, and most importantly, in the minds of employees of the organization — sometimes referred to as human capital. The fact that people carry around a great deal of know-how in their minds, often in the form of tacit knowledge, is underappreciated by most managers. This fact sometimes becomes evident when organizations undergo downsizing and release employees with key tacit knowledge relevant to the organization.

Several organizational authorities have written extensively about what constitutes organizational learning. We have synthesized these into the following five attributes of a learning organization.[40] First, a learning organization develops systematic approaches to problem solving, developing an understanding of what works and what does not work, learning from experience, and learning from the best practices of others. Second, in a learning organization people must override past mental models. This is sometimes referred to as "thinking outside the box." People must become accustomed to trying new things, experimenting. Third, people in the learning organization must develop personal mastery, including developing skills to be open with others. Like many of the approaches to organizational change that we mentioned earlier, communication is key to learning. That communication is critical to the fourth characteristic of a learning organization — transferring and disseminating new knowledge quickly and effectively throughout the organization. Knowledge, information, and skills should not be hoarded or hidden from other members of the organization. Finally, the learning organization should use the learning process and the transfer of information to develop and pursue a shared vision. Table 13.3 summarizes characteristics of the learning organization.

■   **TABLE 13.3**
The Learning Organization

---

1. Develop systematic approaches to problem solving to understand what works and what does not work in the organization.
2. Develop the ability to "think outside the box"; override old, outmoded ways of thinking.
3. Develop personal mastery of skills.
4. Transfer and disseminate knowledge and information throughout the organization.
5. Develop a shared vision of the organization's world.

Peter Senge, one of the principal advocates of organizational learning, maintains that learning organizations derive competitive advantage from constant learning. Becoming a learning organization involves a transformation in thinking. Members can no longer think that any one person has all the answers. Senge further notes that, "People working together with integrity and authenticity and collective intelligence are profoundly more effective as a business than people living together on politics, game playing, and narrow self-interest."[41]

The Lincoln-Mercury Division of Ford Motor Company has adopted an organizational learning approach.[42] Application of organizational learning to the development of the new Lincoln Continental demonstrated impressive results. The development team saved over $65 million budgeted for fixing engineering glitches by opening up the development process. Because of open communication, sharing of ideas, transfer of knowledge, and other learning tools, the team identified nearly three times as many potential problems early in development when fixing and modifying the design was easier and less costly. The development team was able to resolve conflicting systems problems (e.g., air-conditioning, headlights, power seats, etc.) without the bickering that typically accompanied such problems.

Adopting an organizational learning approach was not without cost for the Lincoln Continental project. The approach collided with the engineering-dominated culture at Ford and created massive chaos. Despite the success of the Continental project, the project manager, Fred Simon, was passed over for a promotion and eventually retired. Thus, although the Lincoln-Mercury Division may have adopted an organizational learning framework, the approach has not yet diffused throughout Ford.

FACILITATING CHANGE

Now that we have explored a variety of approaches to organizational change, we need to consider those factors or conditions that pave the way for change. Researchers and practitioners have identified conditions that make change strategies more likely to be successful. The list of characteristics presented below assumes that the change plan has been clearly developed and documented. This should include a time line for implementation and goals or benchmarks for performance.

TOP MANAGEMENT SUPPORT

For any change strategy to be successful it must garner the support of top management. Without that support, it is likely the lower-level managers will view the change strategy with suspicion. Moreover, it may be risky for managers to pursue actions that lack top-management support. Recall the experience of the Lincoln Continental project manager who adopted an organizational learning strategy that was inconsistent with the general culture at Ford.

STRUCTURAL SUPPORT

The *ambidextrous organization* possesses both organic and mechanistic structural characteristics.[43] Organic characteristics are necessary for the flexibility and creativity required to generate new ideas. Product development teams, research and development departments, or teams and task forces devoted to developing change strategies are given organic characteristics. However, change strategies that effectively diffuse through the organization and become institutionalized (i.e., part of the daily fabric of the organization) require some degree of formalization, standardization, and centralization—all mechanistic characteristics. Although some organizations may simultaneously possess ambidexterity, other organizations achieve similar results by switching from organic to mechanistic as they go through the process of first developing a change strategy and then implementing it. One way of achieving this ambidextrous nature on a temporary basis is through the use of teams or task forces with specific responsibility for developing and implementing the changes.

CHAMPIONS

We already noted in discussion of innovations the role of a champion to oversee the project and to fight for it with others in the organization. A champion is an enthusiastic supporter of a proposed change. A champion can be critical to the successful development and implementation of any type of change strategy. The champion can answer questions, remove roadblocks, and persuade those who resist.

COMMUNICATION

Change does not occur in a vacuum. People need to be informed about the nature of proposed change and how that change is likely to affect them.[44] Resistance, confusion, and anger can be minimized with clear and timely communication about the nature and impact of proposed changes. These communications can include meetings, videos, documents, and briefing sessions.

RESOURCES

Although there are stories of organizations successfully pulling off changes or innovations with very limited resources,[45] these stories are the exception rather than the rule. Change is risky for an organization, and underfinancing a change strategy merely increases the risk. If an organization is going to expose itself to the risk and uncertainty associated with change, it should provide adequate resources, including personnel, equipment, facilities, consultants, and money.

Resources are a two-edged sword, however. Often an organization in need of change lacks a generous supply of resources. On the other hand, we discussed the notion of *slack resources* earlier in the text. Slack may provide a cushion for experimenting and taking risks. However, an abundance of resources may also lull an organization into complacency, and it may fail to perceive the need for change.[46]

SUMMARY

We began this chapter by noting that change is simply the alteration of the status quo. That simple statement belies the complexity and difficulty associated with changing organizations. In this chapter we have described various characteristics of change, mapped the change process, described a wide array of types of change, and discussed ways to facilitate change. Along the journey through this material and throughout the text as a whole, we have repeatedly noted that change is endemic to organizations. That is, whether planned or unplanned, radical or incremental, change is experienced by organizations as a result of their being open systems. At the same time, forces exist in the organization that attempt to maintain stability and to fight against change. Moreover, we have noted that change typically has a ripple effect—changing one aspect of an organization often necessitates (or even causes) change to other parts of the organization.

The primary focus of this chapter was on planned organizational change—those changes that are intentional and formally planned. The normal progression through organizational life cycles and the natural political activities in organizations also produce unplanned and unintended change.

Planned changes vary on the continuum between incremental changes that involve minor modifications or adjustments to radical or framebreaking changes. As change strategies become increasingly more radical, they become riskier and typically are more difficult to implement.

We noted that the previous twelve chapters provide an outline for the types of changes that organizations can adopt. The first type of change we identified was changing the organization's goals and strategies. These changes may include identification of new markets, new products, new internal practices, or new guidelines for employee conduct. People in the organization can be changed in several ways. Examples include recruiting new employees, training existing employees, and changing compensation or benefit plans to alter motivation. Organizations often implement change through new products and services; however, the success of new product and service strategies is quite low. Many organizations are adopting new technologies as part of change strategies. These include an array of advanced manufacturing technologies (AMT), team approaches to tasks, and refining existing technologies through process mapping. One of the oldest types of change strategies is the assortment of techniques that come under the heading of organizational development. These techniques focus on the social nature of organizations and attempt to change people's attitudes and behaviors toward other people in the organization. Techniques include survey feedback, process consultation, and team building. Structural and design changes are attempts to alter the division of labor and bases for grouping people together in the organization. Organizations are moving in the direction of flatter, decentralized, networked structures and designs. In discussing cultural change, we introduced Total Quality Management (TQM) as an example of a total system change in an organization that involves a basic change in the values, norms, beliefs, and expectations that are at the foundation of the organization. Finally, we introduced organizational learning, not as a change strategy, but as a different way of thinking about an organization. The learning organization is really an organization that should be flexible and responsive enough to undergo continuous change.

The last section of this chapter identified five aspects of organizations that can facilitate the change process. These include top-management support, an ambidextrous structure, change champions, communication of intent, and the availability of resources. Although these factors will likely facilitate change, there is no guarantee that changes will be accepted or will result in the desired outcomes.

Throughout this text, and especially in this final chapter, we have focused attention on the changing nature of organizations. The information technology revolution (inexpensive computing and telecommunications devices) has laid the groundwork for the emergence of new types of organization. We are seeing the emergence of the virtual organizations and the federal organizations we discussed in Chapter 8. This will probably be only the beginning of the changed nature of organizations as we head into the twenty-first century. The very nature of jobs and careers is changing radically. Regardless of what form new organizations take, this text should provide you with the bases for understanding organizations and organization theory.

Questions for Discussion

1. What is change? What parts of an organization are affected by change?
2. How can change be managed?
3. What is the difference between incremental and radical change? Why is this an important distinction?
4. Why and how does change pose a dilemma to organizations? What do you think are the likely consequences for an organization that does not change? Why?
5. Why do you think that many change efforts fail or fall short of their objectives?
6. Select one type of change that you think would be appropriate for your college or university. Design a brief plan for introducing this change, including diagnosis of the problem(s) it is intended to solve.
7. Some critics of organizational change have suggested that most of these change efforts (e.g., TQM, reengineering, organizational learning) are just fads. Based on what you have learned in this text, why do you think organizations often "jump on the bandwagon" for the newest fad?
8. What is meant by organizational learning? What is new and different about this concept compared with other change strategies?

CASE: FORWARD, MARCH!*

When you think of the U.S. Army, you probably think of a rigid, top-down hierarchy in which generals pass orders down the chain of command to privates in the field. Your impression is an accurate one — of the former U.S. Army.

Since its magnificent triumph in Desert Storm, the Army has been undergoing what amounts to cataclysmic change. No longer is it the same old army by any means. From Desert Storm came a commitment to self-examination and reevaluation that is typically seen in the industrial world. But some have ventured to state that the Army is ahead of this type of "industrial rebirth" thinking. Chains of command now are not the only way by which information, and even suggestions, flow through the organization. The definition of *customer* has been restructured to mean *the enemy* because it requires, according to Army Chief of Staff, General Gordon Sullivan, elimination, the ultimate customer service that the Army can render.

This new Army is a product of its crowning success, the Gulf War. Although the casual observer would count that conflict as a most efficient, effective, and even rewarding one, to General Sullivan, it revealed woeful inadequacies in the basic core technology of his organization. World War II communications equipment and protocol and poor inventory control piqued Sullivan's attention and desire to instill not only a spirit of innovation in his members, but to also actually make the changes that such a spirit can produce.

General Sullivan was faced with the same problems and obstacles — chief among them budget cuts and downsizing of his organization — that are everyday occurrences in

*This case is based on the following article: Lee Smith, "New Ideas from the Army (Really)," *Fortune* (September 19, 1994): 203–204, 206, 209, 211–12.

industry. A one-third cut in the budget and a resulting reduction (from twelve to ten divisions) in the size of troop numbers was accompanied by new missions (Somalia and Haiti) and by a macroenvironment that was anything but placid. This came on the heels of a major success, Desert Storm, after which one might expect the Army to bask in the light of its triumph.

Instead, the Army has responded with an unheard-of technique — that of a public review of maneuvers involving all ranks from private to general. This approach is highlighted at the National Training Center in California. There, mock battles are fought, videotaped, and critiqued in unabashed honesty by lower ranks as well as by top brass. This is a revolutionary way of doing business in the Army, and there are not many businesses that not only invite such frank interchange from all ranks but, indeed, require it as does the Army.

This combination of philosophy and protocol is enabling the Army to become a learning organization in its truest sense. Instead of rehashing old battles and taking what might perhaps be a false sense of pride in accomplishment, this new approach to organization has allowed, even forced, generals to think in long-run terms. This behavior is new and will doubtless nurture what General Sullivan fondly calls the Information Age Army. It will surely change the classic definitions of roles and their interrelationships within the traditional U.S. Army. Information, then, is seen as the key to enable a much downsized Army to compete with ones that are several times larger, both in terms of budget and number of personnel.

Desert Storm was the first encounter in which information played so large a part in operations. But with its success with infrared equipment and radar, information also allowed Sullivan to see troubles not so evident before. Unmarked containers carried everything from generators to spare tires and had to be opened to reveal their contents. And there were more supplies than even the most conservative quartermaster could imagine. Troop locations and vital weather conditions were never transmitted to troops in the field because of what might even be called antique equipment. Literally, pencil and notebook were the basic tools of reconnaissance.

General Sullivan wants to instill information technology in the forms of bar codes, satellites, E-mail, video, faxes, and digital messages to address the shortcomings he saw in Desert Storm operations. This, he maintains, is a simple necessity for preparations for the year 2010.

But even more than technology, Sullivan wants to build a new egalitarian theme into the Army, one which invites free-flowing information regardless of its form of transmission. This will require a fracturing of the old Cold War mindset, but with a better educated (the best ever, now) complement of personnel, Sullivan must be optimistic.

Information will allow a much broader pattern of delegation in which each tank commander, for instance, will be on his own, relying on tightly integrated messages rather than on a command for playing the necessary part in a concerted battle plan. This information will, thus, allow every member of a unit to have the same orientation and to be "on the same page" when it comes to the execution of the plan, of which he or she might even have had a part in crafting.

All this will require soldiers who are truly integrated into the Army's culture and philosophy and who are willing and able to participate in the making of all sorts of truly meaningful decisions. Perhaps, as General Sullivan urges, this Army will be like improvising jazz musicians rather than members of a marching band.

QUESTIONS FOR DISCUSSION

1. What type(s) of resistance do you expect General Sullivan will encounter from other members of the Army's top brass?
2. Can the same standards of success be applied to this new Army as were used to evaluate the old Army? Explain.
3. Do you think that General Sullivan's approach would work in the other branches of service? Why or why not?
4. Does the fact that the Army is a crisis-oriented organization make the introduction of innovation more difficult? Explain.
5. How do the concepts of change discussed in this chapter apply to the U.S. Army situation?
6. Is there a danger that too much information can undermine any organization? Explain.
7. If you were General Sullivan, what would be your main arguments for increased budget and personnel for the coming fiscal year?

REFERENCES

1. Louis S. Richman, "When Will the Layoffs End?" *Fortune* (September 20, 1993): 54–56.

2. Richard H. Hall, *Organizations: Structures, Processes, and Outcomes,* 5th ed. (Englewood Cliffs, N.J.: Prentice-Hall, 1991), 193.

3. Bill McKelvey and Howard Aldrich, "Populations, Natural Selection, and Applied Organizational Science," *Administrative Science Quarterly* 28 (1983): 101–28.

4. Michael L. Tushman, Charles O'Reilly, and David Nadler, *The Management of Organizations* (New York: Harper & Row, 1989), 461.

5. Lawrence Gales, Pamela Tierney, and Andrew Boynton, "The Nature of Information Ties and Development of Technology: An Integration of Information Processing and the Strength of Weak Ties," in *Advances in Global High-Technology Management,* vol. 5, Part B, ed. by L. Gomez-Mejia and M. Lawless (Greenwich, Conn.: JAI Press, 1995), 3–29.

   Lawrence Gales, Pamela Porter, and Dina Mansour-Cole, "Innovation Project Technology, Information Processing and Performance: A Test of the Daft and Lengel Conceptualization," *Journal of Engineering Technology Management* 9 (1992): 303–38.

6. Peter Pae, "Big Company Tactics Spur Turnaround at Small Firm," *The Wall Street Journal* (August 15, 1989), B1.

7. J. Brockner, "The Effects of Work Layoffs on Survivors: Research, Theory and Practice," in *Research in Organizational Behavior,* vol. 10, ed. by B. M. Staw and L. L. Cummings (Greenwich, Conn.: JAI Press, 1988), 213–55.

D. Mansour-Cole and L. Gales, "Work Groups and Transition Events: Understanding the Effects of Commitment, Cohesion and Climate on Employee Justice Perceptions" (paper presented at the Academy of Management Meetings, Vancouver, B.C., Canada, 1995).

8. Paul Hersey and Kenneth Blanchard, "Change and the Use of Power: The Management of Change, Part I," *Training and Development Journal* 26 (1972), 6–10.

    David Nadler, "Concepts for the Management of Organizational Change" in *The Management of Organizations*, ed. by M. Tushman, C. O'Reilly, and D. Nadler (New York: Harper & Row, 1989), 490–504.

9. See note 6 above.

10. "The Big Store's Big Trauma," *Business Week* (February 10, 1989) 50–51.

11. Stanley Gault, "Leaders of Corporate Change," *Fortune* (December 14, 1992): 104–14.

12. Stephen H. Wildstrom, "Laptops for the Desktop," *Business Week* (July 3, 1995): 18.

    Stephen H. Wildstrom, "Tony Printer for the Home," *Business Week* (May 15, 1995): 24.

13. M. Tushman, W. Newman, and E. Romanelli, "Convergence and Upheaval: Managing the Unsteady Pace of Organization Evolution," *California Management Review* (1986): 29.

14. E. Romanelli and M. Tushman, "Organizational Transformation as Punctuated Equilibrium: An Empirical Test," *Academy of Management Journal* 37 (1994): 1141–66.

15. Sherman Stratford, "A Master Class in Radical Change," *Fortune* (December 13, 1993): 82–90.

16. H. Mintzberg, "The Pitfalls of Strategic Planning," *California Management Review* (Fall 1993): 32–47.

    R. Moss Kanter, B. Stein, and T. Jick, *The Challenges of Organizational Change: How Companies Experience and How Leaders Guide It* (New York: Free Press, 1992).

17. K. Kerwin, "Rumble in Buick City," *Business Week* (October 1, 1994): 42–43.

    K. Kerwin, "Fixing G.M.: Pages from a Radical Repair Manual," *Business Week* (November 16, 1992): 46.

18. See Brockner in note 7 above.

    See Mansour-Cole and Gales in note 7 above.

    R. Sutton, K. M. Eisenhardt, and J. V. Jucker, "Managing Organizational Decline: Lessons from Atari," *Organizational Dynamics* 14 (Spring 1986): 17–29.

    D. C. Feldman and C. Leana, "Managing Layoffs: Experience at the *Challenger* Disaster Site and the Pittsburgh Steel Mills," *Organizational Dynamics* (Summer 1989): 52–64.

R. L. Daft, *Organization Theory and Design*, 4th ed. (Saint Paul, Minn.: West Publishing, 1992): 473–74.

19. Julia Flynn, "That Burning Sensation at Glaxo," *Business Week* (October 3, 1994): 76–78.

20. Christopher Power, "Flops," *Business Week* (August 16, 1993): 76–82.

   Edwin Mansfield, J. Rapaport, J. Schnee, S. Wagner, and M. Hamburger, *Research and Innovation in Modern Corporations* (New York: Norton, 1993).

21. H. Fersko-Weiss, "The High-Tech Hall of Shame: Products We Have Known and (not quite) Loved," *High Tech Marketing* 63 (July 1987): 36–41.

   S. Wilkinson, "Boom and Bust in Toyland," *Working Women* (September 1988): 110–12, 222–23.

22. See Gales, Porter, and Mansour-Cole in note 5 above.

   Eric von Hippel, *The Sources of Innovation* (New York: Oxford University Press, 1988).

   Lowell W. Steele, *Managing Technology* (New York: McGraw-Hill, 1989).

   F. Axel Johne and Patricia Snelson, "Success Factors in Product Innovation: A Selective Review of the Literature," *Journal of Product Innovation Management* 5, (1988): 114–28.

   Modesto A. Maidique and B. J. Zirger, "A Study of Success and Failure in Product Innovation: The Case of the U.S. Electronics Industry," *IEEE Transactions in Engineering Management* 31 (1984): 192–203.

   See Daft in note 18 above.

23. Donald Gerwin and Harvey Kolodny, *Management of Advanced Manufacturing Technology* (New York: John Wiley & Sons, Inc., 1992).

   James W. Dean, Jr., and Gerald I. Sussman, "Organizing for Manufacturing," *Harvard Business Review* (January/February 1989): 28–36.

24. William J. Cook, "Ringing in Saturn," *U.S. News & World Report* (October 22, 1990): 51–54.

25. Stephanie Overman, "Saturn Teams Working and Profiting," *HRMagazine* (March 1995): 72–74.

   David Woodruff, "At Saturn What Workers Want Is . . . Fewer Defects," *Business Week* (Special Industry/Technology Issue, December 2, 1992): 117–18.

26. David Woodruff, "Where Employees Are Management: Commitment Equals Empowerment at Saturn," *Business Week* (Special Industry/Technology Issue, December 2, 1992): 66.

27. Amanda Sinclair, "The Tyranny of a Team Ideology," *Organization Studies* 13 (1992): 611–26.

28. D. Keith Denton, "Process Mapping Trims Cycle Time," *HRMagazine* (February 1995): 56–61.

    Thomas Stewart, "GE Keeps Those Ideas Coming," *Fortune* (August 12, 1991): 41–49.

29. See Stewart, p. 48, in note 28 above.

30. See Dean, Jr., and Sussman in note 23 above.

31. Richard Beckhard, *Organizational Development* (Reading, Mass.: Addison-Wesley, 1969), 9–14.

    Wendel L. French and Cecil Bell, *Organizational Development: Behavioral Science Interventions for Organizational Improvement* (Englewood Cliffs, N.J.: Prentice-Hall, 1995).

32. Don Bryant, "Action Research and Planned Change," in *Managing Organizational Change,* ed. by Roy McLennan (Englewood Cliffs, N.J.: Prentice-Hall, 1989): 146–47.

33. James Smither, "An Examination of the Effects of an Upward Feedback Program Over Time," *Personnel Psychology* (1995): 1–34.

34. E. Schein, *Process Consultation: Its Role in Organizational Development* (Reading, Mass.: Addision-Wesley, 1969).

35. Based on the following articles: Shari Caudron, "Diversity Ignites Effective Work Teams," *Personnel Journal* 73 (September 1994): 154–63.

    Andrew Martin, "Man Charges Harassment at Sensitivity Training," *Chicago Tribune* (September 8, 1994), C1.

    Daniel Howes, "More Firms Investing in Diversity Training," *Detroit News* (May 19, 1994), E1.

    Melissa Lee, "Diversity Training Brings Unity to Small Company," *The Wall Street Journal* (September 2, 1993), B2.

36. Charles Handy, *The Age of Unreason* (Boston, Mass.: Harvard Business School Press, 1989).

    Thomas A. Stewart, "The Search for the Organization of Tomorrow," *Fortune* (May 18, 1992): 92–98.

37. For example: Rosabeth Moss Kanter, *When Giants Learn to Dance* (New York: Simon & Schuster, 1989).

    Tom Peters, *Thriving on Chaos* (New York: Alfred A. Knopf, 1988).

    William H. Davidow and Michael S. Malone, *The Virtual Corporation: Structuring and Revitalizing for the 21st Century* (New York: HarperCollins, 1992).

    Michael Hammer and James Champy, *Engineering the Corporation: A Manifesto for Business Revolution* (New York: Harper Business, 1993).

38. R. Aguayo, *Dr. Deming: The American Who Taught the Japanese About Quality* (New York: Simon & Schuster, 1990).

J. M. Juran, *Juran on Quality by Design* (New York: The Free Press, 1992).

39. See Aguayo in note 38 above.

See Juran in note 38 above.

James W. Dean, Jr., and James R. Evans, *Total Quality: Management, Organization, and Strategy* (St. Paul, Minn.: West Publishing, 1994).

40. Peter Senge, *The Fifth Discipline: The Art and Practice of the Learning Organization* (New York: Doubleday Currency, 1990).

Henry P. Sims and Dennis A. Gioia, Jr., *The Thinking Organization* (San Francisco: Jossey-Bass, 1986).

David A. Garvin, "Building a Learning Organization," *Harvard Business Review* 71 (1993): 78–91.

Brian Dumaine, "Mr. Learning Organization," *Fortune* (October 17, 1994): 147–57.

41. See Dumaine in note 40 above.

42. Ibid.

43. Robert Duncan, "The Ambidextrous Organization: Designing Dual Structures for Innovation," in *The Management of Organizations*, vol. 1, ed. by Ralph Kilmann, Louis Pondy, and Dennis Slevin (New York: North-Holland, 1976), 167–88.

Edward F. McDonough III and Richard Leifer, "Using Simultaneous Structures To Cope with Uncertainty," *Academy of Management Journal* 26 (1983): 727–35.

See Daft, pp. 271–72, in note 18 above.

44. See Nadler in note 8 above.

45. Tracy Kidder, *The Soul of a New Machine* (Boston: Little, Brown, 1981).

46. Faribouz Damanpour, "The Adoption of Technological, Administrative, and Ancillary Innovations: Impact of Organizational Factors," *Journal of Management* 13 (1987): 676–78.

PART FIVE

Integrative Cases

In this, the last section of the book, we present five integrative cases that illustrate and integrate many of the concepts that have been covered in this text. Each case requires that the reader apply various organization theory concepts in an analytic framework.

The cases are based on actual incidents experienced by real organizations. Questions that follow the cases help the reader focus on key issues. However, these questions do not address all of the issues presented in each case. As you try to answer these questions you may want to think of other important points raised by the case. Expand your analysis to address the broad organizational perspective presented throughout the text.

The cases cover a variety of types of organizations, including U.S. and foreign firms, manufacturing and service companies, and successful, growing firms as well as troubled, declining firms. Each organization faces unique circumstances to which it must respond. Our strategic systems framework should allow you to identify and analyze the important variables involved in order to develop your appropriate strategies.

We have attempted to develop timely and relevant cases. However, we must note that events often preempt our best intentions to present current issues. You should go beyond these cases to see if and how the conditions facing these firms may have changed since these cases were written. What have these companies done? What has changed in the environment?

Wal-Mart Stores, Inc.: So Help Me Sam!*

Pledge to Wal-Mart Customers
   "Every time our customers come within ten feet of me, regardless of what I'm doing, I'll look them in the eyes, smile, and greet them — So help me Sam!"

INTRODUCTION

After Sam Walton got out of the army at the end of World War II, he opened a Ben Franklin department store in Newport, Arkansas — that was in 1950. Nearly forty-five years later the descendant of this one Ben Franklin store, Wal-Mart Stores, Inc., consists of 1,880 Wal-Mart stores, 256 Sam's Wholesale Clubs, 25 Supercenters, and 13 McLane & Western Merchandisers Distribution Centers.[1]

The company went public in 1970 at a share price of $16.50. By the end of 1993 Wal-Mart was the largest retail organization in the United States. Sales that totaled $1.2 billion in 1980 soared to over $55.5 billion by the beginning of 1994. As seen in Figures 1 through 4 on pages 338–391, this phenomenal sales growth is well complemented by comparable growth in net profit, earnings per share, and dividends per share.[2] As is evident, Wal-Mart has been successful in accomplishing its overall strategic goal of maintaining "continued, controlled, and profitable growth."

Although Wal-Mart stores have traditionally been located in rural and semirural areas in the South and Midwest, locations heretofore ignored by competitors such as Sears and Kmart, future expansion is planned for urban areas in California and the Northeast. David Glass, president and chief executive officer of Wal-Mart, said that there was no state in which he would not consider building a Wal-Mart store. International expansion has taken Wal-Mart into Canada and Mexico.

---

*By Erich Brockmann, Florida State University

■ FIGURE 1
Wal-Mart Net Sales

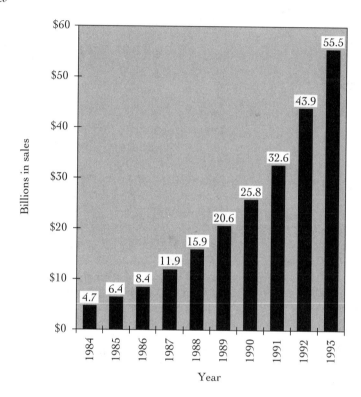

One key aspect of the Wal-Mart success story is the organization's willingness to foster innovation and change. Wal-Mart, Inc., opened DOT Discount Drug Stores in 1983, Helen's Arts and Crafts (named after Sam Walton's wife) in 1984, and Hypermart*USA stores in 1987. New stores are not the only field in which Wal-Mart has experimented. As discussed later in this case, the Wal-Mart organization has used innovative approaches in areas such as employee, customer, and supplier relations; merchandising; distribution; and communications.

Wal-Mart stock is considered by financial experts to be one of the nation's most valuable investments, and the story is often repeated how $4,700 (100 shares) of Wal-Mart stock in 1983 was worth more than $104,200 by 1993.[3] Because Wal-Mart maintained an amazing 44 percent growth rate during the recession years of 1981 and 1982, most analysts claim that the company is "recession-proof."[4] In 1988 *Business Month* declared Wal-Mart one of the five best-managed companies in America while in 1989 *Fortune* claimed that the Wal-Mart organization was one of the five most admired companies in the nation.[5]

Wal-Mart Net Income

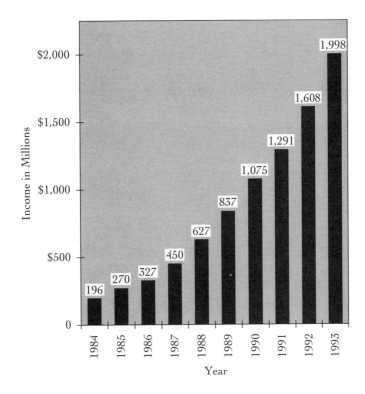

ORGANIZATIONAL STRUCTURE

At the head of the organization sit the board of directors and the chairman of the board, S. Robson Walton. Sam Walton was the titular and official head of the organization until his death in 1992. At that time most of the power and authority had been delegated to the president and CEO, David Glass, and the vice chairman of the board and chief operating officer (COO), Donald Soderquist. After Sam's death, his assets were distributed among his family. However, Glass and Soderquist basically share power and authority in running the Wal-Mart "empire." As president and CEO, Glass is primarily responsible for effecting long-range policies and strategic plans while Soderquist as COO is responsible for administering the organization's day-to-day operations.

Board members also serve on various committees that play integral roles in running the corporation. For the purposes of this case, the most important group is the executive committee, which is charged with executing the decisions made by the board of directors. Walton, Glass, Soderquist, and four other directors, comprise this very

■   **FIGURE 3**

Wal-Mart Earnings per Share

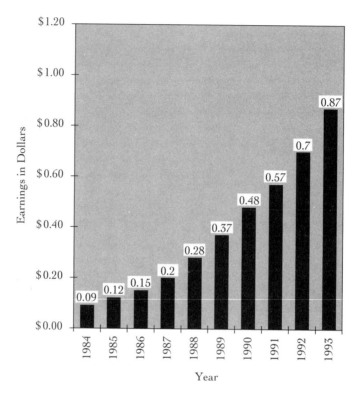

powerful decision-making body. Other executive committee members include the executive vice president and chief financial officer, Paul Carter, and the senior vice president, James L. Walton.

Although the Wal-Mart organization lists its senior officers in its annual report, the reporting relationships and communications channels are deliberately not depicted. According to the public affairs department at Wal-Mart headquarters, the company chooses not to have an organization chart because such a chart would tend to depict rigid relationships that, in fact, do not exist. Open communications—upward, downward, and lateral—typify the Wal-Mart organization. Both individuals and organizational subunits are granted as much authority as possible. Because the senior managers within Wal-Mart are considered "some of the most respected in the discount store industry,"[6] they are delegated the authority and autonomy to manage their respective functions as they see fit, provided that they do so within the decision parameters set by the executive committee.

Figure 5, on pages 392 and 393, shows the senior manager positions and incumbents at Wal-Mart Stores, Inc. The reader should know that the term *operations*, which refers to many positions within the senior managerial ranks, refers to regional operations. Thus, each vice president for operations is a regional vice president to whom individual store managers report.

■ **FIGURE 4**
Wal-Mart Dividends per Share

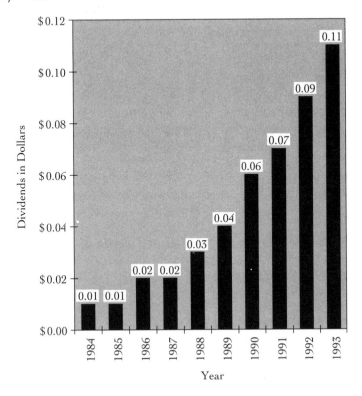

Because Wal-Mart is such a large organization with a very loose organizational structure, the integration and coordination of functions are critical. At the senior level, integration and coordination are partially accomplished by senior managers' visits to the local stores where operations are observed; questions are asked; suggestions are elicited; and so on. At the Bentonville, Arkansas, headquarters it is extremely rare to find even one-half of the senior managers present because most of them are in the field. On Saturdays, senior managers meet with Chairman Walton at headquarters to discuss the previous week's activities and discuss future plans. Also, some lower-level managers are invited to make presentations about a particular merchandising tactic, new products offered, the success of a particular store, and so on. Generally, the range of topics covered at the Saturday meetings includes, but is not limited to, weekly sales, reports on new store construction, distribution center operations, product mixes, and functioning of company information systems. In short, senior managers' visits, combined with the Saturday meetings, do a good job in keeping everybody up-to-date on Wal-Mart activities.

Store visits and Saturday meetings, however, cannot provide the total integration necessary for such a large company. An extremely thick corporate culture, combined

◼ FIGURE 5
Senior Managers Within Wal-Mart Stores, Inc.

Corporate Servant Leaders

Corporate Officers

Founder
Samuel M. Walton
(1918–1992)

President and
Chief Executive Officer
David D. Glass

Chairman of the Board
S. Robson Walton

Vice Chairman and
Chief Operating Officer
Donald G. Soderquist

EXECUTIVE VICE
PRESIDENTS

Chief Financial Officer
Paul R. Carter

President and
Chief Executive Officer,
Wal-Mart Stores Division
William R. Fields

President and
Chief Executive Officer,
McLane Company, Inc.
William G. Rosier

President and
Chief Executive Officer,
Wal-Mart International
Division
Bob L. Martin

President and
Chief Executive Officer,
Sam's Club Division
Dean L. Sanders

Real Estate and Construction
Thomas P. Seay

Supercenter Division
Nick White

Distribution and Transportation
H. Lee Scott, Jr.

SENIOR VICE
PRESIDENTS

Information Systems
Randall Mott

Human Resources
Coleman Peterson

Benefits Administration
Charles Ratcliff

Controller
James A. Walker, Jr.

Store Planning
Ed Nagy

General Counsel and Secretary
Robert K. Rhoads

Co-Founder
James L. Walton
(1921–1995)

VICE PRESIDENTS

Store Planning
Dave Burghardt

Distribution Personnel
John Bell

Distribution
Jimmy M. Wright

Construction
Wayne Cox

Transportation
Larry Duff

Finance
J. J. Fitzsimmons

Assistant General Counsel and
Assistant Secretary
Martin G. Gilbert

Assistant General Counsel
Ronald Williams

Real Estate
Carl Ownbey

Information Systems
Walter Anderson
Rick Dalzell
Kevin Turner

Loss Prevention
David H. Gorman

Marketing and
Sales Promotion
Paul V. Higham

International Construction and
Facility Maintenance
Robert J. Murphey

Risk Management
William E. Newberg

Corporate Affairs
Don E. Shinkle

OTHER CORPORATE
OFFICERS

Treasurer
Terri Bertschy

Assistant General Counsels/
Assistant Secretaries
Sally Strood Varner

Divisional Servant Leaders

Wal-Mart Stores

SENIOR VICE
PRESIDENTS

Merchandising
J. R. Campbell
Vanessa Castagna
David Dible
Lewis Ray Hobbs
John Lupo

Operations
David Jackson
Mel Redman
Kendall Schwindt
Larry E. Williams
Wesley C. Wright

VICE PRESIDENTS

Merchandising
Greg Bailey
Stephen M. Bailey
Brent Berry
Mike Bratcher
William DuBose
Ken Eaton

Don S. Harris
Chuck Kerby
Debbie Kocks
Bill Long
Terry Price
Beth Schommer
Mike Smith
Carl L. White
Jim Woodruff

■ FIGURE 5
Senior Managers Within Wal-Mart Stores, Inc. (continued)

Divisional Servant Leaders *(continued)*

Wal-Mart Stores

Operations
Donald C. Bland
Mike Cockrell
Lawrence E. Fennell
Edwin Fountain
Robert L. Hart
Milburn E. Hudnall
Mike Huffaker
Todd Libbra
Joe Mains
Marianne McDonough
Duane G. Naccarato
Thomas R. Putnam
Rick Russell
Don Swann
Andrew H. Wilson
William Wulfers
Eric Zurn

Inventory Management
Robert T. Bruce

P.O.S. Replenishment
Bryan Banks

Merchandise Planning
Chris Callahan

*Personnel, Training, and
Development*
Maxie Carpenter

Sam's Clubs

SENIOR VICE
PRESIDENTS

Marketing and Administration
Suzanne Allford

Operations
Jim H. Haworth

VICE PRESIDENTS

Merchandising
John Cowgur
Adam DaCosta
Richard L. Jones
John Kusniewski
Bradley W. Link
Brad Thomson
Jerry Duane Wilson

Operations
Randy Edwards
Kenny Folk
Don Hitt
Gary Nebinger
David Simpson
Steve Tiernan

Marketing
Barbara Brown

Membership
Jim McGrath

People Division
Celia Swanson

International

SENIOR VICE
PRESIDENTS

CEO
Millard Barron

CEO–China/Hong Kong
Joe Hatfield

VICE PRESIDENTS

CEO–South America
Arthur Emmanuel

*Vice President — Sam's
International*
Eddie Frail

Supercenter Division

SENIOR VICE
PRESIDENTS

Operations
Mark Schwartz

VICE PRESIDENTS

Merchandising
Donald Cannon
Harold Miller

Operations
Robert Erickson
Leroy Schuetts
Joseph J. Tapper

Specialty Division

Senior Vice President
Thomas M. Coughlin

Vice President, Pharmacy
Clarence Archer
Doug Degn

Vice President, Jewelry
Richard Blickmead

*Vice President and General
Merchandise Manager,
Shoes*
Joe Delacruz

*Chairman and
Chief Executive Officer,
Shoes*
William Hutcheson

*Vice President, Jewelry and
Shoes, Operations*
David York

Operations
Jim Martin

McLane

SENIOR VICE
PRESIDENTS

Administration
Neil W. McCarty

Grocery Operations
Terry McElroy

Logistics and Special Divisions
James L. Kent

VICE PRESIDENTS

Construction and Design
Ronald G. King

Finance and Accounting
R. D. Harger

General Counsel
Michael P. Puryear

*Governmental Affairs
and Taxation*
Kevin J. Koch

*Grocery Operations —
Coastal Region*
Jim Sanders

*Grocery Operations —
Inland Region*
Gary Bitmer

Human Resources
Francesca Souza

Marketing
Roger Grogman

Merchandising
Bill Fendrick

New Market Development
James Leonard

Sales
Jerry Rose

Source: *Wal-Mart Annual Report 1995*, Wal-Mart Stores, Inc., Bentonville, Arkansas.

with the latest information technology, ensures that all Wal-Mart operations are tightly coordinated on a day-to-day basis. We discuss these two aspects of the Wal-Mart organization in other sections of this case.

THE WAL-MART SYSTEM

In addition to structure and culture, which are discussed under subsequent major sections of this case, the Wal-Mart system can be analyzed in terms of (1) types of stores; (2) the distribution network; (3) suppliers; (4) exemplary customer service; (5) communication technology; (6) merchandising and product mix; and (7) employees.

TYPE OF STORES

Wal-Mart Stores, Inc., though renowned for Wal-Mart stores, actually consists of four types of retail outlets. (Helen's Arts and Crafts stores were sold in 1988.)

1. *Wal-Mart Stores.* These stores range in size from 30,000 to 110,000 square feet and are organized into thirty-six departments that offer a wide variety of merchandise, including clothing and shoes, curtains, fabrics and notions, housewares, hardware, electronics, home furnishings, small appliances, automotive accessories, garden equipment and supplies, sporting goods, toys, cameras, health and beauty aids, pharmaceuticals, and jewelry. The average Wal-Mart store stocks between 70,000 and 80,000 items.[7]

2. *Sam's Wholesale Clubs.* Sam's stores range in size from 68,000 to 130,000 square feet and are located primarily in urban areas. Sam's are membership-only, cash-and-carry operations. These stores offer bulk sales of name-brand hard-good merchandise, some soft goods, institutional-size grocery items, jewelry, sporting goods, toys, and tires. The overall objective of Sam's Wholesale Clubs is to maximize volume and turnover and to minimize overhead expenses.[8]

3. *Hypermart*USA.* These extremely large stores average 220,000 square feet. Hypermarts are new on the retail scene and are known as the "malls without walls," supporting peripheral businesses such as hair salons, shoe repair facilities, and health food stores. Approximately one-third of the products sold at Hypermart*USA are grocery items. Big-ticket items, such as furniture, are also offered at Hypermart*USA stores. In addition, these stores carry many more hard-good and soft-good inventory, as well as brand-name clothing, than do the traditional Wal-Mart stores. Two Hypermart*USA stores are joint ventures with Cullum Grocers.[9]

4. *Supercenters.* These stores, which range in size from 95,000 to 150,000 square feet, are a hybrid between a traditional Wal-Mart store and a supermarket. These Supercenters carry a narrower grocery assortment than do the Hypermart*USA stores; thus, they are serviced by Wal-Mart's own distribution system while the Hypermart*USAs must be serviced by external

distributors because of the large array of grocery items they carry. There are currently twenty-five Supercenters in existence, and if they continue to be successful (with gross profit margins of 17 to 18 percent), it is possible that some Wal-Marts will be expanded into Supercenters.[10] The recent addition of a complete deli, fresh bakery, and complementary convenience shops, such as portrait studios, dry cleaners, optical shops, and hair salons, make these Supercenters truly a one-stop center.[11]

DISTRIBUTION

Wal-Mart's distribution subsystem is perhaps the most efficient and effective in the entire retail industry. Using the concept of backward integration, Wal-Mart first builds a distribution center in a rural or suburban area. After the distribution center is constructed, thirty to forty Wal-Mart entities are constructed within a 600-mile radius (although each center is capable of servicing 150 Wal-Marts, Sam's, and so on). Wal-Mart then uses its own fleet of trucks to deliver merchandise to the various stores. For example, at the Cullman, Alabama, distribution center, 1,042 employees work under a twenty-eight-acre roof. Each day approximately 150 outbound trucks are loaded with merchandise for the various stores while approximately 160 inbound trucks from suppliers are unloaded.[12] The immensity of such a center is evidenced by the facts that there are 11 miles of conveyer belts and 190,000 cases of merchandise within each structure.[13] Because all stores serviced by an individual center are within a 600-mile radius, store orders are processed and delivered within a day.

Logistics, distribution centers, and transportation — the Wal-Mart distribution team — are the keys in Wal-Mart's ability to remain competitive. The twenty-two centers, averaging almost 1 million square feet, received and shipped 769 million cases to the stores in 1993. The private fleet permits customized, cost-efficient delivery to the stores, accommodating peak seasonal periods, night deliveries, and accelerated delivery. The 2,500 drivers and 16,000 distribution associates' hard work and commitment to continuous improvement make this investment in centers and equipment pay by improving the in-stock position of the stores and making just-in-time inventory management a reality.[14]

SUPPLIERS

A large retail organization such as Wal-Mart is, of course, one of the largest corporate buyers within the United States. The Wal-Mart organization has recently received a tremendous amount of positive publicity concerning its "Buy American" program. Besides the patriotic aspects of this program, it enables Wal-Mart to secure required quantities of goods at the lowest prices. Wal-Mart has literally saved many small American concerns from going under with this program because, until they started to do business with Wal-Mart, they were being beaten by foreign competitors both in price and quality. In 1992, Wal-Mart challenged Kalikow Brothers, a long-time vendor-partner, to move production of a popular men's shorts back from the Orient to the U.S. By working together, they were able to relocate the manufacturing to a plant in Lake Butler, Florida. Over 125 jobs were added. A second plant has been rejuvenated in the process. Likewise, cooperation allowed a maker of ladies' foundations to bring production back from Haiti and Jamaica.[15]

Wal-Mart works with its American supplier setting up product specifications and design and ensures the supplier that it will buy enough products to keep the supplier in business. Conversely, the supplier guarantees delivery and low price. We should add here that Wal-Mart is renowned in the retail industry for its speedy payment of supplier invoices.

Unlike other large corporate buyers, Wal-Mart does not deal with independent factory representatives; rather, the organization insists on dealing directly with manufacturers' own sales forces. This policy, although unpopular with the thousands of self-employed manufacturers' representatives, saves both Wal-Mart and its suppliers millions of dollars because sales commissions are not paid to independent representatives.

Of course, Wal-Mart does buy goods from foreign manufacturers if American manufacturers are incapable of matching price and quality.

CUSTOMER SERVICE

Wal-Mart is committed to providing the best customer service in all of retailing. Because of its distribution system and supplier relations, customers have the items they want when they want them. Merchandising and distribution experts within the Wal-Mart system identify those items most continually in demand so that they are made part of the basic stock in both the distribution centers and individual stores.

Courtesy and service to the customer are trademarks of the Wal-Mart organization. Upon entering the store each customer is amicably welcomed by an official greeter, usually a retired person. As stated in the Wal-Mart Pledge at the beginning of this case, any employee will stop what he or she is doing to help a customer. And, unlike many of its competitors, Wal-Mart boasts having the fastest check-out service of any retail organization.[16]

To best serve the customer, Sam Walton stressed (and his associates continue to stress) the importance of scanning the economic component of the external environment. Through this scanning process, consumers' spending habits can be forecast and translated into merchandising commitments. Sam Walton stated it best,

> *Sell to the customer what they want to buy. With the changing demographic patterns in the U.S., it will become increasingly more important to know your customers (allot your assortments to fit their needs and sell them what they want to buy). For example, the aging of our population base will require significant adjustments to achieve proper product mix.*[17]

COMMUNICATIONS TECHNOLOGY

State-of-the-art communications technology links together all facets of organizational life at Wal-Mart. Indeed, one could say that Wal-Mart is "married to technology." For example, right after the Saturday morning senior-level management meeting in Arkansas, executives often relay vital information to stores via the company's six-channel communications system. This system, linked to a mainframe computer, is capable of gathering store data on a daily basis, handling credit card transactions, keeping tabs on inventory, and so on. Within the distribution centers, bar codes are read by laser scanners to ensure that the right product goes to the right location in the right quantity. According to CEO Glass,

> *We can talk to every store at the same time as many times a day as we want, and we've dramatically cut our phone costs. We train by satellite. But the biggest advantage is the sharing of merchandising information. A buyer can get on [the satellite system] and say, "These are the new items for Department 16. Here's how you should display them."*[18]

MERCHANDISING AND PRODUCT MIX

When customers walk into a Wal-Mart, Sam's, or Hypermart*USA, they see a tremendous amount and variety of merchandise for sale. In general, the merchandise available is a mixture of heavily discounted name brands and even lower-priced off brands.

Wal-Mart believes in experimenting with new products or merchandising techniques at a few locations before adopting them throughout all stores. The new product sales and/or merchandising techniques are carefully monitored, and should they prove successful, they are then implemented at the other stores.

Since the mid-1980s, Wal-Mart has expanded and upgraded the product mix in its stores to include stereos, televisions, microwave ovens, telephones, and other hard goods. To expand its camera operations, Wal-Mart purchased a film processing plant in 1981.

Because Wal-Mart believes in allowing some autonomy at the store level, store managers have the authority to buy and sell merchandise that reflects consumer preferences in a given area. Examples include crayfish pots in Louisiana stores and school logo items in stores that are located near colleges and universities.

Wal-Mart aims to keep shrinkage at around 1 percent while other retailers typically settle for between 3 and 5 percent.[19] Wal-Mart aims to continue operating as a small company, affirming that every associate is vital and key to the collective success. In 1993, Wal-Mart reduced the operating, selling, and general and administrative expenses as a percentage of sales to 15 percent.

However, the recent ruling that Wal-Mart engaged in predatory pricing could damage its reputation. On October 12, 1993, Judge David Reynolds of Faulkner County Chancery Court in Arkansas found against Wal-Mart for selling items below cost in an effort to drive competitors out of business. Wal-Mart was ordered to stop the practice and to pay about $300,000 in damages to three pharmacies in Conway, Arkansas.[20] Wal-Mart maintains the judge's interpretation of a 1937 state antitrust law that prohibits "trade for the purpose of injuring competitors and destroying competition" was misguided.[21] The trial court misunderstood the legal principles that distinguish a lawful attempt to compete from an unlawful attempt to destroy competition.[22] Wal-Mart is appealing the case in federal court, trying to overturn the state law as unconstitutional.

This is only the beginning of legal woes for Wal-Mart and other megaretailers. In the first congressional probe of the retailing phenomenon that is changing the local markets nationwide, megastores were derided for everything from crushing local competition to altering the product distribution chain. Representative John LaFalce (D, New

York), chairman of the House Small Business Committee, aims to explore the following three routes toward protecting small business from the super chains:

1. increase publicity about expansion of the megastores;
2. curb federal money, such as industrial revenue bonds, that goes toward retail development; and
3. ensure that federal antitrust and banking laws are tough enough and are enforced.[23]

Morrison Cain, vice-president of the International Mass Retail Association, countered with a defense that the big stores seized on technological advances in distribution and logistics, such as checkout scanning, sophisticated inventory processing systems, direct store-to-warehouse and store-to-vendor communications, and just-in-time delivery. To aid the small businesses, Cain suggests that they sell items not carried by the giant discounters, refocus on upscale merchandise, improve store marketing and image, price competitively, and emphasize services that discounters do not provide.[24]

EMPLOYEES

No analysis of Wal-Mart would be complete without a discussion of its employees. All 434,000 Wal-Mart employees are referred to as *associates*, a term that Sam Walton instituted because it implied ownership.[25] Associates are, indeed, owners because each is entitled to participate in a profit-sharing and stock option plan, the benefits of which increase as the employee's length of service increases. For example, after two years' service, the company partially contributes to the stock ownership plan; after three years' service, the company pays for all the stock ownership plan; and after seven years', the employee becomes completely vested, that is, the stock is his or hers outright even if he or she quits Wal-Mart.[26]

A participative management style exists within all Wal-Mart stores. Store managers spend a considerable portion of each day walking around the stores and talking with associates about a variety of matters. The managers listen to suggestions, discuss improvements, and praise liberally for a job well done. Wal-Mart has been fortunate in obtaining a steady stream of innovative ideas from its associates. It is common within Wal-Marts to have task forces, consisting of both managers and hourly associates, to evaluate new ideas and plan for future store operations. This participative management style, in conjunction with the employee profit-sharing and stock ownership plan, is one of the primary reasons why Wal-Mart has obtained the employee commitment that is so vital to long-term success.

INTERNATIONAL

Mexico has been profitable but, just as importantly, a tremendous learning experience. In the joint venture with Cifra, Mexico's largest retailer, Wal-Mart presently has three

Club Aurreras, four Bodegas discount stores, and one Aurrera combination store. Calendar 1993 and 1994 plans called for aggressive expansion of these operations plus the introduction of the first Supercenter in Monterrey and Mexico City.[27] In 1993, Wal-Mart acquired 100 PACE units (to become Sam's Clubs) and 112 Canadian Woolco stores, thus expanding its domain into Canada at a rapid pace.

Wal-Mart is also hedging its bets in Mexico. In October 1994, Wal-Mart announced it will participate in a venture between Dillard Department Stores, Inc., and Cifra SA to open Dillard stores south of the border. This relationship allows Wal-Mart to benefit from the high-end, name-brand apparel that it does not normally stock in Wal-Mart stores. This is one area in which Wal-Mart, for all its strengths, is weak.[28]

ENVIRONMENT

Wal-Mart knows that it can make a difference in combating environmental challenges — pollution, global warming, overpopulation, waste of resources, and others. In partnership with vendors, Wal-Mart now prints all its circulars on recycled paper. Each year it buys more products made of recycled materials and challenges the vendor-partners to find alternatives that are more environmentally friendly. The customers can also help. Therefore, Wal-Mart is collecting motor oil, batteries, and establishing neighborhood recycling centers, often placing bins in the store parking lots. Wal-Mart has sponsored such programs as "Kids For A Clean Environment." In 1993, this international organization had over 30,000 members in local clubs across America. As an ultimate goal, Wal-Mart is opening a unique store in Lawrence, Kansas. It was designed to be environmentally friendly in every way possible. It will serve as a working laboratory for students and become a dynamic experiment in testing new environmental ideas.[29]

THE WAL-MART CULTURE

Concern for the individual, whether the individual be a customer or an associate, is the cornerstone of the Wal-Mart corporate culture. Concomitant with this concern for the individual is open communications. Each store has a Friday morning meeting at which an associate at any level can pose questions and receive answers on subjects such as sales, costs, freight charges, and profit margins. Indeed, there are few corporations that willingly provide this information to their low-level employees.

Promotion to the managerial ranks is often based on performance (although Wal-Mart does hire managers away from competitors or directly after graduation from college). Departmental sales figures are posted weekly, and individuals in departments that regularly outperform the national Wal-Mart average are eligible for bonuses, raises, and promotions.

Wal-Mart's slogan, "Our people make the difference," is more than rhetoric. Chairman Walton firmly believed that by treating associates with respect and by showing them that he (and his senior managers) cared, they would perform with the highest levels of efficiency, effectiveness, and commitment to the organization.

Wal-Mart's culture, in combination with its decentralized and autonomous structure, makes it a most flexible organization. Company officials publicly stated, "We must have a low resistance to change, we must be flexible and willing to adjust rapidly to stay abreast of the competitive environment. We believe that to grow successfully we must continually challenge and test new retailing concepts. We must constantly improve."[30]

One cannot overestimate the role of Sam Walton on the development of this most remarkable corporate culture. Although he was a multibillionaire, Sam Walton was a very down-to-earth person—he drove a 1984 Ford pickup, lived in a modest house, and went quail hunting, his favorite pastime. His work week was normally six days long and included his attendance (in the role of cheerleader) at the Saturday morning senior-level management meetings. During the week Walton traveled to various Wal-Mart entities throughout the South and Midwest where he could be found greeting customers, stocking shelves, or running a cash register.

Walton was an inspiration to his associates, and they often felt as if they worked for Sam Walton, not Wal-Mart Stores, Inc. As one popular journal described the energetic chairman, "He's a little bit Jimmy Stewart, handsome with halting, 'aw shucks' charm. He's a little bit Billy Graham, with a charisma and persuasiveness that heartland folks find hard to resist. And, he's more than a little bit Henry Ford, a business genius who sees how all parts of the economic puzzle relate to his business."[31]

IMPACT ON RURAL AMERICA

Not all has been rosy for Wal-Mart. Its expansion into the American Northeast has hit a wall of rural resentment. As Wal-Mart attempted to roll out its franchises, it was accused of sucking commerce off "Main Streets," thereby destroying traditional retailers that had served their communities for generations. Wal-Mart's counterargument was that the abundance produced in the form of more jobs, consumer savings, and expanded trade more than offset the loss of "Main Street" life and that it seemed an incidental price to pay.[32] Some particular examples follow.

In 1991, after Wal-Mart announced that it was entering Maine with twelve stores, the Bath, Maine, Chamber of Commerce split into two factions—one for and one against the giant's entry. The splinter group decried that "Wal-Mart is a threat to every small business in Bath. That's not to say it's going to put everyone out of business, but there are certain things you have to do or else it'll kill you."[33]

Wal-Mart's muscle helped repeal the "blue laws" in Maine that prevented major retailers from operating on Sunday. Now the local merchants must match Wal-Mart's time-and-a-half pay and extend their operating hours to compete. This adversely affects the local way of Sunday-life, which is filled with churchgoing and ice fishing. Wal-Mart did succeed in opening several stores in Maine. However, on top of the initial resentment, it experienced operating problems. It had trouble paying bills as regularly as the company prides itself on doing, and employees were dissatisfied when they were sent home early or laid off in order to control costs.[34] Even when a new store was successfully planned, failure still followed. For example, after being granted a commercial zoning approval in the summer of 1992 by Greenfield, Maine, the town council was petitioned by residents to put the zoning issue to a referendum. The referendum ultimately reversed the zoning approval.[35]

Several attempts to soothe ill feelings met with little success. Ken Stone, a professor of economics at Iowa State University, who specializes in retail trade and rural development is the keenest student of Wal-Mart. In the spring of 1992, he attempted to advise the downtown merchants not to compete directly with Wal-Mart, but rather to specialize and carry harder-to-get and better-quality products; emphasize customer service; extend business hours; advertise more; and work together. Wal-Mart followed suit with its own sponsor. In the summer of 1992, Wal-Mart sent Don Shinkle, vice president of corporate affairs, to Maine for two weeks to soothe groups of local merchants. Neither Stone nor Shinkle was very successful.[36]

Wal-Mart had even less "success" when it entered Vermont. Twice between 1990 and 1994 Wal-Mart failed to gain appropriate zoning approval for stores in St. Albans, Vermont. The city's anti–Wal-Mart campaign is being led by John Finn, a former state senator, who claims, "We're going to keep fighting the buggers."[37] The big fear is the view that Wal-Mart has become a metaphor for the larger commercial culture that is clearly alien to a state whose greatest contribution to retailing is the gift shop and whose most successful foray into American big business has been Ben and Jerry's, the iconoclastic ice cream maker. Vermont has one of the most stringent land-use laws in the country. Any large project, the law states, must not only be approved at the local level, but must also be evaluated by a district commission on ten criteria. Couple this with an attitude of "big is bad" and an environment in which an honest-to-goodness socialist can still win elected office, and it is obvious why Wal-Mart is having trouble. Even the marketing firm Claritas, which breaks down consumers into dozens of distinct groups based on tastes and demographics, says that Vermont is home to the country's largest concentration of what are called New Ecotopians. They are consumers with above-average education who are technology-oriented and civically active. They are more likely than other Americans to make bread from scratch, drive a jeep, watch the Learning Channel and read *Outdoor Life* and *American Health*.[38] Nationally, New Ecotopians make up 1 percent of the population. In Vermont, they make up 20 percent.

In an effort to make tentative peace in its continuing battle, Wal-Mart is making heroic efforts. It has proposed dropping its standard megastore-on-the-edge-of-town approach and instead building unusually small stores in appropriate downtown locations. Wal-Mart continues to battle such slanders as "sprawl-mart," which was levied by the National Trust for Historic Preservation after the organization declared the entire state to be endangered. Don Shinkle, vice president, responded in the letters-to-the-editor section of the *Washington Post*, "Wal-Mart started in small-town America, and because of this, will always strive to uphold the values and traditions of small-town America."[39] The Vermont governor offered to assist in accelerating the permitting process if Wal-Mart proves to be sincere in its proposals.[40]

In another state, Wal-Mart continued its efforts. In the Massachusetts town of Westford, the battle has been brewing since the spring of 1993. On one side is a group of residents sporting red T-shirts proclaiming, "STOP WAL-MART." The thirty-member anti–Wal-Mart committee is worried that local merchants will be forced out of business. So far, 4,000 people (of the 9,000 voters) have agreed with them. Wal-Mart has been bending over backward to gain acceptance. It went so far as to hire a biologist and station him at the construction site to ensure that migrating tree frogs can get to a breeding pond behind the proposed building.[41] Even this didn't help, and Wal-Mart eventually canceled its attempts to build a store there due to intense organized opposition by what it felt was a small, but obviously vocal, group of individuals.[42]

Both sides have data to back up their positions. The proponents state that Wal-Mart enhances existing merchants due to a spill-over effect that brings more business to the area. The opponents worry that Wal-Mart drives the locals out of business because the small-guy can't compete. In a study of the effect of Wal-Mart on Iowa towns, local businesses had higher sales due to increased traffic and the spill-over effect.[43] Conversely, when looking at sales of small specialty stores, another study found a loss of market share ranging from 2 to 44 percent.[44]

FUTURE CHALLENGES

As Wal-Mart progresses through the 1990s, most analysts and observers believe that it will face three main challenges — size, competition, and the changing leadership.

SIZE

Wal-Mart has recently entered into heretofore "virgin" territory. Its stores have spread into California and the Northeast. In 1993, it earmarked $3 billion for capital expenditures to support 110 new discount stores, 20 Sam's Club additions, 5 Supercenters, and 4 distribution centers. In addition, the company will expand or relocate 70 discount stores and upgrade another 65 to the Supercenter's format.[45] Sam's plans for calendar 1993 included a record 65 new clubs and 20 relocation or expansion projects. Reconfiguration and new club prototype designs are planned as well. Major emphasis is being placed on better understanding the merchandise needs of the business members and improving member service along with creating a new level of excitement in merchandise presentation. Wal-Mart stores' expansion broadened coverage to 45 total states, adding Connecticut, Idaho, Maine, Massachusetts, Montana, Oregon, and the territory of Puerto Rico. Future expansions will target Hawaii, Rhode Island, and Washington.[46]

Communications must be enhanced as Wal-Mart opens new stores and enters new territories; that is, new stores should be linked immediately to the mainframe and satellite systems that currently connect all stores to the Arkansas headquarters.

As Wal-Mart reaches saturation levels in urban areas, it will have to focus on rural areas. If the experience in the Northeast is any indication of the future, Wal-Mart will have to vary its strategy.

COMPETITION

Wal-Mart has been most successful in dealing with and beating its competition. It is now the world's largest retailer.[47]

As a result of its successes, Wal-Mart's competitors have implemented new policies that promise to increase their market share. For example, Sears turned to a policy of "Everyday Low Prices," included name brands in its merchandise array, overhauled its distribution system to make it more efficient, lowered its overhead costs, and cut back on its huge bureaucracy.

Kmart, the other main competitor, has upgraded its merchandise, appearance, and advertising efforts and aggressively cut its prices to keep Wal-Mart from encroaching upon its market share. In addition, Kmart has decided to join the high-tech age with its own computer and satellite system. Former Chairman Antonini of Kmart claimed, "Our vision calls for the constant and never-ceasing exploration of new modes of retailing so that our core business of Kmart stores can be constantly renewed and reinvigorated."[48] To compete directly with Wal-Mart's Hypermart*USA stores, Kmart entered into a partnership agreement with Bruno's supermarket chain to form markets to be called American Fare. However, Kmart has struggled to keep up.

CHANGE IN LEADERSHIP

Throughout its amazing history, Wal-Mart Stores, Inc., has thrived under the leadership of its founder, Sam Walton. Regarding Sam Walton's departure, CEO Glass commented, "There's no transition to make because the principles and the basic values he used in founding this company were so sound and so universally accepted."[49] Although this is true, Sam Walton was the rudder of the Wal-Mart ship, and he appeared on the cover of every major business publication at least once. Moreover, Sam Walton epitomized the American dream in a way that other famous entrepreneurs, such as Donald Trump, Ted Turner, and Leona Helmsley, do not. Walton's personality and his connection to Wal-Mart are parallel to the way that Walt Disney's persona is connected to his company. After Disney's death in 1966, his company floundered for many years until it was revitalized in the mid-1980s by the new chairman and CEO Michael Eisner. So far, Wal-Mart seems to be avoiding a similar decline.

There is no doubt that Wal-Mart is one of the preeminent retailing organizations in the United States, if not the world. If it can continue to usher in new ideas and maintain the heralded loyalty shown by both customers and employees, the organization could thrive well into the twenty-first century. Growth and size, however, should not become ends in and of themselves. In the words of Sam Walton, "Being number one would be nice, but we are more concerned about continuing to do what we do best and to be the best at what we do."[50] S. Robson Walton, Sam Walton's replacement, has reiterated the small town philosophy. "Our commitment to be the low cost provider of merchandise to our customers has never been greater . . . Our focus has been to take care of our customers, take care of one another by treating folks as they want to be treated, embrace innovation and change, and then address growth opportunities as they present themselves. The pursuit of quality, not quantity through continuous improvement must remain our objective."[51]

Questions for Discussion

1. What are some of the factors that contributed to Wal-Mart's success?
2. Describe the organizational structure of Wal-Mart.
3. Describe Wal-Mart's distribution system.
4. What environmental conditions will challenge Wal-Mart's continued success?
5. Discuss the company's impact on rural America.
6. What are Wal-Mart's three main challenges?

REFERENCES

1. Wal-Mart Annual Report (1993), 4–5.

2. Ibid.

3. Ibid.

4. Gene Marcial, "Why Wal-Mart Is Recession Proof," *Business Week* (February 22, 1988): 146.

5. John Huey, "Wal-Mart: Will It Take Over the World?" *Fortune* 19, no. 3 (1989): 52.

   "Wal-Mart Stores Penny Wise," *Business Month* 132, no. 5 (1988): 42.

6. Arthur Thompson and A. Strickland, III, "Case 29: Wal-Mart Stores, Inc.," in *Strategic Management: Cases and Concepts* (Plano, Tex.: Business Publications, Inc., 1987), 951.

7. Wal-Mart Stores, Inc., Securities and Exchange Commission, Form 10-K, Fiscal Year Ending January 31, 1993.

8. Ibid.

9. "Bush and Retailers: What's Ahead?" *Chain Store Age Executive* 65, no. 1 (1989): 16–17.

   Iris S. Rosenberg "A Hit in Europe; Tried Once in the United States. Here We Go Again!" *Stores* 70, no. 3 (1988): 54–84.

10. "Wal-Mart Rolls Out Its Supercenters," *Chain Store Age Executive* 64, no. 12 (1988): 18–19.

11. See note 1, page 2, above.

12. See Huey in note 5, page 56, above.

13. Ibid.

14. See note 1, page 3, above.

15. See note 1, page 21, above.

16. See note 1, page 3, above.

17. Joan Bergman, "Saga of Sam Walton," *Stores* 70, no. 1 (1988): 140.

18. See Huey in note 5, page 54, above.

19. E. O. Welles, "When Wal-Mart Comes to Town," *Inc.* 15, no. 7 (1993): 78.

20. Staff reporter, "In 2 Towns, Main Street Fights Off Wal-Mart," *The New York Times* (October 21, 1993), A16.

21. J. Ramey, "Wal-Mart Files Appeal on Loss Leader Ruling," *Daily News Record* (April 27, 1994), 10.

22. Ibid.

23. Joyce Barrett, "Capitol Hill Turns Up the Heat on Discount Retailers, Congress Lashes Out at Big Stores for Hurting Small Business," *Daily News Record* (April 11, 1994), 10.

24. Ibid.

25. See note 19 above.

26. See note 6, page 947, above.

27. See note 1, page 3, above.

28. Bob Ortega, "Dillard, Wal-Mart and Cifra in Venture to Open Department Stores in Mexico," *The Wall Street Journal* (October 17, 1994), B9.

29. See note 1, page 22, above.

30. See note 1, page 3, above.

31. See Huey in note 5 above.

32. See note 19, pages 76–88, above.

33. Ibid.

34. Ibid.

35. Staff, "Business Briefs: Wal-Mart," *The Wall Street Journal* (October 21, 1993), B4.

36. See note 19, pages 76–88, above.

37. M. Gladwell, "Wal-Mart Encounters a Wall of Resistance in Vermont," *Washington Post* (July 27, 1994), A3.

38. Ibid.

39. D. E. Shinkle, "Small-Town Supporter," *Washington Post* (July 5, 1993), A15.

40. Bob Ortega, "Wal-Mart Offers to Build Small Stores in Effort to Open Outlet in Vermont," *The Wall Street Journal* (August 11, 1994), B8.

41. S. L. MacLachlan, "Small Towns See Wal-Mart as Mixed Blessing," *The Christian Science Monitor* (September 14, 1993), 9.

42. Staff reporter, "Wal-Mart Cancels Store in Massachusetts Town," *The Wall Street Journal* (September 17, 1993), B7.

43. See note 41 above.

44. See note 19, pages 76–88, above.

45. Value Line Reports (May 27, 1994).

46. See note 1, page 2, above.

47. See note 45 above.

48. Francine Schwadel, "Attention K-Mart Shoppers: Style Coming to This Aisle," *The Wall Street Journal* (August 9, 1988), B6.

49. See Huey in note 5, page 61, above.

50. See "Wal-Mart Stores Penny Wise" in note 5 above.

51. See note 1, page 3, above.

Daewoo Group*

Daewoo, one of the Big Four *chaebol* in South Korea, is an industrial and service conglomerate that is active in trading, shipping, construction, telecommunications, financial services, hotels, manufacturing (including automobiles, auto parts, electronics, appliances, computers, and defense products), and heavy industries (including diesel engines, locomotives, construction equipment, industrial vehicles, aerospace, and shipbuilding). Daewoo Corporation, the major unit in the group, has a network of over 100 branch offices and subsidiaries and deals in around 3,500 products in over 160 countries. The company has aggressively expanded its global market through joint ventures all over the world.[1] Americans may be familiar with Daewoo through the cars the company has produced for General Motors under the Pontiac LeMans name. The following overview of Daewoo Group highlights the unique Korean organizational form—the *chaebol*—and an organization of growing importance worldwide.

HISTORICAL AND POLITICAL BACKGROUND

Daewoo's success is inseparable from South Korea's rapid transformation in the latter half of the twentieth century from an agrarian country racked by a long history of hostile invasions and lacking essential resources to a land where a centrally planned "economic miracle" has become a fact of life. Korea was divided by the Allies after World War II, and North Korea inherited all the country's natural resources in the territory north of the 38th parallel. Less than two years after the withdrawal of U.S. peacekeeping troops in 1948, North Korea, with a far stronger military force, began the Korean War. Peace was eventually restored in 1953, and the South Koreans, with the continuing fear of foreign invasion providing a powerful incentive, searched for economic prosperity. However, that search for prosperity was difficult. South Korea

---

*Prepared by Haesun Baek, Florida State University.

entered the 1960s with a crippling trade deficit and a domestic market too poor to support indigenous industries.

The current era of Korean industrialization and modernization began in 1961 after the downfall of the Syngman Rhee government. To boost development, the new government intervened to increase access to resources, promote exports, finance industrialization, and provide protection from competition. In the 1970s, Korean industrial policy added a new dimension — in exchange for loyalty to the government, specific individuals and companies were granted financial support and favorable treatment by the government. This led to the growth and consolidation of most of today's leading *chaebol*.[2]

The *chaebol* is a distinctive organizational form found in Korea. (See Chapter 8 for an extensive discussion of the *chaebol* and a comparison of it to other organizational forms.) *Chaebol* are largely family-based collections of large and diverse companies with extensive cross ownership and family ties.[3] The continued operation of a *chaebol* has depended on active government support and acceptance. The *chaebol* typically has one central leader, such as Woo-Choong Kim at Daewoo, who has nearly absolute authority. The relationship between the leader and the rest of the organization is paternalistic; the leader typically displays great concern for the welfare of the employees. *Chaebol* have a high degree of centralization, with centralized planning and control, oversight, and decision making. The *chaebol* leaders demonstrate a highly entrepreneurial orientation, with emphasis on ambition, vision, and political skills. *Chaebol* accounted for over 60 percent of Korea's GNP in the 1980s.[4] South Korea has more than fifty *chaebol*, but the Big Four, Hyundai Group, Lucky-Goldstar Group, Samsung Group, and Daewoo Group, dominate the economy.

It is important to emphasize the relationship between government and the success of the *chaebol*. Beginning in 1962, the South Korean government instigated a series of five-year plans and forced the *chaebol* to aim for a number of basic objectives. The government has played a key role in the creation and support of the *chaebol* as part of the national economic policy. In common with their Far East competitors, Hong Kong and Taiwan, South Korea's government has relied on a strategy that focuses attention on the importance of exports as the method to decrease the country's balance-of-trade gap and to strengthen domestic production. It is against this economic and political backdrop that Daewoo began its rise at the onset of the second five-year plan in 1967.

In order to understand Daewoo's meteoric rise, it is necessary to appreciate the place of the *chaebol* as the main method of implementing economic strategies. Government and politics have played key roles in paving the way to success for each of the leading *chaebol*. Incentives have been offered in the form of massive subsidies, apparently unlimited cheap credit, and protection against foreign competition. On the other hand, Daewoo has been forced to take over ailing companies and to enter industry sectors that the company would have preferred to leave to more appropriate competitors.

In some cases, the government has taken purely political action with respect to a *chaebol*. The power of the government can be illustrated by the fate of the Kukje Group. In 1985, the company, then the seventh largest *chaebol*, offended the military government of Chun Doo Hwan and was forced into bankruptcy. Kukje's error was its failure to support Chun Doo Hwan's pet rural development program called the New Village Movement.[5]

COMPANY HISTORY

The Daewoo Group was founded by Woo-Choong Kim, the current chairman, in 1967, and the company owes much of its success to its chairman. Although the initial capital investment in the company was a modest $18,000, Kim and his colleagues built Daewoo into a twenty-company group with $25 billion in annual sales by 1993.[6] Woo-Choong Kim is known to work 100-hour weeks and has not taken a vacation in over thirty years.[7] Until recently, Kim was known and admired for his hard work and dedication. He was also recognized as a modern folk hero in Korea. Early in the 1980s, he turned over a personal fortune estimated between $40 and $50 million to an independent medical and cultural foundation.[8]

Daewoo began trading in 1967 at the start of the second five-year plan and benefited from government-sponsored cheap loans by borrowing based on potential export profits. The company concentrated on the labor-intensive clothing and textile industries that provided high profit margins, while utilizing South Korea's major asset—its large workforce. A factory was set up in Pusan, an industrial city, and in 1968, 3.6 million shirts were made there each month. Daewoo contributed to South Korea's growing exports, which grew at a 38.6 percent annual rate during this period.[9]

GROWTH

The third and fourth phases of Korea's economic development ran from 1973 to 1981. The country's most significant resource, its supply of labor, was in high demand. However, competitors from Malaysia and Thailand began to erode Korea's comparative advantage in labor-intensive production as wages increased. The government responded by concentrating on mechanical and electrical engineering, shipbuilding, petrochemicals, and construction. This change in emphasis was designed to continue Korea's export-led expansion and to provide domestic industries with parts that previously had to be imported. A home-based defense industry was also a priority as plans were announced for the total withdrawal of the U.S. peacekeeping force.

Daewoo moved into construction, serving the New Village program to develop the country's infrastructure and, in a farsighted move, the rapidly growing African and Middle Eastern export markets. During this period Daewoo achieved its general trading company (GTC) status and received significant investment help from the Korean government. Subsidized loans and strict import controls aroused the anger of competing nations, but the *chaebol* were in need of protectionist policies if they were to survive this period of world recession, triggered by the oil crisis of 1973.

Government policy forced Daewoo into shipbuilding, an industry in which Hyundai and Samsung were better suited because of their greater expertise in heavy engineering. Kim's reluctance to take over the world's biggest shipyard at Okpo in 1980 is well documented, and his comment on the Korean government indicated a growing frustration as his entrepreneurial instinct was being stifled. However, Kim soon saw Daewoo Shipbuilding and Heavy Machinery earn a reputation for competitively priced ships and oil rigs that were often delivered ahead of schedule.

The 1980s were a decade of economic liberalization for Korea. Small private companies were encouraged, and Daewoo was forced to divest two of the textile companies that had contributed to its success. Protectionist import controls were loosened, and the government no longer practiced positive discrimination toward the shipbuilding industry. These moves were instigated to ensure an efficient allocation of resources in a free market and to force the *chaebol* to be more aggressive in their dealings abroad.

Today, the Daewoo Group consists of twenty principal member companies linked together in a complicated system of cross holdings. The group is involved in extensive international trading, with business interests in North America, South America, Europe, Africa, and Asia. The major company in the group is Daewoo Corporation, formed in 1981 by the merger of Daewoo Group's then-separate trading and construction companies. It traces its roots to the founding of the group in 1967 as a small-volume textile exporter. Table 1 shows the various divisions of the Daewoo Group.

JOINT VENTURES AND OVERSEAS EXPANSION

Daewoo responded to the challenge by establishing a number of joint ventures with U.S. and European companies. Kim's philosophy for the 1980s was that finished products would eventually lose their national identity as countries cooperated in design and manufacturing before exporting the goods to another country. In 1986, Daewoo Heavy Industries launched a $40 million Eurobond issue in order to expand exports of machine tools, defense products, and aerospace interests. The president of the company, Kyung Hoon Lee, hoped that the money would enable his company to move away from simply licensing products from abroad and to enter a new phase of complementary and long-term relationships with foreign companies.

The fifty-fifty joint venture with Sikorsky Aerospace illustrates the benefits of operating in partnership with a U.S. company. Daewoo started by building S-76 helicopters from parts imported from the U.S. and gradually began to produce these parts in Korea. As the Korean government has always regarded the defense industry as being of utmost importance, Daewoo received generous government subsidies to establish new factories. By the end of 1988, Daewoo had enough confidence in the skills it had learned in the Sikorsky project to announce that it would begin work on civilian helicopters and airplanes, which would be priced considerably cheaper than those produced by its U.S. counterparts.

Daewoo has used other methods to capture foreign markets. With excellent experience in turning around faltering companies in Korea, Daewoo acquired a controlling interest in the U.S. ZyMOS Corporation as a means of gaining the technical knowledge necessary for expanding into semiconductor design and manufacturing. Subsidiaries producing goods abroad, rather than acting as sales agents, have been established. The mid-1980s saw an increased emphasis on the motor vehicle industry. Although the government, fearful of arousing protectionist sympathies in its foreign markets, was reticent in announcing its ambitions publicly, it was clear that Korea was aiming to become one of the world's major car exporters before the end of the decade. The Japanese yen's rise also helped make Daewoo's already cheap exports even more attractive. Daewoo was not deterred by the difficulties inherent in setting up the required high-technology

■   TABLE 1
Daewoo Group Companies

Business Area	Company
Construction and trading	Daewoo Corporation
	Keanganam Ent. Ltd.
	Kynungnam Metal Co., Ltd.
	Daewoo Engineering Co.
Heavy machinery	Daewoo Heavy Ind., Ltd.
	Daewoo-Sikorsky Aerospace, Ltd.
	Daewoo Precision Ind., Ltd.
Electronics and electrical	Daewoo Electronics Co., Ltd.
	Daewoo Carrier Corp.
	Daewoo Electric Motor Ind., Ltd.
	Orion Electric Co., Ltd.
	Daewoo Electronic Components Co., Ltd.
Telecommunications	Daewoo Telecom Co., Ltd.
Automotive	Daewoo Motor Co., Ltd.
	Daewoo Automotive Components, Ltd.
	Koram Plastics Co., Ltd.
	Daewoo HMS Industries, Ltd.
	Dongheung Electric Co., Ltd.
Shipbuilding	Daewoo Shipbuilding & Heavy Mach., Ltd.
	Shia Shipbuilding Co., Ltd.
	Daewoo ITT Engineered Products, Ltd.
Financial	Daewoo Securities Co., Ltd.
	Daewoo Research Inst.
	Daewoo Investment & Finance Corp.
Chemicals and petroleum	Korea Steel Chemical Co., Ltd.
	Pungkuk Oil Co., Ltd.
Miscellaneous	Dongwoo Development Co., Ltd.
	Sorak Development Co., Ltd.

Source: Adapted from Richard M. Steers, Yoo Keun Shin and Gerardo R. Ungson, *The Chaebol: Korea's New Industrial Might* (New York: Harper & Row, 1989), 67.

production lines and relied on the experience gained in other parts of the group to set up sophisticated computer systems in a relatively short period of time. Korea's automobile industry ranked as the seventh highest car exporter and the sixth largest car manufacturing in the world, while the domestic and overseas demand for automobiles kept growing.[10]

DIVISIONAL STRUCTURE

The twenty-eight member companies in Daewoo Group are engaged in many diverse activities. Following are descriptions of the major companies and their operational activities.

DAEWOO CORPORATION

Daewoo Corporation is the trading and construction arm of the Daewoo Group Korea, a diversified manufacturing and services enterprise ranked among the world's fifty largest industrial business by *Fortune's* Global 500. As the group's flagship company, Daewoo Corporation has investments in and management links with other companies in the group.

In trading, Daewoo Corporation serves the manufacturing companies of the Daewoo Group, other manufacturers in Korea and abroad, and customers and suppliers in more than 100 countries. The company structures and executes complex multicountry trade, arranges project financing, and is active in countertrade. It provides both buyers and sellers with local market intelligence derived from a global network of its branch offices and subsidiaries. Daewoo Corporation promotes investments overseas by Daewoo Group companies and is a partner in international resource development projects. Daewoo Corporation has a network of over 100 branch offices and deals in around 3,500 products with over 160 countries. The key sources of export revenue include machinery, aircraft parts, steel, chemicals, electronics, appliances, and telecommunication equipment.

Daewoo Corporation is active at home and abroad in the construction of civil and architectural works, industrial plants, and development projects. The company has successfully completed construction assignments throughout Asia, North and South America, Middle Asia, and Africa.

DAEWOO HEAVY INDUSTRIES, LTD.

Daewoo Heavy Industries, the second largest member of the group, is involved in the manufacturing of diesel train engines, construction equipment, rolling stock, machine tools, industrial vehicles, and defense industry. Daewoo Heavy Industries has entered such areas as factory automation and system engineering, aerospace products, and new materials.

In the highly competitive market for machine tools, Daewoo has established an extensive dealership network in many countries to ensure steady expansion of sales of machine tools in the U.S., Europe, Asia, and Australia. In the area of construction equipment, Daewoo-brand excavators, forklifts, and skid-steer loaders have earned a wide reputation for their performance from overseas customers.

DAEWOO MOTOR CO., LTD.

Daewoo Motor Co. produces a variety of motor vehicles such as passenger cars, buses, heavy trucks, and special purpose vehicles. The company currently exports sedans, buses, and trucks to more than 100 countries. Daewoo was the first Korean automobile manufacturer to receive the International Standard Organization (ISO) 9001 certificate of quality for all processes, ranging from design to quality assurance.

Daewoo Motor Co., with Daewoo Corporation, has been promoting overseas production facilities, sales networks, and product localization programs. As a result,

Daewoo is constructing new plants in Uzbekistan, the Philippines, Iran, India, Vietnam, Romania, and China.[11]

The fifty-fifty joint venture with General Motors was initially one of Daewoo's most profitable links with a foreign company. In 1987, 247,000 Pontiac LeMans were built, and the car, based on a design by GM's German Opel division, was initially well received in the U.S. market. Demand for the LeMans soon faltered, and the joint venture ended in 1992 due to the problems of Korean policy toward foreign investment, the volatile domestic labor situation, red tape and government discrimination, and the piracy of technology transferred in the country.[12]

Despite the GM divorce, Daewoo's new vehicle exports rose in 1993 due to the big gains in South America and Asia.[13] Daewoo Corporation has established new local sales subsidiaries in Algeria, Chile, Venezuela, Colombia, the Philippines, and Thailand.

Daewoo is now promoting new model development for the European market in 1995 and for the North American market in 1996. For the coming century, Daewoo plans to become one of the world's top ten automobile manufacturers. Daewoo is continuing to promote expansion of overseas production plans to achieve its goal.

DAEWOO ELECTRONICS CO., LTD.

Daewoo Electronics produces various electronic and electric home appliances, electronic components, personal computers and peripherals, and home automation products. The company rapidly assumed the leadership position in the domestic high-tech electronics market, and its efforts in this area have been spreading to other nations as well.

Daewoo has production plants in Northern Ireland, China, France, Mexico, and Myanmar (Burma) for local production in electronics and home appliances, while it has major distribution centers and networks in the U.S., the U.K., France, and Germany.

DAEWOO SHIPBUILDING AND HEAVY MACHINERY, LTD.

Daewoo Shipbuilding and Heavy Machinery, Korea's second largest shipbuilder, suffered heavy losses in the late 1980s for two reasons: workers' demands for pay raises and sales of ships made at a loss to keep a steady supply of orders. The rapidly appreciating won (the Korean currency) and the bankruptcy of U.S. Lines in 1986 exacerbated the situation, which led to a crisis at Okpo shipyard. The Korean government's intervention and Kim's personal efforts turned around the company, and a profit was realized by 1992. The company won about 25 percent of worldwide shipbuilding orders in 1993. Most of the important orders it has are for the new generation of containership.

DAEWOO TELECOM, LTD.

A growing international name in switching and transmission, terminals, fiber optics, and cables and computers, Daewoo Telecom has exported over 600,000 personal computers to the U.S.

DAEWOO AUTOMOTIVE COMPONENTS, LTD.

To meet increasing demands for automotive parts and components, the company has expanded factory automation systems and now can supply major components for domestic and foreign carmakers.

DAEWOO SECURITIES CO., LTD.

Daewoo Securities is maintaining the lead among Korean securities in terms of market share and stock trading volume. The company also began investment consulting services with the establishment of Daewoo Capital Management Co., Ltd.

DONGWOO DEVELOPMENT CO., LTD.

Dongwoo Development Co. is in the tourism and leisure industry. Dongwoo has a management agreement with Hilton International for the operation of two major hotels in Korea, the Seoul Hilton Hotel and Kyongju Hilton Hotel. The Sonje Museum of Contemporary Art, located next to the Kyongju Hilton, is also under company management.

CULTURE

Daewoo has developed a unique culture among the competing *chaebol*. The company name means "Great Universe." In pursuit of the great universe, Chairman Kim has imbued the company with a spirit that combines elements of creativity, challenge, and sacrifice.[14]

Daewoo's culture can be summarized by a philosophy called Daewoo Spirit.[15] This spirit consists of a commitment to:

- *creativity* — creative thinking by people who are not afraid to consider and to try new approaches to meeting client needs;
- *challenge* — establishing high corporate and personal goals, working to achieve them, and seeing business problems as opportunities for further growth; and
- *sacrifice* — self-sacrifice to achieve long-term objectives that will result in the betterment of society for current and future generations.

Employees note that there is real substance to these values and that they guide employee behavior on the path to success. Along with the above-noted values, Kim espouses the notion of coprosperity whereby the company provides value to employees, customers, suppliers, partners, and the country as a whole.

However, the traditional work ethic that helped Korea reach economic prosperity has been threatened as workers have begun increasingly violent protests against years of long hours and low pay. After two workers at Daewoo Shipbuilding and Heavy

Machinery, Ltd. committed suicide in the 1980s, Kim devoted the better part of two years to develop a unique program to mend management-labor relations. He kept close to workers and their families and talked with them about work- and family-related matters. He used a similar approach to deal with autoworkers' problems after GM cut ties with Daewoo's automobile manufacturing unit.

Daewoo Motor Co., like its competitor Hyundai Motor Co., is requiring managers, including company presidents, to work on the assembly line. The company also gives assembly workers a chance to be promoted to the management level. These new policies aim to improve management-labor relations as well as help managers understand the difficulties and problems on the assembly line.

MANAGEMENT

Daewoo management's beliefs cannot be separated from Chairman Kim's personal beliefs, although Daewoo differs from other *chaebol* in that Kim is not perceived as an autocratic leader. He delegates tasks to well-trained managers and industry task forces. However, if a major crisis occurs in a company, Kim will devote his attention to that company until a solution is found.

Kim emphasizes the importance of self-sacrifice and hard work as motives to succeed in business.[16] He believes that young graduates from a country's best universities should dedicate themselves to adding value to society, possibly by inventing and producing what their nation and the world needs. The development of a sophisticated service sector is vital to emerging global economies such as Korea's.

Daewoo benefits from skilled management and is determined to attract the best domestically educated and expatriated young Koreans to guide the firm into the next century. Daewoo spends $6 million each year sending graduates abroad, usually to the U.S., so that they can further their studies and return with skills to lead effective research and development efforts.

Daewoo's strength includes a flexible and open-minded approach to new opportunities and experience in establishing joint ventures with foreign companies. The company's wide range of industries means that risks can be taken without fear of collapse of the whole group, and the synergy between different subsidiaries can be exploited to the benefit of the whole corporation.

COMPETITION

Korea is dominated by a small number of *chaebol* that manufacture almost everything, because trade restrictions limit what can be imported into Korea. For example, a 100 percent tariff on imported cars keeps Koreans buying Hyundai and Daewoo models. These restrictions have benefited Korean industry because they have forced the nation to strengthen its manufacturing infrastructure. Korean products are often perceived as being of lower quality than Japanese and Taiwanese products, but Koreans are working hard to change this image. More Korean companies are receiving ISO-9000 certification for their products, indicating that they comply with a European standard designed to assure the quality of suppliers. ISO-9002 ratings are for following quality guidelines in the product design process, and ISO-9001 certification is the most all inclusive, covering everything from design and manufacturing processes to inspection and after-sales services.[17]

As a result, Daewoo competes with other *chaebol* in every product and service it produces. In the domestic automobile market, Daewoo competes fiercely with Hyundai Motor Co. and Kia Motors Corp. The three companies released new models in early 1994: Hyundai's new subcompact Accent, Daewoo's luxury model Arcadia, and Kia's subcompact Avella.[18] As Samsung is about to enter the crowded car market, competition is expected to intensify. Samsung and Lucky-Goldstar are the major competitors in electronics and electric appliances. Hyundai and Ssanyong are competing with Daewoo in heavy industries and construction.

However, international demands for free trade, such as the General Agreement on Tariffs and Trade (GATT), are forcing the Korean government to open its markets. Soon, the *chaebol* will no longer enjoy the Korean government's protectionist import controls. Daewoo Group is already operating in a stagnant global market and is increasing its R&D expenditure to be more internationally competitive. Korean President Kim Young-Sam met with the chairmen of Samsung, Lucky-Goldstar, Daewoo, and Ssanyong groups in late 1993. As a result, the *chaebol* have banded together to increase the global competitiveness of Korean products.[19]

FINANCE

In order to bring innovation and flexibility to the dynamic world market, Daewoo enlarges its capital supply sources by diversifying its method of securing funds, including leasing and deferred payments. Daewoo has been able to reduce financing costs as well by streamlining and improving its basic capital procurement programs. Daewoo issues convertible bonds, bonds with warrants, medium-term notes, and other capital instruments to secure a long-term and stable supply of funds.[20]

Although Daewoo has relied on the domestic capital market for long-term funds, it is also looking abroad to tap new and low-cost sources of funds. It has raised funds successfully overseas for large foreign investments projects. In 1993, Daewoo Corporation and Daewoo Electronic Co. made a total of four international issues of convertible bonds and commercial paper; 75 million Swiss francs worth of convertible bonds in the Swiss market for a motorway project in Pakistan; $70 million worth of commercial paper in New York; $75 million worth of convertible bonds in London for its automotive plants in Uzbekistan and Vietnam; and $50 million worth of convertible bonds in the Eurobond market for projects in Pakistan and Malaysia.[21]

STRATEGIES

Daewoo launched its Vision 2000 program to implement a groupwide globalization campaign. The campaign includes foreign joint-venture production facilities, investing in foreign facilities, establishing sales and local subsidiaries, and localizing component production and other operations. The campaign is aimed at strengthening Daewoo's international competitiveness and streamlining the network of coordinated production, sales, and distribution. The campaign also contributes to local economic development. Daewoo expects to increase its foreign subsidiaries to 250 in 1995 and to 330 in 2000.[22]

Kim proposed in his speech to the 1993 *Business Week* Asia Symposium of Chief Executives in Shanghai the formation of an Asian Enterprise Council to promote greater pan-Asian cooperation. He emphasized the threat to Asian economic development due to increased trade restrictions among advanced nations and stressed that pan-Asian cooperation would counter potential restrictions on the region. He claimed that the time had come for Asian nations to maximize and share such advantages as large labor forces, abundant natural resources, and large production capabilities. He proposed a "Made in Asia" label that would be the result of interregional cooperation in technology, production, and marketing. Despite the difficulties of forming such a regional system, Kim argues that such a system would contribute to greater international cooperation and economic growth rather than create confrontations in the region. He emphasized the importance of China's role in a proposed cooperative system based on China's tremendous potential as a producer, a consumer, and a contributor to the foundation of common prosperity and cooperation throughout the Asian region.

Kim, himself, travels vigorously to promote joint ventures, investments, and other projects. He traveled to at least thirty different countries in 1993, including nine trips to China, six to Japan, five to Russia, and five to Uzbekistan.

While Daewoo struggles to improve its image of poor quality, it has shifted its focus from industrial nations to the third world markets.[23] Daewoo also backed away from several projects in Russia, discovering the myriad difficulties that hinder business activity there.

Harsh tax penalties, contradictory rules, and onerous environmental regulations have prompted Daewoo to switch its emphasis in Russia from investment to sales. However, Russia is $400 million behind schedule in paying back a loan from Korea.[24]

Other moves made by Daewoo include the introduction of home appliance products that it claims are environmentally and biologically friendly and the hiring of several foreign experts. Ulrich Bez, who led research and development efforts at both Porsche AG and Bayerische Motoren Werke (BMW) AG, was hired as research director, and Pat Farrel was hired to head its advertising team and launch a marketing campaign in the U.K. Russian engineers were hired to help develop a 100-seat turboprop transport aircraft that will be commercially available by 1998.[25] Daewoo also is developing a plan to counter possible trade limitations imposed by the North American Free Trade Agreement and by the European Economic Community.[26] Daewoo Electronics established eight international subsidiaries to develop local production, research, sales, and service networks.

TECHNOLOGY

In order to boost international competitiveness, Daewoo Group established the Institute for Advanced Engineering (IAE) in 1992. IAE combines research collaboration among industry, educational institutions, and research organizations. The institute is the group's technology think tank to implement Daewoo technology, which includes three key strategies and directions for technical development: maximum competitiveness through first-class development, development of domestic and international technology networks, and technical managerial system development.

IAE is currently developing mid- and long-term plans and strategies for goals to develop technology in four strategic areas, to pioneer advanced industrial development in Korea, and to set a firm foundation for the Daewoo Group's long-term growth. The four core areas of R&D are electronic signal processing for electronic imaging and mobile telecommunications, manufacturing technology for industrial automation and manufacturing processes, electric power systems for nuclear power systems, and integrated gasification combined cycle power generation systems and other futuristic energy production facilities.

In 1993, Daewoo Group received eight ISO certificates and one GS (German Standard) certificate as the group endeavored to meet international recognition for quality products and systems based on advanced technology. The certificates received by Daewoo were the following: ISO-9000 for color and black-and-white TV tubes and for monitors (Orion Electric Co.); ISO-9001 for its ships and offshore structures (Daewoo Shipbuilding and Heavy Machinery); GS for skidloaders (Daewoo Heavy Industries); ISO-9000 for construction management systems (Daewoo Heavy Industries); ISO-9001 for its production system in a microwave oven plant (Daewoo Electronic Co.); ISO-9002 for production processes (Euro Daewoo, a Belgium subsidiary of Daewoo Heavy Industries); ISO-9001 for all its personal computers (Daewoo Telecom); ISO-9001 for its complete line of numerical control lathes and machining centers (Daewoo Heavy Industries); and ISO-9001 for all of its passenger cars, the first in Asia.[27]

TOWARD THE FUTURE

Daewoo entered the 1990s facing more problems. The company is heavily leveraged. This may in part be because it has not marketed itself as well as its competitors Hyundai, Lucky-Goldstar, and Samsung. Some of Daewoo's major markets are stagnant, and expenditures on R&D must be increased if the company is to remain competitive. Continuing labor unrest and changes in government policy add to Daewoo's worries. The tight link between government and the *chaebol* is now coming back to haunt Daewoo.

The most recent, and perhaps most damaging, charge is that chairman Kim allegedly paid $13 million in campaign contributions to former president Roh Tae Woo in exchange for a large government contract to build a submarine base.[28] Chairman Kim will likely face extensive questioning regarding Daewoo's role in propping up the Roh Tae Woo government and suppressing dissent. It appears that an increasingly democratic Korean society will no longer tolerate this sort of collusion between government and the *chaebol*. Meanwhile, Kim continues to explore new ventures for Daewoo. As news of the investigation and Roh's arrest broke, Kim was in Poland discussing a possible Daewoo automobile assembly venture.[29]

Questions for Discussion

1. Which environmental factors have been critical to Daewoo's emergence as a major force in Korean and world business?
2. How are Daewoo's structure and mix of divisions different from that in a typical U.S. or Japanese firm? How are they similar? (Think about companies like Ford, General Motors, Toyota, or Nissan.)
3. As the Korean economy matures and the Korean people gain a greater share of the economic well-being, what could happen to the Daewoo culture?
4. If you were the head of Daewoo, what potential problems or events would raise significant concerns for you? Why? What actions could you possibly take to lessen the impact of those problems or events?

REFERENCES

1. Daewoo Corporation, "Daewoo: A Global Company for Trading, Manufacturing and Resource Development," (Seoul, Korea: Daewoo Corporation, 1993).

2. Richard M. Steers, Yoo Keun Shin, and Gerardo R. Ungson, *The Chaebol: Korea's New Industrial Might* (New York: Harper & Row, 1989), 27–28, 66.

3. Benjamin Gomes-Casseres, "State and Markets in Korea," Harvard Business School case 9-387-181 (Boston: President and Fellows of Harvard College, 1987).

   See note 2, pages 37–46, above.

4. Laxmi Nakarmi, "South Korea's New Destination: The Wild Blue Yonder," *Business Week* (September 11, 1989): 50.

5. See note 2, pages 42–43, above.

6. Andreas Loizou, "Daewoo Group," *International Directory of Company Histories*, ed. by Thomas Derdak (New York: St. James Press, 1991), vol. 3, page 457.

7. See note 2, page 66, above.

8. See note 2, pages 66–69, above.

9. Woo-Choong Kim, "Every Street is Paved with Gold," *Success* 39, no. 8, page 62.

10. Ron Corben, "Carmakers on a Roll, but Pressures Grow," *Journal of Commerce and Commercial* (August 9, 1994): 9A.

11. Suman Dubey, "Daewoo Motor Plans to Manufacture, Sell Automobiles in India," *The Asian Wall Street Journal Weekly* 16, no. 24 (1994), page 19.

    Richard Johnson, "Daewoo to Build Cars in Vietnam; GM, Chrysler Eye Deals," *Automotive News* (March 14, 1994): 6.

    "Daewoo Makes Romanian Deal," *The New York Times* (February 16, 1994), C9.

    Oles Gadacz, "Daewoo Builds in Philippines," *Automotive News* (October 11, 1993): 2.

    "Daewoo Group's China Venture," *The Wall Street Journal* (September 27, 1993), A9.

"Auto Venture Planned in Iran," *The New York Times* (July 8, 1994), C14.

12. "Foreign Investment," *Business Korea* 10, no. 4 (1992): 7.

13. Oles Gadacz, "Daewoo Boosts Exports Despite GM Divorce," *Automotive News* (October 11, 1993): 16.

14. See note 2, page 69, above.

15. Oles Gadacz, "Korean Executives Work on Assembly Line," *Automotive News* (May 30, 1994): 48.

16. "Daewoo's Chairman Accents Self-Sacrifice," *Business Korea* 11, no. 10 (1994): 47.

17. John C. Dvorak, "Seoul Man," *PC Magazine* 13, no. 1 (1994): 91.

18. "Launch of New Models Intensifies Competition," *Business Korea* 11, no. 10 (1994): 32.

19. "President Kim Warms up to Chaebol Leaders," *Business Korea* 11, no. 6 (1993): 40.

20. Daewoo Corporation Annual Report (1993), 6.

21. "News From Daewoo," *Highlights* 3, no. 13 (1993): 13.

22. Mi-Young Ahn, "Terrific Trio Lead Revival: Daewoo Has Pulled Itself Out of a Pit of Despair. Now . . . ," *Asian Business (Hong Kong)* 30, no. 8 (1994): 12.

23. Steve Glain, "Strategic Move; Daewoo Group Shifts Its Focus to Markets in the Third World; Korean Giant . . . ," *The Wall Street Journal* (October 11, 1993), A1.

24. Jeff Lilley, "What Is to Be Done? South Korean Companies Find Russia a Quagmire," *Far Eastern Economics Review* 157, no. 24 (1994): 77.

25. Namju Cho, "Korean Appliance Makers Find Peddling Green Pays," *The Asian Wall Street Journal Weekly* 16, no. 27 (1994), 6.

    Oles Gadacz, "Bez Brings Porsche Skills to Daewoo's Ambitious Plans," *Automotive News* (June 6, 1994): 51.

    Alex Benady, "Daewoo Lists Ad Trio for 20m Pounds Sterling UK Assault," *Marketing* (August 4, 1994): 1.

    Steve Glain, "South Korea Imports Russian Engineers in Quest to Develop Export Quality Commercial Aircraft," *The Asian Wall Street Journal Weekly* 16, no. 8 (1994), 18.

26. Sang-Kyun Chun, "Establishing an International Presence," *Business Korea* 11, no. 2 (1993): 43.

27. See note 21 above.

28. Nicholas D. Kristof, "Seoul Ex-Leader Taken in Custody in Kickback Case," *The New York Times* (November 17, 1995), A1, A8.

    "Former South Korean President Charged in Scandal," *Chicago Tribune* (November 17, 1995), 4.

29. Ibid.

■ C A S E 3

General Motors: From Riches to Rags to . . . *

In August of 1994, *Motortrend* magazine published a comparison of several luxury automobiles: the Lexus GS300, the Mercedes-Benz C280, and the recently introduced Aurora from General Motors' Oldsmobile Division. The two imports were chosen to represent the best Japanese and European cars in this class. In what can be best described as a surprise outcome, the Aurora was chosen as best overall.[1] *Road and Track* concurred when it hailed the Aurora as the "Dawn of a new day at Oldsmobile."[2] Since their introduction in the spring of 1994, the Aurora and its two-door variant, the Buick Riviera, have surprised and impressed both their target buyers and the automotive press.

What makes this event so surprising and important is the widely held belief that General Motors, long the dominant force in both U.S. and world automotive markets, had lost its edge. GM's domestic market share had dropped from 47 percent in 1979 to 34.7 percent in 1989.[3] It was perceived as producing lackluster, look-alike vehicles of mediocre quality and tepid styling. Customer satisfaction had for a long time lagged well behind that of the Japanese and European competitors. Understanding how General Motors first gained, then lost, and is now attempting to regain ascendancy leads to several organizational questions. How and why did GM fall from the top? What changes took place that led to an organization that could now produce these and other exciting vehicles? What are the lessons of General Motors' experiences? As a case study in organizational theory, General Motors illustrates almost any principle within the discipline. However, some issues are more prominent than others: (1) how history repeats itself; (2) how environmental change drives technological change that, in turn, must lead to structural change; and (3) how changes in the level of competition drive internal organizational change. These principles are best understood by first recalling the early days of General Motors.

---

*Prepared by Thomas Debbink, University of Cincinnati.

1908–1920: TWO STRIKES AND YOU'RE OUT

On September 8, 1908, William C. Durant formed a holding company, General Motors, under which he organized his growing interests in several pioneering automobile firms. Within eighteen months, General Motors took over effective control of several independent companies: Buick, Oldsmobile, Cadillac, Oakland (later to become Pontiac), six other automobile companies, three truck firms, and ten parts and accessory companies. Ten years later, driven by Durant's relentless and single-minded strategy of acquisition, General Motors had grown to be the fifth largest industrial enterprise in the United States.[4] Durant's basic strategy was the same one that had made him successful as a carriage maker. Through extensive vertical integration, he would own his critical suppliers and would thus reduce uncertainty surrounding acquisition of components. With upstream integration to ensure his parts supply, he pursued downstream control though the acquisition of the retail sales and distribution network.[5]

Unfortunately, Durant, for all his talent at acquiring the key components of this future automotive giant, paid little or no attention to making it work in a coordinated fashion. Division managers, who were often legendary entrepreneurs themselves, were left to run their own operations, with little or no coordination of products, schedules, production, inventories, or marketing. Only the grace of booming demand for cars allowed this confused amalgam of manufacturing operations to continue. When a slight downturn in the market occurred in 1910, Durant could no longer pay his suppliers or workforce and was forced to seek financial help from several banks. This humiliated the swashbuckling entrepreneur who saw bankers as visionless, myopic thorns in his side.[6] To protect their interests, the banks rescued Durant but forced him out of General Motors' management.[7] The bankers attempted to create a management structure to govern and coordinate the divisions, but they were thwarted in their efforts by the same fiercely independent division managers that Durant could not control.

By 1916, Durant was back in charge and continued his vertical integration strategy through acquisition of more component manufacturers. In 1920, history repeated itself when a market downturn precipitated a crisis within GM. Again, the organization was crippled by massive inventories and uncontrolled capital spending. The price of GM stock plummeted, and after spending over $90 million of his own money to support the price of GM stock, on November 20, 1920, William Durant was forced to resign as president of General Motors.[8] In an attempt to restore the confidence of the financial community, Pierre du Pont, a respected businessman, was persuaded to come out of retirement to head the company.

1920–1925: FROM CHAOS TO COORDINATION

One of the first actions of the board of directors under du Pont was to approve a plan for General Motors' organizational structure that had been formulated by one of the division managers, Alfred Sloan, Jr. Sloan's plan was founded on two principles. Seeking to promote product innovation and competition, the plan dictated that division general managers would have complete autonomy in operating decisions. Each of the major divisions was to be an independent profit center, with the general manager's compensation largely influenced by its division's profitability. To counteract the potential ill effects of this autonomy, the second principle stated that decisions regarding corporate policies would be the exclusive purview of the central headquarters staff.

The twin principles of decentralized operating decision making and centralized policy formation became the foundation for corporate governance at General Motors and, by imitation, at hundreds of other firms.[9] The structure included provisions for standardized accounting procedures, controls on capital spending, and the establishment of several oversight committees at the corporate level. Interestingly, as part of the implementation of the structure, the division heads of Oldsmobile, Oakland, Cadillac, and Chevrolet were fired.[10] Their replacements were undoubtedly less inclined toward defying centralized control.

Sloan also introduced a new marketing structure that gave clear definition to each of the company's brands. The idea was that Chevrolet and Pontiac would produce entry-level vehicles; Oldsmobile and Buick would offer progressively fancier cars; and the height of luxury would be produced by Cadillac. Thus, while Ford focused on reducing cost and price through high-volume production, GM followed a strategy of market niche differentiation. The concept was embodied in the phrase "a car for every purse and purpose."[11] As consumers became more affluent, they could make sure their friends knew it by progressing from a Chevrolet, to a Buick, and possibly, even to a Cadillac.

By 1925, the structure and marketing strategy that would see the corporation through the next six decades was in place. That this strategy and structure were successful is best reflected in GM's average return on net worth of 20.7 percent, twice that of all manufacturing in the thirty years following World War II.[12] With a market share often approaching or exceeding 50 percent, GM could basically dictate the rules by which Ford and Chrysler would play. They, in effect, ran the game. A number of favorable circumstances made this possible. Continuously improving prosperity within the U.S. automotive market created a pool of upwardly mobile consumers who responded well to the strategy of trying to move the buyers progressively upmarket. Further, the postwar industrial devastation of the rest of the world effectively created an isolated U.S. market that was only internally competitive. This combination of a ready market and a less competitive industry did not encourage the automakers to pursue expensive and radical product, process, or organizational innovations. Essentially, the basic structure of cars remained unchanged from the thirties until the late seventies. Thus, the same organizational structure that was effective in 1925 continued to work well into the seventies.

1973–1991: THE DINOSAURS' FIRST SNOWFALL

As students of organizations, we are bound to wonder how General Motors, for years heralded as one of the best-run companies in the world, could be so totally paralyzed in the face of the changing environment it faced in the seventies and eighties. In a sense, that is a question that answers itself. The noted strategic scholar, Michael Porter, has said, "the number one enemy to companies is the quiet life—long periods of rest and stability."[13] It is precisely GM's success and market power that led to its inability to deal with change. GM's fabulous success had led to the accumulation of unprecedented levels of organizational "slack." Just as a bear's fat allows it to effectively ignore the winter's cold, GM's slack allowed it to ignore the changing environment. But if the winter lasts longer than expected, the bear may run short of fat. In GM's case, slack began to run out in the 1980s.

In 1910, there were more than 200 firms making and selling automobiles in the U.S. By 1930, there were fewer than 25, and the largest 7 accounted for 90 percent of the sales. From after World War II until the early seventies, Ford, Chrysler, and GM shared 90 percent of the market.[14] As such, they could basically set the rules for competition. GM was the unquestioned leader of this automotive oligopoly. Ford and Chrysler would follow GM's price leadership, and all three could pass along their costs to the final customer because of the lack of significant foreign competition. General Motors, leveraging its market power and vertically integrated structure, became one of the most powerful organizations in the world. When the president of General Motors, "Engine" Charlie Wilson, stated in 1952, that "What is good for the country is good for General Motors and vice versa,"[15] his thoughts reflected a corporate culture steeped in arrogance and contempt for the outside world. During this period of steady market growth, Americans preferred ever-larger, more powerful cars, and GM was only too happy to fulfill this need. Everyone "knew" there wasn't any money to be made in small cars; so they were content to concede a small part of the market to the likes of VW and Renault.[16]

Throughout the sixties and early seventies, consumers' taste in cars began to evolve. Not only were people more concerned about gas mileage, environmental issues, and safety, they were of the growing opinion that the automakers were not as socially responsible as they should be. Ralph Nader, in his attack on GM's Corvair, led the charge in creating a negative public image of General Motors. GM's response of hiring a private investigator to see if it could discredit Nadar bespeaks the arrogance of top management.[17] The Vega, introduced as an import fighter and touted as "the small car that does everything well," didn't do much of anything well. Utilizing unproven engine technology and a bare-bones approach to engineering design, General Motors managed to produce a car that was almost guaranteed to rust out and/or burn oil excessively within 50,000 miles. Consumers were disgusted. The fact that GM sold millions of Vegas between 1970 and 1976 reflects the lack of alternative choices in the market at that time. The culture of arrogance is understandable; GM could build shoddy cars inefficiently and simply pass on both the vehicle and the cost to its customers.

All domestic auto manufacturers faced a variety of problems throughout the seventies and eighties. Increased government regulations called for cleaner, safer, more efficient cars. Consumers were becoming increasingly sensitized to the industry's performance in areas of social responsibility and ecology. Two particularly significant changes were the increase in gas prices precipitated by the Arab oil embargo of 1973 and the increased competition from Japanese vehicles. The refusal of the Arab states to ship oil following the Arab-Israeli War of 1973 drove oil prices to previously unimagined levels. In 1971, the price of oil was $2.10 a barrel. By 1981, it was $34.00.[18] The energy crisis vaulted gas mileage over features like power and styling in car buyers' minds almost over night. In an industry where it took five to six years to create a new vehicle, this was a problem. The base technology utilized in cars really hadn't changed much since the

1920s. Almost all cars were designed with a body attached to a separate frame, with a front engine driving the rear wheels. It was not very efficient, but it was durable and easy to build. If the automakers were to respond to people's interest in gas mileage, it became apparent that the basic vehicle design would have to change. Front-wheel drive, though more complex and foreign to the Big Three, offered equal passenger and luggage room in a smaller, lighter car. To further reduce weight, it was apparent that unibody construction, wherein the vehicle body supports the vehicle rather than relying on an independent chassis, would have to be used.

General Motors introduced its first front-wheel drive cars, the Chevrolet Citation and the Pontiac 6000, in 1980. The next generation of smaller front-wheel drive cars, the Cavalier and Sunbird, was introduced in 1982. Although the cars were reasonably well received by the market, they had been extremely difficult to bring to market. Part of the difficulty was due to the degree of cooperation required to produce a front-wheel drive versus a rear-wheel drive car. Previously, one group would design and build the chassis, engine, and transmission while another did the body. Furthermore, all the GM car divisions had independent staffs for these functions. At one point there was a total of nine design-and-build centers for engines alone.[19] Although vehicle assembly was coordinated by one division, General Motors Assembly Division (GMAD), there was little or no cooperation across divisions. This had been a bit of a problem with rear-wheel drive cars, but with front-wheel drive cars it was a showstopper. The difficulties in trying to design, engineer, and build new designs within the old organization structure were undeniable.

In 1982, Jim McDonald, then president of GM, initiated a study to create a new structure for the organization. In January of 1984 after exhaustive study and validation of its plans by the best consultants available, GM initiated its first major structural change in over sixty years. The six car divisions, along with the separate body division were merged into two major groups: Chevrolet, Pontiac & GM of Canada (CPC) and Buick, Olds & Cadillac (BOC). CPC would focus on smaller to midsize vehicles while BOC would build larger cars. (Wags inside the company quipped that CPC actually stood for "cheap plastic cars" and BOC for "big old cars.") Thus, increasing gas prices led to a change in product technology that necessitated a change in organizational structure.

The second major shock to the U.S. auto industry was what has become known as the "Japanese invasion." Toyota's initial attempt to sell cars in the U.S. market in 1955 was a disaster. The small, underpowered vehicles were ill equipped for America's high-speed roads and harsh climate. It would be seven more years before it would return with its first successful vehicle, the Corona.[20] The share of the American car market held by foreign manufacturers rose from 15 percent in 1972 to 27 percent by 1981.[21] U.S. auto executives were incredulous. It is said that "the eye cannot see what the mind will not perceive." As a group they couldn't imagine that people would actually buy small imported cars in large numbers. They blamed high oil prices and insisted that Americans would soon tire of their fascination with Toyotas, Hondas, and Nissans and return to the fold, as it were. Years of complacency and conservativism had blinded them to the fact that the market they were selling to was becoming truly competitive. Consumers gleefully defected from U.S. vehicles to purchase and extol the virtues of Japanese products. The U.S. manufacturers' oligopoly was over and, like dinosaurs experiencing their first snowfall, they were befuddled. Nothing in their corporate upbringing had given them a frame of reference for interpreting these changes. Japanese labor cost advantages or the actions of the Japanese government were two of the more popular reasons to which the success of these foreign cars was attributed.[22] It is little wonder that an organization such as GM, which didn't even have a consumer market research staff until 1985, would be out of touch with its customers.[23]

Thus, in the mid-eighties GM was beset by the double problems of having to restructure itself and deal with a newly competitive market. It was ill-equipped to tackle either. The 1984 reorganization was a disaster. Over the years, GM's bureaucracy had grown like an intricate coral reef. Getting anything done within the complex web of approvals and committees was almost impossible. Those managers who could really get things accomplished were those who understood how to circumvent the system. What *was* accomplished was done through an informal competence network.[24] The effect of the reorganization was to "kick over the ant hill" of this competence network. The organizational deck was so thoroughly shuffled that people no longer knew who to contact to get anything done. General Motors was essentially frozen for eighteen months while the organization tried to rebuild its competence networks.[25]

As mentioned, GM never fully understood its customers in the seventies and early eighties. Similarly, top management didn't understand its own internal culture. Years of steady growth and market leadership had bred a culture in which there was no reward for taking a risk and every penalty for failure. To say that the culture was risk averse would be an understatement of monumental proportions. Success was assured by supporting one's boss at all times and not bringing up any problems for which there was not an existing solution, hence, the carefully scripted executive meetings where the rule was "No Surprises!".[26] This type of a culture, while supportable in a predictable, benevolent environment, is utterly unable to deal with radical change. That this culture was not understood was reflected in the fact that there was a conscious decision, led by the financial staff, that the 1984 reorganization would not deal with the approximately 3,000 people within the corporate staffs. Unfortunately, this was also the group most wedded to the entrenched, dysfunctional culture.[27] Although some people associated with the reorganization understood that the problems were both cultural and structural, organizational charts proved to be more easily altered than people's thought paradigms.

1990–1992: OLD DOGS TRY TO LEARN NEW TRICKS

On August 1, 1990, Robert Stempel took over as chairman of the board of General Motors. Stempel, a career-long "car guy" promoted his long-time friend and colleague, Lloyd Ruess, to the job of president. The board allowed this promotion but rather conspicuously displayed a lack of confidence in Ruess by withholding the traditionally added title of chief operating officer. The board would never develop confidence in Ruess, and as will be seen, this undoubtedly contributed to Stempel's eventual demise.

Stempel's tenure as chairman was turbulent at best. The organization lurched from one crisis to another in a desperate attempt to regain its effectiveness before the investment community could realize the true magnitude of its troubles. GM's market share had fallen from an industry-leading share in the high forties to only 36.1 percent—the lowest it had been since the Great Depression. It took GM thirty-five labor hours to assemble its recently redesigned midsized cars, whereas Ford could assemble its new Taurus in just eighteen.[28] The company's continued financial success was based on contributions from the European operations: its data systems subsidiary—EDS; its defense subsidiary—Hughes; the financial arm—GM Acceptance Corporation; and most dangerously, some rather questionable accounting changes that had been made during the late eighties. Conspicuously absent from this profitable group was the North American Operations, the core of its vehicle-making business. Furthermore, General Motors' "good news culture"[29] prevented the organization from honestly and openly dealing with its problems. This "good news culture" grew out of a habit of punishing the bearers of bad news. It is little wonder that the more savvy managers learned early in their careers not to bring up a problem for which they had no solution. As though his challenge wasn't great enough, the day after Stempel took over as chairman, Iraq invaded Kuwait, an act that would eventually lead the U.S. into the Gulf War and seriously diminish the car market for the next six months.

Undaunted, Stempel set about the task of reviving the organization. In November of 1990, he bit a long-overdue bullet and took a write-off against earnings of $2.1 billion to cover the cost of closing seven assembly plants. Clearly, an organization that only had 36.1 percent of the market did not need the productive capacity that it had when its market share was 45 percent. The Gulf War had driven the auto market to its deepest slump since 1982. In February of 1991, Stempel was forced to announce a 47 percent cut in GM's common stock dividend. He also slashed executive bonuses and continued with plans to cut 15,000 people from GM's salaried staff by 1993. Despite these actions and other pronouncements about change, the board was unconvinced that the strategy would work.

Throughout 1991, the outside members of the board of directors became increasingly concerned and vocal regarding the lack of action. This represented a complete departure from the traditional GM board that had been more given to blindly ratifying management's proposals than trying to truly understand the business. GM's North American Operations had lost a mindnumbing $12.5 billion in 1991. In terms of cash flow, GM had bled *$462,000 an hour* for the entire year. Its market share had dropped to 35 percent from 45 percent just seven years earlier.[30] Most of all, the optimistic assurances of top management had taken on a thoroughly hollow ring. As the year wore on, the news only got worse. In November, the Standard and Poor's credit rating agency announced that it was considering snatching away GM's top drawer A-1 credit rating for its commercial paper. This move would significantly increase GM's capital costs and thereby its operating costs. By December, it was clear that the stock market had lost confidence in GM's leadership. General Motors' common stock hit a four-year low. In an effort to rebuild the market's trust, on December 18, 1991, Bob Stempel announced that GM would close twenty-one North American factories and eliminate 74,000 jobs over the next three years. This event became known as the "Christmas Massacre."[31] Although it was a bold statement, it had come too late and too reluctantly to appease the board. In January 1992, the outside members of the board of directors began to meet separately. They were increasingly convinced that the current management team did not possess the thinking to create the changes that would revive General Motors.

Stempel was not comfortable with the board's detailed interest in the company's affairs. GM boards had grown so complacent and detached that "It seemed more likely that Elvis would be found alive than that GM's board would stage a revolt against management."[32] But that was exactly what was happening. Inspired by corporate governance guru, Ira Millstein, John Smale, an outside director and former chairman of the board at Procter & Gamble, began to conduct detailed interviews with about twenty members of top management. His findings were shocking. On March 22, 1992, he reported to the outside directors that GM had a yawning quality gap with its competitors; it was by far the least efficient manufacturer; GM was far slower at developing new products; and it wasn't evident that Stempel's plans for a remedy would fix the problems. That was enough. The board resolved to act. In April, the outside directors forced Stempel to demote Ruess, along with two other long-time financial managers, Alan Smith and Bob O'Connell. They installed Jack Smith, then director of the hugely successful European operations, as president.[33] In telling his long-time friends the bad news, Stempel reflected his own lack of understanding about the situation at GM and the board's resolve. He remarked, "They've panicked. They're being totally unreasonable."[34]

Jack Smith wasted no time in making sweeping changes. Just as in the early part of the century, the individual divisions had become completely focused on their own operations. Cooperation among divisions was lacking. And just as Sloan did some seventy years earlier, Smith centralized decision making. To accomplish this, he created a fourteen-person strategy board to make all important decisions. This "fully functioning decision making body" was a far cry from the old GM committees wherein nothing was suggested that hadn't been preapproved by everyone in the room.[35] The strategy board meetings were characterized by lively and often contentious debate. Smith strongly promoted benchmarking as a process to compare GM's products and their costs with those of other manufacturers to determine where improvements could be made. Further, he did away with the old system of individual divisions as profit centers. In the future, there would be only one profit center, the North American Operations, and it would report its financial results separately from the rest of the corporation. No more hiding behind the profitability of the other operations. Again echoing Sloan's changes in the early twenties, Smith sought to leverage GM's market strength with its suppliers. Smith installed Ignaki Lopez, a firebrand Spaniard, as director of purchasing and centralized the purchasing functions. Lopez sought to repeat the success he had had in reducing GM's purchased parts cost in Europe by aggressively leveraging GM's volume with its suppliers. Contracts were torn up and rebid for almost everything. (Lopez later ran afoul of both GM and the law when he moved to Volkswagen and was accused of stealing trade secrets from GM.) Finally, in an effort to rationalize the confused and often overlapping product lines, Smith pushed the reduction of the number of vehicle platforms from twelve to five. Any future product proposals would have to demonstrate that they fulfilled a unique market need within the corporation's portfolio. This was an attempt to avoid one car division "stealing" sales from another.[36]

While Smith fomented a whirlwind of change, Stempel seemed shocked into paralysis. In a report to the outside directors in June, Smale reflected delight with Smith but stated, "Bob Stempel doesn't show any signs of being a change maker."[37] Stempel seemed to be too mired in the old GM model of the world and thought that things would get better if given enough time. They always had in the past. He had a plan in place and couldn't understand why the board wouldn't leave him alone. His attempt to distance himself from the board only made matters worse. Lacking any clear communication from Stempel regarding plans to address some very urgent problems, the board concluded that there was no plan. During one meeting with Smale, in response to a very urgent question, Stempel replied that he didn't have a worst-case scenario response, because it wouldn't be realistic. In that moment Bob Stempel sealed his fate.[38] Soon the media caught wind of Stempel's lack of standing. Rumors started to fly that he would be replaced. All the media hype along with the internal distraction it created were hampering General Motors in accomplishing its tasks. Toward the Fall, it became obvious to even Stempel that his relationship with the board was an irretrievable loss. On Friday, October 23, 1992, Bob Stempel, age fifty-nine, having spent thirty-five years with GM, tendered his resignation. No chairman since William Durant, seventy-two years earlier, had ever been dumped. But no chairman since Durant had been faced with such radical environmental change, armed with such a totally unprepared executive staff.

PROGNOSIS: EXTINCTION OR SURVIVAL; CAN DINOSAURS ADAPT?

Throughout the eighties GM continued to lose market share and its wealth. Its loss of market share between 1982 and 1992 amounted to a revenue loss of about $13 billion in a normal car-buying year.[39] In 1992, GM only made money on one vehicle, $28 per unit on full-sized trucks. Contrast that against losses of almost $4,000 per unit on the high-volume Saturn cars.[40] Although GM was profitable in the third quarter of 1994, it continued to lose money on the core North American Operations. The financial market has not failed to notice, particularly when Ford and Chrysler are prospering. GM has launched new versions of its bread-and-butter vehicles but only after costly delays due to manufacturing and quality problems. While Chrysler developed its new Cirrus in thirty-six months, it took GM almost forty-eight months to bring its new Cavalier to market.[41] GM continues to be the high-cost producer in the industry. In late October 1994, GM stock dropped 16 percent in ten days, a clear signal that the market is disappointed with its performance.[42]

Recent events have undoubtedly been like a slug of Jolt cola for top management. Although their latest products have struck a chord with buyers and the automotive press, the product design people seem to have written a check that the production side of the business can't cash. The Aurora/Riviera production facility in Lake Orion, Michigan, was only able to produce 4,000 vehicles in the first four months of production. Some of the problems are due to suppliers, which were selected by Lopez based on low price, that subsequently have not performed. Parts shortages and quality problems plague production of the newly introduced Chevrolet Lumina and Monte Carlo. Although production started in February of 1993, by June, GM had only reached 66 percent of its targeted production rate of 4,500 vehicles per week. This loss of production has been estimated to have cost GM $1.5 billion in lost revenue.[43]

Clearly, GM has made monumental structural changes over the last decade. That these changes have not been effective in revitalizing the North American Operations is reflected in Maryann Keller's observation, "GM North America has a long way to go before it reaches the point where it has placed all the right people in the right jobs. Until it does, it can't begin to realize its potential."[44] GM's future success and very existence hinge on whether or not it will be able to effectively adapt to its environment; to effect those organizational and cultural changes that will allow it to prosper.

Questions for Discussion

1. Organizational inertia is the tendency for organizations to continue on in well-worn patterns of behavior. How has General Motors' inertia helped or hurt it? Are there other organizations that have been hampered by or have benefited from inertia?
2. Power and politics seem to be greater at different times in organizations. When would you expect the greatest amount of politicking within General Motors, during the fifties and sixties, or the eighties and nineties? Why?
3. Organizational design (structure) is often driven by different forces. What were the forces that drove General Motors' design in the twenties? And/or the eighties?
4. What was the interplay between technology of the final product and organizational structure at General Motors from 1925 until the mid-seventies?
5. The changes that Jack Smith made were similar to changes that Alfred Sloan made when he came to power in 1920. What was similar in the environment that called for the same changes at two completely different times?

REFERENCES

1. R. Paul, "Aurora Takes on the World," *Motortrend* (September 1994): 74–82.

2. K. Zino, "1995 Oldsmobile Aurora," *Road & Track* (July 1994): 91–95.

3. P. Ingrassia, and J. B. White, *Comeback: The Fall and Rise of the American Automobile Industry* (New York: Simon & Schuster, 1994).

4. A. D. Chandler, *Strategy and Structure: Chapters in the History of the American Industrial Enterprise* (Cambridge: M.I.T. Press, 1962), 115.

5. See note 4, page 117, above.

6. L. R. Gustin, *Billy Durant, Creator of General Motors* (Grand Rapids, Mich.: William B. Eerdmans Publishing Company, 1973).

7. See note 4, page 120, above.

8. See note 5, page 281, above.

9. See note 4, page 134, above.

10. See note 4, page 141, above.

11. See note 4, page 145, above.

12. P. R. Lawrence and D. Dyer, *Renewing American Industry* (New York: The Free Press, 1983), 31.

13. Richard L. Daft, *Organization Theory and Design* (St. Paul, Minn.: West Publishing, 1992), 222.

14. See note 12, page 27, above.

15. M. Keller, *Collision: GM, Toyota, Volkswagen and the Race to Own the 21st Century* (New York: Doubleday, 1993), 115.

16. John D. Debbink, Vice President and Group Executive (Retired), General Motors Corporation, personal communication, September 1, 1994 to December 30, 1994.

17. G. S. May, ed., *The Automobile Industry 1920–1980* (New York: Facts on File Inc., 1989), 179.

18. B. Nussbaum, *The World After Oil* (New York: Simon & Schuster, 1983), 62.

19. See note 16 above.

20. See note 15, page 122, above.

21. See note 12, page 19, above.

22. M. Keller, *Rude Awakening: The Rise, Fall and Struggle for Recovery of General Motors* (New York: HarperCollins, 1989), 89.

23. See note 22, page 2, above.

24. See note 22, page 118, above.

25. A. Taylor, "U.S. Cars Come Back," *Fortune* (November 16, 1992): 52–85.

26. See note 22, page 106, above.

27. See note 22, page 105, above.

28. See note 25 above.

29. See note 3, page 154, above.

30. See note 3, page 278, above.

31. See note 15, page 39, above.

32. See note 3, page 290, above.

33. See note 3, page 298, above.

34. See note 3, page 297, above.

35. See note 3, page 302, above.

36. A. Taylor, "GM's $11,000,000,000 Turnaround," *Fortune* (October 17, 1994): 54–74.

37. See note 3, page 304, above.

38. See note 3, page 308, above.

39. See note 25 above.

40. General Motors Corporation, internal communication.

41. K. Kerwin, "Vapor Lock at GM," *Business Week* (November 7, 1994): 28–29.

42. G. Stern, "GM's Luster Has Dimmed, Say Analysts," *The Wall Street Journal* (November 1, 1994), C1–C2.

43. G. Kobe, "Slow Launches Costly to GM, Chrysler," *Automotive Industries* (December 1994): 34.

44. M. Keller, "GM's Problems," *Automotive Industries* (December 1994): 13.

IBM: The Elephant Learns to Dance*

IBM—the letters create an image of professionalism and superior competence in most people's mind. Consistently rated as the number one company in the world by *Fortune's* ratings of corporate reputation, IBM's 1993 ranking dropped to 265. IBM is a huge organization, the largest computer company in the world. Some critics have asserted that its huge size hurt the organization in the mid-1980s when the computer industry, in general, went into recession. But during the period from 1991 to 1993, when other computer companies bounced back from this slump and reached record earnings, IBM struggled along, posting record losses of $2.86, $4.97, and $8.10 billion in 1991, 1992, and 1993, respectively.[1] To many observers, IBM's poor performance was not just a consequence of its size and bureaucratic culture, but also of the organization's inability to forecast the customer's demand and its decentralized, ineffective information systems. This inefficiency was caused by a great deal of overlap between the product and service groups, which had their own decision-making responsibilities since the reorganization in 1988 under then-CEO Akers' regime.[2] IBM's product development was slower, and its costs were much higher than those of competitors.

To reverse this trend, the new chairman and chief executive officer of IBM, Louis V. Gerstner, implemented a sweeping structural reorganization of his company, starting with cost cutting in March 1993. As a result, expenses dropped faster than revenues. A modestly profitable, but smaller, IBM is already in sight. Gerstner's deep cleaning and restructuring of IBM have caused the organization to become more in tune with its environment, closer to its customers, and more adept at rapidly developing and marketing new products.

The events at IBM provide an excellent laboratory for the study of organizations and organizational change. This case examines recent changes of IBM from five perspectives: (1) environmental; (2) technological; (3) cultural; (4) strategic; and (5) structural.

---

*By Haesun Baek, Florida State University.

■   **TABLE 1**

IBM Annual Report 1994

(Dollars in millions except per share amounts)	1994	1993
For the year:		
Revenue	$ 64,052	$ 62,716
Earnings (loss) before income taxes	$ 5,155	$ (8,797)
Income taxes	$ 2,134	$ (810)
Net earnings (loss) before change in accounting principle	$ 3,021	$ (7,987)
Per share of common stock	$ 5.02	$ (14.02)
Effect of change in accounting principle*	$ —	$ (114)
Per share of common stock	$ —	$ (.20)
Net earnings (loss)	$ 3,021	$ (8,101)
Per share of common stock	$ 5.02	$ (14.22)
Cash dividends paid on common stock	$ 585	$ 905
Per share of common stock	$ 1.00	1.58
Investment in plant, rental machines, and other property	$ 3,078	$ 3,232
Average number of common shares outstanding (in millions)	585	573
At end of year:		
Total assets	$ 81,091	$ 81,113
Net investment in plant, rental machines, and other property	$ 16,664	$ 17,521
Working capital	$ 12,112	$ 6,052
Total debt	$ 22,118	$ 27,342
Stockholders' equity	$ 23,413	$ 19,738
Number of regular, full-time employees	219,839	256,207
Number of stockholders	713,060	741,047

*1993, cumulative effect of Statement of Financial Accounting Standards (SFAS) 112, "Employers' Accounting for Postemployment Benefits."

ENVIRONMENTAL IMPERATIVES

When Gerstner took over the helm at IBM in 1993, the company had two big problems: (1) delays in shifting from mainframe business to smaller machines; and (2) IBM's bureaucratic and lethargic culture.[3] The company refused to believe that its key mainframe business would be eclipsed by smaller machines. That is, IBM failed to recognize and take into account fast changes in the external environment that were directly affecting all aspects of the computer industry. Also, the company chose a closed system of promotion in which the route to the top of the organization was through sales, marketing, and finance—not technology. Moreover, promotions often depended more on one's political skills than on real achievements. Many industry experts claimed that the company had to cannibalize the mainframe business in a managed way in order to create smaller, high-powered products. The company needed someone who could make a fresh start and change the company dramatically.[4]

COMPETITION

Notwithstanding IBM's decades-old consistent leadership in its industry, a multitude of competitors, both domestic and foreign, had been able to successfully attack IBM's dominance. Indeed, just the number of organizations in the world associated with the computer industry is a mind-boggling 75,000.[5] These rivals, consisting of large hardware and software companies, personal computer manufactures, and suppliers of single components such as processors, have presented significant threats to IBM, particularly in two highly specialized niches, or marketing opportunities. For example, IBM's core mainframe business that traditionally delivered the highest profits has been sliding while the sales of PCs have been booming. IBM represents about 80 percent of the market, but total worldwide mainframe shipments plummeted to 2,800 units in 1993 from 4,700 in 1988.[6] IBM and its competitors—Unisys Corp., Amdahl Corp., and Hitachi Data Systems—have tried to stem the tide by cutting prices even before cutting costs. Now they are reworking the machines' insides, borrowing technology from smaller machines that have cut into mainframe sales. Unisys has updated its mainframe line with modern chip-based technology and has made it more compatible with other computers. Psychologically, it has gone even further, calling the machines "enterprise servers" instead of mainframes. Now IBM is making its own move, belatedly, rivals say, ". . . to reposition the mainframe for the new world of clients/server computing, which uses a fast but cheap central computer to link platoons of powerful PCs."[7] IBM's mainframe sales, although continuing to decline, were down only about 10 percent in 1994 instead of the 50 percent as IBM expected. IBM's new mainframes use an advanced technology called parallel processing that links together anywhere from a handful to scores of microprocessors, similar to the fingernail-sized "brains" of personal computers. Traditional mainframes use bipolar processing boards the size of a phone book. Because the new machines are based on less expensive PC technology, they cost less to make and profit margins are higher. Early signs seem to be promising for the new line.[8]

In the personal computer field, IBM's sales revenue hit $9.7 billion in 1993—just shy of the $10 billion generated by mainframes and minis. But that doesn't help the profit picture. Indeed, PCs yield less than half of the profit margin of big computers. The competition in the PC market is fierce, and as companies scramble to achieve consumer sales volume, the PC business is consolidating and margins are shrinking. In 1994, the top ten manufacturers captured about 70 percent of the market, up from 63 percent in 1993. Increasingly, the battle is between Compaq, IBM, Apple, Packard Bell, and a few ambitious wanna-bes like AST Research, Dell Computer, Gateway 2000, and Taiwan's Acer. In the second quarter of 1994, IBM had only 8 percent of the U.S. market share while Compaq had 15 percent; Apple, 11 percent; and Packard Bell, 9 percent. IBM dropped in U.S. market share to fourth place from a near-tie for number one in 1993. This is attributed to its chronic problem of miscalculating demand for its personal computers and the lack of applications programs for its own operating system, OS/2.[9] IBM is in a weak position because Microsoft and Intel, the reigning standard setters, are expected to maintain their roles and buttress their hold on the market by speeding the development of user-friendly technology—unless these two giants encounter new problems with delayed software development or faulty chips.

INDUSTRY FORCES

During the mid-1980s, IBM neglected to consider certain forces that were significantly changing the entire computer industry. For decades, IBM (and other computer companies) developed computers and proprietary items that were unique machines incompatible with the company's other products. In recent years, however, computers are being increasingly used as strategic tools for integrating and processing all types of information from a variety of different machines—mainframes, midsize computers, and PCs. This means that different computers, regardless of size or make, must have common hardware and software standards for the machines to interact successfully with each other.

IBM has been tardy in developing a set of engineering and software specifications that will enable IBM devices to work with other machines, regardless of size or make, within the framework of a coordinated, holistic information-processing network. Thus, IBM's new move is to standardize the PowerPC as basic hardware and Workplace as the core software. IBM has been trying to solve a persistent problem by (1) eliminating the huge incompatibilities across its product lines; (2) relocating resources from mainframe software projects to Workplace; and (3) marketing a coherent software message.[10] For example, IBM's new AS/400 minicomputers face growing competition from PC networks as well as midsized computers that use Unix software, a more "open" design that works with different brands of hardware and software. To address these concerns, IBM released a new version of the AS/400's operating system that enables some programs written for Unix computers to run on AS/400s. IBM also provides ways to connect PCs and Apple Computer's Macintosh models to AS/400s.[11]

CUSTOMERS

IBM's drop in performance during the mid-1980s can partially be explained by the company's arrogance toward its customers. For example, when an IBM customer delivered his company's specifications for a computer system that IBM did not currently have, IBM salespeople would suggest that there was something wrong with the customer's specifications. In short, IBM had become product driven, rather than customer driven, and this attitude opened the door for IBM's competitors who saw the opportunity presented by the gap between what IBM customers wanted and what IBM customers got.

When Louis Gerstner took charge of IBM in early 1993, he realized right away that the company's failure in the past to capitalize on the fast growing client/server market was the single most important mistake IBM had made in the last decade.[12] With the new client/server networks' capability to run on both powerful hub computers, or servers, as well as on desktop clients, many mainframe computer customers are switching to PCs.[13] It is clear that PCs are the computer industry's driving force in the 1990s. The customers want PCs that can be used as easy as appliances. To appeal to this broader, technologically less sophisticated market by building a strong brand image and developing small but distinctive features is becoming more critical than ever.

With the 1994 Annual Report, IBM stressed its customer service orientation. As Figure 1 shows, throughout the report each section is highlighted by a reference to a customer group. The only word on the cover of the report is *you*.

FIGURE 1

IBM Is Customer Oriented

"You.
You are facing the future.
You are an executive on a task force.
You are a radiologist working late.
You are an automotive engineer in Russia.
You are a parent on a mission.
Whatever your needs, we're working with you."

Source: IBM Annual Report 1994.

TECHNOLOGICAL INNOVATIONS

The IBM organization has long been renowned as a leader in technological innovation. The main technological challenge facing IBM and other computer companies in the mid-1980s was to make computers simpler and easier to use.

After the company's reorganization in 1988, each product and service group became responsible for its own product development, manufacturing, and marketing operations. This move created destructive competition and overlap between the various product and service groups and made technological development extremely inefficient. IBM's profit margin was far below that of its competitors because of its high cost, and its product development was lagging because of its inefficiency. Only 5 percent of the Research Division budget was used for software and services research, while 40 percent was used for the basic physical science research.[14]

Now, under Gerstner's direction, the researchers are being brought into everything from product planning to corporate strategy setting to focus on short-term and cost-effective development. Software and services research uses up nearly 25 percent of the Research Division budget. Researchers are leaving the ivory tower to work more closely with IBM operating units, with outside customers, and with partner companies.[15]

For easy transition and more applications, IBM plans to use PowerPC as the basic hardware for all computers it produces. The PowerPC is a new microprocessor chip that IBM codeveloped with Motorola Inc. and Apple Computer Inc. in 1992. IBM plans to spread these speedy PowerPC microprocessors throughout the IBM line while marketing a large scale scientific computer using dozens of chips. IBM's AS/400 minicomputers, based on PowerPC technology and unveiled in May, 1994, have received positive feedback from users and industry experts. The AS/400 has significantly enhanced hardware and software, giving a more Unix-type functionality. It has new software that can more easily work with other computer brands and types while offering an easy transition to PowerPC. The AS/400 series has been one of IBM's star performers, giving an acceptable profit margin. In addition, for 1995 IBM is working on new editions of the OS/400 operating system, variations of its integrated database software, and the AS/400 PC compatibility program, which will handle in-cabinet enhancements to support PowerPC type-systems.[16,17]

Another challenge to IBM is to consolidate all software development around a common "microkernel," a form of software even more basic than an operating system that would work on everything from PCs to mainframes. The company calls this high-stakes gamble "Workplace Technology." A single microkernel would be used across different product lines and, with the addition of "personality" software, would mimic existing operating systems, such as the OS/400 of IBM's AS/400 minicomputers. Gerstner hopes to create a more cohesive IBM that reintegrates nearly autonomous business units and encourages them to rely more on IBM technology. He pushes all IBM units to build new designs around the PowerPC chip and send them out the door with more IBM software.[18] Unfortunately, IBM has been very slow to bring desktop PowerPC units to market.

In late 1994, IBM introduced a new version of its graphical interface software OS/2 Warp. It can use four different applications and a clock under three different environments including OS/2, DOS, and Windows.[19] Its features are believed to be comparable to Microsoft's Windows 95 (which reached the market in late 1995), and it beat Microsoft to market by nearly nine months. However, OS/2 has yet to develop much market momentum. There are few applications designed to exploit OS/2 features, and Windows has become a de facto industry standard for software developers.

ALLIANCE WITH APPLE

To overcome these disadvantages, IBM has undertaken a bold plan as part of an urgent effort to salvage its faltering PowerPC strategy. The plan is to form a broad alliance with Apple aimed at developing a common hardware platform that would run both Apple and IBM software programs. The goal is to make a machine that will run the operating systems for Mac and Windows to boost hardware sales. While IBM is selling a workstation line based on the PowerPC, Apple has introduced a line of PowerPC-based Macs, but they aren't compatible with the PowerPC machines planned by IBM. Each side pushed the other to adopt its technical approach. That left IBM struggling to convert its OS/2 operating system, which now is installed in 5 million Intel-based PCs, compared with the Macintosh's 15 million for the desktop PowerPCs. IBM is running late on OS/2 conversion for PowerPCs. Embracing the Macintosh system might give the company a more popular option and alleviate one of the biggest problems faced by both IBM and Apple: the flight of software developers away from the Macintosh and IBM's OS/2 operating system to the Windows/DOS operating system. The two long-time rivals are expected shortly to sign a series of complex cross-licensing agreements aimed at making their PCs more compatible. IBM would gain rights to the Macintosh operating system.[20]

CULTURE

No discussion of IBM would be complete without a discussion of its heralded thick culture, that is, the homogeneity of beliefs, values, and behavior patterns throughout the organization.

The founder of IBM, Thomas Watson, Sr., set three main values for the organization: (1) loyal and happy employees; (2) customer service; and (3) striving for excellence. These three cornerstones of the IBM culture have basically remained steadfast throughout the organization's life, although they have needed to be fine-tuned and augmented from time to time to "keep the elephant dancing," so to speak.

Thomas Watson, Jr., the son of the founder, served as IBM chairman from 1956 until 1971. Among Watson, Jr.'s, most notable achievements was his decentralization of the IBM organization to enhance innovation and push decision making down to the lowest possible level. Previously, under his father's tutelage, IBM had become a very functionalized and formal bureaucracy.

T. Vincent Learson, who served as the IBM CEO in the early 1970s, was primarily responsible for encouraging different product groups within the company to bring forward proposed designs and compete against each other in a "shoot-out." As intended, this decision enhanced internal competition, which resulted in IBM's producing the finest and most innovative products for the market. Again, as we shall discuss later in this case, this particular aspect of the IBM culture is being revitalized by the recent reorganizations.

Frank Carey, who served as CEO from 1973 to 1980, did little to enhance the more positive aspects of the IBM culture. This was not because of any shortcomings on his part. Rather, IBM was plagued during Carey's tenure by several federal antitrust suits that caused IBM to become very conservative in product innovation and diversification.

John Opel, the IBM chairman and CEO from 1980 to 1985, set out to reinforce two cornerstones of the IBM culture—customer service and a striving for excellence. Although Opel's efforts met with initial success during the early 1980s, the realities and changing conditions of the environment, discussed previously, forced his resignation in 1985 and the ascendancy of John Akers.

John Akers served as the IBM chairman and CEO from 1985 to 1993. His major achievement was the fundamental reorganization of the company to participate in the fast changing worldwide computer industry. His reorganization of the company in 1988 was an attempt to make IBM a decentralized, innovative, and customer-responsive organization. He created more autonomous and responsive businesses for each division, resulting in a lack of communication and overlap of research projects among divisions. He failed to take aggressive action required by the rapidly changing marketplace—with customers' growing preference for small computers and open systems, and growing value on software, services, and integration skills. Instead, he emphasized the key mainframe business whose revenue declined more than 50 percent in 1994 from 1989.[21] He also failed to change IBM's bureaucratic and lethargic culture to serve the client/server computing industry.

Louis V. Gerstner, the IBM chairman and CEO since April 1993, is struggling as he tries to change the ingrained IBM culture. As an outsider, he faces a difficult challenge trying to instigate sweeping changes in a company whose corporate culture has remained the same for seventy years. As part of the reorganization effort, Gerstner plans to eliminate an additional 35,000 jobs and accelerate the product delivery schedules. Previously, the company formally avoided involuntary layoffs and took a team approach in product development, often missing shipping dates to retest systems. However, lower profit margins since the mid-1980s have forced company officials to rethink corporate policies. As he struggles with losses and downsizing, Gerstner is also working to stem a spate of departures of key personnel. IBM lost some very good people in 1993.[22] The company is offering more performance bonuses to employees at all levels and is encouraging managers to stay in close touch with their workers so they don't get demoralized. Meanwhile IBM has been recruiting. IBM has hired more executives than ever before from the outside. One critical barrier that Gerstner faces, however, is that many employees and managers (40 percent by an internal survey) do not accept the need for change.[23]

STRATEGY: SIZE AND DOMINANCE

Until its reorganization, IBM pursued a strategic objective of being the largest and most dominant force in the information-processing industry. Being the "big guy" meant that IBM could afford to spend $5.4 billion in 1987 on research, development, and engineering efforts, which is more money than the total revenues of all but 75 of the top 500 *Fortune* companies.[24] Being big meant that IBM could develop, manufacture, and market its products in every information-processing category, from giant mainframes to small PCs. Being big meant that IBM would have the resources that would enable it to be the low-cost producer of computer products, the low-cost distributor of computer products, and the fastest penetrator of new market opportunities.

For IBM, the bigness part of its strategy meant almost absolute dominance in the industry. Dominance meant that IBM could manufacture proprietary items that gave it nearly total control over its customers. Dominance also meant that IBM could even control its competitors. For years, competitors were forced to live in an environment characterized by fear and uncertainty over what IBM would do next because IBM alone had the resources to determine the future direction of the industry. To get a few crumbs left over from the IBM table, competitors paid IBM dearly in the form of royalties for little bits of patented technology that would enable them to manufacture and sell their own products.

The IBM strategy of size and dominance served the organization well for decades. But the historical success of this strategy also carried the seeds that later blossomed into the distressed situation that IBM found itself in by the mid-1980s. Bigness and dominance can lead to inertia, myopia, and the formation of a stifling and self-serving bureaucracy. Dominance of an industry, in and of itself, can often lead to a contemptuous attitude toward customers and competitors and even toward cherished cultural values, such as service to customers. IBM believed in customer service as long as customers took what IBM gave them.

An organization's strategy should reflect the times in which it lives. The rapidly changing environment in the 1990s has caused IBM to reexamine its former strategy. Thus, in light of the necessity for strategic change, Gerstner embarked upon his six-point plan for the future:

1. to push its core technological innovations across more product lines to sell more components to outsiders;
2. to become a player in client/server computing;

3. to offer network services to large companies;
4. to reengineer the sales force to cut costs;
5. to jump into new geographic markets; and
6. to leverage IBM's size and scale.[25]

Despite efforts to diversify, too much of IBM's revenue (49 percent) comes from hardware. Virtually every IBM hardware market is marked by eroding prices and profits, and there are no signs of a profit rebound. In fact, there is an alarming slide underway in IBM's core large-computer businesses — the product that traditionally delivered highest profit and secured IBM's hold on corporate customers. This hold traditionally generates other revenues from software, leasing, maintenance, and other services. The minicomputers, which have been delivering the biggest chunk of hardware profits lately, could be the next trouble spot. Analysts expect that minicomputers are going to go off a cliff the way mainframe sales have.[26] IBM deemphasized the mainframe business and shifted its emphasis on the fast-growing client/server market of networked PCs.[27] The Research Division also focuses on software and system design, not such base-layer hardware as superfast semiconductors. Sales and licensing of all sorts of component technology will add $3.6 billion in 1994. The second quarter revenue from technology sales in 1994 was up 400 percent over a year earlier, or 100 times growth rate for the entire company. However, the gross profit margin was slender, around 10 percent, which is about one third of IBM's overall gross profit margin.[28]

To leverage IBM's size and scale, IBM has cut 170,000 jobs worldwide, starting before Gerstner arrived. In addition, plans are to lay off 35,000 more employees as this case is being written and to accelerate product delivery schedules. During 1992 and 1993, IBM's write-offs for restructuring were over $20 billion. Those write-offs are starting to do what IBM intended them to do — reduce expenses so that the company can return to consistent profitability in the brutally competitive and ever-changing computer marketplace.[29]

Gerstner's deep cleaning and restructuring, rather than gutting and renovating, is working surprisingly well. Expenses are dropping faster than revenues. Profit margins have stabilized; the stock has begun to climb; and the company posted $1.8 billion net income for the first three quarters of 1994 after having suffered three consecutive years of losses. By mid-1994, the company had $10.8 billion in cash and showed a willingness to make acquisitions (e.g., Lotus), which signals a rebound in self-confidence after several years of multibillion dollar losses, layoffs, and declining market share.[30]

STRUCTURE

To understand the reorganization of IBM under Gerstner, it is first necessary to understand the company as it existed in the late 1980s. Prior to restructuring, IBM beefed up its sales and marketing force by adding nearly 16,000 individuals to ensure that customers' needs were met in a timely and efficient manner.[31] During restructuring, sales and marketing were among the first areas cut. Following are brief descriptions of the product service groups under the IBM U.S. umbrella as they existed during that time.

- Application Solutions. This group contained the marketing divisions and worked with IBM's customers to develop solutions for their total information processing needs. In addition to providing traditional marketing and sales services, individuals within this group worked with customers on projects such as systems integration and application development. This group provided coordination services between IBM and those independent companies that helped IBM with the development, marketing, and installation of its products.
- Programming Systems. Software, programming languages, and application development software were developed by this group. Most important among the group's tasks was the responsibility for developing IBM's System Application Architecture (SAS), a set of specifications that will create standard user, programming, and communications interfaces across all the different IBM systems.
- Communications Systems. All of IBM's communications products and services, including controllers, modems, connectivity, and network management software were developed in the Communications Systems division. Basically, the group worked to develop means that would enable IBM customers to manage global communications networks.
- Enterprise Systems. This group was responsible for all of IBM's System/370 products, which included its most powerful mainframes as well as a midrange computer, the 9370, which was in demand by the same customer groups using the most powerful mainframes.
- Application Business Systems. IBM's midrange line, except for the IBM ES Processor 9370 computer, was the responsibility of the Application Business Systems group. In addition to product similarity, the customer base for this group's products was also uniform, for example, small- and intermediate-sized businesses with similar data processing requirements.
- Personal Systems. This group handled the products with which the typical consumer is most familiar, IBM's line of PCs. In addition to PCs, Personal Systems developed office workstations and displays.
- Technology Products. Technology Products had across-the-line responsibility for developing logic and memory technology in addition to developing electronic packaging used for all IBM products.

Certain other organizational units, in addition to those noted above, were also important parts of IBM. Although the focus of this case has been on changes in the product and service groups, which are the core of IBM operations, the other organizational subunits should be briefly discussed to acquaint the reader with the full gamut of IBM's businesses and its structure. The three IBM World Trade units were responsible for the support of IBM sales and service operations throughout the world. The Research Division, which reported to the senior vice president for science and technology, conducted broad-range scientific research that can have potential importance for the company. IBM Credit Corporation, which reported to the senior vice president for corporate finance and planning, offered financing of IBM products to customers at competitive rates. Information-processing and control systems needs of U.S. government agencies were handled by the Federal Systems Division. The primary responsibilities of the Real Estate and Construction Division were site acquisition and facilities construction. The International Business Units (IBUs) and Strategic Business Units (SBUs) were the independent and semi-independent units discussed earlier that had as their purpose the innovative application of technology to new products.

Prodigy Services Company was a partnership between IBM and Sears, Roebuck and Company. Prodigy is an on-line network and e-mail system that supplies myriad electronic information opportunities that include news, sports, weather, stock quotes, bulletin boards, and on-line business transactions for personal computer users. Science Educational services was handled by IBM's Research Associates subsidiary. The unit was responsible for development, production, and marketing of various educational services for schools and colleges throughout the world.

Gerstner's first moves upon coming to IBM were to appoint former PC chief James A. Cannavino as senior vice president for strategy; sell IBM Federal Systems to defense contractor Loral for $1.6 billion; combine client/server computing, mainframes, minicomputers, and workstation "servers" into a single group; and hire former Nabisco marketer G. Richard Thoman to run IBM PC Company and push it further into the customer market.[32] Hiring Thoman was Gerstner's effort to rattle IBM's entrenched culture and inject some consumer-marketing savvy. Further, IBM PC Company underwent a massive reorganization to fix weak spots in its product line following the unexpected resignation of President Robert J. Corrigan. Richard Thoman assumed the responsibilities. IBM PC departed from the autonomous management system and has become more tightly linked with IBM. Instead of hiring a new president, the roles of four existing top executives (four new general managers) were expanded. The team's top priority is to solve the company's supply-and-demand imbalances.[33]

Gerstner's reorganizing efforts continued through a major restructuring of the entrenched IBM sales system. IBM set up fourteen industry areas and granted broad powers to their chiefs.[34] Moreover, IBM filled half of the top posts in the U.S. with recent hires from the consulting industry. Such a move is remarkable for a company with a historic policy of promoting only from within—especially when it comes to its prized sales force. The biggest impact could occur outside the U.S. where the formerly autonomous heads of IBM country organizations could see their power diminished. Seventy to 80 percent of IBM Europe's business will be handled by a new industry sector team.[35] These are just some of the most obvious structural changes. Change at IBM under Chairman Gerstner appears to be a gradually unfolding process. Clearly, more changes are in process as this case is being written.

CONCLUSION

Will all the changes work for IBM? Can it change its culture and integrate functions across autonomous units? Only time will tell. The market has reacted finally to these changes. IBM stock has climbed from the low $40 range in 1993 to the mid $90 range in 1995. Of course, this is still far below the $225 stock of the mid-1980s. But IBM appears to be on the way back. The elephant may learn to dance after all!

Questions for Discussion

1. How do diverse product goals affect the structure, operations, and culture of IBM?
2. How could IBM have prevented the problems it had in the mid-1980s? Use as many organization theory concepts as you can in answering this question.
3. Describe in detail how IBM's new strategy must be complemented by an organization design-culture "fit."
4. How would you evaluate IBM's new structure? Specifically, briefly describe the appropriate integration devices that you would suggest to coordinate the various groups of the new structure?
5. Evaluate customer input as a means of monitoring the environment.
6. Speculate on how the changing international scene and customer's roles in the decision-making function might affect IBM's strategy and cultural network.

REFERENCES

1. IBM Annual Report (1993): 21.

2. Stratford Sherman, "Is He Too Cautious to Save IBM?" *Fortune* (October 3, 1994): 78.

3. Judith H. Dobrzynski, "IBM's Board Should Clean Out the Corner Office," *Business Week* (February 1, 1993): 27.

4. Ibid.

5. IBM 1988 Annual Report (1988): 2.

6. Bart Ziegler, "If Mainframe Computers Are Dinosaurs, Why Is IBM Creating a New Generation?" *The Wall Street Journal* (April 4, 1994), B1.

7. Ibid.

8. Bart Ziegler, "Vital Signs: Decline in IBM Mainframe Sales Is Slowing," *The Wall Street Journal* (September 12, 1994), B3.

9. Bart Ziegler, "IBM Sells Out New Aptiva PC; Shortage May Cost Millions in Potential Revenue," *The Wall Street Journal* (October 7, 1994), B4.

10. Amy Cortese, "IBM Rides into Microsoft Country," *Business Week* (June 6, 1994): 111.

11. Craig Stedman, "IBM's AS/400 Earns Some Respect," *Computerworld* 28, no. 24 (June 13, 1994): 95.

12. Laurie Hays and Bart Ziegler, "IBM Chairman Offers Analysts Sober Forecast," *The Wall Street Journal* (March 25, 1994), B2.

13. Evan Schwarz, "Finally, Software That Slays Giants," *Business Week* (March 15, 1993): 96.

14. Peter Coy, "Is Big Blue Still on Research? You Bet," *Business Week* (May 16, 1994): 89.

15. Ibid.

16. See note 11 above.

17. Ira Sager, "Lou Gerstner Unveils His Battle Plan," *Business Week* (April 4, 1994): 96.

18. See note 10 above.

19. Charles Babcock, "Slender Debut of Personal OS/2," *Computerworld* 28, no. 23 (June 6, 1994): 6.

20. Laurie Hays, "IBM in Talks to Cover Costs of New Linkup with Apple," *The Wall Street Journal* (October 20, 1994), A3.

21. See note 17 above.

22. Laurie Hays, "Gerstner Is Struggling to Stem Desertions of Top Talent as Morale Tumbles at IBM," *The Wall Street Journal* (August 27, 1993), B1.

23. Laurie Hays, "Gerstner Is Struggling as He Tries to Change Ingrained IBM Culture," *The Wall Street Journal* (May 13, 1994), A1.

24. Peter Coy, "IBM Discovering That the Rules of the Game Have Changed," *Tallahassee Democrat* (October 9, 1988), 1D.

25. See note 17 above.

26. Ibid.

27. See note 12 above.

28. Ira Sager, "IBM Knows What to Do with a Good Idea: Sell It," *Business Week* (September 19, 1994): 72.

29. David Kirkpatrick, "IBM: Nice, But No Cigar," *Fortune* (February 21, 1994): 11.

30. Bart Ziegler, "IBM Earned $719 Million in Third Period," *The Wall Street Journal* (October 21, 1994), A3.

31. "Stepping Up the Pace," *Think, A Special Midyear Report* (Armonk, N.Y.: IBM), 7.

32. Ira Sager, "IBM Reboots Bit by Bit," *Business Week* (January 17, 1994): 82.

33. Laurie Hays and Bart Ziegler, "IBM Reorganizes PC Division as Chief of Unit Quits," *The Wall Street Journal* (May 3, 1994), B4.

34. Bart Ziegler, "IBM Plans to Revamp Sales Structure to Focus on Industries, not Geography," *The Wall Street Journal* (May 6, 1994), A3.

35. Ira Sager, "Big Blue Wants to Know Who's Boss?" *Business Week* (September 26, 1994): 78.

■ CASE 5

*Eastman Kodak Responds to a Changing Environment** *

Eastman Kodak is the largest producer of photographic products in the world. It has recently faced the emergence of a number of competitors, primarily Fuji Photo, who have been seizing sizable portions of Kodak's market share in the profitable film and paper industry. This has seriously challenged Kodak and forced it to respond, including by a massive restructuring and downsizing.

Kodak has had its fair share of experience with restructuring in the past. These efforts have been only moderately successful to date. CEO George Fisher realizes that if Kodak is going to experience any growth and become a powerhouse in the developing global economies, additional drastic measures must be taken. Many feel that Fisher must continuously search Kodak's laboratories for innovative products that could provide substantial revenues from untapped markets. Yet, in order for Kodak to become an efficient global competitor, downsizing will also have to play a significant role in Kodak's future. Kodak realizes downsizing is often a knee-jerk reaction by management to bad times and not a cure-all. However, when company profits begin to decrease, there is great pressure for the company to take action that restores faith to shareholders. Downsizing is such an action because it shows shareholders that there is a commitment in the organization to turn things around.

Former CEO Kay Whitmore described Kodak in the 1992 annual report as being a company that is " . . . deep in unique technology, with a world-class workforce, and outstanding product portfolio and powerfully attractive brands." Whitmore also felt that Kodak was " . . . armed and ready to compete successfully with anyone, in any key market, in any nation of the world." These may be accurate descriptions of the innovative and global-oriented Eastman Kodak whose subsidiaries outside the U.S. are responsible for 49 percent of sales and 34 percent of operating profits. Nonetheless, Whitmore saw Kodak's one dominant position in the marketplace severely challenged, and he was unable to refocus the

---

*By Christopher S. Polaszek and Erich Brockmann, Florida State University.

company. CEO Fisher, in the 1993 annual report, also stressed that "Kodak is recognized around the world as a technology leader, with a patent portfolio that is the envy of many, many companies."[1] He also noted the importance of people and that it would take both good people and good products for the company to reach its former heights. It is now up to George Fisher to revitalize Kodak. The following sections highlight the challenges faced by Fisher and Kodak.

THE COMPANY

PERSONNEL

Kodak is an excellent example of an overgrown bureaucracy. Overall, in 1993 the company had 110,400 employees, 57,200 in the U.S. The leadership at Kodak has been extraordinarily insular. The company has spent over a century in Rochester, New York, with its leaders seldom mixing with counterparts from other companies. Many of them were heavily involved in the company and its social events. Consensus had become the norm and confrontation was frowned upon.[2] To shake this up, the board of directors decided to bring in new blood. They accomplished this by attracting George M. C. Fisher. He received a $5 million inducement; a base salary of $2 million, which is to be reviewed annually; 20,000 shares of stock (with restrictions for five years); 1 million stock options; and an $8.2 million loan to make up for his previous employer's (Motorola) stock options, with 20 percent of the principal and all interest to be forgiven on each employment anniversary.[3] Fisher began as a researcher in Bell Labs. He then advanced to CEO of Motorola after he spearheaded its entry into Japan's paging market. He is a self-effacing individual and a passionate adherent to Japanese production and quality techniques.[4] He is the first outsider CEO in the company's 113-year history. Fisher's theory about leadership is:

> . . . *set high expectations, you make sure people are empowered, and have the tools, training and education to get the job done. And then you get out of their way.*[5]

On October 27, 1993, it was announced that George Fisher would replace Kay Whitmore on December 1, 1993—Whitmore had been CEO since June 1990. Whitmore, whose forecasted departure was made official by the board in August 1993, had replaced Colby Chandler, who retired after 40 years of service. Although Whitmore resigned, the announcement stated that the board of directors decided to replace him.[6] Normally, when results are deteriorating as badly as Kodak's were, drastic measures are necessary to halt and turn around the results. The replacement of the CEO, especially with an outsider, is a radical change that creates discontinuity.

BUSINESS SEGMENTS

Kodak has broken its business into segments. These include imaging, information, health, and chemicals (see Figure 1 on page 448). The imaging products are used for

capturing, recording, or displaying an image. They include films, paper, processing services, chemicals, cameras, and projectors. Recent additions to the product inventory
include single-use cameras and photo-compact discs (CD). Sales of imaging products
are primarily through dealers and independent retail outlets. In 1993, this segment had
$7.2 billion in sales.

■ FIGURE 1

Kodak's Businesses, Based on 1993 Revenue

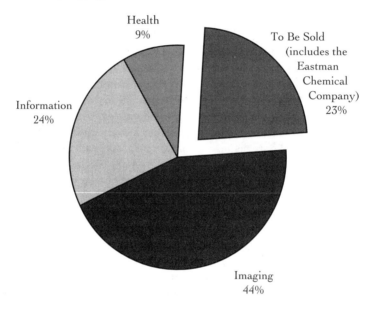

The information segment includes business units that serve the imaging and information needs of business, industry, and government. Its products are used to capture,
store, process, and display images. They include graphic arts films, microfilm, application software, copiers, and printers. The products are distributed through a variety of
channels, including direct sales and leases. In 1993, this segment had $3.9 billion in sales.
    In 1993, the health segment included L&F (formerly Lehn & Fink) Products, a
wholly owned subsidiary that was sold to Reckitt and Colman, Plc., a British food products company, in 1994. It is divided into two product categories: household products
(which include disinfectants, all purpose cleaners, floor-care products, rodenticides, sep-
ticides, deodorants, and hair-care products); and do-it-yourself products (which include
wood stains, and concrete and wood protectors). The products are distributed mainly via
dealers, independent distributors, wholesalers, jobbers, hospitals, and retail. In 1993,
this segment had $5.2 billion in sales. The health sciences portion of this segment deals
with pharmaceutical products and life science chemicals that are sold primarily to other
manufacturers. Its products include X-ray films, processors, image management systems, laser printers, and chemicals for radiography markets. The segment's major contribution to company profits is the Kodak Ektascan Imagelink system that enables
hospital personnel to manage the entire spectrum of electronic and film-based images in

digital form for storage and retrieval, transmission, and manipulation. The clinical products portion of this segment is in alliance with Amersham International of England. This allows development of a decisive presence in the immunodiagnostics segment of the in-vitro diagnostics business. It also has a new jointly-owned company, Amerlite Diagnostics Limited, that specializes in radioimmunoassays, enhanced luminescence assays, and new directions in automated systems and biosensors.

Chemicals, the last segment, is presented here only for a historical perspective (because it is no longer part of the company). It included the Eastman Chemical Company (ECC). ECC became an independent, publicly held company on December 31, 1993, thus ending a relationship that started in 1920. Kodak distributed to existing shareholders all outstanding shares of Eastman Chemical with one share of Eastman Chemical for four shares of Kodak. In 1993, ECC had $3.9 billion in sales.

HUMAN RESOURCES

Kodak is a true believer in the team approach. Its dealings emphasize supplier involvement with in-house personnel. It uses employees for interviewing new prospects and to manage just-in-time inventory. As an example of this empowered culture, in 1989, Kodak gave its black-and-white film division an ultimatum to turn around the dismal financial performance or stop making product. The division had 1,500 employees and 7,000 products. A fifteen-member team of managers led the effort. It changed the division's traditional functional-flow manufacturing to a team-driven work flow. Team Zebra, as the division refers to itself, is now the leading business unit in product quality, customer satisfaction, and overall operating efficiency.[7] Kodak also uses statistical process control throughout its manufacturing and has programs of recognition and reward for both individuals and teams.

QUALITY

Continuous improvement is integral in everything from research and manufacturing to marketing and staff support. To support its continuing quality programs, Kodak has an independent research firm survey more than 10,000 customers annually. Its feedback is incorporated into Kodak's process for improvement.

ENVIRONMENT

Kodak has a split personality when it comes to the environment. It has been recognized by the Environmental Protection Agency (EPA) for its achievements in pollution prevention and energy conservation. It has been found to be "one of the better programs in industry," meeting or exceeding evaluation criteria in all assessed categories by an independent audit of the company's health, safety, and environmental program.[8] The environment is important enough to be monitored by a team led by the CEO. Kodak has eliminated the use of ozone-depleting chlorofluorocarbons (CFCs) and, since the 1980s, has rebuilt or reconditioned Ektaprint copier-duplicators to keep them in use and out of landfills.[9] Kodak is highly involved in product recycling. Recycled paperboard is used in manufacturing the ubiquitous little yellow film boxes. It developed a program to link photofinishers with local companies to recycle the plastic canisters that protect 35mm film. And the Fun Saver cameras allow direct recycling of camera parts into new cameras.

However, not everything is as "clean" as the above facts may lead readers to expect. For example, in October 1994, Kodak agreed to spend more than $60 million to correct environmental problems at its largest manufacturing facility, Kodak Park, in Rochester, New York. The company will also pay a $5 million penalty, as part of a settlement reached with the EPA, for violating federal hazardous waste regulations of the Resource Conservation and Recovery Act. The bulk of the spending will be used to repair leaks and install video inspection devices in the sewage system. Kodak has been under investigation by the EPA since 1988 when the EPA began an inquiry following reports of widespread groundwater contamination. In 1990, New York State collected $2 million in criminal and civil penalties from Kodak for related environmental offenses. Kodak spent $154 million in 1993 for pollution prevention and waste treatment. According to EPA emissions data, Kodak is New York's largest industrial polluter.[10]

GLOBAL INITIATIVES

Kodak is truly a global company. To better communicate with its international markets, it moved the headquarters for the respective international operations closer to the action. The headquarters for overall international operations was recently moved to London. England is recognized as the flagship in international operations and is where Kodak just celebrated the 100th anniversary of its manufacturing operation in Harrow. The international division is divided into three distinct regions. First is the Asia Pacific region with its headquarters in Tokyo. This region consists of Japan, Korea, Taiwan, Hong Kong, China, and the southern portion of Asia, extending to include Australia and New Zealand.

The second region is Europe, Africa, and the Middle East. Kodak recently had this headquarters moved from London to The Netherlands. Operations in this region include a joint venture or BELPAK, in the Commonwealth of Independent States (formerly USSR) and PRIMESTER, a joint venture with the French Rhône-Poulenc.

The third region is Latin America, with its headquarters in Miami, Florida. Kodak has had a manufacturing plant in Guadalajara, Mexico, since 1969 and also has plants in Brazil. Kodak dõ Brasil (the Brazilian subsidiary) developed a distribution center near Saõ Paulo. This distribution center is responsible for importing Kodak products from around the world to be sold in the South American area. A 1993 reorganization combined eleven country organizations into five expanded country operations. Therefore, Kodak created new business opportunities and greatly reduced infrastructure costs. Kodak recognizes that increased competition of global firms is growing.

THE MARKET

In the early 1980s, Kodak was spending billions of dollars on acquisitions with no accompanying increase in earnings realized. At the same time, due to stagnant U.S. film sales and increased competition, Kodak was losing ground in its extremely profitable film and photographic paper business. Kodak's response was to lower prices in order to recapture portions of the market.

CEO Fisher realizes that Kodak can no longer allow competitors such as Fuji to undercut Kodak and further capture market share in the profitable segments, primarily film. Here, Kodak enjoys a gross margin as high as 80 percent, making these products the "golden egg" of the company. In 1993, Kodak's market share dropped in this area. Kodak's main rival in the photographic film and paper segment, Japan's Fuji Photo Film, Inc., was able to capture about 10 percent of this very lucrative market. Many Kodak executives feel that radical changes in the company's marketing approach are needed. Kodak's first reaction to this perception was to concentrate its product marketing emphasis on lower prices rather than on picture-taking, as it had in the past. However, lowering prices of these products in order to generate increased market share limited Kodak's growth plans. Lower prices restricted the cash flow to finance any expansion in the electronic business, which was necessary to pay Kodak's large debt and to satisfy shareholders by increasing earnings per share. Figure 2 on page 452 shows Kodak's increasing film sales and decreasing revenue.

Kodak's newest area of emphasis is CD imaging, the act of capturing an image in digital form and then having it available on a computer disc (CD). The primary competitors in this area include Apple, Philips, Pioneer, Sony, Toshiba, and Agfa-Gevaert. The other area Kodak is emphasizing is its printer products/digital pictorial hard copy products. In January 1994, Fisher announced that "copy products business is not for sale, and we have no plans to sell it."[11]

STRATEGIC INITIATIVES

ACQUISITIONS AND DIVESTITURES

Kodak has had a less-than-satisfactory experience with its series of acquisitions and divestitures. While Whitmore was still CEO, he attempted to stem the tide of failure by beginning the divestitures. Eastman Chemical Company (ECC) was divested. It was announced in June 1993 that ECC would spin off to shareholders, creating an entity with 18,500 employees and sales of $3.9 billion. After the announcement, Kodak's share price fell 3 percent because the plan would neither cut Kodak's debt ratio nor enhance earnings. The act was possibly due to the intense pressure Whitmore was feeling to deliver a restructuring plan. It was generally regarded as little more than a public relations response, demonstrating that he was willing to manage the company differently.[12]

■ FIGURE 2
Stagnant U.S. Film Sales . . .

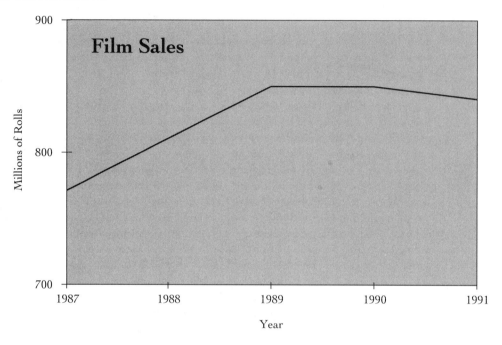

. . . Are Suppressing Kodak's Biggest Line

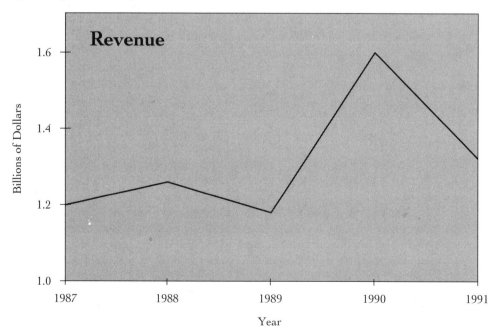

The biggest disappointment in the acquisition strategy was Sterling Winthrop Drug Inc. On February 23, 1988, Kodak acquired substantially all the outstanding common stock for $5.1 billion. Sterling was acquired because of a concern that the basic film business was leveling off, and, at that time, health care was the most lucrative business available.[13] This dive into the pharmaceutical market was a clear departure from the film or image industry. In an attempt to recover and gain the experience it needed, Kodak formed an alliance with Sanofi, a company within the Elf Acquitaine Group, for joint ventures to develop and market pharmaceutical and over-the-counter medicines. The alliance called for three joint ventures: two under the name of Sanofi Winthrop and one under the name of Sterling Health. These were an attempt to internationalize the pharmaceutical area and enhance profits. Neither was very successful, and in May 1994, Sterling was sold. The prescription drugs were sold to Sanofi for $1.7 billion, and the over-the-counter drugs were sold to Smith Kline Beecham for $2.9 billion.[14]

Kodak's U.S. photofinishing operations were combined with those of Fuqua Industries, Inc. in March 1988. The new company, named Qualex, Inc., was the nation's largest wholesale photofinisher, having 70 percent of that market and 28 percent of all photofinishing. Kodak subsequently acquired ownership of Qualex by buying out its 50 percent partner, Actava Group, for $150 million.[15]

Kodak even had its own commercial financial business—Eastman Kodak Credit Corporation (EKCC). Its primary business purpose was to enhance the marketing capabilities of the company by providing long-term product financing to Kodak customers.[16] It was sold to General Electric Capital Corporation on December 31, 1992.

Another divestiture was Atex. It was purchased in 1981 for $80 billion and sold in 1992 for $5 billion. Atex's core business, supplying word-processing systems to newspaper publishers, did not fit well with Kodak's strategy.[17] It had generated little or no profit since its acquisition. The intent was to add imaging capability to Atex products—this never worked. Throughout Kodak's ownership, Atex never developed the earnings needed. Its number of employees was reduced from an original 1,000 to 400 at the time of its sale as a result of attempts to lower costs.[18]

Other sales included Estek, Videk, Interactive Systems, and the Center for Creative Imaging in Camden, Maine. L&F split into two separate groups, household products and do-it-yourself products, that were sold independently.[19] Forstmann Little & Co. agreed to buy the paint, stain, and sealant lines for $700 million. The household-products portion was sold to London-based Reckitt & Colman PLC for $1.55 billion.[20] The Clinical Diagnostics business was sold to Johnson & Johnson for $1.0 billion.

The decisions to sell these business units were revolutionary for Kodak. By selling Sterling Winthrop, L&F Products, and Clinical Diagnostics, which accounted for 23 percent of Kodak's 1993 corporate sales and operating profits, Kodak reversed a decade of failed attempts to diversify and illustrated its determination to recapture prominence in photography. In addition, cash resulting from the sale of Kodak's noncore businesses would dramatically improve its balance sheet and provide the funds necessary to invest in its profitable core imaging industry. Fisher was quoted as saying "Kodak's future calls for nothing less than total commitment to imaging," and that "we were passing up too many opportunities to make small investments because we were so strapped for cash. If we attempted to retain both health and imaging, we would have short-changed both."

STRUCTURE

Whenever restructuring and downsizing of a firm occurs, costs are unavoidable. Kodak's recent series of recovery attempts began with a $1.6 billion charge in 1991. The desirable severance package offered to departing employees was designed to reduce costs by reducing employment, but was so attractive that three times the expected number of employees left the company. Kodak was forced to hire new people to replace them. Ultimately, no improvements to earnings were experienced, and the board of directors slashed Whitmore's bonus by 70 percent, to $140,000.[21] Another $220 million was charged in 1992 to cover severance and early retirements.[22] This was followed by a $538 million restructuring cost in 1993. As part of the restructuring and cost reductions, Kodak recognized that it needed to get the right number of people doing the right job. Therefore, in 1993, it separated 2,000 employees, the first layoffs in ten years.[23] Its ultimate goal was to reduce worldwide employment by 10,000 people by the end of 1994.[24] Separation benefits represented 75 percent of the restructuring costs. These costs are not expected to affect the cash flow because they are being funded primarily by the company's pension plan assets.[25]

By 1984, while the company was developing into a bureaucracy, seventeen autonomous business units had formed, largely within the imaging and information segments. In 1991, Kodak addressed this by forming one consolidated imaging organization to address the costs of decentralization. It made an early retirement offer, and 8,000 employees left the company. In 1992, to improve accountability, the company assigned responsibility for implementing strategies and delivering results to regional managers. As a result, the seventeen previous units were consolidated into five: Asia and the Pacific; Europe, Africa, and the Middle East; Latin America; the U.S.; and Canada.

STRATEGY

In 1987, CEO Chandler believed that the new snazzy technology of electronic imaging was still years ahead of the amateur photographer market. The customers were not ready to pay for the added convenience offered by such a revolutionary product. The company also received a wake-up call initiated by the resurgence of the U.S. dollar on the international currency market. This was a double-edged sword because it both reduced Kodak's income from overseas (which was almost two-thirds of its revenue) while at the same time made it easier for the competition (particularly Fuji) to enter the American market. Kodak made two passes at cutting costs to recover. In 1983, it nudged 8 percent of the workforce out, and in 1987, it cut employment as well as the overall budget by 10 percent.[26]

In 1990, Kodak's goal was to have photographic film continue to be the premier image-capturing medium. To implement this strategy, Chandler made major investments in the core of the company's business. The company built new sensitizing and film base manufacturing facilities and focused on high-volume copiers. Commitment was demonstrated by the formation of the commercial imaging group. This group combined research, product development, and manufacturing efforts, intensifying focus on customers. Therefore, more rapid response to customer requests was available.

In 1992, Whitmore announced that Kodak's strategic intention was to be the world leader in imaging (covering both conventional and electronic imaging).[27] Kodak then announced the photo CD and new digital copier-duplicator to show the world that it had the technology, the will, and the reach to realize its vision. The photo CD was to become the standard of electronic image quality for television display, transmission, and printing. It went to market in 1992. Kodak further increased its investment in research and development related to silver-halide film technology, the company's core competency. Kodak had finally decided to view the world as it is rather than as Kodak might wish it to be—thereby reducing costs. Overall, it reduced manufacturing costs by more than 25 percent in less than five years.

In response to continuing pressure from investors, Whitmore decided to run the company to maximize earnings and the stock price. This was a drastic departure from the company's traditional growth strategy.[28] He backed up his strategy by hiring an outsider as chief financial officer. This was the first attempt at using an outside change agent to enhance the change process. Christopher J. Steffen was a turnaround artist with experience at Chrysler Corporation and Honeywell, Inc. The announcement of his hire caused the stock price to jump 17 percent. His plan was to cut the debt-to-total-capital ratio by 30 to 40 percent from its current 59 percent.[29] The company's previous cost structure was predicated on a return to growth in the core photographic market after its slowdown in the 1980s. This slowdown was assumed to be temporary when, in fact, the core market for Kodak had reached its maturity. This turned out to be the hardest fact for Whitmore to admit.[30]

Success was not yet in reach, and Steffen resigned after only eleven weeks. The main cause was lack of cooperation and a perceived power struggle. Officially, Whitmore stated he was concerned that Steffen was focused on only restructuring finances and was not addressing the larger strategic issues of market growth and new product development. The market reacted by lowering the stock price 11 percent.[31] Steffen was replaced by Harry L. Kavetas. He joined the company in February 1994 and within two months was able to decrease Kodak's debt by nearly $1 billion. He did this primarily by refinancing revolving credit. Kavetas also eliminated approximately $100 million of Kodak's expenses on unneeded real estate.[32]

Even with the divestitures and improved credit rating, Kodak was still sending signals that it had not returned to the desired state. An internal memo of September 20, 1994, stated that the company would freeze hiring until the first quarter of 1995. It would also speed up pending staff reductions and cut research and development expenditures—possibly delaying product introductions. These cost cuts suggested a commitment to meeting earnings targets but were viewed as short-range temporary solutions.[33]

NEW STRATEGY

Kodak's current and future strategy must continue down the road already begun. It needs to continue cost cutting and rightsizing, and return to the growth company of yesteryear. Wall Street analysts figure that 25,000 of the remaining 110,000 employees should be cut. This should be done quickly because a long, drawn out program will further decay morale.[34] Furthermore, research and development costs are 7.9 percent of sales—this is probably too high with money lavished on fruitless projects according to Wall Street analysts.[35]

In light of the changes being made, Kodak cannot lose sight of its program of total customer satisfaction. Continual and relentless focus must be made on quality, reduced cycle time, being first to the market to get the high margins and highest market share, and product and service leadership to the customer.[36]

In the human resources and culture areas, the stage is set for progress. Kodak was one of the first companies to tie executive pay to performance. In 1992 Whitmore required forty executives to hold company stock worth one to four times their base salary—they will have until 1998 to accumulate the required amount.[37] Furthermore, Fisher is the first CEO from outside Kodak. He needs to establish an atmosphere to hold managers accountable. Fisher is not going to continue the slash-and-burn technique. He is going to " . . . get in there and find out exactly what is going on."[38] He intends to go through with the planned layoffs but is more concerned with having the right number of people doing the right high-value work rather than just increasing productivity by cutting the workforce.[39]

GROWTH

Instead of arguing that growth will be 5 or 8 percent, the company is now trying to manage with 2 percent growth. At the beginning of 1993, Whitmore was concentrating on stock price and earnings of the company. He, therefore, was more worried about today and put all his faith in the photo CD.[40] Whitmore poured $1 billion into research and development on electronic imaging, still fretting about the impact on Kodak's regular film technology. The major concern was who will need film, paper, and chemicals if a picture can be captured electronically.

Kodak knows that to increase growth and compete globally, it must continually strive to become an efficient, streamlined and worldwide organization that offers quality products at competitive prices. It can no longer afford to be the "bureaucratic, wasteful, paternalistic, slow-moving, isolated, and beloved" company that it was in the past.

Fisher realizes that growth for Kodak in a global environment will not come easily. Many feel that Kodak will have to transform itself from a chemical company into an electronics company. This is because the chemical business, silver halide photography, is extremely slow growing and is in its mature phase. Additionally, Kodak realizes that electronic imaging is a small, rapidly developing industry that appears to be the wave of the future. Kodak believes that it must develop a strong presence in the electronic imaging industry, which is seen as a severe threat to Kodak's very profitable photographic paper and film business. In general, it needs to focus on core products, continue its commitment to imaging, and build digital technologies.

FUTURE

Kodak's debt rating rose to single A-plus from triple B-plus by Standard and Poor's rating service in October 1994. Its debt is expected to be substantially reduced over the next several months due to proceeds from the sales of its nonimaging health businesses.

Debt reduction is expected to more than offset the loss of operational diversity created by divestitures.[41] Kodak is buying back $4.8 billion worth of debt at a premium. It also plans to unwind its derivatives positions to protect against movements in interest rates that have plagued other global companies.[42]

Kodak's business environmental position was recently improved when Fuji, Kodak's main competitor, agreed to raise its prices under pressure from the Department of Commerce.[43] Kodak had been charging a 25 percent premium for its film, causing it to lose market share because the average customer did not perceive the added value.[44]

A signal of Kodak's restated commitment to electronic imaging is its recent removal from the auction block of KEPS, a Kodak company specializing in color management and process production technology. KEPS went through its own major restructuring recently and had a positive cash flow for the first time in 1993.[45]

However, we cannot lose sight of changes in the international playing field. Kodak must consider the implications of the North American Free Trade Agreement (NAFTA) and the European Economic Community (EEC). It must also be concerned with the fact that a similar alliance could form in the Pacific Rim. The erosion of all barriers to trade (quotas, tariffs, etc.) should lead to the development of a greatly improved and efficient market in which economies of scale can be realized. As a result, greater quality products at lower costs should emerge and Kodak could again capture the position as the number one photography and imaging company in the world.

■ FIGURE 3

Eastman Kodak Consolidated Statement of Financial Position

	December 31,	
(In Millions)	1993	1992
ASSETS		
Current Assets		
Cash and cash equivalents	$ 1,635	$ 361
Marketable securities	331	186
Receivables (net of allowances of $141 and $191)	3,463	3,433
Inventories	1,913	1,991
Deferred income tax charges	435	247
Other	244	219
Total current assets	8,021	6,437
Properties		
Land, buildings, and equipment at cost	13,311	13,607
Less: Accumulated depreciation	6,945	6,843
Net properties	6,366	6,764
Other Assets		
Unamortized goodwill (net of accumulated amortization of $846 and $693)	4,186	4,261
Long-term receivables and other noncurrent assets	1,271	1,473
Deferred income tax charges	481	—
Net assets of discontinued operations	—	1,406
TOTAL ASSETS	$ 20,325	$ 20,341

(continued)

■   FIGURE 3

Eastman Kodak Consolidated Statement of Financial Position (continued)

LIABILITIES AND SHAREOWNERS' EQUITY	December 31,	
Current Liabilities	1993	1992
Payables	$ 3,630	$ 3,127
Short-term borrowings	655	1,732
Taxes — income and other	420	490
Dividends payable	165	163
Deferred income tax credits	40	34
Total current liabilities	4,910	5,546
Other Liabilities		
Long-term borrowings	6,853	5,402
Postemployment liabilities	3,678	760
Other long-term liabilities	1,449	1,508
Deferred income tax credits	79	568
Total liabilities	16,969	13,784
Shareowners' Equity		
Common stock, par value $2.50 per share	948	936
(950,000,000 shares authorized;		
issued 379,079,777 in 1993 and 374,479,114 in 1992)		
Additional capital paid in or transferred from retained earnings	213	26
Retained earnings	4,469	7,721
Accumulated translation adjustment	(235)	(85)
	5,395	8,598
Less: Treasury stock, at cost	2,039	2,041
(48,513,344 shares in 1993 and 48,562,835 shares in 1992)		
Total shareowners' equity	3,356	6,557
TOTAL LIABILITIES AND SHAREOWNERS' EQUITY	$ 20,325	$ 20,341

■   FIGURE 4

Eastman Kodak Consolidated Statement of Cash Flows

(In Millions)	1993	1992	1991
Cash flows from operating activities			
Earnings (loss) from continuing operations before extraordinary item and cumulative effect of changes in accounting principle	$ 475	$ 727	$ (302)
Adjustments to reconcile above earnings to net cash provided by operating activities:			
Depreciation and amortization	1,111	1,202	1,142
Benefit for deferred taxes	(130)	(34)	(201)
Loss on sale and retirement of properties	199	159	125
(Increase) decrease in receivables	(120)	251	(19)
Decrease (increase) in inventories	269	(147)	88
Increase in liabilities, excluding borrowings	243	251	771
Other items, net	567	614	310
Total adjustments	2,139	2,296	2,216
Net cash provided by operating activities	2,614	3,023	1,914

(continued)

■ FIGURE 4
Eastman Kodak Consolidated Statement of Cash Flows (continued)

Cash flows from investing activities	1993	1992	1991
Additions to properties	(1,082)	(1,625)	(1,533)
Proceeds from sale of investments	48	189	33
Proceeds from sale of properties	30	30	52
Marketable securities — purchases	(391)	(159)	(60)
Marketable securities — sales	245	114	102
Net cash used in investing activities	(1,150)	(1,451)	(1,406)
Cash flows from financing activities			
Net decrease in commercial paper borrowings of 90 days or less	(1,438)	(629)	(111)
Proceeds from borrowings assumed by discontinued operations	1,800	—	—
Proceeds from other borrowings	527	476	1,518
Repayment of other borrowings	(592)	(1,184)	(1,207)
Dividends to shareowners	(657)	(650)	(649)
Exercise of employee stock options	175	17	—
Other items	2	2	2
Net cash used in financing activities	(183)	(1,968)	(447)
Effect of exchange rate changes on cash	(7)	(17)	(2)
Net increase (decrease) in cash and cash equivalents	1,274	(413)	59
Cash and cash equivalents, beginning of year	361	774	715
Cash and cash equivalents, end of year	$ 1,635	$ 361	$ 774

Questions for Discussion

1. What are Kodak's major threats? What can be done to combat these threats?
2. Why has an acquisition growth strategy proven to be ineffective for Kodak?
3. What further changes are necessary for Kodak to become competitive in an emerging global economy? How are these changes to be implemented, and how will they affect earnings?
4. What would your next step as CEO of Kodak be? Why?

REFERENCES

1. Eastman Kodak Annual Report (1993), 3.

2. Maremont, Mark, "The Revolution that Wasn't at Eastman Kodak," *Business Week* (Industrial/Technology Edition, May 10, 1993): 25.

3. Securities and Exchange Commission Form 10-K (1993), 52.

4. Maremont, Mark, "To: George Fisher—RE: How to Fix Kodak," *Business Week* (Industrial/Technology Edition, November 8, 1993): 37.

5. See note 1, page 5, above.

6. *Standard Corporation Descriptions* (New York: Standard and Poor's Corporation, 1994), 6912.

7. Dawn Anfuso, "Team Zebra Changes Kodak's Stripes," *Personnel Journal* 73, no. 1 (1994): 57.

8. See note 1, page 18, above.

9. Eastman Kodak Annual Report (1990), 23

10. Wendy Bounds and Timothy Noah, "Kodak Will Settle Government Claims on Environment," *The Wall Street Journal* (October 7, 1994), B4.

11. See note 6, page 6454, above.

12. Mark Maremont, "Why Kodak's Dazzling Spin-Off Didn't Bedazzle," *Business Week* (June 28, 1993): 34.

13. See note 1, page 4, above.

14. *Value Line Report* (New York: Standard and Poor's Corporation, 1994).

15. Ibid.

16. See note 14, page 46, above.

17. Jim Rosenberg, "Eastman Kodak Sells Atex Inc.," *Editor & Publisher* 125, no. 49 (1992): 32.

18. Ibid., page 33.

19. See note 14 above.

20. Jonathan Welsh, "Forstmann Agrees to Pay $700 Million for Lines of Eastman Kodak's L&F," *The Wall Street Journal* (October 17, 1994), A4.

21. See note 2 above.

22. Eastman Kodak Annual Report (1992), 44.

23. Mark Maremont, "Getting the Picture: Kodak Finally Heeds the Shareholders," *Business Week* (Industrial/Technology Edition, February 1, 1993): 24.

24. See note 3, page 34, above.

25. Ibid.

26. Thomas Moore, "Old-Line Industry Shapes Up: Seven *Fortune* 500 Companies Show How Restructuring Can Make the U.S. Competitive Again," *Fortune* 115, no. 9 (1987): 26.

27. Ibid., page 10.

28. Ibid., page 26.

29. Ibid.

30. Ibid., page 25.

31. See note 2, page 24, above.

32. See note 14 above.

33. Wendy Bounds, "Kodak Starts Sweeping Drive to Slash Costs," *The Wall Street Journal* (October 17, 1994), A3.

34. See note 4 above.

35. Ibid.

36. See note 23, page 25, above.

37. See note 23, page 26, above.

38. Laurel Touby, "The Business of America Is Jobs," *Journal of Business Strategy* 14, no. 6 (Nov./Dec. 1993): 24.

39. See note 38, page 21, above.

40. See note 23, page 25, above.

41. Staff Reporter, "Kodak's Debt Ratings Are Boosted by S&P," *The Wall Street Journal* (October 4, 1994), B6.

42. Staff Reporter, "Asset-Backed Security Sales Top $1.4 Billion, Led by Offerings from Dean Witter and Sears," *The Wall Street Journal* (October 5, 1994), C17.

43. See note 14 above.

44. See note 4, page 26, above.

45. Hadley Sharples, "Kodak Restates Digital Aims," *Graphic Arts Monthly* 66, no. 3 (1994): 80.

Name Index

Subject Index